T0291182

'This superb book brings together – in a rigorous and pedagogical way – the academic knowledge and real-world challenges and solutions to the regulation of sectors that constitute an essential part of our economies. In our politically and socially uncertain times, it is particularly useful in thoroughly addressing the efficiency, equity and political acceptability of regulatory systems, as well as their fiscal and institutional constraints.'
Mathias Dewatripont, Professor of Economics, Université Libre de Bruxelles & Honorary Vice-Governor, National Bank of Belgium

'Auriol, Crampes and Estache are great connoisseurs of the theory and practice of regulation. Their book is a rigorous and yet accessible approach to theory combined with a deep knowledge of what really matters in the field. It guides the reader through the various trade-offs faced by regulation and provides the lens to look at the future while benefiting from the field experience and knowledge we have inherited from the past. No one said that getting regulation right was simple, but this book makes it look as exciting and intellectually challenging as it can get. Regulating public services is a must-read for practitioners and scholars willing to understand the regulatory challenges faced by most, if not all, key sectors of the economy.'
Natalia Fabra, Professor of Economics, Department of Economics, Universidad Carlos III de Madrid

'There are few books on utility regulation that are useful to practitioners and academics alike. This book is a much needed exception. It provides a thorough treatment of the conceptual and practical issues faced by regulators and policymakers, including the need to address institutional and political considerations with examples from developed and developing countries.'
Andrés Gómez-Lobo, Professor of Economics, Department of Economics, Universidad de Chile, and Minister of Transport and Telecomunications of Chile (2014–17)

'This extraordinary book should be read by everyone serious about the theory and practice of economic regulation. The authors present the main results from the economic theory of regulation clearly and connect them to a wide range of real issues. This unique breadth should enable graduate students and regulators alike to see what economic theory can and – so far at least – cannot contribute to resolving policy issues. Its lessons should make regulators more careful and economic theorists more willing to tackle important but difficult problems.'
Richard Schmalensee, Emeritus at the Sloan School of Management and at the Department of Economics at the Massachusetts Institute of Technology (MIT)

'This excellent book does justice to its title. It builds a perfect bridge between the theory and practice of economic regulation. Books on economic regulation are often technical and lack examples, case studies and much needed intuition to link theory to practice. This is precisely the great merit of this book: it thoroughly and rigorously analyzes the design and implementation of regulatory tools while simultaneously showing how they are applied in practice. The book delves deep into social, political

and institutional areas that are of paramount importance for a regulator, but are usually bypassed in economic books on utility regulation. And it invites the reader to explore how digitalization, big data and social demands for more and better services will impact the regulator's job. A book not to be missed!'
Tomas Serebrisky, Principal Economic Advisor, Inter-American Development Bank

'This is a powerful and timely book that examines topical industries of public interest, and how to control their power through the lenses of economic regulation, without forgetting institutional, legal, and political considerations. Offering perspectives through both the microscope and the telescope, the book constantly revolves around the three pillars of efficiency, equity, and financial sustainability. The authors are in the unique and authoritative position to write on the theory and practice of regulation based on their experience. A truly fascinating and engaging book that should be read not only by students and scholars interested in the regulation of industries, but also by every person who is concerned with the future of public services.'
Tommaso Valletti, Head of the Department of Economics and Public Policy, Imperial College London, Chief Competition Economist, European Commission (2016–19)

Regulating Public Services

Regulation is one of the tools used by governments to control monopolistic behaviour in the provision of public services such as electricity, transport or water. Technological and financial innovations have changed these public services markets since the 1990s, bringing new regulatory challenges, including technological and financial ones. This book demonstrates that basic regulatory theory and tools can address these new challenges, in addition to more traditional regulatory issues, in both developed and developing economies. The theory covered in the book is robust enough to guide regulators in multiple contexts, including those resulting from the effects of financial or political constraints, evolving market structures or the need to adapt to institutional weaknesses, climate change and poverty concerns that demand regulatory intervention. A bridge between theory and an evolving global practice, this book mobilizes the lessons of the past to analyse the future of economic regulation.

Emmanuelle Auriol is Professor of Economics at the Toulouse School of Economics. Over the years she has received several awards for her research on regulation, industrial organization and development economics.

Claude Crampes is Professor Emeritus of Economics at the Toulouse School of Economics. He has worked as an advisor for energy utilities and regulators in Europe.

Antonio Estache is Professor of Economics at the Université Libre de Bruxelles and a member of the ECARES research centre. Prior to that, he worked at the World Bank for twenty-five years, on public sector policies.

Regulating Public Services

Bridging the Gap between Theory and Practice

EMMANUELLE AURIOL
Toulouse School of Economics

CLAUDE CRAMPES
Toulouse School of Economics

ANTONIO ESTACHE
Université Libre de Bruxelles

CAMBRIDGE
UNIVERSITY PRESS

CAMBRIDGE
UNIVERSITY PRESS

University Printing House, Cambridge CB2 8BS, United Kingdom

One Liberty Plaza, 20th Floor, New York, NY 10006, USA

477 Williamstown Road, Port Melbourne, VIC 3207, Australia

314–321, 3rd Floor, Plot 3, Splendor Forum, Jasola District Centre, New Delhi – 110025, India

103 Penang Road, #05–06/07, Visioncrest Commercial, Singapore 238467

Cambridge University Press is part of the University of Cambridge.

It furthers the University's mission by disseminating knowledge in the pursuit
of education, learning, and research at the highest international levels of excellence.

www.cambridge.org
Information on this title: www.cambridge.org/9781108833950
DOI: 10.1017/9781108987660

© Emmanuelle Auriol, Claude Crampes and Antonio Estache 2021

This publication is in copyright. Subject to statutory exception
and to the provisions of relevant collective licensing agreements,
no reproduction of any part may take place without the written
permission of Cambridge University Press.

First published 2021

A catalogue record for this publication is available from the British Library.

ISBN 978-1-108-83395-0 Hardback
ISBN 978-1-108-98747-9 Paperback

Cambridge University Press has no responsibility for the persistence or accuracy
of URLs for external or third-party internet websites referred to in this publication
and does not guarantee that any content on such websites is, or will remain,
accurate or appropriate.

Contents

Figures

Tables

Boxes

Foreword

Regulating Public Services is a tour de force. It offers a rigorous and up-to-date treatment of the economic theory of regulation while managing to connect this theory with actual policymaking. This is enabled by the double-hatted authorship: Emmanuelle Auriol, Claude Crampes and Antonio Estache have all both extensively contributed to the theory and participated in the design or the evaluation of regulation in developed, developing and emerging economies. The result of their collaboration is an accessible, rigorous and sensible textbook that addresses the key policy issues raised by the design of regulation in a wide range of economic, financial and social contexts. ACE (as the book will be referred to here) also discusses the relevance of their analysis for both private firms and state-owned enterprises, which are still the dominant ownership structure in some industries and in many developing countries.

This economics text on regulation naturally provides a careful coverage of the many ways in which regulation can improve or deteriorate efficiency. ACE presents a detailed overview of the academic literature. It emphasizes the importance of distinguishing between adverse selection and moral hazard in the identification of the optimal design of regulation in a world in which there are significant limitations on the authorities' access to information on cost and demand. The book also delivers solid evidence and multiple anecdotes that facilitate practitioners relating to their own experience and demonstrates the concrete relevance of the theoretical developments.

More generally, ACE provides the readers (academics, students and policymakers) with a user-friendly exposition of how different sources of market failures impact the efficiency of alternative regulatory choices. Each chapter starts with an example or a case study to provide the intuition; the theory is then presented in an accessible way, and the chapter ends with a summary of its main policy implications.

Another feature that makes this textbook somewhat unusual in the field of economic regulation is its emphasis on the need to look beyond efficiency to get regulatory policy right.

First, ACE highlights the regulatory importance of social concerns, such as service affordability and equity among stakeholders. It reminds us that the neglect of this dimension played a role in the rejection of privatization and regulatory reforms in some countries. Moreover, it demonstrates that energy and water shortages are just as relevant in developed as in developing or emerging economies, and yet could be addressed by regulation if there were a political will to do so. ACE shows how the choice of prices, subsidies targeting and contract coverage (as in the case of regulated public–private partnerships when cream skimming may exclude poor users) can all make a difference to the social, and hence the political, viability of a policy. To minimize the risk of negative social outcomes, ACE provides a useful policy-oriented perspective on the options regulators have to manage efficiency–equity trade-offs.

A second original feature of the book is ACE's case for a more careful analysis of the interactions between regulatory policy, fiscal constraints and the capital markets. ACE discusses how the fiscal capability to subsidize enables or limits regulatory options, whether the service providers are public or private. It also explains how capital market constraints can influence the average price required to enable financing when the service provider relies on capital markets to finance its investments. The chapter on the relevance of the costs of capital in regulatory debates is particularly clear on this point.

Third, ACE discusses the importance of the market structure in which the regulated service provider operates for service quality and investment decisions. It shows why the new reliance on competition in regulated industries does not warrant abandoning regulation, but rather makes it more complex. Increasingly, regulators deal with multiproduct monopolies and oligopolies. Part of the added complexity regulators have to account for is also a consequence of new ownership structures, with a growing role for new types of financial stakeholders. This evolution forces regulators to cope with novel forms of collusion and abuses of market power. As argued by ACE, the frontier between regulation and antitrust is increasingly blurred, making the case for additional research. In this context, the authors also suggest that the theory has so far underestimated the regulatory relevance of the evolution of the role of financial intermediaries such as hedge funds, pension funds and other institutional investors, offering yet another research theme.

Fourth, the authors pay specific attention to the relevance of the institutional capacity of the authorities for the optimal design of regulation. As they emphasize, one size does not fit all in regulation. They provide evidence that institutional limitations should be a key driver of the regulatory choice. Modelling institutional characteristics explicitly explains, for instance, why the same sector should not be regulated in the same way in countries as different as Belgium, Brazil, France and Mali. They convincingly argue that, unless institutional limitations are accounted for in the choice of regulatory instruments and processes, regulation will not be able to address market failures. In this dimension, again, ACE delivers a useful guide, as it provides the reader with a pragmatic review of the various sources of institutional weaknesses which can be found in both developed and developing countries, and of the optimal regulatory choice for each type of weakness. In this context, too, ACE is transparent about the limitations of theory and what this means for future research.

Finally, the authors share their views on the future of regulation in a provocative concluding chapter. Their discussion of the main emerging issues provides a fair overview of the main challenges regulators are likely to face to ensure that the production of regulated services meets demand in an efficient, fair and financially sustainable way. The IT revolution and the entry of new players into regulated markets will create new risks and opportunities and alter the way regulated markets will operate, be financed and be supervised. More work on these issues is likely to be performed in the years to come as we learn about the practical relevance of the evolutions. The concluding chapter is a useful start to get the governments and academics to join forces in preparing the future.

Overall, the book should become a popular text in a wide range of academic programmes as it fits with the material usually covered in one or two semesters at the graduate level. It should also be an essential companion to most regulators and their advisors, and all those keen on looking for the key concepts and for ideas to tackle social, institutional or financial issues in developed, developing or emerging economy. As I said earlier, a real tour de force.

Jean Tirole
Toulouse School of Economics
Winner of the 2014 Nobel Prize in Economic Sciences

Preface

Where does this book come from?

This book formalizes our lectures on the economics of regulation to graduate students in various European countries. It also addresses the main concerns identified in our interactions with policymakers, regulators, regulated firms, investors, parliamentarians and members of civil society in developed, developing and emerging countries. The desire to produce a textbook delivering both the analytical rigour needed to present the basic conceptual tools combined with a pragmatic perspective on the usefulness of theory to the design and evaluation of regulatory policies options in a wide range of institutional and political contexts may be what makes this book different, and hopefully useful.

What is the main focus of the book?

The book focuses on the regulation of industries of public interest in a context in which service providers, public or private, operate in imperfectly competitive environments and have more information than the regulators on their cost drivers, consumers and financing sources. The book reviews what the market power and information advantages enjoyed by the regulated firms imply for the quantity, quality, costs and financial viability of services as well as for the fairness with which they are delivered. It highlights the extent to which regulatory solutions need to adapt to the specific information gaps but also to the specific context in which regulation is designed and implemented. It shows how the risks of regulatory failures can be cut when the relevance of institutional, social and political constraints is explicitly accounted for in the choice of the economic regulatory instruments. It also shows how financial uncertainty, corruption or incompetence should matter to the design of regulation.

Who is the book aimed at?

We aim at three main audiences: first, students in economics and public policy programmes; second, academics interested in learning how the concepts are translated in concrete policies; and third, policymakers and their advisers. Therefore, we combine theoretical rigour in the presentation of the concepts with evidence on their relevance in practice. We realize that, despite the many examples, some of the chapters may be hard to read for audiences less analytically inclined. To compensate, within each chapter we try to be as intuitive as possible and to make it easy for those readers less interested in the technical details to skip some of the more challenging maths and yet not lose the main insights on the topic. Moreover, we end each chapter with a summary of the messages the reader less interested in techniques and more concerned with the policy relevance of theory may want to remember.

What are our biases?

The book reflects four biases. First, we emphasize that economic regulation is not just about efficiency. In practice, it is also about the need to continuously arbitrate between efficiency, equity and financial sustainability. Second is the desire to emphasize the relevance of the multiple forms of institutional weaknesses ranging from corruption to a limited capacity to develop, implement or enforce regulation because of constraints on human and/or financial resources or to make long-term commitments to regulation because of complex political contexts. The third bias is our decision to rely on regulated infrastructure activities only in our case studies and examples, even if most of the concepts are relevant to any regulated industry delivering services of public interest. This is because these are the sectors on which we all have direct policy experience. The final bias stems from the fact that the three of us focus on regulation as economists. Yet legal, political and public administration scholars have also made significant contributions to our collective understanding of 'economic' regulation design and implementation. We will refer to some of these insights often, but we cannot do justice to that vast literature. Other authors are more qualified to explain these contributions.

What is the 'pedagogical logic' of the book?

To make the learning process as smooth as possible, the theoretical formalization initially builds on a simple discrete modelling approach before slowly moving on to more complex approaches to illustrate the diversity of tools found in the academic literature but also in the ('best') practice of regulation. The most technically demanding discussions are covered in boxes, in footnotes or in chapter appendices. As mentioned earlier, these can be skipped without losing the main policy content of the core text. Not all conceptual dimensions will be sidelined, however, as technical details are often useful to show both the interest and the limits of some of the policies resulting from assumptions made in conceptual diagnostics of regulatory challenges. This is particularly important in the field since, as we shall see, assumptions are sometimes quite ideological.

How much material does the book cover?

The coverage of the book is not exhaustive. Instead of trying to do justice to all theoretical developments produced by the voluminous literature on regulation over the last forty years, it focuses instead on those relevant to address the most common and most lasting regulatory concerns in practice. Throughout the book we also try to address the regulatory implications of changes in the contexts in which regulation is likely to take place in the foreseeable future. Digitalization, increased awareness of environmental risks and shadow banking, for instance, are already leading to sector-specific regulatory policy changes. We will discuss these changes in different chapters as needed.

Acknowledgements

First, we are grateful to the Belgian National Scientific Research Foundation (Fonds de la Recherche Scientifique or FNRS) for its financial support to Antonio Estache to allow him to spend time at the Toulouse School of Economics and work at the home base of his two coauthors. Emmanuelle Auriol and Claude Crampes acknowledge funding from ANR under grant ANR-17-EUR-0010 (Investissements d'Avenir programme).

Second, we are grateful to Steven Kennedy, our first reader, for going through the book in its rawest version to help us see the margin for improvements in the language and to Joan Dale Lace for her patience with us while editing the final version.

We are particularly grateful to Lisa Bagnoli, Salvador Bertomeu-Sanchez and Rasha Shakra for their careful rereading of the full book and to Mathias Dewatripont, Renaud Foucart, Andres Gomez-Lobo and Richard Schlirf-Rapti for their detailed comments on specific chapters as we were trying to get a sense of the extent to which we could be read by both theoreticians and practioners of regulation. We are also indebted to Tomas Serebrisky of the Inter-American Development Bank for intensive discussions on the policy relevance of the chapter on the future of regulation, which started as a joint think piece for a report on the state of infrastructure that he was leading.

We also want to thank L. Athias, G. Balineau, G. Bel, D. Benitez, J. Bouckaert, O. Chisari, F. Colautti, D. Camos, J. Carbajo, V. Daxbek, M. de Halleux, J. A. Gomez-Ibanez, J. L. Guasch, T. O. Leautier, D. Martimort, S. Saussier, G. Sember, T. Soreide, J. Tirole, F. Trillas, L. Trujillo, M. Vagliasindi, T. Valila, T. Valletti, Q. Wodon and L. Wren-Lewis for useful exchanges on specific issues discussed in the book.

The three of us often talk about our debt to Jean-Jacques Laffont. He died on 1 May 2004 but each of us was lucky enough to learn with him many of the issues discussed in this book. Two of us interacted with him for many years in an academic environment and one of us in policy work during most of the 1990s and early 2000s. In many ways, this book is the result of those interactions. His joint research with Jean Tirole and our many informal discussions made a significant difference to the way we conceptualize regulatory issues and discuss their policy implications.

Of course, it is impossible not to mention our families and their patience and tolerance as they saw us spend more time than expected working on various versions of the book. Emmanuelle Auriol is dedicating this book to François, Mathilde and Lucien.

Symbols

a	Access charge
A	Asset value
AM	Amortization
α	Weight assigned by the regulator to the well-being of the regulated operator in the social welfare function, i.e. $W = V + \alpha\pi$ with $0 \le \alpha \le 1$
β	In finance theory, covariance-to-variance ratio
β_a	Asset β
β_e	Equity β
c	Variable unit cost
c_e	Entrants' long-term generation cost
c_g	Long-run generation marginal cost
C(q)	Total cost of producing q
C'(q)	First derivative of $C(q)$ = Marginal cost of increasing q by 1 unit = C_m
C^{SR}	Short-run costs
C^{LR}	Long-run costs
C_m	Marginal cost
C_M	Average cost
C_x	Sum of the market shares of the x largest firms
D	Debt
Dep_t	Depreciation in year t
Div_t	Dividends in year t
Δ	Variation symbol
ε	The market price elasticity of demand ($\varepsilon = -(\Delta q/q)/(\Delta p/p)$)
ε_{ij}	Cross-elasticity of demand for good i with respect to price pj ($= (\Delta q_i/q_i)/(\Delta p_j/p_j)$)
$\Psi(e)$	Cost of exerting effort e
DWL	Deadweight loss
E	Equity
EW	Expected welfare
e	Effort
F	Fixed costs

γ	Measures the degree of capture of public decisions by the industry ($\gamma \geq 0$)
gr	Expected dividend growth rate
g(x,q)	Production function (also noted as q = f(x))
HHI	Herfindahl–Hirschman Index
$\mathbf{I_t}$	Consumer's income in year t
ID	index of domination
k	Measure of ease with which a regulator can be captured ($0 \leq k \leq 1$)
$\mathbf{K_t}$	Capital stock in year t
L	Lerner Index
$\mathbf{L_M}$	Modified Lerner Index
$\mathbf{L_t}$	Full equivalent employment in year t
λ	Opportunity cost of public funds, i.e. their shadow price
m	Allowed profit margin
$\mathbf{M_t}$	Raw material used in year t
η	Congestion shadow price
NPV	Net present value
p(q)	Inverse demand function, willingness to pay for the last unit of q
p(x)	Price of service x
$\mathbf{p^{be}}$	Price needed to allow firm to break-even
$\mathbf{p^r}$	Regulated price
π	Profit, rent or well-being of operators, depending on context
$\pi\mathbf{(q)}$	Profit function: $\pi(q) = R(q) - C(q)(+ t)$ (+ transfer t if any)
Q	Quantity of product or service
q = f(x)	Production function (also noted as g(x,q) = 0)
q(p)	Direct demand function q(p), quantity demanded at price p
$\mathbf{q^c}$	Quantity in a competitive market
$\mathbf{q^m}$	Quantity in a monopolistic market
$\mathbf{q^r}$	Quantity associated with the regulated price p^r
r	Rate of return
$\mathbf{r_d}$	Cost of debt
$\mathbf{r_{d,prem}}$	Debt-specific risk premium
$\mathbf{r_e}$	Cost of equity
$\mathbf{r_f}$	Risk-free rate
$\mathbf{r_k}$	Cost of capital
$\mathbf{r_j}$	The return for company or sector j
$\mathbf{r_M}$	The average market return
$\mathbf{r_m}$	Market rate
RPI	Retail price index
R(q)	Firms' revenues
R'(q)	First derivative of R(q) = Marginal revenue from increasing q by 1 unit = R_m

$\mathbf{R_m}$	Marginal revenue $= R'(q)$
$\mathbf{R_u}$	Consumers' expenditure on the utility-maximizing level of consumption u
s_i	Firm i's market share
$\mathbf{S(q)}$	Gross surplus achieved by consumers from consuming a volume q of a service
$\mathbf{S'(q)}$	Inverse demand function, willingness to pay for the last unit of q
Sca	Economies of scale
Sco	Economies of scope
σ_{jm}	Covariance of assets j and m
$\sigma^2{}_m$	Variance of asset m
ζ	Probability that the regulator discovers the firm's actual costs
t	Depending on the context:
	• Transfers, which can be positive (subsidies) or negative (taxes)
	• Year of observation for a variable
$\mathbf{t_x}$	Tax rate
T	Tariff
$\mathbf{V(q)}$	Net surplus of consumers
W or W(q)	Social surplus
w	Vector of inputs' prices
$\mathbf{x = (K,L,M)}$	Vector of inputs: K installed capital, L labour, M raw materials
z	Quality z
Z	Ad hoc price adjustment

Abbreviations

ACCC	Australian Competition and Consumer Commission
AS	Adverse selection
CAPEX	Capital expenditure = Investment
CAPM	Capital Asset Pricing Model
DCF	Discounted cashflow model
DEA	Data Envelopment Analysis
EC	European Commission
ECPR	Efficient Component Pricing Rule
EU	European Union
FERC	Federal Energy Regulatory Commission
GDP	Gross Domestic Product
IC	Incentive compatibility
ICSID	International Centre for Settlement of Investment Disputes
ICT	Information and Communications Technologies
ISDS	Investor–State Dispute Settlement
MCF	Marginal cost of public funds
MH	Moral hazard
MRT	Marginal rate of transformation
MS	Merchandising surplus
NPV	Net present value
OECD	Organisation for Economic Co-operation and Development
OPEX	Operational and maintenance expenditure
ORR	Office of Rail and Road
PBR	Performance-based regulation
PC	Participation constraint
Pcap	Price cap
PPIAF	Public–Private Infrastructure Advisory Facility
PPP	Public–private partnership
RAB	Regulated asset base
R&D	Research and development
RES	Renewable energy sources
RIA	Regulatory Impact Assessment
RIIO	Revenue–Incentives–Innovation–Output
RPM	Risk premium model

SOE	State-owned enterprise
SRA	Separate regulatory agency
SSA	Sub-Saharan Africa
TSO	Transmission system operator
TTIP	Transatlantic Trade and Investment Partnership
UNCITRAL	United Nations Commission on International Trade Law
UNSW	University of New South Wales
VIM	Vertically integrated monopoly
WACC	Weighted average cost of capital
W&S	Water and sanitation services

1   Introduction

1.1   Let's Start with Some Intuition

Every time you turn on the light, take a shower or ride on a train, you are using a regulated service. Do you ever wonder how it gets funded? Are you paying for this service as a user or are you paying as a taxpayer? For sure, someone has to pay for it. Whether the service is funded by users or taxpayers, it has to raise enough revenue to ensure it is financially and/or fiscally sustainable. But revenue cannot be the only dimension against which these prices should be assessed. The price should also send the right signal to users. If the price you pay for water is too low, you are likely to stay longer than necessary under the shower. And if the price is lower than the costs involved then water companies may not have a strong incentive to invest. This might not hurt you in the short run, but it could eventually result in water rationing. Farmers may not be able to irrigate enough and as a result food prices might increase. Equivalently, if the price of public transportation is too high or there are no tolls on highways, you may prefer to use your car. Air pollution is likely to increase as a result. And if the price of water or electricity is set high in order to get people to consume less, that may exclude some poorer users, who need the service as much as the richer users (think of water).

Clearly, getting the price right is not simple (and it is even more complex when subsidies are an option to finance the service). Adding to these dimensions the strong role of monopolies (or quasi-monopolies) in the production and delivery of these services explains why, in most countries, electricity, water or transport prices tend to be subject to regulation by the government or a regulatory agency.[1] How theory argues this regulation *should* be done and how policy experience suggests it *can* be done is what this book is all about. In the rest of this chapter, we look in more detail into each of these dimensions before revisiting some of the intuitions more conceptually in the following chapters.

1.1.1   Every Time You Turn on the Light, Take a Shower or Ride on a Train, You Are Using a Regulated Service

Significant investments are needed to allow you to use these services. A firm, public or private, has to invest in the facilities needed to produce the electricity and then rely on

---

[1] Similar characteristics also hold for other public services such hospitals.

transmission lines to bring it close to your location. A firm, maybe another one, has to maintain the local delivery lines to your home to allow you to plug in your phone or laptop safely when it suits you. The water you use to take your shower or to drink has to be pumped from ground sources or rivers. Before you use it, it has to go through expensive treatment facilities to make it safe for consumption. Then it is channelled to your home, often from quite far away, through large pipes which have to be maintained and repaired regularly. Similar investment and maintenance needs apply to the train stations and tracks. The point is that most of the regulated services you enjoy are heavy users of capital and labour and other basic inputs to ensure their operation. Many are also set in public space and rely on complex planning and coordination between the various users of shared public assets, which can include air, land and water assets.

1.1.2   Someone Has to Pay for the Regulated Services

The investment, maintenance and operating costs of regulated services are significant in most circumstances.[2] These cost levels, however, do not only depend on the cost of the physical inputs. Because these services involve long-lived assets amortized quite slowly, they are particularly sensitive to financial costs associated with long-term borrowing requirements. The expected return for public or private banks or investment funds providing or lending the capital is an important cost driver in these activities. These costs show up, somewhere, in the price paid by users or in the subsidies the government needs to allocate to the sector.

If, on average, the price paid by users fully recovers these costs, it is essentially a user fee. But in many of the sectors providing services of public interest, the price is often set below costs. In that case, subsidies are needed and these are financed by current taxes or public sector borrowing (i.e. future taxes).[3] For instance, in most countries, rich or poor, the investments made to ensure that we all have access to water are usually largely paid for by current and future taxpayers rather than users. The price we pay often only covers the costs of operating and maintaining the assets. It seldom recovers the amortization of the investments made. Even more rarely does it reflect the scarcity value of water, which, in an ideal world, should be accounted for in the price we pay for these services. Such formal or informal subsidies make these services more affordable. But, as will be discussed in various chapters, while they are well intended, and certainly necessary for the poorest populations, they also tend to lead to

---

[2] For a given service, costs can differ a lot across service areas since they depend also on factors such as the technology used or on the geographical and geological characteristics of the region in which the service is provided. Building rail tracks in the Swiss mountains is quite different from doing so on the flat lands of the Netherlands.

[3] Some developing and emerging economies rely on a third de facto financing source. In Mexico, for instance, during the 1990s, poor regions started to rely on voluntary community work to maintain roads and thereby reduce the need to depend on cash subsidies. Similarly, in the slums and many poor rural parts of Africa, Asia and Latin American countries, the basic and light repair works on water systems are performed by trained local citizens committed to contribute in kind to the maintenance of what they see as public goods. As a result, studies show that most citizens on earth contribute to public goods, either through the taxes they pay or through their in-kind contribution.

overconsumption by users who do not face the real cost of their consumption and this adds to the demand for underfunded investment.

1.1.3 The Price Paid Needs to Account Jointly for Financial/Fiscal Viability, Efficiency and Equity Concerns

Regulated prices have multiple purposes. Combined with subsidies, they are essential to ensure the long-term economic, social, financial and fiscal viability of the service. The discussions between regulators and regulated firms tend to focus on the role they have in the determination of the financial returns to public or private investors and the residual costs to taxpayers if subsidies are needed. Regulators, and increasingly many stakeholders in civil society, also spend (or at least should spend) time analysing the role of prices in signalling the effects of consumption decisions on the use of natural resources. Many stakeholders think as well about the impact of prices on the affordability of the service, to avoid penalizing the poorest users. Moreover, many analysts highlight that prices have to be fair to tomorrow's stakeholders. It is indeed easy to forget – or to choose to forget! – that if investment is not made today services will not be available tomorrow. From a financial perspective, the prices need to ensure that the investors get a return consistent with the risks they are taking – accounting for subsidies. And from a fiscal perspective, they need to deliver on many policy responsibilities, including accounting for the distortions associated with the need to raise taxes to pay for subsidies, as will be discussed in some detail in subsequent chapters.

Ideally, prices should also account for the difference between the social return and the financial return from the regulatory decisions. For instance, the net costs of environmental externalities should be reflected in the price of the services you are consuming if they are not subject to a specific tax. This is seldom the case. This explains, for instance, why it is still much cheaper to travel short distances by plane than by train.[4] In a nutshell, getting the price right implies addressing the often conflicting concerns of many different stakeholders, including some that are yet unborn.

1.1.4 Pricing Is Influenced by the Strong Role of Monopolies in These Industries

Ensuring that the price of a service accounts for all these concerns would be challenging in any market, but it is particularly hard for industries in which the services are

---

[4] The decision to omit the difference between social and private returns to decisions has dominated many policy activities, and not just regulatory decisions. For instance, most of the private sector development vice presidencies of international organizations work on the assumption that the private returns are a lower bound for the social return. This implies that they rule out the possibility of a negative impact of environmental or other externalities on social welfare when assessing the price of a service. The pricing is usually disconnected from the information provided by the environmental impact assessments required by these organizations for the projects they finance. This disconnection has been a long-lasting debate within these organizations. For now, in practice, the private sector perspective, anchored in a socially costly conceptual omission, continues to define the policy perspectives. This perspective also spills over in debates on the optimal design of regulation of private firms or commercialized state-owned enterprises.

often best provided by local, regional or national monopolies, as is the case for many of the regulated public services. Monopolies are a source of concern if they enjoy enough discretionary margins on their production decisions to underprovide quantity and/or quality and to overcharge. Monopolies also enjoy an informational advantage over all other stakeholders that they can use to influence the setting of prices or quantities to their benefit. For instance, they know more about their actual costs, and their potential cost savings from changes in technologies or improved management efforts, than consumers do. They can use the informational advantage to inflate their costs report and hence secure higher compensation for their services than they deserve, as a way of increasing their profits.

Regulation needs to arbitrate between all these concerns, and it is not simple. It has to account for the fact that not all participants have access to the same information and that the abuse of market power is a serious threat in these sectors in most countries. This is why, historically, the price of basic services has usually been, directly or indirectly, controlled by the State in some form. In other words, *this is why the prices charged by monopolies are typically being regulated*. Regulation is needed to minimize the risks that the de facto power a firm has over a market is not abused to the disadvantage of users (domestic and industrial) or taxpayers.[5]

1.1.5   What Does Regulation Deal With?

Ultimately, in very broad terms, regulation could be defined as a policy tool used to ensure efficient price, quantity and quality outcomes in utilities services that are fair to all stakeholders when markets on their own fail to do so. And this applies whether the tool is implemented by a national, regional or local public authority. In practice, regulation ends up being an essential policy tool. To make the concept as practical as possible, it may be useful to point to some of the most basic questions it is expected to address when competition is limited:

What is a fair price?

How can a price possibly be fair to all stakeholders?

Should it be based only on the level of costs claimed by the service providers?

Is the cost data reported by the firms the right one to compute the price?

How much margin is there in adjusting quality to influence cost levels and hence prices?

How are prices, subsidies and expected returns connected?

How well are social concerns and externalities accounted for in prices?

---

[5] The same concerns apply if the market is only catered by a few firms able to collude (i.e. if the market structure is an oligopoly), and in that case regulatory rules also need to be designed to make sure that an incumbent or a group of incumbents do not manage to block potential entrants to the market.

How is investment taken into account in short-term regulation?

How much does the nature of consumers and investors matter to the way prices are set?

Should regulation be implemented by the government or by an independent regulator?

Should regulation be local, national or international?

Does the prevalence of corruption in a country influence the answer to these questions?

More generally, is the answer to these questions the same for developed and developing or emerging economies?

By the end of the book, you should have an informed view on how to address each of these essential questions because the economic theory of regulation offers answers, or at least guidance, on how to deal with them. In many cases, there are various ways of answering any of the questions. In each chapter, we summarize the options available to regulators suggested by theory and practice, as well as the limits of our collective knowledge on these issues, and therefore the need for future research.

1.1.6 The Choice of the 'Optimal' Regulation Also Depends on the Institutional Context

The degree of adoption of technical guidelines and rules derived from theory varies significantly according to the specificities of the informational, institutional and political environments in which regulatory interventions have to be designed and implemented. The preferred approach to regulation depends on the extent to which countries trust markets and institutions involved in the design, financing, implementation and enforcement of regulation. When trust among consumers, taxpayers and firms is strong, rule-based regulation tends to prevail over politically driven regulatory decisions. When trust is weak, political solutions tend to prevail over technical rule-based decisions, often deepening the distrust of many stakeholders.

The option to be somewhat flexible with rules may be useful when significant economic shocks such as brutal devaluations, changes in interest rates or social crisis hit a country, making extreme policy reversal such as renationalization less likely. But it also makes the regulatory process much more subject to political interference and sensitive to electoral cycles. For instance, a change in government can lead to price freezes resulting in financing gaps despite commitments to cost recovery made by the previous political administration. This is what happened in 2001 in Argentina, for instance. It led to legal battles between the government and service providers that were sorted out by international arbitration courts, sidelining national regulators and over-ruling previous regulatory commitments.

The dual characterization of countries between rules versus discretion is clearly extreme. Many countries sit somewhere in the middle of the trust ladder and of the scope for discretionary leverage to change rules. Moreover, regulatory preferences can be a moving target as they tend to evolve over time with the political context. But as discussed throughout the book, the risk of abuses resulting from the difficulty of achieving full protection of regulators from undue political interference is serious in any country.[6] When regulators are not independent and free from political pressure, they can indeed be pushed to adjust to changes in political preferences.[7] This is true whether the country is a young, unstable democracy or an old, established one.

Some of the instability of regulation is the result of ideological fads. For instance, less than thirty years ago, when the privatization wave started with the British reforms, nobody focused on the fact that the privatization of a public electricity or railway company could actually mean the acquisition of a national public enterprise by the public enterprise of another country.[8] Hardly anyone really worried about this possibility in the 1990s when Prime Minister John Major cleared the transformation of the sector. In 2019, in a context in which the British population had voted to exit the European Union and the perceived German influence on the region, the fact that Deutsche Bahn (DB), the national German railway company, controls five British rail services (through its Arriva subsidiary acquired by DB in 2010) had become an issue in regulatory discussions.

In addition to the effects of ideological swings on preferences, there are also more technical reasons why countries may differ in their choice of design and practice of regulation. For instance, size matters. Mali's regulatory challenges are quite different from those Brazil has to address. And those Portugal must deal with are quite different from those of the United States, Canada or Australia. In other words, the regulatory needs and constraints of a small market are not the same as those of a much more complex large market in which regions have a lot of autonomy to decide on how they regulate. Market size defines the distribution of regulatory responsibilities across government levels and sometimes across government agencies within the same government level. Market size defines the margin a country has to attract domestic and international private financing. It also often impacts the level and composition of demand. Differences in income levels may explain differences in the willingness to pay versus the ability to pay and demand different regulatory designs. Circumstances and context clearly matter too, as illustrated throughout the book. But before getting into the technical details of what can be learned from economic theory and policy

---

[6] Full independence does not mean that regulators are not subject to audits and accountability. The design of regulatory institutions is discussed in detail in Chapter 14.

[7] Not all changes are politically driven. The fast-changing digitalization of many regulated industries is leading some regulators, notably in the transport sector, to consider adaptive regulation. The evolution of the legislation adopted by various countries to frame the use of autonomous public transport vehicles is anchored in 'soft laws' designed to make the adaptation of rules easy enough to match the fast-evolving technologies. These soft laws are more flexible than the stricter approaches used in technologically more stable environments. They also allow the industries and the regulators to converge towards realistic and fair regulatory standards in a much more transparent way.

[8] See Clifton et al. (2006, 2016) for a detailed discussion of this phenomenon in Europe.

practice, it is useful to set the stage in broad terms.[9] That is the main purpose of this first chapter.

To complement the intuitive discussion, we provide some basic statistical information on the relative and absolute economic importance of infrastructure industries to show how large the stakes are in terms of affordability, investment needs and associated costs across the world. Next, we summarize the main case for regulation made in the economic literature. This is followed by a first discussion of the continuous gap between the theory and practice of regulation and the need to reconcile the two more systematically to account for a more realistic sense of what regulation can and should deliver. The need for more pragmatism in the development of theories and a faster adjustment capacity is reinforced by a brief discussion of the evolution of the context in which regulation is expected to deliver, suggesting that theory continues to lag behind rather than lead real-world discussion on some key issues. The chapter concludes with an overall presentation of the content of the book and a discussion of how it can be used in different ways by the diversified audiences interested in regulation.

1.2 Some Basic Statistical Evidence on the Importance of Regulated Services

One of the main challenges for the design of regulatory policy is the need to work with partial or incomplete data on the various economic characteristics of the sector. It is, indeed, often only when frequency and duration of traffic jams explode, when a bridge collapses or when there is a significant power outage that additional audits are conducted to collect the data that would have helped identify the risks of technical failure well ahead of the incident. Despite these limitations, there is enough data collected by national governments and international organizations to demonstrate that the services provided by regulated industries are economically, socially and politically important. For instance, we know how much consumers spend on infrastructure services – that is, the sum of expenditures on electricity and gas, information and communications technologies (ICT), transport (including ownership of vehicles, their use and the use of public and private transportation) and water and sanitation (W&S) services. We also have a good sense of how much countries actually invest against how much they need to invest in these activities to sustain growth and meet demand. Any of these indicators illustrates the importance of these services and can be used to highlight the role of regulation in the effective delivery of public services. In what follows we focus on household infrastructure expenditures and investment in the sector.

---

[9] While this book takes an economics perspective on regulation, the legal public sector management and political perspectives are just as important. They will only be addressed in this book when they point to dimensions ignored by economists in their assessments. For useful sources to give a better sense of these approaches, see, for instance, Baldwin et al. (2012), den Hertog (2012), Gomez-Ibanez (2006), Levi-Faur (2011) or Lodge and Wegrich (2012).

1.2.1   How Much Do We Spend on Infrastructure as Consumers?

This is an important question, as how much we spend on a regulated service is one of
the core indicators used to assess the extent to which regulation accounts for social
concerns. It turns out that we all spend a lot on these regulated services and that some
income classes end up spending a lot more than others in relative terms, as will be
discussed in detail in Chapter 9.

In 2017, on average, depending on where we lived, between 16% and 26% of our
total consumption expenditures went to pay for infrastructure.[10] For developed economies, the differences across countries varied from around 16% for Australians on
average to around 25% for American and European households. Canadians were
closer to Europeans at about 22%. For developing, emerging and transition economies, the range was somewhat narrower than for developed economies. The average
household spend on all infrastructure services was between 16.3% in South Asia and
21.7% in Latin America.

For a vast majority of families, this is a significant share to allocate to services that
are hard to compress, in particular for the middle- and lower-income classes. This is
also a big part of the reason why these services are so politically sensitive at all stages
of development. To make this relevance as concrete as possible, think of what it would
mean if the costs of these services were cut by, say, 10–20% because regulation
managed to make the service providers become more efficient. It would be equivalent
to an increase in the total purchasing power of families of 1.5–5%. This is significant
and can come from various sources, ranging from improvements in the management
of regulated companies leading to cuts in operational costs to the adoption of cheaper
technologies. Chapter 10 will show that the equity payoffs of these efficiency gains
can make a difference to the political viability of regulatory reforms, but this requires a
design of regulation which ensures that the gains are shared fairly. The basic data on
expenditure shares allocated to regulated services suggests that the efficiency–equity
trade-off should be a core focus of the design of regulation at all stages
of development.

To get a more precise sense of the relative importance of these trade-offs across
sectors, it is useful to take a look at the disaggregated expenditure data. Once again,
the most obvious observation is the strong heterogeneity across countries and regions.
Nevertheless, it is on transport (including all expenditures linked to vehicle ownership) that people spend the most. In developing, emerging and transition economies,
on average, in 2017, households spent from 6.7% of their income in South Asia to
12% in Latin America on this sector. Energy absorbed from 4.5% of the household
expenditure in Sub-Saharan Africa (SSA) to 6.9% in Eastern Europe. ICT expenditures vary from 3.2% in Sub-Saharan Africa to 4.4% in Eastern Europe. Finally,
W&S absorbs from 0.4% of income in South Asia to 1.5% in the Middle East.

---

[10] The data for Organisation for Economic Co-operation and Development countries is from the OECD
website on household expenditures and the data for developing and emerging economies is from the
World Bank household expenditure website. All of the data is for the year 2017.

Table 1.1 Order of magnitude of share of total household expenditures in infrastructure services

	Total infrastructure (%)	Electricity and gas (%)	ICT (%)	Water & sanitation (%)	Transport (%)
Developed economies	16.2–26.5	2–7.5	2.2–4	1.2–4	10–11
Developing and emerging economies	15–25	4.5–6.9	3.2–4.4	0.4–1.5	6.7–12

Source: Authors' compilation from various sources.

In developed economies, the patterns were somewhat different. As in the rest of the world, transport dominates with on average 10–11% of household expenditure but the share spent on energy is also quite significant. In Europe, for instance, it stands on average at 7.5%. And the share spent on W&S in this region is also much larger at about 4%. At 3–4%, Europeans' expenditure on ICT is closer to the figures noted in poorer regions. Australia is somewhat of an outlier since its households spend on average only about 1.2% of their disposable income on W&S, 2% on energy and 2.2% on ICT (it is in the average range for transport at 10.2%).[11]

Table 1.1 summarizes these figures to make the comparison across country groups and sectors easier. If the shares noted in developed economies serve as a leading indicator of what is the likely evolution of expenditures in developing and emerging economies, the demand for energy and water should be expected to grow the most. This is consistent with the evolution of demand resulting from the fast-emerging middle class in these regions. This is not a minor concern in practice since both are central to the debates on the environmental sustainability of growth.

Regulation is not neutral to the evolution of these shares and what they imply for the environmental sustainability of household infrastructure consumption. The expected evolution means that the regulatory pressure is likely to have to adapt, and possibly increase, as demand management becomes a necessity, unless new resources and technology solve the problem. For now, the most likely scenario is that demand is going to be rationed unless regulators come up with politically sustainable ways of managing it. In Europe, the European Commission has been pushing for a national regulator to take on the challenge. In all cases, regulated prices (including subsidies) and the definition of harmonized standards will be central to the solution but there is evidence that not all countries will adapt at the same speed. In the USA, states differ in the pace at which they adapt, mainly based on local needs. For instance, California has a long tradition of being ahead of other states in testing and mainstreaming regulatory innovations to improve the sustainability of water and energy consumption, simply because these resources are scarce locally. States with more abundant resources are less keen on using regulation for conservation and optimal rationing.

---

[11] UNSW City Futures Research Centre (2019).

Overall, while the data reviewed so far is useful to highlight the social and political relevance of regulation, it ignores some of the other concerns that regulators must address. One of these is the impact of regulatory decisions on investment levels. It is frequently the case that the apparently high costs stated by regulated firms hide higher profit margins allowed by creative cost accounting and corporate financing practices. This implies that getting a firm, public or private, to cut costs is equivalent to cutting its profits. If, in the process, the efficiency gains demanded by regulators cut too much into these profits, its incentive to invest or its ability to do so may also decrease. Unless this can be compensated by subsidies, service coverage and quality may drop. This is why it is also important to track the evolution of investment, subsidized or not.

1.2.2   How Much Do Countries Invest in Infrastructure and How Much Should They Spend?

Tracking investment is needed to assess the extent to which there is a fair regulatory treatment of current and future generations of consumers. Regulatory decisions designed to protect the weakest users in the short run may not always have the intended consequences in the long run. This can be avoided in the design of regulation. For now, however, the investment data available at the global level suggests that there is a regulatory failure. Investment in many regulated industries is lagging demand in most countries of the world. This lag tends to penalize the poor in the short run and all users in the longer run.

Consider the case of infrastructure investment.[12] Since the mid-2000s, a large number of estimations conducted by consulting firms and multilateral organizations such as the World Bank and the regional development banks suggests that investment levels have ranged from less than 1% of GDP in some of the most developed economies to 10% in some of the developing countries with the lowest initial infrastructure asset stocks or with the strongest commitment to develop their capacity (notably China). The levels for most developing countries are actually much lower: their infrastructure investments are estimated at about 4% of GDP on average. In most cases, these figures are well below what is needed to meet the demand for these services that is expected to come from economic growth. These needs are summarized in Table 1.2. The growing middle class in developing and emerging economies may not get what it wants even if it is willing to pay for it. This is why it is important to make sure that the incentives to invest to meet the growing willingness to pay are one of the mandates assigned to regulation.

The regulatory challenge is not minor. According to the World Economic Forum, if investment trends follow the current paths, the world is expected to face a US$15 trillion gap in infrastructure investment by 2040.[13] That is close to 20% of the world's GDP in 2018 to be spread over a twenty-year period, with much higher gaps in the

---

[12] For a review of the evidence on the social rate of return of investment in infrastructure see Pender and Torero (2018)

[13] www.weforum.org/agenda/2019/04/infrastructure-gap-heres-how-to-solve-it/

Table 1.2 Annual investment needs per sector and country group between 2020 and 2035 (ranges as share of GDP)

	Total infrastructure (%)	Electricity (%)	ICT (%)	Water & sanitation (%)	Transport (%)
Developed economies	3–7.5	1–2.5	0.5–1	0.5–1.5	1–2.5
Developing and emerging economies	7–12	3–4	0.5–1.5	1–1.5	2.5–5

Source: Authors' compilation from various sources.

figures for developing regions than for OECD countries. But this does not mean regulators in the OECD should not worry about investment. Many OECD countries are relying on outdated water pipelines, excessively polluting energy sources and transport networks biased against shared mobility. For now, they are also rationing investment and hence future consumption of these services. In most countries, governments tend to underestimate the importance of the costs of operating and maintaining the assets. Without maintenance, services will usually fail to match the level promised at the time the investment was made. And in some cases, the consequences can be quite dramatic, including killing people, as when trains derail, flood walls break or bridges collapse.[14] When prices are too low, maintenance falls, as discussed in Chapter 9. In many countries, the maintenance budget should be as high as the investment budget on an annual basis if service standards are to be met.

This insufficient investment and maintenance performance at the global level, and across country types, illustrates how decisions tend to be biased towards the short run rather than the long run. And this has an impact on regulatory preferences. Political preferences focus attention on the price level of public services and/or on the subsidies going to the sector, instead of focusing on the need to increase revenue to pay for investment. Such short-term preferences can translate into indiscriminate efforts to cut costs. This is also politically attractive since the consequences of poor maintenance tend to have to be addressed much later, possibly by other political administrations. From a technical viewpoint, the bias also reflects an underestimation by many regulators of the scope to rely on creative pricing, and subsidy design options, to deliver pricing strategies that are both politically and financially sustainable. These options are quite well established in the academic literature and some countries have been open to adopting them, as discussed in Chapters 7 and 8.

Without a regulatory mandate to push firms (whether public or private) to make the right investment decisions and regulatory decisions that ensure the proper financing of investments, neither public nor private firms are likely to make them. This is particularly damaging in countries where the poorest are excluded from service due to the

---

[14] The collapse of a bridge linking the east and west of the city of Genoa in Italy killed forty-three people in August 2018. All the evidence points to a long-term lack of maintenance by the private company contracted for it. The emerging legal battles turn around the human cost of financial savings intended to increase profit margins.

lack of investment, as illustrated by the low access rates in low-income countries. For now, while high-income countries enjoy access rates close to 100% for electricity and for W&S, SSA stands at less than 40% for electricity, 68% for water and 30% for sanitation. And it is the wealthier households that have access to the public utilities services. On some dimensions, the poor regions of rich countries are just as bad as some of the poorer countries. For instance, access to safe sanitation is a problem for every one of the poorest regions of the world, including within Europe.

In developing countries, these gaps mean that when international organizations make the case for investment increases, they are pushing for regulatory fairness in the treatment of all citizens. But the call for change has not been having much impact in national political circles. Many governments are keen to promise change, but few are taking the investment and regulatory decisions that will make a sustained difference in a wide range of regulated industries. This is why the case for market-based financing solutions continues to be popular. While the evidence shows that hardly more than 10% of the needs are eventually financed by private sources, the promise and the partial efforts buy time and reduce the need to wait for fiscal support.

A similar conclusion could be reached from a diagnostic of the actual financing of the significant investment needed to implement the energy transition in most OECD countries. As of 2019, for instance, few countries had voted in climate change laws that would trigger adjustments in the regulation of the sector in a structured way, accounting for the needs of both future generations and today's poor. The regulatory tools are there, as will be shown throughout the book. This lack of action often reflects strong political constraints. For instance, the attempt by the French government in 2018 to increase the price of petrol and diesel in order to reduce its use and fight global warming (and collect new taxes) was met by strong popular opposition, in the form of the 'Gilets Jaunes' (yellow jackets) movement. Trying to internalize the welfare of future generations is a tricky business if it means reducing the welfare of today voters.

1.2.3   What Does This Data Mean for Regulation?

The data on only two of the indicators of interest in the evaluation of regulatory policy effectiveness suffices to argue that there is a case for various improvements in the practice of regulation. First, markets need more and better regulatory incentives to invest, as will be analysed in Chapter 11. The massive sectoral restructuring implemented over the last three decades throughout the world, including deregulation and privatization reforms, has failed to deliver the right incentives to invest. The private sector is not going to fill the investment void, especially in poor countries. Public money will continue to be needed in most regulated sectors and in particular in the poorest countries. Second, social concerns need to be dealt with more cautiously. In most countries of the world, where these services are actually delivered they represent such a significant share of expenditures that there is a case for regulators to track the evolution of affordability more systematically. This should also be on the agenda of regulators, as discussed in more detail in Chapter 9. Yet as we shall see, these concerns have often failed to attract the attention they deserve, in theory as well as in policy circles. As discussed next, short-run (static) efficiency concerns tend to dominate research in regulated industries, even if the growing case for environmental concerns is producing a fast-growing volume of research on their investment implications.[15]

1.3   Efficiency at the Core of the Main Academic Economic Case for Regulation

In the academic economic literature, the inefficiency risks associated with monopolies, and highly concentrated market structures, largely drive the case for regulation of public services. At the very broad level, this literature identifies two main policy concerns. The first is linked to the choice of technology to make the most of the size of the market to be catered to. The second is related to the need to mitigate the risks of abusive exercise of market power allowed by the differences in access to information by the various stakeholders. The producers of these services tend to have the upper hand in their interactions with consumers and regulators. This is because they have access to more and/or better information on the supply and demand characteristics of many of the markets that are delivering public services, as discussed at some length in the book.

The 'size argument' is the oldest one in the academic and policy literature. When there are significant scale and scope economies to be captured in the production and delivery of the service, it is efficient to allow a monopoly to take over the market rather than relying on competition. In other words, it makes sense to adopt an integrated production and service delivery structure as long as it is more efficient for one firm to produce the public service(s) than two or more firms.[16] And this is supported by the evidence available on the empirical assessments of scale and scope economies across the regulated sectors.

For the water sector, for instance, Saal et al. (2013) surveyed about twenty years of empirical studies measuring scale economies and validated the case for a significant degree of vertical or horizontal integration. They found solid evidence of vertical scope economies between upstream water production and distribution. They also

---

[15] To see this, check the tables of contents of the main academic publications focusing on regulated industries in the last five to ten years (i.e. *International Journal of Industrial Organization, Journal of Regulatory Economics*, the *Review of Industrial Organization*, the *Review of Network Economics* or *Utilities Policy*). Most of the papers focus on efficiency and it is only occasionally that equity or financial/fiscal sustainability are the main topic of a published paper. For empirical papers, this can be explained by the poor coverage of poverty-related data in databases of interest to regulated industries. For theoretical papers, it could be considered as an indicator revealing the dominant research preferences of the profession.

[16] This does not mean that the authorities have to give up on competition, since when competition *in* the market fails, competition *for* the market offers an alternative. This competition is usually anchored in auctions designed to allow the potential future monopolist to reveal as much as possible on their willingness and capacity to cut costs as part of their bidding. But this should best be discussed as part of a review of auction theory or procurement theory, which would go beyond the scope of this book.

found evidence of scale economies, although only up to certain output level. Abbott and Cohen (2017) reached equivalent conclusions from a survey of the railway industry. Cost efficiency gains from vertical integration tend to be more common than losses but depend on predictable factors, including the range of services provided (e.g. passengers versus freight) and the intensity of track use. And for the electricity sector, the survey by Meyer (2012a) suggested that the switch from vertically integrated firms prevailing in the sector prior to the reforms of the 1980s–2000 to more complex market structures with unbundled services (in the hope of making the most of competitive options in the sector) did not improve efficiency enough to offset the losses of coordination gains from vertical integration. For the United States, for instance, Meyer (2012b) estimated the cost increase from an unbundling of generation to be between 19% and 26%, 8% and 10% for separation of generation and transmission, and 4% for the separation of transmission alone. For Europe, Gugler et al. (2017) estimated the added costs associated with vertical unbundling of the sector at around 14% for the medium-sized utilities and over 20% for large ones.

At first sight, this research shows that the initial case for reforms designed to unbundle large, vertically integrated monopolies underestimated the payoffs to intra-firm coordination and overestimated the gains from competition. One of the reasons why the empirical results are biased against unbundling is that reformers underestimated the importance of regulation. The level and quality of regulation both matter in practice and drive the optimal choice of an organizational form. Failure to assess the ability of a country to implement a specific form of regulation determines the quantity and quality of services, as discussed at length in Chapter 14.

To tease your curiosity, consider the evidence accumulated since the mid-1990s for a wide range of countries and sectors on how the efficiency gains achieved through reform were passed on to users. Despite the common focus of the narrative on reforms highlighting efficiency gains, there is significant evidence that, when the opportunities for competition were realistic and unbundling the historical monopolies was desirable but demanded residual regulation, the regulatory models adopted by most countries failed in various ways to ensure that firms delivered the potential efficiency gains or at least passed them on to consumers through lower prices. The residual market power achieved by the many monopolies serving local, regional and national markets often continues to be excessive and many of these firms still manage to capture most of the efficiency gains achieved by the reforms.[17] The point is that the case for regulation is as strong under a vertically integrated monopoly as it is in a structure in which residual local, regional and national monopolies continue to enjoy market power that can lead to efficiency losses. The scope for market power by a monopoly is thus still the main

[17] In many instances, some of the gains were also captured by the fiscal authorities. In Latin America, for instance, the significant cost reductions achieved from the restructuring of the sectors were shared by firms and tax authorities, which increased tax rates of these services or introduced new taxes, often local, as in the case of regulated telecoms services, or regional, as in the case of electricity services. In some ways, this implies that taxpayers also gained from reforms, although in many countries some of the tax revenue had to be used to compensate for the increase in unemployment resulting from the reforms, since a large share of the efficiency gains were achieved by staff reductions (e.g. Estache et al. 2004).

reason why regulation is needed and the evidence suggests that this necessity is hard to overestimate.

The second major justification of regulation by academic research emerged in the late 1980s. It also focuses on efficiency. It became 'academically mainstream' with the Laffont and Tirole (1993) textbook that synthesized research produced since the early 1980s on the risks of efficiency losses due to information asymmetries. As mentioned earlier, firms know their costs and clients better than anyone else (including the regulator). The only other agent that may know almost as much as an incumbent may be another firm operating in a comparable market. Unless regulators intervene, there is little reason for a monopoly to reveal enough information to check if there are abuses leading to inefficiencies in the production decisions. This is why many regulators spend significant resources trying to approximate the cost and consumption information they need to make fair assessments of the regulated market. In most cases, these efforts are insufficient to obtain detailed data, but they are usually good enough to allow regulators to develop processes to shift the burden of proof for relevant information onto the regulated firm.[18]

The effectiveness of these regulatory processes drives the extent to which the market will fail and abuses take place. Most of these processes are associated with insights that can be credited to the continuous (economic) academic push for the need to recognize that access to information matters in many ways, none of them simple. Since the breakthrough started by Laffont and Tirole (1993), many other excellent surveys or textbooks have contributed to the dissemination of the theoretical insights as these were improving, including Train (1991), Armstrong et al. (1994), Newbery (2000), Crew and Kleindorfer (2012), Vogelsang (2002), Crew and Parker (2006), Armstrong and Sappington (2007), Joskow (2007), Robinson (2007), Sherman (2008), Baldwin et al. (2012), Decker (2014), Rose (2014), Tirole (2015), and Viscusi et al. (2018 in its fifth edition).[19] Until Jean Tirole, of the Toulouse School of Economics in France, was awarded the 2014 Nobel Prize in Economics for his work on regulation, most of the insights summarized by these textbooks were largely reserved to technical specialists of regulation. The Nobel prize awarded to Tirole managed to increase the profile of research in the field and the transparency of some of

---

[18] The Australian regulators may be among the most effective at doing this data digging. But more importantly, they are amazingly transparent about their processes and the background work done to inform their decisions. For more details, see the Australian Consumer and Competition Commission or ACCC (www.accc.gov.au/). It is an exceptionally useful resource. Tracking the evolution of their perspectives provides a window on the historical evolution of the approaches to regulation in OECD countries. It includes a series of punchy, well-informed publications clearly interested in making sure that regulatory decisions in Australia are anchored in frontier knowledge in theory and in practice. For developing countries, the World Bank Public–Private Infrastructure Advisory Facility (PPIAF) is doing an equivalent job in collaboration with the University of Florida.

[19] We do not list here the sector-specific books that also deal with regulation, but Finger and Jaag (2016) or Florio (2013a) would be good sources as they discuss or illustrate in specific chapters the sector-specific relevance of regulatory issues. They focus on developed economies, however. As much as possible, we provide illustrations throughout the book which show that many of the concepts and their implications are also relevant in developing and emerging economies.

the various perspectives on the topic.[20] These provide most of the material covered in Chapters 2–6.

This early research has focused on the many ways in which information asymmetries can distort the supply, pricing and investment decisions as well as demand in regulated markets. A quick look at the tables of contents of the various textbooks covering the topic shows that there has been less interest in financial viability or increased accountability generated by regulatory solutions to the initial information gaps. And there has been even less interest in the distributional effects and political viability of regulatory solutions. Yet, as the world is finding it hard to recover from the series of global crises that started in 2008, these concerns have risen to the top of the policy and political agenda in many countries. Politics needs economics to deliver more ideas to address some of the negative distributional effects of public services reforms that have been much more clearly exposed in the post-crisis years, as discussed in Chapter 9.

1.4   When Politics Meets Standard Regulatory Economics Equity Shows Up

While mainstream regulatory economics emphasizes efficiency, political speeches tend to focus more on equity. In many countries, the promise of freezing, or at least capping, the price of electricity has become a standard campaign promise (e.g. the promise was made by all left-leaning parties in the 2019 Belgian parliamentary election). A cynical interpretation is that this is because equity buys more votes than efficiency. A gentler, fairer perspective would argue that accounting for the social effects of regulation makes regulatory pricing decisions more politically and ethically acceptable. This makes them easier to implement and sustain. In practice, these dimensions are thus more important to consider than often recognized by economic academic and policy research.[21]

Some are likely to argue that poverty and equity concerns are seldom accounted for in regulation because they are best addressed through well-targeted subsidies to be included in the fiscal policy agenda. Allowing price regulation to focus on efficiency would thus be reasonable: two tools for two goals. As we shall see in Chapter 9, this is not a realistic perspective in a world in which fiscal constraints are often too binding to address the social mandates. Yet these mandates are important for the viability of reforms aimed at improving both efficiency and equity.

Besides these differences in perspective in the proper use of policy instruments to achieve two goals, there is a second important reason why academic research may not have dealt well enough with poverty concerns. This is linked to the increasing role of

---

[20] Tirole (2017) himself contributed significantly to the efforts to increase the very concrete relevance of this research in a book aimed at non-specialist audiences.

[21] This is even if they can lead to undesirable side effects. For instance, lower energy prices do not favour reductions in consumption of energy produced by highly polluting sources. Somehow the environmental effects of social policies are seldom considered by politicians and only poorly documented by regulators.

ideology in the definition of regulatory preferences. It is not easy to deal with these concerns because ideology changes often turn policy goals into moving targets. Consider, for instance, the evolution of perceptions on the desirability of privatizing public enterprises or nationalizing private ones.

From the early 1980s to the mid-2000s, the main assumption was that private providers would be able to do anything better than public providers. And this included the assumption that they would do better at meeting the needs of the poor, for instance.[22] To allow private firms to make the most out of their potential, politicians, supported by many economists, started to argue that deregulation was essential.

This narrative was built on two main ideas. First, technology would make it easier to maximize the opportunities to increase competition and limit the role of residual monopolies to the activities for which competition is not a cost-effective option for users or taxpayers, or an efficient one from a technical perspective. Second, the long record of failures by public enterprises provided enough case studies to fuel a growing global mistrust in public authorities. Government failures were seen as riskier than market failures and this stimulated a global effort to try to limit the role of the public authorities to a supervisory role. This role would be split between independent regulatory and anti-trust agencies whenever possible. Self-regulation of large public utilities was no longer politically easy to sell (even if, as discussed in Chapter 14, politicians have been quite good at continuous interference with the independence of the agencies).

But there has also been an evolution since the late 1990s. Over time, the relative importance of anti-trust has increased and in many countries the role of regulators has become more focused on narrower residual monopolistic activities and the coordination of activities with other national regulators on well-targeted matters (e.g. the definition of access rules and prices for common facilities). In many of the poorer countries, the regulator's role has been limited to the supervision of network industries while local alternative technologies have been left to local communities or to agencies concerned with rural needs.[23]

During that period, regulation has also evolved because of the increased scope for trade-in-services, including traditionally regulated services. This increased the need to consider supranational regulation as an option to minimize the risks of national distortions of investment opportunities that can cut costs. The debate is not settled as many countries are fighting to maintain full sovereignty and secure access to basic

---

[22] The term 'privatization' has been overstretched in many discussions. As discussed by Bortolotti and Faccio (2009) or Florio (2013a, 2014), reforms counted as privatizations were either (i) a simple change in legal status (the mandate of public firms was refocused to allow them to be 'commercialized') or (ii) a limited transfer of ownership to private partners, with the public sector maintaining control of the board through a majority share or a de facto veto right on key business decisions. This control has, however, been increasingly difficult as the leverage of new private partners has increased since the early 2010s, as discussed in Chapters 7 and 15.

[23] Torero (2015) provides an insightful discussion of the multiple dimensions to consider when developing rural electrification strategies. Many of the issues raised are typically underestimated when designing electricity regulation.

services in a world of increasing political instability. This is one of the cases made by pro-Brexit advocates.

The tide may now be turning, as seen in recent reports and decisions in Europe since the late 2010s. Consider the United Kingdom. This is the country that launched the ideological preference for market-oriented solutions to any market failure in the late 1970s and served as a model around the world in the following thirty or so years. In 2018, its National Audit Office, an independent but official watchdog, released a report providing evidence of the lack of credibility of the assumption that market-based solutions will do better than public solutions (National Audit Office 2018). This was then followed within a few months by an equivalent assessment by the European Court of Auditors (2018). Since in many ways the dominating ideology tends to influence the research agenda, it is likely that research on how to make public enterprises more effective and how to tackle equity concerns will start benefiting from new research on a systematic basis.[24]

A third, subtler, way in which political perspectives are now influencing econo-mists is in communication strategy. Across political parties the communication of regulatory preferences benefits from careful narratives building on selected examples and anecdotes rather than robust empirical and technical assessments. In many ways, these communications strategies have fuelled ideological cycles regarding the way regulation has to be assessed, designed and implemented.

For many audiences, the political marketing is much more effective than the very technical approach adopted by many regulatory experts. Case studies and anecdotes are indeed useful and the literature disseminated by international organizations offers many of these to illustrate technical insights. The 'best-practice' approach helps 'non-technical' readers get a much more concrete and intuitive sense of the challenges than many econometric and other complex technical studies favoured by the economic academic literature. This is why, throughout this book, and despite a clear technical bias in the presentation of theoretical results, we rely on examples to set up the technical discussions. We try to leave the most complex technical insights to footnotes and boxes, which may only be useful to readers as interested in theoretical develop-ments as in the policy-oriented arguments of the book. For the sake of completeness, we also provide many references to the academic literature to ensure that the intuition provided by case studies and anecdotes is complemented by more robust statistical evidence.[25]

---

[24] See Clifton et al. (2019) for a useful short discussion of the renationalization of public services, in particular local public services, and the interpretation of what appears to be quite a widespread phenomenon for some services.

[25] Despite their usefulness in terms of communications, anecdotes and case studies often fail to give a full sense of the actual technical and political complexity of a problem. Unless there are multiple coherent and robust approaches pointing in the same direction, doubt is allowed. This is basically what the Condorcet Jury implies for the many situations in which only partial evidence is available. The Condorcet Jury states that majorities are more likely than any single individual to select the 'better' of two alternatives when there exists uncertainty about which of the two alternatives is in fact preferred. For a conceptual presentation in the political context, see Austen-Smith and Banks (1996).

1.5   When Theory Meets Practice

As for most policy areas, the practice of regulation is typically more complex than its conceptualization. It involves a number of predictable challenges that need to be considered before jumping from theory to actual regulatory decisions. Some are technical and require the measurement of specific dimensions, including the efficiency levels and their changes since they need to be shared in theory between producers, users and taxpayers. Many other financial and social indicators are also needed to be able to decide on trade-offs between the social, financial and political goals imposed on regulators. This quantification seldom takes place at the required level of detail. According to the OECD (2019), in 2017 only three of the twenty-eight member countries of the European Union had the obligation to quantify the costs and benefits of new regulations.[26] As we shall see, the skills demonstrated by regulators to conduct these assessments vary a lot across countries and sectors, but this in itself is an essential insight.

This matters because a fair share of the regulatory failures can be traced back to the underestimation of the relevance of the differences in institutional capacity across countries and/or sectors.[27] These differences are too often ignored by mainstream approaches to regulation, resulting in sometimes misleading standardized policy recommendations. This is also something we try to address in the book, in Chapter 14. For instance, regulation in a corrupt country should not be modelled on regulation in a country in which all economic actors comply with laws and regulations. The British system is unlikely to work in Tanzania, Mongolia or Paraguay. Academic research is getting better in its ability to account for these institutional differences and is much better than it was twenty years ago. But we still have a long way to go in our understanding.

A third challenge is the need to actually account for processes and managing the time it takes to get things done much more seriously than is often the case in economic publications.[28] Processes have not really made it into mainstream economic regulation textbooks, yet they are one of the key reasons why things get done slowly in regulation. For instance, firms and regulators need to agree on the method to be used to estimate efficiency levels. They need to agree on the terms of the interactions of the

---

[26] OECD (2019) includes a chapter reviewing the practice of Regulatory Impact Assessments (RIAs) in Europe. RIAs are used in many OECD countries to organize the assessment of the positive and negative effects of proposed and existing regulations. They are supposed to be evidence-based but in practice they focus on compliance with processes. They are also often perceived as too sensitive to methodologies and assumptions that are not tested. Carrigan and Shapiro (2017) argue that they sometimes appear to be 'used to justify decisions already made, rather than to inform those decisions'. Despite these limitations, they are important to highlight administrative and legal aspects. From an economic policy perspective, they do not allow an assessment of the relative importance of trade-offs between the various policy goals in quantitative terms.

[27] See Deller and Waddams (2015) for a discussion of European experiences and Estache and Wren-Lewis (2010) for a survey of the evidence in developing countries.

[28] See Estache and Martimort (2000) for an early survey covering all key types of processes in the context of infrastructure regulation.

firms with financial markets (e.g. should leverage be controlled, should dividends be controlled?). All these interactions need to follow due diligence and it may take from six months to two years depending on the complexity of the situation. During that period, many things can happen. This also needs to be accounted for in the design of processes.

Another reason why these processes can be slow and complex is that they often involve multiple government units. The degree of complexity of the interactions between these units makes a difference to the optimal choice of regulation. This choice needs to account for an extremely broad set of dimensions, such as the distribution of regulatory rights among these units, including at different levels of the government, the specific objectives assigned to each unit, the timing and sequencing of the various steps demanded by a regulatory intervention, the voting procedures used to pick managers, the duration and scope of control of different regulatory bodies, and the design of the communication channels within the regulatory hierarchy.[29] A failure to address these influences is bound to over- or underestimate the effective impact of incentive-based regulation on regulatory outcomes.

While we will not deal in detail with all the day-to-day constraints of regulation, we will remind you of their relevance. Unless these constraints are accounted for, the odds of regulatory failures increase. There are disagreements between the various research fields on their degree of importance but, in many cases, keeping processes as simple as possible is a good strategy. The more complex they are, the more likely it is that those with the most resources will grasp an unfair share of the efficiency gains. This might work to their benefit for a while, but not when it becomes an identified pattern. And this brings us back to the need to consider the political viability of regulatory decisions as much as their short-term and long-term efficiency impacts.

1.6   Is Academic Research Lagging or Leading Regulatory Practice?

Until the 1990s, it could be argued that regulatory practice was lagging theory. Most regulators were focusing on controlling the rate of return on assets. They largely took costs, including investment costs, stated by regulated firms for granted, which means that incentives for regulated firms to improve their efficiency levels were not really included in the design of regulation, even if efficiency losses were a central focus in academic research on regulated industries. Since then, efficiency has also risen to the top of the regulatory agenda in practice. The ideological switch pushing policymakers to trust markets more than governments explains the trend towards deregulatory policies that continues to prevail in many countries and among many international organizations. In many ways, this ideological commitment could be credited or blamed (depending on your personal ideological perspective) for the systematic efforts

---

[29] Researchers focusing on transactions costs have also emphasized these dimensions, see for instance Spiller (2010, 2011).

to limit the scope for regulation to infringe on individual freedoms and on business freedom.

But ideology has not only changed regulation; it has also changed the perception of what is needed in regulation. After the reign of overactive public enterprises since World War II, politicians with strong ideological convictions on the superiority of the private sector persuaded the OECD countries first, and some of the emerging countries next, to switch to the reign of the all-powerful private enterprise as a provider of public services. But ideology was not the only driver of the change. The demand for regulation and the nature of this demand also changed because of other factors that should not be underestimated. And some of these changes also influenced academic research.

The three main sources of change that have contributed to transform the theory and practice of regulation are:

(1) A technological revolution.
(2) A financial sector regulation revolution.
(3) The globalization revolution.

1.6.1   On the Technological Revolution

Technology matters to regulated industries as much as it matters to any industry. But the various public services are highly heterogeneous in their ability to benefit from technological innovation. The telecoms sector is a clear leading outlier (consider the growing number of things you can do with your smartphone that nobody could have imagined in the mid-1990s). Mobile technology has been disruptive. It allows providers to operate on a much smaller scale than with fixed lines. It has justified the deregulation of the sector and the move towards regulated competition, generally overseen by antitrust authorities. The deregulation 'example' of telecoms has sometimes been used to justify deregulation in other public utilities. Yet some of them did not experience significant innovations, not to mention disruptive ones. For example, at the other extreme of the innovation spectrum, the W&S sector is a clear laggard despite major improvements in desalination and data management techniques. It is not too surprising that the public utilities that did not benefit much from technological progress are still the responsibility of state-owned enterprises (SOEs) in many countries, especially in developing ones. For electricity distribution, the share of countries with a public enterprise in charge was 62% in 2017 (Küfeoğlu et al. 2018)). In the W&S sector in 2018, in a sample of 174 countries, 55% did not have any significant private participation in the ownership of their main utilities and only 22% had managed to get at least some private investment when they had agreed to some form of public–private partnership (Bertomeu-Sanchez and Estache 2019). In many of those with private participation, the contract was signed at a city level rather than at the national level, suggesting that the relative importance of large-scale public operators in a given country is actually much greater than 55%. For developing countries, the domination of SOEs is even clearer. In a panel covering 1990–2002 and collected by

Gassner et al. (2009), it was found that only 15% of the 977 water utilities in their sample were not SOEs.

But focusing on ownership and market structures underestimates the many other, subtler, ways in which innovations have been making a direct difference in the operation and management of all public services.[30] For instance, the digitalization of these sectors is starting to make a big difference and matters just as much to the optimal design of the regulation of public services. The explosion of information (the big data phenomenon) is changing the way providers can optimize their supply as well as the way in which they can practise price discrimination. For instance, ICT improvements have allowed competition in wholesale electricity (electronic auctions), increased the control of flows in all networks and facilitated metering and billing (with smart meters). Many of these changes may result in the questioning of some of the regulatory decisions that were once considered to be best practice, as will be discussed in the last chapter of this book.

Innovation is, however, not the only engine of technological change in these industries. First, technology also changes because preferences change. The most obvious change in preferences, largely driven by consumers in the last 10–15 years, is linked to environmental concerns. The transport and energy transformation are part of that agenda and meeting this evolving demand implies many changes in the optimal design of regulation of the concerned sectors as well. Here also, progress has been slow.

1.6.2   On the Financial Sector Revolution

Changes in both the demand and supply side of the global financial markets have impacted on the way services traditionally operated and financed by the public sector are now being financed and regulated. The financial sector is ultimately where the ideological and technological changes translate into concrete opportunities and challenges for regulated industries and for regulators. This ability to influence the regulated industries keeps evolving and is part of the challenges regulators have not yet been able to internalize, as will be seen in Chapters 7 and 12. This essential role of the financial sector has become possible for at least a couple of clear reasons.

The first is that the deregulation of the financial industry created an explosion of savings and liquidity in the 1990s. This explosion eased somewhat the rationing in financing of a sector in which the investment needs were growing while fiscal support was increasingly binding. And all this happened in an environment in which financial market integration also accelerated. Access to private funds to finance public services has progressively become a credible complement to traditional public financing options for many countries, although not for all countries and not for all types of investments, as will be seen in Chapters 7 and 12. For many, however, there was the

---

[30] Musacchio and Lazzarini (2014) show how well public enterprises compete with private firms with similar strategies and objectives. Florio et al. (2018) find that these firms can behave as any private firm when trying to acquire other firms, focusing on 'shareholder-value maximization' motives.

hope that they would find a way to use this excess supply of savings and liquidity to help close the historical financing gap. At the same time, it gave the financial actors input into the design of regulation, more often informally than formally.[31]

Second, the deregulation of the sector has also unleashed a significant creativity in the production of financing tools, which increased the leverage of the financial actors in negotiations. In the context of infrastructure, this became clear with the development of the use of project finance techniques as part of the financing strategy for investments in regulated industries. The new techniques have been welcomed by many governments, but it has also led to significant regulatory concerns over time. A common one is the increased incentive for cream skimming which reduces the scope for cross-subsidies within a sector.[32] Often the packaging of projects leaves the high-profit-margin operations to the private investors and maintains the high costs and low or negative margins in the hands of the public sector. The extensive use of the technique has also revealed the incompatibility between the short-term return concerns of private investors and the long-term perspective on payoffs from long-lived assets that governments and users tend to focus on. Any disagreement ends up increasing the average price expectations. This is usually reflected in a risk-sensitive cost of capital or in extensive public sector guarantees rebalancing sector costs from users and investors to the taxpayers. It is impossible not to address these issues in some details in this book. And we will do so in a chapter focusing on the interactions between finance and regulation (Chapter 7), but also in the discussion of the additional changes to come resulting from the evolution of the number and types of actors in the financial markets. The growing role of shadow banking is indeed already having an impact, as discussed in the last chapter of this book.

1.6.3   On the Impact of Globalization

Since the end of the cold war countries worldwide have engaged in a substantial restructuring of their economy. Former communist countries implemented massive privatization and deregulation programmes to make the transition from a planned to a market-based economy. To create a fully integrated economic zone, European member states opened all their markets, including their public utilities, to EU competitors, which generally implied deregulating, corporatizing and privatizing several national monopolies. In other OECD countries and in developing and emerging economies, the move towards deregulation and privatization was generally part of a broader agenda of reforms known as the 'Washington Consensus'. As a result of these global structural reforms the role of the State in the sector is now weaker than it was thirty years ago. National governments in many cases lost direct control over essential

---

[31] The contract signed by governments with private operators typically included many of the concerns of the underlying private financing sources. Often, the relevant clauses dramatically constrained the regulatory options, as should become clearer in Chapter 7, where risk allocations are discussed.

[32] Cross-subsidies, as discussed in Chapter 9, can be a useful tool when fiscal constraints are limiting the scope to rely on the often more desirable direct subsidy approach to financing specific needs.

infrastructures and public utilities. In contrast, firms, both national and multinational, and institutional investors such as pension funds, have become key players. It increased the case for a careful look at regulation. In many instances, the effectiveness with which it has been implemented did not meet the expectations of the reformers.

The internationalization of experience also increased the political dimensions of regulation since some of the big international players are also often part of an explicit or implicit industrial policy in their home country. This implies that when they operate outside of their borders they can also count on the political support of their government. One of the outcomes is that regulatory conflicts called for an institutional solution capable of reconciling differences in perspectives on the role of regulation (e.g. how much discretionary power should be granted to regulators implementing general principles against how much to specify in a regulatory contract to limit discretionary powers). International arbitration has been the solution adopted in general. But the solution was also often seen as increasingly politicized.

This has been one of the issues raised in the context of international trade agreement that covers trade-in-services, for instance. The ease with which large global firms could call upon an international court would turn national regulators into minor actors. Consider the debates on concerns for the protection of public services at the centre of some of the tensions between Europe and the United States in the negotiation of the Transatlantic Trade and Investment Partnership (TTIP). The resolution of regulatory conflicts impacting the profitability of regulated industries is one of the sources of divergence. The US and European regulatory traditions in public services are quite different. As of 2016, the official European Commission (EC) position is that, in case of conflict, national rules will prevail and US companies will not be allowed to sue for loss of profit. This is a bit less credible than it seems at first sight, because one of the mechanisms for arbitrating disputes is known as Investor–State Dispute Settlement (ISDS), which essentially, in practice, is a form of international private arbitration. This form of arbitration can overrule many national decisions made by a regulator. That is a political and social problem.[33]

This implies that there is a layer of regulation above national regulation because the TTIP proposals de facto allow an appeal of national decisions to supranational arbitration. This could disempower national regulatory agencies. For anyone familiar with conflicts between governments and private operators and investors in infrastructure services in developing countries, this sounds familiar. In the last twenty-five years, regulators have frequently been overruled by arbitrators, sometimes fairly, sometimes not so fairly. This large number of conflicts illustrates the difficulty of getting regulation right in an environment in which technology and the number and the type of stakeholders keep evolving.

---

[33] To calm the concerns over this possibility, in mid-2015 the European Commission proposed two additional options: a multilateral investment court – e.g. the World Bank's International Centre for Settlement of Investment Disputes (ICSID) and the United Nations Commission on International Trade Law (UNCITRAL) – and a bilateral appeal body with seven judges. The EU suggests that, in case of conflict, investors would be free to select their preferred approach.

1.7   Conceptually, What Are the Sources of These Regulatory Failures?

The failures of any organizational mechanism must be assessed in reference to the objectives assigned to this mechanism. For instance, because market mechanisms are based on egoistic behaviours, they cannot reach the level of production of common goods expected by the members of a community. This market inability is well identified by the economists, for example when they consider environmental concerns. It can be corrected in different ways, all of them requiring the intervention of a public authority, a form of regulation. The regulatory options to solve an environmental crisis associated with a specific firm cover a wide range of actions. The most drastic solution is the nationalization of the faulty industry. A softer one is the allocation of tradable property rights or the introduction of use taxes. Equivalent crises can arise for non-environmental reasons, as will be shown in the book. These include mistargeting support to the poor, underinvesting to meet the needs of future generations or under-supplying a quality standard.

For many reasons that the book will help to identify, none of the regulatory patches suggested by theory or acquired in practice can fully fix the problem. It would thus be tautological to systematically refer to regulatory failures when the regulation cannot fully bridge the gap between the market and the optimal frictionless outcomes. By contrast, the performance of a given regulatory mechanism can be usefully measured relative to the results pledged by its designers. With this benchmark, any discrepancy can be tagged as a failure.

One can imagine testing the performance of a regulatory mechanism in comparison with alternative mechanisms. This definition is not perfect either, since, as we will show repeatedly in the book, regulation is multidimensional and, in most cases, when a mechanism outperforms a rival one in one dimension (say efficiency), it is at the cost of a lower performance in another (say equity). This is why, throughout the book, when we conclude that 'regulation has failed', it should be understood as the failure of a regulatory mechanism to close the gap between its designer's specific public commitments and the measured outcomes. This is, in many ways, also how arbitration courts and auditors tend to assess regulatory failures by a State. They boil down to identifying non-compliance with contractual commitments.

1.8   How Will the Book Cover the Issues?

The big-picture story on the gap between practice and academic research discussed earlier is not representative of the full range of issues that need to be addressed across countries. The wide range of cross-national differences in regulatory and legal preferences explains why there are so many different ways of taking on a similar challenge. Moreover, the practice has also evolved in very different directions around the world. Anglo-Saxon countries (i.e. Australia, Canada, New Zealand and the United Kingdom) and the Nordic countries have adopted regulatory processes and tools signalling a steady commitment to accountability for economic and financial decisions. In most other countries, regulatory decisions often reveal, instead, a preference for ignoring possible trade-offs between short-term political concerns and long-term economic, social and environmental needs when they represent a short-term political risk. These differences are interesting per se, but we cannot deal with all of these in the context of this book.

To limit the coverage, while still doing justice to the diversity of issues revealed by these different experiences, we have decided to focus the book on the *economic* regulatory role of the State. This includes the usual discussion of the incentives to be built into regulation as well as the scope for fine-tuning price level and structure in any of the services. But it also covers subtler dimensions such as the relevance of the choice of market structure for the optimal design of regulation. In addition, the book addresses explicitly the relevance of the financial markets and institutional constraints on the optimal choice of market structure and hence of regulation through their effects on risk perceptions. This is an often underestimated, yet crucial dimension in the practice of regulation.

Although the legal implementation of many of the policy and regulatory choices made for each sector is important, they are not covered here in detail. They will, however, often be referred to through this text because they are central to the way the sector actually works. They also explain differences across countries, and sometimes across sectors within a country, in the degree of coherence between the economic intentions of the law and the outcomes.

1.9   The Structure of the Book: A Readers' Roadmap

After this introductory chapter, the fourteen remaining chapters are organized in four main blocks. The first block, composed of Chapters 2–5, covers basic concepts of microeconomics required to understand the rest of the book, and the two canonical models of regulation. The second block, Chapters 6–9, deals with the crucial issue of price setting in regulation and what it implies for regulators in terms of finance tools. The third block, Chapters 10–12, enriches the analysis by studying multi-product monopolies, including quality and investment issues, as well as the regulation of oligopolies. The fourth block, Chapters 13–15, covers advanced topics, including the moving frontier between regulation and anti-trust, institutional quality, and finally the implications of the IT revolution and behavioural economics in regulation.

The book is constructed in such a way that it can be used to teach at different levels. The main intended audience is economists with at least a core training in microeconomics. To make the book as helpful as possible for academic use, the different topics are addressed in fifteen chapters, each equivalent to what is usually covered in a three-hour lecture. We have also tried to make the book useful for professional training for new regulators or for regulators wishing to develop additional conceptual skills. That is why the level of technical detail can be easily adjusted to match the needs of these different types of audience by simply skipping the more analytically demanding sections. This is possible because difficult concepts are always presented in two steps. We illustrate them first with the help of simple numerical examples. Then we develop the conceptual discussion of the issues at stake. In every chapter, the most demanding technical parts of the book are either in boxes or in an appendix, which can be dropped without losing much on the policy insights. We provide a road map so that both audiences can be addressed easily with the book.

Introduction. Chapter 1 is the introduction to the book and should be useful to all. It offers a brief review of the most 'popular' views on the role of economic regulation and of the distance between theory and practice. We show that this distance is partially due to the fact that theory is often trying to catch up with a fast-moving real world and that policymakers have a much broader agenda than recognized by the majority of academic economic research on regulation.

Core concepts and canonical models of regulation. Chapters 2 and 3 are a primer in industrial organization. They cover standard microeconomics concepts necessary to understand the rest of the book. These chapters should therefore be covered in detail for advanced bachelors students and professionals. For masters and PhD students, they can either be covered very quickly in class, read at home or simply skipped. Chapters 4 and 5 present the canonical models of regulation, first in a situation of complete information (Chapter 4) and then in a situation of asymmetric information (Chapter 5). These are the key concepts of the book. More specifically:

- Chapter 2 summarizes the normative framework anchoring the theory of economic regulation at the most basic level. It serves as a reminder of some of the essential concepts used in economics and explains how concrete these are in analysis of regulation in practice. It should be helpful to practitioners in particular because it shows that many of the theoretical concepts can actually be measured, an essential dimension to be able to take informed and fair decisions.
- Chapter 3 then explains how monopolists get their market power and manage to use it without regulatory supervision. To regulate well, it is necessary to understand all stakeholders. Since the regulated firms are central to many of the distortions likely to hurt efficiency and fair allocations of resources, it is essential to get a good 'operational' perspective on what drives the decisions by this central actor. This chapter presents the Lerner index, a key concept used throughout the book to understand intuitively how laissez-faire monopoly prices and regulated prices impact on the markets of public services.
- Chapters 4 and 5 complement each other. Chapter 4 summarizes the theories of optimal regulation when the regulator has all the information needed to make efficient decisions. Chapter 5 shows what happens to the optimal regulation design when the regulator has less information than the regulated firm on costs and demand. The two chapters also remind the reader that the theories of the optimal design of regulation have initially been designed to consider the viewpoint of both public and private firms in their interactions with a regulator. Since dealing with asymmetric information can be challenging technically, Chapter 5 is in two parts. In a first part, intended for all readers, the cost imposed on regulation by asymmetric

information is illustrated with the help of a simple example. This part delivers the main results and intuitions at the core of the regulation literature, in a simple way. The second part is more technical as it presents the general case. It is intended for a more advanced audience and can be skipped by policy-oriented readers and bachelors students.

Prices and finance. Chapters 6 and 7 also need to be thought of as complementary. Chapter 6 focuses conceptually on the relevance of regulation for efficiency outcomes and on average prices. Chapter 7 shows how these theoretical concepts are put into practice. More specifically, it explains how the financial management of the regulated firms internalizes the incentive issues identified by theory. Chapter 6 summarizes the main results covered by the theoretical research of interest to any academic audience, while Chapter 7 covers familiar ground for a professional audience, which is often ignored by theoretical research on regulation. Linking the two is useful to both types of audience, although one might insist more on the former or the latter, depending on the orientation of the class. Chapter 8 focuses on allocative efficiency and non-linear pricing; Chapter 9 on redistribution and equity concerns. These chapters are intended for all. The most technical discussions are in boxes. More specifically:

- Chapter 6 explains the various models used to get to an average price that allows firms to break even and compares their incentive effects. It emphasizes the comparison between the 'old' rate-of-return approaches and the use of prices caps. But it also briefly summarizes the evolution of the practice towards a hybrid form of regulation combining these two approaches. It focuses on productive and cost efficiency.
- Chapter 7 may be unusual in a book on economic regulation. It emphasizes the essential role of finance in the implementation of regulatory principles to foster productive efficiency. It shows the central and concrete role financial concepts play, or should play, in defining a reasonable expected rate of return for both public and private regulated firms. It summarizes how many of the insights of the traditional approaches to the optimal design of incentive regulation can be internalized in relatively simple financial models used by many regulators around the world.
- Chapter 8 considers the heterogeneity of the demand side. It focuses on allocative efficiency and summarizes when and how to use non-linear pricing options, emphasizing the various forms of price discrimination and their effects. In particular, it shows that price discrimination, even though politically condemned and sometimes legally banned, can be an efficient way to cover the costs of the regulated operators. Price discrimination is useful to manage demand and to reach different goals, but it must be closely monitored because of the risk of market power abuse and regressive discriminating tariffs.
- Chapter 9 is also somewhat unusual in a textbook on regulation as it discusses the pricing tools that the regulators have to comply with in their equity mandate. It goes through the different available options to address social concerns in the context of regulatory policy design and implementation. This chapter is accessible

to all. It can be used independently, in a development class, for instance, or in a class on social policies, to illustrate the options available to ensure access and affordability in public services.

On the multidimensionality of production decisions and the scope for regulated oligopolies. The first part of the book focuses on single-product monopoly and deals with choices such as effort to reduce costs, information revelation and price structure. However, regulated firms are typically dealing with multidimensional products and services in deconcentrated economic environments. In this third block, we enrich the initial analysis to cover other types of decisions regulated firms make, including choosing quality (Chapter 10) and investment (Chapter 11). We then address the consequences for regulation of the fact that regulated firms are also often operating in complex oligopolistic structures and managing several products (Chapter 12). More specifically:

- Chapter 10 discusses the various dimensions of quality and the margin available to regulators to ensure that the quality delivered meets its demand. For regulated firms, an easy way to comply with cost-reducing requirements is to lower the quality of the service they provide. Their performance should thus also take quality into account, as long as it can be verified.
- Chapter 11 summarizes the theoretical and empirical literature on the effects of regulation on investment decisions. It highlights the gaps between the insights of theory and those produced by empirical research, emphasizing the relevance of contextual and institutional dimensions identified by econometric studies but sometimes omitted by theoretical research. It also emphasizes the role of access pricing in the sharing of capital costs. The most technical parts of the chapter are in boxes.
- Chapter 12 considers the various situations in which the regulators need to monitor multi-product firms and discusses why the substitutability or complementarity of products makes a difference to the optimal regulatory choice. It also analyses the scope and limits of some form of deconcentration by comparing the relative merits of monopolistic to oligopolistic regulated market structures. It discusses mixed oligopolies, self-regulation and public–private partnerships.

Advanced topics. The last part of the book covers topics that are emerging in regulation or are key to its evolution. Chapter 13 focuses on the link between anti-trust and regulation and on the moving frontier between the two. Technicalities are relegated to boxes. Chapter 14 looks into the institutional dimensions of the regulatory process. It is accessible to all. Chapter 15 concludes. More specifically:

- Chapter 13 discusses the ways in which traditional regulation needs to tackle new sources of possible abuses of market power. Increasingly complex ownership structures seem to characterize many firms as the role of hedge funds, pension funds and other institutional investors grows in regulated industries. Access pricing in formerly vertically integrated structure and competition in network industries are also analysed.

- Chapter 14 reviews the various sources of institutional weaknesses and explains how these should influence the optimal regulatory instruments choice. This is the chapter most relevant to understanding why there are so many regulatory failures, which in turn explains why market failures can last. It is particularly relevant to anyone interested in designing regulatory policies in developing and emerging economies but also in OECD countries requiring significant governance and institutional reforms.
- Chapter 15 concludes with a look at the future of regulation. It discusses the main emerging issues and changes in the way regulated markets operate, are financed and are supervised, thanks to the IT revolution and the insights of behavioural economics. It is non-technical and intended for all.

1.10   Summing Up

- Regulated services are costly to operate and maintain. They demand heavy investments to deliver services for extensive periods of time. Both types of expenditures have to be funded for the sector to be able to deliver.
- Investment needs in infrastructure average 1–2% of GDP (about 4–8% in developing or emerging economies).
- For all income groups, in all economies, regulated services represent 14–26% of household expenditures.
- The price of these services coupled with subsidies should be recovering the costs of meeting demand.
- When setting the price of the various regulated services, the regulator usually needs to address multiple goals:
  - ○ Financial or fiscal viability
  - ○ Efficiency
  - ○ Equity
  - ○ Institutional viability
  - ○ Political viability.
- Most of the common regulatory decisions have an impact on the extent to which each of these goals are achieved, e.g.:
  - ○ Should the financing of the services rely mostly on users or on taxpayers?
  - ○ Should the regulator favour more efficiency or equity?
  - ○ Should the regulator favour short-term or long-term goals?
- The fact that the technological characteristics of some services justify their production and/or delivery by monopolies or quasi-monopolies and that the demand for these services can be quite difficult to adjust implies a risk of abuse of market power by these firms; this drives the original case for the regulation of the price of these services.
- In view of the nature of the trade-offs and the social risks of abuse of market power, regulation is not only an economic decision but also a political one and it needs to account for the specific institutional context in which the decision is taken.

- Since the institutional, political and social contexts evolve, regulation has to have some flexibility to adjust to the changes, while still providing enough protection guarantees to all stakeholders.
- For many of the key decisions, economic theory provides useful guidelines, but in some dimensions, theory still has some way to go to become fully operational in the practice of regulation.

2 Defining a Theoretical Normative Benchmark

This chapter reviews the normative framework regulatory economists use to anchor conceptually their assessments of the performance of a sector dominated by a monopoly.[1] That normative framework, whether made explicit or held implicit, is useful to understand what regulation is expected to deliver. To some readers this may serve as a refresher of many basic concepts with an emphasis on their use in the context of regulation. For others, it highlights the seed of many of the more complex developments discussed throughout the book. It provides the core conceptual approach typically used in economics to decide on the extent to which a government needs to regulate a service provided by a single firm. This, in turn, will help assess the extent to which the regulator is managing to get the provider to do its utmost in the interest of all stakeholders (i.e. users, investors and taxpayers).[2]

By going through the basics of the way regulatory economists tend to look at regulation, the chapter highlights the core dimensions underlying the recurring policy debates on regulation. Many of these discussions on the proper design of regulation started with the debates on the privatization of activities which have traditionally been operated by public enterprises. State-owned utilities, many of them monopolies, were transferred to the private sector on the assumption that 'the market' is more rational and better able to manage these firms. Chile was the leader of these transformations in the 1970s, under the Pinochet dictatorship. It was followed by the United Kingdom under the Thatcher administration in the 1980s.[3] In both cases, regulation played a somewhat low-profile role, but was already quite an important part of the agenda. It was also part of the debates on the desirability of privatizing.

---

[1] Competition authorities follow a similar framework to conduct their core assessments, although they tend to focus on a single goal (efficiency), increasingly with an emphasis on what it means for the well-being of consumers' welfare, whereas the expected scope of action for a regulatory agency can be much broader.

[2] Many of the results extend to the cases in which the services are provided by oligopolies. This is discussed in more detail in Chapter 13.

[3] As explained by Bel (2006, 2011), the first major wave of privatization of the twentieth century of traditional large-scale public monopolies started in Italy under Mussolini, where life insurance, telephone networks and tolled highways were privatized (some of them after having been nationalized only a few years earlier). Germany followed in the 1930s under the Nazi administration, which sold off steel, mining, banking, shipyard, shipping lines and railway enterprises. Noteworthy is that, in both countries, it was done under a tight regulatory control, as in the rest of the economy, which often included major political interference with management decisions.

The long-lasting nature of the debate, and its implications for the evolving perception of the role of regulation, is nicely illustrated by the tense discussions that took place as recently as 2018 in England, where the European privatization wave started, between the Conservative and Labour parties on the need to consider the renationalization of the water and railways services. These debates result, among other factors, from unhappiness with deteriorating services and recurring strikes (in the case of railways sector) and excessive dividends paid by underinvesting operators and increasing prices charges on consumers (in the case of the electricity and water sectors).

Of particular interest in the context of this book is the fact that the arguments made by the English Labour party in favour of nationalization included claims about the incompetence of the regulators, in addition to the limitations demonstrated by some of the private operators. They argued that self-regulated public providers would deliver better for less, i.e. that they can be more efficient in meeting a wide range of goals, including the social goals. In contrast, conservative politicians highlighted their distrust of the public sector's ability to deliver efficiently and expressed their concerns with the financial unsustainability of the multiplicity of goals assigned to these firms, including service obligations. They essentially argued that well-designed regulation should be able to ensure that private operators are more effective overall. While these debates tend to enjoy solid media coverage, they are often more ideological than technical.[4] And you will realize, as you go through the book, that ideology is often distant from facts in industries in which a single or a few firms enjoy significant market power. Real life is not only more complex than theory, but also much more complex than ideological interpretations of economic challenges imply.

The academic view on these issues is that neither regulation nor nationalization is a panacea in increasing return to scale sectors (i.e. in sectors where the average cost declines as the size of operations increases). But these debates are interesting because they reveal the multiplicity of goals a regulator is expected to consider. The concerns used to justify the privatization of many public monopolies in the 1990s and those used to justify nationalization since the early 2010s in many countries reveal that the debate is not only about efficiency. The effectiveness of service provision and its regulation is also assessed against financial/fiscal goals (Chapter 7) and social/equity (Chapter 9). They clearly need to be accounted for in the development of theoretical and practical regulatory options. However, the diversity of perspectives revealed by these debates also highlights the importance of separating ideology from facts in the identification of the desirable form of service provision and supervision. As we will see throughout the book, the optimal choice depends much more on context, constraints and on consumption and production preferences than is often recognized by policy and political discussions. They also depend on the specific policy objectives assigned to the regulatory mandates among those identified in the previous chapter.

---

[4] In January 2018, the *Financial Times* published a series focusing on the failure of privatization and regulation in the United Kingdom. See, for instance, Ford and Plimmer (2018).

Our discussion will focus, initially, on efficiency, reflecting the bias of the economic literature on the topic. Indeed, efficiency is the first concern of regulation policy as derived from theoretical frameworks – defined as an allocation of resources that will produce a quantity of goods or services maximizing social surplus. We will address the equity, fairness, financial viability and transparency concerns in later chapters. We will show that they are just as important as efficiency and often imply politically challenging trade-offs. For now, however, we will look at what it takes to ensure efficiency in a market run by a monopoly, defined as a single provider operating without competitors. Whether the monopoly is public or private, it will enjoy significant market power. The leverage granted by this market power may show up in many ways. To keep the discussion simple, we will assume that the main focus is on maximizing profits.

In practice, this perspective is often framed as: *What must be done to reduce the impact on output and prices of the monopoly's market power?* To judge the extent to which a regulatory correction may be needed, one must compare the output the monopoly is willing to deliver with what would be achieved if the market had been competitive. This approach is generally consistent with the idea that any observed outcome has to be assessed against a benchmark – either an ideal or a real situation. Regulatory policy often takes as its desirable benchmark the efficiency level that would be achieved from competition (without any externality).[5] A subtle but crucial assumption built into the idea of benchmarking is that all economic agents have full information on the choices they must make. Any deviation from this ideal situation – whether resulting from service providers' decisions, mistaken market corrections or the decisions of public authorities not to correct imperfections – can be expected to decrease efficiency.

Observed (and measured) inefficiency should trigger State intervention only to move the activity towards a more efficient outcome. One common mistake is to assume that the State can and should restore efficiency. Without any externality, if the market for a private good fails to deliver an efficient outcome, then nobody can, as any public intervention is both costly and imperfect. At a very general level, this intervention can take two main forms in public services. The State can intervene by regulating a private provider or it can provide the service itself, usually through a public enterprise and sometimes more directly through the activities of a Ministry. Note that the public provision option also implies the need to regulate, but often governments tend to rely on self-regulation by public providers.

In theory, the choice of intervention will depend on the consequences for the various stakeholders of distortions from the ideal (efficient) outcome. In practice,

---

[5] Keep in mind that the competitive benchmark can come from various types of competition. Competition may be in the market or for the market (as in the case of auctions) when competition in the market is limited. When multiple firms can potentially provide the good or the service of interest, the outcome of competition in the market is the usual benchmark. Monopolies are often associated with situations in which one provider is selected from the few firms with the potential to provide a service. In this case, a competitive bidding process mimics the effects of competition and identifies the most efficient provider. The outcome of the competition for the market is then to be used as the desirable regulatory benchmark.

the choice is a bit more complex, since intervention may be driven by how the consequences of distortions are distributed among stakeholders and political preferences tend to be the main driver. But we will ignore that at this stage of the discussion.

For now, since we have chosen to focus on efficiency, our main concern is to assess the *size* of the distortion that results from having to rely on a monopoly. To make that assessment, we first must review how efficiency and competition are related, after which we can move on to review the basics of supply and demand under the assumption that all stakeholders have full information. These steps will help us establish a formal modelling of costs, demand, profit maximization and social welfare. The broad concepts are likely to be a reminder for many readers, but in the process we will highlight points that figure prominently in policy debates on the regulation of monopolies.

2.1 Efficiency as a Driver of Regulation

From a strict economic perspective, the concern for efficiency covers various dimensions. They include efficiency in production, investment and consumption. In practice, it is often cost efficiency that governs discussions on resource allocation in regulatory processes. Actually, the concept is somewhat more encompassing: a decision is said to have achieved Pareto efficiency when there is no other decision that would improve the well-being (or 'utility', to use the conventional terminology) of some stakeholders without reducing that of others. This definition implies that, at a minimum, decisions should produce more utility to consumers than it costs them to consume and that it should account for winners and losers.

The multidimensionality of the concept of efficiency makes it a complex concept to work with in practice, but irrespective of the specific source of inefficiency, it is useful to remember that the inefficiency confronting regulators can be categorized in either one of the two following categories:

- Inefficiency *by excess* – that is, when a given action produces less utility than its cost.
- Inefficiency *by default* – when an action that would generate greater utility than it costs is not undertaken.

These inefficiencies may derive from: (i) a lack of rationality by the decision-maker (e.g. failing to use all available information to make the right decision to consume, produce or invest); (ii) biased or incomplete information (e.g. when stakeholders do not share what they know with others or manipulate the reporting of information); (iii) restrictions that limit the decision-maker's authority (e.g. cultural, religious or legal limits); or (iv) restrictions on the decision-makers' objectives that lead them to focus only on a subset of agents (e.g. the rich or the poor, but not both).

These behavioural and institutional drivers of inefficiency are ignored by the simplest version of normative economic theory reflected in basic textbooks. The basic theory argues that optimal resource allocation should be determined by an authority that is rational, benevolent, omniscient and omnipotent – that is, in practice, by a 'good' government or regulator. A public agency with these four attributes would choose to maximize the well-being of all stakeholders (*benevolence*) by fully understanding their preferences and the available technologies (*omniscience*), without any legal or regulatory restriction (*omnipotence*) and without making mistakes (*rationality*).

Clearly, these are strong assumptions. In Chapter 14, on institutional weaknesses, we will see how non-benevolence can affect regulatory design. We will also discuss the policy implications of limited rationality in later chapters. But for now, we will work with the optimistic institutional assumption, which has the advantage of providing a useful benchmark for an optimal policy.

So, ultimately, what does efficiency imply? Assume that the focus of regulatory decisions is a volume q to be produced (e.g. kilowatt-hours, kWh, of electricity, cubic metres of water, passengers to carry); that the welfare of the users achieved by the consumption of q is $S(q)$ and that the cost of producing q is $C(q)$. You may remember from basic economics that the best allocation is determined by the level of q that maximizes the level of welfare net of the cost of producing q – that is, by the q that solves max $S(q) - C(q)$.

One challenge with this formula is the need to come up with a satisfactory way to measure the 'welfare' generated by the consumption of q units of the good or service produced. In other words, how would a regulator quantify the positive or negative effects of the changes in consumption entailed by its decisions (or lack thereof). The reason why this is a challenge is that 'utility' or 'happiness' are subjective and cannot be measured directly. Economic theory circumvents this difficulty by looking instead at how much people are willing to pay to obtain a certain amount of a commodity. This is relatively easy to estimate in monetary terms through surveys or through analysis of behaviour. Economists refer to this monetary amount as the *gross consumer surplus*. A measure of gross consumer surplus is the sum of all the maximum prices consumers are willing to pay to buy each successive unit they are offered. The *net consumer surplus* is the sum of the difference between the maximum prices consumers would be willing to pay to obtain the commodity and the prices they actually pay. Intuitively, it seems reasonable to expect that the more they have already consumed, the less they will be willing to pay for additional units, hence the lower the additional surplus that will be achieved by an increase in consumption.

To be able to quantify the surplus, regulators (and service operators) start with the identification of the *demand function*. This function yields, for each price, the maximum quantity that consumers are willing to buy at that price, or symmetrically, for each quantity, the maximum price that consumers are willing to pay. As a consequence of the decreasing additional surplus, in general, demand functions are downward sloping (which reflects the fact that higher price leads to lower consumption for so-called normal goods and services), and that income and prices of other goods affect the specific demand that results from the estimation.[6]

---

[6] Many other variables can influence demand – among them weather, time of day, user characteristics and regulatory design. We'll discuss this in more detail later.

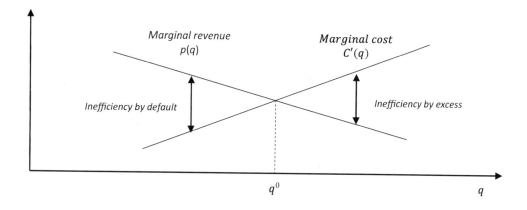

Figure 2.1 Efficient volume of activity

Formally, this is usually developed as follows. Let us define the gross consumer surplus associated with a purchase of $q \geq 0$ units of the commodity as the sum of the prices consumers accept to pay for x units up to q that is, $S(q) = \int_0^q p(x)dx$.

The basic microeconomics behind many economic evaluations links the optimal quantity to the marginal cost of delivering that quantity but also to consumers' marginal propensity to pay. Formally, the optimal quantity q^0 is achieved when marginal propensity to pay for the commodity (i.e. the incremental surplus derived from obtaining one more kWh of electricity or one more cubic metre of water) and marginal cost (the incremental cost of this additional production) are equal: $S'(q^0) = p(q^0) = C'(q^0)$.[7]

As Figure 2.1 shows, producing a quantity q such that $q > q^0$ is inefficient by excess since the price that consumers are willing to pay for the extra production of electricity or water or other public service is lower than its cost: $S'(q) = p(q) < C'(q)$. Inversely, any decision q such that $q < q^0$ is inefficient by default. This is because $S'(q) = p(q) > C'(q)$: some units whose value is greater than their cost are not produced.

In a dream world, a brilliant, rational, fully informed, empowered, accountable and benevolent regulator or public service provider would know exactly the value of q^0 (i.e. how much to produce to make every stakeholder as happy as possible). But history has never been able to produce any such 'enlightened leader' who delivers goods and services that efficiently. This is one of the reasons why so many regulatory decisions are often frustrating and why some argue that decentralizing decisions on resource allocation to markets or to structures that mimic the functioning of markets

---

[7] Analytically, $S'(q)$ is the first derivative of the surplus function $S(q)$, and $C'(q)$ is the first derivative of the cost function $C(q)$. The implicit assumptions needed to come up with the optimal output are that the utility function is increasing and concave, which is true with most goods and services, while the variable cost function is increasing and convex. This produces a decreasing marginal utility function and an increasing marginal cost function in q.

may be more desirable. The choice ends up betting on the odds of markets failing against regulators or governments failing.

The regulatory challenge is enhanced by the number of actors to consider in the design of policies. Conceptually, the discussion so far has focused only on two of the key stakeholders of a market: (i) users or consumers and (ii) suppliers or producers. This ignores the possibility of other stakeholders such as taxpayers, workers or investors. It is a useful simplification at this stage, but we will have to address it later. To make things even simpler in our quest to identify an ideal benchmark, we also assume that these two types of agents are rational and perfectly informed – the first group about their preferences and the second group about their technologies.[8]

What must be kept in mind at this point is that users target their consumption q_u so as to maximize their net surplus:

$$\max_q (S(q) - R_u(q)) = \int_0^q p(x)dx - R_u(q) \tag{2.1}$$

where $R_u(q)$ represents spending on q. Similarly, producers select the production q_c that maximizes their profit:

$$\max_q \left(R_c(q) - C(q) \right) \tag{2.2}$$

where $R_c(q)$ represents their gross revenues from sales.

The solution to these two optimization problems provides the benchmark quantity we are seeking. Users optimize their consumption when their marginal surplus, $S'(q) = p(q)$, matches their marginal spending on q, $R'_u(q)$. In other terms, when $S'(q_u) = R'_u(q_u)$. Producers optimize when their marginal revenue, $R'_c(q)$, matches their marginal cost, $C'(q)$, that is, when:

$$R'_c(q_c) = C'(q_c) \tag{2.3}$$

An equilibrium benchmark quantity, q, is achieved when the two parties agree on quantity and price, that is, when $q_u = q_c$.

If the sellers' revenue function and the buyers' expenditure function match and are proportional to the quantity exchanged, the market is said to be perfectly competitive. In other words, in a competitive market, $R(q) = pq$, where p is the unit price not dependent on the quantity consumed by each single user or the quantity produced by each single firm. Then, the firms' marginal revenue is the same as consumers' willingness to pay. So, when competition works in a market economy in which consumption and production decisions are decentralized to individual agents, the price reveals both the marginal cost to the consumer and the marginal utility to the producer. At that price, the quantity produced and the quantity demanded are the same: $q_c = q_u = q^O$; the results is: $S'(q_u) = p = C'(q_c)$.

---

[8] In Chapter 15 we will discuss the relevance of the assumption of rationality and how removing it can prove quite useful to regulators.

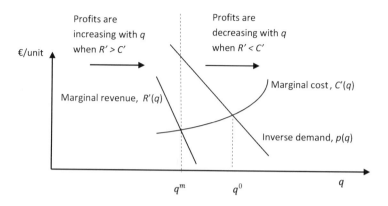

Figure 2.2 Competitive and non-competitive equilibria

This is illustrated in Figure 2.2 by the intersection of the marginal cost and the inverse demand function at point q^O. Pricing at marginal cost thus delivers the efficient outcome in this market because it maximizes the surplus of the interaction between producers and consumers. It cannot be improved upon to the satisfaction of all stakeholders. This is the main argument driving the case for marginal cost pricing often made in policy speeches for technical audiences.

It is a useful but unrealistic benchmark for the kind of market we are interested in. For one thing, it assumes that agents are not able to manipulate prices. If they can, the result does not hold. Indeed, for laissez-faire to lead to efficiency, consumers and producers must view prices as exogenous to their individual calculation, since the equilibrium prices are supposedly determined by the comparison of *all* individual plans. In a context in which any individual or coordinated action allows some agents to control either the volume of purchases or the selling price, as in a monopolistic market structure, the market outcome will be inefficient. For example, as we will detail in Chapter 3, the equilibrium quantity can be $q^m < q^0$ because the marginal revenue of the firms is below the consumers' marginal expenditures. An overly concentrated structure among suppliers will also lead to inefficiency. Both situations involve interference with competition. This is why economists, including regulatory economists, are so concerned with barriers to entry, concentration and abuses of dominant position and why monitoring these risks is often part of the mandate of regulatory agencies, in addition to being the central concern of competition agencies. Efficiency is thus clearly central to regulatory decisions.

2.2 Why the Basics of Supply and Demand Really Matter in Practice

The next step in understanding the importance of the benchmark and of deviations from the 'ideal' outcome is to focus on what, exactly, drives supply and demand. Prices and income are the usual suspects in economics, even if behavioural economics is broadening the menu of options, as discussed in Chapter 15. For now, we will focus on the need to quantify the sensitivity of supply and demand to prices and income as these may be essential to monitor whenever the scope of interference with normal competitive behaviour is at issue. To see why this matters in regulation, it is useful to distinguish between the consumer and producer perspectives.

On the consumer side, prices and income are well-established decision drivers of final demand since they determine the budget constraint under which households try to maximize their utility from the consumption of different available commodities.[9] In practice, it is important to remember that there is also sensitivity to the availability of substitutes of the good or service of interest. These sensitivities are summarized in measures discussed in every basic textbook: the 'elasticity' of demand to the prices of the good or service of interest (direct elasticity), the elasticity to the price of substitutes (cross-elasticity) and the sensitivity to income. As for industrial consumers, the output (approximated by production data and sometimes by employment) is the relevant activity indicator, so that the elasticity of input demand to output plays a role similar to the elasticity of demand to income for the household. The direct price elasticity, the cross-price elasticity and the income/output elasticity are important measures to many regulatory decisions, sometimes much more so than in regulatory and policy debates.

Estimating the elasticity of demand is unavoidable when assessing the impact of changes in price and income linked to policy decisions and anticipating possible strategic behaviour on the part of producers and consumers. Think of the differences across income groups in the residential consumption of electricity or water that is caused by price changes. The evidence suggests that the demand for water or electricity is 'price inelastic' for the poor. They do not consume much to begin with and they cannot cut their consumption even when the price increases.[10] The opposite holds for the richer populations, who can decide to wash the car or water the garden less often.

Demand elasticity is also needed to address concerns about the risks of a single supplier, or a small number of suppliers, exerting excessive control over a specific activity and abusing this market power to reduce the level of output delivered in the sector and increase the average price.[11] Such occasions arise, for example, when authorities must assess the acceptability of joint bids in an auction for the right to provide an essential service, such as transportation or water services, where the case for scale economies may or may not be as strong as argued by the firms bidding jointly.[12] Similar concerns arise when authorities must decide whether to accept or

---

[9] Consumer theory is based on the analysis of choices. The utility function is an ordinal concept used to order consumption baskets between 'better' and 'worse'. Each individual must choose among several consumption options under a budget constraint. Under the optimal consumption scheme, the ratio of the marginal utility of any two commodities (known as the marginal rate of substitution) is equal to the ratio of their prices. In addition, the budget constraint is binding. Demand unfolds from this set of equations.

[10] See, for instance, Estache and Wodon (2014) for evidence on the African experience.

[11] Demand elasticity is key to the definition of the reference market (or relevant market) when assessing these risks.

[12] Joint bids are not a good idea when they restrict potential cost savings by reducing competition for the market. But they may be in the interest of users even when they imply less competition, as we will see when we start accounting for risks and assessing their effects on the costs of financing investments.

Table 2.1 Average price and income demand elasticity

				Price elasticity		Income/output elasticity
Electricity	Short run	Total:		0.1–0.8	Total:	0.4–0.6
		Industry:		0.2–0.6	Industry:	>0.5
		Resident:		0.1–0.8	Resident:	<0.5
	Long run	Total:		>0.5	Total:	0.4–0.9
		Industry:		0.2–0.6	Industry:	0.5–0.6
		Resident:		0.1–0.8	Resident:	0.2–0.9
Water	Short run	Industry:		0–1.3	Industry:	0.2–0.4
		Resident:		0.25–0.75	Resident:	0.2–0.3
	Long run	Resident:		0.01–1	Resident:	0.1–0.4
Land transport		Passenger:		0.1–1.2	Passenger:	0.2–0.4
		Freight (tkm):		0.2–2	Freight:	0.5–1.5

Source: Authors' compilation from multiple sources (reported in absolute value; they are negative for prices and positive for income).

Note: Most direct price elasticities are negative since the quantity demanded and the price vary in opposite directions. However, they are generally presented under a positive format because the important information is their absolute value, not their sign.

reject a proposed merger. The impact on consumers' welfare depends on how sensitive consumers are to the price increase that might result from a poorly regulated merger or alliance, which generally depends on the existence of substitutes. Whenever a firm enjoys sufficient market power, it will have an incentive to charge more and produce less (see quantity q^m in Figure 2.2). And price elasticity of demand is one of the drivers of this market power. The lower this elasticity, the higher this market power, as will be discussed later.

Table 2.1 provides a sense of the value of these elasticities for the major public services.[13] They give a range of values based on studies covering both developed and developing economies. They distinguish between price and income or output elasticities, between short and long run and between types of consumers. Ranges are only indicative as they report results from studies which are not comparable.

We see that the dispersion of the elasticities characterizing residential users tends to be larger than for non-residential users. In general, also, there is no clear pattern on the average levels across user types and across sectors. This heterogeneity serves as a reminder that summary tables can only be indicative and complemented by more case-specific research when measures need to be used in specific regulatory decisions. And when this is done, it is important to account for the drivers of the differences observed. They may include dimensions as diversified as age, education, weather, family

[13] Note that elasticities are ratios of relative variations, such as $(\Delta q/q)/(\Delta I/I)$ for income elasticity (i.e. q is quantity and I income). Consequently, they are pure numbers independent of how consumption, prices and income are measured. They essentially measure whether consumption q varies by more or less than 1% when the independent variable (e.g. income) varies by 1%.

composition, housing characteristics, tariff structure, time of day of consumption or size and sector of the business.

Note that the time dimension is particularly interesting in a policy context. The long-term elasticity with respect to income/output and prices tends to be higher than the short-term elasticity for all sectors because the agents can more easily adapt their behaviour to changes in the economic environment. Long-term elasticity is particularly relevant to investment decisions because it directly affects the financial and social return on those investments. Short-term elasticity is often quite relevant when considering the equity consequences of pricing changes and income subsidies. In practice, most studies do not distinguish between short- and long-term elasticities.[14]

On the supply side, the key is to get a good sense of the impact of any given policy on the production decisions. This means that production costs, which depend on technology choices, must be quantified. Supply decisions are linked not only to technology and its associated costs, but also to the strategic possibilities that the market's structure offers. This must be kept in mind in any attempt to increase competition in a market. The scope for strategic interactions changes with the nature of the market. In electricity, for instance, allowing one generating company to also own a transmission company will increase the risks of distorting the market to the extent it allows the transmission company to favour the generating company to which it is related.

While these basic concepts are central to many regulatory decisions, they tend to focus on a snapshot of the market that regulators are dealing with. They also assume that today's information is a good proxy for tomorrow's. In practice, this is often not the case in regulated industries, in which investment decisions imply a long-term commitment by operators and depend on expected future demand.[15] This brings us back to the importance of demand elasticities. It also forces us to keep in mind that, as long-term elasticities can be quite significantly higher than short-term elasticities, this difference is likely to impact on key investment and operational management decisions in the real world. In recent times, for instance, the electricity sector has discovered that the increasing public support for renewable sources of energy has been decreasing the demand for non-renewable sources at a level which was not anticipated by many investors less than ten years ago.

In sum, it continues to be essential to gain a solid quantitative sense of the basic demand and supply functions. But it is also important to keep in mind that firms' options and decisions are a moving target not always easily reflected in the basic quantitative modelling. This will become increasingly clear as we go deeper into the theory and in the challenges of its implementation.

---

[14] For more details, see, for energy, Fouquet (2014), for water, Sebri (2014), and for land transport, Dunkerley et al. (2016) and Litman (2010).

[15] Forecasting demand is actually quite a big business. Within the academic literature, it is much more studied in the context of transport than in the context of utilities, however. See, for instance, Salling and Leleur (2015).

2.3   How Are Firm Revenue and Price Elasticity Related?

Recognizing the relevance of the elasticity of demand to price and income (or output) for the viability of investment and production decisions is thus important but not enough in many applied regulatory contexts. In practice, regulators will also often confront the need for a more precise discussion to clarify concrete questions such as how much difference this elasticity will make to the revenue impact of a given change in prices. This further emphasizes the necessity of having a good sense of the specific local market being analysed.

To understand how revenue and price elasticity are related, let's denote by $q(p)$ the demand function for a product or service and by $R(p) = pq(p)$ the revenues of the firm. A variation of price Δp will have the effect:

$$\Delta R = q\Delta p + p\Delta q \Rightarrow \frac{\Delta R}{\Delta p} = q + \frac{p\Delta q}{\Delta p} = q[1 + (\Delta q/\Delta p)(p/q)] = q(1 - \varepsilon) \quad (2.4)$$

where $\varepsilon = -\frac{\Delta q/q}{\Delta p/p}$ denotes the direct price elasticity of the product or service.

Given that $\Delta R = q(1 - \varepsilon)\Delta p$, to increase its revenues, the firm must:

Raise its price if $\varepsilon < 1$
Lower its price if $\varepsilon > 1$

But when a firm is operated to maximize profit, $R(p) - C(p)$, we saw earlier in Equation (2.3) that the firm should set its price and output so that marginal revenues and marginal costs are equated:

$$\frac{\Delta R}{\Delta p} = \frac{\Delta C}{\Delta p} \quad or \quad \frac{\Delta R}{\Delta q}\frac{\Delta q}{\Delta p} = \frac{\Delta C}{\Delta q}\frac{\Delta q}{\Delta p} \quad (2.5)$$

Using the result on the driver of marginal revenue $\Delta R = q(1 - \varepsilon)\Delta p$ and rearranging the terms yields

$$q(1 - \varepsilon) = C'(q)\frac{dq}{dp} \quad (2.6)$$

Since the marginal cost is positive, $C'(q) > 0$, and since with a normal good $dq/dp < 0$, we deduce that $\varepsilon > 1$ in markets in which profit maximization is the main driver of the production decision, without service obligations or other constraints on output and investment levels.[16]

This is normally the case in deregulated markets in which consumers can choose among many service suppliers or when service substitutes are easily available – as in the long-distance transportation or mobile phone sectors, for instance. This is also why, in these markets, when analysts talk about inelastic demand, they are actually

---

[16] A normal good or service is defined as a good or service whose demand increases as the consumers' income rises.

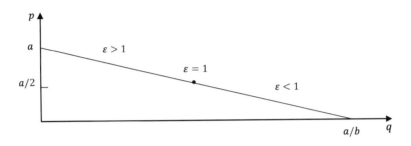

Figure 2.3 Demand price elasticities

referring to demand elasticity slightly above 1. Very elastic demand can be close to infinite if the good under scrutiny has perfect substitutes.

In contrast, if a product is a necessity and has no real substitute, as is often the case in regulated industries such as water and energy, consumers cannot easily respond to changes in price. A good example is short-term electricity consumption: consumers depend on their industrial or household equipment, and they cannot 'escape' immediately if prices increase. In this case, ε is very low and price regulation is required to prevent vendors from setting very high prices.

As shown earlier, most common estimates of the price elasticity of demand for public services suggest that these services are not very sensitive to price changes (i.e. elasticities < 1). This means that price increases in regulated firms tend to translate into higher revenue, while price decreases translate into lower revenue.

Knowing the average elasticity is often useful only to gauge whether or not an insufficient quantity, excessive price or excessive profit issue exists. But to make firm- or sector-specific decisions at any specific time, it is important to remember that for most demand functions, the precise value of ε changes with the value of the initial observation point. For example, if demand can be approximated by a linear function, $p = a - bq$, where a and b are positive coefficients, since $dp/dq = -b$, we obtain $\varepsilon = p/(a - p)$. In other words, the elasticity increases with price p as illustrated by Figure 2.3.

To many readers, it may be quite intuitive to find that many consumers are less sensitive to price changes when initial prices are low but become much more sensitive as prices rise high enough to have an impact on their purchasing power. This is one of the insights used by regulators concerned with the environmental impact of excessive consumption. They rely on demand management to reduce consumption, as is the case for water and electricity.

2.4 On the Underestimated Regulatory Relevance of Income Elasticity

The need to assess the income elasticity of demand – that is, the effect of a 1% change in income on the relative variation of the quantity demanded by households – is crucial to regulatory decisions related to essential public services in any context in which poverty is, or may become, an issue and in which the social ladder leads to significant increases in income levels. Developed and developing countries provide recurring examples of these phenomena.

In developed economies, since the 2008 crisis, poverty rates have tended to increase and this has given reasons to regulators to be concerned with the affordability of basic public services. This has been a major concern in the European Union for instance. In the United Kingdom, the energy regulator has imposed a cap on the amount operators can charge some of the poorest consumers.[17] When making these types of regulatory decisions, it is important to gauge the extent to which lower incomes will reduce consumption of the basic essential public services. When this elasticity of demand to income is reaching extremely low levels, regulators are tempted to increase price control or service obligations.

In many developing countries, in contrast, sustained long-term growth has translated into the growth of a middle class, thus raising average income levels. In this alternative situation, the main concern is to compute how much consumption will expand with growth in average income. And consumption of electricity, transportation and water increases with income. This matters because the answer will inform decisions about the investments the sector will have to make to cater to the needs of the population. The concern for increases in income also appears when governments rely extensively on income subsidies to reduce poverty.

Most regulated services are likely to be 'normal' goods, as suggested by Table 2.1. An increase in income will lead to a rise in demand for those goods across subsectors and across regions.[18] Table 2.1 also shows that in the water industry this elasticity is greater for developing countries than for developed countries. In practice, there are many other factors driving elasticities. Table 2.1 shows that it is different according to the user types (residential versus non-residential). Additional sources of differences include demographic, geographic or subtle economic factors likely to influence specific demands. In transport, for instance, age, lifestyle, cultural preferences, parking opportunities and costs, walkability or safety can all be relevant as well. Any of these may be of relevance to regulatory decisions.

2.5 How Broad Are the Uses of Elasticities in Business and Policy in Practice?

The various dimensions of the elasticity of demand are used much more frequently to weigh policy decisions than is sometimes recognized in textbooks and casual policy assessments. Politicians have a good sense of the extent to which price (in)elasticity is

[17] To be more precise, users of a domestic prepayment meter who are typically poor will be protected by a safeguard tariff (or 'price cap'), which essentially limits the per-unit price operators can charge them.
[18] An inferior good or service is characterized by a negative income elasticity of demand: an increase in income will lead to a fall in the demand and may lead to changes to more 'luxurious' (superior) substitutes.

politically sensitive and more so in sectors considered to be basic needs such as water. For instance, one of the most common arguments used to renationalize privatized water companies is that the private operators have not been sensitive enough to the basic necessity characteristic of the services they are providing.

This is not to say that business decisions are not influenced by elasticities. Their values are quite well internalized in business decisions. Assessing elasticities as precisely as possible enables firms to understand how revenue will be affected by changes in their own or their competitors' prices. Business actors are also quite focused on the opportunities to make the most of differences between users' sensitivities to prices to target their pricing decisions. The use of elasticities to decide on pricing strategies is a common implicit or explicit source of disagreement between operators and regulators, but they are instrumental to the possibilities of relying on price differentiation techniques such as those discussed in Chapter 8. The challenge for a regulator is to ensure that they are used in the interest of all stakeholders and not just as a way to increase the rent for service providers.

Elasticities are also of interest to a wide range of policy analysts expected to anticipate the payoffs or risks of new policies. For instance, when a government decides whether to subsidize renewable energies or water savings programmes, it must compute how high the price subsidy will have to be if it is to have an impact. If the subsidy budget is limited, the likelihood of having an impact may be very low if price elasticities are low; in such cases the authorities may want to look for alternative policy instruments, in particular non-price instruments.

Similarly, the income elasticity of demand is quite useful in gauging the evolution of demand for technologies according to income classes or according to a country's average income. For example, it may reveal the feasibility of switching from dirty to clean technologies in energy or transport. The profile of demand for traditional heating and cooking sources in developing countries demonstrates that these commodities can be considered as inferior goods.[19] With increases in income (but only with such increases), users are likely to switch to modern technologies. The specific interest of a regulator is the speed at which this switch takes place, given a certain rate of income growth. We will return later to the role of elasticities in policy to explain how it is used to assess market concentration.

Income elasticities are also quite useful when pondering the evolution of a market and its implications for the financial viability of an operator. Specifically, elasticity computations are commonly used to derive a first-order approximation of the ability of regulated firms to deliver on their service or investment obligations. When revenue is needed to finance investment, a reduction in users' ability to pay may imply a lower ability of operators to finance investment.

The point of this section is that elasticities matter a great deal in practice. They matter more than recognized by casual observers of the challenges of regulation. This

---

[19] In economics, an inferior good or service is a good or service that sees its demand drop/rise as the consumer's income increases/decreases. This is the opposite of what is observed for normal goods or services.

should become clear as the discussions become more technical in the book. They have to be used in a wide variety of contexts. Just as importantly, they are not too difficult to approximate for assessing the impact of policies. Information on prices and quantities for a set of consumers having a range of abilities to pay is quite simple to collect. And very simple techniques are available to turn this basic data into first-order approximations of elasticities (Box 2.1).

Failing to develop a good sense of these elasticities poses the risk of over- or underestimating reactions to policy changes. It may also lead to underestimating the

---

Box 2.1 The Easy Estimation of the Price and Income Elasticity of Demand for a Public Service

The two simplest specifications for demand are linear and log-linear forms. The first assumes that elasticities change with the level of consumption, as in Figure 2.3, whereas the second assumes that they are constant. When price and quantity observations cover a wide range of values, elasticities are likely to vary, so a linear specification with its varying elasticities is usually a better choice. If the sample data are concentrated over a narrow price (and quantity) range, a constant-elasticity specification may be a better choice.

The easiest solution to get a quick idea of the relevant elasticities is to estimate a log-linear demand function. In that case, the demand function is written as a Cobb–Douglas function, $q = \alpha p^{-\varphi} p_s^{+\gamma} I^{\omega}$, where q is the quantity of service demanded, p is the price of the service demanded, I is consumer income, p_s is the price of a substitute service or provider (if there is one), and φ, γ and ω are, respectively, the elasticities of demand with respect to the price of the service, of a possible substitute and to income.

To get direct estimates of the elasticities from the log-linear demand function, the easiest way is to convert the expression to natural logarithms:

$$ln \; q = ln \; \alpha - \varphi \; ln \; p + \gamma \; ln \; p_s + \omega \; ln \; I$$

A basic econometric estimation of this model yields a sense of the three main elasticities of interest (φ, γ and ω). The fact that they are assumed to be constant has to be kept in mind when conducting policy analysis. If a more detailed assessment is needed, an alternative specification is the linear form.

In the linear case, the coefficients on each of the explanatory variables measure the rate of change in quantity demanded as the explanatory variable changes, holding all other explanatory variables constant. In this case, the formal demand specification is $q = \alpha - \varphi p + \gamma p_s + \omega I$. The estimated demand elasticities are then computed, based on the initial constant elasticity estimations, as

$$\varepsilon_{qp} = \varphi \, p/q, \varepsilon_{qp_s} = \gamma p_s/q \text{ and } \varepsilon_{ql} = \omega I/q$$

This approach provides a better sense of the changes in elasticities that take place as prices and incomes change. In cases where it is important to understand how different income classes may be affected by a policy, it allows a quick comparison

> **Box 2.1** (*cont.*)
>
> of income elasticities for poor, middle-income and rich consumers without having to rely on detailed household surveys, which may not be available.
>
> A number of additional assumptions are needed in practice to make these elasticities reliable, but they concern more technical econometric concerns that go beyond the main focus of this book. In practice, the simple approaches discussed here are often used to simply get a first-order quantitative measure of the relevant elasticities. Ideally, they should be validated with more careful approaches, including structural models that account for both the demand and supply sides of the market.

differences between short- and long-term reactions. In regulated industries, such failures can translate into oversupply or rationing. More generally, ignoring the relevance of elasticities increases the odds of worsening the efficiency, equity or financial viability of an activity.

2.6 How Do Regulators Look at Technology and Production beyond Elasticities?

The price and income elasticities of demand are essential to understand the deadweight loss consequences of key pricing decisions or to assess the efficiency payoffs and/or limitations of taxes or subsidies in regulated industries.[20] But they do not provide quantitative measures of the extent to which a regulated firm is doing what it can to make the most of the resources it controls and of the technological options it can pick from. Once more, the regulatory solution is to try to produce some benchmark against which the observed performance can be compared.

There are a few reasons why this is a bit tricky. The first is that the heterogeneity of options on the supply side raises the risk of oversimplification in the modelling. The goods and services delivered by the firms of any sector are, indeed, the result of a production process that may vary across firms. Each activity is characterized by its own technology, which can be modelled analytically to summarize how it combines the various inputs involved in delivering the final product. The second reason is that the assumption that all relevant information is available to all stakeholders is difficult to accept. For now, we stick to it and see how it helps us generate a useful benchmark for the production side. But we will have to revisit this assumption.

Let's start with the representation of technology. There is a great diversity of technologies in some activities and hardly any in others. Electricity can be produced

---

[20] A deadweight loss can be defined as a cost to society resulting from a market failure. From a more technical perspective, it corresponds to a loss of economic efficiency linked to an excessive price or insufficient quantity or quality consumed or produced. As we'll see in Chapter 3, in the context of monopolistic market structures, it corresponds to the loss of surplus resulting from the ability of the monopoly to produce less and charge more than a competitive market would deliver.

in many ways (thermal, nuclear, hydro, solar, wind) but there are not too many ways of pumping water from the ground or from rivers, although there are many techniques to clean it, transport it and actually deliver it. How much water needs to be treated depends on the strength of the stream flow of the river into which wastewater is put. How much to spend on the dredging of a port depends on the depth of the sea where the port is built and on other natural characteristics of the sea at that location. There is no general predictable pattern for technology.

When accounting practices are reasonable in the regulated sector under study, a look at the cost accounting of any firm is an easy way of appraising the diversity of inputs that can be used in a given activity, since most inputs have to be paid for and need to be reported in the accounting system. If accounting data is not available or is too poor, engineers are often the main source of information on the production process to be analysed. In addition, finding matching cost data from international best practice is relatively easy, even if it must be purchased since it is usually produced by private consulting firms. The point is that benchmarking production processes to get a sense of 'best practice' is usually not too difficult, as discussed next.

2.7 How Are Production Processes Modelled?

To keep things manageable, the production process considered in regulatory discussion is typically modelled to account for a broad aggregate of inputs, such as labour, machinery and raw materials. This is the usual production function discussed in basic microeconomics classes. This function is a formalization of the process that allows the inputs to be transformed into a final output. In a subset of the regulatory literature, this function is also known as the 'production frontier' to emphasize the fact that it yields the maximum output that is technologically feasible.

Formally, it is a function, $q = f(x)$, that describes the maximum output, q, that a firm can produce using any particular set of inputs, x.[21] If the firm relies on three factors, say capital (K), labour (L) and raw materials (M), then x is the vector of inputs needed to produce the output $q : x = (K, L, M)$. The approach to the formalization of complex production processes may look straightforward, but it is more demanding and subtle than the simple general expression above suggests. Why? Because how details on inputs, technology and time are accounted for matters a great deal.

Details on inputs matter. The number of inputs to be separately modelled is a pragmatic decision that depends on the policy issues being analysed. For instance, if

---

[21] To be able to conduct more formal assessments, this production function must comply with a number of characterizations, including (i) non-negativity: the production of positive output is impossible without a positive input; (ii) non-decreasing in x or monotonicity: additional units of an input will not decrease output (if the production function is continuously differentiable, monotonicity implies that all marginal products are non-negative); (iii) concave in x: any combination of the inputs will produce an output that is no less than the linear combination of the outputs from these input levels. If the production function is continuously differentiable, concavity implies all marginal products are non-increasing (under the well-known law of diminishing marginal productivity).

some inputs are subject to price control and defined by complex negotiations rather than markets (e.g. the number of employees negotiated with unions) or if some are imported and hence subject to specific related risks and taxes, it may be useful to have a clearer picture as to how these factors enter the production process.

Technology matters. The choice of the specific form the function will have is even more important since it is the economist's approximation of the production technology. The extent to which combinations of inputs and outputs can be changed through management decisions must be assessed so as to measure the scope for substitution. How well this can be done depends on the specific functional form assumed for the formalization of the production process, as explained in Box 2.2. The most recent literature relies on flexible functional forms which do not require major assumptions on these dimensions and reflect the actual degree of substitutability as well as the effectiveness of the production process and hence of the technology adopted.

Time matters. The previous discussions have already emphasized the relevance of time. We will have occasion to return repeatedly to the time dimension, because many regulated assets are long-lived and many changes and shocks can occur over time. For now, our concern is simply to note that the subtle implications of time are not always reported in policy or academic publications. The scope for changes in the efficiency of a producer is quite different in the short and long run. Many analysts implicitly assume that the production function is set for the long run. This is not a major issue for industries or firms relying on long-lived assets that are seldom replaced. But it can be more problematic for industries in constant evolution owing to research and development and to the rationalization of technical choices. This is obviously the case for the telecoms sector, where the broadband speed offered to the public has been increasing steadily over the last ten years. Ignoring time dimensions when they are relevant can thus lead to an underestimation of the margin for change and hence the margin for payoffs to users (and taxpayers, if the activity is subsidized).

2.8   How Does Efficiency Appear in Production Diagnostics?

Conceptually, a desirable benchmark to which actual performance can be compared will be such that a production efficiency level computed for that market structure or for a firm cannot be improved upon once all the constraints that managers cannot affect have been taken into account. In practice, this means that a firm (and by extension society if the firm is a monopolistic service provider) cannot do better than the benchmark.

What does it mean that it cannot be improved? For a given combination of outputs, for a given technology and for every set of inputs available, the scope for improvement may be limited because the production of one output cannot be increased without a decrease in the production of at least one other, or without increasing the use of at least one input. And this has to be assessed at the lowest possible cost in purchase and use of each input. This may seem quite restrictive, but it is useful to keep in mind that we are looking for a benchmark. Production benchmarks are typically impossible

---

Box 2.2 Using Production Data to Approximate Scale Economies in an Industry

The easiest 'actionable' functional form for $q = f(x)$ is the Cobb–Douglas: $q_t = AK_t^a L_t^b$, where q_t is the output at time t, and K_t and L_t are total assets and full-time-equivalent employment, respectively, in the same period. K_t increases with investment over time, corrected from depreciation of assets, and L_t changes with staff recruitment, firing, voluntary withdrawal and retirement. A, a and b are the constants that, when estimated, describe the quantitative relationship between the inputs (K_t and L_t) and output (q_t). The sum of the constants $a + b$ determines returns to scale. That is, $a + b > 1$ implies increasing returns to scale (i.e. doubling K_t and L_t provides an output that is more than doubled), while $a + b = 1$ implies constant returns to scale (the output and inputs vary in the same proportion). These are the two possibilities when all inputs are adjustable, typically in the long run. In cases in which one of the inputs is fixed (e.g. capital in the short term), there is also the possibility of decreasing returns to scale, which would be observed if $b < 1$.

Taking logs, we get the following log-linear form: $ln\ q_t = ln\ A + a\ ln\ K_t + b\ ln\ L_t$.

This expression makes it easy to estimate econometrically the key coefficients (a and b). This functional form is easy to work with, but it imposes strong assumptions, including unit elasticity of substitution between K and L, which does not really account for the broad range of substitution options in some regulated industries.

The most common alternative functional form used in the literature, the *translog* function, avoids this restriction but is more complex to estimate and subtler to interpret. It has a flexible functional form that permits the partial elasticities of substitution between inputs to vary. For the comparable two-factor case, the translog production function is:

$$ln\ q_t = A + a\ ln\ K_t + b\ ln\ L_t + (c/2)(ln\ K_t)^2 + (d/2)(ln\ L_t)^2 + e\ ln\ K_t\ ln\ L_t$$

where A, a, b, c, d and e are all parameters that can be estimated from data on the firm over time. They can also be estimated from a sample of n firms ($i = 1, \ldots, n$) in a single year:

$$ln\ q_i = \beta_0 + \beta_K\ ln\ K_i + \beta_L\ ln\ L_i + (\beta_{KK}/2)(ln\ K_i)^2 + (\beta_{LL}/2)(ln\ L_i)^2$$
$$+ \beta_{KL}\ ln\ K_i\ ln\ L_i$$

This can then be used to estimate the production elasticity for any firm to an input $j = K, L$ as $\varepsilon_j = \beta_j + \beta_{j1}\ ln\ K_i + \beta_{j2}\ ln\ L_i$ and the scale elasticity for firm i as $\varepsilon_i = \varepsilon_{Ki} + \varepsilon_{Li}$.

The econometrics are a little more complex for the translog, as are the efforts needed to come up with elasticities, but the effort usually yields gains in precision and many software programs are now quite good at guiding their users through these estimations. In sum, the translog function is easier to use than it seems.

dreams rather than statements of reality. The wedge between dream and realism can actually grow as time goes by. For instance, if technology is likely to change, more options open up. The same set of outputs may be obtained from different sets of inputs, and thus from different levels of expenditure.

Whether technology is likely to change or not, any deviation from the ideal situation should show up in a sector or firm diagnostic as inefficiency (that is, as a welfare loss to society). When a country has divided the mandate to deliver the regulated service to various local monopolies, the benchmark can often be common to all firms, accounting for local specificities. This approach then allows a ranking of the firms according to their level of inefficiency and a comparison of their perform-ance. This will come in handy when trying to set up concrete differentiated policy decisions, as discussed later.

Of course, matters are not that simple. It is hard to know the details of the costs and production structure of any firm, and of regulated firms in particular, since they have a strong incentive to keep this information hidden. But to appreciate the importance of deviations from the benchmark linked to information gaps or other distortions, it is essential to understand how benchmarks anchor discussions of efficiency and other performance diagnostics.

A benchmark production or cost function is, indeed, probably the most concrete measure government agencies can hope to have when conducting diagnostics, judging whether a firm might be able to improve cost savings, or determining whether the decision of two firms to merge will lead to efficiency gains in the interest of consumers. Such a benchmark is necessary, moreover, when estimating the margin for improving scale and scope economies – that is, for lowering costs by bringing together the production of one or several products or services. It quantifies the extent to which larger plants actually lead to a more efficient use of resources. It is also quite crucial when assessing ex post the effectiveness of restructuring and deregulation of public services so as to learn from mistakes. The key question in these discussions is whether gains from increased competition would offset any losses in economies of scale or scope caused by unbundling vertically or horizontally integrated firms.

If production efficiency cannot be measured for some reason, it becomes relatively easy for a regulated operator to question any policy or regulatory decision regarding its production or pricing choices. The alternative in such cases is to rely on any data that might be available on the cost side of the business. In the standard competitive benchmark, looking at production and cost is equivalent – provided some reasonably moderate mathematical assumptions are respected (to be able to switch between the results from the production to the cost data and vice versa).[22] The two approaches

---

[22] The possibility of drawing equivalent conclusions from switching between cost and production functions is discussed in basic microeconomics textbooks as the concept of duality between cost and production. The use of theoretical results allowing the switch from production to cost when assessing efficiency and other performance dimensions of a firm is actually not quite so rigorous when firms do not function in perfectly competitive upstream markets. This is only one of the many corner-rounding techniques used in applied economics. But it is a salient issue in interactions between economic advisors to regulators and those advising regulated firms.

serve as each other's backup in policy analysis, and one is often preferred to the other depending on data availability. Both approaches can also be used to assess the many dimensions of efficiency that may interest regulators and competition agencies.

2.9 What If We Looked at Efficiency from the Cost rather than the Production Side?

As noted in the preceding section, when cost data is more readily available than production data, the efficiency issue has to be tackled on the cost side, which can be relatively easily available if standard cost accounting practice has been imposed by the regulator on the operators. This is often more intuitive to non-specialized analysts than it is to specialists, since lay observers often find production technologies difficult to analyse. In countries where cost-reporting laws are well designed (such as Australia, Canada, the United Kingdom and the United States) or when regulators have imposed cost accounting rules on the operators, whether public or private (such as Brazil, Chile, Mali, Niger or Peru), it is quite common to assess efficiency from the cost side.

Under this approach, an efficient firm minimizes the costs of producing the set of outputs it generates so as to enhance its competitive position or to increase its profits. From the users' (and hence the regulator's) perspective, the focus is on making sure that the firm produces a specific level and combination of regulated outputs at the lowest possible cost. This will eventually lead to the lowest possible average price for the service if the regulator uses the information properly.[23]

To determine this minimum cost, a *cost function* mirroring the production function discussed earlier is needed. This cost function, also known as the 'cost frontier' in some terminologies, is the functional relationship, $C(q)$, between the outputs that the firm can produce and the minimum amount of spending, wx, needed to produce those outputs, with x, the set of inputs, and w, their unit prices. It thus combines the technological information of the production function with the accounting information of the spending function to generate an optimized direct relationship between outputs and expenditures.

Formally, this can be expressed as follows. The firm is said to acquire its set of inputs x at unit prices w at a cost of wx. If its production process links the inputs x and the outputs q by means of the technology, $g(x, q) = 0$, then, by definition, the cost function is the relationship between the outputs and the expenditure, at fixed input prices: $C(q) = \min(wx) \text{ s.t.} g(x, q) = 0$.[24]

Any deviation from the solution to this problem translates into wasteful expenditures (i.e. higher costs than necessary). Concretely, once the cost function reveals the

---

[23] For reasons that we will explain in Chapter 5, this joint focus by operators and users on cost minimization changes when information is not transparent and regulators need to decide with some degree of uncertainty on the actual performance of the operator.

[24] Note that the cost function should be written $C(w, q)$ since variations in the input prices play an important role in the calculation of cost coverage.

acceptable level of expenditures for each level of output and given the assumed technology, we compare the observed costs to the ideal costs to reach a conclusion about the level of inefficiency of current practice.

Estimating or calculating this cost is not terribly complex given some basic data on the volume of inputs for various levels or combinations of outputs, and on the price of each input.[25] Even if such data is scarce, there are tricks to get around the informational gap, including databases on standardized input prices and technological ways to identify best-practice outputs. This is particularly useful when working on regulated industries in which the informational gaps are actively maintained by regulated firms. But these tricks exist only to pass on to producers and service providers the burden of proof on costs. If they are not happy with the assumed costs, they have an incentive to provide more accurate data.

Box 2.3 presents a common form of cost function, the translog, which is also used to assess the production function (Box 2.2). To offer the reader a more formal presentation of the same function in its application to cost data, Box 2.3 is a bit more general than Box 2.2.

2.10   Some Insights on How to Use Cost Data to Develop Policy Intuitions

The visual presentation of the cost function in Figure 2.4 conveys that the expected efficiency level is linked to the production level, something that is not always obvious from the formal expressions of these functions. But this simple intuition is essential if one is to appreciate the importance of benchmarking exercises that compare non-competitive market structures to the competitive benchmark. To see this point, consider the case of a firm or a sector responsible for a single product. The average total cost simply reports the evolution of $C_M(q) = C(q)/q$ as production increases, where $C(q)$ is the total cost and q is the single output level. This is usually easy to calculate when the firm is specialized in one service (or when the analyst assumes it is so as to make things simple). In many cases, this is represented by a U-shaped curve (labelled average total cost, C_M, in Figure 2.4). In the same figure, the average fixed cost (F/q) is declining, to reflect the fact that the cost of the fixed asset needed to support production can be distributed over a larger output as output increases. At any output level q, the average total cost is the sum of $AVC = (C(q) - F)/q$, the average variable cost, and F/q, the average fixed cost: $C_M(q) = AVC + F/q$.

The larger the market size, the greater the scope for decreases in the unit cost of activities. The drop in unit cost, combined with the less-than-proportional growth in

---

[25] If an econometric approach is used to estimate the cost function, it requires an *estimation* of the coefficients that weight the variables or shift the function. If a non-linear optimization technique is used, the costs are *computed* rather than estimated. The first approach is known as *parametric* because it is based on the estimation of parameters derived from an explicit production function. The second is known as *non-parametric* because it does not require the specification of any particular functional form to describe the efficient frontier. The debates in the profession as to which method is most reliable are ongoing.

Box 2.3 Two Common Cost Functions

Cobb–Douglas or Constant Elasticity Cost Function

It is one of the most common formal expressions of the relationship between costs, on the one hand, and outputs and input prices, on the other. For an output q and a vector of input prices w, it takes the form $C(w, q) = Aq^k w_1^{a_1} w_2^{a_2} \ldots w_n^{a_n}$ where A, k, and $a_i > 0$ are constant, and where $\sum_{i=1}^{n}$. The k and the a_i are quite useful in practice, as they measure the elasticity of cost to output and input prices respectively. They can be readily estimated by rewriting the expression as follows: $\ln C = \ln A + k \ln q + \sum_{i=1}^{n} a_i \ln w_i$.

Translog Cost Function

The translog cost function is much less rigid in its assumptions about the relationships between variables and hence provides more precise information. The translog cost function allows elasticities and marginal costs to vary flexibly with the level of outputs and prices. Flexibility comes from the fact that the function includes both first- and second-order terms in all variables. It allows for varying degrees of returns to scale and density as firm size varies. This is why it is often a good approximation of the cost functions associated with production functions. Thus, if the exact functional form of the production function relevant to the firm or the sector is not available, the translog is a sage option for the functional form of the cost function. In the context of regulated industries, it can also be useful to accommodate both economies and diseconomies of scale. It takes the form:

$$\ln C = a_0 + a_q \ln q + \sum_{i=1}^{n} a_i \ln w_i + \frac{1}{2}\sum_{i=1}^{n}\sum_{j=1}^{n} a_{ij} \ln w_i \ln w_j$$

$$+ \sum_{i=1}^{n} a_{qi} \ln q \ln w_i + a_{qq}[\ln q]^2$$

with q as the level of output and w_i as the price of input i.

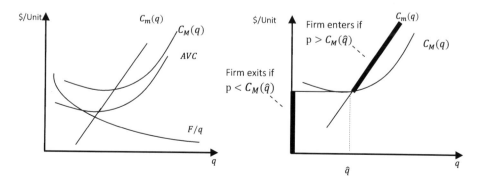

Figure 2.4 Firm entry and exit and cost functions

variable costs (owing to the effects of learning and standardization), is what propels concentration in these sectors. The output level associated with the declining part of the average total cost, $C_M(q)$, is the one a regulator tends to be interested in. This is what the regulator wants to be able to measure when estimating cost functions.

But it is not the only cost dimension of interest for a regulator. Marginal cost (i.e. the cost of the last unit produced) is just as important. The marginal cost, $C_m(q) = C'(q) = \Delta C / \Delta q$, where Δ represents the change in the variable, is almost as easy to approximate from basic data (e.g. how much more it costs to build an extra kilometre of road, or to connect an extra neighbourhood or family to a water network). When the market is competitive and there is free entry, marginal cost is equal to average cost $C_m(\hat{q}) = C_M(\hat{q})$, which corresponds to the point where the average cost is minimized.[26]

In the industries we focus on in this book, the average cost of production is usually declining over a substantial range of output, so that the marginal cost usually is below the average cost until production capacity is almost at the maximum. In these industries, the marginal cost tends to be relatively low and stable (i.e. flat graphically) as discussed in the next chapter. Because of these characteristics, the total cost function is often represented in textbooks on regulation as $C(q) = F + cq$, which leads to an average cost function $C_M(q) = F/q + c$. This average cost function represented in Figure 2.5 is appealing because it captures simply how economies of scale shape cost functions. It is therefore useful, at least until congestion occurs and leads to increases in total average costs.

In Figure 2.5, for all levels of production, the average cost, $C_M(q)$, decreases, which reflects economies of scale or increasing returns. The higher the fixed cost component F (e.g. a water treatment building, an electricity transmission line, an airport or a port terminal), the more likely that economies of scale or increasing returns to scale will be observed. Such economies of scale are typical of the physical infrastructure of most public services.[27] These cost functions provide a first view on one trade-off faced by regulators (and detailed in the next chapter): the optimal output is q^0 and the price should be c, but $c < F/q + c$ so that operators would incur financial

---

[26] This implies that if the price is to be set to recover costs, pricing at marginal cost is the right decision in theory. In practice, it also matters that pricing at marginal cost in a competitive environment should provide a fair return on capital. This return is the outcome of an arbitration across all investment opportunities, not just those in the sector. Whatever pricing rule is derived for a non-competitive environment, it has to account for an equivalent fair return to capital, and this requires an explicit link to the financing strategy of the operators, something that is largely ignored by standard microeconomic theory.

[27] More precisely, the case for large firms in infrastructure services and in many other public services comes from sub-additivity in their cost function. In terms of economies of scale, this means that if all firms have the same cost function $C(q_i)$, with $i = 1, \ldots, k$ firms, and if the public service output is $Q = \sum_{i=1}^{k} q_i$, a cost function is strictly sub-additive if $C(Q) < C(q_1) + \ldots + C(q_k)$. One firm produces the entire output at lowest cost compared with any allocation of outputs between two or more firms. In terms of economies of scope, it is less costly to produce several products or services in the same firm than to separate them. If a and b are two products (e.g. parcels and letters in postal services), $C(q_a, q_b) < C(q_a, 0) + C(0, q_b)$.

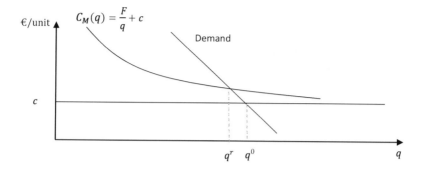

$$C_M(q) = \frac{F}{q} + c$$

Figure 2.5 How fixed (F), marginal (c) and average costs (C_M) relate to output (q)

losses; at q^r, the operators break even, but $q^r < q^o$ which means there is a deadweight loss.

For a given technology, efficiency also depends on the size of operations, then on the demand for the product or service. Demand will therefore affect efficiency and will have to be accounted for in any diagnostic, even if some of the quantitative tools tend to disconnect the demand and supply sides of a business. For instance, when the economy slows down, traffic tends to slow down as well. In Figure 2.5, the demand curve is shifted leftwards. For toll road or railways operators, this means that their roads and trains will be less used than they could be. Their production capacity will be underused because demand has dropped. Since the transport infrastructures are built to cater to a given demand, any slowdown will reduce the efficiency performance of these infrastructures. Supply efficiency is indeed linked to demand.

2.11   Summing Up

- Regulators can benchmark the performance of a service provider in terms of the level of output it delivers and the average price it charges when information on demand and on costs is accessible to all stakeholders.
- Conceptually, regulatory policy often takes as its desirable benchmark the efficiency level that would be achieved from competition (without any externality).
  - Efficiency is thus a central concept in the theory of regulation. Its detailed definition and specific measurement is at the core of the practice of regulation which shows up in the large literature on the estimation of cost and production functions.
- In practice, the common economist's benchmarking approach to assess distortions in efficiency is to compare the output and price outcomes to those that would be achieved under perfect competition. This requires a solid diagnostic of both the demand and the supply side of the market.
- For the consumers' side, regulators should collect the information needed to allow an assessment of the price and the income elasticity of demand. This information

can be used to gauge the risks of abuses by the monopolist of its market power, including the risk that it will set prices at levels that are unaffordable to some users and reduce quantities enough to impede access by others.

- For the supply side, the regulator needs to collect enough data on costs and/or on production to be able to assess the size of the performance gap of the operators when compared to a perfect competition benchmark or to some other best practice benchmark.
- In the public service industries (e.g. electricity, water and sanitation, railways, roads or telecoms) based on large infrastructures, the average cost of production is usually declining over a substantial range of output, and the marginal cost is below the average costs over that same range of output. Then marginal cost pricing entails financial losses to the operators.

3   Thinking Like a Monopoly about Price and Output

This chapter discusses how the cost characteristics of monopolies influence the determination of optimal prices and quantities of goods and services and how regulators need to internalize these characteristics in the way they design regulation. For now, we assume that regulators are able to observe the firm's cost and to estimate a cost function. They find that the sector is characterized by high upfront investment costs, low marginal costs and declining average costs linked to significant scale economies.

Understanding how monopolies 'think' is important because they are overrepresented in many public services, as seen in Chapter 1. In infrastructure in particular, the cost characteristics are such that only a few firms can survive and, in many cases, the market should remain under the control of a single firm – a monopolist – to be able to lower average costs as much as possible. This is why most countries have a single company running the railways or airport infrastructures, regional electricity transmission lines or water pipelines network. The high investment costs needed to deliver the service are a barrier to entry for potential alternative suppliers.

We are no longer within the realm of the competitive benchmark case discussed in the previous chapter. It would make little sense to have multiple companies bringing parallel water pipes to your home simply to allow you to have the choice. In this case the activity is a *natural monopoly*.[1] Despite low marginal costs, the large upfront capital costs create barriers to entry. They limit the optimal number of participating firms in the market. In the monopoly case, the demand to the firm is the whole market demand, which to some extent makes regulation simpler. This is the case we focus on for now.

In practice, there is a trade-off between the gains from scale economies that can be achieved by relying on a single provider and the risks of welfare losses stemming from the strong bargaining power this monopolist will enjoy. Addressing this trade-off is one of the roles of a regulator. If the monopolist is allowed to capture all the gains from the scale effects, society may not be better off than it was under a more

---

[1] An industry can be defined formally as a *natural monopoly* if the technology is such that any vector of outputs will cost less when produced in one single firm than if it is shared among several firms, whatever the sharing rule. In the single-product case, it is equivalent to economies of scale or decreasing average cost. If the industry supplies several products, the natural monopoly definition necessitates a combination of conditions on economies of scale and economies of scope (see Box 2.2).

competitive environment. This is why the government needs to consider influencing the choices made by the monopolist if that ends up being the preferred market structure. To design the government's intervention, however, it is essential to understand the business decisions of the monopolist, including its optimal production and pricing strategy. This starts with a better formal appreciation of the relevance of the time dimension in industries requiring large and lumpy investments and of the way in which short- and long-term incentives differ for a monopolist.

3.1 On the Relevance of the Time Dimension in Industries with Large Fixed Costs

One of the main defining characteristics of many regulated industries is their necessary large upfront investments. Their levels are selected to meet the needs of both current and future users. These investments are usually labelled CAPEX in the applied regulation literature, short for capital expenditure. The fact that they have to cater to a forward-looking assessment of demand is what introduces a time dimension in the optimization process. The implications are wide-ranging, but from a practical viewpoint their main impact is that these assets need to be maintained as well as possible to ensure that their actual asset life and use is consistent with their intended life and use.

The total costs needed to deliver the services on a day-to-day basis, including maintenance costs, are labelled OPEX, short for operational and maintenance expenditures in the applied regulatory literature. These OPEX drive the marginal costs covered in the theoretical literature. Their remarkable characteristic from a regulatory viewpoint is that they differ in the short term and the long term. This difference stems from their sensitivity to the volume of production in practice. Whether the demand increases fast or not makes a difference to these OPEX. Maintaining a road with high traffic does not imply the same marginal costs per kilometre as maintaining a road with low traffic. The OPEX cost will therefore vary in time as traffic evolves. This insight needs to be used in a wide range of regulatory contexts discussed in this chapter and the following ones.

For now, to illustrate the policy relevance of the OPEX and CAPEX concepts in practice, we will focus on analysing whether a monopoly has overinvested or underinvested in production capacity for a given demand forecast. This is a common and often misunderstood issue in regulated industries. Roads to nowhere or empty regional airports are just as common around the world as highly congested roads and airports at any given point in time. But they can be explained by two factors. First, they can be the outcome of poor ex ante assessments of the potential size of the market – i.e. the long-term demand forecast. Second, they can also be indicators of the relevance of the time dimension to be considered when conducting sector performance diagnostics, that is the need to distinguish between costs in the short and in the long term.

The quality of long-term demand forecast is hard to underestimate when conducting regulatory diagnostics over long periods of time. It drives the size of the investment to be made. And this is particularly important in the context of regulated industries because one of their characteristics is that capacity additions (i.e. new investments) are often indivisible as they cannot be gradually increased as demand grows. Investments need to be lumpy. Engineers are quite keen to point out that underestimating size can be costly. For instance, it is a lot more cost-effective to build a three-lane road to meet long-term demand rather than to start with two lanes and add a lane when traffic congestion starts to appear on the two-lane option. The problem is that the fear of underestimating often leads to overestimation, which can also lead to a waste of money. For instance, building a regional airport hoping that it will attract low-cost airlines can be quite irrational when there is no tourism industry in the region. Many provinces in Spain made that mistake in the 1990s.[2]

These overoptimistic forecasts are common as they provide an easy way to justify ex ante investments for any government with short-term electoral concerns in mind. Infrastructure inaugurations are usually well covered by the media and this makes a difference in the voting booth. This is often what explains overinvestment or mis-guided investment, known as white elephants or roads to nowhere. These are indeed quite common in both developed and developing economies.[3] Forecast manipulation is one of the ways in which public decisions can be distorted for private interests in regulated industries. But there are other ways in which the high concentration of market power in these industries seems to facilitate these distortions. Some are legal because rules and regulations are imperfect. But others boil down to corruption. Some of the main ways in which the private interests of actors with significant market power in infrastructure can penalize the public interest are summarized in Box 3.1.[4]

The time frame of the diagnostic is just as relevant to regulatory decisions and often better internalized in the theory supporting regulatory decisions than in its practice. Indeed, analysts should expect to observe performance differences between similar projects at different stages of their life because there are differences between short- and long-term marginal costs. When assessing the performance of a toll road operator, for instance, in the early years of the asset life, analysts should expect scale efficiency to be lower than in the longer run simply because it takes time for traffic to reach its steady-state long-term level. But while overcapacity prevails, they should also expect the short-run marginal cost to be lower than the long-run marginal cost because the road is underused. In the longer run, when traffic has picked up, road congestion will be more common, and the short-run marginal cost will tend to be higher than the long-run cost while scale efficiency may have improved. On the other hand, when traffic never picks up, this should provide a good indication of the likelihood that the

---

[2] Aeropuertos Espanola's y Navegación Aérea (AENA), a public firm attached to the Ministry of Transport, manages forty-six commercial airports in Spain. Over 20% of these airports do not offer flights on most days of the year. Traffic is well below forecast since in 2016, seventeen had fewer than 160,000 passengers per year, including eight with fewer than 5,000 passengers per year, although none was built to cater to fewer than 300,000 passengers per year (AENA 2017).

[3] Bel et al. (2014) document the extent of the problem in Spain for instance. Flyvbjerg et al. (2003; Flyvbjerg 2017) have documented a much broader set of cases in their assessments of the failures of mega-projects.

[4] For more details see Rose-Ackerman and Søreide (2011) or Soreide (2014).

Box 3.1 The Doors to Corruption in Industries with Market and Political Power: The Case of Infrastructure

The first door to corruption is linked to the process followed to restructure a sector. This includes revisiting the role of planning and of the regulatory function. If, in the restructuring process, planning is reduced to a strict minimum then it allows the vision of the sector to be a moving target matching short-term political preferences and those of the industry lobbies. Similarly, regulation, even if assigned to a new institution separated from the sector's ministry, can be subject to political interference or to capture by regulated industries. And the risk is particularly high if the regulated firms enjoy both market and political power. For many countries, these two important institutional weaknesses largely explain why demand and costing can so easily be instrumentalized both ex ante and ex post in regulation decisions and audits.

Financing strategies open a second door to corruption. When public and private financing actors have their preferences for partners under various types of public–private partnership (PPP) schemes, it can distort costs in significant ways. In many countries, the case for such preferences is justified by a desire to support national champions. This may seem to be a reasonable form of industrial policy in some countries, but from the viewpoint of consumers or taxpayers, it often boils down to potentially corrupt strategies which can lead to higher than necessary costs. For developing countries, this is one of the ways in which the old-fashion tied aid continues to exist.

The third door to corruption is procurement. There is ample literature on how large operators can influence their design and enforcement. Piga (2011), for instance, summarizes many of the key issues in the context of OECD countries. Estache and Iimi (2011) raise equivalent issues for developing countries and Nag (2013) provides a fairly detailed country-specific case study of Indian railways. Auriol and Blanc (2009) provide the equivalent for water and energy in Sub-Saharan Africa. Kenny (2010) provides a useful discussion of how much the construction phase of any public investment is open to corrupt practices. Kenny and Musatova (2011) also show how often procurement issues can be used as red flags for the risk of corruption in infrastructure. And Guasch et al. (2016) show how easily contract renegotiations can be manipulated to favour large incumbents. Most of these papers find that the victims of the tricks tend to be users, taxpayers and excluded potential entrants.

Source: Estache (2014).

---

operator has overinvested and that without some government support, the short-run marginal costs will become financially unaffordable for this operator. The gains from scale efficiency will never show up because of a lack of traffic.

The risks of inconsistencies in the assessment of efficiency related to the timing of investment have been quite well documented empirically for regulated industries. For instance, Cambini and Rondi (2010) have shown for a sample of EU energy utilities from 1997 to 2007 that the investment behaviour of incentive-regulated firms can be negatively impacted by unclear assessment rules of the relevance of timing in the definition of regulatory goals. Transitory inefficiency may be confused with operational efficiency. How perverse the impact of the confusion is depends on how regulation is implemented in practice (Vogelsang 2010). Unfortunately, goal-setting without consideration of intertemporal effects is still common, even if it has generated and continues to generate much academic research (e.g. from Färe and Grosskopf 1996 to Fallah-Fini et al. 2013). The main policy implication of this research is that blindly penalizing a firm for the short-run underuse of its investment is irrational if it ignores the difference between the short- and long-term marginal costs associated with an asset. Alternatively, ignoring a failure to improve the scale-efficiency performance as time goes by can also be irrational if it is the outcome of an overoptimistic demand forecast.

3.2 The Fading Distinction between the Monopolist's Short- and Long-Term Incentives

This discussion so far has shown that, in practice, the relevance of the time dimension can be quite a challenge for regulators. But technology is changing the nature and the dimensions of the regulatory challenge. The promise of scale economies has weakened in many regulated industries and this implies that the difference between the short and the long run may slowly be fading away for some new investments. Smaller power generators, water treatment plants or satellites are all making size matter less than fifteen to twenty years ago in these industries. The growing role of digital solutions is also making it easier to use smaller capacities more effectively.

The lower relevance of size implies a growing irrelevance of time but they also imply new transitional challenges. Indeed, if for new investment the shorter asset life reduces the risks associated with poor demand forecast, the risks are still highly relevant for older investments not yet fully amortized. The changes are also increasing the scope for relying on competition in the market between smaller scale operators and this also demands a coordination of regulatory strategies between old and new investments. Despite their practical relevance, these transitional issues will not be dealt with here as their analytical treatment is much more complex than the level adopted in this book. We will focus instead on showing how much the growing ability of firms to adjust their capacity to the speed at which demand is growing is likely to influence the behaviour of some of the monopolists. This is likely to be a concrete concern for regulators in the coming years as the energy and transport transition towards environmentally friendlier options is being implemented.

To be able to assess analytically the difference between the short- and long-run perspective in the old and new technological context, we need to account for the changes in the production process. Moreover, we need to be able to quantify the extent to which the cost of producing a given volume with fixed equipment (short-run cost) is higher than the cost that would be incurred if the capacity could be adapted to suit the production to be undertaken. Finally, we also need to be able to account for the fact

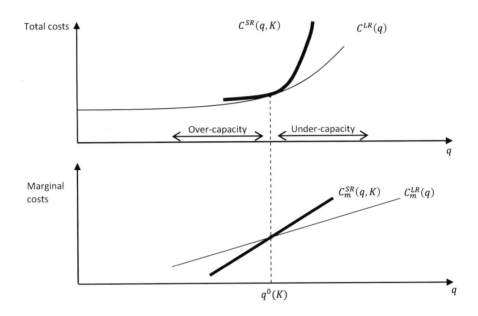

Figure 3.1 Short- versus long-run costs

that when installed equipment is ample (overcapacity), producing an additional unit is not very costly. In contrast, when equipment is limited (undercapacity), increasing production with that equipment is much more expensive in the short run than in the long run, when equipment could be adapted to the desired change in output.

Graphically, it is easy to see in Figure 3.1 that only when the output corresponds to the installed capacity is the short-run marginal cost equal to the long-run marginal cost. Box 3.2 provides a more technical illustration of the relevance of the difference between the short- and long-run costs and what they mean for a regulator trying to assess the extent to which there is over- or undercapacity.

From a regulatory policy perspective, this discussion suggests that it makes sense to start planning new investment when the short-term costs associated with an increase in output comes to exceed the matching long-term additional cost linked to the increase in production. Up to that point, the production capacity is being underused. From that point forward, however, it makes sense to consider investing to increase production capacity. This is straightforward enough, but we also know that part of the story has to be linked to the way the firm will be able to price these services.

3.3   How Does Long-Term Size Impact on Optimal Pricing?

When assessing the pricing scheme of a monopolist, the regulator needs to keep in mind the incentives that drive the way in which this monopolist makes its decision.

Box 3.2 Short-Run and Long-Run Cost Functions

Assume that the production function is of the Cobb–Douglas type with constant returns to scale: $q = (LK)^{1/2}$, where q is the output (e.g. the number of letters circulated by a post office), K is the capital invested (e.g. the number of vehicles) and L is the other inputs (e.g. the number of employees at the post office).

In the long run, all inputs can be adapted so that the cost function is obtained by solving $C^{LR}(q) = \min (wL + rK)$ subject to $q = (LK)^{1/2}$, where w and r are the unit costs of the two types of inputs. To keep things simple, assume that $w = r = 1$. Given the symmetry of the production function and the unit cost of the inputs, the solution is given by $L = K = q$ so that $C^{LR}(q) = 2q$. Then the long-run marginal cost is obtained by taking the derivative of the cost function with respect to output, $C_m^{LR}(q) = dC^{LR}/dq = 2$.

In the short run, the installed capital K is fixed. Only L can be adapted to the level of output q. By inverting the production function, we have $L = q^2/K$ so that the short-run cost function is $C^{SR}(q, K) = wL + rK = (q^2/K) + K$, and the short-run marginal cost is $C_m^{SR}(q, K) = \frac{\partial C^{SR}(q,K)}{\partial q} = C^{SR'} = 2q/K$.

First, observe that $C^{SR}(q, K) - C^{LR}(q) = (q - K)^2/K$. This means that the short-run cost is greater than the long-run one for all values of q, except when the output is just equal to the installed capacity since when $q = K$ then $C^{SR}(q, K) = C^{SR}(q, q) = C^{LR}(q)$, i.e. the long-run cost is the envelope of the short-run costs.

As for marginal costs, $C_m^{SR}(q, K) - C_m^{LR}(q) = 2(q - K)/K$. This difference is 0 again if and only if $q = K$.

This implies that: (i) in the case of undercapacity, i.e. if the firm must produce more than the output corresponding to the installed capacity (i.e. $q > K$), the short-run marginal cost is greater than the long-run marginal cost and (ii) in the case of excess capacity (i.e. $q < K$), the opposite holds.

And this means keeping track of a number of predictable theoretical insights. You should remember that the short-run marginal cost tends to be quite low as compared to the average cost in the sectors we are interested in. This is largely driven by a high fixed cost associated with the high investment levels needed to deliver a service (e.g. rail tracks and rolling stock to transport passengers and freight, water pipes and transmission lines to bring water and electricity from its source to your home). If this high fixed cost accounts correctly for the demand forecast and hence for the time horizon the firm wants to work with, it should be intuitive to many of the readers that marginal cost pricing is not going to give the right incentives to the monopolist to make production and investment decisions in the interest of society. Imposing marginal cost pricing to mimic the competitive benchmark would lead to negative profits since the high fixed costs would not be recovered. In other words, prices driven by marginal costs would not cover average costs.

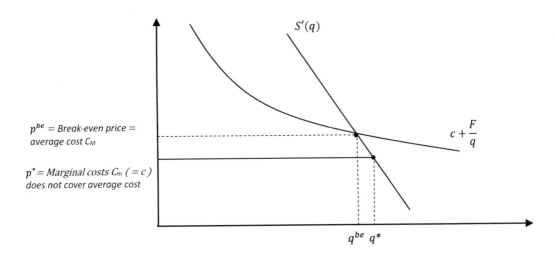

Figure 3.2 The general unsuitability of marginal cost pricing in public services

The easiest solution to ensure that prices cover costs would be to set the price equal to the average cost. Any price below that would be too low to cover costs and if the authorities are trying to attract private operators to take over the business, it is unlikely to be successful since the returns to any investment would be insufficient to cover the full costs.[5] The difficulty for the regulator is that allowing the operator to charge a price higher than the marginal cost implies that the output will be lower than under the competitive benchmark and at least some consumers with willingness to pay higher than marginal cost will not be served. With marginal cost pricing the firm incurs financial losses; with average cost pricing a fraction of the potential consumer's surplus is lost.

The challenge for the regulator is to be fair to all parties involved. Most of the common wisdom focuses on the risk of abuses by the monopolist (the risk of excessive prices). These risks are real and deserve the full attention of regulators. But the risk of scaring away potential operators is just as real if they cannot be guaranteed to achieve a reasonable rate of return, whether the operator is public or private. If pricing cannot ensure profit, there is no option but to rely on subsidies. Subsidies are actually quite common in regulated industries in both developing and developed countries. The British Railways sector, for instance, despite its privatization, has continued to operate with significant subsidies since the mid-1980s, as discussed for instance in Office of the Rail Regulator (2017).

To get a more analytical perspective on this discussion, consider Figure 3.2 which describes a situation in which the demand is linear and the cost of production of the good or service is composed of two parts, a proportional variable cost and a fixed cost: $C(q) = cq + F$. The fixed cost is the basic infrastructure used to produce the public

---

[5] This discussion assumes that the long-run marginal cost is not equal to the long-run average cost. That is, we are not in a situation of constant returns to scale.

service in question (whether rail tracks, transmission lines, or water pipes). The variable costs are linked to the inputs used, which depend on the level of service provided. A large share of these inputs is linked to the wage bill and to the basic raw material (such as electricity for rails, raw water for water services, and oil or coal for the generation of electricity).

Remembering that the demand curve is the marginal surplus of consumption of the service, $S'(q) = p(q)$, the figure shows why pricing at marginal cost c would result in an output level q^* for which the average fixed cost F/q would not be recovered. The financing gap under marginal cost pricing is thus the average fixed cost. More specifically, $C_M(q) = C(q)/q > c = p^* = C_m(q)$.

Unless the operator is subsidized, a price $p \geq p^{be}$ is the only path to a balanced budget, as p^{be} corresponds to the break-even point, i.e. the point at which the operator incurs neither profit nor losses. This can be seen more formally by solving the following constrained-optimization problem with respect to production q: max $S(q) - pq + \pi(q)$ subject to $\pi(q) \geq 0$, where $\pi(q)$ is profit. The matching production level is derived from the binding constraint $\pi(q^{be}) = 0$. Then, $S'(q^{be}) = p^{be} = c + \frac{F}{q^r} > c$. The solution is indeed that, for a single-product producer, only average cost pricing allows it to balance the budget. This pricing rule also alleviates (but does not eliminate) the loss of welfare caused by the operator's need to recover costs by reducing the incentive to cut production so as to increase profits.

This does not imply that marginal cost pricing is not useful to the implementation of regulation. For instance, wholesale electricity markets employ marginal cost pricing to ensure cost-effective dispatch so that generators are compensated at least for their operational costs. But to ensure that total revenues are sufficient to cover the fixed and variable costs of providing reliable services and justify investments to cater to future demand, regulation will need to come up with other revenue sources which will add up to the revenue from marginal cost pricing. In the energy sector, this is often achieved by imposing complementary fees such as prices on capacity market or capacity payments.

From a regulatory policy perspective, the discussion so far has two main implications. The first is that for the monopoly to be able to break even and to have an incentive to make the right level of investment to meet future demand, the regulator has to allow total cost recovery. Short-run marginal cost pricing alone in these industries cannot guarantee cost recovery. The available additional options should lead to a combination of tools that try to maintain the efficiency payoff of marginal pricing as well as the financial sustainability of the operations provided by average cost pricing. These combinations can take multiple shapes, as will be discussed in more detail in Chapter 8. They may also include subsidies, as discussed earlier.

A second implication is that the analysis of the optimal pricing decision should be computed in net present value terms. This is the most effective way of ensuring that users do pay some part of the CAPEX needed to cater to their future needs. This also implies that the sum of producer and consumer surpluses and any constraint accounted for would have to be formulated in net present value terms. This has a number of technical implications which will be covered in Chapter 7 on the ways finance and regulation interact. For now, we will continue to think through the issues in static models. We will show in Chapter 15 how much the internationalization of financial concerns reintroduces time and hence dynamic concerns quite explicitly in the implementation of regulatory decisions.

3.4   What Would Be the Welfare Consequences of Not Regulating a Monopoly?

Monopolies are not popular in the media. The 2018–21 debates in many European countries on the need to regulate Amazon, Google or Facebook for instance illustrate nicely the fear they can inspire. The criticism is also quite common when monopolies control specific public service activities, in particular every time prices have to increase, even when these increases are justified by increases in raw material costs. Prices are the focus of criticism today, but in the 1970s the criticisms focused on the inability of public monopolies to improve energy, railways or telecoms services. This is, to some extent, what made the case for deregulation easy at the time. But the public debates on the pros and cons of these monopolies are often more ideological than informed. And this is unfortunate since there are concrete ways of documenting and quantifying the welfare consequences of relying on concentrated market structures and of failing to regulate them properly.

The following discussion analyses the circumstances under which granting a firm control over a market is likely to be bad for the users when no regulatory intervention is considered. This should increase the transparency of the risks associated with the need to rely on a monopoly. The theory reviewed so far has hinted at the fact that monopolies have a negative welfare effect as compared to the competitive benchmark when no government intervention is considered. But it has not yet demonstrated how much the distribution of the welfare losses between the various stakeholders matters to the perception of the desirability of monopolies. The following analysis shows that this distribution may not be as predictable as sometimes argued in the media, for instance, and this should be part of the concerns to be addressed in the design of regulation.

The dominating perspective reported in basic microeconomic textbooks and in the media is that a monopolist may be able to make excessive profits at taxpayers' and consumers' expense, while producing too little. This view is supported by ample evidence accumulated since the global wave of deregulation in public utility services launched in the 1990s.[6] More recently, there has been a recurring debate as to whether deregulation had gone too far in giving up the scope for scale economies. This concern has been quite clear in the rulings evaluating the request to authorize mergers designed to recover the efficiency gains allowed by larger operational sizes. Most of the

---

[6] For instance, for a discussion of the US electricity reform experience see Borenstein and Bushnell (2015) and for a global perspective on the historical evolution of the deregulation around the world see Clifton et al. (2011).

research on mergers has suggested that, indeed, efficiency gains have been the outcome of larger size but a lot of this research also showed that when market power was increased in regulated industries, both prices and profits were likely to increase (e.g. Sonenshine 2016). The net effect of combining higher efficiency with higher market power is, however, unpredictable as it varies across cases.[7] Few industry studies, if any, accounted for the quality of regulation or of regulatory agencies when conducting the diagnostics. Yet regulation and the ability of regulators to make the right decisions ensure that the effects of scale are greater than the effects of market power.

In most cases, if the regulator has a good sense of the shape of demand and of the cost function, it is relatively easy to get a good quantitative measure of the risks of abusive pricing or financially unsustainable pricing and hence of the negative welfare consequences of under-regulating the monopoly. But details matter, as discussed next.

If the demand curve points to a quantity of output at which the price rises above the total average cost, the firm is charging a price that recovers more than its variable and fixed costs. This is the textbook case illustrating the negative welfare effects of monopolies and the fact that the main losers are the users (or the taxpayers if subsidies are part of the equation). Real market circumstances could actually be different. If the demand curve points to a price–quantity combination at which the price is equal to average costs then there is no extra profit. The monopolist simply recovers its costs and achieves a normal profit, which can be set at any level (including zero) by the regulator. However, if the demand curve points to price–quantity combination for which the price is below average cost then the monopolist is not fully recovering its fixed and variable costs. If the price is below short-run average costs, it does not recover even its variable costs. In those cases, there is also a welfare loss but the firm, or the taxpayers in case of public ownership, is the loser. This is not a fantasy situation. It could result from a switch in preferences. For example, travellers could switch from toll roads to rail in response to a campaign designed to promote the use of public transportation. Or they could switch from public to private transport in the aftermath of a terrorist attack. A shift in long-run costs following cuts in subsidies for outdated technologies or political pressure to keep prices low in public firms could have similar effects.

This intuitive discussion shows that, if left unregulated, the monopolist may fail to cater to the current or future needs of consumers simply because it may charge too much, forcing the users to consume less than they would want to or it may charge too little to cover the investment costs needed to meet the future needs, as is often the case with public utilities in developing countries. But it also shows that if left unprotected, it can also be facing significant financial risks, for instance from unexpected changes

---

[7] It is ironic to note that the private deregulation wave of the 1990s designed to ease entry in the regulated industries explains the wave of mergers in the 2000s. Indeed, once established the new entrants quickly looked for ways to reduce entry by newcomers and the scale effects allowed by mergers were an easy barrier to entry.

in demand or political interference. In this case, the market power mostly serves to mitigate the risks.

Ultimately, any of the outcomes is driven by the firm's effective market power, i.e. its control over the market. It is thus important for regulators to have a quantitative view of this power in the preparation of regulatory diagnostics. First, it matters because it allows the regulator to have a sense of the actual strength of the bargaining power of the firm rather than a view based on perceptions which can easily be instrumentalized by some of the stakeholders. Second, it matters because it has implications for the choice of regulatory interventions. One of the most common approaches to assess market power, the Lerner index (Lerner 1934), is discussed next because it is anchored in some of the basic measures we have discussed so far: the elasticity of demand and the marginal cost.

3.5   Assessing the Importance of Market Power

Before arguing that a firm (or a reduced number of firms) enjoys too much market power, it is necessary to assess this market power quantitatively and to do so accounting for some of the essential characteristics of the market the firm caters to. This is useful to get a sense of the extent to which a regulator should intervene with the way the firm operates. To do so, we start with the benchmark in which the regulator does not intervene initially in a market served by a single supplier.

Assume that the customers of an unregulated monopoly consume up to the point where they are being charged their marginal propensity to pay for the service:

$$p(q) = S'(q) \tag{3.1}$$

which is referred to as consumers' 'willingness to pay' or 'inverse demand function'. Let us further stipulate that demand is a decreasing function, due to decreasing marginal utility.[8]

$$p'(q) = dp/dq = S''(q) < 0. \tag{3.2}$$

This is a function linking price and quantity in a negative relationship.

Assume also that costs are $C(q)$, that the monopoly's revenue is $R(q) = qp(q)$ and that the monopoly's profit is simply the difference between the two:

$$\pi(q) = R(q) - C(q) = qp(q) - C(q) \tag{3.3}$$

Under these assumptions, the choice of the private monopoly will be to produce the quantity q^m so that $qp'(q) + p(q) - C'(q) = 0$: that is, it will produce until marginal revenue equals marginal cost. This expression is equivalent to $p(q) - C'(q) = -qp'(q)$.

---

[8] For normal goods and services, the marginal propensity to pay decreases as consumption increases because needs are gradually saturated.

Dividing right and left by $p(q) = p$ yields:

$$L = \frac{p - C'(q)}{p} = \frac{1}{\varepsilon} \tag{3.4}$$

where $\varepsilon = -\frac{p}{qp'(q)}$ is the elasticity of demand with respect to price defined in Chapter 2.

The ratio $L = \frac{p - C'(q)}{p}$ is known as the Lerner index. It measures the percentage of extra profit the firm can earn per unit sold on top of the marginal cost. The Lerner index is always between 0 and 1. A monopolist seeking to maximize profits will never be on the inelastic part of the demand curve (i.e. $1 > \varepsilon$) and will thus produce only to meet a demand with elasticity such as $1 \leq \varepsilon \leq \infty$. This is because the private monopoly equates marginal cost with marginal revenue. Since marginal cost is positive, the same is true of marginal revenue. And for this to happen, demand elasticity to price must be greater than 1.[9] This being said, what really matters to appreciate the risks of market power is how much greater it is than 1. At the monopoly equilibrium in Equation (3.4), we see that the higher the demand elasticity ε, the lower the firm's market power since consumers can easily escape from price increases by decreasing consumption or switching to close substitutes. In other words, being a monopoly does not necessarily guarantee strong market power.

When the price elasticity of demand is very large, for instance because good substitutes for the product are available, the Lerner index is small. Then, the price charged by the unregulated monopoly is closer to marginal cost. And the closer is the outcome to what is observed in a competitive market, which is characterized by $L = 0$, since the elasticity is infinite in that case, and $p = c$. In this situation, the market power of the operator is nil. For a railway company, for instance, a low L is observed when the users can rely on other transportation means such as buses or cars to reach their destination. The railway company enjoys a monopoly in railway services, but not on transport services. This is one of the reasons why regulators tend to be unhappy when the same owner seeks to operate several modes of transport on the same routes.

By contrast, when the price elasticity of demand is small, as in the case of water services for instance, the Lerner index is large. This means that the unregulated monopoly's mark-up is commensurately large. The unregulated monopoly's pricing strategy implies that some consumers are excluded from trade, which is by definition inefficient. This explains that the laissez-faire monopoly generates a deadweight loss, i.e. a loss to society as compared to what would be observed if there had been the technical and policy option to provide the service in a competitive market.

Figure 3.3 illustrates this result in a linear demand/cost example. The declining linear demand $p(q)$ represents consumers' propensity to pay for the commodity. The lowest flat line represents the constant marginal cost function, $C'(q) = c$. The monopoly rent is $(p^m - C_M(q^m)) \times q^m$. Whenever $p(q) > c$, there is a gain from trade (i.e. producing more): then, producing $q^m < q^*$ is inefficient. Since the

---

[9] Formally, $qp'(q) + p(q) = C'(q) > 0 \Rightarrow -\frac{p(q)}{qp'(q)} > 1$.

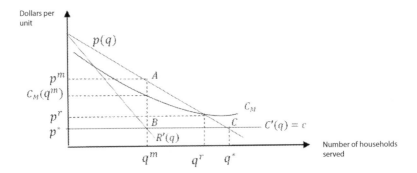

Figure 3.3 Measuring the deadweight loss from unregulated monopoly

marginal revenue function is lower than the demand function for any value of q, $R'(q) = qp'(q) + p(q) < p(q)$, the quantity that equalizes marginal revenue and marginal cost, q^m, is lower than the quantity prevailing under the competitive case, q^*. That is, it is less than the optimal quantity that equalizes propensity to pay (marginal surplus $p(q)$) and marginal cost $C'(q) = c$. This difference in quantity drives the deadweight loss. In Figure 3.3, it is measured by the triangle ABC (known as the Harberger triangle in the public economics literature).

Intuitively, this can be explained as follows. The deadweight loss comes from the fact that when the laissez-faire monopoly chooses its price to maximize its profit, it is unable to capture the entire consumer surplus generated by its trading activity. The monopoly does not know the individual propensity to pay for the good or service it is supplying, and therefore cannot tailor its prices individually to collect it all. It therefore chooses a price that is high enough to make its markup optimal (i.e. to maximize its profit), sacrificing some consumers in the process. This loss is a deadweight loss because the excluded consumers are willing to pay more than what it costs to produce the commodity but less than the monopoly price. If the monopoly could tailor its price individually it would choose to serve these consumers as well (see Chapter 8 on price discrimination). But since it cannot, some of the gain from trade is lost for all.[10]

With a monopoly, therefore, we know that we will encounter a degree of inefficiency. And the size of this inefficiency can and should be quantified so as to provide an explicit target for regulators seeking to protect the interests of consumers without discouraging the monopoly from producing enough output to satisfy demand. One way to quantify the deadweight loss is to measure how much consumers would have been willing to pay to consume the unproduced units, minus the cost of producing them. And this implies once more that the regulator needs to have a good sense of the demand.

At this stage it is useful to distinguish distributional and efficiency issues as both are relevant to regulation. To understand the difference, assume that in a sector the

---

[10] And from a distributional viewpoint, this is a particularly politically sensitive issue since it is likely that those with a lower ability to pay are also the poorest households.

demand is fixed at Q (i.e. it is totally inelastic) if price is below a maximum threshold, and 0 beyond this threshold. In this case the monopoly can impose the maximum price without losing customers, or reducing the quantities sold. The monopoly's behaviour is not creating a deadweight loss but it creates an unbearable situation as it abuses its power to extract rents from the people. This creates a distributional problem, and this problem is more serious for inelastic (i.e. uncompressible) demand, than for elastic demand (i.e. for commodities with good substitutes).

How sensitive this demand is to prices is what drives the size of the distributional problem and the deadweight loss, linked to the inefficient supply level preferred by the monopoly. The distributional problem is small when the elasticity is high, and is high otherwise. The more sensitive demand is (that is, the flatter the demand curve or the higher its elasticity), the less market power the firm has to increase prices. By contrast, if demand elasticity is small, the relative importance of market power is great. If the demand is more rigid (that is, if the demand curve is steep or its elasticity low), the firm needs only to cut production a little to get a higher price. Alternatively, it can raise its price without cutting too much into sales.

So far, we have discussed the Lerner index for a monopoly. However, an adjusted Lerner index is also quite commonly used when the market can be served by a few firms rather than a monopolist. The adjusted version is discussed in Box 3.3: with competitors strongly reactive to its price changes, a dominant firm enjoys a mitigated market power.

3.6   What Does Market Power Imply for Regulation?

The challenge of ensuring the regulation of public service monopolies is linked to market power since this market power influences the relative bargaining power of the operator and the regulator. Regulation boils down to ensuring that output and prices are as close as possible to the competitive outcome without threatening the financial viability of the operators or overburdening taxpayers (if subsidies are involved). However, getting firms to produce more when this is likely to reduce their profits is not an easy goal.

The most common way to achieve this is either public ownership or, in the case of privatization, to increase the number of firms active in a sector. But if the techno-logical characteristics of the sector are such that a single provider (or very few) is the more rational way to organize production, competition will have to be managed differently. In this context, it simply means that competition *for* the market has to take the place of competition *in* the market. A well-designed auction asking firms to bid for the right to be the sole provider of the service should indeed deliver the right output–price combination.[11]

---

[11] When the government cannot observe private costs, competitive bidding is likely to be a better method of selecting contractors than a series of bilateral negotiations. See, for instance, Bulow and Klemperer (1996).

Box 3.3 The Lerner Index with a Fringe of Competitors

When the regulator has to deal with a small number of operators rather than a monopolist, the Lerner index can be adjusted to account for the relevance of differences in market shares and for the fact that the users can have a stronger elasticity to the price of a specific firm than it has to the market price.

Let $q^o(p)$ be the supply by a fringe of competitors when the regulated firm fixes price p. It is an increasing function.

The dominant firm solves $\max_p p \times \left(q(p) - q^o(p)\right) - C\left(q(p) - q^o(p)\right)$. From the first-order condition $(p - C')\left(q' - q^{o'}\right) + (q - q^o) = 0$, we can write the link between the Lerner index $L = \frac{p-C'}{p}$ and the market characteristics (elasticities and market shares) as $L = \frac{s}{\varepsilon + (1-s)\varepsilon^o}$.

The drivers of the modified Lerner index are the regulated firm's market share $\left(s = (q - q^o)/q\right)$, the market price elasticity of demand (ε) and the elasticity of the fringe supply $\left(\varepsilon^o = pq^{o'}/q^o\right)$ which measures the percentage change in the amount supplied by competitors due to a 1% change in the dominant firm's price.

Higher values of this index indicate greater market power. It increases when the dominant firm's market share increases, market price elasticity of demand falls, and/or competitors' supply elasticity falls. But the expression also shows that the impact of an increasing market share can be offset if the two elasticities increase as well. Conversely, a firm with a low market share can enjoy strong market power if the two elasticities are also very low.

Source: Adapted from Landes and Posner (1981).

To be effective, the competitive bidding process must be able to help the authorities identify the operator with the lowest available costs. If the process is well designed, it induces potential vendors and contractors to reveal their true costs to procurers, which in theory should enable governments to procure regulated services at a minimum cost. In practice, however, this mechanism does not always work well, particularly for infrastructure projects, as they are highly customized and technically complicated. Furthermore, some selection procedures are vulnerable to risks associated with institutional weaknesses, such as the risks of collusion between the bidding firms and corruption of the public representatives or the politicians in charge of allocating the market to one operator.

Corruption can occur at all stages of the delegation of public services to private operators, as mentioned earlier (Box 3.1). Quantitatively, a survey conducted by PwC and Ecorys (2013) on behalf of the EU shows that corrupt procurement processes continue to be a significant issue in Europe for public services. In a sample of eight EU countries, the survey finds the highest probabilities of corruption in the construction of wastewater plants (22–27%), rail (15–19%), roads (11–14%) and airport runways (11–13%). The overall direct costs of corruption in public procurement in 2010 ranged between €1.5 billion and €2.3 billion, about 19% of the estimated value of tenders for

Table 3.1 Frequency of renegotiations in PPPs

Geographical area	Sector	Renegotiated contracts (%)
Latin and Caribbean America	All sectors	68
	Electricity	41
	Transport	78
	W&S	92
United States	Highways	40
France	Highways	50
	Car parks	73
United Kingdom	All sectors	55

Source: Estache and Saussier (2014).

public expenditures on works, goods and services published in the EU electronic tendering system in the eight EU member states covered by the survey.

Although corruption is a serious problem, trying to combat it through a set of rigid rules can be counterproductive. Poor design of procurement is often a serious limitation on the extent to which governments can make the most of the opportunities offered by PPPs.[12] For instance, countries such as the United Kingdom are now avoiding organizing auctions for their public utilities with awarding criteria based on the lowest price. This design, although a priori more transparent, was found to often lead to implementation delays and cost overruns, and eventually to contract renegotiations between the government and the regulated firm. Similarly, Estache and Iimi (2011) show, for a large sample of developing countries benefiting from World Bank and Japanese aids, that public sector procurement rules often tend to limit or distort competition in public markets to deliver infrastructure needs, such as roads or water and sanitation facilities. The inefficiency associated with the limitations of the process represents at least 8% of the infrastructure needs of the developing world discussed in Chapter 1 – and much more in countries in which corruption and incompetence combine to allow inflated costs.

Contracts in regulated industries tend to be quite frequently renegotiated, as indicated by Table 3.1. Most of the studies analysing these renegotiations show that they have an impact on cost efficiency. Most of the time, this impact is negative – i.e. costs become higher. Thus renegotiations reduce the cost savings expected from the competition *for* the market, as shown early on by Guasch et al. (2014) for instance. And most of the studies also show that the poor design of regulation is an important reason why the efforts to rely on auctions to minimize costs fail. And by now it should be clear to all readers that when regulation fails, rents, costs and prices are likely to be higher than they should be. Quality may also be set at the wrong level (too much or too little). Finally, renegotiation can hide corruption. The winner underbids its competitors with the help of the corrupt public authority and later 'renegotiates' the terms

---

[12] We will examine PPPs in Chapter 12.

of the contract with generous overruns, which are not subjected to competitive bidding or public scrutiny.

3.7　How Hard Should the Regulator Fight to Trim Monopoly Rent?

Since, in practice, regulation fails when the regulator lacks the bargaining power needed to negotiate with the operators they are supposed to regulate, a sense of the specific dimensions of the operations of a monopoly that will influence this bargaining power may help. In Chapter 5, we will see that the balance of power depends largely on information asymmetries and the regulator's determination to reduce them. We will also see that the regulator may have to leave significant rents as a result of these asymmetries. These rents are often going to be more rational than basic microeconomic textbooks document. But even so, the rent tolerated can be excessive. To assess the effectiveness of whether regulation works or not, it is useful to start with an estimation of the size of the rent that would prevail in the absence of regulation. This is the benchmark against which the outcome under regulation will be compared to assess the performance of regulation.

Intuitively, it is easy to anticipate that the size of the rent is central to the regulated firm's incentives to bargain with the regulator. This is explicit in Figure 3.3. But the same applies to the regulator. A larger rent is usually associated with a larger welfare loss, and a larger payoff to society if the regulator manages to increase its bargaining power. Any regulatory failure to control the size and the distribution of the rent implies a higher welfare loss.

Before entering into the bargaining process, it is essential to estimate the stakes, i.e. the size of the potential welfare loss. The information required boils down to the data on costs and demand discussed in Chapter 2. We have already established that the cost data can be approximated reasonably well from standard accounting data. As for demand, there are many techniques available to estimate the public's willingness to pay for a product or service. They range from surveys of the customers of specific firms to econometric estimations from aggregate data on the sector. The challenge is not overwhelming; it simply takes time and commitment.

The regulator then needs to have a sense of the price that would prevail under competition. The easiest way to determine this is to rely on the cost function discussed earlier to assess the marginal cost, since $p^* = c$ under a competitive environment. Once this price is known, it is easy to put a value on the quantity that would prevail under competition, by matching demand and marginal cost.

The regulator also needs to determine the quantity that would be supplied by an unregulated monopolist and the price it would charge. To do this, it can rely on theory to figure out how monopolists select their price and output level. Once again, the cost function is a valuable tool since it can be used to compute economies of scale and scope which are essential to approximate the optimal level of output. From the demand function, it is then possible to derive the monopolist's price, which is such that the monopoly's marginal revenue equals its marginal cost. The Lerner index can then be used to estimate the mark-up the firm is expecting to apply if it controls the market.

We know that the monopolist will charge a higher price than the price a competitive market would deliver. And we know that this is linked to a lower quantity being produced. In practice, it is not difficult to collect data on these basic variables. And this means that it is quite easy to compute a rough value for the deadweight loss imputable to monopoly behaviour and use it as a benchmark to assess how much of an impact price regulation can have for society.

Often, it is useful to try to normalize this value (i.e. view it in relative terms) to get a sense of the extent to which the measure of the deadweight loss is large or small. Two common ways to normalize it are by relying on the firm's profit or, in the case of very large firms, on the nation's GDP. Benchmarking deadweight loss with GDP is particularly useful because it allows politicians to highlight how regulation sizes up against other issues they have to tackle. In some cases, it can be more effective to normalize estimates against tax revenue or expenditure, notably when a regulated industry is heavily subsidized. If the size of deadweight loss is small compared with the relevant benchmark, one need not worry too much. The best strategy in such cases is to let the monopolist set its prices and quantity. But if the loss is sizeable, a greater commitment to regulating the sector is called for. For many regulated industries, the evidence reviewed by Schmitz (2012) suggests that there are reasons to be worried.[13]

In the case of public services, it is easy to anticipate that welfare losses without regulation, or without solid regulation, are going to be large. The monopolist has more leverage than it would with many other services because demand is less elastic. This implies that the threat of rent extraction tends to be quite significant (although with substantial variation across countries and sectors, reinforcing the case for country- and sector-specific estimates). The poorer the initial conditions, the less elastic the demand is likely to be and hence the greater the social/political loss of getting regulation wrong. According to McKinsey (2016), today the world invests some $2.5 trillion a year in the transportation, power, water and telecom sectors but this is falling short of demand. From 2016 to 2030, the world needs to invest about 3.8% of GDP, or an average of $3.3 trillion a year in these sectors to support the expected growth rate. So, while the sector is already big, the demand is quite strong and particularly inelastic for the poor regions and for the countries committed to invest to make the sector more environmentally friendly. If poor regulation allows firms to inflate costs by 20–40% in the sector, it implies that the investment needs are inflated by 0.8–1.5% of GDP. These losses are likely to be at least twice as large in developing countries because, for the foreseeable future, their annual investment needs are closer to 8–10% of GDP.

---

[13] During the late 1950s and early 1960s, the consensus, influenced by Harberger (1954), was that the social costs of monopoly were minor. This vision was challenged by Mundell (1962) and by Leibenstein (1966) based on concerns with the methods used by Harberger. It is only since the mid-2000s that new views on the size of the welfare losses linked to monopolies have started to emerge. For details, see Schmitz (2012).

This is a reasonable first-order approximation of the welfare loss of having to live with poorly regulated infrastructure service providers with significant market power.[14] And this is high enough to warrant making an effort towards improving regulation, if only to better stimulate cost savings. Ultimately, the fairness to society of the outcome of the regulatory bargaining process depends on the quality of regulation and on the political commitment to design and implement a regulatory regime that can exploit opportunities to maximize social welfare.

3.8   Summing Up

- To a large extent, public services tend to be delivered by natural monopolies which can serve consumers at lower cost than any combination of two or more firms.
- Since the assets used to produce many of these public services tend to be long-lived, the short- and long-term marginal cost of production differ and their relative size informs on the extent to which an operator has overinvested or underinvested in production capacity.
- When there is overcapacity, the short-run marginal cost is lower than the long-run one; when there is undercapacity, the opposite holds.
- For a monopoly to have an incentive to make the right investment levels to meet future demand, average cost pricing is the most obvious solution; however, it leads to an underprovision of the service as compared to the competitive benchmark.
- One way in which the efficiency concerns of the regulator and the financial sustainability of the operator can be reconciled is through the allocation of subsidies to the operator to compensate for the loss linked to imposing marginal cost pricing.
- All realistic pricing strategies create deadweight losses resulting from overcharging as compared to a competitive benchmark, but the size and the distribution of these losses depend on the relative importance of the efficiency gains a monopoly can achieve from its size versus its market power; these two effects work in opposite directions and the net effect has to be assessed case by case.
- When the regulated industries are characterized by long-lived assets demanding upfront lumpy investments, pricing decisions should be computed in net present value terms.
- Technological change is reducing the need to rely on lumpy investments to meet future needs and this leads to transitional issues in regulation since the optimal pricing strategies are different when investments are lumpy. Even if new investment is not lumpy, most countries still need to amortize old, lumpy ones.
- As a rule of thumb, the more sensitive demand is (that is, the flatter the demand curve or the higher its elasticity), the less market power a firm has to increase prices.

---

[14] Chisari et al. (1999) relied on a general equilibrium model of Argentina to assess the rent generated by poor regulation of the privatized utilities. They came up with a lower bound of about 2% of GDP. Most of the rent was being paid by the poorest income classes. Additional examples of regulatory uses of general equilibrium models are available in Chisari (2007).

By contrast, if demand elasticity is small, its market power is large. When demand is more rigid (that is, elasticity is low), the firm can raise its price without cutting too much into sales. It creates a problem of rent extraction from the captive users that is socially unbearable.

- To reduce market power, regulators can introduce competition *for* the market to compensate for the lack of competition *in* the market, but the difficulty of designing the required bidding process is easy to underestimate and mistakes can make things worse.

- Many of the empirical studies of experiences of competition for the market point to implementation failures linked to design and institutional weaknesses, including corruption, which results in excessive cost, prices and profits, and insufficient quality.

- Welfare losses of regulatory failures in the public utilities sector range from 1% to 1.5% of GDP.

4 Regulating a Monopoly with Full Information

Now that the case for regulation has been made, the next challenge is to decide *how* to regulate. This used to be a simple question, but that is no longer the case. And this is a relatively recent realization as, until the early 1990s, regulation followed the simple broad ideas discussed in the previous chapter. It was essentially about coming up with an average price that would cover all of the monopoly's costs (accounting for subsidies) and include a fair rate of return, thus ensuring its financial autonomy. Everyone knew that the solution was inefficient from a social welfare perspective but it was largely accepted as a fact of life. In many countries, when the average price was producing a rent, this rent was often used to justify the public ownership of monopolies. Making this rent available to the Ministry of Finance was endorsed by many if it could be used to cut taxes and protect taxpayers. And if the government preferred to protect users and keep prices close to marginal costs, the allowed regulatory pricing strategy would simply have to focus on minimizing the need to rely on subsidies to finance the business and impose the least possible burden on taxpayers.

This view of regulation ignored that the bargaining process surrounding the regulatory proceedings is a complex game subject to manipulation by investors, politicians or other stakeholders (e.g. specific users or workers). And unless the regulator internalizes the complexity of this game, it is unlikely to be able to minimize the welfare losses associated with monopolistic production. This is because the operators, whether public or private, will often enjoy enough bargaining power to make the most of their market power. The existence of the high welfare losses mentioned in the previous chapter demonstrates that regulators were not very good at playing the game until the early 1990s.

Regulation has since changed and regulators appear to have learned, at least to a certain extent, but, as we will see, the game continues. The difference is that the rules of the game, and in particular the relevance of the bargaining power as a driver of the regulatory outcome, has now been internalized in the design of regulation. This has been possible because academics, notably David Baron, Jean-Jacques Laffont, Martin Loeb, Wesley Magat, Roger Myerson, David Sappington and Jean Tirole, have been able to reframe the discussions of regulation, highlighting the differences in access to information on cost and demand across stakeholders as drivers of regulatory outcomes.[1]

---

[1] For a more technical survey of the history of the progress of these theories, see Laffont and Tirole (1993) and Armstrong and Sappington (2007).

The earlier models assumed, naively but analytically conveniently, that all relevant information was public. Removing this assumption makes a significant difference to the way the design of regulation needs to be thought through. To see this, we will review two of the models that have had the biggest impact on the way we think about regulation today: Baron and Myerson (1982) and Laffont and Tirole (1986, 1993). They reframed the regulatory games played by public and private enterprises in a significant way. In what follows, we first look at how these authors model the regulatory game, and key drivers of the outcomes such as costs and objective functions, when regulators are assumed to have full access to firms' information. In the next chapter, we will see how these results change when they factor in various sources of information asymmetry and what this means for the optimal design of regulation.

4.1   Modelling the Cost Functions of the Regulated Firms

As should be clear now from the earlier chapters, the way costs are accounted for and in particular the way they are modelled is central to the regulation of firms in the industries we are interested in here. Differences in context or in focus may explain why academic or policy diagnostics model costs differently, even if the main regulatory policy concerns are similar. In practice, differences may come, for instance, from uncertainty on the technology used by the firm, on the maintenance costs of the assets or on efforts made by the firms to make the most of the technologies they rely on.

The two seminal papers on the topic, Baron and Myerson (1982) and Laffont and Tirole (1986), deal with different contexts and informational constraints. This is apparent in the differences in the way they model marginal costs. In Baron and Myerson (1982), the marginal cost of the regulated firm is constant but unknown to the regulator. In Laffont and Tirole (1986), the marginal cost of production is variable as its value depends on the efforts made by the firm's management to minimize it. The regulator observes the total costs (e.g. the accounting cost) but is unable to observe these efforts.

For Baron and Myerson (1982), the regulator's main challenge is to minimize the information gap on the costs so as to be able to set the regulated price at a level fair to both investors and consumers/taxpayers. The monopolist's fixed costs are known to the regulator but the level of constant marginal cost is only known to the firm. This model is particularly relevant for the regulation of private firms, where the shareholders put strong pressure on management to minimize costs as they care only about return on investment and seek to maximize their monetary rent.

That David Baron and Roger Myerson are American economists is not incidental to their focus: the American context is likely to have influenced their vision of how to formalize regulation. Indeed, in the United States, most regulated firms are private (although not all – e.g. many airports are still public). This ignores some of the challenges specific to public enterprises, including the strong political interference with the management of these firms which may influence the efforts to cut costs. Yet

Box 4.1 shows that, in most countries of the world, regulated public service providers have long been, and continue to be, operated as state-owned enterprises (SOEs).[2] This public ownership and operation adds a number of concerns to the regulatory agenda for firms focusing on maximizing profits. For instance, in many countries there is often a preference to rely on more workers than required by an assessment based only on profit maximization, simply because it contributes to reducing unemployment or underemployment in difficult social contexts. This wider view of the regulatory agenda is easier to address with the comprehensive approach developed by Laffont and Tirole.

For Laffont and Tirole (1986), the regulator's main challenge is to minimize the rent obtained by slacking off, while understanding that effort is costly and not easy for the regulator to observe or measure.[3] The regulator observes realized total costs, but not the effort put into cost-reduction by the firm (a post-contractual hidden effort problem). Allowing the regulated firm to slack off results in inflated costs and hence prices. The regulated firms' rents in this setting are thus not exclusively monetary. They can also take the form of lower demands on the firm's workers and management than would prevail in competitive private companies, and other forms of cost inefficiencies that influence final prices and/or subsidies (expensive company cars and phones that workers can use for personal needs, high representation budgets, privileged service pricing and use for relatives, longer paid holidays than in unregulated private industries, etc.).

Highlighting how information asymmetries affect monopolies' cost calculations, including when the regulated firms are public enterprises or subsidized private enterprises, is one of the main contributions of the theories of regulation of French economists Jean-Jacques Laffont and Jean Tirole.[4] Their vision was consistent both with the private regulated monopolies prevalent in Anglo-Saxon countries and with the natural laboratory offered by the dominating role of public providers of utilities services in Europe at the time they were developing their theories. Many of these providers have now been at least partially privatized, but the role of SOEs in the delivery of public services continues to be important around the world, as shown by Box 4.1.

The Laffont–Tirole model is more realistic than the Baron–Myerson model because it applies to a much broader range of situations, including for private firms, where the Baron–Myerson assumption of unobservable costs is unrealistic. This is the case when regulated private firms operate in countries in which audits can be used to produce at

[2] Clifton et al. (2006, 2016) provide useful additional historical perspectives on the evolution of SOEs.
[3] Conceptually, Laffont and Tirole (1986) builds on Baron and Myerson (1982) which had innovated the discussion of regulation by introducing the relevance of the fact that information on costs could not be observable. Laffont and Tirole's (1986) more general framework makes the discussion more applicable to concrete policy in many ways. For more details on the comparison, see for instance Bolton and Dewatripont (2004).
[4] Their theory became known in the 1980s as 'the new theory of regulation'. It has since become mainstream but still is occasionally referred to in the literature as 'new'. Jean Tirole won the Nobel prize in economics in 2014, in part for this work.

Box 4.1 On the Economic Size of State-Owned Enterprises

According to the OECD (2015a), a state-owned enterprise is any corporate entity recognized by national law as an enterprise in which the government exercises ownership and control. Quasi-corporations, which are autonomous commercial activities carried out inside the general government sector, should be considered as SOEs if they are financially autonomous and charge economically significant prices.

As recently as 2017, the OECD conducted an inventory of the relative importance of public enterprises in a sample of forty countries as of the end of 2015. This information, which is summarized in Table 4.1, is available in OECD (2017b). SOEs in the sample area are highly concentrated in the network industries and the financial sector. Together, the electricity and gas, transportation, telecoms and other utilities sectors account for 51% of all SOEs by value and 70% by employment. The financial sector accounts for 26% of all SOEs by value, making it the largest individual sector by this measure.

In the sample, SOEs incorporated according to company law are the predominant corporate form, representing 92% of all SOEs by value and 84% by employment, and about half (by value) are listed on national stock exchanges. SOEs incorporated according to enterprise-specific legislation are an increasingly less common corporate form, accounting for only 8% of all SOEs by value and 16% by employment as of 2015, a significant drop from the value observed a few years earlier by the OECD.

According to Estache (2020a), the latest data available specific to regulated industries (2015–18) suggests that for electricity distribution (for a sample of 175 countries), only 7% had a purely private operator and 30% were mixed ownership. For water and sanitation (for a sample of 175 countries), the proportion of firms with at least some private investment was 22%. For transport, 97% of airports and 95% of rail operators are public (including 29% mixed ownership). The relative importance of private firms is the strongest in the port sector with 78%.

Table 4.1 Public enterprises in a sample of forty countries

Measure	Number of firms	Number of employees (thousands)	Value of enterprises (US$ billions)
Primary sectors	215	508	263
Manufacturing	225	842	143
Finance	291	769	621
Telecoms	64	392	109
Electricity & gas	220	816	502
Transportation	313	1 739	437
Other utilities	231	3538	164
Real estate	106	32	85
Other	802	602	82
Total	2,467	9,238	2,408

Source: OECD (2017b).

least some data on total costs whether the firm is public or private. More importantly from a policy point of view, it is particularly useful when considering the regulation of public firms for which cost audits – although often not in sufficient detail – tend to be quite common to minimize the risks of corruption.

To see how the differences on the cost side between the two models make a difference to the design of regulation, it is necessary to get into a somewhat more technical discussion. The next couple of sections show the main modelling similarities and differences. Let's start with the main similarity: they both assume similar objective functions for the regulator. More specifically, both modelling approaches assume that the regulator maximizes a weighted sum of the users' and taxpayers' surplus (that is, the regulator is utilitarian).

4.2   The Objective Function of Regulation

A social objective (or welfare) function is a description of the set of objectives that the social planner maximizes in order to determine the socially optimal policy.[5] With the utilitarian objective, the planner maximizes a weighted sum of individual utilities. On top of the politically risk-taking choice of the weights, this requires comparing interpersonal utility levels, and summing them up, which does not always make sense. However, in the case of regulation, this comparison is relevant because agents' utilities are simple numerical measures of their gains from trade (i.e. taxpayers' and consumers' surplus and firms' profits). In terms of equity, maximizing this sum implicitly assumes that it will be possible, later, to redistribute surpluses so as to raise everybody's welfare, for instance through subsidies and taxation. However, the traditional regulation literature, which focuses on efficiency issues, generally does not detail this redistribution process. Chapter 9 will discuss how social concerns and redistribution issues can concretely be internalized by regulations.

The regulator needs to take into account the interests of multiple stakeholders, i.e. investors, consumers and taxpayers in the simplest versions of the models. This implies that the regulator's objective function must: (i) internalize the profitability constraint of the regulated firm and (ii) simultaneously protect the interests of consumers and taxpayers (if subsidies or dividends are involved). Profitability has to be considered quite broadly. For private firms, it corresponds to the usual rate-of-return concept relevant to any private activity. For public firms, it corresponds to the need for the firm to produce enough revenue to deliver the services for a given level of subsidies.

The new insights provided by these models were particularly interesting when they were first published for many policy and technical reasons. Since most of these

---

[5] There are two broad classes of social objective functions in economics. The first one, which is also the most popular, is utilitarian. The second is the maximin. It is often referred to as a Rawlsian social welfare function, with reference to Rawls (1971). It aims to maximize the welfare of the most disadvantaged individuals.

reasons are still relevant today in many settings, it is useful to discuss them in some detail from a modelling perspective. For instance, they put the spotlight on the details of the monopoly's revenue. These are relatively easy to characterize and eventually measure. Moreover, in both the Baron–Myerson (1982) and Laffont–Tirole (1986) models, the monopoly does not discriminate in pricing, so that the focus is on the average price. This is just as relevant from a policy perspective as the specific price paid by the various types of consumers.

Formally, all this can be expressed as follows. If the quantity produced and sold is q and the price $p(q)$ is negatively related to the output level, the monopoly's gross revenue from sales is the amount that consumers will have to pay for q, i.e.

$$R(q) = p(q)q \qquad (4.1)$$

But this is only part of the monopolist's surplus since it can also get subsidies or pay transfers t from/to the government. This implies that, given the production costs $C(q)$, the total monopolist's surplus is:

$$\pi = p(q)q + t - C(q) \qquad (4.2)$$

This π is also known as the 'rent' the firm receives by virtue of being the monopoly supplier.

Gauging consumers' interest can be trickier. This is why its computation is usually simplified. In most regulatory models, consumers' well-being is assumed to come only from consumption of services. Formally, this can be expressed as follows. Consumers' *gross* surplus from consuming a quantity q of the good is the sum of their willingness to pay for each unit up to q:

$$S(q) = \int_0^q p(q)dq \qquad (4.3)$$

In regulation theory, what makes consumers happy is to consume as much as possible, accounting for the price charged for each unit of consumption, $S(q) - R(q)$, where $R(q)$ is the total bill paid by consumers for q units of the commodity. This is not an anecdotal observation. As will be seen in detail in Chapter 8, it is not uncommon in regulated industries to see operators practising price discrimination. In practice, regulators are also increasingly considering price discrimination as they seek to slow consumption of water or energy, for instance, or to discourage the use of private cars. For now, we'll focus on the average price and will return to the impact of price discrimination on the consumer surplus in Chapter 8.

The final stakeholder identified in the simplest version of these models is the taxpayer. Estimating its interests can also be challenging. Taxpayers may well be unhappy to discover that they are being taxed to subsidize a monopoly service provider, so that raising an amount t in taxes represents a cost to society that is greater than the face value of the tax might suggest. Indeed, raising taxes impairs the efficiency of the economy. In economics, this damage is expressed as the *opportunity cost of public funds*, $\lambda \geq 0$. It is also known as the *shadow cost of tax financing of an activity*.

The disutility for taxpayers of having to subsidize public services in the amount of t is given by $(1 + \lambda)t$. Essentially this means that as taxes rise the taxpayers' welfare falls at a rate of $1 + \lambda$. Conversely, welfare rises for every reduction in the need to rely on subsidies to finance public services. In particular, welfare rises when the monopoly pays taxes (i.e. when 'subsidies' are negative). Although the specific figure depends on each country, the available evidence suggests that the opportunity cost of public funds is around 0.3–0.5 in developed countries and greater than 1 in developing economies (see Box 4.2).[6]

Now that the interest of all stakeholders has been matched against quantitative outcome indicators (i.e. consumers', taxpayers' and producers' surplus), the next step is to discuss how the regulator adds them up. Since in the standard models, the monopoly is assumed not to be price discriminating, its gross revenue is determined by a single price, i.e. $R(q) = p(q)q$. The users' net surplus is the surplus from consumption, $V = S(q) - p(q)q$ and the (variation in) surplus of taxpayers is $-(1 + \lambda)t$. In the end households, which most of the times are both consumers of the public service and taxpayers,[7] are left with:

$$V - (1 + \lambda)t \tag{4.4}$$

Consumers are assumed to maximize their welfare. This implies that demand is determined by equating the marginal surplus to the price, i.e. $S'(q) = p$. It is useful to keep this in mind because it tells us that the price is how the regulator approximates the gains from marginal increases in production – i.e. in terms of benefits to consumers.

Assume for now that the regulator is benevolent – that is, that it cares only about the well-being of the operator, measured by π, of consumers, measured by V, and of taxpayers, measured by $(1 + \lambda)t$. Assume also that the regulator has no unrelated private agenda – for instance, it cannot be corrupted or faces no conflicts of interests, as will be discussed in Chapters 5 and 14. In this case, the social welfare function that the regulator is assumed to maximize can be expressed as follows:

$$W = V - (1 + \lambda)t + \pi = [S(q) - p(q)q] - (1 + \lambda)t + [p(q)q + t - C(q)] \tag{4.5}$$

Or in simplified form:

$$W = S(q) - C(q) - \lambda t \tag{4.6}$$

This simply equates society's welfare with consumers' welfare, accounting for production costs and distortions linked to the need to finance subsidies through taxes. In

[6] The fact that tax systems are more distortionary in developing countries than in developed economies would suggest that there is a stronger case to rely on user fees in developing economies. But such a conclusion disregards the disproportionate limitations on ability to pay in developing economies and the degree of importance of the redistributive role of the tax system, despite tradeoffs between efficiency and equity. The main alternative is to rely on cross-subsidies, as discussed in Chapter 9.

[7] Note that a fraction of households are also shareholders of the operators and can receive dividends from the producers.

Box 4.2 Opportunity Cost of Public Funds versus Marginal Cost of Public Funds

The opportunity cost of public funds and the marginal cost of public funds are the two concepts commonly found in the literature on how to weigh the taxpayers' surplus in the context of public services provided by regulated monopolies. The two concepts are different, though the difference is not always acknowledged in policy or academic discussions.

The concept of the *marginal cost of public funds* (MCF), drawn from the public economics literature, refers to the social cost incurred by a marginal increase in a tax. There are therefore as many MCFs as there are tax instruments. In an optimized tax system, these are equalized; in an inefficient system, they are not. An intuitive measure of a tax system's inefficiency is the variance of its MCFs. Typically, that variance is large in poor developing countries (Auriol and Warlters 2012). The literature on regulation relies on estimates of MCFs in advanced economies to assess the value of λ.

The *opportunity cost of public funds* is a short-term concept, relevant to the regulation of firms in financially constrained governments. Governments typically pursue multiple objectives – such as the production of public goods, the regulation of non-competitive industries and the control of externalities – under a single budget constraint. Because that constraint is typically binding, the opportunity cost of public funds, defined as the Lagrange multiplier of the government budget constraint, is strictly positive. Concretely, increasing subsidies of regulated services means decreasing the production of other essential public goods (such as national security or law enforcement) and of commodities that generate positive externalities (such as health care and education). Alternatively, it means increasing the level of taxes or debt. For instance, taxing general profits to finance public service investments may reduce incentives to invest in the rest of the economy and dim the prospects for general growth. Similarly, taxing labour income to finance public services may reduce the ability and incentives of workers to consume and to work, which would also affect growth. All these actions have a social cost, which must be weighed against the social benefit of subsidization. The opportunity cost of public funds is higher when, everything else being equal, government revenue is lower. Tax revenue as a proportion of GDP is typically much lower in developing countries than in rich countries, so the opportunity cost of public funds is typically much higher in the former (Auriol and Warlters 2005, 2012).

In poor developing countries, the relevant concept is the opportunity cost of public funds, as their tax systems are usually fairly inefficient owing to the size of the informal sector and the difficulty of raising taxes.[8] In this case subsidizing public utilities implies tough arbitrage.

---

[8] The average value of MCFs is not necessarily large, but its variance is. This is due in part to the presence of a large (untaxed) informal sector, which tends to increase the variance of the MCFs (Auriol and Warlters 2012).

this simplification, the regulator is assumed to assign the same weight to the well-being of operators and users.[9]

Rewriting Equation (4.2) to isolate t, we get $t = \pi - p(q)q + C(q)$. Substituting this value in Equation (4.6) and simplifying yields the objective function of the benevolent utilitarian regulator:

$$W = S(q) + \lambda p(q)q - (1 + \lambda)C(q) - \lambda \pi \qquad (4.7)$$

Note that the regulator's objective, W, increases with sales revenue:

$$\frac{\partial W}{\partial (p(q)q)} = \lambda \geq 0 \qquad (4.8)$$

This result can be somewhat counter-intuitive at first sight and certainly quite controversial since higher prices suggest lower welfare for consumers. However, there is a rational explanation. In regulation, if the price is too low, subsidies are needed to meet the firm's participation constraint. And since there is a shadow cost to tax financing, i.e. $\lambda > 0$, the regulator should prefer to finance the service through user fees rather than subsidies. In other words, with $\lambda > 0$, raising taxes to pay for the subsidies implies a burden on society which cannot be ignored when deciding on the optimal policy. Symmetrically, being able to tax the regulated firm, rather than subsidize it, represents a relief for taxpayers and a benefit for society with a shadow value of λ.

In countries with abundant natural resources or a tax system able to produce revenue with very few distortions in investment, labour supply or consumption decisions, relying on subsidies may not be a bad option for some services. But in countries without these characteristics, subsidies should not be the preferred option. The more distortionary taxes are in a country, the more the regulator should try to get the operators to rely on user fees rather than on subsidies in the interests of total social welfare.

Since the 1990s, the common wisdom has been that relying on user fees is easier to do when the service providers are private since they are expected to be less subject to pressure to make concessions on these user fees than public providers.[10] It has also

---

[9] A more general formulation would recognize that a regulator may assign different weights to the welfare of operators and consumers. Setting aside taxes and subsidies, this can be modelled as $W = V + \alpha \pi$. If the regulator cares more about consumers than about the operators, α will be $0 \leq \alpha \leq 1$. If $\alpha = 1$, it means that the regulator cares only about efficiency and does not intend to use regulation to deal with equity issues between operators and consumers. Finally, if $1 \leq \alpha$, it means that the regulator cares more about the firms' rents than the consumers' surplus, as this occurs when the regulator is captured by the industry (see Chapter 14). And for regulators interested in the distributional consequences across user types, it is easy to create two or more categories of users to track the extent to which users with different abilities to pay may be impacted by regulatory decisions. Assuming that only the willingness to pay matters may be misleading, as mentioned in the previous chapter.

[10] This common wisdom is evolving as there are many examples of situations in which the private firms have been forced to reverse price increases under political pressure. In most cases, this has been compensated, by lower maintenance and/or adjustment to the timing of investments when subsidies were not an option. In extreme cases, the solution has been to nationalize the services, as was the case in Bolivia or Mali, for instance.

been one of the arguments made to stimulate the privatization of public services. But it has also led to many debates on the social and political sustainability of the economically rational solution.

To many participants, the theoretical conclusion has been, and still is, quite difficult to accept and quite difficult to sell politically. The idea that choosing user fees for services provided by private operators over tax-financed subsidies is welfare-enhancing continues to be hard to accept for many poor countries and increasingly led some who first adopted it to renationalize the privatized utilities.[11] A common perception is that privatization is bad for the poor and often for the middle class too. Most large audience discussions of the issue omit that this flows from the narrow and highly distortionary tax bases characterizing many poor countries. Just as importantly, they also ignore that regulated public service providers can rely on more specific pricing techniques and subsidies design to ensure that the poorest are protected, as discussed in Chapter 9.

In practice, the provider ownership and the cost recovery strategy decisions are usually more ideological than technical. Opponents of privatization will underplay the role of tax distortions while those in favour will inflate them. This should be settled empirically through a quantification of all the key variables, including some which have not been picked up in this simple model. For instance, the health payoffs of access to clean water are easy to underestimate. This is one of the reasons why the case for subsidies designed to keep water prices low for a reasonable level of water consumption is easily made in policy debates. Subsidizing public transport to tilt the relative price of transport against the use of private cars is another instance in which the case of subsidies reflects concerns (i.e. health or pollution externalities) not accounted for in this simple model.

A second, less controversial, contribution of the model is that it makes the risks for a society of poor regulation quite explicit. Bad regulation allows an excessive rent, π (i.e. by allowing excessively high prices or subsidies), and this is bad for a society's welfare, W, as can be seen:

$$\frac{\partial W}{\partial \pi} = -\lambda < 0 \tag{4.9}$$

The higher the social cost of public funds, the higher the welfare costs of a regulation too generous for the regulated firm.

In sum, the objective functions used by these authors, and many more since, are quite broad but somewhat exclusive. For instance, they ignore environmental costs, which have become a major policy concern since the original papers were written. For most firms, internalizing these costs is not part of the optimization process for

---

[11] In practice, regulators working in dedicated agencies are not authorized to raise taxes to subsidize firms, or to tax them to subsidize taxpayers. Decisions to subsidize/tax regulated firms must be approved by the government. Regulators are therefore obliged to internalize that subsidizing public utilities is socially costly, when at all feasible.

operators, unless required by regulation. In practice, the disconnection of environmental considerations from regulation is a very serious issue to which we will return,
because integrating environmental costs into the regulatory mandate can change the
optimal design of regulation in surprising ways.[12]

For now, let's focus on seeing how this approach to modelling objectives that is
common to both Baron–Myerson (1982) and Laffont–Tirole (1986) can be combined
with their different approaches to modelling costs to discuss the optimal design of
regulation for different types of firms.

4.3   Baron–Myerson (1982) and the 'Ideal' Regulation of Private Monopolies

Private firms focus on profit; their negotiations with regulators largely aim at maximizing their monetary rents. Key to those negotiations is the fact that the firms know
more about their costs than does their regulator. Because of this information asymmetry, to which we will return in much more detail, regulators do not really know
whether they are dealing with a low-cost or a high-cost firm. This is one of the ways in
which the adverse selection you may have seen in your microeconomics classes shows
up. Persuading the regulator that the company's costs are higher than they really are
and using that to secure higher tariffs for regulated goods or services is the simplest
way to maximize profits.

To see this more formally, consider that the total costs of a monopolist producing a
quantity q of a good or service for domestic consumption can be expressed as the
following function:

$$C(q) = cq + F \qquad (4.10)$$

The cost depends on c, a firm-specific characteristic representing its underlying
marginal cost, as well as on F, a fixed cost which is unrelated to output. F is the
CAPEX discussed in Chapter 2. It covers all investments. c essentially reflects the
extent to which the marginal cost of the regulated firm is high or low and also drives
the size of the OPEX. Two firms may differ in their marginal cost c for different
reasons, the most obvious being that they may have adopted different technologies.
A given operator might depend on an old technology that may no longer be cost-
effective, leading to technological inefficiency. However, bad (i.e. high) c may also
reflect the fact that local operators are stuck with institutional constraints such as
wages and employment levels negotiated by the government for all workers and all
public service companies. These costs may be higher or lower than market rates and
comparable costs in other similar countries, and there is not much that local operators

---

[12] This is one of the emerging dimensions to consider in the modelling of the firms' objective functions, as
many are internalizing environmental concerns in their objectives as a response to growing societal
pressure to adopt corporate social responsibility perspectives as part of their regular business activities.
Many regulated firms are now highlighting this in their marketing strategies.

can do about this. Instead, the input choices of local operators are shaped by these agreements, leading potentially to allocative inefficiency.

The cost of imported inputs subject to a long-term contract is another common source of cost inefficiency reflected in c. A common case in point is the oil or natural gas needed to generate electricity or the basic chemicals needed to treat water. Once more, these factors, over which the operator has little or no control in the near term, explain why costs are higher than one could expect. A final illustration is linked to changes in exogenous input costs over time (summer against winter) or space (rural against urban). The regulator needs to know about them because it will influence their view on what a reasonable price should be for the monopolist.

A key characteristic of these two cost dimensions is that they are outside the firm's control, at least in the short to medium term. They reflect the current technological characteristics of the operator. Moreover, they are not related to the level of effort of the firm's managers. Since the management's goal is to maximize the firm's rent (the difference between revenue and cost), it will maximize its efforts to achieve the lowest possible cost. In Baron–Myerson's world, this cost-minimization problem is a black box: the firm's marginal cost is fixed at c.

This cost structure also implies that the total average cost, $C_M(q) = c + F/q$, is greater than the constant marginal cost, $C'(q) = c$, since $F/q > 0$. Therefore, the sector is characterized by increasing returns to scale and is incompatible with perfect competition and marginal cost pricing, as discussed in Chapter 2.

We deduce that with a cost structure of the Baron–Myerson type, in a situation where the operator may be able to collect subsidies (for instance to pay for some expensive parts of a network that the firm would not be able to recover through user fees), the surplus of the regulated operator (Equation 4.2) is:

$$\pi = p(q)q + t - cq - F \tag{4.11}$$

The main focus of the regulator is to design a scheme that will maximize W as defined in Equation (4.6) under the constraint that a private operator is willing to serve the market. This is not as simple as it may look.

In Baron–Myerson's world, one of the basic challenges of regulation is to come up with a regulatory framework that provides some incentive for the (private) monopolist to enter a market and stay in it. This means that the optimization process has to account for what is known as a *participation constraint*. This constraint is such that the monopoly's surplus must be no less than what it could earn by moving to some other industry or country (i.e. exiting the regulated market) here normalized at 0: $\pi \geq 0$.

The participation constraint implies that the following must be true: $p(q)q + t \geq cq + F$. This simply means that the revenue from users' fees and subsidies has to be larger than the sum of the variable and fixed costs that the firm has to take on to be able to run the business. This is not an unreasonable implication and it is consistent with the demands made by potential investors in regulated industries in the real world.

What is less realistic is that, for now, we still assume that the regulator can observe the firm's costs (i.e. that the access of information is not asymmetric for the regulator and the regulated firm). This is because we are still focusing on the benchmark case where the regulator has full information on all variables of interest. Substituting the cost $C(q) = cq + F$ into the welfare function in Equation (4.7) yields:

$$W = S(q) + \lambda p(q)q - (1 + \lambda)(cq + F) - \lambda \pi \qquad (4.12)$$

under the constraint that the firm breaks even, $\pi \geq 0$. By virtue of Equation (4.9), the regulator wants to minimize the firm's rent, π. To maximize W, the first thing to do is to fix π as low as possible without violating the participation constraint $\pi \geq 0$. The result is that $\pi = 0$.

This then leaves us with the decision as to how much the monopolist should produce and charge in an environment like this. Since the optimal price is driven by the optimal quantity (and symmetrically), this is decided by optimizing W with respect to q, as the regulation theoretical literature focuses on quantity.

Substituting $\pi = 0$ in Equation (4.12) and differentiating with respect to q leads to the following:

$$\frac{dW}{dq} = S'(q) + \lambda p(q) + \lambda p'(q)q - (1 + \lambda)c = 0 \qquad (4.13)$$

Recall that $S'(q) = p(q)$. Hence, the first-order condition (Equation 4.13) can be rewritten as:

$$p(q) - c = \frac{-\lambda}{1 + \lambda} p'(q)q. \qquad (4.14)$$

Dividing the left and right sides of the equation by $p = p(q)$ yields:

$$\frac{p - c}{p} = \frac{\lambda}{1 + \lambda} \frac{1}{\varepsilon} \qquad (4.15)$$

where ε is the price elasticity of demand (see Chapter 2) and $p - c$ is the markup over the marginal cost incurred by the firm when it is required to increase output.

Equation (4.15) is essentially an upgraded version of the Lerner formula discussed in Chapter 3 (Equation 3.4. It accounts for distortions linked to the balance between the public and the private financing of the firm (and the sector more generally). This formula is generally known as the Ramsey–Boiteux formula, to which we will return in Section 4.5. For now, it is simply useful to remember that it can be seen as a third way of setting prices in a regulated environment in which revenue has to cover costs. It complements the marginal cost pricing cum subsidies and the average cost pricing options discussed in Section 3.3. Allowing the operators to set the price according to the elasticity of demand while accounting for the distortions that would result from the need to subsidize consumption is actually quite common in practice.[13]

---

[13] If the elasticity of demand (ε) falls, the need to subsidize may increase to avoid the distributional consequences of the associated price increase. The regulatory decision is not a simple one since more subsidies may also imply more distortions associated with the need to tax in order to finance the subsidies. In situations and models in which there are at least two types of consumers with different

It is worth noting that in the Baron–Myerson model, when $\lambda = 0$, the optimal regulated price is the marginal cost of the firm: $p = c$. This result is intuitive. If the regulator does not put a positive weight on the taxpayer surplus, it chooses a price (or alternatively a quantity) that maximizes the consumer surplus. We have already shown in Chapter 2 that this is achieved by setting the price of the commodity at marginal cost c and that the resulting gap between costs and revenue can be compensated by subsidies. In other words, the subsidies are there to cover the fixed cost, hence $t = F$ since the cost of public funds is nil.

Symmetrically, when $\lambda \to +\infty$, then $\frac{\lambda}{1+\lambda} \to 1$, and the regulated price converges to the laissez-faire monopoly price suggested by the Lerner index in Equation (3.4), which is driven by the elasticity of demand. This is what standard microeconomics textbooks teach on the optimal pricing strategy for a private monopoly. If we use the figures mentioned in Section 4.2, i.e. λ between 0.3 and 0.5 in developed countries, the regulated mark-up $\frac{p-c}{p}$ should be between 20% and 30% of the non-regulated one. In developing countries, the regulated mark-up should be between 50% and 60% of the private monopolist's. This helps understand the necessity to differentiate policies according to the level of development.

More generally, the expression shows how the allowed markup, expressed as a share of the price, is limited by the elasticity of demand as well as by the distortions associated with subsidies. It suggests that any markup higher than that suggested by the formula implies an excess rent for the operator. Any lower markup implies that the distortions imposed by taxation are not accounted for properly in the decision to subsidize production (hence consumption) of the public service. This is not immaterial. When price controls are linked to subsidies, the economic prospects of the country are likely to be affected if the taxes raised to finance subsidies distort economic choices (see Box 4.2). Such concerns are at the core of debates over the relative merits of user fees and tax-financed subsidies to pay for public services.

Ultimately, one of the key lessons of the Baron–Myerson model, which is sometimes underplayed, is the growing imperative to account for the distortions linked to subsidies. This imposed a major change in the way monopoly pricing needs to be considered. Failing to take those dimensions into account can lead to a suboptimal or counterproductive use of scarce public resources – a serious economic mistake when fiscal constraints matter. Symmetrically, ignoring the impact on social welfare of laissez-faire monopoly pricing by focusing too narrowly on the operator's financial concern can also be a politically serious mistake.

Just as importantly, the model shows that, depending on the value of λ, a narrow approach to pricing may lead to underestimation or overestimation of the markup that would produce an optimal price. Simply simulating various levels of λ in the formulae shows that the higher λ is, the less incorrect the Lerner markup is for a given demand elasticity. In other words, the higher the distortions introduced by taxation, the wiser it

elasticities of demand and income constraints (i.e. rich and poor), it is important to consider the trade-offs associated with the need to subsidize the poor if these have a lower demand elasticity. This shows that distributional considerations are relatively easy to deal with within these basic models.

is to allow the monopolist to self-finance through higher markups and then tax its excess profits, referred to as rents, which have a shadow value of λ.

Despite its many significant insights for the design of regulation in practice, the model also has its weaknesses from the viewpoint of a regulator looking for concrete solutions. One of the main frustrations is that, while the improved version of the Lerner index in Equation (4.15) continues to recognize the importance of the demand side, it also supposes that the regulator knows the firm's marginal costs. Yet, in practice, regulators are likely to be uncertain about those costs. In many instances, they will be unaware (or not fully aware) of the technological and institutional constraints on the firm, the main drivers of c.

What this means is that regulators, long worried mostly about estimating demand elasticity to make sure monopolists were financially sustainable but not abusing their power, now also need to analyse costs in detail. They must also estimate a cost function that is precise enough both to permit an assessment of the importance of inefficiencies as drivers of profits for a given markup and to produce a sense of the extent to which overreliance on subsidies may damage the rest of the economy and its prospects. We will deal with this problem after presenting the second canonical model of regulation.

4.4   Laffont–Tirole (1986): A Unified Framework to Study the 'Ideal' Regulation of Monopolies

When regulation is not solely, or even primarily, focused on narrow monetary considerations such as the operator's sustainability or even the consumer surplus, it must classify costs in terms of their degree of 'manipulability'. This standard concern in the regulation of both private and public monopolies highlights the importance of paying attention to the details of cost drivers.

It is particularly interesting to use in the context of public monopolies (i.e. the SOEs), as one recurrent problem in their regulation is their tendency to make decisions that lead to higher-than-required costs (i.e. inefficiencies). The most common examples of this tendency are (i) overstaffing to create public jobs when unemployment is high; (ii) tolerance for low productivity associated with outdated business practices; and (iii) sluggish responses to evolving consumer needs that may require major organizational changes within the firm. If the regulator is not fully informed about how hard the managers of the firms try to address these weaknesses, it is said to be facing a moral hazard problem.

The Laffont–Tirole (1986) framework makes it easy to account explicitly for such cost drivers in addition to the risk of adverse selection issues identified by Baron–Myerson. Their trick is to explicitly add an effort variable in the modelling of costs.[14]

---

[14] Keep in mind that for pedagogical reasons, we focus here on the usefulness of the Laffont–Tirole model in the evaluation of the regulatory needs of public enterprises. The model is also quite useful for private monopolies, for which moral hazard concerns are realistic.

They stipulate that production costs depend on three factors: c, a firm-specific characteristic representing its underlying costs; e, the effort expended to decrease marginal cost; and F, a fixed cost unrelated to output.[15] Formally, we obtain the following function:

$$C(q, e) = (c - e)q + F \tag{4.16}$$

This approach to modelling costs shows that there are two potential sources of cost inefficiency but they differ in an essential way. As in Baron–Myerson (1982), c reflects those costs that the firm cannot change in short to medium term because they are rooted in its technological characteristics. In contrast, e represents costs that the firm can affect – largely through management and operational decisions. In practice, these are usually the costs that the firm can cut by improving efforts to use technology better. And when comparing two firms with the same technology, it explains why they can have different costs simply because they use the technology differently. Baron–Myerson ignores this dimension but, according to Laffont–Tirole, this e is what the regulatory game focuses on since all other cost dimensions can be audited and are hence harder to manipulate.

In this vision of the regulatory game, the operator has an incentive to manipulate the signals sent to the regulator (often embedded in accounting data) in order to appear to be making good-faith efforts to minimize costs. Auditing is supposed to offset this incentive and to help the regulator make essential distinctions between, and judgements about, a firm's cost and behaviour. This distinction is needed because e can be linked to inefficiency just as much as c, but dealing with these two sources of inefficiency will demand different regulatory actions. Technology (i.e. c) is linked to technical standards determined to meet the demand while accounting for budget constraints. They are best dealt with from an engineering perspective. Effort levels are linked to a much more heterogeneous set of dimensions. For example, managers may be able to cut costs by switching suppliers, renegotiating contracts, training the employees or improving core operations such as maintenance of the assets used to respond to service outages, interactions with consumers to reduce delinquency and collect unpaid bills, and basic financial management to minimize costs. This is much more complex to deal with in many ways. It also makes the audit of firms much more demanding for both the regulator and the regulated company.

The model assumes that putting in the extra effort to improve cost management is a source of stress for firms. Conceptually, this translates into the recognition that exerting effort e causes the firm a disutility of $\Psi(e)$, which grows more than proportionally as effort increases ($\Psi' > 0, \Psi'' > 0, \Psi''' \geq 0$). This is not an accounting cost, or what analysts usually think of when they discuss monetary costs, but, from the

---

[15] See Laffont and Tirole (1993), Armstrong et al. (1994) and Armstrong and Sappington (2007) for detailed presentations of models in this type.

operator's perspective, it is a factor when deciding how hard to try. This implies that the total cost function $C(q)$ used to derive the regulator objective function in Equation (4.7) for the Laffont–Tirole firm is:

$$C(q, e) + \Psi(e) = (c - e)q + F + \Psi(e) \qquad (4.17)$$

The emphasis placed on cost so far reflects a genuine concern of regulators wishing to do their job well. However, the regulator's job also entails understanding the revenue side of the operator's business, since revenues are just as important as costs in determining whether profits are excessive, insufficient or just about right. Attending to this side is particularly important in cases where the financial viability of the firm may well depend on a subsidy t to be provided by the government, as is often the case for publicly owned service monopolies.

For such entities, the initial revenue assessment depends on sales. Just as in the Baron–Myerson model, for a given cost level, revenue from sales is pq, where p is the average price level and q the total volume of output sold.[16] This model recognizes, as did Baron–Myerson, that subsidies can matter. Indeed, in practice, for many publicly owned service providers, revenue also depends on the willingness of the government to provide transfers to cover the total costs of the firm, both OPEX and CAPEX.[17] The real concern for regulators is thus the extent to which the firms undercharge in various ways, which is tantamount to demanding subsidies. These demands usually concern the CAPEX and are quite common for public enterprises delivering transport and W&S services.

Combining the information on total revenue $p(q)q + t$ with the information on the full costs of producing and making the effort to do so given by Equation (4.17) provides the regulator with the firm's net profits. For Laffont and Tirole it is crucial to keep in mind that welfare includes not just financial profits (with subsidies taken into account), but also the costs, $\Psi(e)$, associated with making an effort to cut accounting costs. Accounting costs can be audited, effort cost cannot.

Once all these costs have been accounted for, the monopolist's profit, π, from Equation (4.2), can then be expressed as:

$$\pi = p(q)q - (c - e)q - F - \Psi(e) + t \qquad (4.18)$$

In this specific model, the public firm's welfare is thus defined by the size of the rent, π, it can achieve from being the monopoly supplier. And, as in Baron–Myerson, the firm's participation constraint is still such that $\pi \geq 0$.

---

[16] Keep in mind that this is a simplification, since, in real life, a firm may decide to charge different prices to different users – that is, to practise price discrimination (see Chapter 8). The average price is thus nothing more than a weighted average of the various prices charged to different groups of users.

[17] Laffont and Tirole (1993) talked about transfers that could be positive (subsidies) or negative (taxes). This terminology is still dominant in the literature on economic regulation, whereas the public policy literature relies more on an explicit use of the concepts of subsidies and taxes.

As in Baron–Myerson, the benevolent regulator (one immune from political pressures) maximizes the social welfare function, internalizing the social cost of subsidies. In this context, accounting for non-monetary cost drivers, the total welfare function is expressed in Equation (4.6). Substituting in Equation (4.6) the total cost function $C(q)$ by its value from Equation (4.17), $C(q, e) + \Psi(e)$, yields:

$$W = S(q) - (c - e)q - F - \Psi(e) - \lambda t \tag{4.19}$$

Assuming that all variables are known to the regulator and all other actors, and that both the regulator and the operators are able to commit fully to their service and subsidy obligations, the regulatory process will come up with a price and subsidy mix. First, since taxes hurt the economy $(\lambda > 0$, then $dW/dt = -\lambda < 0$ as shown in Equation 4.9), t must be fixed at its lowest value without violating the constraint $\pi \geq 0$. Then, as in Baron–Myerson case, $\pi = 0$. As long as the participation constraint is met, it is better to increase prices and cut taxes than to cut prices and offer a larger subsidy to the firm. Injecting $\pi = 0$ in Equation (4.18), we deduce that:

$$t = -p(q)q + (c - e)q + F + \Psi(e) \tag{4.20}$$

Substituting this value in Equation (4.19) yields the regulator objective function under full information:

$$W = S(q) + \lambda p(q)q - (1 + \lambda)[(c - e)q + F + \Psi(e)] \tag{4.21}$$

Full access to information also implies that the regulator is able to measure effort and can penalize slacking whenever it is detected (e.g. by reducing subsidies). The consequence of this full access to information is that the level of effort is optimal and any cost inefficiency that produces minimal marginal cost higher than is desirable can be imputed only to the technological and institutional constraints of the firm. More specifically, optimizing W in Equation (4.21), the effort exerted by the firm will be efficient no matter what the technological and institutional constraints are, if:

$$\Psi'(e) = q \tag{4.22}$$

In other words, the optimal effort must provoke a marginal disutility, $\Psi'(e)$, just equal to the marginal gain of decreasing the unit cost of producing quantity q. The remaining challenge is thus to pick a quantity, q, or alternatively a price, $p = p(q)$, that maximizes the social welfare function, recognizing that both profits and the consumer surplus depend on quantities, and accounting for the binding operator's constraints on participation.

Formally, recalling that $S'(q) = p(q)$, the optimization of W in equation (4.21) with respect to quantity $(dW/dq = 0)$ leads to the following expression:

$$\frac{p - (c - e)}{p} = \frac{\lambda}{1 + \lambda} \frac{1}{\varepsilon} \tag{4.23}$$

This is almost the same formula as in Baron–Myerson (see Equation 4.15). The difference is the expression for marginal cost. Since Laffont–Tirole accounts for the effort level, it allows the analysis of a broader range of situations which typically characterize SOEs. It can also be relevant to private providers of public services when conducting a performance diagnostic for a private monopoly operator in cases where levels of effort can be used to mislead regulators about true costs.

4.5   What If There Is No Possibility of Subsidizing? Ramsey and Boiteux to the Rescue

If the government cannot or will not subsidize the public or private monopoly but requires it to balance its budget, we know that marginal cost pricing is not an option since it would lead to a financing deficit. In such a case, the monopolist will have to move away from the first-best optimum (i.e. the price–quantity combination that would be produced by marginal cost pricing). This is necessary to generate the resources needed to pay for both OPEX and CAPEX. We have already seen that average cost pricing is a likely option when the service provider delivers a single product.

To suit such circumstances, the Ramsey (1927) and Boiteux (1956) 'second-best' pricing solution mentioned in Section 4.3 offers an attractive, pragmatic option. Equation (4.15) maximizes total welfare under the condition of non-negative profit (i.e. that the firm is allowed to enjoy financial autonomy because subsidies are not possible). This is the same upgraded Lerner formula we have already encountered, but in this expression λ now measures the burden of the self-financing requirement that weighs against the firm (i.e. it is the Lagrange multiplier of this constraint, also known as the *shadow price* of the budget constraint).[18]

This shows that it may be efficient to allow the firm a certain amount of market power to gather the funds it needs to function rather than forcing it to rely on a costly financing strategy such as borrowing in capital markets. This is a very current debate in an environment in which many potential sources of financing in capital markets have much shorter time horizons than those needed to finance long-lived assets. Infrastructure is increasingly attracting institutional investors such as pension funds, insurance companies and hedge funds looking to diversify their fixed income portfolios. What makes these actors different is that they tend to be looking to get a spread premium over the price the operators would have to pay for a more traditional loan or bond. If this spread is excessive and if the alternative borrowing options are limited, Ramsey–Boiteux pricing indeed has to be attractive. The main challenge is a political one. It requires explaining to users that the impact on the fees they will have to pay may actually be lower under Ramsey–Boiteux than it would be if the firm had to rely on a hedge fund to finance its activities.

---

[18] In this approach, λ is endogenous to the firm's optimization problem – that is, determined by the calculation. In the former paragraphs, we had the same formula, but λ was exogenous. In that case, the business receives outside financial assistance to balance its accounts, but subsidies of this sort suppose a fiscal levy on taxpayers and entail a social cost measured by λ. In a nutshell, λ is exogenous when reasoning with subsidies and endogenous when reasoning with a balanced budget constraint.

So far, we have assumed a single-product monopoly, or a monopoly facing homogeneous demand. In the real world, however, public utilities face different types of consumers (e.g. urban–rural, domestic–industrial) and typically sell differentiated commodities (e.g. electricity in different voltages, transportation of different types or speeds). Yet it is not unusual in practice that the monopoly delivers multiple products catering to heterogeneous customers, as will be discussed in more detail in Chapter 11. Many water companies collect and treat sewage as well as supply water. Many railway companies provide suburban and long-distance passenger services as well as freight services. When it delivers various goods or services, more options are available. In particular, it can apply different prices to different type of consumer.

For a given market structure (once all the possible scope for restructuring to make the most of opportunities for competition has been accounted for), assuming k different types of products or consumers, then, for each product $i = 1, \ldots, k$ having a marginal cost c_i, a price p_i should be set such that:

$$\frac{p_i - c_i}{p_i} = \frac{\lambda}{1 + \lambda} \frac{1}{\varepsilon_i} \tag{4.24}$$

This is the same upgraded Lerner formula we have already encountered. However, in this expression λ still measures the burden of the firm's self-financing requirement, while c_i is the firm's marginal cost for product $i = 1, \ldots k$ and ε_i its price elasticity of demand.[19] It will vary depending on circumstances and the approach taken.

The Ramsey–Boiteux solution states that a monopoly firm should impose, for each of the products or services it delivers, a price markup that is linked to the inverse of the price elasticity of demand. The higher the elasticity of demand for the product or service, the smaller is the price markup – and vice versa. This is similar to the Lerner conditions already discussed several times, but it excludes any concern for tax-related distortions since firms are expected to be financially autonomous. This also explains why the same monopoly may be allowed to rely on different markups for different types of uses or users. It also explains why Ramsey–Boiteux pricing is quite popular among some of the regulated companies such as mobile phone companies.

To minimize the market power of the monopolists implied by the Ramsey–Boiteux principle, many regulators seek to increase competition (via restructuring) in the various markets in which the firm is active. This is because greater competition is associated with greater demand elasticity for any specific firm and hence makes it easier to mitigate the risks of market power abuses.

The challenge of Equation (4.24) is to explain that according to Ramsey–Boiteux, the more inelastic the demand for product or service i, the more efficient it is for its price to differ from the marginal cost. Thus, if demand for service i is very elastic, the change in demand resulting from a price change, Δp_i, will be high in absolute value – and the welfare loss will be significant. Then, p_i is to be set close to c_i if ε_i is large and at high value if ε_i is small. This can be quite politically sensitive even if it is in the best

---

[19] If demand i has substitutes or complements, ε_i is the super-elasticity, that is, the relative variation of demand taking into account all the indirect reactions provoked by a 1% change in price (see Chapter 11).

interest of users in an environment with limited fiscal capacity and high business risk perception, as may be the case in many developing economies or developed economies managing a fiscal crisis.

We know that deviation from marginal cost pricing obviously leads to a loss for society, and there are trade-offs in which the regulator can minimize these losses. Now, in addition, we have learned from the Ramsey formula how the trade-offs work between distortions. One must balance the distortion between the services provided by the firm as a result of their respective elasticities, ε_i, and the distortions reflected in λ. An equilibrium must be established between the social costs of non-marginal cost pricing, on the one hand, and, on the other, of the fiscal distortions caused by the need for a subsidy if prices are set below average cost.

The result is important in terms of the assessment of the optimal markup, but we will see in Chapter 8 that it is also essential to justify specific pricing strategies. Indeed, if the same product or service is sold in different markets (that is, if $c_i = c$ for all $i = 1, \ldots, k$, and the demand elasticities are different), the Ramsey–Boiteux principle clearly indicates that price discrimination is efficient. However, since it is often the case that poor people's demand for basic regulated public services (such as water or electricity) are more inelastic than the demand of rich people, the efficient economic solution 'fix a high price for poor (and a low price for rich) households' is hardly sustainable on political grounds. This is why pricing options merit their own chapter.

4.6 Accounting for Politics: A First Quick Look

So far, we have tried to identify how pricing should be influenced by the cost and demand characteristics of the market. The political viability of some of the technical dimensions has been a recurring theme, but we have not dealt squarely with the political pressure to which the monopoly provider may be subject because of the nature of the services it is providing. Nor do we have to deal with the way providers can apply pressure in their negotiations with regulators to rig the regulatory game. Yet this is particularly important in the industries we are discussing.

It is not uncommon for politicians to impose operational restrictions that increase costs, such as superfluous hiring, costly domestic technology, high-cost contracts with politically connected suppliers or favouring underperforming national champions. Governments supporting a national nuclear or coal industry may prefer to go for thermal installations than for renewable options and operators may use such preferences to make a case for subsidies. The case is particularly easy to make if politicians wish to ensure that the political favours do not show up in the prices paid by consumers or if prices would have to be increased too much to be politically sustainable. In such cases, creative subsidies and other types of transfers are used to shift some of the bill from consumers to taxpayers.

Such political interference in the regulatory process is one of the reasons why many academics argued early on for independent regulatory agencies (e.g. Estache 2020a).

Truly independent regulators operating in a dedicated agency are better placed than regulators working within a ministry to oppose political demands to maintain prices at inefficiently low levels by relying on costly public subsidies. This independence also reduces the risks of capture by special interests and, in particular, the regulated company. Independence needs to be put in place jointly with accountability. Regulators need to be held accountable for their decisions to ensure that the risks of selective under-enforcement of rules and those of excessive regulation are minimized.

In practice, this academic suggestion to increase the degree of independence of the regulator has been translated into the decisions by many governments to create separate regulatory agencies, i.e. separate from the Ministries covering the sector to be regulated. This institutional change was supposed to reduce corruption and, more generally, undesirable political interference with the performance of the regulated firms. In Europe, the leader was the United Kingdom (e.g. Majone 1994, 1996, 1997; Thatcher 2002, 2011). However, the model was also broadly followed for developing countries (e.g. Bertomeu-Sanchez and Estache 2018 for the water sector; Foster et al. 2017 for electricity).

The early academic evaluations of the effectiveness of these governance changes supported the hope that the separate regulatory agencies (SRAs) would help meet the goals of regulation and improve service coverage and quality as well as overall welfare. For instance, Andres et al. (2007), Cubbin and Stern (2006), Gassner et al. (2009) and Vagliasindi (2012) described the potentially positive effects of independent regulators on investment in developing countries for various infrastructure sectors. By the late 1990s, however, the evidence was becoming less conclusive, as suggested by Parker and Kirkpatrick (2012) in their survey. The main explanation is that agencies are never fully independent. In Europe, Busuioc (2009), for instance, shows that the actual level of autonomy of such agencies is below the autonomy provided by formal legal rules. Likewise, Cambini and Rondi (2017) recently concluded that political interference largely persists within the EU, with the negative consequence of decreasing investment. Similar conclusions have been reached for developing countries. Moreover, even government changes are often characterized by changes in the staffing of regulatory agencies to increase the odds that regulatory decisions match political preferences when conflicts arise.[20]

The point of this brief comment on political interference in regulation is that any discussion of the regulation also needs to consider the risks of non-benevolence of some politicians and some regulators. Most of the initial theory assumed benevolence on all parts. Firms were not lying about their costs, and regulators and politicians cared only about the public interest. Changing these naïve assumptions is one of the main contributions of the modern theory of regulation. This, in turn, implies that regulatory

---

[20] In March 2018, the French government launched a major reform of the railways sector. Most of the debates have focused on the reduction of protection to the next generation of employees of the sector. But one of the items with the most immediate impact on the sector was the proposal to take away from the rail regulator the right to veto some of the price decisions by the incumbent which could reduce competition in the sector.

designs have to account for the quality of information as well as for the quality of institutions. The next chapter will look into this as it considers the ways in which information asymmetries and absence of governmental benevolence influence the optimal design of regulation.

4.7   Summing Up

- Regulation is a complex game subject to manipulation by investors and politicians. Unless the regulator internalizes the complexity of this game, it is unlikely to be able to minimize the welfare losses associated with monopolistic production.
- To benchmark the consequences and risks of the regulatory game, an analyst needs to have a good understanding of what the outcome in prices and quantities would be if the game were played under full information on cost and demand by a benevolent regulator.
- Baron and Myerson (1982) focus on the risk of high markups linked to asymmetric information on the production technology and hence on costs; Laffont and Tirole (1986) add the risk of cost overruns linked to asymmetric information on the effort levels produced by the operators (i.e. stemming from poor management practices).
- Baron–Myerson (1982) is useful to analyse the optimal regulation of efficiently run private monopolies for which maximization of profit, and therefore cost controls, is paramount, while Laffont–Tirole (1986) is useful to design the regulation of any type of monopoly for which institutional or management characteristics are just as important as technological ones. In addition to private enterprises, this typically includes SOEs since these tend to be much more subject to political interference than their private alternatives.
- Optimal regulation needs to consider the possibility of constraints on the fiscal capacity of the sector. Combined with the need to recognize that without subsidies monopolies have to enjoy financial autonomy to be able to deliver the services, it leads to an upgraded Lerner index: the optimal price level, when cost can be observed, depends on the elasticity of demand and on the opportunity cost of public funds. In countries with highly distorted tax systems or with little fiscal capacity, user fees may impose lower costs on society.
- Any discussion of the regulation also needs to consider the risks of non-benevolence of some politicians and some regulators. This could impact on the effectiveness of regulatory designs as much as any information gap on cost and demand.
- To reduce corruption and political interference, many governments have created separate regulatory agencies. Despite this institutional change, political interference largely persists, with the negative consequence of decreasing investment.

5   Regulating under Informational Constraints

When a regulator possesses inadequate information about the operator providing a public service its task is a lot more complex than basic textbooks suggest. In the real world, it is not only the information asymmetries about costs levels or demand that matter, but also budget constraints, fiscal distortions and governance weaknesses. Ignoring these dimensions when setting prices would be at best naïve as it is usually not good enough to link them to elasticities in demand as the simplest theory argues.

Setting the wrong price carries serious risks, beginning with finding no qualified firms willing to provide the service. Where regulators do not know operators' technical capacity, they can easily confuse low- and high-cost ones. A low bidder with inferior technical capacity may well prove less economical than a higher bidder with greater capacity. On the other hand, a high-capacity firm may pretend to be less competent simply to have a chance to increase its profit margin if it knows all other potential service providers are much less competent than it is. Given these challenges, it is no easy task for regulation to meet its primary goal of ensuring the public utility service at a fair price to users and a fair return to operators.

What this chapter will show is that, ultimately, regulators must 'pay' to access the information they need, which can go well beyond the rent that was part of the average cost pricing approach assumed to be unavoidable in the old days of regulation and under an assumption of full information. This fee for information is known in the academic literature as the *information rent*. It will eventually be paid either by the consumers or the taxpayers to the benefit of the operator, who will enjoy larger profit.

The issue is politically sensitive either way. It is difficult to explain to consumers and taxpayers – that is, to voters – why they must live with the idea of paying operators for the information regulators require. However, it is one of the consequences of information asymmetries and the various institutional weaknesses commonly found around the world. The two simple benchmark models reviewed in the previous chapter are useful to illustrate how optimal regulation may be adjusted to minimize these consequences. Since this discussion is pulling together much of the theory used to analyse misunderstood dimensions of regulatory design, it may be useful to start with a simple example. It is selected to highlight the challenges that regulation is expected to address.

5.1   Challenges Linked to Cost Information Asymmetries: An Example

Suppose a government wishes to increase the production of water in a city which has encountered a significant population growth due to massive rural–urban migration. The demand for water has exploded because of this migration and the risk of water rationing has been a concern for many citizens and business users. The regulator has commissioned a series of economic studies to assess users' willingness to pay and the social surplus associated with a lower risk of water rationing. It has also commissioned technical studies to get a sense of the groundwater available and the difficulty of accessing it. The technical studies suggest that, depending on the technological skills of the firm, it will either be profitable to extract a great deal of the groundwater or an amount that would probably be seen as a disappointment but would be just enough to reassure consumers. There are thus two scenarios: a good (low-cost) case and a bad (high-cost) case.

The economic team is next asked to turn the technical information into economic and financial information. Which leads to the following diagnostic: if the firm's technology is inefficient/high cost, the unit cost is $c^h = 2\$/$unit. If it is efficient/low cost, the unit cost is $c^l = 1\$/$unit. There are two possible levels of exploitation here: the water company will be able to extract a large quantity of $\bar{q} = 2{,}500$ units yielding a social surplus of $S(\bar{q}) = $ US$ 5,000 or it will be able to extract $\underline{q} = 625$ units yielding $S(\underline{q}) = $ US$ 2,500. This suggests that the marginal increase in surplus from an increase in production is declining but is still quite significantly positive. To keep the exposition simple, we assume that the fixed-cost investment needed to increase capacity is observable and financed by a public subsidy or aid.

It is up to the regulator to set the price p per unit of output so that the water company can generate enough revenue to recover the full variable costs of the water production. The regulator wants to make sure that it is not too generous, but without running the risk of violating the participation (profitability) constraint of the operator. It does not want to be faced with a situation in which no firm expresses interest in the project. To ensure that this scenario does not occur, it needs to offer enough to persuade at least one reasonably qualified operator that it will be able to cover its costs.

To follow the standard practice of economic analysis, the economic team first looks at what the optimal regulatory decision would be if the regulator were able to access all the information available (i.e. the full information benchmark). It then explores what happens to this optimal choice when some key information gaps cannot be closed.

The full information benchmark. If the regulator has full information, they will know if the firm has high-cost/inefficient or low-cost/efficient technology. If the firm is high cost $\left(c^h = 2\right)$, consumers will be better off with the smaller output level of $\underline{q} = 625$.

If the firm's technology is low cost $\left(c^l = 1\right)$, it is efficient to order $\bar{q} = 2{,}500$ units of water because the net social surplus is higher than if the contract requires it to supply only $\underline{q} = 625$. Indeed, ordering the lower volume of water implies $S(\underline{q}) - c^l\underline{q} = 2{,}500 - (1 \times 625) = $ US$ 1,875, which is lower than the welfare consumers would gain from a high-volume contract, $S(\bar{q}) - c^l\bar{q} = 5{,}000 - (1 \times 2{,}500) = $ US$ 2,500. If the regulator wants to pay the minimum to be able to meet the participation constraint of the firm, it needs to reimburse the costs associated with the production of the high volume of water. Since the scenario with a water volume of 2,500 units from a low-cost firm is associated with a unit cost of US$1, the regulator will have to allow the firm to recover US$2,500, and this implies a unit price of $p(c^l) = $ US$1. This is not surprising since, in this simple problem, pricing should be at marginal cost, which is also equal to the average variable cost.

If the firm is high cost $(c^h = 2)$, consumers will be better off with the smaller output level of $q = 625$. This is because they will obtain a net surplus $S(q) - c^h q = 2{,}500 - (2 \times 625) = $ US$ 1,250 which is greater than if the high-cost firm has to produce a larger output $S(\bar{q}) - c^h\bar{q} = 5{,}000 - (2 \times 2{,}500) = 0$. And the firm will recoup its cost with $p(c^h) = $ US$2.

The information asymmetry case. Now assume that the regulator does not know whether the firm is efficient/low cost (c^l) or inefficient/high cost (c^h). One option is to resolve the uncertainty by allowing the firm to select from a menu offering the two contracts that would prevail under perfect information. Under the first contract, T^h targeted at firm h, the firm is committed to deliver a quantity of $q = 625$ units for an authorized cost recovery of $ 1,250 (or a selling price $p(c^h) = $ $2). Under the second, T^l targeted at firm l, it is committed to deliver a quantity of $\bar{q} = 2{,}500$ for an authorized cost recovery of $2,500 (or a selling price $p(c^l) = $ $1). The firm is then allowed to select the contract that best suits it.

If the firm is inefficient $(c^h = $2)$, it will choose the small quantity with high unit price (contract T^h) because its net profit is: $\pi(c^h, T^h) = [p(c^h) - c^h] q = (2 - 2) \times 625 = 0$, while if it chooses the high quantity with small unit price (contract T^l), its net profit is: $\pi(c^h, T^l) = [p(c^l) - c^h]\bar{q} = (1 - 2) \times 2{,}500 = -2{,}500 < 0$. Contract T^h is also the best option for society when the firm is inefficient.

The bad news from a social welfare viewpoint is that, under this menu approach, the efficient firm $(c^l = $1)$ will also choose the 'small' contract because, for the efficient firm, it implies:

$$\pi(c^l, T^h) = [p(c^h) - c^l] q = (2 - 1) \times 625 = 625$$
$$\text{which is larger than } \pi(c^l, T^l) = [p(c^l) - c^l]\bar{q} = (1 - 1) \times 2{,}500 = 0$$

The efficient firm would be quite irrational if it were to offer to produce the maximum output. This in turns means that the government is less likely to be able to minimize the risk of water rationing in the near future than it would have been in a full-information world.

The example illustrates two key lessons from the modern theory of regulation. The first is how easy it is for an efficient firm to take advantage of the regulator's lack of knowledge or of information since it can make more money by pretending to be inefficient. More specifically, it pays to lie when the regulator is incompetent or limited. When an efficient firm's real costs are lower than those of potential competitors, the efficient firm can make a profit by lying and producing the output that would be optimal for the inefficient firm. The outcome is the usual monopoly result: output is too low and the price too high. Hence, the regulator is back to square one and must devise another regulatory design in order to get the various types of firms to reveal their true type.

The second key lesson illustrated by the example is that society pays a very high cost for the failure of regulators dealing with firms in a monopolistic position to build information obligations and incentives into regulatory designs. Any uncertainty occasioned by political interference or regulatory incompetence provides an opportunity to argue about costs. The game is quite predictable: the operators will have an incentive to claim costs higher than the actual costs. The challenge for the regulator then is to try to assess the wedge between the claimed and actual costs. The problem can be partially mitigated by introducing incentive mechanisms, as discussed next. But a more comprehensive solution will require regulatory accounting rules, as we will discuss later in the chapter.

5.2   How Can a Regulator Induce Providers to Be Honest about Costs?

Mechanism design looks for system-wide solutions allowing the implementation of economic decisions involving multiple self-interested agents, each with private information about their preferences and skills. It has proven to be quite helpful in explaining why the efficiency of market mechanisms may differ under different institutional contexts. It has also been quite useful in improving the match between regulatory needs and regulatory designs, accounting for the differences in incentives of the various agents involved. It is only by trying to understand the incentives for operators to lie, that the regulators will be able to minimize their occurrence.

On the question of how to get an efficient provider to reveal its type and to produce the socially optimal output (a high volume of water, in the example earlier), the regulator needs to understand the opportunity cost of being honest. Transparency is just as bad for the operators as opacity is for consumers and taxpayers. The regulatory design must balance these perspectives. What the most pragmatist theorist argues about is that, unless the regulator has the resources to monitor service providers (and enforcement has a cost, which consumers or taxpayers will have to pay),[1] it may be useful to consider providing an incentive for operators to be truthful. In practice, this means rewarding them for their honesty. That is, the final price paid for the service includes an amount to compensate the provider for revealing its cost – which can be seen as a reward for integrity – in addition to the production cost.

---

[1] A regulator can increase efforts to reduce information asymmetries through more frequent audits and penalties. But it is always limited in implementation due to their cost and the need to deal with the operator's participation constraint.

5.3   How Should a Reward for Integrity Work?

The price of honesty can be assessed by analysing the differential payoffs of being honest and of hiding information from a regulator. The difference in payoffs is the value of information. To induce truth-telling, the regulator must pay a price that is linked to the operator's opportunity cost of revealing the truth. In the water example, to persuade the provider to choose the appropriate contract (and thus to produce the efficient quantity $\bar{q} = 2,500$), the regulator must promise the low-cost firm to allow a price such that $(p^l - c^l)\bar{q} \geq (p(c^h) - c^l)q$, that is, a profit at least equal to US$625, or alternatively a unit price of $p^l = $ US$1.25. This implies an 'information rent' paid to the efficient provider of US$0.25 per unit, to guarantee that the higher output is provided. This amount is exactly what the operator would have won by pretending to be inefficient.

In other words, to dissuade the operators from lying about their costs, it is sufficient to offer them – when they reveal the truth – what they would have won by lying. Reducing the reward for lying is therefore a way for the regulator to reduce the cost of asymmetric information. And we will see in Section 5.5 that the regulator can influence the operator's incentive to lie by changing the quantities to be produced by an inefficient operator – for example, by reserving the right to lower the quantities to be produced, or even in some limited cases, to shut down production altogether whenever the operator claims a high cost.

Alternatively, the regulator might choose to ignore the fact that there might be a low-cost provider among the possible service providers. If a low-cost provider gains the market, the drawback of this solution is a loss of efficiency combined with the appropriation of undue rents. The choice between the different options depends on how much the regulator knows about the real value of the production cost and its statistical distribution – that is, in our water example, how likely it is that a firm is a low-cost operator.

Finally, note that the incentive contract targeted at the efficient firm $(\bar{q} = 2,500 \text{ units}, \ p^l = 1.25)$ may be impossible to implement. Indeed, if the information rent is to be paid through a subsidy, the cost of public funds discussed in Box 4.2 would create a welfare loss. Then the regulator must trade off the sectorial gains and the tax costs of the incentive policy. Alternatively, relying on a pricing policy requires the firm to charge a selling price $p^l = \$1.25$ instead of $p(c^l) = \$1$. But if demand is elastic, at this higher price, consumers will demand a quantity lower than $\bar{q} = 2,500$.

5.4   Where Do Information Gaps Come from and How Can They Be Bridged?

Most of the information gaps faced by a regulator are products of adverse selection and moral hazard, two concepts many readers are likely to have been exposed to in their basic microeconomics classes when studying market failures. To better appreciate how regulatory strategies might counter these failures, it is useful to consider how the related issues emerge in practice in the context of regulatory design.

Adverse selection (AS) arises from differences in access to pre-existing information between a regulator and a firm. Many of these differences find their source in poor or mismanaged accounting practices. Giving too much margin to the regulated industries to report and allocate costs will generally lead to firms optimizing the level and type of information they are willing to report. This is why modern regulatory practice is so keen on issuing regulatory accounting guidelines which minimize the risks of mismatches between the reporting offered by the firms and the reporting needed by the regulator. The data reported should be detailed enough to allow the regulator to answer some basic questions. For instance, is a firm high cost or low cost? innovative? competent and technically up to date? polluting? safe?

The answer to any of these questions depends on how well the regulator can characterize the firm and its costs. In both the Baron–Myerson and Laffont–Tirole models, this is what the c is all about. It is thus the conceptualization of the many 'real-life' dimensions. In principle, c should be modelled as a continuum ranging from best to worst practice. To make the analysis as simple as possible, however, academic researchers often rely on a binary modelling of c whereby, as in our water example, the firm is either low cost, $c = c^l$ (occurring with a given probability), or high cost, $c = c^h$ (occurring with the complementary probability). Even though c cannot actually be controlled by the firm (at least in the short to medium term), regulators need to learn its value to make sure a firm is not setting prices higher than it should by simply pretending to be a higher-cost firm than it actually is.

Within the framework we are relying on here, most of the risks of 'fake information' are observed on the OPEX side of the business and on misstatements of consumers' preferences which drive demand and determine the output to be produced (hence revenue). To illustrate how concrete the theoretical treatment of these risks is, consider the market for mass transport. The provider knows if a bus or train is old and unreliable or new and safe, but the user knows this only after buying a ticket and riding on that specific bus or train. Until then, the user can only forecast their experience based on expected quality across the market. The provider of a high-quality service may not be able to convince a prospective user that its services are of high quality, but it will charge a higher-than-average fee. The provider of a low-quality service, meanwhile, would be happy to sell its services at an average price. Thus, users are likely to end up adversely selecting the lowest-quality services (at least until there is enough collective experience to reduce the information asymmetry). All this implies that adverse selection generates inefficiency since there is a serious possibility that good service providers will leave the market. Consumers and taxpayers will have to deal with those that remain.

One could think that good accounting and audit practices, and sound technical expertise and benchmarking, should help to close the information gap between the regulator and the operators. This is true to some extent. However, there are limits to what auditing and expertise can do, simply because some part of the costs is determined by the firm's action, as discussed in Section 5.6.

Moral hazard (MH), the second type of risk we will consider, arises from a lack of information about firms' actions. No matter how good or bad the technology is, a firm can try to reduce its cost. How hard the firm tries to control costs deals with the MH side of regulation. This is what the *effort* variable e is all about in the Laffont–Tirole model. The Laffont–Tirole model acknowledges that some cost auditing is possible for the regulator (i.e. it assumes that the regulator can observe the total variable cost ex post), but this audit is not sufficient to control the composition of the regulated firm's costs.

Certain business practices can help a low-cost firm mimic a high-cost one. For example, it is common to see firms try to rely on complex networks of unregulated subcontractors, while using transfer-pricing techniques to inflate the costs of service delivery. Transfer pricing is a common approach to fake costs and hence allows firms to inflate costs artificially. It is common for regulated firms to outsource basic business needs such as client management software, core technical services or even raw materials to some affiliate firms. This allows regulated firms to inflate costs in high-tax countries and declare revenues on the part of the business in low-tax countries for instance. And in the process, this allows them to claim high average costs where the final price is set. To reduce the incentive to rely on these practices, some regulators have been quite aggressive. For instance, the UK water regulator, Ofwat, has issued specific guidelines on transfer pricing in the sector. It has also occasionally imposed fines for infringements of its rules in the reported regulatory accounting returns. The idea is not to block outsourcing of part of the regulatory mandated activities but to block the manipulation of prices which can be used to 'fake costs' and hence inflate prices and returns. In most of these cases the regulator's main complaint was that the water operators had not undertaken competitive market testing of the outsourcing contract values.

Similarly, certain accounting practices make it difficult to assess moral hazard. For instance, if maintenance records are not up to date or precise, it is hard to gauge what firms are doing to minimize the risk of service failures such as power outages or train derailments. Moreover, firms will make decisions that are inefficient but profit-maximizing if they expect regulators to turn a blind eye. Consumers who can pay for a more dependable service will do so, allowing firms to increase profits without increasing service quality across the board. Where the risk of moral hazard is serious, controlling prices is not enough. The simplest and most effective illustration may be the extent to which the resources allocated to maintenance of assets (e.g. roads, transmission lines, water pipelines, train tracks) are consistent with the maintenance expected to take place at the time the investment was made. If a regulated firm knows that there are some dimensions of a service that users cannot control, such as quality (see Chapter 10), and maintenance is central to this, it is likely to try to adjust its efforts in ways that cut costs but maintain profit margins (at least in the short run). Besides, cuts are often made in maintenance, leading eventually to service failures and the need for repairs. When this happens, delivering a given level of service comes at a greater cost to society – users in particular. And that greater cost is not only financial. The point is that if the regulator lacks access to information on a firm's specific level of effort, a firm can cut costs in the short run to increase profits. Years later, when rehabilitation is needed, it will often be done as part of a renegotiation of the initial agreement, a renegotiation that is likely to penalize users and taxpayers more than firms. It is not uncommon to see major rehabilitation costs being used to increase a firm's asset base. This has implications for the average tariffs in regulated industries, as we shall see later.

The discussion so far has focused on the supply side of the business, but the demand side also affects the size and nature of moral hazard risks and consequences. If demand is relatively elastic, as in the case of transportation where users can choose between various modes, a low level of effort by a train operator to meet the demand of its potential users will lead to a switch to other modes. Since railways costs are linked to demand, the lack of effort to meet demand will increase costs. This in turn increases prices, which leads the market to shrink to an inefficient level, whereas at the right price demand would have been higher. In a context in which the environmental sustainability of transport options is a growing worry, the large number of strikes linked to key public transport systems in countries such as Belgium or France is a source of concern.

Similar issues arise when demand is inelastic such as for water or telecommunications in rural areas served by a single provider. In that case, the market size does not shrink, but users pay higher prices (unless taxpayers cover the cost through government subsidies). This illustrates that inefficiencies from a lack of effort come in multiple shapes and sizes, but they are still inefficiencies. And while basic models of regulation do not really deal with equity concerns, it should also be clear that the social incidence of these inefficiencies deserve a close look. The victims of higher prices and fewer options are not necessarily those who can afford it the most.

Whether the sources of information asymmetry are AS or MH driven, both theory and practice suggest that the risks they imply justify the time spent by regulatory designers trying to anticipate them. Both theory and practice also reveal the limits of the tools available to reduce the distortions and rents linked to information asymmetries. The limitations should not be an excuse not to try to minimize them. To do so, the regulator's agenda is clear, if not simple. If the main goal is to counter the risk of moral hazard, regulation should give the operators significant incentives to cut costs – and to demonstrate their effort to do so. To counter adverse selection risks, regulation should give the operators the assurance that they will be able to make rents when they are efficient. As in many other policy topics, sticks for bad behaviour and carrots for good behaviour are both part of the regulatory policy toolkit.

For now, let us look at a relatively simple regulatory model to appreciate how theory can help in thinking through the challenges faced by regulators and identifying specific and well-targeted solutions. We will assume (as did Baron–Myerson and Laffont–Tirole) that the fixed cost, F, discussed in the earlier chapters is common knowledge to all stakeholders, including regulators and consumers. This means that they all know how much it costs to build a road, a water treatment station, or a new transmission line. This might seem ambitious, but it is not unrealistic. A public entity providing a public service goes through a procurement process when deciding when and how to invest in increased service coverage or quality. A private firm, too, goes through this process. A regulator needs to know the value of regulated firms' assets, including those added by new investments. So, deriving a reasonable estimate of the value of F is not an impossible task. The real informational challenges are elsewhere, and to see where they come from it is useful to start the discussion with the simple AS model.

5.5 Modelling Adverse Selection Risks

To get a sense of the economic significance of adverse selection and what it implies for regulatory design, we will start with a simple framework (à la Baron–Myerson) with two types of firms: low cost identified by l and high cost identified by h. We begin by comparing the rent of the two types:

$$\pi^l = p(q^l)q^l + t^l - c^l q^l - F \tag{5.1}$$

$$\pi^h = p(q^h)q^h + t^h - c^h q^h - F \tag{5.2}$$

Whether the firm relies on a low-cost (c^l) or a high-cost (c^h) technology with $c^l < c^h$, it must achieve profitability, accounting for the possibility of transfers/subsidies t by the government. This brings us to the participation constraint (PC):

$$\pi^l \geq 0 \text{ if the firm possesses low-cost technology } c^l \tag{5.3}$$

$$\pi^h \geq 0 \text{ if the firm possesses high-cost technology } c^h \tag{5.4}$$

Perhaps the most puzzling insight to be gained from this set of equations is that the high-cost firm (with a poor technology that results in a high OPEX in practice) enjoys a non-negative rent. Why would the government allow a high-cost firm to collect a profit, as required by Equation (5.4)? If the alternative is to run the risk of finding no operator to provide the service or of relying on another operator with an even worse marginal cost, c, then working with a firm with a high-cost c^h may indeed be a good idea. This in part explains why a new, high-cost private operator may be chosen over a public operator with a long record of poor performance. But it is not an easy sell. Indeed, users and taxpayers have a hard time connecting poor performance to positive rents, and understandably so. Thus, it is all the more important for regulators to ensure that the firms choosing to participate in the market decide on a price level that is in the interest of society at large. This is not just about political selling; it is key to minimizing conflict.[2]

In the context of the Baron–Myerson model, the rent is the outcome of bargaining between the regulator and the operator. Since the regulator cannot observe the firm's

---

[2] Although the political implications of regulatory decisions are outside the scope of this book, they are essential: cooperation and sustained communication among all stakeholders is necessary to reduce information asymmetries.

cost, it needs to check if an efficient firm (that is, one characterized by c^l) lies and pretends to be high cost (c^h) to maximize its rent. As we have seen, efficient firms may claim to be inefficient (or hide their efficiency) so they can produce the low quantity associated with an inefficient provider – and thus gain a higher rent per unit produced. One way for the regulator to get a better sense of an operator's cost is to pay experts or specialized consulting firms for information on its productivity. Alternatively, it can use information on costs from other similar producers. Such benchmarking is costly of course, but it is done in practice when the stakes are high enough. For instance, some international organizations, such as the World Bank, finance engineering audits of assets before they are privatized or restructured in order to minimize ex post risks of costs and technical data manipulation by the new operators. We will come back to the issue of benchmarking in various chapters.

This brings us to the incentive compatibility constraint (IC), which is needed to make sure that neither type of firm will have an incentive to pretend to be the other type.[3] We know that, unless forced to be honest, a low-cost firm (c^l) will pretend to be high cost in order to claim an extra per-unit rent. Formally, the IC constraint can be expressed as follows:

$$\pi^l \geq p(q^h)q^h + t^h - c^l q^h - F \quad \text{for the low-cost firm} \tag{5.5}$$

$$\pi^h \geq p(q^l)q^l + t^l - c^h q^l - F \quad \text{for the high-cost firm} \tag{5.6}$$

where π^l and π^h are defined in Equations (5.1) and (5.2) respectively. In Equation (5.5) the right-hand side is the profit of a firm endowed with cost c^l when it produces and sells q^h, and receives a subsidy t^h, both dedicated to the firm with cost c^h. The interpretation of Equation (5.6) is similar concerning the firm with a cost c^h.

However, not all constraints in Equations (5.3)–(5.6) are simultaneously binding, as demonstrated in Box 5.1. Only the participation constraint of the high-cost firm in Equation (5.4) and the incentive constraint of the low-cost firm in Equation (5.5) are problematic. Indeed, it is always possible for a low-cost firm to pretend to be high cost, and hence secure a higher markup, that is, $\pi^l = q^h \Delta c$ where $\Delta c = c^h - c^l$. But it is not possible for a high-cost firm to claim to be low cost. If it claims to be low cost, it will get a low per-unit price and run a deficit. Similarly, it is easier for a low-cost firm to break even than it is for a high-cost firm. Here lies an important lesson for regulators. Where there is asymmetry of information, the binding constraint is not the same for high- and low-cost firms.

---

[3] In the more technical academic literature, this would be interpreted as a situation in which each firm will reveal its type truthfully. This is based on the 'revelation principle' and linked to the use of the revealed preferences in the interpretation of observed behaviour. In that literature, the challenge of regulation is to specify incentive constraints to push agents to make the right choices. It is thus essential to make sure that if the regulator wants the firm to do the right thing, regulation has to stimulate the right choices.

Box 5.1 Incentive Compatibility Constraints in the Adverse-Selection Case

$T(\hat{c}) = (\hat{q}, \hat{t})$ represents the contract proposed to a firm announcing that its unit cost is $\hat{c}$. If its real cost is c, its net profit is $\pi(\hat{c}, c) = p(\hat{q})\hat{q} + \hat{t} - c\hat{q} - F$, with $\hat{c}, c \in \{c^l, c^h\}$. The contract $(\hat{q}, \hat{t})$ is incentive-compatible if and only if $\pi(c^l, c^l) \geq \pi(c^h, c^l)$ and $\pi(c^h, c^h) \geq \pi(c^l, c^h)$. Adding these two constraints and rearranging provides a necessary condition for incentive compatibility (IC):

$$\pi(c^h, c^h) - \pi(c^h, c^l) \geq \pi(c^l, c^h) - \pi(c^l, c^l)$$

If we substitute the π functions with their values and simplify, this is equivalent to $(c^h - c^l)(q^h - q^l) \leq 0$. Given that $c^h > c^l$, we deduce that a necessary condition for incentive compatibility is $q^h \leq q^l$. With demand decreasing in price, an equivalent necessary condition for incentive compatibility is $p^h = p(c^h) \geq p^l = p(c^l)$.

The regulator faces four constraints (two participation constraints PC and two incentive compatibility constraints IC):

$$(PC_h) : \pi(c^h, c^h) \geq 0 \text{ and } (PC_l) : \pi(c^l, c^l) \geq 0$$

$$(IC_h) : \pi(c^h, c^h) \geq \pi(c^l, c^h) \text{ and } (IC_l) : \pi(c^l, c^l) \geq \pi(c^h, c^l)$$

It turns out that these constraints are not all binding at the same time. The only two binding constraints are (PC_h) and (IC_l). Indeed, let (PC_h) bind so that $\pi(c^h, c^h) = 0$, which is equivalent to a transfer $t(c^h) = c^h q^h + F - p(q^h)q^h$. Substituting $t(c^h)$ in the binding (IC_l), $\pi(c^l, c^l) = \pi(c^h, c^l)$, yields $t(c^l) = (c^h - c^l)q^h + F - p(q^l)q^l + c^l q^l$. It is then easy to check that substituting $t(c^l)$ in (PC_l) yields $\pi(c^l, c^l) = (c^h - c^l)q^h > 0$. In other words, if (PC_h) and (IC_l) bind, then (PC_l) holds. Similarly, substituting $t(c^l)$ and $t(c^h)$ in (IC_h) yields $(c^h - c^l)(q^h - q^l) \leq 0$, which is true as long as $q^h \leq q^l$. In other words, if (PC_h) and (IC_l) bind and $q^h \leq q^l$, then (IC_h) holds.

Applying the fact that $\pi^h = 0$ and $\pi^l = q^h \Delta c$, which implies that Equations (5.3) and (5.6) are not binding, with some reorganization of the equations to isolate the key variables of interest, the four constraints just identified are simply equivalent to:

$$t^h = c^h q^h + F - p(q^h)q^h \tag{i}$$

$$t^l = c^l q^l + F - p(q^l)q^l + q^h \Delta c \tag{ii}$$

$$q^l \geq q^h \tag{iii}$$

Condition (i) implies that the transfers/subsidies to the high-cost firm cover any of its costs that are not covered by revenue from sales, while condition (ii) implies that the low-cost firm's transfer covers its costs that are not covered by its revenues from sales but also allows an information rent, which is linked to the cost advantages implicit in its technology, $q^h \Delta c$. Finally, condition (iii) states that the low-cost firm should not produce less than the high-cost firm, which is quite intuitive as regards efficiency.

We can now use these constraints in the regulator's optimization process. Let v be the probability that a firm is low cost and $(1 - v)$ that it is high cost. The regulator's primary goal is to optimize the expected total social surplus, that is:

$$EW = vW^l + (1 - v)W^h \tag{5.7}$$

where $W^k = S(q^k) - c^k q^k - F - \lambda t^k, (k = h, l)$ is from Equation (4.6) in Chapter 4.

It needs to be optimized with respect to the quantities under the constraints (i) to (iii). Substituting t^h from (i) and t^l from (ii) into W^h and W^l respectively yields:

$$EW = v\left(S(q^l) + \lambda p(q^l)q^l - \lambda q^h \Delta c - (1 + \lambda)\left(c^l q^l + F\right)\right)$$
$$+ (1 - v)\left(S(q^h) + \lambda p(q^h)q^h - (1 + \lambda)\left(c^h q^h + F\right)\right) \tag{5.8}$$

Observe that q^l only appears in the first line of Equation (5.8). Then, for a low-cost firm, c^l, the solution to this problem (that is, $dEW/dq^l = 0$) is the same as in the benchmark case of complete information:

$$\frac{p^l - c^l}{p^l} = \frac{\lambda}{1 + \lambda}\frac{1}{\varepsilon^l} \tag{5.9}$$

This result is referred to in the literature as 'no distortion at the top in the regulatory contract'.[4] The most efficient firm (i.e. the low-cost firm) does not suffer from a distortion of its production as compared to the benchmark of complete information.[5] By contrast, observe that q^h appears in both lines of Equation (5.8). Then the solution for the high-cost firm (that is, $dEW/dq^h = 0$) is distorted and this distortion is quite predictable:

$$\frac{p^h - c^h}{p^h} = \frac{\lambda}{1 + \lambda}\frac{1}{\varepsilon^h} + I \tag{5.10}$$

where $I = \frac{\lambda}{1+\lambda}\frac{v}{1-v}\frac{\Delta c}{p^h} > 0$.[6]

Since I is positive, the price p^h in Equation (5.10) is higher than under complete information, which implies that the demand is lower than in our benchmark case. The price p^h is also higher than the price p^l, which implies that condition (iii) is satisfied: $q^l \geq q^h$. The quantity to be offered by the low-cost firm is higher than the quantity to be offered by the high-cost firm, but the difference between the two levels of output is sensitive to the odds estimated by the regulator for each of the operator's technological capacity (that is, to the probability that it is high or low cost), as well as to other variables influencing its likely cost level. And this can be approximated quantitatively since it is captured by the optimal distortion I in Equation (5.10), which increases with the ratio $\frac{v}{1-v}$ (that is, the distortion increases with the probability that the firm is low

---

[4] A lot of the academic research looks at regulation as a contract between various stakeholders and hence the use of regulatory contracts in many of the papers that have contributed to the development of this field.

[5] For readers interested in generalizations of these results, see more advanced textbooks such as Laffont and Tirole (1993) or Bolton and Dewatripont (2004).

[6] Note that Equation (5.10) is an interior solution. When the high-cost firm is shut down, the result no longer holds.

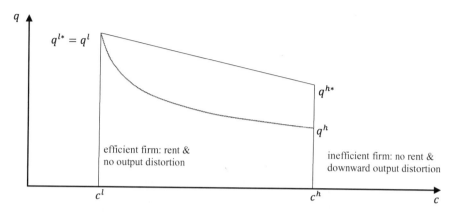

Figure 5.1 Optimal regulated quantity under symmetric (q^{h*}, q^{l*}) and asymmetric information (q^h, q^l)

cost, v). Everything else being equal, when the probability v converges to 0, the distortion of high-cost firms' production vanishes, demonstrating that this distortion does not have to be directly related to production or demand considerations. It is explained by the size of the informational rent that can be captured by an operator, $q^h \Delta c$. Since it is paid only with probability v, its expected value is $v q^h \Delta c$. So if v is small, there is no need to distort q^h too much. But if v is close to 1, then the regulator will shut down the production of the high-cost firm thus reducing the rent to 0, the value it would have had if a low-cost firm were the incumbent provider. Indeed, the smaller q^h is, the smaller is its rent. It is worth emphasizing that distortion I also increases with the cost differential Δc.

The fact that the information rent of the low-cost firm is proportional to q^h explains why the distortion related to the situation of asymmetric information therefore affects that term. The distortion increases with $\Delta c = c^h - c^l$ because the rent increases with Δc. So, to lower the cost of asymmetric information, the regulator decreases the quantity to be produced by the high-cost firm. In other words, an increase of Δc is matched by a decrease in q^h to lower the cost of the rent. The distortion also increases with v (the probability that the regulated firm is low cost) or, alternatively, it decreases with $1 - v$ (the probability that it is high cost). This is intuitive: if it is more likely that the firm is high cost rather than low cost, then the rent will be given rarely and the scheme of regulation that is implemented will generally be designed for a high-cost firm. Any drastic reduction in the quantity produced by the high-cost firm will hit consumers hard. Everything else being equal, the distortion is therefore moderate when v is small, and large when v is large.

Figure 5.1 shows the optimal regulated quantities for c^l and c^h, both in the benchmark case of symmetric information (q^{h*} and q^{l*})[7] and in the case of asymmetric information (q^h and q^l). The high-cost firm collects no informational rent (its participation constraint is binding, so that $\pi(c^h) = 0$), but suffers a downward distortion of its production scheme $(q^{h*} > q^h)$. By contrast, the low-cost firm enjoys an

---

[7] q^{h*} is the solution to the maximization of Equation (5.8) when $v = 0$.

information rent (the rent that led it to behave truthfully is $\pi(c^l) = (c^h - c^l)q^h > 0$) and undergoes no distortion of its production scheme $(q^{l*} = q^l)$.

The moral of the story is that having to live with adverse selection entails a predictable social loss, and it explains the very large estimations of distortions linked to often overoptimistic demand forecasting practices. To discourage the most efficient type of provider from pretending to be inefficient, the regulator is forced to depress the production of the less efficient one. If a low-cost firm claims to be high cost, then it will be 'punished' by low production. Yet even high-cost firms generate a surplus, and cutting their production imposes a cost on society. Ultimately, what regulation will achieve is a reduction in the production of the inefficient firm and this, in turn, will reduce the rent achievable by the efficient firm. And it will also stimulate this efficient firm to increase its output to maximize its profits.

The correction needed to account for information asymmetry thus has the advantage of allowing the low-cost producer to deliver a lot, thereby reducing its incentive to overestimate its costs. This strategy is a good one, even if second-best, because it reduces the expected cost of providing a commodity when access to information is asymmetric. Since information gaps are common in real life, the first-best solution is seldom a realistic one, and second-best solutions are both expected and desirable outcomes in these environments.

There are two key points here and both can be quite politically sensitive in practice. The first is that the regulator has no choice but to give some of the operational surplus to the provider. In other words, in real-life situations – where access to information is asymmetric – the regulator, the consumers and the taxpayers must accept the need to pay an information rent, at least temporarily. Few regulators or politicians are likely to organize press conferences to explain that they have decided to allow a high profit rate to a public service supplier because it was needed as a result of an information gap they could not resolve. Yet their decision would be rationally based on the discussion in Section 5.5. This may partly explain the high dividend levels observed among privately owned regulated industries – although it is unlikely to be the only factor driving these levels, as discussed in Chapter 7.

In a detailed diagnostics analysis of dividends pay-outs (i.e. the ratio of dividends to net income), Damodaran finds level for utilities as high as 100.9% in the United States, 190.6% in Europe and 223.1% in emerging markets.[8] These pay-outs produced dividend yields (i.e. annual dividends per share divided by the share price) of, respectively, 3.61% 3.28% and 1.85%. These yields were well above average in developed economies but below for emerging economies.[9]

The second point is that to reduce the social cost of this rent, the regulator should, when possible, cut the size of the output that high-cost firms are allowed. It may seem unfair, but it is more efficient than giving all operators, irrespective of cost, the same

---

[8] From 'Dividend Fundamentals by Sector (US)', http://pages.stern.nyu.edu/~adamodar/New_Home_Page/datafile/divfund.html (as at 12 March 2021).

[9] The level of dividends has become a source of tension in the United Kingdom, leading to suggestions to renationalize some of the regulated industries. See for instance Bertomeu-Sanchez and Estache (2019).

treatment. And this is also likely to be quite a political challenge if, for instance, the high cost is linked to high employment levels and the reduction in output is associated with reductions in jobs. This is one of the debates many national railway companies in Europe are trying to avoid. It boils down to trading off the interests of users, or taxpayers if the service is subsidized, with those of workers. Few politicians or regulators are keen on taking this on.

The essence of this discussion is that accounting for the importance of information and of the associated adverse selection risks is quite essential when designing regulation. Within the modelling approach followed so far, the simplest way of doing so is to correct the usual pricing formula. In the case of a single-product firm, this can be done by including a correction, as described in Equation (5.10), where I is an indicator of the provider's 'information rent'.[10] This correction is thus the main concrete policy recommendation to emerge from this analysis of cases where the regulator is concerned with adverse selection.

5.6   Modelling Moral Hazard Risks

The discussion so far has focused on the problem of adverse selection in circumstances under which access to ex ante information (in the form of estimated forecasts) is asymmetric. But, in practice, actual (ex post) data are just as important and as complex as hinted at in the earlier discussion of poor accounting practices. They are also more complicated to handle because they are somewhat of a moving target. Adverse selection involves differences in marginal costs (c), which are exogenous. Moral hazard, meanwhile, involves effort (e), which is endogenous. By adding this to the Baron–Myerson model, Laffont–Tirole provide a wide range of new insights relevant to the optimal design of regulation.

Considering the many ways in which an operator may be tempted to play its advantage under conditions of information asymmetry, the regulator must figure out what proportion of the firm's costs are controllable in the short term, posing the moral hazard risk (e), and what proportion is not, posing the adverse selection risk (c). The exercise starts with the available information on accounting costs, which can be used to assess the final marginal cost, $c - e$. However, unless clear regulatory accounting guidelines force the operator to classify costs into those inclined to decrease with effort and those not, the regulator cannot properly distinguish c from e. That is, unless the regulator manages to make this distinction between low- and high-cost firms, there is a scope for both types of firm to pretend to be what they are not.

The regulators will therefore have to satisfy two incentive compatibility constraints. As explained earlier, they are needed to make sure that neither type of firm will be tempted to pretend to be the other type but instead will reveal its type truthfully. This is where concerns about moral hazard kick in. Any attempt to simultaneously satisfy participation

---

[10] For a detailed analysis, see Laffont and Martimort (2002).

constraints and incentive compatibility constraints raises issues linked to the costs of improving efforts. When the costs of effort are accounted for, pretending to be a high-cost firm allows the low-cost firm to reduce its effort, which it views as a disutility denoted by the increasing and convex function $\Psi(e)$. Pretending to be a high-cost firm therefore generates an informational rent of $\Psi(e^h) - \Psi(e^h - \Delta c)$, since the firm can reduce its effort and still appear to be cost-efficient at the pretended high-cost level, c^h.

Similarly, in the case of pure adverse selection examined in Box 5.1, the participation constraint binds for the high-cost firm, whereas for the low-cost firm it is the incentive compatibility constraint that binds, as shown in Box 5.2 (Laffont and Tirole 1993). In this case, while the high-cost firm will again receive no rent, $\pi^h = 0$, the low-cost firm will receive the rent $\pi^l = \Psi(e^h) - \Psi(e^h - \Delta c)$ required to meet its IC. This means that the markup and the subsidies built into the optimal pricing formula will have to be computed based on the high-cost firm, at least for a while, to ensure participation.

Since this rent effectively comes out of public funds, either in the shape of public subsidies or more perniciously in the shape of reduced taxes, it costs society $\lambda[\Psi(e^h) - \Psi(e^h - \Delta c)]$. The regulator now must live with this information rent, but also needs to ensure that the markup allowed is not larger than what is needed to meet both the participation and the incentive compatibility constraints. This is largely what determines the mechanisms that the regulator must devise to control operators in a non-competitive environment.

The regulator must maximize the expected social surplus under four constraints of two types: (PC$_l$) and (PC$_h$), and (IC$_l$) and (IC$_h$). The four constraints are simply equivalent (see Box 5.2) to the following three conditions:

$$t^h = C(c^h)q^h + \Psi(e^h) + F - p(q^h)q^h \tag{i}$$

$$t^l = C(c^l)q^l + \Psi(e^l) + F - p(q^l)q^l + \Psi(e^h) - \Psi(e^h - \Delta c) \tag{ii}$$

$$e^l \geq e^h \tag{iii}$$

Condition (i) implies that the transfer to the high-cost firm simply covers its cost (net of sales to the market) so that $\pi^h = 0$, whereas condition (ii) implies that the low-cost firm's transfer covers its cost plus an information rent, so that $\pi^l = \Psi(e^h) - \Psi(e^h - \Delta c)$. Condition (iii) implies that the high-cost firm is never tempted to pretend to be low cost.

We can now use these constraints in the regulator's optimization programme. Recall that v is the probability that a firm is low cost (and $1 - v$ that it is high cost). As before in Equation (5.7), the main regulation goal is to maximize the expected total social surplus: $EW = vW^l + (1 - v)W^h$, under the constraints (i)–(iii). Substituting t^h from (i) and t^l from (ii) into W^h and W^l respectively, yields:

$$EW = (1 - v)\left(S(q^h) + \lambda p(q^h)q^h - (1+\lambda)\left((c^h - e^h)q^h + F + \Psi(e^h) \right) \right)$$
$$+ v\left(S(q^l) + \lambda P(q^l)q^l - \lambda\left(\Psi(e^h) - \Psi(e^h - \Delta c) \right) - (1+\lambda)\left((c^l - e^l)q^l + F + \Psi(e^l) \right) \right)$$

$$\tag{5.11}$$

Box 5.2 Incentive Compatibility Constraints in the Moral Hazard Case

The regulator can observe the ex post cost $C = c - e$ but it cannot distinguish between the two components c and e. Then, if the firm with initial cost c pretends it is $\hat{c}$, it must exert the effort e such that $c - e = \hat{c} - \hat{e}$ where $\hat{e}$ is the effort exerted by a firm with initial cost $\hat{c}$. Then $e = \hat{e} + (c - \hat{c})$, which provokes the disutility $\Psi(\hat{e} + c - \hat{c})$ where $\Psi(e)$ is an increasing and convex function representing the cost of exerting effort e. The resulting rent is $\pi(\hat{c}, c) = p(\hat{c})\hat{q} + t(\hat{c}) - C(\hat{c})\hat{q} - \Psi$ $(\hat{e} - (\hat{c} - c)) - F$ with $\hat{c}, c \in \{c^l, c^h\}$ and where $C(\hat{c})$ is the ex post variable cost observable to the regulator through auditing.

The contract $(p(c), C(c), t(c))$ is incentive-compatible if and only if:

$$\pi(c^l, c^l) \geq \pi(c^h, c^l) \text{ and } \pi(c^h, c^h) \geq \pi(c^l, c^h)$$

Adding these two constraints, a necessary condition for incentive compatibility is:

$$\pi(c^h, c^h) - \pi(c^h, c^l) \geq \pi(c^l, c^h) - \pi(c^l, c^l)$$

Substituting π by its value and simplifying yields:

$$\Psi(e^l + \Delta c) - \Psi(e^l) \geq \Psi(e^h) - \Psi(e^h - \Delta c)$$

Given that $\Delta c = c^h - c^l > 0$ and $\Psi'' > 0$, we deduce that a necessary condition for incentive compatibility is $e^h \leq e^l$. The regulator now faces four constraints (two participation constraints and two incentive compatibility constraints):

$$(PC_h) : \pi(c^h, c^h) \geq 0 \text{ and } (PC_l) : \pi(c^l, c^l) \geq 0$$

$$(IC_h) : \pi(c^h, c^h) \geq \pi(c^l, c^h) \text{ and } (IC_l) : \pi(c^l, c^l) \geq \pi(c^h, c^l)$$

It turns out that these constraints are not simultaneously binding. As in the case of pure adverse selection, the two binding constraints are (PC_h) and (IC_l).

Let (PC_h) bind so that $\pi(c^h, c^h) = 0$, which is equivalent to:

$$t(c^h) = C(c^h)q^h + F + \Psi(e^h) - p(c^h)q^h$$

Substituting $t(c^h)$ in the binding (IC_l) constraint, $\pi(c^l, c^l) = \pi(c^h, c^l)$ and simplifying yields:

$$t(c^l) = \Psi(e^h) - \Psi(e^h - \Delta c) + F + \Psi(e^l) - p(c^l)q^l + C(c^l)q^l.$$

Substituting $t(c^l)$ in (PC_l) then yields:

$$\pi(c^l, c^l) = \Psi(e^h) - \Psi(e^h - \Delta c) > 0,$$

since the cost of effort $\Psi(e)$ is increasing.

In other words, if (PC_h) and (IC_l) bind, then (PC_l) holds. Similarly, substituting $t(c^l)$ and $t(c^h)$ in (IC_h) yields:

$$\pi(c^h, c^h) = 0 > [\Psi(e^h) - \Psi(e^h - \Delta c)] - [\Psi(e^l + \Delta c) - \Psi(e^l)] = \pi(c^l, c^h)$$

which is true as long as $e^h \leq e^l$.

In other words, if (PC_h) and (IC_l) bind and $e^h \leq e^l$, then (IC_h) holds.

Maximizing with respect to the quantity q^k, the solution to this problem (i.e. $dEW/dq^k = 0$) is the same as in the benchmark case of complete information for both $k = l, h$:

$$\frac{p^k - (c^k - e^k)}{p^k} = \frac{\lambda}{1 + \lambda} \frac{1}{\varepsilon^k} \qquad (5.12)$$

We deduce that, for a given elasticity level, if $c^k - e^k < c^{k'} - e^{k'}$ then $q^k > q^{k'}$ or alternatively that $p^k < p^{k'}$. In other words, a firm with an ex post observable lower marginal cost will be allowed to produce more than a firm with an ex post observable higher marginal cost.

Given the ex post observability of the cost $C(c) = c - e$, the effort level e can be included in the regulation contract. Then, maximizing with respect to e^l (i.e. $dEW/de^l = 0$), we obtain:

$$\Psi'\left(e^l\right) = q^l \qquad (5.13)$$

So, there is no distortion for the low-cost firm (a reappearance of the 'no distortion at the top' result). By contrast, observe that e^h appears in the two lines of Equation (5.11). Then, the solution with respect to effort $\left(dEW/de^h = 0\right)$ is distorted for the high-cost firm:

$$\Psi'\left(e^h\right) = q^h - H \qquad (5.14)$$

where $H = \frac{\lambda}{1+\lambda} \frac{\nu}{1-\nu} \left[\Psi'\left(e^h\right) - \Psi'\left(e^h - \Delta c\right)\right] > 0$. Since H is positive and $\Psi(e)$ is increasing and convex, all else being equal (that is, for a fixed q^h), effort e^h is lower than under complete information (that is, $\Psi'\left(e^h\right) = q^h - H \leq q^h$), implying that the ex post cost of the firm is higher than under the benchmark case of complete information. Since the marginal cost of the high-cost firm is higher, the quantity it produces, q^h, is distorted downwards. Alternatively, its price p^h is higher than under symmetric information.

Finally, in the symmetric information case, we had $e^{l*} > e^{h*}$ by Equation (4.22) since $q^{l*} > q^{h*}$ and $\Psi'' > 0$. In the case of asymmetric information, the low-cost firm produces its first-best effort and its first-best quantity, contrary to the high-cost firm, which produces less of both (in particular $e^{h*} \geq e^h$). We deduce that the second-best condition (iii) is satisfied: $e^{l*} = e^l > e^{h*} \geq e^h$. This in turn implies that $c^{l*} - e^{l*} = c^l - e^l < c^{h*} - e^{h*} < c^h - e^h$, and therefore that $q^l = q^{l*} > q^{h*} > q^h$.

Since distortion H occurs only as a function of the regulator's effort to lower the cost of asymmetric information, it increases with ν, the probability of a firm being low cost. As in the pure adverse selection case, if the odds that the firm is low cost are high, then the information rent will be paid often, and it is important that it be reduced. But discouraging the most efficient firm from choosing a contract designed for the other type of firm involves a significant distortion of the high-cost firm's effort. By contrast, if the odds that the firm is low cost are very low, then the information rent is not of major concern. Distorting the high-cost firm's effort would do little to reduce the rent, which is rarely paid but involves a large social cost by reducing the production level and increasing the production cost of the high-cost firm.

The abstract optimal contract derived above can be implemented via a menu of linear contracts, $t(c^k) = a^k + b^k C(c^k)$ with $k = l, h$. Each linear contract involves a fixed payment, a^k, and a variable element, $b^k C(c^k)$, which covers a fraction of the audited cost $C(c^k)$. These two terms (a^k, b^k) are such that each type of firm – low cost and high cost – can self-select the contract designed for its type. The efficient firm (that is, the low-cost one) chooses the contract in which it receives a large fixed payment (that is, a^k large), even though only a small fraction of its ex post cost may be reimbursed (b^l small). This 'fixed-price' contract leads the low-cost firm to produce the first-best level of effort, since it will be able to claim all the profit yielded by its effort. By contrast, the inefficient firm chooses a contract under which a large fraction of its ex post costs will be reimbursed (that is, b^h close to 1). Such a 'cost-plus' contract, with a large b^h and a small a^h, does not encourage the firm to engage in a high level of effort as it does not benefit from it, but it does effectively discourage the low-cost firm from pretending to be high cost. Thus, the distortion of the high-cost firm's effort is compensated by a lower information rent for the low-cost firm.

The case of moral hazard is usually the most challenging for regulators. In addressing moral hazard, the regulator should have two main concerns. First, how far should regulation go to reduce firms' incentive to do less than their best? Second, what combination of incentives and penalties will be most effective in persuading operators to deliver? It is generally hard to determine how much room for manoeuvre the regulator might have to force a firm to adopt more efficient technology or intensify its efforts to cut costs. This problem is particularly salient in state-owned enterprises or other public entities involved in public service delivery. Since the issue can be analysed only after the fact, any regulatory decision needs to be based on an assessment of outcomes. But these outcomes may be driven by the degree of an operator's effort as much as by other (random) factors unrelated to effort. This is why regulatory theory suggests that the optimal regulated price should incorporate the following two dimensions: First, a fixed fee, which encourages the firm to exert greater effort as any cost reduction is a benefit when payment is fixed. Second, a payoff to the firm proportional to the observed ex post costs and based on the observed production decision to moderate the firm's exposure to random shocks and other risks it cannot control. But the theory clearly implies that to preserve incentives, this reimbursement of costs should only cover part of the ex post audited costs. Finally, to encourage the firms to reveal their type of cost truthfully, the regulator should offer a menu of contracts spanning from pure fixed price to pure cost-plus. If the menu of the contracts is designed adequately, the most efficient suppliers will pick fixed-price contracts, while inefficient ones will select contracts with a higher share of ex post cost recovery.

In practice, this is doable. It takes a relatively simple form and it is also quite common, as we will see in the next chapter. Since it is relatively simple to separate cost drivers into (i) inputs that operators cannot control and (ii) those they can, the cost-recovery guarantee should cover only the first group of costs. This is what justifies partial rather than full pass-through of costs to users or taxpayers as a way of protecting the operator against random input shocks. The fact that not all cost changes are passed through ensures that the firm is exposed to some residual risk and has some incentive to make an effort to manage that risk. Otherwise, it would have to absorb at least part of the consequences of not trying hard enough to maintain its assets properly.

Ultimately, moral hazard is a fact of regulatory life. But it is hard to deal with. What the theory reviewed here suggests is that partial coverage of moral hazard risks is often the best regulatory strategy. Theory is, however, more courageous than practice. Indeed, many regulators are reluctant to impose too much risk on the operator so as to ward off the threat of bankruptcy, the ultimate participation constraint! (see Box 5.3). This leads to overprotection of investors and users and underprotection of taxpayers, since subsidies are often the instrument of last recourse to finance poor management of risks. The undesirable consequences of excessive efforts to protect firms from bankruptcy are many. For instance, a guarantee of overprotection can result in overinvestment in quantity and/or quality. The practical challenge is to decide how partial the coverage should be, knowing that the higher the coverage, the higher the risk of distortions in investment and production decisions. In practice, the degree of coverage depends on the regulators' sensitivity to the threat of bankruptcy, on a political preference to minimize the risk of bankruptcy, and on how the financial markets assess this risk. These problems are explored later in this book in Chapter 7.

Box 5.3 Alternative Modelling of Moral Hazard

How to design the regulation contract when the effort variable can be verified neither directly nor indirectly by the regulator? The regulator can only impose obligation concerns on the outcome, not the means to carry it out.[11] For example, the operators of electricity networks can be incentivized to spend a lot on security with rewards that depend on observed blackouts, whatever the causes.

To illustrate the trade-offs faced by the regulator, consider the case where there are two possible states of nature: in the 'good' (or 'bad') state, the net surplus takes a high (or low) exogenous value. The probability in the good state is a function increasing with the effort of the operator. As in Laffont–Tirole, the firm incurs a disutility increasing with the effort level. Clearly, there exists an optimal level of effort that maximizes the net welfare by equating the expected increase in surplus and the marginal disutility due to more effort.

Assume now that we must delegate the decision on effort to the operator. In this framework, effort does not guarantee a good outcome, it just makes it more likely. The bad outcome remains possible despite an intensive effort by the agent. Symmetrically, the outcome can be good even if the agent did not exert a high level of effort. Then a crucial question is how much of the risk should be carried by the operator?

---

[11] For a recent survey, see Macho-Stadler and Pérez-Castrillo (2018).

Box 5.3 (*cont.*)

When information is symmetrical, if the firm is risk averse and the regulator is risk neutral, the regulator should carry all risks, which means paying the same to the firm whatever the observed state of nature. Clearly, this is optimal only if the level of effort can be monitored by the principal. In contrast, if the effort level can be chosen by the firm without being known by the regulator, the firm is better off when picking the lowest feasible level of effort. To incentivize the firm, remuneration must be contingent on the outcome: the contract must stipulate that the firm will receive more if the outcome is 'good' than if it is 'bad'. Then there is a trade-off between the optimal sharing of risks (with full insurance of the firm) and promoting the optimal level of effort (with differentiated payment).

In the second-best contract designed to internalize the opportunistic behaviour of the firm, the payment it will receive in the case of a 'bad' state of nature can be very low, even negative: instead of being rewarded, it will incur a penalty. This means that the firm can face financial difficulties in the case of a bad outcome, even if it has done its best. This can be dissuasive ex ante, i.e. the regulator may find no candidate willing to enter the industry. To solve this problem, the regulation contract must contain a 'limited-liability' clause. Here is an additional trade-off. The higher the floor payment, the lower the incentive to engage in effort.

In California, the state holds electric utilities responsible for wildfire damage caused by their equipment, even though the companies have scrupulously complied with safety rules, such as the pruning obligations. This so-called inverse condemnation doctrine is an extreme application of the moral hazard bias: since the safety effort is not verifiable, the regulated firm must pay for the consequences. Pacific Gas & Electric Company (PG&E), the biggest Californian electricity utility, declared bankruptcy in January 2019, citing $30 billion of potential liabilities arising from its role in causing deadly wildfires.

5.7 The Underestimated Role of Accounting and Benchmarking in the Quality of Regulation

In our model (and in practice), the regulator must work with an estimated value of c (usually derived through a benchmarking exercise). In the best-case scenario, the approximation is reliable and able to reveal the distribution of c, thus identifying an acceptable markup over marginal cost. The assessment of the distribution of c is crucial to the quality of regulation. If the regulator makes mistakes in its evaluation, either no operator will be willing to provide the service, or they will take very large, unjustified rents. This concretely means that regulators must have a good technical knowledge of the industry and of the production options. But this is not the only concern. Regulators must also worry about the distortions that may be caused by raising taxes to cover any financing gap occasioned by the effort to avoid ceding any excess rent to the firm. To minimize the cost of expertise, regulators should build and share the technical information on cost distribution at the sector level, through international benchmarking and best practices. For both adverse selection and moral hazard, a good approach is to rely on relatively accessible information on the costs of comparable activities. That can then be used to assign a set of probabilities to various cost outcomes, depending on the risks of adverse selection and moral hazard. The regulator then has a lower and an upper bound within which the true cost lies. Trying to narrow down the estimate is one of the main goals of the technical component of modern productivity analysis used to assess best-practice production costs and methods.

Public service websites that post comparisons of sector performance and prices have a similar purpose. Otherwise uninformed users may consult these data, and their newly gained knowledge may be used to mitigate the risk of moral hazard. The instrument is not perfect, though, since firms can sometimes too easily manipulate the information generated for these sorts of public comparisons. But the information made available this way is increasingly well analysed by consumer associations offering the results of their assessments on the web and some of these comparisons are accredited by the regulators themselves.[12]

It is also useful to emphasize the role of accounting data in narrowing information gaps. Transparent auditing, both of estimates and of actual data, significantly diminishes the negative effects of adverse selection and moral hazard. But effective auditing requires a level of commitment still lacking in many regulatory settings. Pick almost any energy, water or transportation regulator around the world and visit its website. Search for regulatory accounting guidelines tailored to the information requirements of regulations. The odds of finding useful data are only high for a few members of the OECD.[13] Basic accounting data produced by most countries is not designed to address information gaps specific to the regulation of non-competitive service providers.

A handful of developing countries have also organized relevant guidelines in response to conditions imposed by lenders to utilities or transport companies, but they are the exception rather than the rule.[14] In some countries, the evidence of poor cost-accounting practices in key public services is associated with corruption (OECD 2015a). The resulting lack of transparency complicates the task of a regulator trying to distinguish good from bad firms along a wide range of criteria. It also leads to higher-than-necessary costs in the sector – a result observed around the world. In 2016, Spanish authorities found that several firms had been willing to pay a 3% 'fee' to political parties to win large-scale infrastructure contracts. Within a few years, researchers will be able to document the return on this 3% 'investment', knowing that it has already been paid by users and taxpayers. In Wallonia, the mostly French-speaking part of Belgium, major public service providers inflated costs to cover salaries up to five times higher than top civil servants are allowed. Similar stories

---

[12] E.g. for Belgium, www.energyprice.be/ or for Australia, www.energymadeeasy.gov.au/

[13] Australia, Canada, England, Ireland, the Netherlands, New Zealand, Norway, Scotland or Sweden.

[14] Brazil, Colombia, Ghana, Ivory Coast, Mali, Mexico, Peru and South Africa are examples of countries with quite different legal and accounting traditions relying on accounting guidelines for regulatory decisions in at least some of their regulated industries.

could be told for many countries. Adverse selection and moral hazard must be anticipated in the design of regulation – particularly in the rules that determine which firms may bid for the right to provide a public service. Very basic, practical decisions on standard business practices, including accounting rules, will decide the magnitude of adverse selection's effects. One of the benefits of increased transparency around the existence of unethical players in the sector is to make 'clean' firms and regulators more aware of their identifying characteristics – and to encourage good firms to signal the qualifications that distinguish them from the pack as a complement to the information that can be provided through honest regulatory accounting practice. This, too, is what information campaigns, led by service providers, aim to achieve as they reveal business information to users and regulators that otherwise would remain uninformed. Such information includes concrete commitments such as reimbursement guarantees to users when service fails to meet the promised quantity and quality standards.[15]

These insights are significant improvements over the simple idea that monopolists should be forced to charge a price based on marginal cost and that the government should cover the financing gap through subsidies. But even the most forward-thinking contemporary analysis is still quite naïve and can be gamed to the disadvantage of consumers and taxpayers. The cost signals that a government receives may be distorted by the government's own dysfunctions. These may be the result of disagreements between Ministry and regulator on which actions to prioritize. Or they may be the result of collusion between regulator and operator, meaning that the government is fed incorrect information. Because the internal organization and allocation of tasks across government is an important element of regulatory design, it is useful to consider the complexity of the institutional characteristics of a regulatory function. We shall return to that point in Chapter 14. One aspect we want to discuss now is the issue of commitment.

So far, we have focused on a static environment, where the regulatory decisions impact on an operator in a once-and-for-all interaction. This is inaccurate in public utilities and infrastructure because most roads, railway lines, water-treatment facilities and transmission lines are used for twenty-five to fifty years. This longevity is a challenge for regulators, as many of the cost and demand drivers are likely to fluctuate over the lifecycle, adding uncertainty to the original information gaps. For instance, in environments where there are concerns such as the need to deal with climate change and the increasing 'green' consumer sensitivity, firms make continuous technological improvements. These are not really picked up with the static view of their activities as discussed here. They may thus be more likely to be low cost thanks to these continuous efforts to improve than they may be willing to claim. Symmetrically, operators need to recover the fixed investment costs of long-term assets. From an incentive point of view this also distorts the revelation game analysed earlier.

[15] We'll return to commitment issues when we discuss investment and institutional weaknesses in Chapters 11 and 14 respectively.

The very basic approach to making the most of the information collected to design an optimal regulation must be enriched to take into account dynamic concerns. Laffont and Tirole (1993) showed that an observation made by Weitzman (1980) also applies to regulated firms. Specifically, when a regulatory decision is based on the observation of both current and past production, firms will internalize the fact that any improvement in their performance will only produce a temporary payoff but demand a permanent increase in efforts. This is known as the 'ratchet effect' in academic research and in its most extreme forms it is also sometimes discussed in the context of regulatory expropriation risks. When firms believe that they are functioning in a regulatory environment in which this effect is present, they will have a much lower incentive to reveal their hidden potential for a short-term payoff. And this, in turn, demands a stronger effort by regulators to get firms to reveal their potential to produce more or cut costs. In the Laffont–Tirole model, this means that the low-cost firms would have to be allowed a larger rent in a dynamic context with repeated interactions than without the presence of a ratchet effect. Typically, one could hope to pay the informational rent only in the first period. In subsequent periods, once the firm has revealed its information, it is tempting to impose the first-best contract. Yet if the firm anticipates this reversal to first-best contract, it will not reveal its cost truthfully in the first period. In other words, the simple static contract studied earlier is not incentive compatible in a dynamic context with lack of commitment.

One of the practical ways in which the ratchet-effect risks can be minimized is by providing some guarantees to the firms that they will be able to retain the payoffs to their efforts long enough. To be effective, this guarantee must be credible: the operators must believe that the regulator will not renege on its commitments. This is less likely to occur when the regulator is under the direct control of the government, which might unexpectedly cut prices or reduce subsidies for electoral reasons. This will, for instance, be the case if the operator makes a large profit or if the consumers protest against much-needed price rises.[16] Independent regulatory agencies can more easily and credibly commit to consistent regulation and pricing schemes. In environments in which the risk of regulatory renegotiations imposed by political considerations on using the information gained from observing realized costs is high, the ratchet effect is likely to be the strongest. In other words, it will lower the odds of an effort by firms to cut costs, improve quality or achieve any type of regulatory goal which implies a burden in the future on the regulated firm. This will impact on both OPEX and CAPEX. Indeed, the effort levels are not only linked to cost-effectiveness in operating the assets. It could also impact on the choices of technologies to be used to deliver the public services. For instance, the Averch–Johnson effect mentioned in Box 5.4 is more likely to be noted when the ratchet-effect risks are significant.

---

[16] For a detailed discussion of examples in the context of European toll roads, see, for instance, Albalate (2014), and for a broader discussion in the Latin American context, see Rovine (2014).

Box 5.4 What Is the Averch–Johnson Effect?

Averch and Johnson (1962) provide one of the first empirical illustrations of the biases associated with an excessive trust in the information provided by regulated operators when they are guaranteed to recover their costs. Their model looks at a profit-maximizing monopoly with a production function $q = Q(K, L)$ where q is production, K is the capital invested with an opportunity cost of capital s, and L is its employment level paid at an average wage of w. For the sake of simplicity, ignore any amortization. If the monopoly's price is set by its inverse (market) demand $p = p(q)$, its profit can be expressed as $\pi = R(K, L) - wL - sK$ where $R(K, L) = p(Q(K, L)) \times Q(K, L)$.

How can the average price be controlled? Until the 1980s, the most common approach was to focus on the rate of return to capital. The regulatory challenge was to pick a realistic return r. It had to at least cover the firm's opportunity cost of capital s but it also had to be lower than the rate of return that could be achieved by the firm if it were left unregulated. The constraint faced by the firm was $\frac{R(K,L)-wL}{K} \leq r$. To maximize profit under this constraint we have to write the Lagrange function $R(K, L) - wL - sK + \lambda [wL + rK - R(K, L)]$, where λ is the shadow price of the constraint.

Solving the problem and rewriting the first-order conditions yields the regulated firm's marginal rate of technical substitution of capital for labour, $\mathrm{MRT}_{KL} \equiv \frac{Q_K}{Q_L} = \frac{s}{w} - \frac{\lambda(r-s)}{(1-\lambda)w}$, with Q_i as the marginal product of Q with respect to each factor $i = K, L$. It shows that as soon as $r > s$, the regulated firm would not set the rate of substitution equal to the ratio of the market input prices (s/w) as is usual for a cost-minimizing firm. More precisely, with $0 < \lambda < 1$, $\mathrm{MRT}_{KL} < s/w$ for the equilibrium level of q, the regulated firm uses more capital relative to labour than a cost-minimizing firm would. In other words, firms regulated through a control of their rate of return will overinvest.

5.8 Summing Up

- Pretending that costs are higher than they actually are allows operators to charge prices higher than those needed to satisfy their participation constraint, thereby generating a rent to be paid by consumers or taxpayers.
- The information gaps faced by a regulator are products of adverse selection and moral hazard. Under adverse selection, the regulated firm has private information on cost or demand characteristics it cannot modify. By contrast, moral hazard concerns hidden endogenous effort the firm can exert to increase quality or decrease costs.
- Regulators must pay an information rent to access the information required for designing the regulation contract. The issue is politically sensitive because the 'fee' for information increases the operator's profit and it will be paid either by the consumers or the taxpayers, that is, by voters.

- The information rent should only be abandoned to the most efficient firm that is induced to produce the first-best level. The least efficient firm should produce below the first-best output and receive no rent.
  - If there are multiple types, efficiency will only be achieved 'at the top', and some rent will be earned by all those with someone below them.
- Moral hazard risks impacting cost should be only partially covered. The higher the coverage of the ex post audited cost, the higher the risk of distortions in production decisions.
- A good approximation of the optimal regulation mechanism is to offer a menu of linear contracts where the reward varies with the audited cost: efficient firms will choose the contract with a high fixed payment; inefficient firms will prefer the contract that reimburses a large fraction of their cost.
  - This menu reduces the information rent of the efficient firm.
- Unless the regulator audits all costs and assesses the extent to which they are reasonable, information rent is likely to be quite high. Improving accounting practices is an efficient way to limit the information gap.
- Regulators have to worry about the distortions that may be caused by raising taxes to cover any financing gap occasioned by the effort to avoid ceding any excess rent to the firm.
- To avoid the ratchet effect regulators have to be able to credibly commit to a path of contracts.

6 Regulatory Rules to Set the Average Price

Complaints by users that regulated electricity, transport or water companies are charging excessive prices and that they are making excessive profits are common and well covered in the media. For instance, in January 2018, many Australian newspapers noted that the average electricity price in the previous year had increased six times more than the average hourly wage or the average consumer price index (roughly 12% against 2%). Users were unhappy and very effective at voicing their dissatisfaction. Unsurprisingly, regulated companies can be just as vocal in arguing that their allowed prices are set too low. European railway companies illustrate this powerfully since many, if not most, have long argued that, at the ongoing average prices and subsidy levels, they can only break even if the volume of traffic increases significantly and there are not too many strikes interrupting the revenue flows. In other words, their lament is that most of the time, at current prices, they are likely to lose money.

Similar debates take place throughout the world across sectors and they need to be taken seriously as they often reflect genuine concerns, by both consumers and producers. Of course, they reflect some degree of strategic bad faith in the context of price negotiations. However, they also often free-ride on common broad misunderstandings among opinion makers on what prices should reflect, especially the relevance of many sources of uncertainty.

To have a better sense of how average prices would be dealt with if practice matched theory, this chapter shows how the insights from theory can be turned into acceptable concrete operational price-setting approaches. The chapter emphasizes the importance of conducting a good diagnostic of the major information asymmetry concerns the regulator will have to tackle as it influences the optimal design of price regulation. It starts with a review of the ways in which details on costs influence, or rather should influence, prices.

6.1 Which Costs Drive Prices?

Prices clearly need to reflect reasonable financial and economic costs, once subsidies have been accounted for. However, they also need to mirror the impact of informational asymmetries discussed in Chapter 5. Uncertainty on costs and management efforts matters to prices. Most regulators know they need to live with only limited access to detailed data on operating expenses and capital expenditures – the c and the F in the model presented in the previous chapter, which add up to the production costs. But they also know that the price-setting process can be used to acquire more information. The best regulators, ex post, are those allowing profit levels consistent with participation and incentive compatibility constraints and not much more. And the worst are probably those unable to avoid service rationing simply because the regulatory designs do not account for these constraints and allowed profits do not cover all the expenses needed to deliver an output level consistent with demand, a situation typically found in developing countries with publicly owned operators. This is what recognizing the relevance of participation and incentive compatibility constraints means in practice.

If the price of oil or salaries increases, the final price of electricity or train rides will have to increase.[1] However, if the regulated firm initially has a better knowledge of its cost levels and structure, or any other information bias, this will also have to be picked up in the way prices are set. Conceptually, these biases justify a rent, which is nothing more than the price consumers and/or taxpayers need to pay to get the regulated firm to reveal some of the missing information. The stronger are the biases, the greater is the rent likely to be, and hence the higher the average price. And this is one of the reasons why it is important for regulators to minimize informational biases.

Politically, this is a sensitive issue. To many observers, this rent feels like an unacceptable excess profit. Yet it can, and should, boil down to a short-term or temporary price to pay to get access to the information the producers would otherwise want to hide. Once it has been cashed in by the service providers, the regulator has learned something new about their costs. This closes the information gap. The future size of the rent that must be paid by users and taxpayers is hence smaller. The observed rent (i.e. the revenue not driven by reasonable costs) is a good proxy of the margin the regulator has to impose a cost cut in the following price-setting negotiation. If the firm anticipates this reduction, it will have fewer incentives to cut costs in the first place and will try to hide its true value from the regulator to secure some information rents in the next period too. This ratchet effect is inevitable in long-run relationships such as regulation of public utilities where contracts and prices are renegotiated regularly.

It typically takes three to five years for this rent to be turned into a cost reduction passed on to users and taxpayers. However, this assumes that the regulator is both competent and empowered to make regulatory decisions without political interference. This is often an issue which we will also discuss in Chapter 14 on institutional capacity. It makes decisions on the choice of the optimal price-setting mechanism more complex. Moreover, it is complex enough even when regulators are competent, benevolent and credible. In this dream situation, regulators can rely on various options

---

[1] Oddly enough, many observers seem to be more concerned than regulators that, when these inputs prices fall, the final prices do not drop as fast as they should. This is important to appreciate, but it is more the result of non-technical characteristics of regulatory processes which we will deal with more in the discussion of institutional weaknesses in Chapter 14.

to ensure the fair distribution of realized efficiency gains across stakeholders. All approaches are anchored to relatively simple (not simplistic) and transparent rules translating the complex theoretical formulae into operational ways of regulating any firm. Simplicity and transparency tend to ease accountability, and accountability tends to stimulate effectiveness. That is the main focus of this chapter.

To illustrate the diversity of ways in which these rules can be set, the chapter starts with a review of the international practice of regulation in the electricity distribution activity. This experience is then used to conceptualize the various ways in which regulation can be implemented to address both participation and incentive compatibility constraints. It concludes with a discussion of the ways in which the various design options should ideally be matched against the informational biases to minimize their burden on users and taxpayers.

6.2   How Do Regulators Actually Regulate Prices?

Although theory leads to a simple classification of approaches, a careful look at the practice of regulation shows that there is some heterogeneity revealed by the way different regulators implement the basic theoretical rules. Consider the way European regulators controlled the prices of the electricity distribution companies to make sure they did not make unjustified profits in 2017. Some regulators relied on actual or benchmarked costs to set the access prices, some relied on a pre-set maximum price or revenue. The reason can be political but there are also some sound economic justifications. In the costs of electric distribution, there are roughly three thirds: (i) costs imposed on the operator, such as high voltage transmission network fees and local taxes; (ii) partly controllable costs (e.g. amortization and financial charges, energy losses) and (iii) controllable costs (in particular operation of lines and transformers, meter reading).

For category (i), a mere reimbursement should be the rule since the operator cannot change these costs and they are verifiable by the regulator. Actually, there is neither adverse selection nor moral hazard in this group. Category (iii) encompasses the maintenance and repair of the distribution infrastructure as well as the measurement of the network usage. Most of these expenditures are not verifiable by the regulator. Consequently, they are not directly contractable because the effort to cut them is not observable. However, the regulator can collect ex post data from automatic devices (smart meters) and organize a reporting by clients on the number and duration of power cuts (System Average Interruption Duration Index, SAIDI, and System Average Interruption Frequency Index, SAIFI).[2] To tackle this moral hazard problem the most efficient tool is a fixed reward accompanied by penalties based on the number of outages. The risk is that the operator goes bankrupt because poor weather

---

[2] The Council of European Energy Regulators (CEER) publishes comparative data on SAIDI and SAIFI in twenty-seven European countries. 'CEER Benchmarking Report 6.1 on the Continuity of Electricity and Gas Supply. Data update 2015/2016', Ref: C18-EQS-86-03, 26 July 2018.

conditions and forest fires provoke many long power cuts and casualties in spite of a high level of effort.[3] Finally, category (ii) is in between. For example, energy losses are unavoidable on physical grounds, but they can be financially compensated more or less efficiently.

The distribution companies also face highly heterogeneous geographical conditions, depending on whether they operate in urban or rural zones, on plains or in mountains, with or without rivers to cross, and so on. Then, even though there are many electricity distribution companies in the same jurisdiction, comparing their relative performances to design a pricing mechanism is not an easy thing as many characteristics are idiosyncratic. This diversity explains the lack of homogeneity observed in the regulatory schemes applied to electricity distribution operators.

Setting prices based on observed costs is favoured by Greece, Luxembourg and Switzerland. In contrast, the United Kingdom imposes a maximum regulated price with some additional restrictions linked to profit levels rather than to costs. A variation on this approach limits revenue rather than prices and has been adopted by Austria, Belgium, Denmark, Finland, Germany and Portugal. The last form of regulation observed in Europe's electricity distribution is the reliance on national or international cost benchmarking to assess the authorized costs. This is the approach adopted by the Netherlands and Norway, for instance.[4]

This diversity of approaches can also be observed within a country for the regulation of retail and/or distribution prices when states or provinces enjoy significant autonomy. In Australia, electricity retail prices are controlled by state regulators in all states except Victoria, where prices are set competitively. In the United States, the prices are set by public utility commissions (PUCs) equivalent to the Australian state regulatory agencies. The PUCs all rely on a cost-of-service approach. The differences in prices across states reflect differences, first, in authorized and recognized historical costs and, second, in allowed predetermined profit level added to the cost set through a process called a 'rate case', which, as in Australia, varies across states. Similar differences are noted in Canada and India. In contrast, in Brazil, all electricity distribution companies are regulated by ANEEL, the national energy regulatory agency, which sets their tariff levels.

6.3   Classifying the Forms of Regulation

The diversity of approaches noted in the practice of regulation suggests the need for some form of classification. In academic literature, the forms of regulation that guarantee cost recovery are known as cost-plus. Cost-plus is sometimes referred to

---

[3] Pacific Gas and Electric Company (PG&E) filed for bankruptcy on 29 January 2019. The Californian energy supplier, which was valued at more than $25 billion at the beginning of November 2018, was, mere months later, only worth $4 billion following suspicions of responsibility in the fires that ravaged northern California, killing eighty-six people and destroying 15,000 homes.

[4] For a comparison of the differences in the use of benchmarking across countries, see for instance Burns et al. (2006).

as low-powered incentive regulation since, as we have seen in Chapter 5, it does not give much incentive to the regulated firm to cut costs. Any excess costs would automatically be passed on to the users through a higher than needed average price. Therefore, it is also sometimes known as fixed-margin regulation. Since the fixed margin is usually computed as a guaranteed rate of return on the assets, it is also often referred to as the rate-of-return regulation.[5] Yet another label used for this approach is flexible price regulation, since this form of regulation leads prices to adjust to costs quite fast.

The main conceptual alternative to the cost-based approaches focuses on imposing a limit on prices or revenues. These forms of regulation are known as price cap or revenue cap. These approaches are also known as high-powered incentive regulatory mechanisms. This is because any difference between the allowed and the actual price or revenue defines the profit level achieved by the company. In the case of price caps, for instance, the greater the effort to cut costs, the higher the margin between the allowed price and the realized cost. This approach is also known as fixed price regulation since prices are set, and it is up to the regulated firm to adjust costs if it wants to increase its profit margin. As shown in Chapter 5, this gives a strong incentive to the operator to cut costs.

The third type includes alternative forms of regulation that often serve as a complement to the other forms, as well as various hybrid forms that combine various types of regulation. The description of the electricity distribution examples illustrates a form of regulation known as yardstick competition or benchmarking regulation. It relies on observations of cost data available from comparable firms. This data can be used to benchmark the performance of any individual operator. Benchmarking is used to identify any excess in cost claims made to justify lower than required effort (moral hazard risks) and therefore higher prices. It can also reveal any private information, such as under-maintenance of assets, that a regulated firm may be trying to hide. It is because this form of regulation uses the available cost information from comparable operators that could be competing for the market as a yardstick to assess the incumbents' costs that it is known as a yardstick competition or benchmarking regulation. All the terminologies characterize the same form of regulation focused on performance comparisons. Their diversity simply reflects the preferences of the various authors in the specific context in which they are used but without significant analytical implications.

Yet another alternative form of regulation often observed in practice relies on a combination of the cost- and cap-based approaches. They are known as hybrids. Their main characteristic is their heterogeneity, as there are many ways of combining the first three types of regulation. Most essentially, they allow prices to reflect costs but also include some assessment of the share of costs that could be cut by improving

---

[5] Essentially, the regulator allows the regulated firm a revenue which is the sum of its OPEX, the amortization (AM) of its past CAPEX and a margin computed as the allowed rate of return (r) applied to the value of the capital assets (K) used to produce the service (which comes down to an evaluation of the current economic value of the investments made in the past). Formally, $R = r.K + OPEX + AM$

management or stimulating innovations. They imply that the regulator implicitly or explicitly computes, for a set profit margin, an acceptable profit level based on acceptable costs. This estimated profit is then contrasted with the observed profit based on claimed costs. Since the acceptable or regulated profit tends to be lower than the observed one because claimed costs are inflated, the main regulatory decision is to decide how much of the excess is to be retained by the firm as a function of the informational rent the regulator is willing to allow. Together with cap-based measures, hybrid regimes are also known as performance-based regulatory regimes. Among the most common example found in the academic literature, it may be useful to highlight profit sharing or sliding scale regulatory mechanisms. In these approaches, the allowed average regulated price is only partially responsive to changes or is triggered by specific realized cost levels and the triggers are defined ex ante in the regulation.

Table 6.1 summarizes the formulae underlying the main regulatory approaches observed in practice. *RPI* is the retail price index that reflects the overall rate of inflation in the economy, *X* is the agreed-upon improvement in efficiency the firm should be able to achieve and *t* refers to the specific period at which the assessment is being made. In the case of yardstick competition, *i* refers to the specific firm being assessed and *j* to all the firms to which this firm is compared, as will be explained later. It shows how the allowed average price (p) or total revenue (R) can be linked in different ways to:

- average total costs (C_M);
- average operational expenditure $(OPEX)$;
- amortization (AM);
- an allowed profit margin (m) or rate of return (r);
- the value of the assets (K);
- ad hoc factor (Z) accounting for costs linked to exceptional circumstances (e.g. improving security facilities or dealing with the consequences of a major weather-related disaster) or quality investment;
- differences between observed and acceptable profits $(\pi - \tilde{\pi}$, where π are the profits observed and $\tilde{\pi}$ are the profits the regulator has authorized and the share, α, of this difference that can be retained as a rent by the regulated firm).

Table 6.1 Price- or revenue-setting mechanism observed in regulatory practice

Regulatory approach	
	Cost-based formulae
Cost-plus	$p_t = (1 + m)C_{M(t-1)}$
Rate of return	$R_t = OPEX_{t-1} + AM_t + rK_{t-1}$
	Cap-based formulae
Price cap	$p_t = p_{t-1}(1 + RPI_t - X_t) + Z_t^p$
Revenue cap	$R_t = R_{t-1}(1 + RPI_t - X_t) + Z_t^R$
	Other formulae
Benchmarking/yardstick	$p_i = (1 + m)\left(\sum_{j\neq i} \frac{C_{Mj}}{(n-1)}\right)$ or $p_i = (1 + m)\left(\sum_{j\neq i} \frac{OPEX_j}{(n-1)}\right)$
Hybrid	$R_t = R_{t-1}(1 + RPI_t - X_t) + \alpha\left(\pi_{t-1} - \tilde{\pi}_{t-1}\right)$

The formulae all assume that there is no transfer by the government to cover any part of the costs. They are easy to adjust if there are subsidies since this boils down to lower costs and hence lower revenue requirements. The various expressions also show that there is usually a one-year time lag between the price and the cost measure used to set the price. Many rely on formulae based on costs forecasts, but the costs forecast is generally also based on past costs – though usually corrected for expected improvements in efficiency linked to better uses of technology or better management efforts. This is one of the characteristics of hybrid forms of regulation which try to stimulate performance while sending the signal to the regulated firms that their costs will be recovered as long as they reflect a reasonable standard.[6]

6.4 Why Is There Such a Diversity of Regulatory Approaches?

We will go through a more technical discussion of the various formulae later in the chapter. For now, it may be useful to discuss conceptually what drives the diversity of regulatory approaches across countries, and sometimes within countries. It largely reflects differences in the extent to which the informational gaps have been recognized by the authorities and in the way regulators have chosen to address the distortions they have identified. Two regulators with different access to information on comparable firms may choose different regulatory strategies.

Other factors, such as the institutional characteristics of the countries or the sectors, contribute to the observed diversity of strategies. These include political preferences, poor skills to assess the biases and their sources, fads or copy-cat approaches to the choice of regulatory models (i.e. picking price caps, because everyone else does, and information and expertise are available). It is likely that the actual choice is the result of a combination of any of these factors. Therefore, 'one size does not fit all' in regulation.

Differences in these dimensions within countries may also lead to differences in regulatory preferences across sectors. Moreover, over time, differences in biases may evolve and it makes sense for the regulation of the same sector or firm to be different at different points in time in the same country. Gaps and distortions evolve and so does regulation. These differences in informational circumstances and preferences explain why the optimal allowed average price or revenue would have to vary across firms in a given sector.

In the following chapters, we will show how to quantify all these very pragmatic insights. For now, what is important to keep in mind is that the various approaches adopted all internalize that, for as long as information asymmetries matter, the average price or allowed revenue also needs to include a reasonable rent level that matches their informational advantage. Unless this is done (and we will see how this is done in practice in the next chapter), at least for a while, the regulated firm is likely to supply

---

[6] For a clear and insightful comparison of these methods, see Burns et al. (2003).

less (in quantity and/or quality) and possibly invest less than it should from a social welfare perspective. It could also simply pull out of the business if it has the option to do so and does not get a reasonable rate of return on its assets.

Getting this average price or the allowed revenue right is thus not straightforward in practice. Most importantly, as for any policy, there are winners and losers from the imperfections of regulation implementation. Countries focusing on realized costs tend to favour the interests of service providers. This will usually include the suppliers of capital to finance the operations but often also workers since, in many industries, wage bills can represent a large share of costs and automatic labour costs pass through are usually favoured by unions.[7] Those focusing on price or revenue limits are more likely to claim to be concerned with the interests of users and taxpayers. And if this means that labour and capital costs need to be compressed, so be it.

The clear identification of the winners and losers is particularly important when trying to convince all actors to move from one regulatory regime to another, and the regulator needs to help identify those most likely to block the change – typically those most likely to be hurt by it. For instance, when a regulated sector is getting ready to face more competition, as is the case for the railways industry in Europe as of 2019, the sector's workers realize that in the short- to medium-run, there is a good chance that labour costs will be pushed down. This means fewer jobs or lower wages and most likely both. From a regulatory perspective, this explains why labour unions are less keen on moving from cost-plus to price or revenue caps since it would shift the regulatory regime towards more protection of consumers and taxpayers and less protection of workers. This is part of the reason why France and Belgium have been through recurring railways strikes in 2017 and 2018. It illustrates that regulation is also challenging because it is not socially or politically neutral.

It is worth emphasizing that real life is much more complex than we can discuss within the scope of this book. Multiple issues are usually at stake simultaneously when a regulatory reform is being considered. But the basic simple categorization of regulatory preferences used in theoretical research has proven to be useful in understanding the major incentive issues played out in practice. Understanding the sources and size of informational distortions goes a long way towards deciding which one of the regulatory design options summarized in Table 6.1 to pick in order to achieve the highest social welfare payoff.

6.5   Reconciling the Diversity of Observed Regulatory Approaches with Theory

A lot of the evidence available suggests that the practical choices of regulation often do not lead to as many improvements in the efficiency of public service delivery as argued by theory. This evidence collected over the last thirty years or so suggests that regulation has largely been effective at protecting the joint interest of consumers,

---

[7] For the UK rolling stock operators, the wage bill represents around a third of the total operational costs.

suppliers and taxpayers when it worked as a complement to competition as in the telecommunications sectors. It has been much less effective at protecting all stake-holders when the scope for competition was limited, as in the water and sanitation sector, for instance. And in the other sectors, the evidence is at best mixed, with stories of both successes and failures.

The mixed evidence has (at least) two possible explanations. First, the regulatory choices made in practice are not consistent with the informational distortions characterizing the sector. Second, the translation of the theoretical insights into feasible and implementable regulatory tools is not robust enough to deal with simultaneous distortions which are each best targeted by a different regulatory approach. Any feasible regulatory approach is likely to be imperfect because it demands a judgement call on the relative importance of the various types of distortions. Unfortunately, because we usually do not have enough regulatory tools to tackle all issues simultaneously, regulatory strategies are unlikely to be perfect most of the time.

These imperfections have significant implications. The first is that residual distortions are the norm rather than the exception in regulated industries. Information asymmetries are, notably, unlikely to be corrected fully. For instance, regulatory mechanisms will not force firm managers to care more about consumers than for their own careers. The image of managers working only in the public interest is nice, but unrealistic, if their private incentives are not aligned with those of the public through the design of regulation. Regulators may try to reduce adverse selection and moral hazard, but there is no known regulatory mechanism so far that has achieved second-best perfection. Some argue that nationalization of all regulated public services may be the way out. But there is also a lot of evidence that the implementation of that solution suffers from its own set of informational biases, including a lack of effort to control costs, as illustrated by the Laffont and Tirole (1986) model. These distortions can just as well lead to underperformance. Context and constraints matter to the ranking of the options as solutions to regulatory imperfections, and much more so than suggested by the frequently ideological debates on the optimal degree of intervention of the public sector.

The second implication of regulatory imperfections is that any design will fail to provide comparable protection to all stakeholders since different distortions will hit various groups of actors differently (i.e. lack of investment is likely to hurt future consumers more than today's and excess prices will benefit investors, workers, or both, more than consumers). Thus, how the regulator sets the average price will determine which stakeholder is best protected, and there will be winners and losers. Recognizing the fiscal and social implications of these distributional effects ex ante is essential to the choice of the optimal form of regulation since that drives its political sustainability.

6.6   How Useful Is a Theory That Accounts Only Partially for Informational Biases?

The difficulty of covering all sources of bias, including political and social bias, is such that theory has so far been unable to produce perfect implementable regulatory mechanisms. Does this make theory useless? In our view, the answer is no. Theory helps anticipate the nature, direction and intensity of biases. Biases are indeed a lot more predictable than sometimes recognized by politicians commenting on the effects of regulation. When society chooses to protect workers or shareholders rather than consumers, a regulatory advisor has the tools to design a regulation that delivers on this vision, and vice versa. More generally, theory has shown that there is a match between the ranking of regulatory tools and the ranking of stakeholders' interest.

To make the most of the theoretical insights when deciding which regulatory strategy to adopt or how to fine-tune an existing strategy, while minimizing imperfections in the design of regulation, solid diagnostics of the extent to which the regulatory choices match the specific sources of informational distortions will always help. Moreover, when the time or the resources to do a detailed assessment are missing, getting a first conceptual idea of the likely effects and effectiveness of various regulatory price-setting options is a good start. Ignoring this boils down to increasing the odds of designing regulation imperfectly. Worse, it can lead to the wrong regulatory strategy.

When regulators want to protect the interests of users and taxpayers, the main goal is to get the regulated firm to cut costs as much as possible since it is hoped that lower costs will eventually be translated into lower prices or lower subsidies. This is one of the most common justifications for the adoption of the price or revenue cap formulae reported in Table 6.1. This sounds good when the regulator suspects a moral hazard problem (e.g. the firm relies on too many underused workers). But if the real issue is an adverse selection problem (e.g. the equipment is too old or insufficient), caps may be counterproductive. For instance, it is unrealistic to try to get a 1980 water treatment station to function as effectively as a 2021 unit. Just as is trying to get an old vehicle to be as energy efficient as a recent one. In these cases, when the regulator is too harsh in setting the average price, simply because the firm's technology does not allow for much margin to cut costs, a financing gap is likely to emerge. The firm may not be able to break even although it increases the efforts to minimize costs and to maximize sales. In this situation, the firm has no alternative but to underdeliver output in the short run and/or to underinvest in the long run (i.e. fail to meet the future demand). It is the only way to meet the participation constraint.

If the regulator is more worried about the risks of underinvestment to improve current or future quality and/or to ensure a sufficient service to the future generations of users than about the moral hazard risks, it makes sense to adopt a regulatory design which guarantees that prices will cover the costs. For instance, because investing in a transmission line in a zone prone to earthquakes or floods is quite risky, private financing sources are more difficult to obtain without government support than in a zone without any exposure to natural disasters. To increase the odds of obtaining financing and minimizing the risk of underinvestment, the cost-plus or rate-of-return formulae in Table 6.1 makes sense. The challenge here is not to be too generous in setting the average price. This regulatory mistake would eventually allow the regulated firm to charge as if it were unregulated. And this would indeed bring the output and investments back to levels which called for a regulatory intervention to begin with since it imposed a welfare burden shared by today's and tomorrow's consumers while overprotecting the firm.

These two extreme situations illustrate the difficulty of getting it right and, most importantly, they illustrate that, for a regulator as for most policymakers, pragmatism and the willingness to make decisions where there are trade-offs are essential skills. In most real-life cases, all types of risks and concerns are likely to be relevant simultaneously. Since technology and knowledge keep improving, there will usually be at least some margin for cost savings in the interests of users. Moreover, since the investment needs are likely to continue to be significant as a result of the growing demand for most regulated services, there will always be a need to protect investors. The protection of the investors' interests is largely required by the lumpy nature of the investments needed to deliver the regulated services. These tend to be amortized quite slowly and, without some commitment by the regulator to ensure this amortization is possible for the long run, the participation constraint is likely to kick in quite fast and investment is unlikely to match the needs.

It is because both concerns are often justified jointly that many countries end up relying on some hybrid forms of regulation which combine some cost recovery commitment to protect the operators with some price limits to protect consumers and taxpayers. The weight to be assigned to the two extreme options in the design of these hybrid solutions has to be decided from a good diagnostic of the relative importance of the adverse selection problem (i.e. having to live with a high-cost firm because of its technological characteristics or because of its high investment requirements) and of a moral hazard problem (i.e. being stuck with a 'lazy' operator or an operator under strong political or social pressure not to try too hard to cut costs, in particular when a big part of these costs are linked to excessive employment levels).

To get a better sense of how the various forms of regulation will have to be designed to deliver what is expected of them, it is useful to return to a more technical discussion of the various regulatory design options introduced in Table 6.1. We will focus on cost-plus, price caps and various hybrids and benchmarking approaches. In the process, we will highlight the different names under which each of these approaches are known in an industry which has proven to be quite creative in terms of labelling regulatory schemes.

6.7 Cost-Plus/Fixed-Margin/Rate-of-Return Regulation

Until the 1980s, prices were set so that they would reflect ex post costs, provide a constant margin over costs or ensure a reasonable rate of return on assets invested to deliver the services. As shown in Table 6.1, the simplest way of guaranteeing that costs will be recovered is to pick a formula for the average price which allows the regulated firm to collect the sum of the average costs plus a fixed margin over these costs. This implies that the regulator has a view of what constitutes a reasonable cost and a reasonable margin. Therefore, it is more suitable in sectors with mature technology and little innovation, as information on costs is readily available.

The main advantages of this form of regulation can be summarized as follows. First, since it guarantees the recovery of reasonable costs, including investments, it minimizes uncertainty for investors. This may be one of the most relevant characteristics of the approach in high-risk environments. It is quite helpful when the regulator wants to reduce uncertainty on the viability of a regulated business or investment. It guarantees public or private shareholders of the regulated firm a 'fair' return, that is, one roughly equivalent to the average return on capital across the entire economy, corrected for a premium specific to the industry concerned. This is why it makes sense in countries characterized by a high-risk premium in the financial markets to rely on cost-plus or rate-of-return regulation. Indeed, when risks are high, whether they are driven by business, regulatory or political concerns, the odds of having access to capital markets to finance investment and operations expenditures shrink, leading to undersupply or underinvestment, unless the regulatory regime ensures the recovery of costs.

Another way of ensuring that business and/or investment are not rationed is to focus on the value of the assets needed to deliver the service. As indicated by the rate-of-return regulation formula reported in Table 6.1, all the investments made by the regulated firm (net of amortization for depreciation) define the asset base, and the regulatory regime is designed to ensure that the regulated firm is guaranteed to enjoy a positive rate of return consistent with the risk levels encountered. The asset base is the 'rate base'. In terms of cash, which is often the main focus of investors, the larger the rate base, the greater the volume of cash authorized, and hence the profit allowed. In practice, the allowed rate of return is equivalent to a constant margin, m. Price can fluctuate with unit costs either by a constant cost differential as illustrated in Figure 6.1 or by a proportional differential as in Table 6.1. This also guarantees that profits and returns are stable.

Ignoring for now the issues of financing risks, this approach has several drawbacks which need to be recognized and compared to its advantages when conducting a full diagnostic of its potential in any specific context:

- *It demands an ability to conduct an initial evaluation of costs and of the asset base.* If the regulator is not able to conduct audits or to come up with comparable cost and valuation data for similar firms, it must rely on the information provided by the

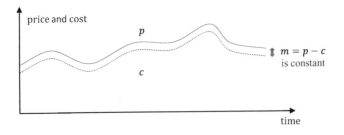

Figure 6.1 Evolution of the profit margin over time under cost-plus regulation

operator. This can be quite complex in many public services. In the water sector, for instance, many pipelines are underground, and their state and maintenance requirements can be quite hard to assess. In that context, since the firm wants to be able to maximize profit (e.g. cash to maintain high dividends in the case of a private firm, managerial excesses and workers' privileges in the case of a public firm), the easy solution is to inflate initial cost and asset value estimates as much as possible. This is what allows the operator to charge higher tariffs and hence generate more cash (private firm) or compensate for overstaffing and slacking (public firm). The same problem applies if the margin is calculated as a rate of return on old and new assets. In this case, the asset base becomes the strategic variable that operators hope to inflate.

- *It increases the risks of distortions in spending decisions* by interfering with firms' natural inclination to minimize investment in quantity and quality (i.e. capital expenditure, in contrast to operational expenditure). Indeed, another way of inflating costs and increasing revenue is to spend on so-called white elephant projects (large, expensive projects for which there is little demand). This is one variant of the Averch–Johnson effect summarized in Box 5.4, or overinvestment owing to rate-of-return or cost-plus regulation. It may also manipulate specific cost components such as depreciation to inflate costs when it is convenient.
- *It increases the moral hazard risks.* Even where the regulator has exact knowledge of the costs involved, cost-plus regulation does not give the operator any incentive to cut them. Overstaffing is one of the most common indicators of this bias, especially in public firms. Underuse of bargaining options for basic input prices (e.g. wages, oil, electricity and other basic inputs) is another illustration of the ways in which poor efforts to cut costs are commonly observed.
- *It raises a problem of management of obsolescence* for assets that become partially or fully useless due to technological or regulatory drastic changes. Should their costs still be covered, and for how long?

6.8   Cap-Based Regulation

As explained in the discussion of the intuition on the challenges of regulation under information asymmetry in Section 5.1, regulation needs to reduce the incentive operators have to claim costs higher than the actual costs. Cost-plus regulation has proven not to be able to address these perverse incentives. This section discusses the various cap-based instruments available to reduce the negative effects of cost information asymmetry. It also highlights their weaknesses.

6.8.1   Price-Cap Regulation

Fixing a maximum price, or cap, is widely credited to Littlechild (1983) as the main alternative to cost-based regulation. The idea is that by fixing, ex ante, a maximum average price for a regulated service, the regulator can encourage the operator to

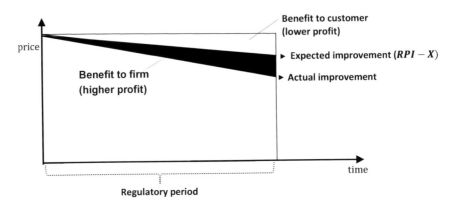

Figure 6.2 Price-cap regulation

improve its operational performance in terms of cost management. It is by lowering costs that it will be able to increase its profit margin. There is no guarantee that costs will always be recovered since they may occasionally be higher than the price cap. But on average, they should allow cost recovery if the participation constraint is to be met. The extension of the capping idea came somewhat later and raised some specific issues. But before getting to that, it may first be useful to highlight the benefits and risks associated with price caps.

An easy way to think through how price caps work is to analyse how they are implemented in practice during two successive regulatory periods. During the first period, the regulator does not know enough details about the actual costs of the firm and sets a maximum price for the regulated service which accounts for an estimated improvement in efficiency that the firm should be able to achieve. Since the period can last from three to six years, a common solution is to have a declining cap during that period. The idea is to allow the consumers to benefit increasingly more over time from the expected efficiency gains that the firm should be able to achieve (see Figure 6.2). During this period, however, the firm continues to keep part of the efficiency gains assumed by the regulator (the X in the $RPI - X$ formula in Table 6.1). But it also gives an incentive to the firm to continue to work hard at improving efficiency since for as long as the X is set, any difference between the actual efficiency gain and the X comes down to additional profit for the firm. This type of regulation is better suited for sectors where technology is evolving so that costs are declining (e.g. learning by doing).

This price cap is likely to guarantee a positive return. This return can be quite generous if the regulator is not very good at coming up with an X that matches the actual efficiency improvements the firm should be able to achieve. In the second period, the information on costs revealed by the first-period interactions between the regulator and the firm allow the regulator to have a better sense of the extent to which prices can be cut. A new price cap, including a new X, is then set. It starts at a cost level closer to what the actual improvements observed reveal. This new price cap is once again set, to guarantee a positive gross return, and continues to give an inventive to cut costs. However, it does not guarantee a positive net return; this is quite different from the cost-plus approach, which guarantees a return, including in an environment where there is uncertainty on the actual cost level.

In most developed countries, where regulatory accounting standards are relatively high, when price caps are first adopted they are based on information on observed past costs, estimations of recent costs or on some international cost benchmark. In some countries without a good accounting tradition, as is sometimes the case in developing and emerging economies, international cost benchmarks provide the initial information set.

The change in the cap decided at the beginning of the second period is usually based on a correction for inflation or changes in the productivity of the firm or the sector. The regulator decides how much of the estimated productivity gains must be shared with users and taxpayers. Occasionally, caps can also account for exceptional circumstances. For instance, the growth in concerns for terrorist risks has forced airports or nuclear power stations to install additional security equipment. The cost of these additional requirements can be factored into a price or a revenue cap. That's what the Z factor in Table 6.1 represents.

In most countries, whether developed or developing, the price reviews take place every three to six years and during the period in between two reviews the regulated firm can keep the difference between the capped price and realized costs. This means that the relationship between the costs of production and the prices of the regulated services is not subject to a tight control by the regulator during a predictable and relatively long period. It is simply monitored to allow the regulator to learn about the firm's costs. Any difference between cost and price cap is thus a profit during that period and this is why the approach is supposed to alleviate the moral hazard risks. It is because a firm can keep any profits obtained via cost reductions relative to the price cap during the review period that price cap regulation is expected to increase production efficiency. Over time, prices do adjust, though their adjustment is constrained by changes in input prices (the consumer price index, a wholesale price index, or any index that can be used to assess inflation in the sector).

Because the regulator must ensure that the regulated firm does not lose money, the level of the cap must account for uncertainty regarding some or all of the regulated business's costs, as well as opportunity costs. In other words, the regulator must recognize the firm's *participation constraint* – that is, its need for an incentive to participate in the market. Whether the participation constraint is met or not largely depends on the choice of the value for X, the efficiency correction. If it is set too high, the firm may not be able to recover its costs. In contrast, if it is too low, the firm is allowed to make excess profits on the back of users and/or taxpayers.

Although the discussion has so far largely focused on the price cap imposed on a single service, in practice, the regulator can set a cap for a basket of the regulated services provided by the firm. This allows the firm to increase prices of some services while cutting the prices of other services to stay within the average cap limit. In practice, a regulated firm often delivers multiple products (e.g. water and sanitation, freight and passenger transport, fixed and mobile phone lines). In this case, the price cap must be designed to impose an upper limit on the weighted average of the price changes corrected for the expected efficiency increase X. In its most basic form, this is done by relying on the following formula:

$$\frac{\sum_i \left(p_{i,t} q_{i,t-1}\right)}{\sum_i \left(p_{i,t-1} q_{i,t-1}\right)} \leq 1 + RPI_t - X_t \qquad (6.1)$$

where $p_{i,t}$ is the price in period t and $q_{i,t-1}$ the quantity of the good or service i in period $t-1$; RPI_t is the price index that reflects the overall rate of inflation in the economy and X_t is the agreed improvement in efficiency the firm should be able to achieve. Note that the formula in Equation (6.1) is a price cap and not a revenue cap (analysed in the next section) since the quantities are the same in the numerator and the denominator (those of period $t-1$) contrary to prices.

6.8.2   Revenue-Cap Regulation

A revenue cap limits the total revenue received by a regulated firm. Like a price cap, it is adjusted to account for inflation and an efficiency factor. Depending on the circumstances, it can focus on variable revenue (i.e. ignoring fixed costs) or total revenue instead. And a variable revenue cap can apply to average revenue or to a panel of revenue sources only.

From an incentive perspective, a revenue cap works the way a price cap works in the sense that they both stimulate the regulated firm to cut costs, since the firm captures the cost savings. But there are several significant differences between the price cap and revenue cap. The first is the allocation of the volume risk. Under a price cap, the firm bears the volume risk (e.g. traffic in transport or telecommunications, physical sales in energy and water services). Under a revenue cap, this risk is passed on to users (or taxpayers, if there are subsidies or excise taxes) and can be passed on through prices since the focus is pq and not just p. If demand q is lower in one period, users (or taxpayers) will simply pay more per unit of consumption to allow the firm to reach the revenue cap in future periods. This possibility of shifting risk is a new source of moral hazard not found under a price cap. There is no reason for a firm to try to improve demand (for, say, bus or rail transport), since the revenue is guaranteed. A second important difference applies to sectors in which demand is uncertain. In that case, the revenue-cap mechanism does not favour users or taxpayers unless their demand is very inelastic and regulators are concerned that the service may not be delivered if the firm's risk perceptions exceed its participation constraints. A third difference stems from the greater freedom in setting prices when the regulated firm delivers multiple goods and services allowed by revenue caps. This additional freedom makes it easier for firms to try to manipulate their sales margins depending on the risks of entry or competition in the various segments in which it is operating.

A fourth difference leads to a subtler perspective on the relative desirability of price and revenue caps. Revenue caps can lead firms to try to get their users to reduce consumption as a way of cutting costs and increasing margins for a given revenue target. This may be bad news when cutting demand is perceived as an imposed rationing by users craving for higher levels of consumption. But in a context in which demand management is important, for environmental reasons for instance, this risk may be welcome. But it also means that the management of environmental concerns through revenue caps may lead to higher rents for the regulated firm. Better instruments may be available and could be more effective.

6.8.3   The Drawbacks of Cap-Based Regulation

Despite their numerous advantages, and ignoring for now some of the issues already raised, the approaches based on caps also suffer from several drawbacks:

- *They increase the adverse selection risks.* Since the regulator must set prices to ensure that the participation constraint is met, the sector must bear the full cost of adverse selection risk.
- *They can potentially increase rents, as a temporary rent is the instrument used to stimulate incentives.* This has two additional implications:
  - It reduces allocative efficiency, at least temporarily.
  - It impacts the role of prices as a signal to manage demand, which can be quite a serious issue if prices are expected to be a key instrument to deal with environmental concerns or congestion problems for instance.
- *They increase exposure to specific cost- and financing-related risks.* Since revenue and prices are not connected to costs, and in some countries and some context costs can be subject to exogenous shocks, the approach implies a much stronger exposure to risks and uncertainty than cost-based approaches.
- *They increase the risk of undersupply of quantity.* In risky environments, firms may be wary of making an investment with no guaranteed return since the price will not be adjusted for shocks. This is consistent with the observation that firms operating under caps tend to be quite selective in their investment commitments. This is especially true in high-risk environments (e.g. in some developing countries, during times of crisis and in certain volatile sectors), and it may slow service expansion or improvements quite significantly.
- *They also increase the risks of undersupply of quality.* Ignoring costs fully boils down to ignoring the risks that at least some quality dimensions are likely to be cut to increase the profit margins.
- *Their effectiveness is likely to be limited in time in the absence of innovation.* When first launched, a cap-based regime is expected to factor in the scope for improvements in efficiency. But at some point, the scope is likely to be limited and unless the regulated firm is controlled well enough for its ability to deliver on quality and on quantity, the only way to continue to achieve cost savings mimicking efficiency improvements is to cut both dimensions.

6.9   Other Forms of Regulation

While cost-plus/rate-of-return and cap-based regulation dominate the theoretical discussions, in practice there are other forms of regulatory options. Some complement the
mainstream forms of regulation discussed in Sections 6.7 and 6.8. This is the case of
benchmarking/yardstick regulation. Others are hybrid forms combining cap-based and
cost-plus mechanisms. Yet others are creative solutions adopted in some regions of the
world. They deserve to be highlighted as they could be considered complementary to
the more traditional regulatory mechanisms. Each of these options are discussed next.

6.9.1   Benchmarking/Yardstick Regulation

Benchmarking/yardstick competition is a different type of high-powered incentive
regulation which takes advantage of the existence of similar operators (e.g. a network
of local monopolies such as hospitals or water distribution networks). It is often used
as a complement to other forms of price regulation. The regulator compares the
performance of a regulated company with that of similar firms and uses the average
(or the best) performance in the sample as a benchmark for allowed prices or other
performance dimensions. The mechanism is commonly expressed as a benchmark
price:

$$p_t^i = (1+m)\frac{\sum_{j\neq i}C_{Mt-1}^j}{n-1} \tag{6.2}$$

where i is the firm being regulated, $j = 1, \ldots, n, j \neq i$ are the firms to which the
regulated firm is being compared, m is the profit margin allowed by the regulator and
C_{Mt}^j is the average cost of each firm j at time t in the benchmark sample. Therefore
yardstick regulation combines a cost-plus element to fix the benchmark with a fixed
price element as the benchmark is unrelated to the firm's own cost.

To see how this can be used in assessing the revenue, let q_t^i be the quantity
produced by firm i at time t. Then the revenue of the firm is

$$R_t^i = (1+m)\left\{q_t^i\sum_{j\neq i}C_{Mt-1}^j/(n-1)\right\} \tag{6.3}$$

As with price-cap regulation, care must be taken in the implementation of yardstick
regulation. Attempts at yardstick regulation are almost always criticized by the
regulated firm based on 'special circumstances' that render its comparison with other
firms inappropriate. While these criticisms are generally driven by self-interest, even
elaborate and complex comparisons will be unlikely to fairly compare different
enterprises across all circumstances. Consequently, a degree of subjectivity must be
employed when implementing yardstick competition. The firms used in the benchmark sample must either be ideally similar in technology, cost and operating conditions or at least regulated efficiently enough to account for differences in operating
conditions (e.g. age of the assets and differences in population density of the areas
served and in customers' wages, access to credit, taxes and so on).

Basically, yardstick competition is a good regulatory solution when the regulator faces a moral hazard problem and there is no adverse selection among the firms to regulate or in the reference sample. It can be a useful solution in many circumstances but there are also risks in relying only on this approach because it can end up turning into an overly aggressive contest between firms that can be counterproductive when they are heterogeneous and the least efficient already do their best. Box 6.1 explains

---

Box 6.1 How Are Productivity and Efficiency Changes Measured?

Measuring productivity (the ratio of observed output to observed inputs) or efficiency (a ratio of observed values of inputs and outputs to their optimal values) in the context of regulation is necessary to ensure that consumers get a fair share of cost savings that can be achieved by monopoly and that the regulatory demands made on operators to improve their performance are realistic. More specifically, regulators often need to be able to measure: (i) potential minimum inputs needed to produce given outputs; (ii) efficient costs levels to recover or (iii) the impact of input or output price distortions that the regulated firm may not be able to control. In addition, they also choose to be able to compare performance across operators when they rely on yardstick competition as part of their regulatory toolkit to check on the competitiveness of individual operators or of a sector.

There are three approaches to producing a measure of productivity or efficiency changes: (i) price-based or quantity-based index numbers (PIN); (ii) data envelopment analysis (DEA) and (iii) stochastic frontier analysis (SFA).

An index number is a real number that measures changes in a set of related variables. It can be used to measure price and quantity changes over time as well as to measure differences in the levels across firms. Price index numbers can refer to consumer prices or more complex combinations of input and output prices. Quantity index numbers can be used to measure changes in quantities of outputs produced or inputs used by a firm or industry over time. Their main advantage is that they are relatively easy to compute. Their main disadvantage is that they only give a very aggregate perspective on performance and its evolution. A popular index in regulatory discussions is the Tornqvist index (expressed in log-change form). It is a weighted geometric average of the relative quantity or price in two different periods with weights given by the simple average of the value shares in these two periods. It gives a quantitative proxy for the overall growth rate achieved by a firm or a sector that can easily be calculated from observed empirical data without having to estimate cost or production functions. Their main drawback is that they say nothing on the performance drivers – allocative versus technical versus technological drivers of (in)efficiency. This decomposition requires relying on either of the other two methods.

Data envelopment analysis is a linear programming method that constructs a non-parametric production frontier by fitting a piece-wise linear surface over the observed data on outputs and inputs to create the 'best performance frontier'. The distance to this frontier is used to measure the degree of inefficiency of the firms

Box 6.1 (*cont.*)

below the frontier. The efficiency of a firm is calculated in terms of scores on a scale of 0–1 with the frontier firms receiving a score of 1. Depending on the regulatory issue, the distance can be assessed in terms of the wasted amount of inputs or the potential output that could be produced given the level of inputs. DEA can be used to distinguish the allocative and technical efficiency of the firms. The main advantage of the method is that it can be used to identify a set of peer firms (efficient firms with similar input and output mixes) for each inefficient firm and it is relatively easy to compute for multiple outputs and inputs. It requires few assumptions on the frontier. It can be sensitive to the quality of the data, to outliers and to sample size, although recent technical developments are suggesting ways to minimize the risks.

Stochastic frontier analysis regroups a set of econometric techniques used to estimate production or cost functions. The (in)efficiency measure is derived from an analysis of the error term. The deterministic portion of the specification represents the frontier of maximal output for a given set of inputs. The error term has two components: the stochastic symmetric error term and the inefficiency term which measures the systematic departure from the estimated frontier. Its main advantage is that it can account for important control variables that can be used to assess the relevance of key policy variables (such as the type of regulation adopted) and can deal with outliers. Its main disadvantage is that, as always in econometrics, the results are quite sensitive to the choice of the functional form, to sample size and to specific assumptions on the error terms characteristics and the specific estimation technique.

For more details, see for instance Grifell et al. (2018) for a recent update of on the theoretical research in the field or Coelli et al. (2003) for a simple introduction to the use of the measures in regulated infrastructures.

how this type of regulation relies on a wide range of fairly advanced techniques. As discussed in Cherchye et al. (2018), these techniques have significantly improved recently but there are still many issues to be sorted out before they can turn benchmarking into a tool that can be used on its own. For now, it is usually a useful complement to other forms of regulation.

Sunshine regulation is, in many ways, a complement to yardstick competition designed to improve the accountability of regulated operators for their performance. The regulator makes the results of performance diagnostics, typically comparative ones, publicly available ('sunshine regulation') and follows up with aggressive communication campaigns to shame the poorly performing firms and congratulate the good ones. In Europe, the approach has been used quite effectively by Dutch and Portuguese water regulators. One of the early assessments of this form of regulation showed that in the Dutch political and institutional context, sunshine regulation of the water operators was effective in leading to small price cuts for water combined with sustained and substantial economic profits (De Witte and Saal 2009). The approach has also been effective in the regulation of health care and education (Bevan and Wilson 2013).

The approach has clear potential payoffs in a world in which social media are quick to report bad or good news. But it is far from being without faults. For instance, it can be less effective if there is enough margin for the regulated operators to actively use information advantages or biases when reporting the information. This can influence consumer behaviour as much as regulators' evaluations.

6.9.2   Hybrids and Other Forms of Regulation

While pure cost, cap-based and benchmarking formula are important regulatory options, in practice, regulators have commonly adopted hybrid forms of regulation. And some have been relying on creative adaptations of these more standard approaches. An example is the reliance on the efficient model firm as a form of benchmark used in various Latin American countries to produce a specific type of price cap, as discussed in Box 6.2.

Box 6.2 Regulation by Benchmarking through the 'Efficient Model Firm'

Since the early 1980s, several Latin American utilities regulators have adopted a form of regulation centred on the idea that the efficient firm could be modelled based on the available best practice. The original idea is usually credited to Chile, which first used it in the 1980s for the electricity sector (Bustos and Galetovic 2002, 2006), but Grifell-Tatje and Knox Lovell (2003) discuss an equivalent approach adopted by the Spanish regulators in the 1990s and defined as an 'engineer' model.

As suggested by Gomez-Lobo (2006), this efficient 'model' firm (*empresa modelo eficiente* in Spanish) is the answer to the following question: 'if we had to design from scratch a firm that would efficiently meet the expected demand, what would that firm look like and how much would it have to charge to be financially sustainable?' In practice, as argued by Gomez-Lobo (2006) and Grifell-Tatje and Knox Lovell (2003), this is indeed essentially how an engineer advising the regulator would or should look at the problem. From an economic perspective, the approach can be interpreted as a form of yardstick regulation in which the yardstick is an 'ideal' efficient firm. However, a significant difference is that with yardstick competition the regulator can use observable costs from other firms in the industry while with the efficient model firm the regulator or its advisors need to have the knowledge to build the most efficient firm.

In the efficient model firm approach, this firm is modelled based on the assumption that it functions with the best technology and the best effort level possible, which allows an estimation of the 'ideal' minimum cost for a specific quality standard. Since the firm has to be financially sustainable, the average price is based on the net present value of the cash flows that can be generated from the capital

Box 6.2 (*cont.*)

stock at time 0 (updated if needed to account for technological changes). This implies that the average price has to be based on the minimum long-run average cost accounting for the original undepreciated value of the assets. In some ways, this implies that the initial similarity with yardstick regulation can now be interpreted as well as a price cap (Gomez-Lobo and Vargas 2002).

In practice, the modelling of costs is quite detailed. The efficient model firm accounts for the context since it corrects for geography and demography, for instance. It also accounts for technological constraints such as network design and administrative characteristics (degree of decentralization of commercial and administrative operations and digitalization of data treatment). As explained by Gomez-Lobo (2003), it follows a bottom-up approach to cost modelling in contrast to the bottom-down approach adopted in models inspired by the UK approach of benchmarking.

Bustos and Galetovic (2006) offer a good overview of the limitations of the approach, notably with respect to the incentives to update technologies when technological changes are frequent and the regulator decision on the time allowed to amortize the investment is uncertain as a result of a lack of credibility of the regulators. Gomez-Lobo (2003) also emphasizes the uncertainty over the relative importance of the various sources of information asymmetries. Indeed, in this regulatory approach, the regulator has to have enough knowledge of the firm and the context in which it operates to be able to model the 'ideal' firm. In practice, however, this is usually done by external consultants unlikely to have enough detailed information on the efficient configuration of assets and operational costs. And unlike the yardstick or price-cap approach, there is little incentive for the firm to reveal its efficient costs.

In their detailed empirical assessment of the Spanish experience, Grifell-Tatje and Knox Lovell (2003) conclude that indeed the engineer perspective can lead to superior network design and these combined with lower input prices can lead to cost savings. However, in a credible revenue cap regime, managers can do a better job exploiting the incentive to be cost-efficient.

In sum, this approach can be quite helpful in some contexts, in particular when adverse selection is a major issue. But it may not be able to assess the scope to reduce moral hazard when this issue is the most important of the two main types of information asymmetries.

These hybrid options are largely consistent with the insights of theory when sources of uncertainty are important. Conceptually, the hybrid forms of regulation are classified as second-best solutions. They correspond to the idea that, in highly uncertain environments, regulators should offer a menu of contracts with a predictable profile to allow service providers to pick what suits them best and, in the process, reveal their type. Each contract should be composed of a negotiated fixed payment and a variable one proportional to ex post costs. A contract specifies the share of the ex post observed costs that are reimbursed. Within this menu, the firm will choose the option that maximizes its profit. A firm that expects a large ex post cost is likely to prefer a contract with a low fixed and high sharing part. Another way to structure this is to get the firm to accept a low guaranteed return, in exchange for a commitment by the government to take on any cost overrun. In contrast, a firm expecting low costs would be willing to live without guarantees but demand the right to keep any profit, whatever its level, in exchange for a larger fixed payment. In other words, high returns are the expected outcome of high cost uncertainty.

In practice, hybrids reflect these theoretical insights by linking the regulatory rules to explicit assumptions the regulator imposes about cost and revenue levels as well as cost- and revenue-sharing arrangements. These assumptions are used to produce a theoretical revenue, for instance. Working with a theoretical revenue, operation cost or financing cost may be important to consider if it appears that the firm could be tempted to follow risky or costly operational or financing strategies to increase its profit margin. Working with assumed revenue can also be quite useful when there is a suspicion that the firm has been relying on transfer pricing to distribute costs across locations, to conduct fiscal optimization strategies, or simply to inflate the costs on specific inputs it buys from its own subsidiaries.

One of the advantages of hybrid approaches is that they may increase competition to provide the regulated service. They allow a firm with low-cost technology to offer its services in an auction for the right to control these services when it is convinced that the cap component of the hybrid will ensure a high return. And for a high-cost technology, it provides solid enough guarantees that the authorized revenue will allow its costs to be recovered.

In practice, menus will be designed using predictable criteria, including (i) the authorized cost level; (ii) the acceptable margin around that cost level; (iii) the tolerance for additional related business activities (to allow some degree of cross-subsidies); (iv) the rewards for honesty and (v) the penalties for dishonesty. Using these criteria, regulators have designed a wide range of adaptations of both price-capped and cost-plus regimes that elicit truthful sharing of key information, thereby reducing the risks of cost inflation.

The following examples illustrate the diversity of ways to deal with moral hazard and adverse selection. They share significant similarities with price caps, but there are a few notable differences in the context in which they are most likely to be desirable.

Profit sharing (also called *sliding scale* or *earnings sharing*) is a form of regulation adopted when the responsiveness of user prices to changes in actual costs must be smoothed or minimized. The regulator defines a profit (or rate of return) range within which the firm is free to keep all earnings. Profits or returns outside this range are split between the regulated firm and its clients in accordance with clearly defined quantitative rules. In practice, this means that the users share with the regulated firm the consequences of fluctuations in profits and returns. For example, if profits are higher than allowed, users enjoy lower average prices. If profits are too low, users pay a higher average price to reduce the drop in profits. This type of mechanism may be expressed as:

$$R_t = (1 + RPI_t - X_t)R_{t-1} + \alpha \left(\pi_t - \tilde{\pi}_{t-1} \right) \qquad (6.4)$$

Here, R, RPI and X are defined as before; π_t is the realized profit; $\tilde{\pi}_{t-1}$ is the profit level defined by the regulator in the preceding period, and α is the profit-sharing factor. Similar approaches can be used to smooth or even cap dividends for instance, or to ensure a cost sharing to additional unpredictable but required improvements in quality or rehabilitation when a regulated firm can be subject to environmental or other types of shocks.

Disconnecting dividends and prices. Another situation of interest is one in which prices and dividends need to be managed jointly. A hybrid form of regulation can be used to avoid the perverse temptation of increasing prices simply to pay more dividends, as happened in the British water sector in the 2010s. In this case, one possible trick is to allow the firm to pay dividends inversely proportional to the average price of the service it is providing. This approach had already been used in England in the nineteenth century and may enjoy a revival in an environment in which private operators are tempted to be more concerned with shareholders than with consumers.

Profit-sharing rule between workers and shareholders. A third context of increasing interest in policy circles is one in which the regulator has reasons to be concerned about the fairness of the treatment of the firm's workers or with the necessity to maintain more workers than needed as part of a negotiation with the unions, while at the same time pushing firms to minimize costs. In the first case, the concern is that profits are passed on to dividends while workers' salaries are pushed down. In the second case, the opposite holds, and the wage bill becomes so high that, for a given regulated price, the return to investors is kept lower than required to maintain the attractiveness of the sector. In these situations, one approach is for the regulator to manage the split of surplus profits between shareholders and workers. Both owners and workers thus have an incentive to improve efficiency. The scheme can be adopted only for a limited time, as in the case of a price cap, to allow the regulator to eventually pass on some of the gains to users or taxpayers.

These examples show that, ultimately, hybrid forms of regulation are the outcome of creative solutions to minimize specific informational gaps. Part of the creativity is the ability to focus on specific performance dimensions in the design of incentives to be built into the formulae. For these forms of regulation to be effective, the goals must be based on dimensions of firm performance that are easy to monitor technically (such as quality of service or expansion of coverage). This is particularly useful when accounting or financial data is not reliable, as is often the case when cost-accounting practices are poor or not enforced. With specific performance targets, progress towards the goals is simply linked to an explicit system of financial rewards and penalties. This is why, just like cap-based regulation, hybrid forms are also known as performance-based regulation (PBR) approaches (see Box 6.3). Their focus is more on the *what* than on the *how*.[8]

---

[8] While tempting, the approach can be misleading, as is the case when the regulator sets goals that are not aligned with profit-making objectives such as environmental or social targets.

Box 6.3 The Move towards More Performance-Based Regulation (PBR)

Over the past twenty-five years, the tendency has been for regulators to try to link more systematically their evaluation to specific performance indicators. Multiple versions of PBR have been developed around the world. Many countries are also adopting the approach to stimulate the adoption of more environmentally friendly technologies. This is because it can be designed to stimulate innovation by operators without giving up on the need to deal with the increased demand for a service.

Maybe the most creative, or at least the highest profile, PBR approach launched in recent times is the 'RIIO' approach adopted in Britain. RIIO is short for Revenues = Incentives + Innovation + Outputs. It brings together the 'IIO' elements into an eight-year price-monitoring plan anchored into an extensive set of performance measures matched by financial incentives to get operators to try hard to deliver and to penalize them when underperforming. More technically, it is essentially an enhanced revenue-cap mechanism linking allowed revenue to specific output targets. The main motivation of the adoption of this ambitious new approach to regulation is the desire to focus *jointly* on six specific output targets: safety, environmental impact, customer satisfaction, consumer vulnerability protection, connection speed, reliability and availability.

The approach is quite process oriented as it puts stakeholders at the heart of the decision-making process (rather than the regulator only, as earlier approaches usually did) and is anchored into a fair degree of planning on interactions. Doing so takes time to develop and to implement. The purpose is noble since it is expected to stimulate innovation to reduce service costs for current and future consumers while maintaining service quality. The approach was first introduced in 2013 for electricity and gas transmission (RIIOT1) and gas distribution (RIIO-GD1). It was then adopted for electricity distribution (RIIO-ED1) in 2015. At this stage, it is still too early to have robust evidence on its effectiveness. There is, however, already a sense of some of the main changes it brings to the way regulation is likely to be implemented as more countries follow the lead.

The most obvious change contributed by RIIO may be the effort to improve accountability. What makes the approach more accountable than the traditional price or revenue caps is that the actual return is explicitly linked to delivery performance. Moreover, the regulator is also expected to assess performance much more precisely than in the past to highlight any specific issues in terms of cost efficiency and the extent to which investment needs are being addressed. Accountability is further reinforced by a shift in the burden of proof to demonstrate that costs are efficient over the long term. This burden is now on the regulated firm.

It is worth pointing out that there is something in this approach for the regulated firms as well. Indeed, it provides a broader range of options to innovate in cost-cutting and improve long-term performance. This may imply an increase in the risk levels the firm has to take on, including some they may not be able to control directly (e.g. when the regulator gets targets wrong because the historical information is poor).

Hybrid form of yardstick competition. Regulators have adopted yardstick competition as a substitute of price-cap regulation when the operators are sufficiently homogenous. When they are heterogeneous yardstick competition can still be used as a complement to the cost-plus form of regulation. If some components of cost are common to all operators, despite their heterogeneity, the regulator can reimburse this common part based on yardstick competition and the idiosyncratic part based on cost-plus. In other words, the fixed part of the hybrid contract is computed based on benchmarking. The most efficient firm will pick the fixed payment, while the most inefficient one will favour a contract that reimburses most of the ex post costs.

6.10   In the End It Is All about Matching Information Asymmetries with Regulation

From the discussion so far, it should be clear that for regulation to be as effective as possible, its design needs to ensure a match between possible mechanisms and sources of information asymmetry or biases. The starting point of any decision on the choice of a regulatory regime, whether when writing a new contract for a specific project or renegotiating an existing contract, should be a diagnostic of the relative significance of moral hazard and adverse selection.

If the concern associated with the information gap is a moral hazard problem in the form of low levels of effort to cut costs, then cost-plus regulation is clearly not a good idea. This is a common situation in regulated industries in which operators rely on outsourcing to carry out some activities without a clear specification of time or input intensity in the delivery of the subcontracted activities. In that context, guaranteeing a net return is unlikely to encourage significant efforts towards cost savings. Price caps or fixed prices based on benchmarking would probably be more effective in forcing operators to exert themselves and, in the process, reveal the true costs of operating their business, thus helping to close the information gap. But this will only work if quality is clearly specified and the price level is neither too high nor too low.

On the other hand, cost-plus regulation is a good option if the concern associated with the information gap is an adverse selection problem, or if risks are high because of exogenous factors. In developing countries, for instance, investors can be quite uncertain about the size of the market they will be able to reach, and this may make them hesitant to invest without a guaranteed return. Price caps could end up limiting the actual returns if a small volume of sales impedes grabbing the payoffs to scale economies. Cost-plus regulation, instead, ensures that regulated firms will be compensated for all the costs of production they incur – after audits, of course, to ensure the accuracy of data. The downside is that there is no incentive to cut costs, including those associated with high levels of risk. Hybrids that combine a fixed but partial reimbursement with an additional reimbursement based on audited costs will provide greater incentives to regulated firms to cut costs. Sharing business risks between firms and users/taxpayers is essential to encourage efficient management and production.

The problem now is that the two sources of information asymmetry are often correlated while regulation tends to be focused on one or the other, as mentioned earlier. For instance, the cost savings achieved by price caps may not be as great as expected if the cap is set too high (for fear of not meeting the participation constraint). This makes the problem of adverse selection worse since it ensures that high-cost firms (those with poor technologies) are still 'invited' to deliver their service, which in turn leaves a lot of rent to the low-cost firms (those with the most cost-effective technologies) simply because the regulator is uncertain what type of firms they are facing. It must ensure financial viability even if it turns out that the firms interested in delivering service are high cost. Thus, while a fixed-price incentive solves the moral hazard problem, it increases the risks of having to face the full costs of adverse selection. An efficient provider which keeps all the benefit of its cost reduction in the form of rents is not optimal from a social perspective. What matters from a distributional point of view is how much users and taxpayers pay for a service of a given quality, not how much it costs to produce it.

Similarly, guaranteeing recovery at any cost level reduces incentives for a firm's management to exert optimal (if any!) effort. The outcome is that consumers end up paying higher prices than they would if the firm had been better managed. It is also likely that some rent will be accrued by the firm and its managers to the extent that they can manipulate perceptions of effort and mislead regulators regarding their actual level of costs. Thus, while the adverse selection problem can be solved by a straight-forward cost-plus mechanism, the costs associated with moral hazard will make themselves felt.

Also, consequences must be considered across several overlapping but distinct dimensions. Good intentions in one may have perverse effects in another. For instance, in the context of climate change, adopting cost-plus regulation may favour the adoption of new, cleaner technologies by investors uncertain about the market's evolution. However, this introduces its own set of biases. It will, in effect, make the upgraded capital cheaper relative to labour and therefore induce the firm to substitute capital for labour. This may not be the best solution where unemployment is high.

In sum, if the main concern is underinvestment in quality or quantity, then flexible mechanisms, such as cost of service, cost-plus or rate of return, are attractive. Therefore they end up being favoured in high-risk environments, such as some developing countries, once the regulators have been able to develop a reasonable idea of actual costs. It is useful to keep in mind, however, that firms are then allowed a full pass-through of costs to the final user (or to the taxpayer if the service is being subsidized). So, from the point of view of users and taxpayers, timely investment and good service quality come at the cost of higher average prices (or subsidies).

In contrast, if the main concern is a lack of managerial effort to cut costs for existing services (a typical situation in public firms, where low productivity and overstaffing are a recurrent problem) or uncertainty about these costs, capping the service price (or imposing a dynamic price cap) can get a firm to reveal if it is indeed an inherently high-cost firm. This is one reason why price caps are often used in times of transition, such as when a new project is being considered or a sector has just been restructured. They buy the regulator time to conduct necessary cost audits, and the firm to restructure and make rent out of it.

The practice of regulation is internalizing these insights. Information gaps and biases have multiple sources. Moreover, the menu of policy concerns and constraints that regulators need to address are increasing as social and environmental issues are becoming standard items on the regulatory agenda across countries and sectors. This multiplicity of dimensions is progressively leading regulators to rely more on explicit performance indicators as a way of increasing accountability for specific policy targets, as explained in Box 6.3.

6.11   Summing Up

- The optimal form of regulation of the average price depends on the relative importance of the various sources of information asymmetry influencing the cost levels (i.e. adverse selection issue versus moral hazard issue).
- No matter what the main source is, theory provides two main insights that hold, irrespective of the main source of distortion:
  - The average regulated price needs to include a temporary payment to cover the price the regulator must pay to get the missing information and this price should be seen as an additional cost.
  - Regulators should set up a menu of desirable contracts and allow the firms to self-select the contract type that best matches their capacity and risk-taking preferences; good firms (low costs) tend to prefer fixed-price contracts and bad firms (high costs) tend to prefer cost-plus.
- There are three main approaches to setting the average price in practice: cost-plus, price caps and hybrids. Various forms of performance benchmarking can be useful complements to close the informational gap on costs and to shame poor performance (sunshine regulation).
- In practice, most countries are evolving towards hybrid forms of regulation emphasizing the need to account for the multiplicity of regulatory goals and informational constraints.
- The multiplicity of experiences adds up to a menu of options of designs regulators can pick from according to context and circumstances.

7   Linking Regulatory Theory to Practice through Finance

The previous chapters focused on theoretical guidelines on how to regulate the pricing of public services to ensure a fair treatment of users, taxpayers and producers. This chapter explains how regulatory practice has turned these conceptual guidelines into operational ones thanks to tools borrowed from finance theory and practice. The link is a necessary one, since behind every producer there is an investor or a lender concerned with a return on their capital and the allowed average price ends up having to be consistent with the allowed average return expected by these financial stakeholders, whether private or public.

Finance theory and practice offers a methodology allowing a quantitative assessment of the rate of return to the capital (K) used by a regulated firm that can be fair to all stakeholders. This return will be implicit in the average price allowed. It is the translation in regulatory practice of the concept of opportunity cost of capital, r, discussed in Chapters 5 and 6. Just as importantly, the implementation of the methodology leads to technical interactions between regulators and regulated firms that help reduce information asymmetries in regulated industries. The specific rates of return adopted in these decisions are the outcome of these interactions and end up driving the average price that regulators will accept as part of the regulatory processes.

The approach is not fool-proof, as we will see in this chapter. It is anchored in many imperfect and often subjective decisions negotiated between the regulators and the regulated firms. It is also subject to many academic and policy debates and most are unresolved.[1] But it beats imposing returns and average prices without justification. This is why it deserves a somewhat detailed discussion in this book.

The chapter is far from covering all of the issues regulators have to deal with in practice when deciding on the fair rate of return.[2] But it offers a broad enough overview of the challenges encountered in the actual regulatory processes. Throughout the chapter we link the insights offered by this practice to those derived from the earlier theoretical discussions.

---

[1] See for instance, Fernandez (2019) for a harsh criticism of the use of the cost of capital concept in the practice of regulation.

[2] For more details in the context of transport and utilities regulation see, for instance, Alexander et al. (2000), Beecher and Kihm (2016), Morin (1994), Villadsen et al. (2017) or Wright et al. (2018).

7.1   A Bit of Intuition on Business Finance Practice to Begin With

7.1.1   The Big Picture

In any activity, including regulated activities, the financial (or fiscal) viability of cost, production and pricing decisions is an essential dimension to quantify. In the design of regulation, it is also one of the main drivers of the participation constraint, if not the main one. To assess viability, regulators rely on detailed financial models allowing a fairly precise comparison of costs and revenue.[3] The costs C_t that are accounted for are those typically recorded by standard cost accounting practice, eventually adjusted to meet the efficiency requirements imposed by the regulator. They include operational costs ($OPEX_t$), new investments ($CAPEX_t$) and the depreciation/amortization of assets used in the activity (AM_t):

$$C_t = OPEX_t + CAPEX_t + AM_t \tag{7.1}$$

In these financial models, revenue R_t boils down to the product of the volume of sales (q_t) and of the average price allowed by the regulator (p_t):[4]

$$R_t = q_t.p_t \tag{7.2}$$

Let's consider the case in which the regulator takes a forward-looking perspective on the business since this is now the approach adopted by most regulators.[5] If the value of the assets (K) is known, if this information is tracked on a cash basis rather than an accrual (accounting) basis, and if this is done in net present value (NPV) terms over a specific price review period T, the rate of return on the capital K can then easily be inferred from Equation (7.3):[6]

---

[3] For an example, see www.ipart.nsw.gov.au/Home/Industries/Special-Reviews/Regulatory-policy/IPART-cost-building-block-and-pricing-model, where the New South Wales Independent Pricing & Regulatory Tribunal (IPART) presents a simplified but quite detailed Excel version of models used to set regulated prices.

[4] In this simple version of the model, we assume that the firm receives no subsidies. The modelling process can easily be adjusted to account for subsidies when this is relevant in a specific country or sector. In that case, the modelling needs to distinguish between gross revenue and revenue net of subsidies.

[5] The alternative is to look at past costs and allow firms to recover these costs. But in a world in which financing investments is quite important in regulatory decisions, it is common for equity investors and lenders to assess the extent to which pricing will ensure that future OPEX and CAPEX will be recovered. This is one of the most common themes of discussions in project financing, for instance. This explains why considering forward-looking costs and revenues is the preferred approach in modern regulatory debates.

[6] To decide on T, the regulator needs to justify the beginning and the end point of the evaluation period. The beginning point of the stream of costs and revenue estimates should be the year in which the regulatory decision begins to have an effect. The end point is usually decided to allow the regulator to account for the expected life of the main assets used in the regulated activity. These estimates are usually reviewed in the next three to six years and updated as needed when significant events that can influence costs, revenue or financial conditions take place (e.g. an exchange rate crisis or a significant increase in the price of a major input).

$$NPV \text{ of total net cash flows} = \sum_{t=1}^{T} \frac{R_t - C_t}{(1+d)^t} = K \times r \qquad (7.3)$$

where d reflects the discount rate adopted for the computation of NPVs in regulatory decisions and capital K is the value of the capital stock or assets used in the production activity. This is essentially what is covered by the value of the regulatory asset base (RAB) usually discussed in regulatory practice.

The *rate of return* is thus simply the ratio of the *NPV of cash flows* to the value of K (= RAB):[7]

$$r = NPV \text{ of total net cash flows}/K \qquad (7.4)$$

This K is assessed as the sum of the value of total debt used to finance the activity (D) and the equity allocated to finance the activity (E), i.e.

$$K = D + E \qquad (7.5)$$

The equation does not say anything about the ownership of debt and equity. Both could be public or private. The main difference is that, when the financing sources are private and when the financial returns are insufficient, the capital eventually gets reallocated to more profitable activities. When the financing sources are mostly public, as in the case of many state-owned enterprises, the 'return gap' is often compensated by subsidies (or by a rationing of services) while this is less systematic when the capital is private. These fiscal effects are part of the assessment of the overall financial viability of the activities in the detailed modelling conducted by regulators.

The combination of Equations (7.1)–(7.5) provides a simple yet relevant insight into the context of regulation. Most importantly, they imply that the ideal allowed rate of return is simply the cost of capital (i.e. how much it costs to compensate lenders, D, and investors, E). The precise value of this cost of capital is central to the interactions between regulated firms and regulators. Indeed, if the rate of return derived from Equation (7.4) does not cover the cost of K, it means that the net cash flow allowed by regulators, based on the sales forecast, is too low for the costs incurred. It is likely that the firm will then be reluctant to make the necessary investments or even to continue the regulated activity in some cases, notably if there is no scope to compensate through subsidies. In other words, the participation constraint is likely to be binding. If the derived rate of return is higher than the cost of K, it means that profits are larger than needed to convince the firm to stay in business. The net cash flow generated by the activity produces a rent paid by consumers (or taxpayers if unnecessary subsidies are involved).

Formally, if the cost of capital is r_k, the rule of thumb to be followed to assess the financial viability of the business and hence to guide regulatory decisions, is as simple as

$$r \geq r_k \qquad (7.6)$$

---

[7] K is usually the symbol used in theoretical papers on regulation, while RAB reflects the terminology used in the practice of regulation. The RAB is always considered in monetary terms, while the K sometimes reflects the physical value of capital.

To be 'just and reasonable', the regulator needs to try to be as close as possible to $r = r_k$ when: (i) it decides on the allowed average price (which drives R_t in Equations 7.2 and 7.3) and (ii) it assesses the efficiency of costs and the timing of investment decisions. When this is the case, the resulting allowed rate of return guarantees the financial viability of the business as well as its creditworthiness to be able to finance future investment needs. At the same time, it protects consumers from the risks of abuse in pricing by the service provider to achieve a higher r_k than the rate of return required to ensure financial viability.

This very synthetic presentation of the basic financial equation commonly used in regulatory processes provides a number of early insights to keep in mind when assessing regulatory decisions. First, it allows the computation of the order of magnitude of the return the investors can expect to obtain in a regulated industry for a given asset value and cash-flow level. This estimation is useful whether the owners and lenders are public or private since both managers should be accountable for the returns on the resources allocated to the business, whether these resources are public or private. Second, it shows that, for a given cost of capital r_k, the main interactions between the regulated firms and the regulator will focus on detailed components of the cash flows to ensure that the allowed rate of return is sufficient or not excessive. The relevant data is relatively easy to obtain since, for most firms, the cash-flow data is produced routinely to manage the operational side of the business, based on assumptions about the allowed average price or the current average prices.

If the initial estimation of the allowed rate of return is below the level that maintains the equality in Equation (7.4), there will be a discussion on the specific sources of cash flows to adjust. This always includes a detailed evaluation of cost levels and timing. Indeed, in practice, the revenue side is often too politically sensitive to allow a significant margin for change. The negotiation between the firm and the regulator is more often than not about whether to cut or delay expenditures to match costs and revenue to produce the desirable rate of return. In the opposite situation, if the initial estimation of the allowed return is excessive, the allowed cash flow needs to be reduced. For a given demand level, Equation (7.3) shows that this can be done by cutting the average price or by speeding up investments for instance. Both are politically attractive.

7.1.2   The Details

Now that the basic financial management ingredients of regulatory decisions have been identified, it is useful to try to dig into the details that lead to a fair rate of return. This usually starts with a detailed identification and audit of the cost and revenue drivers in the accounting and financial reports.[8] The precision with which the cash-

---

[8] Keep in mind that this discussion is about regulated costs. Getting access to the right data can be complex. This is because many regulated firms are involved in both regulated and unregulated activities. Ideally, the two types of activities need to be unbundled via complex regulatory accounting rules that distinguish the cost and revenue of the two types of activities. None of these rules is totally objective, and so no assessment of returns will be precise (e.g. Rodriguez-Pardina et al. 2008). Getting it wrong implies that there is margin for spill-overs from the unregulated to the regulated side of business.

flow sources can be analysed depends on the reporting standards adopted by a country or a sector.[9] When these standards are good, they produce most of the necessary data and it is relatively easy to close the data gaps from minor additional more targeted audits. When the data is unreliable, regulators need to look into alternatives to end up with a quantitative evaluation of all the key variables, if the capture of the regulatory process by the regulated firm is to be avoided. The level of detail needed can be schematized as follows.

Costs, C_t. The values of OPEX and CAPEX[10] during year t are relatively easy to obtain from standard sources or with assessments of these values based on best practice.[11] They are also easy to adjust to account for the efficiency requirements imposed by the regulators.[12] In contrast, the valuation of the depreciation of the assets is often trickier. Conceptually, depreciation is simply computed as the difference between the initial investment K_0 (the asset value at the beginning of the period) and the final asset value K_T, assessed at the end of the regulation period. In practice, the specific value depends on the valuation approach adopted by the regulator at the beginning of the regulatory period. It can be based on replacement value, market value or other more complex approaches.[13]

The sum of the cost components to be accounted for during a specific regulatory period (T) is then:

$$\sum_{t=1}^{T} \frac{C_t}{(1+d)^t} = \sum_{t=1}^{T} \frac{OPEX_t + CAPEX_t}{(1+d)^t} + K_0 - \frac{K_T}{(1+d)^T} \tag{7.7}$$

This cost equation provides a simple, relevant, quantitative perspective on the revenue required by the regulated firm. From the firm's perspective, it sets the lower bound for this required revenue. From a regulator's perspective, it identifies all the variables to audit or benchmark to ensure that the firm is not misleading the evaluation process. But it imposes a new challenge for the regulators. Indeed, it highlights the need to have a view on the discount rate, as will be discussed in detail in the next section.

The NPV of revenue, $\sum_{t=1}^{T} R_t/(1+d)^t$. This computation is often more complex because only part of the data can be collected from standard accounting and financial

---

[9] Data requirements are usually specified in detailed regulatory accounting guidelines as discussed in Groom et al. (2008).

[10] OPEX and CAPEX are net of any subsidy provided to the firm.

[11] When expenditures are based on a bottom-up approach, the individual cost items used are those recorded by the firm in its accounting books. When expenditures are based on best practice, they can be validated through simple external comparators or more complex yardstick comparison which can be used to assess efficiency costs.

[12] This can be done either by using the authorized cost only or by adding a correction factor accounting for the efficiency gains expected and their timing.

[13] The value of existing assets is usually based on historical costs, replacement costs or current value or value in use, which usually reflects the net present value of future net cash flows expected from the business. In practice, picking the right valuation can be particularly challenging for industries with long-lived assets in which technology evolves fast. When technology changes fast, the market value of assets can be quite different from their historical accounting value.

sources and it thus leaves some more margin for subjective evaluations. The volume of sales is not always available with sufficient precision and has to be estimated.[14] The forecast is derived from a formal, usually econometric, estimation driven mainly by: (i) the income of potential users of the service (including the risks of unemployment, for instance); (ii) prices (more precisely, users' willingness to pay); (iii) service quality and (iv) the alternatives available to users. If any of these factors changes for some reason, the volume of sales or demand estimated will over- or underestimate the market size, i.e. q_t in Equation (7.2). This can have a significant impact on the final regulatory decisions since demand drives the optimal size in businesses in which scale economies matter to costs. Inflating demand will lead to underestimating average costs and vice versa, and this will eventually be reflected in the regulated prices and returns.[15]

The average price, p_t. This is even more complex to deal with as it is a weighted average of the prices charged to the various uses and users of the service. The weights are supposed to be based on the forecast of the specific volumes of sales to each group of uses and users. This is rendered more difficult by the fact that the average price is often de facto controlled by the regulator to ensure the fairness of returns. Reaching an agreement implies an iterative process between firms and regulators. We will discuss this process as part of the presentation of the financial modelling of the regulated activity at the end of the chapter, when we explain how the average price and the rate of return interact.

Once the costs and the revenue side are well audited by the regulator, it is usually convenient to insert the cost and revenue equations into a spreadsheet such as Excel. Relying on such a basic data-processing tool makes it easy to simulate the effects of policy, management or financing decisions. For instance, if an operator stops maintaining its assets, this means that the NPV of $OPEX_t$ is lower than it should be. If costs are lower, the allowed revenue should also be lower than if maintenance had been as scheduled initially. For a given demand level, this means that the average price allowed to the regulated company should be lower if maintenance is cut. Since the allowed revenue and costs are interactive, it is easy to get an estimation of the drop in price that accounts for the drop in cost from a simple simulation in the Excel spreadsheet of Equation (7.7).[16] Similarly, if a new technology emerges or if the policymakers decide to impose changes in quality standards (i.e. the adoption of cleaner technologies), the residual asset value K_T will be damaged, the OPEX are likely to be different and both will impact on the required revenue. Equation (7.7) also

---

[14] The estimation and forecast of the volume of sales (i.e. physical demand) is an industry in itself for which many consulting firms have developed very profitable expertise.

[15] For a discussion on demand forecast inaccuracies in the transport sector, see, for instance, Skou Nicolaisen and Driscoll (2014).

[16] This is easily seen by playing with the model www.ipart.nsw.gov.au/Home/Industries/Special-Reviews/ Regulatory-policy/IPART-cost-building-block-and-pricing-model produced by the New South Wales Independent Pricing & Regulatory Tribunal (IPART).

helps quantify this impact. More generally, whenever markets evolve for any reason, the revision of costs and revenue can be measured to inform regulatory decisions and updates. Under cost-plus and rate-of-return regulation, this tends to be done quite frequently, often annually. Under other regulatory regimes, the resetting is done every three to six years depending on the sector and country.

In practice, the financial regulatory models based on the basic equations just introduced tend to be quite detailed. Many regulators (but not all) make these models transparent to ensure the intelligibility of their decisions and increase the accountability of all stakeholders.[17] This transparency is also highly effective in reducing information asymmetry and hence improving the odds of efficient, fair and sustainable regulatory decisions.

7.2   What about the Discount Rate?

The discount rate is where the links with finance theory and practice appear more explicitly. We have focused on the 'real' dimensions needed to assess the rate of return (i.e. costs and sales all estimated in constant prices to avoid distortions associated with disagreements on inflation forecasts). Since revenues and costs are spread over time, it would be wrong to simply add all of the expected revenue and costs without taking account of the timing of their materialization. How this is done influences the assessment of the required revenue over the duration of the regulatory assessment period. This is what makes the choice of the discount rate to be adopted in the NPV calculations so important. There is, however, a wide range of approaches adopted in practice, as illustrated by Box 7.1.

If firms were indifferent between getting revenue and spending now or later, adding up the annual values would be fine to assess the net revenue. But they are not indifferent. Firms usually prefer to get all the revenue as fast as possible and often try to delay or spread costs as much as they can without hurting the business. This is what the discount rate internalizes. It corrects revenues and costs for differences in timing. The further in the future the revenue and costs are expected to occur, the more they should be discounted. This is reflected by the discount factor calculated from the discount rate with the formula $(1/(1+d)^t)$ in Equations (7.3) and (7.7), where 't' measures the number of years in the future that the revenue or costs are expected to occur.

In today's regulatory practice, the discount rate is expected to reflect the 'opportunity cost of capital' as estimated by investors. This is the r_k we discussed in the context of Equation (7.6). To account for the relative importance of the two financing sources (debt D and equity E), this cost of capital is computed as a weighted average of the cost of D (r_d) and the cost of E (r_e) where the weights reflect the shares of debt

---

[17] For instance, see www.ofwat.gov.uk/regulated-companies/price-review/2019-price-review/data-tables-models/, which provides all the details on the approach adopted by the water regulator in England.

> **Box 7.1** Examples of Approaches to Discounting Cash Flows Used around the World for Public Policies
>
> There are multiple measures of the discount rate around the world. In the United Kingdom, it is 3.5% for projects up to thirty years and then drops progressively to 1%.[18] In France, it also varies with the duration of the projects. It is 4% up to thirty years, decreasing to 2% beyond thirty years. A risk premium, specific to each project, is added according to its macroeconomic sensitivity and systemic risk; when the macroeconomic risk is unknown, the recommended rate in France is 4.5%.[19] In Australia, the discount rate used in project analysis varies with the type of sector and region. Until recently, it was 4% for goods and services in traditional core public service delivery areas, for which the benefits are hard to assess in monetary terms (e.g. education, public health and justice). It is 7% for most infrastructures as the benefits tend to be easier to assess. For other projects, the decisions are on a case-by-case basis. But Australians have been debating the choice of the discount rate, partially as a result of the evolution of financial markets conditions.[20] In the United States, it varies with the extent to which a regulatory decision impacts on the consumption decisions. When it directly affects private consumption (e.g. through higher consumer prices for goods and services), the discount rate is 3%.[21] Otherwise, it is 7%.[22]
>
> Roughly speaking, these differences reflect the two main approaches to estimating the discount rate used in policy decisions. The first main approach adopted in public policy practice comes from the financial economics literature. It takes a private investor's viewpoint rather than society's. In this perspective, the discount rate should reflect the 'social opportunity cost of capital'. The alternative approach comes from the public economics literature and focuses on the welfare of all stakeholders in society, current and future. It is quite common in the conduct of purely public project evaluations. It sets the discount rate at the value at which the population assesses the degree of preferences for current consumption over future consumption.[23] This is known as the 'social rate of time preference'. There are many disagreements on how to assess it, but formal estimations have long ranged between 1% and 4%. The countries adopting this approach tend to rely on low discount rates in the evaluation of their public policies returns.

---

[18] See www.gov.uk/government/publications/green-book-supplementary-guidance-discounting
[19] See www.strategie.gouv.fr/sites/strategie.gouv.fr/files/atoms/files/10_fs_discount_rate_in_project_analysis.pdf
[20] See www.aph.gov.au/About_Parliament/Parliamentary_Departments/Parliamentary_Library/FlagPost/2018/October/Discount-rates
[21] See https://obamawhitehouse.archives.gov/administration/eop/cea/factsheets-reports   [22] See ibid.
[23] With the increase in environmental concerns, many authors have argued for an approach accounting also for the elasticity of the marginal utility of consumption with respect to income and the expected growth rate of consumption with respect to income as suggested by Ramsey (1928). This tends to lower the discount rate to be adopted.

Table 7.1 Average value of the key variables defining the r_k for the Damodaran representative sample of firms

	WACC = r_k (%)	r_e (%)	r_d (%)	Leverage (D/D+E) (%)
Environmental and waste services	8.2	9.8	4.6	25.2
Green and renewable energy	7.4	12.4	5.4	59.4
Power	4.5	5.9	3.6	44.3
Telecom (wireless)	6.5	10.2	4.6	53.7
Telecom services	6.9	9.9	4.6	47.1
Transportation	7.6	9.5	4.2	29.8
Transportation (railroads)	14.3	17.4	3.6	21.2
Utility (general)	3.6	4.3	3.6	41.6
Water utilities	4.5	5.2	3.6	30.1
Total market	**7.0**	**9.4**	**4.6**	**40.0**
Total market (without financials)	**8.2**	**9.9**	**4.6**	**25.7**

Source: www.stern.nyu.edu/~adamodar/New_Home_Page/data.html (as at 20 December 2019). For more details see Damodaran (2020).

and equity in total capital K.[24] This weighted average is also known as the weighted average cost of capital or WACC. Formally, it is expressed as:

$$r_k = WACC = \frac{r_d(1 - t_x)D + r_e E}{D + E} \tag{7.8}$$

where t_x is the corporate tax rate (indeed interest on debt is tax-deductible).[25]

To provide a sense of the order of magnitude of the variables discussed so far, Table 7.1 presents the estimations of their average value for 2019 for a sample of firms from sectors usually subject to some form of regulation. They are produced by A. Damodaran on his widely quoted website. They assume a risk-free rate of 2.7% and a risk premium for equity of 5.96%. These are based on a representative global cross-sectoral sample of 7,209 firms (including 415 in infrastructure sectors).

For this large sample, the r_e ranges from as little as 4.3% for general utilities firms to 17.4% for railroad companies for a market average of 9.4%. The dispersion of the r_d is more limited since it spreads from only 3.6% (for a large number of sectors) to 5.43% for green and renewable energy firms for a market average of 4.6%. The leverage ranges from 21.2% for railroads to almost 60% for green and renewable

[24] Retained earnings are a third financing option. This is ignored here for simplicity.
[25] This takes the financing structure (i.e. the ratio of D to E) as given. If left unregulated, the optimal financing structure is actually endogenous. The regulated firm will adjust a number of tax, regulatory and other legal dimensions that may influence the relative cost of debt and equity. A discussion of this endogeneity goes beyond the principles we want to highlight in this chapter, but the issue is quite important to keep in mind.

energy firms for a market average of 40% and a much lower average of 25.7% when financial firms are excluded.

While the Damodaran data is useful as a benchmark, it is only indicative. Each regulator needs to make a decision on each of the variables included in Equation (7.8). These are discussed with the regulated firms and this is one of the reasons why regulatory processes include often quite heated negotiations between firms and regulators. The technical debates have recently been reviewed in a paper on the WACC in regulated industries by Wright et al. (2018). The next sections summarize the main challenges associated with the assessment of each of the variables defining the WACC. The discussion also shows the extent to which there is margin for discretion as none of the measures is fool-proof.

7.3   How to Assess the Cost of Equity

The cost of equity, r_e, used in Equation (7.8) may be the variable subject to the most intensive debates in regulatory processes. Among the various approaches suggested by finance theory to assess the cost of equity r_e (i.e. the return expected by investors), regulators have tended to focus on three: (i) the capital asset pricing model (CAPM); (ii) the discounted cash-flow model (DCF), also known as the Gordon dividend growth model and (iii) the risk premium model (RPM).[26]

In their most basic forms, they can be synthesized as follows. In the CAPM model, r_e is the sum of a risk-free rate, r_f, and a market premium adjusted to account for the sector- or firm-specific risk. In the DCF model, r_e is the sum of the dividend yield and its growth rate. Finally, in the basic risk premium model, r_e is simply the sum of the interest rate on bonds (r_d) and an equity-specific risk premium which can be negotiated or estimated (e.g. it can be inferred from a cross-section of allowed returns or from realized accounting returns).

Since the CAPM model is the most common in regulatory discussions outside of the United States but is also quite popular in the American regulatory tradition, we'll focus on this one only. But it may be useful to go through the brief discussion of the DCF approach in Box 7.2 since this approach is popular in the United States among national and state regulators. Elsewhere, it is sometimes considered as a complement to the CAPM model (notably in the energy sector). One of its main advantages is that it is less data-intensive than the CAPM but it raises many issues, as discussed in Box 7.2. The RPM is mentioned here because it can be useful in countries in which capital markets are still small. It is seldom used in regulation outside of this context.

One of the advantages of the use of the CAPM approach in actual regulatory discussions is that it relies on an explicit link between investment and risks in its assessment of one of the key components of the cost of capital. It usually beats most of the alternatives available to assess the cost of equity and the required return on equity

---

[26] Other approaches often discussed or considered include the Fama–French three-factor model and arbitrage pricing model.

Box 7.2 Assessing the Cost of Equity with the Dividend Growth Model

The model is also known as the Gordon dividend growth model.[27] In its most basic form, it assesses the value of a stock or share simply as the present value of future dividends:

$$p_0 = \frac{Div_1}{\tilde{r}_e - gr} = \frac{Div_0(1 + gr)}{\tilde{r}_e - gr}$$

where p_0 is the current price of the common stock/share, Div_0 is the current dividend, Div_1 is the expected dividend, $\tilde{r}_e$ is the return required by equity investors, and gr is the expected dividend growth rate. In practice, $\tilde{r}_e$ is also the cost of equity: $\tilde{r}_e = r_e$. Rearranging terms and replacing $\tilde{r}_e$ with r_e yields:

$$r_e = \frac{Div_0(1 + gr)}{p_0} + gr$$

The approach's simplicity stems from the fact that the cost of equity can be estimated from a directly observable value for p_0, an observed or estimated value for Div_0 and gr. Both Div_0 and gr can be estimated and simulated based on the evidence available from similar firms in other countries or handling similar projects.[28]

The fact that a model is simple does not mean it is without problems. Damodaran (2020) notes that dividend growth may not match growth in earnings. Moreover, the expected growth rate of a firm may not converge with that of the economy over the long run. If the regulated firm is expected to grow faster than the economy, on average, a solution is offered by the two-stage dividend growth model. This other model allows for a non-constant growth rate for a short period of time, followed by a stable growth phase. This model is used by the US national energy regulator (the FERC), for instance.

---

in regulated industries because it forces the regulators to look into risks in quite a systematic way. This is a significant advantage in an environment in which information asymmetries are the norm.

Conceptually, the CAPM starts from the assumption that investors pick the portfolio with the lowest variance consistent with the level of expected return on equity

---

[27] This model dominated regulatory decisions in the United States and Canada in the late 1960s and early 1970s.

[28] For instance, D_0 can be calculated as the initial market value of the FTSE All-Share index multiplied by the observed 'cash yield', where the cash yield is made up of (i) a dividend yield; and (ii) a buy-back yield. The dividend yield is the value of periodic cash dividends received by equity holder. Buy-backs are the company's repurchases of equity from investors as an alternative form of cash return for investors which is also measured annually by the FTSE index.

(i.e. 'mean-variance' efficient portfolios). Formally, the resulting return on equity is a weighted average of the risk-free rate (r_f) and the market return (r_m):

$$r_e = \beta_{ej}\, r_m + \left(1 - \beta_{ej}\right)r_f \tag{7.9a}$$

Usually, to highlight the relevant market risks defined as the difference between the market rate and the risk-free rate, this is expressed as follows:

$$r_e = r_f + \beta_{ej}\left(r_m - r_f\right) \tag{7.9b}$$

where r_f is the risk-free rate, $\left(r_m - r_f\right)$ defines the market risk premium and β_{ej}, known as the 'equity β', is a measure of non-diversifiable risk of the equity (i.e. the regulated firm) defined as:

$$\beta_{ej} = \sigma_{jm}/\sigma_m^2 \tag{7.10}$$

where σ_{jm} is the covariance between the yield of share for firm j and the general market return, σ_m^2 is the variance of the market's return and β_{ej} is the resulting systemic risk of share for firm j with respect to the total market. In other words, the expected (required) rate of return for the asset is proportional to its covariance with the market.

If the return on j is uncorrelated with the market, β_{ej}'s value is 0 and the cost of equity is the same as the risk-free rate. If the regulated business is as risky as the market, $\beta_{ej} = 1$. If its value is greater than 1, this means that the business is riskier than the market. This is the case for transport stocks, for instance. They tend to have high βs because they are much more sensitive to changes in market conditions such as the degree of intermodal competition. If the equity β is less than 1, the business or the project is less risky than the market. This is the case for many regulated utilities. Their β is usually expected to be lower than 1 because their stocks tend to move more slowly than market averages. Table 7.2 reports the β values estimated by Damodaran in his database for the sectors we are interested in. It confirms that β has a low value for power, water and utilities and a value greater than 1 for most of the other sectors.

The β_e are generally stable for firms that stay in the same industry. However, a firm's β can change because of new product lines, new technologies, deregulation or re-regulation, including of the allowed financial leverage or simply because of the relative importance of fixed and variable costs. For instance, higher fixed costs in relation to variable costs (quite common in regulated infrastructure industries) magnify the effect of business cycles on β.

When the stability assumption is credible, a common, easy way of estimating the β of the firm or sector j is through a simple linear regression:

$$r_j = a + \beta_{ej}r_M + u \tag{7.11}$$

where r_j is the return for company or sector j, r_M is the average market return, a is the intercept of the regression, u is the error term and β_{ej} is the measure we are looking for. The coefficient of determination R^2 of the regression provides an estimate of the proportion of the risk (variance) of a firm that can be attributed to market risk and $(1 - R^2)$ estimates the share that can be attributed to firm-specific risk.

Table 7.2 Damodaran's estimation of the equity βs for his large representative sample of firms

Sector name	β
Environmental and waste services	1.19
Green and renewable energy	1.62
Power	0.54
Telecom (wireless)	1.26
Telecom equipment	1.09
Telecom services	1.22
Transportation	1.14
Transportation (railroads)	2.47
Trucking	1.22
Utility (general)	0.27
Utility (water)	0.42
Total market	**1.12**
Total market (without financials)	**1.21**

Source: www.stern.nyu.edu/~adamodar/New_Home_Page/data.html (as at 20 December 2019).

Additional control variables are often needed to control for the various sources of instability in βs. These controls are also often needed when working in countries or sectors undergoing regulatory or other economic or political-structural changes. Although general practitioners tend to use daily data for five years of historical data to estimate β values, there is quite a lot of margin on this dimension. For instance, recent regulatory decisions in the United Kingdom have favoured daily data from a single year. Many regulatory processes are refining the estimation approach since the basic regression assumes a constant β_{ej} estimate which is not appropriate given the time-varying nature of the true β_{ej}.

When this approach is not an option, for instance because the regulated firm is not quoted on the stock market, values from comparators are used.[29] These comparators may be firm-specific (including estimates from another quoted firm in the same industry or country) or industry-specific (the industry's β is considered a proxy). The interpretation of the β can be challenging because it reflects many types of risks.

Equity βs reflect the fundamental business risk faced by a firm. It normally also reflects its financial risk but how well this last risk is reflected depends on the capital structure. For example, a company with a higher leverage has greater volatility in returns to equity holders. This is because debt holders have a prior claim on cashflows. • This is accounted for by the equity β. In that case, it may be useful to correct for differences in financial risk premia across comparators resulting from differences in financial structure across these firms. This effect can be addressed by working with the

[29] Some are not listed simply because they are owned by the government but in other cases, including in many developing countries, it is because there is no local stock market and the firms are part of the international activities of larger groups.

Table 7.3 Equity versus asset β estimates for regulated public services in the United Kingdom

Sector	Year	Equity β	Asset β
Airports	2014	1.10–1.13	0.50–0.56
Electricity distribution and transmission	2017–18	0.93	0.93
Rail network	2013	0.95	0.37
Telecoms	2018	0.95	0.65
Water and sanitation	2018	0.76–0.78	0.31–0.37

Source: UK Regulators' websites consulted in June 2019.

asset β (also known as the levered β since it accounts for both debt and equity) rather than the equity (or unlevered) β:

$$\beta_a = \frac{\beta_d(1 - t_x)D + \beta_e E}{(1 - t_x)D + E} \tag{7.12}$$

where $(1 - t_x)D + E$ is the after-tax value of the company, D is the interest-bearing debt, E is the market value of equity, t_x is the marginal (corporate) tax rate[30] and β_a is the company's risk (without considering the financial effect). If the risk of debt, β_d, is zero, the asset risk, or the risk of the shares without leverage, becomes:

$$\beta_a = \frac{\beta_e}{1 + (1 - t_x)\dfrac{D}{E}} \tag{7.13}$$

When compared to an equity/unlevered β, an asset/levered β has a value closer to zero since it has less volatility due to the differences in the tax advantages of debt. Table 7.3 provides a snapshot of the asset and equity βs for regulated industries in the United Kingdom.

Note that in some contexts, the equity β, β_{ej}, can be negative if $\sigma_{jm} < 0$. This is because the business performs well (poorly) when everything else does poorly (well). When this is the case, the expected return is lower than the risk-free rate. The gold-mining industry is a good illustration and this is explained by the fact that gold is a 'refuge' asset in times of crisis. In regulated industries, the negative correlation can be observed when concerns (e.g. environmental or safety) are leading some firms relying on outdated technologies to do worse than suggested by an otherwise reasonable global market perspective. This is what happens to some of the firms producing only carbon-intensive energy sources.

Note also that the categorization of risks imposed by the CAPM approach can be quite useful as it parallels the risk assessments conducted during regulatory debates or

---

[30] This approach is anchored in Modigliani and Miller (1958), who defined the value of a levered firm (that is, *Debt* + *Equity*) as the value of the firm unlevered, i.e. the value of the firm without any debt plus the present value of the tax shields due to debt financing, assuming perpetual debt and ignoring any bankruptcy or distress costs accompanying debt financing.

investment project preparations.[31] A risk may be (i) unrelated to the specific regulated activity and linked instead to changes at the global financial market level (e.g. the uncertainty in stock markets linked to the tensions between the United States and China under the Trump administration) or (ii) specific to the regulated activity (e.g. risks associated with the price of sector-specific inputs). This is relevant to the returns to be allowed by the regulator. For instance, an equity investor should not expect any additional return linked to the specific risk, since it can protect itself by adequately diversifying its portfolio. The investor can, however, claim compensation, or an expected return, for taking on risks linked to the sector. Investing in electricity in a given country can be riskier than investing in commercial real estate simply because regulation is less predictable in one sector than in the other.

7.4 What about the Measurement of the Other Key Components of the WACC?

Most of the other key components are easier to deal with in principle. Although, as the discussion will show, each component leaves significant room for negotiation between a regulator and a regulated firm. We focus on the risk-free rate (r_f), the equity risk premium $(r_{e,prem} = r_m - r_f)$ needed to assess the cost of equity (r_e), the cost of debt (r_d), the risk premium ($r_{d,prem}$) needed to assess the cost of debt contracted by the regulated firm, the leverage and, finally, the tax rate to be considered. Whenever necessary, we highlight how the choice of a specific measure can distort the assessment of the desirable allowed rate of return.

The data sources may vary across sectors and countries, but there are usually enough to be able to come up with a proxy as needed, at least for the most common variables. The following discussion summarizes these sources and refers to the choices made by some of the regulators most often used as references in regulatory practice.[32] In the process, it highlights the fact that the measurement challenge is often more complex in developing and emerging economies than in OECD countries.

The risk-free rate. In developed economies, the risk-free rate r_f is usually approximated by the return on tax-free government bonds. There is no agreement on what the term of the tax-free bond should be, however. For example, the Dutch energy regulator relies on the three-year average yield of ten-year Dutch and German government bonds. The English water regulator uses the average of the normal ten-year British government bonds and the average of real yields obtained from nominal and index-linked bonds at the twenty-year horizon. In developing countries, the proxy is typically a US, UK or French government bond.

---

[31] Besides the usual risks associated with the macroeconomic context in which a firm is operating, the risks to cash flows faced by a firm may be project-specific or linked to an industry-specific competitive context. They may also be associated with the fact that the firm is exposed to fluctuations in the exchange rate for some of its costs and some of its revenue.

[32] This is clearly not a substitute to the detailed discussion available from textbooks specializing in valuation and investment finance.

The choice of the time horizon for the chosen bond rate is not an innocent question. Longer-term bonds have higher returns, and this will affect the estimated cost of capital. The case for using a long-term bond centres on the long life of the assets associated with most public service commitments. Some argue for short-term bonds as they match better the life of the risk-free asset with the length of the price control period (three to six years). There are arguments for both options. Whatever choice is made in the end, it should be consistent across firms and across time.

The cost of debt. This is the future cost faced by a regulated firm funding part of its operations from lenders and creditors. The return they require can be estimated in three main ways. First, it can be extrapolated from the equivalent cost of new debt issued by comparable regulated companies or for the same company operating in other markets. This is a direct estimation using market yields. Second, it can be approximated by adding an expected, debt-specific risk premium $r_{d,prem}$ to the risk-free rate based on a survey of professional opinions in the field:

$$r_d = r_f + r_{d,prem} \tag{7.14}$$

The risk premium is the additional compensation demanded by creditors, since the probability of default is higher than that implicit in the risk-free rate. This method has been traditionally used in the United Kingdom and France. Third, the cost of debt can be derived from the historical embedded cost of debt recorded by the regulated firm or a sample of firms, a method referred to as a portfolio approach or trailing average.

In practice, regulators often work with a range of estimations since each of the three methods involves various assumptions that need to be internalized as part of the sensitivity analysis. However, when possible, the third method is avoided because it is backward-looking and does not reflect the market conditions the operator is facing. Nor does it provide enough incentive for the regulated firm to cut financing costs. Instead, it guarantees an automatic pass-through of these costs to customers, since tariffs eventually reflect the cost of capital, including the cost of debt.[33]

The equity risk premium. Within the CAPM, the risk premium boils down to the difference between the return on a diversified portfolio and the risk-free asset: $r_{e,prem} = r_m - r_f$. A specific way of deriving this difference is to rely on long-term historical data of the differential return on shares against long-term government bonds in a sample of comparable markets. For example, European regulators often rely on comparison with neighbouring European markets.

---

[33] The data challenge does not stop here, however. For instance, the discussion has so far ignored two issues that may be of particular interest to developing and emerging economies and to smaller or more fragile firms in OECD countries. The first issue is the relevance of the term structure of the corporate debt to consider. Short term is normally not included in the cost of corporate debt computation. However, when firms are unable to access medium- to long-term debt and renewable short-term debt is the only debt available, it has to be included in the debt computation. A second issue is the choice of comparators when there are no firm-specific bonds. There are two main options. The debt premium can be based on data from a similar regulated environment. Alternatively, it can be based on data from similar firms with a similar credit rating. These two approaches may also be combined.

The measurement challenge does not stop here. When comparing the risk-free asset and the relevant market index, the regulator needs to make a few decisions which will impact the final assessment of the cost of capital and hence the allowed rate of return. The first may be to decide whether to look forward or back. Looking back (that is, the historical approach) is the most common: the expected returns are approximated using the average of past realized returns. But how far back should the analysis go? One element to consider is the relative stability of the market in which the regulated firm is operating. The more unstable the market, the longer the time period needed for analysis. The forward-looking approach is the alternative when there is no historical data or when data is not reliable. In this case, the DCF model presented in Box 7.2 is often the way to go since it does not require much data and most of it can be estimated from exchanges with the regulated firm. An alternative is to rely on surveys of investors, portfolio managers and other experts. The various approaches can also be used as robustness checks to cross-validate the results.

A third concern is the need to be able to deal with common specific data issues. This itself raises a number of questions. First is how to define the set of firms to include in the market portfolio. Most of the time, it is relatively easy for regulators in developed economies to come up with a representative portfolio. For developing countries, this is harder to put together; regulatory estimations tend to be based on US or UK data, just as in the case of bonds. This is clearly not an ideal option, but it is often the only one. The second major question is whether the historical mean should be arithmetic or geometric.[34] If future returns are highly uncertain but need to be assessed anyway, an arithmetic average offers an unbiased forecast of the value of a repeated number of observations of a random variable. If future returns cannot be assessed and there is a sense that there is a serial correlation of returns over time, a geometric average has the advantage of implying a reversion to the mean and may be more reliable.[35] The main concern with the geometric average is that it is always lower than the arithmetic average, and this difference is a common source of conflict between regulators and firms.

Leverage. This is the ratio $D/(D+E)$, which is usually relatively easy to obtain from multiple sources, starting with the firm's accounting books. In theory, the higher the leverage, the lower should be the cost of capital. This is because the cost of equity is normally higher than the cost of debt since equity is considered riskier. However, this decreasing relation between the leverage and the cost of capital does not seem warranted in regulated industries, as seen from the evidence summarized in Box 7.3. This is an important topic of discussion in regulated industries since leverage has been steadily increasing in the regulated sector. The potentially strong effects of capital structures on the cost of capital, and hence on the authorized rate of return, have led some regulators to rely on an assumed, or notional, leverage rather than an actual one. For instance, regulators in the United Kingdom, the Netherlands and Belgium's

---

[34] $\overline{x_a} = \frac{1}{n}\sum_{i=1}^{n} x_i$ is the expression for the arithmetic mean, while $\overline{x_g} = \sqrt[n]{x_1 x_2 \ldots x_n}$ is the equivalent expression for the geometric mean.

[35] The reversal to the mean implies that a stock price tends to move to the average price over time.

Box 7.3 How Leverage (i.e. Gearing in the UK Terminology) Matters

Since the late 1970s, research in the United States suggests that regulated rates of return (and prices) tend to increase rather than fall with leverage in contrast to what theory predicts (e.g. Hagerman and Ratchford 1978; Ovtchinnikov 2010, 2016; Spiegel 1994; Spiegel and Spulber 1994, 1997). A possible explanation is that this effect is induced by regulators out of concern for financial distress. Regulated firms know that regulators are concerned with the risks of financial distress. This is why they are willing to allow a higher cost of capital when a firm shows strong leverage. Bortolotti et al. (2011) find similar evidence for European countries.[36]

These results have very concrete implications. For instance, once a regulated firm becomes too highly leveraged, it may no longer be able to finance its operations with debt at a reasonable cost, and the higher premiums it must pay for debt may end up offsetting the tax savings from the higher debt ratio. This is important to consider in any credit-risk assessment. The greater the reliance on debt, the farther the credit rating may slip and the greater is the likelihood of increases in the cost of capital. Ultimately, the optimal capital structure – i.e. the one that minimizes the weighted average cost of capital – is firm- and time-specific and should be assessed as such in regulatory processes.

Flemish region use a notional leverage level. This is a response to the concern that the use of the actual leverage of regulated firms to set the WACC would give an incentive to these firms to increase their leverage to abnormal levels. In general, the notional leverage is based on the average of a comparator sample, normally, the same sample used to estimate the asset β.

Taxation. Equation (7.8) shows that taxes matter to the financing decision. This is the result of the fact that debt and equity are generally not subject to the same tax treatment. In most tax systems, the cost of debt (the interest paid) is tax-deductible. This implies that debt financing is cheaper than suggested by the cost of debt, r_d, only. The tax benefit of deductibility in terms of the WACC has to be weighted by the share of debt financing of the capital of the firm (D/K where $K = D + E$). To help make this discussion of the tax relevance more transparent, it may be useful to rewrite this WACC Equation (7.8) somewhat as:

$$r_k = WACC = (1 - t_x).(D/K).r_d + (E/K).r_e \tag{7.15}$$

The 't_x' of Equation (7.15) is the top marginal tax rate paid by the regulated firm on its profits. In Belgium, for instance, for a large firm, the statutory rate was (almost) 34% until 2018. Then, $(1-t_x)$ was 0.66, which means that if the interest rate is 5%, the

---

[36] Bortolotti et al. (2011) find for their sample a greater leverage for private firms than for state-controlled firms and that this greater leverage is correlated with a higher regulated price for private firms, but not for state-controlled firms.

effective cost of debt is only 3.3%. The higher is the marginal tax rate, the lower is the effective cost of debt. The higher is the interest rate, the more attractive is the tax shield allowed by tax deductibility.

Relying on the marginal tax rate is the easy solution, but it may be misleading. This is because the tax rate that the firm will face in the future may be much lower. Many analysts prefer to rely on the effective average tax rate computed from the firm's balance sheet. The effective rate accounts for the many tax-reduction opportunities firms generally try to internalize. In Belgium again, the effective corporate tax rate paid by the largest companies has long been well below half of the statutory tax rate.

A word on inflation. Variables such as the risk-free rate are expressed in nominal terms and thus include expectations for inflation. To maintain consistency, nominal cash flows must be discounted using a nominal cost of capital, whereas real cash flows should be discounted using a cost of capital estimated in real terms. To get this real cost, regulators must account for the effects of inflation on each relevant variable. For instance, to switch from a nominal discount rate to a real rate, the following relationship is used:

$$1 + real\ rate = \frac{1 + nominal\ rate}{1 + expected\ inflation\ rate} \tag{7.16}$$

More generally, the conversion from a nominal WACC to a real one is done as follows:

$$real\ WACC = \frac{1 + nominal\ WACC}{1 + expected\ inflation\ rate} - 1 \tag{7.17}$$

A first challenge in setting up this computation is choosing the inflation index. Consumer price indices (as opposed to producer price indices) are commonly used when inflation forecasts are based on past inflation rates. But when a regulator wants to assess future inflation without reference to the past, to better align with theoretical guidelines, there are three common options: (i) relying on independent forecasts of inflation published by central banks, the European Commission, or the International Monetary Fund; (ii) relying on surveys of professional forecasters conducted at regular intervals to produce a 'market consensus' estimate of inflation expectations or (iii) approximate inflation expectations based on the difference between yields on conventional debt and yields on index-linked debt (in cases where a government relies on index-linked debt).

A final important observation is that risk perceptions are linked to the specific type of regulation adopted. For instance, a price cap imposes a higher risk on the regulated firm, as discussed in Chapter 6. Instead, under a cost-plus (or rate-of-return) regulation, the investor's risk is low, since any negative shock will be directly passed through to consumers via a change in tariffs. The differences between these two regulatory systems affect the non-diversified risk reflected in the β. Therefore, the β value tends to be higher under a price cap than under a cost-plus (Alexander et al. 1996).

7.5   How Should Regulators Compute the WACC?

The discussion on the measurement challenges shows that coming up with a WACC to be used in regulatory decisions is not as simple as theory suggests. We just saw that almost all of the variables defining the WACC (as identified from Equation 7.8) are subject to discussions. For instance, the allowed return will depend on whether the regulator relies on actual or notional debt, on the real or the nominal version, or on the term structure of bonds used to compute the cost of debt and the risk-free rate. The main decision margins are summarized in Figure 7.1.

In practice, one of the key issues on which regulators tend to disagree is the way taxes are accounted for. Some prefer to rely on the after-tax cost of capital, others rely on the before-tax cost and others yet prefer to deal with tax issues only partially. Even if the three approaches are supposed to be equivalent because all end up imposing adjustments to the measurement of cash flows, in practice they are not.

Conceptually, they simply offer different ways of computing the NPV of the tax liability. But in practice, this equivalence seldom holds as a result of the complexity of the tax systems and the endogeneity of key dimensions, such as the tariff structures and the scope for tax arbitration. This complexity increases when a regulated firm offers different services subject to different tax treatments. Ultimately, the extent to which a regulated firm (and its clients) is favoured or penalized by a specific approach ends up being unpredictable, at least as precisely as needed. Their specific computations are as follows.

The 'pre-tax WACC' is normally calculated as:

$$pre\text{-}tax\ WACC = \frac{D}{K}.r_d + \left(1 - \frac{D}{K}\right).r_e.\frac{1}{1 - t_x} \tag{7.18}$$

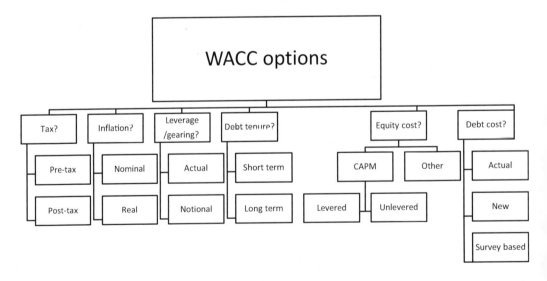

Figure 7.1 On the diversity of options to get to a WACC

where the notations are as earlier, i.e. D/K is the leverage or gearing level, r_d is the cost of debt calculated before tax, r_e is the cost of equity, normally computed after tax, and t_x is the tax adjustment factor used to convert the after-tax cost of equity to a before-tax figure. If, as is the case in most countries, interest on debt is tax-deductible, a correction factor for taxes needs to be applied to r_e only. The correction factor, $1/(1 - t_x)$, known in the literature as a 'tax wedge', ensures that the after-tax return is enough to meet the before-tax return on equity expected by investors. This tax wedge can make quite a difference. For instance, if the statutory corporate income tax for large firms is 34%, it implies a correction of 51% (since $1/(1–0.34) = 1.51$).

The vanilla WACC, one of the most common calculations of WACC used by regulators, is calculated as:

$$vanilla\ WACC = \frac{D}{K}.r_d + \left(1 - \frac{D}{K}\right).r_e \tag{7.19}$$

where the notation are the same as for Equation (7.18). It gives the rate of return on capital after corporate tax and any tax credits have been accounted for elsewhere in a firm's cash flows. One of the reasons why this version of the WACC is popular in regulation is that it avoids the need to consider whether interest payments are tax-deductible or not.[37] This avoids having to deal with some of the complexity of tax arbitration opportunities.

The fully post-tax WACC is calculated as:

$$fullypost\text{-}tax\ WACC = \frac{D}{K}.r_d.(1 - t_x) + \left(1 - \frac{D}{K}\right).r_e \tag{7.20}$$

This option is used when the regulator wants to avoid making an allowance for the tax deductibility of interest payments. This is why the approach is also known as the 'after-tax WACC'. It really means the WACC net of the debt tax shield. It builds the tax deductibility of interest payments into the cost of debt by multiplying the gross cost of debt by a correction factor representing the tax shield. This measure can differ across regulated firms if the effective tax rates on their debts differ.

There is no consensus on which approach is the best one. This is why, in most countries, the regulators end up computing the three WACC measures and discussing the optimal choice as part of the regulatory process, as illustrated in the UK case for various sectors summarized in Table 7.4. The ideal choice is contextual.[38] The main advantage of the pre-tax WACC is that it simplifies the process of price setting by addressing the issue of taxes upfront and avoids the possible risks of tax-related differentiated treatment of firms associated with the post-tax WACC. The vanilla WACC is the best choice when it is necessary to avoid the complexities resulting from the constant tax-arbitration decisions made by any firm given the opportunity to

---

[37] Note that the tax treatment of interest payments affects the capital structure. How differences in capital structure in turn affect the vanilla WACC, however, is unclear. Robustness checks are used to decide this question case by case.

[38] For a helpful discussion on the optimal choice of WACC, see OXERA (2015).

Table 7.4 Recent cost of capital decisions by British sector regulators

	Symbol or equation	Airport (Heathrow) October 2013 (%)	Gas June 2017 (%)	Electricity June 2017 (%)	Water December 2017 (%)	Telecoms March 2018 (%)
Cost of debt (pre-tax)	r_d	3.2	1.63	2.45	1.33	3.90
Risk-free rate	r_f	0.5	1.25	1.25	−0.88	2.90
Equity risk premium	$r_{e,prem}$	5.75	5.25	5.25	6.31	6.30
Equity β	β_{ej}	1.1	0.77	0.61	0.77	0.8
Asset β	β_a	0.5	0.4	0.38	0.37	0.39
Cost of equity (post-tax)	r_e	6.84	5.29	4.45	4.01	7.90
Gearing/ leverage	D/K	60	55	45	60	30
Tax	t_x	20.2	20.0	20.0	17.0	17.0
Pre-tax WACC	(7.18)	5.35	4.32	3.80	2.83	7.90
Vanilla WACC	(7.19)	4.66	3.73	3.18	2.40	6.70
Fully post-tax WACC	(7.20)	4.30	3.46	3.04	2.27	6.50

Source: UK Regulators' Network (2018), Cost of Capital – Annual Update Report, 4 June.

do so. Just as importantly, it does so while being fair to both firms and users. In particular, from a users' perspective, it avoids the upfront charges assumed by consumers under a pre-tax WACC. It is also more efficient since it is less likely to distort investment decisions.

In some contexts, however, the pre-tax WACC may be a better choice despite some of its limitations. For instance, when there is a need to speed up investment decisions, the distortions characterizing this WACC measure may be helpful. Since profit tends to be lower than average in the early phases of an activity and higher later, inflating the forecast return by allowing a higher-than-necessary tax allowance in the short run may give an incentive to overinvest in the early years. This may imply short-run inefficiency but end up being a smart decision for the long run if demand speeds up, as is often the case in fast-growing economies when the middle class starts becoming significant.

The key insight here is that it is not only the choice of the regulatory regime that influences investment decisions; it is also the choice of the WACC adopted to assess the allowed rate of return.[39] In view of the difficulty of dealing with the complex tax treatment of firms characterizing many countries, the choice of how much to adjust the WACC for tax (and inflation) can have significant impacts on the operational and investment behaviour of the regulated firms. For instance, it may influence their

---

[39] Chapter 11 will discuss in detail how regulation influences investment.

financial viability and their financing choices. Perfection is unlikely and so pragmatism with respect to the relatively easily anticipated biases the regulators want to favour will tend to drive the choice of the specific WACC.

In the end, the experience suggests that the ideal option to drive the regulatory decisions depends on the context. In theory, it should not make a difference to the average prices that the firm will be allowed to charge since all the real variables determining the net cash flow will have to be adjusted to account for the tax treatment. In practice, some minor differences often arise because of the difficulty of adjusting all the variables as precisely as needed to the complexity (and many loopholes) of the tax systems.

7.6   What Does This All Mean for the Average Price of the Regulated Service?

The next challenge regulators need to address in the 'real world' is the need to ensure a transparent link between the WACC they have decided to adopt and the average price that they will allow the regulated firms to charge. To make things as simple as possible, let's assume that the firm only sells one product and only charges one price. In practice, we know, as will be discussed in Chapter 8, that regulated firms tend to rely on price discrimination and, as will be discussed in Chapter 12, that they often deliver multiple regulated and non-regulated products. This makes the computations a bit more complex but does not change the way in which the WACC and the average price are to be linked.[40]

The simplest way to establish the link is to insert the revenue from Equation (7.2) into the NPV of total net cash flows in Equation (7.3) and to rely on the WACC that has been estimated following the procedure just discussed as the measure of the allowed rate of return and of the discount rate.[41] This leads to:

$$Authorized\ NPV\ of\ total\ net\ cash\ flows = \sum_{t=1}^{T} \frac{p_t q_t - C_t}{(1 + WACC)^t} = K \times authorized\ WACC$$

(7.21)

As soon as the regulator has an estimation of costs, of demand and of the WACC, it simply needs to set p_t to get to a net cash flow such that the equality holds. In other words, the average price for the regulated service is set by the regulators to ensure that the allowed rate of return is consistent with the allowed cost of capital. This is roughly how the regulatory financial models produce an estimation of the average price consistent with the authorized WACC. If the average price suggested by the regulated

---

[40] Essentially, the average price is the weighted average of all the prices charged by the firm and the weights are the specific quantities associated with each use and each type of product.

[41] Any of the WACC definitions will yield the same results for the optimal average price provided the definition of costs and revenue is consistent with the definition of WACC applied and the tax rate used to adjust the required post-tax return to the required pre-tax return is the effective tax rate paid by the entity.

firm is higher than the one implicit in Equation (7.21), it leads to a rate of return higher than the authorized WACC and needs to be reduced. The adjustment is in the opposite direction if the allowed rate of return initially estimated is lower than the cost of capital.

Average prices are thus central to the regulatory process in ensuring the match between the *RoR* and the p_t in modern regulatory practice. And this conclusion is valid whether the regulatory regime adopted is high-powered or low-powered. If the regime relies on a price cap, then p_t is the maximum value for the average cap. And if, for political or other reasons, the regulator needs to set the cap at a lower level, it simply means that the regulated firm will have to cut costs or broaden demand to be able to ensure a match between the rate of return and WACC. If the regime relies on a markup over costs (i.e. cost-plus pricing), this markup will be defined by the difference between the price needed to ensure that the rate of return and the WACC are equal, accounting for the cost forecast.

The various equations discussed so far form the basis of the financial regulatory model that regulators sometimes offer in free access, as in Australia or the United Kingdom. This makes it easy to run various simulations covering topics commonly discussed in regulatory evaluations. For instance, it is quite easy to assess the relevance for the optimal average annual price of changes in the evolution of demand over time (i.e. changes in the specific values of the q_t between periods 1 and T). Alternatively, for a given demand forecast, the impact on the average price of changes in any of the expenditure categories can easily be measured.

7.7   The Use of Financial Tools in Regulation Is Not Fool-Proof

It is important to emphasize that the financial modelling discussed in this chapter suffers from various limitations. Some are particularly important to keep in mind during the process leading to the assessment of the authorized WACC and matching average price.

First, we have seen that any regulatory model is anchored in several subjective decisions. For regulators to ignore their scope for discretion puts the efficacy of their efforts at risk. That risk justifies consultations, hearings and other similar means of estimating in a transparent way any key regulatory variable. Processes matter much more than hard-core theory often recognizes.

Second, some of the modelling can be somewhat simplistic on some dimensions if not enough attention is paid to details that should be easy to deal with. For instance, if the estimated market size, q_t, for the business is overestimated, the average price needed will be underestimated since it assumes scale economies that are not material-izing. In that case, the revenue collected will not match the revenue required. This is a common issue in some regulated industries, in particular transport, where overopti-mism in forecasting demand is a common way of making projects look better than they really are (e.g. Flyvbjerg 2008). This ex ante optimism bias is also one of the main factors behind requests to renegotiate contracts in regulated industries (e.g. Guasch et al. 2017).

Third, these models ignore tax distortions when deciding whether user fees or subsidies should be relied on to recover costs. The higher the distortions linked to taxes, the stronger the case to rely on financial markets, for instance through public–private partnerships, to finance investments in regulated industries. The comparison between the opportunity cost of raising public and private funds argued by theory is unfortunately seldom done in regulatory practice and this is a significant shortcoming that can be addressed as part of the regulatory negotiation process.

Fourth, these models ignore the relevance of the possible consequences of various types of institutional limitations on the optimal choice of regulation and financing strategies. The internalizing of institutional limitations requires that government conducts objective assessment of its institutions and links these to the choice of a regulatory framework. This is not yet a standard practice either. Many countries overestimate their ability to handle the regulatory tasks and many are unwilling to recognize that corruption or administrative inefficiency is a major problem in their country.[42] This makes them underestimate the governance and institutional payoffs to the adoption of regulatory practices forcing the transparent quantification of the key factors influencing the regulatory decisions and their outcomes.

Finally, if the design of the model is only anchored in financial considerations, it may underestimate industry- and firm-specific goals (and matching decision margins). For instance, the goals and constraints of a commercialized public firm will often differ from those of a purely private firm, as will their rate of return. The models should be designed to allow assessments of the relative achievements of all the regulatory goals. Efficiency and financial/fiscal viability are usually well dealt with, but equity and intergenerational concerns are often granted a lower priority or simply ignored. Yet any of these goals is relatively easy to model. As in many other policy contexts, all it takes is the political will to give the proper mandate to the regulator.

7.8 Summing Up

- Finance theory and practice drive the translation of the theoretical approaches to regulation into operational guidelines.
- The guidelines define a financial model based on a few basic equations used to assess the net present value of all the allowed costs and demand-related variables faced by the regulated firm and the resulting allowed rate of return.

---

[42] Although this bias is starting to be addressed. In 2018, for instance, the African Development Bank produced an Electricity Regulatory Index that measures the level of development of regulatory frameworks in fifteen African countries and examines their impact on the performance of their respective electricity sectors. See www.afdb.org/en/news-and-events/african-development-bank-launches-first-electricity-regulatory-index-for-africa-18250/

- o The cost component accounts for the expenditures needed to meet all services, investments and quality obligations imposed on the service providers, net of any possible subsidies.
  - ➤ Costs can be assessed at either their observed or at their efficient level depending on the regulatory guidelines adopted.
- o The demand forecast is typically based on long-term needs to be able to identify the investment requirements of the sector.
- The discount rate used to assess the net present value of costs and revenue is the cost of capital allowed by the regulator.
  - o The cost of capital is estimated as a weighted average cost of capital (WACC) of equity and of debt, with the weights reflecting the relative importance of the two sources of financing.
    - ➤ The cost of equity is usually based on the capital asset pricing model (CAPM).
    - ➤ While the cost of debt is usually determined as the sum of the risk-free rate and of a firm-specific risk premium.
  - o The cost of capital is used to set the upper bound for the allowed rate of return.
- The average price for the regulated service should be set to ensure that the allowed rate of return is consistent with the allowed cost of capital.
- Financial concerns are only a piece of the regulation jigsaw. They must be complemented by institutional and environmental considerations.

8   Non-Linear Pricing in Regulation

So far, we have emphasized two of the dimensions associated with price setting in regulated industries. The first is its relevance to the regulated firms' incentives and in particular to the optimization of their efforts to minimize costs. The second is its role in ensuring that budget and participation constraints are met, more specifically in ensuring that the rate of return is consistent with the cost of capital faced by the firm. Both dimensions focus on the average price. But there is more to pricing, as most of us know as consumers.[1]

Checking the website of any rail company shows multiple prices for the same trip, depending on the age of the travellers, their income group, the lead time of the trip or many other characteristics identified by service providers as potentially useful to increase their revenue and possibly their profits. Actually, the website of any public service provider offers the same complexity. Mobile phone service providers differentiate the unit cost of phone calls according to the volume of calls made but also with a client's willingness to rely on the same company to use its internet services and possibly its TV and fixed-line services. Even electricity and water companies, which offer quite homogeneous products and services, change their prices with consumption levels. Some charge for a connection fee to cover fixed costs, some build the fixed costs into the consumption charges.

These are all examples of price discrimination. Price discrimination exists when two similar products which have the same marginal cost to produce are sold by a firm at different prices (Armstrong 2006). More generally, price discrimination refers to all pricing schemes such that differences in prices do not accurately reflect the difference in costs, e.g. first-class against economy-class tickets on the same flight. They should not be confused with price differentiation. Unlike price discrimination, differentiated prices reflect differences in production costs. Price differentiation does help limit congestion problems.

These pricing techniques illustrate the regulated firms' detailed understanding of the heterogeneity of demand in the markets they are serving and often controlling quite tightly. The scope for price differentiation and discrimination and their use by service providers is the focus of this chapter. More specifically, the chapter revisits some of the basic concepts learned in introductory microeconomics and goes through

---

[1] For useful complementary overviews of pricing theory see Brown and Sibley (1986), Berg and Tschirhart (1988) and Wilson (1993).

a reasonably detailed discussion of the broad pricing techniques used by the regulated firms. These techniques can be used for profit maximization, as in the case of price discrimination, but also for productive and allocative efficiency goals (e.g. consumption smoothing and peak-load management in case of congestion).

The chapter shows that in order to distinguish between the right and the wrong in the pricing differentiation and discrimination decisions adopted by regulated firms, it is essential for a regulator to understand the way they use their freedom to set prices for specific consumer groups or specific usages. This is because the service providers that we are interested in enjoy some market power. Regulators need to be able to assess the extent to which there is a risk of abuse that would demand their intervention. And to appreciate this risk, it is useful to examine in more detail the ways in which firms set their prices.[2]

8.1   How Many Pricing Details Does a Regulator Need to Deal With?

To make the discussion as simple as possible, let's focus on a single regulated firm with the average price set over a specific regulatory period (say three to five years, as is increasingly common) in such a way that the firm can achieve a rate of return consistent with its cost of capital. Let's also assume for now that the service provider cannot rely on subsidies and that prices must be set to recover costs. In this context, the key pricing decision is the decision by the regulated company to differentiate the price of the service it is providing across users and uses. This is what the price structure is all about and it requires that users be unable to trade among themselves. Price discrimination is possible only when there is no chance of arbitrage among customers. It is defined by the various prices, discounts or rebates associated with a given set of products and services. It seems reasonable to expect that most providers will design this structure to produce a revenue consistent with their profit goals. In practice, the use of price structure is also part of the action plans derived from firms' broader business strategies which include forward-looking dimensions such as market penetration or market segmentation. We will not discuss these broader goals as they are usually more the concern of competition agencies and policy negotiations with sector ministries than of the regulatory mandate.[3] However, they can be important when assessing price structures.

[2] The other main pricing issue that regulators need to focus on is related to the fact that regulated industries are usually delivered by networks which can be shared by several providers. Think of different railways companies sharing the same tracks. The addition of a user of the common facility brings benefits to both private (to the new user) and public (to the client of this new user). This increases competition and improves the prospects for final consumers of lower prices. The key question is how to price the access to the common facility to make sure these benefits are not being captured by the owner of the common facility that allows the network to function. This important issue is discussed in Chapter 11.

[3] And there can be divergent views between regulatory agencies and competition authorities concerning the degree of freedom competing operators should be allowed in terms of price discrimination. For the case of retail prices in the British electricity industry, see Crampes and Laffont (2016).

From a strict regulator's perspective, as we will see in Section 8.4, the main mandate includes the monitoring of the coherence between the price structure and the average price. The price structure should not lead to an average price above the one identified as fair by the regulator. And it is also up to the regulator to check that the price structure does not lead to unjustified exclusion of some users, undersupply of some services and excess supply of some others. This is part of the efficiency–equity trade-offs regulators are expected to track. The final related mandate is the need to ensure that the various ways in which prices are differentiated do not lead to consumption levels or expenditures incoherent with the country's environmental and social goals. Excessive discounts on water or energy use for large consumers can be consistent with decreasing average cost but could have damaging environmental consequences if they lead to abusive uses of ground water reserves or excessive emissions by thermal generation plants.

To highlight the role of price discrimination in regulated industries while keeping the discussion relatively simple, the chapter focuses on a somewhat static description of the role of pricing. But it is important to recognize that, as a result, the chapter underemphasizes the relevance of some of the consequences of the price structure for investment and consumption decisions over time. Price structures can be manipulated to create short- and long-term rents and to influence the way in which these rents are shared between stakeholders. The decision by a regulator to allow the regulated firms to differentiate prices across users at a given point in time or over time clearly has an impact on the odds of ensuring a fair welfare outcome in the long run. Yet in practice regulated firms enjoy a great deal of freedom in setting prices. For instance, in the United Kingdom, only some of the rail fares one sees on the web, such as season tickets on most commuter journeys, some off-peak return tickets on long-distance journeys and anytime tickets around major cities, are controlled by the regulator. The latter estimates that only 40% of rail fares need to be regulated as the rail companies compete with other transport modes for most of their services.[4]

Ultimately, the regulator needs to have a view on many details to decide how much discretionary power to leave to the regulated firm. And the number of details to consider in order to make the right decision highlights the difficulty of switching from theory to practice. But to get to a fair assessment of price-discrimination practice, it is essential to conceptualize the way firms would exploit the opportunity of serving several markets. It provides a healthy distance to the many practical details that tend to blur the key underlying incentives in environments in which firms are dealing with heterogeneous users and uses of their services.

8.2 How Are Average Prices Set When Firms Cater to Several Markets?

To understand the additional margins producers have to make profit when they serve several markets, it is useful to revisit the result derived in Chapter 2 that, without any

---

[4] For more details, see www.nationalrail.co.uk/times_fares/ticket_types/83871.aspx

regulation, a monopolist delivering a single product or service will charge according to the elasticity of demand it is facing (Ramsey–Boiteux pricing).[5] This result is useful as a starting point but needs to be actualized to take into account the growing demand heterogeneity of regulated markets.

A rail company caters to domestic and international travellers. It caters to passenger and freight demand. A phone operator sells mobile and fixed lines, and internet or TV services. Water companies sell both water and sanitation services. One operator may provide services in various cities or regions of the same country. In Belgium, for instance, an electricity company sells services in three regions (Brussels, Flanders and Wallonia) each with a different regulator and set of regulations. But the vehicle fleet sent out to fix outages is common to all three regions, suggesting that a portion of the production cost is likely to be common to several of the user groups.

In an environment in which public and private regulated firms produce several goods or services, the optimal pricing strategy is likely to be more complex than the simple Ramsey formula. To see how multi-production affects the average price an unregulated producer would like to charge, it is useful to revisit the simple equation as follows. Let's start by looking at how a private monopolist would set prices in a more complex market and compare it to the optimal pricing decision by a public monopoly facing the same market.

The private monopoly case with common cost and independent demands. Consider a private monopoly selling the same good in two separate independent markets, tagged 1 and 2. It sells the quantities q_1 in the first market and q_2 in the second market, but produces the services needed in these two markets jointly so that the production costs are driven by the total output (i.e. $C(q_1 + q_2)$) Let $p_1(q)$ and $p_2(q)$ be the inverse demand functions, since the firm could be setting different prices in the two markets. The monopoly's optimization problem is to choose the quantities q_1 and q_2 that maximize:

$$\Pi(q_1, q_2) = p_1(q_1)q_1 + p_2(q_2)q_2 - C(q_1 + q_2) \tag{8.1}$$

The solution is:

$$p_1 + p_1'(q_1)q_1 = p_2 + p_2'(q_2)q_2 = C'(q_1 + q_2)$$

It can be rewritten by using the definition of demand elasticity for market: $j = 1, 2, \left(\varepsilon_j = -\frac{\Delta q_j}{\Delta p_j} \frac{p_j}{q_j} \right)$

$$\frac{p_j - C'(q_1 + q_2)}{p_j} = \frac{1}{\varepsilon_j} \tag{8.2}$$

---

[5] We also saw that when the monopolist gets subsidies, the optimal price will have to reflect the opportunity cost of public funds but, since we ignore subsidies in this chapter, it is just important to remember that, when ignoring the distortions related to the taxes needed to finance subsidies, all prices are likely to fail to reflect the real costs the consumption of a services imposes on society. In other words, ignoring the cost of public funds leads to overconsumption.

Rearranging the expression in Equation (8.2) yields $p_1\left(1 - \frac{1}{\varepsilon_1}\right) = p_2\left(1 - \frac{1}{\varepsilon_2}\right) = C'(q_1 + q_2)$. The equality between marginal cost and marginal revenue in each market is just an extension of the old pricing rule in Equation (3.4). More interesting is the equality between marginal revenues. This results in

$$\frac{p_1}{p_2} = \frac{1 - \dfrac{1}{\varepsilon_2}}{1 - \dfrac{1}{\varepsilon_1}} \tag{8.3}$$

Equation (8.3) shows that it makes sense for an unregulated private monopolist to differentiate prices on the basis of demand elasticity. For example, if $\varepsilon_1 > \varepsilon_2$ then, after profit maximization, $p_1 < p_2$. Compared with uniform pricing, price discrimination increases the benefit of the private monopoly because demand responds more to a small change in price in market 1 than in market 2. The firm can use prices, taking into account the responsiveness of demand and the fact that average costs are sensitive to the output level, to set quantities in each market to maximize its profits.

The public monopoly case. What if the firm was a public firm concerned with maximizing social welfare rather than a private firm focused only on maximizing its profit? Let $S_j(q_j)$ be consumers' gross surplus in market j as defined in Chapter 2. By construction, the marginal willingness to pay in market j (that is, the demand function) is obtained from the derivative of the surplus function: $p_j(q_j) = S_j'(q_j)$. Since we focus on normal goods so that $p_j(q_j)$ is decreasing in q_j, the surplus is an increasing concave function. This means that more production generates more surplus, and that the increase in surplus generated by each additional unit becomes smaller and smaller.

In this context, if one neglects public finance issues (i.e. taxpayers' surplus), the public monopoly chooses q_1 and q_2 that maximize the net social welfare (in contrast to profit in the case of a private monopoly):

$$W(q_1, q_2) = S_1(q_1) + S_2(q_2) - C(q_1 + q_2) \tag{8.4}$$

The solution is:

$$S_1'(q_1) = S_2'(q_2) = C'(q_1 + q_2) \tag{8.5}$$

which entails marginal cost pricing:

$$p_1(q_1) = p_2(q_2) = C'(q_1 + q_2) \tag{8.6}$$

For a public enterprise focused on consumers' surplus, pricing the service at marginal cost for the entire business across the two markets is the efficient choice. In contrast to the result obtained for a private monopoly, no price discrimination is likely to be found to be desirable in this context. But this result omits that, in the industries treated here, technology tends to exhibit increasing returns to scale. This implies that marginal cost pricing will lead to financial losses unless the difference between price and marginal costs is compensated by subsidies.

But what if the public firm faces the same restriction on subsidies as the private monopoly? With this in mind, let's reconsider the optimization problem for the public firm but add the obligation of balancing the budget:

$$\text{max } W(q_1, q_2) \text{ subject to } p_1(q_1)q_1 + p_2(q_2)q_2 - C(q_1 + q_2) \geq 0 \qquad (8.7)$$

The interesting case is obviously when the balancing constraint is binding: $q_1(p_1)p_1 + q_2(p_2)p_2 = C(q_1(p_1) + q_2(p_2))$. The optimization leads to a new version of the so-called Ramsey–Boiteux prices discussed in Chapter 2 and detailed in Chapter 4 (Boiteux 1956; Dierker 1991). The price in each market needs to account for the elasticity of demand but also for the extent to which the budget is tight, as discussed in Chapter 4. If the tightness of the budget constraint (i.e. the extent to which marginal cost pricing would create a financial loss) is measured by $\gamma = \frac{\lambda}{1+\lambda}$ where $\lambda \geq 0$ is the Lagrangian multiplier of the financing constraint, we see that $0 \leq \gamma \leq 1$. The Ramsey–Boiteux price in market j is:

$$\frac{p_j - C'(q_1 + q_2)}{p_j} = \frac{\gamma}{\varepsilon_j}, \quad j = 1, 2 \qquad (8.8)$$

Rearranging this formula, the price in markets $j = 1, 2$ is $p_j = \frac{C'(q_1 + q_2)}{1 - \frac{\gamma}{\varepsilon_j}}$.

Taking the ratio between the prices in markets 1 and 2 leads to an equation similar to the one obtained for the private monopoly in Equation (8.3):

$$\frac{p_1}{p_2} = \frac{1 - \dfrac{\gamma}{\varepsilon_2}}{1 - \dfrac{\gamma}{\varepsilon_1}} \qquad (8.9)$$

When budget constraints on public operators are binding, therefore, price discrimination makes sense from a social welfare viewpoint. The public firm must use the same signal as the private firm, namely elasticity. In practice, this also means that, to recover its costs, the firm must charge consumers more than the marginal cost. The main difference between public and private firms is that the margin is smaller for the former and that this difference is driven by the size of γ. Despite this difference, overall these results show that price discrimination will often be desirable from both a private and a social welfare perspective.[6] The next question is thus whether all forms of price discrimination are equally acceptable from a regulator's perspective. To be able to address this concern, it is useful to understand the various ways in which price discrimination can be implemented.

---

[6] This discussion reflects the economists' view of price discrimination through the lens of social welfare. Many antitrust lawyers prefer to look at price discrimination from a perspective of fairness or in terms of its impact on competition instead, which can result in disagreements on the desirability of price discrimination. For a more precise discussion see Gifford and Kudrle (2010).

8.3   The Three Broad Types of Price Discrimination

Economic theory suggests that price discrimination is likely to be an option any time a firm (i) can identify different submarkets in which different users or uses are characterized by different willingness to pay and different demand elasticities and (ii) has some control over the price it can charge to specific users or uses, i.e. any time the operator has enough market power on some segment of the market. Theory also shows that, for the option to be sustainable, the firm betting on price discrimination must be able to prevent consumers in one group selling to consumers in the other to profit from price discrepancies between the two submarkets. But this is usually relatively easy to manage technically in regulated industries as they generally require some physical infrastructure for service delivery.[7]

In markets with these characteristics, analysts have identified three broad types of ways in which firms discriminate on price. They are typically labelled by degree. In first-degree price discrimination, the focus is on consumers' willingness to pay; in second-degree discrimination, it is on the quantity consumed; and in third-degree discrimination, it is on grouping consumers according to the elasticity of their demand.

Under *first-degree price discrimination*, the firm charges each consumer in its market a different price for each unit they consume. This price is based on what the consumer is willing to pay. If the firm can practise this form of price discrimination (also known as 'perfect price discrimination'), the profit captured by the operator is equal to the total surplus of trade (that is, it captures the entire consumer surplus). Each consumer is charged exactly what they are willing to pay to obtain (rather than forgo) the service. Note that a perfectly discriminating monopolist produces more than a 'regular' monopolist, as seen in Figure 8.1.

Figure 8.1 compares the level of surplus and its distribution in the usual monopolistic market (right-hand panel) and in a market in which the monopoly can perfectly discriminate (left-hand panel). It shows that a perfectly discriminating monopolist produces the same quantity (q^*) as under perfect competition since it manages to price each unit of output at the maximum a consumer is willing to pay until it reaches the competitive price, p^*, paid only by the marginal consumer. The main differences between the two situations are the level of surplus and its distribution. Without price discrimination, there is a deadweight loss (DWL) on the right-hand panel in Figure 8.1 not present on the left-hand panel. In that pricing approach, the consumer and the producer share the residual surplus. However, when the monopoly can adopt a first-degree price-discrimination strategy, this DWL disappears, but the surplus is now totally captured by the monopoly. The surplus left to consumers (light grey) is nil. This contrasts with the polar case of perfect competition in which the consumer surplus is maximal and the firm's profit is limited to infra-marginal rents.

---

[7] It is much more difficult in international trade where exporters find it hard to block parallel trade.

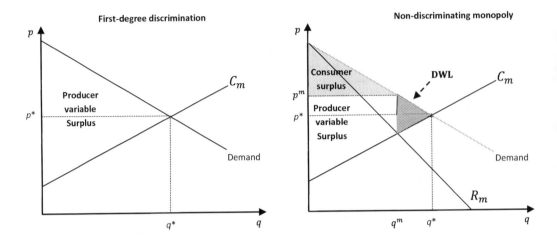

Figure 8.1 First-degree price discrimination

This allows the perfectly discriminating monopolist to make much higher profits than a regular monopolist, since it captures the consumer surplus in full. Better yet, it produces up to a level at which there is no more deadweight loss. This means that, from an efficiency point of view, the outcome is quite desirable. The downside is the effect on equity, since there is even less consumer surplus than under a non-discriminatory monopoly. In theory this downside could be mitigated through taxation of the firm's rent and a redistribution of tax revenue among users. In practice first-degree price discrimination never occurs due to asymmetric information on consumer propensity to pay for the service. Yet it offers a useful benchmark. It shows that discrimination per se is not a problem. The problem arises when discrimination is not perfect, in which case it creates distortions.

In the theoretical literature, one way to illustrate how first-degree price discrimination could work in practice is to consider a two-part tariff. Users of type i are charged a lump-sum fee, A_i, for the right to access the service and then a price per unit consumed, p, so that the tariff is: $T_i(q) = A_i + pq$. If the monopolist wants to reap all the consumer surplus, price, p, must be set at the marginal cost, $p^* = C'(q^*)$, and the fixed charge, A_i, must be set at the net surplus of consumer i.

Based on this theoretical discussion, it may be unclear to policymakers whether a two-part tariff is a type of first-degree price discrimination that allows the service provider to capture all consumer surplus or not. The firm is assumed to set the fee and the consumption charge to maximize its profit. To this end, the firm should set the charge equal to the marginal cost (to maximize the net consumer surplus, $W(q) = S(q) - C(q)$, and capture the consumer surplus through its access fee. This looks good on paper but is quite misleading. When there are two different demand curves for two types of users (in practice there are thousands of different types of users), the service provider needs to charge each type a different access fee to be able to extract all the consumer surplus. But this would be quite hard to do in practice.

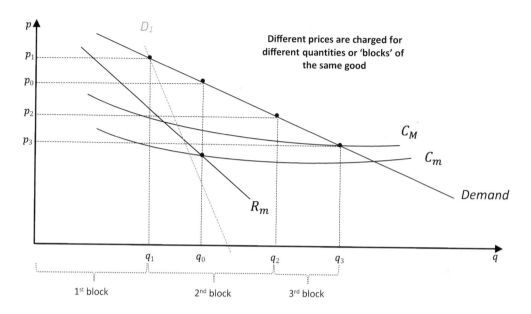

Figure 8.2 Second-degree price discrimination (the decreasing block-pricing case)

First, the firm will struggle to determine exactly how much each type of consumer is willing to pay. Second, even assuming it can manage to overcome this asymmetric information problem, it will find it politically difficult to charge each user a different fee with the sole purpose of extracting all their surplus. It is usually forced to grant the same access to all and must charge given pools of users (e.g. residential, industrial) the same access fee. The fee extracts less than the full consumer surplus from those consumers most able to pay. Under a two-part tariff of this type, perfect price discrimination is thus not enforceable.

As of today, first-degree price discrimination is implemented nowhere. It requires an impossible level of information on consumers' willingness and ability to pay and a politically unsustainable prices structure. But the emergence of big data and similar tools that track the preferences of consumers across a wide range of consumption types, including for public services, is likely to gradually reduce the practical limits of this theoretical concept in many regulated industries. The political constraint will remain, however – it will still be hard to charge individualized prices for public services.

Second-degree price discrimination. When the firm has limited information on consumers' profiles, it can still discriminate using the quantity demanded as a proxy of preferences. It can charge different prices for different blocks of consumption quantities or bundle products to be sold at a package price. Figure 8.2 provides an illustration in the case of decreasing blocks. Without price discrimination, the monopoly set a uniform price of p_0 and the quantity q_0 will be sold. With price discrimination, the output will increase to q_3 and three different prices will be charged (p_1, p_2 and p_3), one for each consumption block. The first block is made up of a small quantity, q_1, and a price, p_1, higher than when the monopoly is not discriminating. For the second and third blocks in this example, the price is lower.

This pricing approach allays political concerns, since consumers select the contract they prefer from a menu of possibilities, here from blocks: $(q_1, T_1 = q_1 p_1)$, $(q_2, T_2 = q_1 p_1 + (q_2 - q_1)p_2)$ or $(q_3, T_3 = q_1 p_1 + (q_2 - q_1)p_2 + (q_3 - q_2)p_3)$. They are free to choose what suits them best. If you want to travel by train, for example, you may be able to buy a single ticket at full price or pay a fixed fee and then buy tickets at a discount over a given period. The decision depends on whether you plan to travel regularly, in which case the second option is preferable, or rarely, in which case the first option is best. Figure 8.2 represents consumers with a large demand, so their best option (i.e. to maximize their surplus) is to pick contract 3 and consume q_3. By contrast, type 1 consumers, represented with the demand D_1, would choose contract $(q_1, T_1 = q_1 p_1)$. If the contracts (i.e. the blocks) are badly designed, different types of consumers might end up choosing the same contract. When contracts cannot be allocated based on verifiable characteristics (e.g. residential, industrial), second-degree price discrimination demands a design of incentive compatible tariffs (i.e. so that consumers select the tariff designed for them). This generally means that the affluent part of the demand gets an informational rent.

Moreover, this form of price discrimination requires that a firm be able to closely monitor the level of services consumed by an individual buyer. For public utilities, monitoring means metering, which is even easier to implement with new technologies such as smart meters. It is becoming simple to distinguish between various types of consumers and consumption patterns. The ability of improved data treatment is also changing the precision of price targeting to make the most of users' willingness to pay. For regulated firms, this has an impact on how much to invest in information to yield higher profits than the uniform pricing would.

Second-degree price discrimination is quite common in regulated industries. For electricity or water, for instance, users are charged different prices depending on the quantity consumed or on the type of usage (industrial or domestic). In doing so, utilities can be quite effective at using the theoretical insights. This is why some electricity utilities charge more for the first block of consumption. They know the first consumption units are essential, and therefore demand is more inelastic. However, after this initial consumption level, demand is less essential and becomes more price-sensitive. Therefore, the tariff level drops. This approach to pricing can make a significant difference across consumers, as seen in the data collected quarterly by the British energy regulator, OFFER. In the first quarter of 2018, the smallest non-residential consumers paid on average a bit over 14 cents per kWh, about 20% more than the somewhat larger users and about 40% more than the very large and extra-large ones.[8]

---

[8] Department for Business, Energy and Industrial Strategy (2018), Quarterly Energy Prices, P 36, https://assets.publishing.service.gov.uk/government/uploads/system/uploads/attachment_data/file/720379/QEP_Q1_2018.pdf

Second-degree price discrimination is not only about increasing profits; it can also serve other purposes, including efficiency. In particular, it facilitates the revelation of hidden willingness to consume. In Figure 8.2, picking the contract (q_3, p_3) is equivalent to a commitment to be a loyal customer. If many consumers choose this contract – a subscription if time is involved – the firm is encouraged to invest.

Second-degree price discrimination can also be helpful when the regulator wants users to consume more of a certain good or service. In that case, it can implement 'decreasing block pricing' as in Figure 8.2 – that is, charging less per unit when larger quantities are consumed. This is quite common to stimulate the use of public transport, for instance. Note that decreasing block tariffs can also help firms maximize profit, to the extent that their costs drop at higher levels of consumption.

This popular strategy is not without problems. If badly designed then decreasing block pricing can easily lead to equity concerns when essential inelastic demand becomes unaffordable to the poorest consumers. At the other extreme, it may lead to excessive consumption. For example, there may be bottlenecks in transport, and scarcity of primary sources, such as water. In the case of electricity, producers may come to rely on polluting energy sources at the margins to decrease the risk of outages or try to ration energy when production capacity cannot be adjusted in the short run.

To meet environmental concerns or to avert bottlenecks and outages, increasing blocks may be favoured by regulators. But these may violate the principle that prices should reflect the costs of serving consumers, in particular in an industry with economies of scale. In sum, the trade-offs between various forms of efficiency as well as between efficiency and equity should be present in the mind of regulators as they assess the desirability of this particular form of price discrimination.

The most common form of second-degree price discrimination trying to account for these trade-offs is the two-part tariffs mentioned earlier, whereby the service provider charges an entry fee as well as user charges that reflect discounts for buyers of larger quantities. This practice is not equivalent to first-degree price discrimination, contrary to what practitioners sometimes think, because the firm is offering a menu of contracts to consumers, who freely select from among them. If the firm wants different types of users to choose different contracts, it must make sure that the contracts carry appropriate incentives, exactly as when a regulator wants a low-cost firm to select the contract designed for it. It implies that conditions of asymmetric information distort the optimal non-linear prices for a single type of consumer, as studied earlier.

For instance, if there are only two types of users, one with more ability to pay and the other with less, typically the one who consumes more will get the best unit price (because of marginal cost pricing) and a fixed charge lower than that user's capacity to pay. By contrast, smaller users will pay a fixed charge equal to their capacity to pay and a unit price distorted upwards (that is, greater than the marginal cost). Thus, the quantities made available by contract to smaller users are not consistent with marginal cost pricing. This approach is therefore less efficient than first-degree, or perfect, price discrimination, since the operator ends up selling less than it would with full information. It also implies a welfare loss due to the reduced consumption of the small users. Actually, the price-maker faces the same type of incentive compatibility

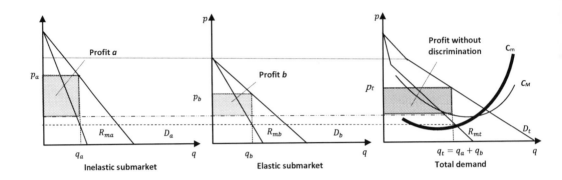

Figure 8.3 Third-degree price discrimination

constraint as the one we have detailed in Chapter 5 in the game played by a regulator and a regulated firm.

Third-degree price discrimination occurs when firms are able to split the market for a particular good or service into easily identifiable groups and then charge each group a different price. If the firm is maximizing profits, it follows the inverse elasticity rule with respect to each group, as we have seen in Equation (8.2). Thus, when a firm is able to split its market into two or more groups, it is quite easy to use differences in the price elasticities of demand to come up with different prices for customers in each group.

Figure 8.3 shows how this takes place when there are two groups of consumers. Allowing the service provider to charge separately in the two markets increases the firm's profit overall even if it does not change the total output level. This is because the output is reallocated between the two markets. Total marginal revenue is greater than is obtained when the firm ignores the possibility of differentiating the two markets. The profit margin is, as expected, significantly greater in the least elastic markets. And this comes at the cost of differentiating the price paid for access to service across consumer groups.

The group with the low demand elasticity (group *a* in Figure 8.3) pays a higher price than without discrimination and the group with the higher demand elasticity (group *b* in Figure 8.3) enjoys a lower price. Note, in our illustration, that total production is the same under both scenarios. This is because, when demand is linear, third-degree price discrimination does not increase total consumption. However, with non-linear demands, it will often lead to a higher output, which is a necessary condition for third-degree price discrimination to increase the total consumer surplus in the economy. Under any of the production outcomes, the monopolist enjoys a higher profit level.

The change in price paid by different groups of users or uses can have quite challenging consequences which need to be considered by a regulator because it may lead to undesirable net distributional effects. Since the low-elasticity groups benefit from uniform pricing, but the high-elasticity groups do not, the net welfare effects depend on the extent to which the positive effect offsets the negative one. If low-elasticity groups, which are the big losers of third-degree price discrimination, are the poorest consumers and represent a large share of the market, the net social impact of this form of price discrimination would be regressive. And this is a situation in which regulators are unlikely to be willing to support requests for third-degree price discrimination in this market. In some industries and in countries in which the scope for subsidies is quite limited, this risk needs to be balanced against its potential financing payoff. It can indeed be supported if the additional revenue is earmarked to help finance increases in overall capacity. It can also help cut the cost of capital since risk premia are likely to be lower as there is evidence of an increased capacity of the sector to produce the cash flows needed to finance the investment.

In practice, for this form of discrimination to be feasible, the service provider must be able to distinguish various types of consumers by verifiable characteristics. Knowing the extent to which the elasticity of demand changes with characteristics such as geography, age, time of use, type of use, income, social status and so on is thus essential. An example is the difference in the elasticity of demand for electricity or water between the north and the south of a country. Others are the difference between young and old consumers or between rural or urban users. The challenge is to quantify these differences in order to be able to differentiate the market as precisely as possible. As with other forms of price discrimination, the provider must be able to prevent the resale of the good or service across groups. For example, a rail operator must make it impossible for someone paying a discounted fare to resell the ticket to someone expected to pay a higher fare, which is achieved through some kind of identification card.

Although this form of discrimination is increasingly common in regulated industries, it can be quite controversial. For instance, airports have long used the origin of flights to differentiate landing charges. This got Heathrow into trouble in 2011 when it was sued by some airlines. The airport lost and was found guilty of using discriminatory practices against domestic flights.[9] Similar discrimination cases have been rejected by courts in France and Spain where the authorities were trying to favour national airlines (see Silva 2017).

8.4 How Much Should Regulators Support Price Discrimination?

As in so many regulatory issues, the case for supporting or impeding price discrimination is not simple. This chapter shows that it can have positive effects when it allows market sizes to increase, which is good for efficiency. It can also allow some consumers to enter markets they would otherwise not have been able to afford and this is an important equity payoff since it reduces exclusion. For instance, it can allow service suppliers to cater better to lower-income consumers or rural users or any other

---

[9] CAA, Investigation under Section 41 of the Airports Act 1986 of the structure of airport charges levied by Heathrow Airport Limited – CAA decision, Civil Aviation Authority, London, 2014.

groups with a lower ability to pay. But just as importantly, some forms of discrimination can have negative effects. From a strict efficiency viewpoint, price discrimination can be quite undesirable if it does not lead to an increase in market size and consumers' coverage. It can also have undesirable equity payoffs if it allows firms to penalize the low-income groups with inelastic demand and modest consumption levels as they will end up paying higher markups than larger, and often richer, consumers. It might also be used by incumbents to exclude potential competitors which will eventually penalize all users by preventing market development.

In general, regulators and competition agencies try to balance the different perspectives by comparing the extent to which the total output under price discrimination is higher than under a single price monopoly and by considering the winners and losers of the specific forms of discrimination adopted in the pricing structure. In addition, they consider more dynamic concerns such as the extent to which the additional profits associated with discrimination can help finance investment needs as well as research and development expenditures, which is increasingly important in industries in which environmental concerns are pushing firms to consider new technologies. From a fairness viewpoint, the assessments also consider the extent to which it can be used to finance cross-subsidies between different classes of users without having to rely on fiscal support and without reducing competition.

Without regulatory supervision, price discrimination allows an operator to end up with an average price that is higher than that needed to achieve the fair rate of return to match the cost of capital. The trick for the regulator is often to support the creativity of the firms they regulate in coming up with diversified tariff structures to be used to recover costs in a non-competitive public service. But this can be risky. Indeed, the regulator needs to ensure that it is done in a way that minimizes the risks that the firm ends up capturing most of the additional surplus generated by its pricing creativity. It also needs to minimize the risks of abusive prices or of reducing an operator's incentive to minimize costs. For instance, if it leaves a room for cross-subsidies, there is a room to inflate costs in such a way that average costs end up higher than they should be.[10]

Overall, price discrimination has to be considered as a possibly desirable regulatory instrument. But this has to be done formally and quantitatively. In addition to its undesirable fairness and efficiency effects, any misjudgement of the distortions associated with price discrimination can be quite damaging for the regulator's reputation and could increase the concern for its capture by the regulated firms. In turn, this may lead to much more challenging political situations than usually discussed in economics textbooks.

These political risks are quite visible in the debate on the acceptability of the new technologies used to document the heterogeneity of consumers – information needed to refine the use of price discrimination. Surveys of pricing practice suggest that firms are increasingly trying to come up with price structures which are more value-based

---

[10] Cross-subsidies occur when users of high-cost services pay less than the cost of the service designed for them, with the difference being recovered through a price hike imposed on users of low-cost services.

than cost-based (see e.g. Lambrecht et al. 2012). Recent research also shows that service providers are now much better able to account for the heterogeneity of consumers and consumption both in tastes and in price sensitivity than they were less than five years ago (Colombo 2018).

A good illustration of this change and of the debates on its desirability is the emergence of strong lobbying by service providers to increase the scope for smart metering. While the potential payoffs to the suppliers are quite clear, the payoffs to users are more uncertain. A July 2018 report by the 'Cour des Comptes' (France's public accounting office) argued that the smart-meter programme was likely to be more beneficial for the utility company in charge of most electricity distribution (Enedis) than for consumers.[11] A growing number of European countries have expressed similar concerns (although often more linked to the health risks associated with this technology). While the debate is not settled at the time of this writing, it certainly illustrates that the romantic passion for opening the access to private consumption and behavioural information is not universal. Limits are likely to be adopted in many countries, and this will probably have an impact on the views of regulators on the desirability of some forms of price discrimination.

8.5 On Price Differentiation and Its Benefits

Unlike price discrimination that basically consists in charging different prices for goods or services that costs the same to supply, differentiated prices reflect differences in production costs. Price differentiation is hence encouraged by the authorities when it helps to smooth consumption and therefore limit congestion problems and the need to invest in peak-load capacity. In other words, they are encouraged to improve productive and allocative efficiency.

To illustrate the social gains from price differentiation, we consider two important theoretical examples from the electricity sector: peak-load pricing and state-contingent prices. Since they are theoretical, the examples yield insights applicable to other sectors as well.

Peak-load pricing.[12] When demand regularly runs up against the entire installed capacity of a given set of infrastructure, it needs to be managed because peaks pose a threat to service quality. When roads get congested during holidays, travellers spend extra time in their vehicles. During rush hour, rail commuters will have a hard time finding a seat on the train.

Similar issues arise in the power sector. Because electricity is not storable on a large scale, it must be produced at the same time it is consumed. To accomplish this, producers must install capacity that will be combined with primary energy (natural

---

[11] www.ccomptes.fr/sites/default/files/2018-01/07-compteurs-communicants-Linky-Tome-1.pdf

[12] Boiteux's (1960) approach to the peak-load problem has become the basis for further work in this area. Unfortunately, his contribution, published in French in 1949, had little or no impact outside of the French academic world. But its impact in France, and especially in Electricité de France, was quite immediate.

gas, coal, uranium and wind, for example) to generate electricity.[13] The primary fuel is a private good. That is, it is destroyed to supply consumers with electricity within a given time frame. By contrast, the production capacity has some characteristics of a public good since it will be used repeatedly over time. Whereas the primary fuel is to be included in the price paid by each user, the way to pass through the capacity cost is far from obvious. Peak-load pricing, or congestion pricing, is used to align these two disparate elements of the equation.

To see how it works, it is useful to consider the elements of a sector diagnostic. Since, in the case of electricity, there is at the moment no possibility of stocking, the modelling is as follows. Let K denote the capacity to be installed at the unit cost r. The quantity to produce and consume at date t is q_t. We assume that c is the variable cost of producing 1 kWh and is constant over time.

We need to be able to reflect the fact that consumers value electricity differently at different times of the day (day versus night-time) or in different seasons (winter versus summer). To do so, we rely on the linear modelling expression $S_t'(q) \equiv p_t(q) = \alpha_t - q$. It represents the marginal surplus from electricity consumption at time t. In this expression, α_t is the maximum willingness to pay for the first unit of electricity and varies with time (i.e. day or night, winter or summer) since the demand for electricity is not the same at all times.

Let us first consider a case in which capacity K is to be used within a given time period where demand does not change (no need for the time index). The first-best investment and pricing policy is then (i) to invest up to the point where marginal surplus is equal to the *long-run* marginal cost, $S'(K) = c + r \Rightarrow K = a - (c + r)$; (ii) to produce up to capacity $q = K$ and (iii) to set the price of electricity at the long-run marginal cost $p = c + r$.[14] Under this policy, the consumer surplus is maximum under the constraint that firms recover their cost.

Let us now assume that K will be used for two periods of equal duration: During the lifespan of K, demand will be high (i.e. peak) at period H but low (off-peak) at period L $(a_H > a_L)$. Because charging different prices at H and L could be (wrongly) viewed as discriminatory or because consumers do not have smart meters allowing them to react to time-varying prices, a regulator could be tempted by $p_H = p_L = c + r/2$, motivated by the equal duration of the use of K. This results in $q_L < q_H \leq K$, which is financially unsustainable since $(p_L - c)q_L + (p_H - c)q_H - rK = \frac{r}{2}(q_L + q_H - 2K) < 0$. Then, getting rid of the constraint $p_{II} = p_L$, we can determine the investment and pricing policy by maximizing the social surplus:

$$\max_K -rK + \sum_{t=H,L} \max_{q_t} [S_t(q_t) - cq_t] \text{ subject to } q_t \leq K, \quad t = H, L.$$

---

[13] Since electric energy cannot be stored, production is determined by a Leontief production function: $q = \min$ (K (the capital installed), f (primary energy (i.e. coal, sun)). In other words, this means that in a windfarm, for instance, if there is no wind, $q = 0$, no matter the size of K.

[14] Obtained by solving $\max_{q,K} -rK + S(q) - cq$ subject to $q \leq K$.

Box 8.1 How do peaks influence optimal capacity?

To consider the effects of peaks, the problem to be solved is: $\max_K -rK + \sum_{t=H,L} \max_{q_t} [S_t(q_t) - cq_t]$ subject to $q_t \leq K$, $t = H, L$ with H the peak time, L the off-peak time and K the installed capacity.

Designating μ_t as the non-negative Lagrange multiplier of the capacity constraint at period t, the Lagrange function is: $L = -rK + S_H(q_H) - cq_H + S_L(q_L) - cq_L + \mu_H(K - q_H) + \mu_L(K - q_L)$.

Assuming strictly positive outputs and capacity, the first-order conditions are: $\frac{\partial L}{\partial q_t} = S_t'(q_t) - c - \mu_t = 0$ ($t = H, L$) and $\frac{\partial L}{\partial K} = -r + \mu_H + \mu_L = 0$ plus the complementary slackness conditions $\mu_t(K - q_t) = 0, t = H, L$. From the condition $\frac{\partial L}{\partial K} = 0$, we see that μ_H and μ_L cannot be simultaneously nil. Then, $q_L < q_H < K$ is not a solution. We thus have two possibilities:

(a) $q_L < q_H = K$ then from $\mu_L = 0$ and $\mu_H = r$ we obtain $S_H'(q_H)|_{q_H=K} = c + r$; $S_L'(q_L)|_{q_L<K} = c \Rightarrow K = a_H - (c + r)$; $q_L = a_L - c$

(b) $q_L = q_H = K$ then $\mu_L > 0$ and $\mu_H > 0$ imply $\mu_H + \mu_L = r$ and $S_H'(K) + S_L'(K) = 2c + r \Rightarrow K = \frac{a_H + a_L - (2c+r)}{2}$

For the second case to hold, we need $q_L = a_L - c > K = \frac{a_H + a_L - (2c+r)}{2} \Rightarrow r > a_H - a_L$

For more details see Leautier (2019).

As shown more precisely in Box 8.1, we may end up with two possible situations, each one requiring a different optimal price:

- If $r \geq a_H - a_L$, $q_H^* = q_L^* = K^* = \frac{a_H + a_L - 2c - r}{2}$: we have permanent saturation of K.
- Otherwise, $q_L^* = a_L - c < q_H^* = K^* = a_H - c - r$: the capacity K is saturated only by peak demand.

The pricing policy that makes it possible to decentralize this allocation is:

- $p_H^* = c + \frac{r}{2} + \frac{a_H - a_L}{2} > p_L^* = c + \frac{r}{2} - \frac{a_H - a_L}{2}$, if $r \geq a_H - a_L$.
- $p_H^* = c + r > p_L^* = c$, otherwise.

We see that it is optimal to charge different prices at H and at L, whatever the discrepancy between the two periods, $a_H - a_L$, relative to the cost of capital, r. Charging a higher price at the peak effectively limits demand and saves installed capacity. When peak demand and off-peak demand are not very different, the off-peak price also helps finance equipment (since $p_L^* > c$) but is less than the theoretical long-run marginal cost (since $p_L^* < c + r/2$). By contrast, when the capital cost is not very high and/or willingness to pay is very different ($a_H - a_L$ is large), then consumers at peak are charged for the entire capacity cost on top of the energy cost, whereas those at off-peak times must pay only the energy cost.

It is important to note that this peak-load pricing policy is not a case of second-best policy in which the same product (obtained at the same cost) is sold at different prices, as in the Ramsey–Boiteux system. Here, given the installed capacity, the marginal cost is different at periods H and L. Also note that because capacity K is determined to maximize welfare, the off-peak/peak prices are a first-best option that also balances the firm's budget.

State-contingent prices. Fluctuations in demand and uncertainty of supply are at the heart of the electricity industry's business model. They can be analysed with models similar to that used for peak-load pricing, but where time is replaced by physical conditions (rain, average temperature and so on). More recently, as renewable sources of energy (which fluctuate by season, among other factors) are increasingly used to produce electricity, state-contingent pricing is quite useful to account for variation in inputs and demand.

In the following example, we forecast demand based on historical data and assume a mix of electricity sources, intermittent (wind, solar energy) and non-intermittent (fuel, gas, coal). Since the wind (or solar) power plant has a zero operating cost, it must be dispatched before the thermal plant, which is responsible for residual demand. This residual demand is intermittent, since it is the difference between the gross demand and the intermittent energy supplied by the wind or the sun.

The main difference from peak-load pricing is that the magnitude of the intermittent residual demand is endogenous, depending on the installed capacity of the intermittent source. Yet the pricing of intermittent energy shares some similarities with the standard peak-load model. In both cases, prices should reflect the cost of capacity when used.

Assume there are two states of nature, which are random. In the first one, denoted w, wind/sun blows/shines with frequency v. Then, in the second state, $\bar{w}$, that occurs with frequency $1 - v$, one can only rely on fossil-fuel plants. The marginal cost of producing electricity from wind or solar energy is nil, as long as the wind is blowing or the sun is shining. The problem to solve is as follows:

$$\max_{K_i, K_f} \left\{ v \max_{q_f^w} \left[S(K_i + q_f^w) - c q_f^w \right] + (1 - v) \left[S(K_f) - c K_f \right] - r_i K_i - r_f K_f \right\}$$

$$\text{subject to } q_f^w \geq 0, q_f^w \leq K_f, K_i \geq 0$$

where K_f and K_i (with unit costs r_f and r_i respectively) are the capacity of plants using fossil-fuel (thermal plant) and intermittent sources (e.g. wind, solar), respectively; q_f^w is the quantity to be produced by the thermal plant while the renewables are also producing; and c is the marginal cost of burning fossil fuel to produce one kWh of electricity. Given that they are costly to install, technology f is fully used in state $\bar{w}$ and technology i is fully used in state w. Solving this problem leads to three possible optimal energy mixes:[15]

1   If $\frac{r_i}{v} > c + r_f$, no intermittent source of energy should be installed; all power should come from fossil fuels.

---

[15] For the formal proof, see Ambec and Crampes (2012).

2 If $c > \frac{r_i}{v}$, both technologies should be installed, with the fossil-fuel plant used only when the intermittent source is not available.

3 If $c + r_f > \frac{r_i}{v} > c$, both technologies should be installed, with the fossil-fuel plant making up any deficit that physical conditions have prevented the renewable plant from producing.

This first-best investment and dispatching choice can be decentralized to market actors using the following system of prices, where $\bar{w}$ identifies windless conditions and w the presence of wind sufficient to drive the turbines:

1 If $\frac{r_i}{v} > c + r_f$, $p^{\bar{w}} = p^w = c + r_f$

2 If $c > \frac{r_i}{v}$, $p^w = \frac{r_i}{v}$ and $p^{\bar{w}} = c + \frac{r_f}{1-v}$

3 If $c + r_f > \frac{r_i}{v} > c$, $p^w = \frac{r_i}{v}$ and $p^{\bar{w}} = \frac{c + r_f - r_i}{1-v}$

These prices allow producers to recover their costs, on average.

The above pricing rules show the difficulty of pricing a product that is generated using a mix of heterogeneous technologies. Under perfect competition, each producer (and consumer) need only bid its marginal willingness to be paid (and to pay) for each unit, following which the market commissioner (most likely a software system) will determine the price. But a real-world central planning agency requires comprehensive information on costs and preferences.

Where primary energy sources are intermittent, there is an additional challenge: in cases 2 and 3, the implementation of the first-best option requires prices $p^{\bar{w}} > p^w$, contingent on physical conditions at the production node(s). In the future, smart grids will be likely to convey state-contingent prices to signal scarcity to consumers, encouraging them to adapt their behaviour to this signal. But until it is possible to transmit (and adapt to) such a signal, efficient dispatch is out of reach. The additional constraint $p^{\bar{w}} = p^w$ creates a financial imbalance at the expense of fossil-fuel plants.

8.6   Summing Up

- The average price is essentially set to ensure a fair rate of return to the regulated firm, but it is also the weighted average of the various prices faced by the various types of users where the weight is the share of the specific users in the total demand.
- Which specific prices and which specific weight the average price reflects depends on the forms of price discrimination and price differentiation adopted by the firm.
- Price discrimination requires that consumers cannot re-trade among themselves as the same unit is sold at different prices to different consumers.
- Full price discrimination is unrealistic under current consumption measurement technologies and political constraints.
- Most firms providing public services rely on second- and third-degree price discrimination or some combination of the two.

- Under second-degree price discrimination firms charge different prices for different blocks of consumption quantities or bundled products sold at a package price. Users choose the bundle they prefer.
- Under third-degree price discrimination firms manage to split the market for a particular good or service into easily identifiable groups and then charge each group a different price.
- From a regulated firm's perspective, price discrimination is an effective way of maximizing its share of the surplus produced by its activities.
- From a social welfare perspective, price discrimination can have both positive and negative effects as it can improve or worsen both efficiency and equity: the net effect depends on the specific market analysed and the specific form of price discrimination adopted by the firm.
- Rapid improvements in the technologies available to measure consumption, such as smart meters, imply that firms can implement increasingly precise forms of price discrimination. The increased volume of information on individuals calls for regulators to assess the costs and benefits of increasing the scope for price discrimination.
- Price differentiation, such as peak-load pricing, is a tool to smooth demand and avoid congestion. It is a source of efficiency in regulated industries.

9   Social Concerns in Regulatory Design

Meeting the needs of the poor and reducing inequality in service provision caused by geography, history or other factors are among the social goals that figure prominently in official regulatory objectives and missions. Yet in practice, efforts to address social concerns often come second to other policy goals. In some countries, this might be because regulation is more focused on the financial viability of an activity – and on minimizing costs to maintain or improve viability. In others, it reflects political preferences for other approaches to address social needs and concerns.

Even where concerns for the public good fall squarely within the regulatory mandate and the political preferences, the way those concerns are addressed is often constrained by a limited fiscal scope for subsidies. How social goals are pursued within financial, fiscal and efficiency constraints, depends on context, as well as on available technological and policy options. These dimensions and their interconnections have been addressed in theory as well as in practice.[1]

This chapter synthesizes the extensive academic literature on conceptual options and constraints regulators face when pursuing equity and related social concerns.[2] It also illustrates how regulators address social concerns in the real world while still catering to the efficiency, financial sustainability and political viability dimensions of regulatory interventions. The more conceptual parts of the chapter show how theory can help practitioners address these trade-offs in their day-to-day activities. And, in the process, they also show how good intentions (e.g. to protect the poor) can have predictable perverse effects that can be avoided in the careful design of policies.

The chapter starts with a case study on the evolution of tariff designs for the Californian electricity sector illustrating how difficult it can be to deal with both efficiency and equity concerns. This is followed by a more general discussion of the relative importance of equity and other social goals in the overall regulatory agenda, notably in sectors that involve large-scale infrastructure, using illustrations from current debates in member countries of the OECD and in developing countries.

---

[1] For public services in general, see Amin et al. (2008). The specific case of water is analysed in Nauges and Whittington (2017).

[2] See Bagnoli et al. (2020) for a survey of the quantitative academic evidence on the social impact of privatization and other forms of public–private partnerships resulting from a mistargeting of regulatory interventions.

Next, it provides some recent data on the implicit demand for interventions designed to expand service access and improve affordability. It then moves on to poverty-related diagnostics conducted in the context of regulation. This discussion weighs the options available for targeting service needs identified through the diagnostics. Recognizing that precise targeting is impossible, we provide simple rules of thumb for identifying those who would benefit most from regulatory protection. The final section shows how theory can help avoid the unintended negative consequences of good intentions.

9.1   What Do Social Concerns Mean in Practice? A Look at a Californian Experience

Over the past two decades, California has tried a wide range of designs to manage power consumption while also addressing social concerns and preserving providers' financial viability. Until the 2000–01 electricity crisis, California's utilities relied on an increasing block-pricing system. The second-tier marginal price was 15–20% higher than that of the first tier. One-third of residential consumers were paying only the first (lowest) price because they did not consume enough to reach the second level. This tariff was not high enough to discourage overconsumption and undersupply, which led to the 2000–01 crisis, and it did not really protect the poor.

After the crisis and in an attempt to better protect the poor while simultaneously reducing overall consumption, over the course of fifteen years, California switched to a five-tier, then four-tier, system in which the marginal price increased with the tier index for each utility.[3] Once again, the system was a disappointment, delivering only modest redistribution and efficiency effects. One reason was the system's excess complexity. As shown by Ito (2014), when faced with such a complex pricing menu, consumers responded more to average price than to marginal price.[4] All the efforts to get the marginal price right was, in the end, an ineffective approach to try to help the poor while controlling the overall level of consumption. Indeed, whereas a decrease in consumption was expected, California's reformed electricity tariffs resulted in a slight increase in total consumption.

In 2016 the California Public Utilities Commission responded with yet another reform. It decided to flatten the tiered rate structure by gradually increasing the rates of tiers 1 and 2, and gradually decreasing those of tiers 3 and 4 (CPUC 2017). By March 2016, there were only two tiers left, one below 130% of the baseline, the other above

---

[3] The highest-tier rate was more than twice the lowest-tier rate. More specifically, given a baseline set between 50% and 60% of average residential consumption in a given climate zone, tier 1 included usage up to the baseline, tier 2 usage between 100% and 130% of the baseline, tier 3 usage between 130% and 200% of the baseline, and tier 4 all usage above 200%.

[4] Since an increasing block tariff is essentially a convex function, and a convex function's marginal value is higher than its average value, the effect of increasing higher tier unit pricing on individual consumption should be weaker than assumed in the new pricing structure.

In 2018, the second tier of usage cost 25% more than the first tier of usage. Beginning in 2017, a 'super-user' surcharge was collected from very high energy users (those above 400% of the baseline), and in 2019, residential customers were switched to time-of-use rates. To make sure the reform would not have perverse equity effects, poor households qualified to receive discounts on their energy bills when enrolled in the California Alternate Rates for Energy (CARE) programme. They received a 30–35% discount on their electric bill and a 20% discount on their natural gas bill. It is too early to know if the changes will pay off, but the sequence of changes illustrates the difficulty of addressing social concerns by manipulating prices, in particular when trying at the same time to deal with efficiency issues.

More generally, the experience yields the following insights in the context of this chapter. First, as already mentioned, knowing the specific characteristics of users and usage is essential when designing price discrimination, in particular if the poor are to be protected. Second, it shows that for a complex tariff structure to be effective for both equity and efficiency purposes, customers need to internalize all its dimensions. But when the structure is too complex, however analytically rational it may seem, this is unlikely to happen. When tariffs are complex, customers do not necessarily respond to marginal price, and yet this response is needed if increasing block pricing is expected to improve both equity and efficiency. Third, one of the ways in which the poor may be helped is by giving them an opportunity to self-identify to become eligible for financial support within the sector. When information is scarce, this may also help to cut the risk of mistargeting.

9.2 A Detailed Look at Increasing Block Pricing: Does It Always Help the Poor?

Efficiency requires that prices reflect long-run marginal costs to signal scarcity, but service providers are also expected to cover all costs. When these two goals are achieved, there is a strong possibility that the resulting (efficient) prices will be unaffordable to poor people. One popular solution to simultaneously address social, efficiency and financial viability concerns, favoured in political circles, is to charge poor consumers below cost and to compensate for their consumption by charging rich consumers above cost.

When the poor consume less than the rich, a simple application of this strategy is increasing block pricing. Here, the volumetric price charged for service use increases from one consumption block to the next. Usually the first block corresponds to a 'lifeline' or 'subsistence' consumption level – a minimum quantity provided at a low price or, in some cases, for free. The idea is simple enough and certainly politically attractive when social concerns are high on the political agenda, which may explain why, for the water sector, the global water price survey conducted by Global Water Intelligence (GWI) shows that over 70% of utilities in low- and middle-income countries relied on increasing block pricing.

9.2.1   The Theory

Consider the case of utility consumption (e.g. water, electricity) in a community in which there are two categories of consumers, those with a high willingness to pay H and those with a low willingness to pay L. The difference is illustrated in Figure 9.1 by the two demand functions H and L. At any price level, the Hs consume more than the Ls. For the sake of argument, assume that those with a low willingness to pay are the poor consumers, and those with a high willingness to pay are the rich consumers. Under a linear pricing scheme, both would pay the same unit price, p. At this price, their consumption levels are q_{H1} and q_{L1} respectively.

Then imagine that, instead of the linear pricing rule, the regulator uses the following new pricing rule with two blocks, open to all consumers (Crampes and Lozachmeur 2014):

$$T(q) = \begin{cases} \underline{p}q \text{ if } q \leq \hat{q} \\ \underline{p}\hat{q} + \bar{p}(q - \hat{q}) \text{ otherwise} \end{cases}$$

where $\underline{p} < p < \bar{p}$. This means that type L customers will now face a lower price, while type H customers will face a higher marginal price. Since utility services is a normal good, under this specific pricing rule, type L customers would be expected to increase their consumption to q_{L2} and pay $T(q_{L2}) = \underline{p}q_{L2}$, whereas type H customers would cut it to q_{H2} and pay $T(q_{H2}) = \underline{p}\hat{q} + \bar{p}(q_{H2} - \hat{q})$.

The regulator's challenge is to set $\underline{p}$, $\bar{p}$ and $\hat{q}$ to address three concerns at once: social welfare, operational efficiency and financial viability. As shown by the California utilities example, getting this right is a complex, data-intensive exercise. The regulator needs to know the number of each type of consumer (n_H, n_L) and the elasticity of their demand, and then decide on realistic constraints to be imposed on the pricing system.

Assume that the initial unit price, p, was equal to the average cost, so that the utility was fully balancing its budget under the uniform pricing approach. If the same balancing constraint must hold for two-tier pricing, the values of the parameters that

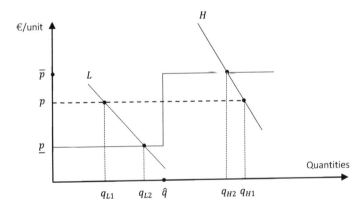

Figure 9.1 Increasing block pricing

regulators need to set must satisfy two constraints: they must guarantee that the financing of the activity is sustainable and that it pushes efficiency in a desirable direction. This second point is particularly important in sectors closely associated with environmental concerns. Cutting water and energy consumption is a critical goal of the demand management pursued using various regulatory approaches. In that sense, many pricing strategies would be deemed successful simply if they led to less consumption in aggregate.

The financing concern can be expressed as: $n_H T(q_{H2}) + n_L T(q_{L2}) \geq p(n_H q_{H2} + n_L q_{L2})$ since p stands for the average cost. It implies that the profit generated by consumption beyond the threshold $\hat{q}$, which is equal to $n_H(\bar{p} - p)(q_{H2} - \hat{q})$, must cover the financial losses due to all consumption below the threshold which is equal to $n_H \hat{q}(p - \underline{p}) + n_L q_{L2}(p - \underline{p})$. If the large consumers are indeed the rich consumers, this is an attractive solution, since it organizes an income transfer from the rich to the poor. For instance, the option is useful in countries or contexts in which limits on subsidies constrain efforts to help the poor gain access to services or require the rationing of access.

Efficiency, i.e. a cut in the overall consumption of all users, is boosted when $n_L(q_{L2} - q_{L1}) \leq n_H(q_{H1} - q_{H2})$. A careful look at the formula hints at the risks associated with the block-pricing tool in practice. In a context in which the share of the population with initially low levels of consumption is much larger than the share with high levels, there is a strong possibility of a net total increase in consumption. More specifically, a net increase is more likely when n_H is small against n_L and/or type L consumers are very price-sensitive as compared with those of type H. This characterization is not uncommon in developing countries. It implies two directions for regulatory action. First, it suggests that the specific block prices are instrumental in minimizing the risks of a perverse consumption effect. Second, and particularly in a developing-country context, it implies that focusing on a static vision of efficiency may be misleading. If the pricing approach allows an increase in the overall level of consumption among the poor, it may actually be good news. More access to safe water has many benefits in regions in which water-borne diseases continue to put children's lives at risk.

The more general implication of this discussion of increasing block pricing is that the importance of detailed data on the characteristics of populations is hard to overestimate. Increasing marginal prices is justified if rich households consume more than the poor. But even if this is generally true, exceptions are common. Indeed, demand for services such as electricity or water depends on several predictable factors. These include the composition of the customer groups and the price elasticity of their demand for service. But outcomes are also decided by supply factors, such as the quality of the equipment installed at consumption locations. In the case of electricity, for the many poor living in badly insulated housing with old refrigerators, unit prices that increase with consumption would be regressive.

9.2.2   The Practice

In practice, the solution is not as simple as it seems. As with many regulatory tools, its implementation is data-intensive. It requires the ability to separate rich from poor. In many countries this is unlikely to be feasible. Few electricity or water operators have access to the income data of their clients. In most countries, asking for this information is illegal. Therefore, regulators often rely on an approximation, which focuses on the separation of low and high levels of consumption. A different unit price is then applied to the two consumption types. And the pricing holds for all consumers, but the implicit assumption is that the poor consume less of the service than the rich. Unfortunately, this assumption turns out to be wrong in many cases.

These insights, counterintuitive for some, have been validated by empirical studies of international experience with the well-intended approach to increasing block pricing. For instance, Nauges and Whittington (2017) show for the water sector in nine OECD countries and four developing countries that, although the correlation between consumption and income is typically (but not always) positive, it tends to be weak. And this is not surprising. In countries in which poor families have a large number of children, and are overcrowded, poor households might use large quantities of water. As a result, Nauges and Whittington (2017) and Whittington et al. (2015) have documented the water sector's failure to ensure that the poor benefit from increasing block pricing. Barde and Lehman (2014) compare increasing block tariffs with means-tested tariffs in the water sector and find that the first distribute more income to the poor than do the second, but that the share of poor consumers benefiting from water subsidies is lower under the first.[5]

Ultimately, all these examples suggest that regulators should not forget how important it is to understand the market they are regulating. Both the demand and the supply sides of the markets matter. These points were evident in the Californian electricity pricing experience discussed earlier.

It is also obvious in a 2013 failed regulatory reform in France, where assistance to the poor has typically been accomplished through means-tested rebates on gas and electricity tariffs charged by the former incumbent utilities.[6] In this case, the reformers had underestimated the legal risks associated with the proposal. This is how events unfolded. In 2013, France decided to adopt a progressive pricing structure for network energy (electricity and natural gas) to both increase efficiency and protect the poor with a design much simpler than the one adopted in California. It was called the 'bonus-surcharge on residential energy consumption'. The bonus (rebate) was to correspond to a price lower than cost, and the surcharge to a price higher than cost. As in California, the proposal had both an efficiency and an equity goal, specifically

---

[5] Not all experiences with means-tested tools are negative. Contreras et al. (2018) analyse the Chilean experience with means-tested subsidies in the water sector over a long period (1998–2015) and find that the incidence of the subsidy is progressive, even if moderate. They do find, however, lasting errors of inclusion and exclusion.

[6] Starting in January 2018, these social tariffs were replaced by an energy check sent once a year by governmental tax agencies to eligible households (www.chequeenergie.gouv.fr/).

(i) to reduce residential energy consumption by giving consumers a clear price signal when use exceeded a threshold and (ii) to provide assistance to the 4 million French households that spend more than 10% of their income on energy.[7]

Conceptually, the system was quite precise. It was based on the preliminary determination of a yearly volume, v, computed for each dwelling, based on the type of heating (electricity, natural gas or local heating network), the geographical location, the number of people in the dwelling, and the consumption per head of the first quartile of most efficient users. Three distinct blocks of consumption were to be applied to this baseline: below v, a bonus (rebate) that could reach 20% on the selling price; between v and $3v$ there was a small surcharge (around 5%); above $3v$, the surcharge could become as high as 50% of the standard price.

In practice, this system was not implemented. It was invalidated by the French constitutional court on the ground that it would have violated the basic principle of citizens' equal claim to public service obligations (equal treatment under the law). Besides the legal aspect, the bonus-surcharge system would have been impaired by high management costs. Indeed, it would have necessitated setting up a specific agency in charge of collecting, processing and maintaining data on individual consumption and computing the bonus and surcharge rates to balance the entire system. Once more, complexity would have been an issue, as was the case in California.

9.3 The Big Picture: Options to Deal with Social Goals in Real-World Regulation

The scope for action in addressing inequality and other social concerns is large, and regulators have been creative in finding ways to proceed. A look at the websites of regulatory agencies around the world reveals a long list of solutions, including social tariffs; cash discounts, rebates and vouchers; price, income and investment subsidies; tax credits; low-interest loans; and guarantees. Conceptually, many of these tools correspond to some form of price discrimination or subsidy (on consumption, production or financing costs). Their aims vary across a wide range of objectives, from covering the costs of serving the basic needs of the poorest to encouraging customers to embrace environmentally friendly technologies.

Price subsidies tend to be the norm in water supply, and these generally benefit residential and agricultural users more than the other consumer groups. In many nations, this form of price discrimination is justified by certain user groups' historical sense of entitlement to low prices, irrespective of the cost of service. Cost-recovery efforts in the water and sanitation sector tend to focus on operational expenditures, extending less frequently to capital expenditures. This means that consumer payments cover the costs of operating and maintaining a network, while taxpayers tend to finance the investments required to develop it. In Europe, for instance, on average,

---

[7] Law no. 2013-312 of 15 April 2013.

only around 80% of the financial costs of water and sanitation activities are recovered. The rest is financed by subsidies provided by national or subnational authorities (Reynaud 2016).

Price subsidies are also quite common in transport, but their targeting is much less specific than in the water sector. For instance, the high level of subsidies afforded to rail transport services and infrastructure do not specifically seek to allay poverty concerns or, if they do, only indirectly. Often, they maintain connectivity from secondary cities or rural areas to urban hubs. Keeping a train station open for just a few passengers per day is not cheap. It is a tough decision, typically justified by a desire to treat all citizens in a similar way, irrespective of where they live. In other contexts, transport subsidies are designed to favour one mode over another. And this motivation is increasing in importance amid growing efforts to mitigate polluting emissions and favour modes of public transport that deliver both social and environmental payoffs. Overall, transport subsidies keep average costs within reach of most consumers, even if the effectiveness of the specific support mechanisms adopted varies significantly across countries.[8]

In many countries, the solutions adopted to further the common good imply giving up on efficiency, at least in part, and often on both efficiency and financial autonomy. Indeed, when prices are lower than costs, consumption can easily become excessive. And efforts to reduce water or electricity consumption have not made it to the top of the regulatory agenda around the world. In transport, by contrast, regulators are concerned with the differences in prices across transport modes. For example, many debates today centre on the need to cut the price of rail travel and increase the relative price of air and road travel to reduce congestion and pollution.

In practice, regulators are often asked to address political goals. The relevance of political concerns to the design and implementation of regulation has been particularly obvious in the process of infrastructure privatization. The price increases associated with privatization were one of the reasons behind the water riots in Bolivia in 2000. Protests followed on the heels of the water sector's privatization in other countries of Latin America as well and, later, in Sub-Saharan Africa (e.g. Mali, Niger and Tanzania) and South Asia (most recently in India, where efforts to increase the private financing of infrastructure have been stepped up in the past decade).

Public reactions to hikes in utilities prices are not limited to developing economies. In Europe, too, water and urban transport costs are politically sensitive. In the United Kingdom, where large-scale water privatization was initiated in 1989, the frequency of user complaints of poor service exploded in the late 2010s (according to OFWAT, the water services regulator). Meanwhile, investors in the sector have been enjoying generous returns. These two factors prompted the regulator to review the dividend policies of service providers to assess whether the sector's management favoured investors over consumers.

---

[8] For a useful overview in the context of urban transport, see Serebrisky et al. (2009).

Some public services are more politically sensitive than others, and regulators are aware of these differences. Clearly, water is particularly sensitive, and the main challenge for authorities is to balance the political risks linked to this sensitivity with the financial and fiscal sustainability of the solutions considered to diffuse public tension. This means balancing the interests of users, taxpayers and investors. Taxpayers tend to be the residual source of financing to mitigate social concerns. Where contracts between the state and suppliers can be renegotiated because of social unrest, a common outcome is the raising of subsidy levels.

Even if authorities often fail to rely on precise assessment of the distortions resulting from explicit or implicit subsidies, most are not blind to the extent of the fiscal costs involved. Often, however, they see these costs as necessary to minimize political tension. A limited scope for subsidies has various implications. First, the sector must rely increasingly on payments from customers rather than taxpayer-funded subsidies.[9] Second, service providers must devise ways to cut costs if they are to avoid an excessive increase in average tariffs. One way of doing this is to lower service quality, delivering a greater quantity within the same budget, but that path can be taken only so far. Third, regulators may try to improve efficiency at a given quality level – for example, by auctioning the right to provide services in a given area. The winner is the provider offering a specific service at the lowest cost. While each of these solutions has different social implications, they all force regulators and operators to strive for efficiency.

Various trade-offs between equity and efficiency are discussed in the rest of the chapter. How much room for manoeuvre a regulator enjoys is limited by the size of the trade-offs involved, since giving up on efficiency imposes other financial and economic costs on society.[10] If these costs become excessive, most economic agents lose, with politically unsustainable results in the medium to long term. Effective targeting of any measure undertaken for reasons other than efficiency is thus essential to protect both equity and financial viability.

Targeting is usually relatively easy to implement when the focus is overall fairness, since this tends to involve broad policy dimensions that are easy to identify (e.g. treating two regions equally). It can be much more complex to implement regarding other social concerns. This is particularly challenging for those concerns demanding the availability and sophisticated processing of extensive data to ensure effective targeting. But in many countries, there is usually at least some basic data to achieve a reasonable level of social targeting effectiveness if there is a political will to implement it. For instance, regulators can rely on poverty diagnostics in the context of their sector, allowing them to identify the extent to which households' lack of service connection is predominantly a matter of access (stemming from a gap in infrastructure investment) or affordability (where households choose not to connect

[9] This is also one of the transformations favoured by policies such as privatization or PPPs.

[10] In regulation, as in many other public policy areas, it is essential to keep in mind the differences between financial and economic distortions. Where subsidies are concerned, the profits and losses reflected in financial accounting concepts ignore that the taxes raised to fund them produce distortions in the overall allocation of resources (recall parameter λ representing the cost of public funds introduced in Chapter 4).

even when access is available).[11] Such diagnostics require geographical data to decide where and when each option applies. In many countries, the detailed data required to carry out this exercise are simply not available. So, various techniques have been developed to minimize the margin of error arising from the use of approximate data. Some of the simplest of these are reviewed next.

9.4   Who Needs Help from Regulation?

When equity and other social goals are on the regulatory agenda, the priority should be to properly target any subsidies, explicit or implicit, built into the regulatory design. This is needed to make sure that benefits are limited to those for whom they are intended. More concretely, good targeting requires tools to measure the twin risks that some of those who need the support may not get it (exclusion error) and that some of those who do get it may not need it (inclusion error).

Measuring these targeting risks is necessary to assess the effectiveness of a support policy. For example, if the exercise reveals that the population benefiting from water subsidies includes both subsistence consumers and swimming pool owners, there is good reason to doubt the effectiveness of the targeting mechanism. Reducing the risks of mistargeting grows in importance as the fiscal resources allotted to help the neediest become more limited.

In practice, public service regulators' first step in picking targeting instruments is to specify the goal sought. Typically, this involves framing the issue as one of access or one of affordability. The difference is important since each may require different levels of fiscal commitment as well as different targeting tools.

In most countries, it is easy to determine whether access is an issue. Countries produce standardized statistics on access rates for most public services. For instance, access to electricity or improved water sources[12] is unlikely to be a major regulatory concern in many countries. Notable exceptions include large areas of Sub-Saharan Africa and South Asia and parts of Latin and Central America where gaps are still significant. Access to sanitation is a much more common problem around the world, including among the poorest regions of some of the most advanced countries.[13] New questions of access are also likely to emerge as technological improvements create new services to be included in the social agenda (such as 'broadband for all'). As economies digitalize, the use of the internet becomes a necessary input into many activities, ranging from banking to teaching to income tax payments. Where

---

[11] See Crampes and Laffont (2014).

[12] Note that where people have access to 'improved' water, this does not imply it is within their home. Hence regulators may still need to work to improve the quality of access as part of any mandate to deal with social and equity concerns.

[13] For instance, the 2020 edition of the EU's Sustainable Development in the European Union Monitoring Report, https://ec.europa.eu/eurostat/en/web/products-statistical-books/-/ks-02-20-202, shows that, in Europe, the share of the population without access to a bath, a shower or indoor flushing toilet in their household was 1.9% in 2018. However, it is 25.6% in Romania and around 9% in Bulgaria, Latvia and Lithuania. Overall, 5.4% of the poor in Europe were in that situation.

Table 9.1 How different are expenditures on public services across income classes (as percentage of income)?

Income group*	Energy (%)		Water and sanitation (%)		Transport (%)		ICT (%)	
	Lowest	Highest	Lowest	Highest	Lowest	Highest	Lowest	Highest
East Asia	5.6	2.8	0.6	0.6	5.2	28.7	1.8	3.4
Eastern Europe	7.5	4.8	0.7	0.5	3.5	16.0	2.7	3.5
Latin & Central America	6.7	2.6	1.2	0.8	5.9	21.7	2.0	3.1
Middle East	5.4	3.2	1.2	1.0	3.8	20.3	1.8	3.6
South Asia	6.7	2.3	0.2	0.4	3.8	28.3	1.9	2.4
Sub-Saharan Africa	4.6	2.9	0.8	1.1	4.3	29.4	1.6	3.8

Source: Bagnoli et al. (2018).
* Lowest income group: ≤50th percentile of the global distribution (below US$2.97 per capita a day at purchasing power parity). Highest income group: ≥91st percentile of the global distribution (above US$23.03 per capita a day at purchasing power parity). Transport includes vehicle ownership.

neighbourhoods or regions lack access to the internet, this is likely to lead to discrimination in other forms of service provision and support.

Getting a sense of affordability is more complex. It starts with an assessment, across income groups, of the amounts households must spend to obtain the public services they need. It ends with an assessment of the extent to which this level of spending, for each income class, is affordable. This exercise is of course particularly relevant for those with the lowest incomes, and its main purpose is to assess the extent to which the price associated with their consumption bundle matches their ability to pay – or if, instead, they have been forced to ration their consumption or even forgo it entirely.

International organizations are a reasonably good source of information on expenditure levels. Unfortunately, the data are not easily comparable across organizations. For instance, the World Bank reports data per 'quartiles', while the European Commission focuses on quintiles. Despite this limitation, the data provided by such organizations are enough to offer a sense of the differences in spending patterns across income groups.[14] Table 9.1 shows that for the developing country dataset, the share of income spent on basic utilities (energy and water) tends to decrease with income, whereas the share of income spent on transportation, including vehicle ownership, and on ICT increases with income.

Similar insights emerge from country-specific studies in developed economies. In 2016, 9.4% of the EU population could not afford to keep their homes warm enough. The problem was particularly significant in Southern, Central and Eastern Europe, reaching almost 40% of the Bulgarians and more than 25% of the population in

---

[14] The World Bank data is not really reported per quartile in the usual sense. As mentioned in the footnote to Table 9.1, the Bank reports the data for population divided into four groups – 0–50, 51–75, 76–90 and 91–100 – which are constructed based on the global distribution of income, and not the within-country-data.

Lithuania, Greece and Cyprus. In the United States, between 2011 and 2013, low-income households spent 7.2% of their total household income on energy bills, a proportion more than twice as high as that of median-income households and three times that of higher-income households. Similar trends were observed in the water sector of OECD countries. According to the British water regulator (OFWAT), 15% of household customers struggle to pay their water and sewerage bills in England and Wales. This is linked to the fact that water and sewerage bills have increased by more than 40% in real terms since the sector was privatized in 1989. The average expenditure in England and Wales is 1.6% of income, yet for the poorest third of households, it rises to 3.7%. Water affordability is also a problem in the United States. Based on 2014 water rates, 11.9% of all households with incomes below US$32,000 allocate more than 4.5% of their income to pay for water services (Mack and Wrase 2017).

Overall, these stylized facts provide two main insights for a regulator concerned with social issues. First, the total share of income that the poor spend on essential public services, such as energy, tends to be higher than for higher-income classes. By contrast, they spend little on less-essential goods and services (such as internet access or transportation), largely because they cannot afford the equipment needed to make the most of the service available (i.e. the very poor are less likely to have a car or a smartphone). Second, in order to assess the extent to which regulatory intervention may be needed, regulators must be able to estimate what share of household income is a 'reasonable' one to spend on a given service. Unfortunately, there is no real solid theory or empirics available to guide this process. In practice, many general guidelines and rules of thumb are used and sometimes enshrined in national legislation, as discussed next. This has implications for the choices to be made when targeting subsidies under tight fiscal constraints. The next step is to figure out how much to support consumption and its affordability.

9.5   What Exactly Does Affordability Mean?

To determine which, if any, consumer groups require support through subsidies, a regulator must get a sense of the consumption that can reasonably be purchased by people with a strong willingness to pay but a limited ability to do so. Most practitioners rely on several rules of thumbs to define a threshold for the share of total household expenditure beyond which affordability is likely to be an issue. These rules tend to be used at a much more granular level than the quintiles mentioned earlier. They can be used, for instance, to get a notion of the extent to which a new pricing structure could inadvertently penalize the lowest income classes for their current consumption levels.

These rules of thumb are summarized in Table 9.2. Based on early studies and occasional updates, they tend to be embraced by international organizations, which have broad exposure to usage trends across countries. Some rules have become quite formal and now are included in international and national policy guidelines to identify the level of spending on services, expressed as a percentage of income, beyond which consumers will eventually have to ration consumption. Alternatively, they can be seen as the dividing line beyond which consumers can be considered 'poor' in terms of their ability to pay for a service.

Table 9.2 Rule-of-thumb affordability thresholds: percentage of income dedicated to utility beyond which poor consumers may have to ration consumption

	Energy (%)	Water (%)	Sanitation (%)	Transport (%)	Infrastructure (including communication services) (%)
Developed economies	10	3–3.5	1.5	None defined	None defined
Developing economies	4–5	3–3.5	1.5	15	20–25

Source: Authors' compilation from various sources.

The most widely recognized threshold is for water supply and sanitation. The World Health Organization has long estimated that 5% of income is the maximum the poor should spend on their water and sanitation needs – 3.5% for water alone. These thresholds are taken as a measure of water poverty in both developed and developing countries. Many countries have made an explicit commitment to adapt their water-pricing policies accordingly. These include high-income economies such as the United States and Northern Ireland; middle-income countries such as Argentina, Chile and Lithuania; and low-income countries such as Kenya, Indonesia and Mongolia. Many other countries that have not made a formal commitment still consider this threshold when setting the pricing structure for their regulated water companies. This explains why, on average, households, whether rich or poor, spend less than the cap, as can be seen in a comparison of Table 9.2 with Table 9.1.

In the case of energy, there is no single widely accepted threshold. Household expenditure caps, where they have been adopted, have differed across developed and developing economies, often to reflect differences in needs (heating requirements are different in Africa and Eastern Europe). In developing countries, spending 4–5% of household income on electricity and gas is a common upper limit. Spending more than this is considered to be evidence of electricity poverty. The comparison of Table 9.2 with the data reported in Table 9.1 also shows that in most regions of the world, the poor allocate more of their income to energy than called for by this rule of thumb, suggesting a regulatory failure to deliver on social concerns in this sector. In developed countries, there is no consensus on the right threshold. In the United Kingdom, the share has been 10% since the early 2000s, but energy regulators are revising it downwards.[15] Smaller shares are used as proxies in other European countries, even if most do not formally trigger regulatory intervention.

---

[15] A household is fuel poor if (i) its required fuel costs are above the national median level and (ii) if meeting its fuel costs would leave it with a residual income below the official poverty line – that is, a disposable income of less than 60% of the national median ('Annual Fuel Poverty Statistics. Report 2016', Department for Business, Energy & Industrial Strategy). This means that some households that are not considered poor in terms of income could be considered poor in terms of how much they need to spend on energy.

How much people spend on transportation depends on too many factors to allow a reliable international standard. Commuters tend to spend more than those who work or attend school close to where they live, and this in turn depends on a variety of factors, such as city planning, available transport options and so on. Cervero (2011) argues that, even if there is no rule of thumb for developed economies, transport spending is becoming a problem that regulators need to consider. He points out, for instance, that in the United States, the working poor spend more than 6% of their income to get to work (against 3.8% for the non-poor). Adding the cost of travel to schools, health-care centres, and grocery stores can explain why some families have to spend more than 20% of their income on transportation (including the cost of owning one or more vehicles). Things are getting worse with the implementation of environmental taxes on fossil fuels that increase the cost of driving old cars. Low-income people who live in zones without public transport services cannot switch to efficient modern cars (electric or hybrids) and protest violently against these non-compensated regressive taxes, as it has been the case in France with the 'yellow jackets' demonstrations in 2018–19.

Another broad rule of thumb recognizes that so-called infrastructure poverty may emerge from the sum of the amounts spent on each subsector. In developing countries, this share is about 15–25% of income (including telecommunications and transportation).

These aggregate data suggest that affordability is a widespread issue. And this is largely validated by more detailed studies, such as those of Estache and Wodon (2014) for Sub-Saharan Africa, Fay et al. (2017) for Latin America, the Asian Development Bank (2017) for Asia, and Deller and Waddams (2015) in the European context.

The main insight for regulators so far is that targeting various types of explicit and implicit support to the poor is not a straightforward exercise; otherwise, affordability would not remain an issue. Moreover, the difficulty of getting it right seems to be increasing. Growing infrastructure poverty problems around the world reflect poor targeting, budget constraints and possibly the wrong choice of support mechanisms. This holds, irrespective of the development level. Regulators must revisit the menu of options considered to support the poor, and gain access to the data needed to improve targeting. The situation calls for a simple way of assessing effectiveness in reaching the poor or other consumer groups that need support.

9.6   The Need to Calibrate Targeting

There are too many ways of implementing targeting mechanisms to do justice to all of them here. The main methods used in support programmes can be grouped into three broad classes of instruments: categorical/group, individual and self-selection, summarized in Table 9.3.

Categorical instruments are divided into two groups, geographic and demographic. They are quite attractive because they are relatively simple to implement. Geographic targeting is common in countries where poor and rich regions are clearly segregated, or where the difference in service between rural and urban areas requires some form of

Table 9.3 Targeting designs

Targeting approach	Specific targeting focus
Categorical	Geographic
	Demographic (e.g. children, students, elderly)
Individual	Actual or proxy means or incomes
	Community (e.g. farmers, slums)
Self-selection	By desired quantity
	By desired quality
	In packages or bundles of quantity and quality selections

correction. Demographic targeting (children, elderly, others) is common in transportation, for instance. Retirees and students get reduced fares in many countries.

Instruments targeted at the individual are probably the best known but are more complex to implement. They are usually also divided into two groups: targeting based on means or income and community-based targeting (e.g. farmers or slums). Income- or means-based approaches are sensitive to the precision with which means and income can be approximated. Tax-based information is often used, but this suffers from well-known limitations, since tax bases tend to be narrower than needed to give a full picture of assets or income. Community-based targeting is quite sensitive to the degree of heterogeneity across communities. Urban gentrification processes, for example, often lead to a combination of low- and high-income populations living in the same neighbourhoods. This is likely to reduce the effectiveness of efforts to allay poverty concerns based on zoning data.

Finally, in the case of self-selected mechanisms, people may sign up on their own for special tariffs, subsidies or other support mechanisms matching their preferences for quantity and quality with their willingness and ability to pay. These presume a high level of sophistication among the targeted populations, and they require regulators and service providers to monitor consumers' uptake and usage closely to ensure that discount packages do not cause providers to lose money.

Understanding these diverse approaches to targeting is useful because it gives regulators some room to match targeting goals with targeting tools. But the diversity of options also indicates that the risks of mistargeting are real. Common sense might suggest that the broader the eligibility criteria, the higher the risk of inclusion (i.e. helping people who do not need it); the narrower the criteria, the greater the risk of exclusion. But such assumptions can be misleading. Robust and carefully calibrated targeting techniques are needed to identify the most effective and efficient policy instruments to achieve specific goals in specific contexts, including data constraints.

As an example, consider the case of subsidies designed to help the urban poor.[16] Most common approaches rely on some form of explicit or implicit subsidies. In theory, support mechanisms can be designed to provide access at affordable prices for

---

[16] We do not discuss the ways in which subsidies are financed. In practice, they can be financed from general revenue, cross-subsidies or special funds.

the poor. But in practice there is no way around prioritizing either access or afford-ability, or the differential extent to which the populations targeted will benefit from the instruments applied. Various approaches are available to implement the inevitable prioritization. They range from complex analysis of poverty incidence and regulatory instruments anchored in general equilibrium models to simple, yet effective, partial targeting performance indicators.

One simple measure of benefit incidence that can be put together relatively easily is suggested by Angel-Urdinola and Wodon (2006, 2012). It has been used in a wide range of country-specific diagnostics.[17] Its targeting performance indicator, denoted by Ω, is simply the share of the global explicit or implicit subsidies received by the poor, divided by the proportion of the population in poverty. When $\Omega = 1$, the support to the poor is proportional to their share of the overall population, and no rebalancing takes place. When $\Omega > 1$, the subsidy distribution is progressive, since the share of subsidies allocated to the poor is larger than this population's share of the total population. And when $\Omega < 1$, the subsidy distribution is regressive, since the share of benefits allocated to the poor is smaller than the proportion of poor in the total population. For instance, suppose 25% of the population is poor and they obtain 50% of the subsidy benefits, then $\Omega = 2$, meaning that the poor are receiving twice as much in subsidies as the overall population – a transfer of wealth.

The indicator Ω can be used to compare the performance of various types of support mechanisms within a sector or across sectors, or within a country or across countries. For instance, if all households benefit from a lower price at lower blocks of consump-tion, all residential users of the service will have access to the subsidy, and therefore Ω will be equal to 1. The share of households receiving the subsidy is then equal to the share of all connected households – and the same holds for the poor. In this case, the social support is not as strong as it could be. By contrast, if the lower prices to be paid for lower blocks of consumption are accessible only to households consuming below the threshold amounts in the tariff structure and if the poor consume less on average than the non-poor, the benefits are greater for the poor than for the non-poor, and $\Omega > 1$. This would deliver a better overall targeting performance of the support mechanism.

Estache and Wodon (2014) shows that the drivers of the targeting indicator can also be unbundled, if necessary, into access and subsidy-design factors. In that case, Ω can be rewritten as: $\Omega = (access\ factors) \times (subsidy\text{-}design\ factors)$. This is useful to get a sense of where the main source of mistargeting might come from.

To compute the value of the *access factors*, the first driver of Ω, two relatively easy-to-obtain indicators are:

- Whether a household lives in an area served by the network, i.e. the rate of connection among the poor to the network.
- And, if the area of interest is connected, whether a household in this area is actually connected to the network, i.e. the rate of connection in the whole population.

---

[17] For an illustration of its use in Sub-Saharan African countries, see Estache and Wodon (2014).

The access factor is thus simply the ratio of these two rates. In Sub-Saharan Africa, South Asia or Central America, the access factor is likely to be less than 1 as the poor have much lower average connection rates than the population as a whole. But these indicators can also be useful in advanced economies in which access to basic services is universal but access to new technologies is not. Access to the internet, access to energy-efficient equipment and access to public transport are all dimensions of interest in the context of social policy. Government or regulatory intervention would be prompted by a political decision to speed up convergence towards universal or at least more encompassing access to these services. In these contexts, one way to assess policy effectiveness is to compute the speed at which the ratio is evolving towards 1.

The second variable affecting the value of the targeting parameter is the *subsidy-design factor*, which accounts for both the share of the population benefiting from subsidies and the size of the subsidies. It represents the ratio of:

- The average benefit from the subsidy among all poor households connected to the network; and
- The average benefit among all households connected to the network, whether poor or not.

As in the case of access, a factor less than 1 indicates poor targeting performance. This may reflect two policy failures. First, it may reflect an insufficient difference between the implicit or explicit subsidy rate applied to the poor and non-poor. Second, it may reflect the fact that the quantities consumed by the population as a whole tend to be larger than those consumed by the poor, so the overall subsidy received by the poor is lower on average than that received by the population as a whole.

Many more dimensions of targeting performance can be measured, but these two examples of simple measures demonstrate that there is little reason not to try to minimize the risks of poor targeting. Their main defect is that they tell the regulator only that something is wrong with the targeting, but they do not specify what went wrong.

9.7   What Can Go Wrong in Regulators' Efforts to Meet Social and Equity Goals?

The next question is why targeting may not be working well in the first place. Once again, experience provides a long list of explanations and hints at possible solutions for a variety of problems. Although the following list of explanations for regulatory failures to deliver on social and equity goals is quite long, it is by no means exhaustive. And even though access and affordability issues and their solutions often overlap, it is useful to discuss them separately for the sake of clarity. Each discussion may be used as a checklist when conducting a diagnostic of the key regulatory decisions.[18] Table 9.4 summarizes the discussion.

---

[18] The following review does not cover situations in which, for fiscal reasons, authorities stop subsidizing an activity and, in so doing, create a situation in which prices must be increased across users to cover costs.

Table 9.4 Potential problems with regulatory efforts to address social and equity concerns

	Access		Affordability	
Instrument	**Problem(s)**	**Possible solution(s)**	**Problem(s)**	**Possible solution(s)**
Pricing design	Excessive access, connection or fixed charges	Rely more on subsidies if fiscally possible Rebalance tariff design between connection and usage charges Cross-subsidies between low- and high-cost users or uses Rethink cost pass-through rules	Under-use of tariff design options or mistargeting of the design choices Excessively simple tariff structures to match the standardization of consumption bundle options Wrong quantification of blocks when block pricing approaches are used	Improve use of price discrimination techniques to make it easier for users to self-select quantity and quality consumption bundles they can afford Reset blocks
Subsidy design	Underused Mistargeted	Increase use and level of subsidies if fiscally possible, otherwise rely on cross-subsidies Conduct quantitative needs assessment and rebalance or retarget as needed	Underused Mistargeted	Increase use and level of subsidies if fiscally possible, otherwise rely on cross-subsidies Conduct quantitative needs assessment and rebalance or retarget as needed
Cost level	Outdated technology Wrong technology Ineffective cost management	Impose an update of technology Match technology with needs and budget constraints Increase the number and type of suppliers Improve incentives for better matching	Outdated technology Wrong technology Mis-management Ineffective cost management	Conduct quantitative needs assessment designed to improve match between technology preferences and willingness to pay Increase transparency of cost accounting Improve incentives for better matching
Quality levels	Insufficient/ excessive quality relative to consumers' needs and ability to pay	Match technology with ability to pay and increase/cut some dimensions of quality if needed	Insufficient/excessive quality Excessive standardization unable to match significant differences in ability to pay	Adjust operational dimensions of quality to match ability and willingness to pay
Service obligations definition	Omitted Underused Mis-specified	Rely on universal obligations but with flexibility in choice of technology to deliver on obligation	Excessive standardization in particular with respect to service options Underestimation of the importance of	Introduce menus of options to allow self-selection Restrict the scope for discrimination in service delivery quality

Table 9.4 (*cont.*)

Instrument	Access		Affordability	
	Problem(s)	**Possible solution(s)**	**Problem(s)**	**Possible solution(s)**
Users' cognitive ability	Too many complex options lead some users to opt out	Simplify enough without giving up on some scope for choice Define menu of options to minimize risks of exclusion	differentiating options when technology allows it at low cost Overestimated ability of users to know what is best for them in terms of price and consumption bundle choices	across users or use types Simplify without giving up on some scope for choice Define menu of options to minimize risks of exclusion

Source: Authors' compilation from multiple sources.

9.8 Problems with Access Rates

Access is often seen as a developing-country problem, one linked to investment. But it is much more common in developed countries than casual observers realize. For instance, access to new technologies in energy, telecommunications and transport is a serious global issue. In most countries, only small shares of users have access to the full range of new technologies that offer opportunities for improvements in service quality and reductions in unit usage costs. This reflects a mismatch between the cost of the investment needed to provide access to the new technologies and users' ability to pay for accessing them (or of the State to subsidize it). This is more complex than a simple question of affordability at the household level. Considering the size of the access gaps and the limited ability to pay user charges across large swathes of population, the adoption of these new technologies may be fiscally unaffordable.[19] This is one of the reasons why so many countries have been unable yet to facilitate a comprehensive switch to greener technologies.

It is also wrong to assume that access gaps can be closed simply by attracting more public or private investment. There are other reasons why access may be restricted, and regulatory design is central to some of them. The failures involving regulation include design defects in tariffs and subsidies, imperfect definitions of service obligations imposed on service operators and excessive quality requirements. To frame these issues in the more conceptual approach followed in the earlier part of this book, regulators may err grievously enough in setting price, cost, quality and service obligations to provoke a rationing of access among some users – and uses – of public

---

[19] The challenges of the technological transformation may also be linked to the difficulty of dealing with unamortized assets (stranded assets) as operators see their replacement as a costly financial waste. More on stranded assets in Box 11.2.

services.[20] And, as is often the case in economics, the four dimensions of price, cost, quality and service are interconnected.

Some of the regulatory issues are quite common and predictable, such as when operators rely on a two-part tariff in which the first part is the connection charge (also known as the access or fixed charge) and the second depends on usage or consumption. Setting the fixed charge too high often excludes low-income users. An extreme illustration is offered by a water services operator in Argentina (e.g. World Bank 1996). The initial regulatory design allowed the operator to charge a monthly connection fee equivalent to 25% of the average income level of the poor – just to get connected and excluding the cost of consumption! In this case, the solution is simple: connection subsidies for new users. But this requires capacity to target the subsidies to those who really need them, which in turn requires a good quantitative diagnostic of the consumption and income characteristics of the users of the service.

Diagnostics, however, does not guarantee that access will be improved. Unless regulators use the information to define and target investment needs, operators may exploit it to adjust their investment plans in a manner that detracts from the public good. The timing and targeting of investment decisions is linked to the prospects of producing income. In project finance, this is part of what is labelled 'commercial risk' and often used to justify a higher cost of capital in regulatory proceedings. For instance, rural areas or slums rarely attract businesses, because such areas entail a high-cost and low-financial-payoff investment (despite the high social payoff). More information without attendant service obligations may give operators a better opportunity for further cream skimming – a risk that must be managed by regulators.

Even when the capacity to subsidize access expansion is limited, solutions may exist within the sector. For instance, regulators may impose cross-subsidies across high- and low-cost users. The case for cross-subsidies often has both a social and equity dimension. Indeed, in many countries, initial connections have historically been highly subsidized. But the subsidies tended to favour firms and higher-income users that, once connected, would consume electricity or other services at profitable levels. Over time, this approach has ended up being fiscally unsustainable, and regulatory mandates now tend to include the requirement that connection costs be recovered from users. Since unconnected users often have lower incomes, the new regulatory mandates imply a regressive financing strategy: the previously excluded must pay for something that the richest users received at a subsidized price or even no cost. One way of correcting this is to have the current users finance at least part of the connection costs of new users, which produces a fairer distribution, over time, of the earlier subsidies.

A subtler problem of pricing design is linked to cost pass-through rules. When regulation explicitly or implicitly allows costs to be passed on to all users, producers have little incentive to match technology choices to the preferences for (or the willingness to function with) lower service quality when the ability to pay for it is

---

[20] See for instance Estache et al. (2006) for a discussion of a common way in which this arises in the context of developing countries.

limited. In practice, excess costs have been linked to regulatory tolerance of production choices that are oblivious to users' needs under circumstances where costs can be passed through (Estache et al. 2002). In some cases, there is little incentive to upgrade the production technology or change it to meet users' preferences, particularly when there is no competition and demand is quite inelastic. In other cases, excess costs can be linked to excessive quality levels tolerated and sometimes demanded by regulators. In this last case, well-intended preferences for the best technologies and/or decisions to standardize supply technologies may have ignored demand concerns and limited ability to pay.

An enthusiasm for unaffordable quality is common in transport, for instance, where the choice between buses, trams and subways has implications for financing urban mobility. Subways are often the best long-term solution but imply unaffordable fiscal commitments and politically sensitive increases in user charges. Buses may be less-efficient solutions but are easier to finance from user charges without excluding those users with a limited ability to pay. And when traffic levels are not significant enough to justify heavy investments in rail, buses also represent a cost-effective way to reduce the exclusion of users based on revenue or location. But authorities often prefer flashier rail-based solutions that are less rational from a financial and economic viewpoint, even when accounting for differences in emissions of pollutants. Also, in the case of a subway the investment is sunk (literally!), whereas bus networks can be easily modified, and the operator can shift its buses to another location if its contract is not upheld.

Adjusting quality may also help accelerate access gains. When it would take too long to build the infrastructure needed to upgrade quality, regulators should consider speedier solutions even if these imply lower quality. For instance, until water distribution companies can provide piped water in developing countries, low-cost local alternatives (such as standpipes and water trucks) may save lives, even if the investments have a much shorter operational lifecycle. This approach is increasingly popular in developing countries, especially when it affords an opportunity to rely on green technologies. The most obvious illustration is solar energy, the cost of which in developing countries with good sun exposure is now slightly cheaper than wind energy and much cheaper than many conventional sources.[21] Also, and importantly, solar panels can be set up within a matter of days in regions unserved by transmission lines. The same is true for wireless telecommunications compared with traditional telephone networks.

These examples show why ensuring that the quality standards built into technology choices are matched against users' ability to pay – and also the urgency of their need – is an essential component of good regulatory practice. This is especially true if the goal is to minimize the risks of sustained access gaps. The key, once again, is to match the mode of supply with the ability to pay – and across all user categories. This implies

---

[21] For instance, in Chile in 2016, the unit price of solar-derived electricity was about half that of coal-based electricity (IRENA 2019). However, in many developing countries, in particular in Africa, the problem of recycling batteries is yet unsolved.

quality standards that are reasonably flexible and, when technologically feasible, an increase in the number and diversity of suppliers.

We will now turn to some subtler ways in which regulatory tools may inadvertently depress access. The first is the definition of the service obligations imposed on the service providers. As mentioned earlier, unless operators are bound by service obligations, they are likely to avoid dealing with customers whom they view as costly and risky, focusing instead on maximizing their return on investment by skimming the cream from their customer base. Where obligatory services are subsidized, authorities facing the need to cut costs often reduce the obligations imposed on operators. This is why rural areas and secondary cities are seeing reductions in rail services. Stopping and starting a train and maintaining a station for just a few passengers per day is indeed not profitable and demands direct or cross-subsidies. A similar explanation holds for a lack of access or lower-quality connections to the internet in rural areas and secondary cities.

9.9   Problems with Affordability

Since the concept of affordability is less precise than that of access, it is more difficult to come up with a clear list of regulatory weaknesses.[22] When related to income alone, affordability may be no more than a pro-cyclical measure of a broader problem with users' consumption capacity, linked to fluctuations in their income. But even in that case, limited affordability may also reflect the poor design of pricing and of subsidies or even of the consumption options offered. It may also reflect excessive costs, linked to inadequate incentives for service providers to minimize them.

The solutions are all quite straightforward in these cases, and most have been discussed in the context of access. Trickier issues are posed by transitions. When authorities switch from tax-financed consumption to user fees as part of a process of commercialization or privatization, affordability may become an issue for users accustomed to subsidies. And, as in the context of access, a poor choice of quality options or poor definition of service obligations may lead to affordability problems as well.

The technical and political ease with which solutions can be identified and implemented depend, as one might expect, on the informational, social and political context. Often, improving price discrimination and its targeting will do the trick. Similarly, when block-pricing approaches are in place, simply resetting the blocks to change the targeting may be enough to improve affordability. Either is relatively easy to accomplish once needs and initial conditions have been assessed, usually building on detailed household and enterprise consumption surveys or on consumption-monitoring processes put in place by operators. The digitalization of monitoring

---

[22] Moreover, these lists are usually done at the sector-specific level, e.g. Gomez-Lobo (2011).

processes (e.g. smart grids) has made it increasingly easy to improve targeting in recent years and should help refine pricing and subsidy designs.

Another solution, often overlooked, is to reduce the quantity–quality consumption bundles offered to users. Historically, consumption bundles were standardized in an industry characterized by economies of scale and scope as a way of cutting average costs. However, it did not guarantee that services would be affordable for the poor. Today, new technologies such as sensors that monitor and control consumption and production are making it easier to differentiate quality along many dimensions. Although such technologies have not yet been deployed to support social policy goals, they can help make basic consumption more affordable without necessarily increasing average costs in a sector. Proposing different quantity–quality bundles might also help reduce targeting inclusion errors as the rich typically prefer high-quality services. They are less likely to choose the subsidized bundle if it comes with a lower quality.

An important example of technology's capacity to ease the matching of quality of supply with users' ability and willingness to pay is the growing reliance on prepayments for consumption made possible by prepaid electric or water meters. Most utilities charge users for consumption at the end of a billing cycle based on information collected via a manual meter reading. New technologies enable a process by which some users pay for their expected consumption. Essentially, users buy a consumption credit, usually in the form of a prepaid card or an access code to be used on a smart meter installed in their dwelling. Once credit is added, consumption is possible, and credit falls with consumption at the average prices built into the user's tariff programme. The system is quite flexible, since consumption credits can be acquired through social services or purchased commercially (e.g. from banks, post offices or designated shops). From the suppliers' perspective, the process saves the costs of the meter reading and paperwork involved in standard billing. Kelsey and Smith (2015) show that switching households to prepaid electricity in South Africa reduced electricity use by 13% or 2 kWh per customer per day, on average. The biggest difference was observed among relatively poor customers. The process also improved revenue recovery, especially from households that would typically pay their monthly bills late.

The process also helps screen users more effectively, since they must identify themselves in order to receive the prepaid cards or vouchers. This does not let regulators entirely off the hook, however. In the United Kingdom, for instance, regulators failed to account for the possibility that providers of prepaid services would not offer the same tariff options as those offered to users with standard meters. Suppliers tended to offer just one tariff level to prepaid customers: the most expensive available. This is something regulators need to monitor if social policies are to be cost-effective and fair. In developing countries, prepaid water service is still being piloted, and there are still many bugs to fix before it can be mainstreamed (Heymans et al. 2014). But it does have significant potential to cut costs while more effectively meeting user needs, and the number of success stories is growing.

Finally, behavioural economics has produced, since the early 2010s, new, simple, non-pecuniary behavioural regulatory interventions, or 'nudges', that may improve efficiency while catering to social concerns. Such interventions have changed behaviours in electricity consumption (Allcott 2011; Buckley 2020) and water consumption (Ferraro and Price 2013; Lu et al. 2019). Most cost little to implement. For instance, simplifying choices and setting default service at the level most likely to fit the poorest users' needs are relatively easy. Robust evidence suggests that too many choices may be as bad as too few, especially for low-income users with less education and less time to spend on assessing options. Indeed, across a wide range of countries users prefer not to decide when choices are too complex and instead go with the default option. In their survey of the literature, Hobman et al. (2016) show evidence for low rates of voluntary uptake of preferred electricity service options in the residential electricity sector. This is not surprising, since household electricity demand, in the aggregate, appears to be relatively price inelastic. But it can have brutal implications: unless regulated, service providers are likely to use this bias to set, as the user default, the combination of price, quantity and quality that produces the highest financial return. Other studies reach similar conclusions for public transport (Garcia-Sierra et al. 2015). Behavioural diagnostics thus help explain why affordability issues can arise in ways not necessarily identifiable using standard approaches to regulatory design. But even without accounting for users' behavioural patterns, standard economic diagnostics can be useful in explaining the anti-social biases built into regulatory decisions, including some widely considered to be pro-social, such as increasing block tariffs, which were discussed at the beginning of the chapter.

9.10   So What?

This brief review of the experience, and the various case studies discussed, suggest that some of the main implementation challenges commonly faced by regulators are relatively predictable. The first is the limit imposed by users' cognitive ability on the complexity for the design of the regulatory tools adopted to achieve social goals. The second is the need to internalize the fact that any regulation, including the best-intended social regulations, must account for the legal system. Credible economic solutions to economic and social problems need to fit into legal frameworks that address issues far beyond sector-specific concerns. And in many countries there are limits on what kind of sector-specific solutions can be adopted, even if these do respond to pressing concerns. Third, the implementation of attractive conceptual solutions can be costly. Unless implementation costs are accounted for as part of the regulatory mechanism, it is quite likely that the adoption of an otherwise conceptually attractive approach will be challenged by those who are expected to pay for it.

It is however crucial that delivery on social concerns is not just a technical or legal matter. It is also a political challenge. Any reform must be politically sustainable rather than simply economically sustainable. And how politically sustainable a reform is often depends on its social viability. If enough voters with sufficient political leverage are unhappy with a regulation, the odds are that it will somehow be challenged. Efforts by France to adopt more efficient and fairer energy pricing systems to address environmental concerns have led to massive social actions. Since the early 2010s, these sorts of actions have led President Hollande to drop a creative road pricing mechanism and President Macron's attempt to increase energy prices has ignited the yellow-jacket rebellion. Yet the policy was marketed as environmentally desirable, which conceptually boils down to an intergenerational equity argument, since its purpose is to protect future generations who do not vote today. This argument had a much lower weight than the short-term social consequences of the reforms. Hollande forgot to account for the unhappiness caused by some regions losing more than others (e.g. Bretagne) and Macron forgot that he was favouring wealthy urban citizens with access to public transportation over poorer suburban and rural citizens without such access. In both cases, the political economy of the reforms had been underestimated. And, as both French presidents learned the hard way, the social impact of reforms is quite central to this political dimension.

In sum, a look at practice shows that, unless the new generation of regulators does a better job at internalizing the accumulated experience, the long history of socially unsustainable regulation leading to crisis will continue to reproduce itself. The spread of energy poverty issues, notably in OECD countries, in addition to the well-recognized energy poverty challenges faced by emerging economies, the global concerns of water poverty and environmental degradation, and the transportation problems faced by the poorest and rural citizens in many countries, all signal regulatory failure in its social dimension. And this at a time when the growing volume of information allowed by techniques such as geo-localization, the improved and more refined monitoring of household expenditures and the increased digitalization of databases should make it easier to target those who need help at the least possible fiscal cost.

9.11   Summing Up

- Evidence accumulated over the last twenty to thirty years shows that the ability to appreciate and account for the magnitude and complexity of the interactions of efficiency and viability, on the one hand, and social concerns (including equity), on the other, continues to be a major challenge for regulated industries.
- Inclusion and exclusion errors are common in public utilities policies aiming at subsidizing the poor. This is for instance the case with increasing block-pricing schemes in water and electricity.
- In many circumstances, the good intentions built into the social agenda must be tempered by a realistic sense of what is financially, technically, legally and politically sustainable.
- With respect to ensuring a fair treatment of the needs of the poor, the regulators will have to be able to distinguish between lack of access and lack of affordability.
  - Affordability has traditionally been more challenging to identify and address but increasingly governments are defining thresholds on the income share that families or individuals should spend on each public service.

- o For both challenges, regulators can rely on a large menu of pricing, direct and cross-subsides, technological or quality options or service obligations to reduce or eliminate the undesirable social biases.
- o The optimal choice depends on the local preference, on the local fiscal capacity and on the implementation capacity of the regulators. And this requires a specific institutional diagnostic.
- o Recent theoretical developments have also shown that regulators should pay more attention to the costly default options often found in menus of service levels, and push for these to be reset so as to maximize the odds of helping those who need it most.
- To ensure that regulation delivers on the social goals to be addressed, regulators must make the most of the growing volume of data available and use it with more rigour to refine the social targeting efforts. To this end:
- o Sector-specific poverty diagnostics are indispensable.
- o Data are needed to provide more precise profiles of whether the poor have access to the service or not; whether they can afford access and usage; whether affordability constraints are linked to income or to biases specific to the sector; and the extent to which service quality matches willingness and ability to pay.
- o They are also useful in conducting the winners' and losers' assessment of regulatory options needed to evaluate their political viability, since the experience clearly shows that this is a sine qua non requirement for the sustainability of regulations.

10 Regulating Quality

Because quality is a key cost driver, it is a crucial, yet sometimes underestimated, topic in regulatory economics.[1] Increasing quality tends to inflate costs, including longer-term costs when it is also more expensive to maintain. For instance, high-speed trains are usually not only more expensive to build but also more expensive to operate than regular trains. Similarly, the more demanding are environmental restrictions with respect to the treatment of sewage, the higher is the cost of technologies to be used in sanitation. From the operator viewpoint, cutting service quality allows them to save on costs, at least in the short run. The most visible examples of cost savings linked to quality include cutting the staffing of repair or client-oriented crews in any public service. At a more technical level, cutting the frequency of scheduled asset maintenance is a common way to reduce short-term costs, even if often less visible, but with long-term consequences since it speeds up the need to rehabilitate or replace assets.

Regulating quality can be quite challenging. This is because it is multidimensional, not always objective and hard to verify, both ex ante and ex post. Therefore, mis-targeted regulatory interventions are going to be more common than social welfare would demand. But there are many ways in which regulation can reduce the risk of mismatches between the demand for quality and its supply.

Trade-offs between costs, quality levels and the odds of mis-targeting are to be expected. But they are reasonably easily identified. The main challenge is to take the time to identify the options, the sources and margins for error, and to cost them to ensure that trade-offs, and their consequences for consumer prices and subsidies, can be quantified as precisely as possible.

The purpose of this chapter is to review the main insights from theory and practice on the design of regulation aimed at assessing and influencing the level of quality delivered by regulated companies. It shows that, while aiming at perfection is an unrealistic goal in quality regulation, controlling it is easier than the complexity of the challenge would suggest.

---

[1] For a useful early survey see Sappington (2005).

10.1   What Does 'Regulating Quality' Mean in Practice?

The most obvious characteristic of quality in regulated industries may be its multidimensionality. This is the case for roads, for instance. The definition of road quality includes technical dimensions such as the network's maintenance requirements or their ability to withstand unexpected weather conditions. It also includes more service-oriented dimensions such as the availability of lanes during rush hours, the average speed at which travel takes place or the speed with which potholes are repaired. Any of these dimensions require some degree of monitoring and each of them may demand some intervention at a cost to road operators. And these will eventually get passed on to users if roads are financed by tolls or to taxpayers if they are financed through subsidies.

This has been internalized in the design of the regulation of highways networks in the United Kingdom. In 2010, an independent review of the government's approach to managing the road network concluded that operating and development costs were excessive and funding insufficient. After some intense debates, the country decided in 2013 to turn the highway agency into a separate government-owned company interacting with the Ministry of Transport, Highways England. The company was expected to oversee about 2% of the total road length of the country, but around a third of all motor vehicle traffic. Highways England works in fixed funding periods of five years, called Road Periods, and is expected to implement the Road Investment Strategy during that period. The transformation became formal in 2015 and the land transport regulator, the Office of Rail and Road (ORR) was mandated to monitor the performance of this new company. The regulator's mandate includes the monitoring of the quality of highways and of the services highways provide to users and identifying potential improvement areas, including investment needs.

To produce the performance indicators, ORR compares the whole strategic road network with other road operators or organizations. Best practice is then benchmarked nationally, and this benchmark is validated through international comparisons. ORR focuses on five key quality performance indicators. Two are based on objective quality measures, such as lane availability, or share of incidents cleared within an hour. Three are more difficult to measure and have to rely on more subjective indicators, namely road users' satisfaction, work done to minimize average delays and proportion of pavement requiring no further investigation for possible maintenance.

These quality benchmarking exercises provide a wide range of insights. They can show that, on some dimensions, road management is working fine. However, when performance is not meeting expectations, they can be used to target regulatory decisions. For instance, the 2017 assessment suggests that a reasonably competitive road operator could potentially make annual operating productivity gains of around 0.6–0.9% which need to be considered as part of the assessment of the financing requirements of the sector. But since benchmarking can ignore local specificities, the assessment had to be complemented by a more detailed audit of real unit operating costs. Benchmarking is only one component of the 'information revelation' effort expected from the regulation of quality. As we saw in Chapter 5, it works mainly when the costs of different operators/firms are reasonably comparable.

Overall, the British case illustrates that the assessment of the quality performance of a regulated activity can be quite structured and transparent. And it is needed to minimize the risk of suboptimal quality delivery by service providers. It also shows that the diversity of quality measures can be quite a challenge to monitor. Relying on a combination of subjective and objective measures and benchmarks reduces the difficulty of tracking all quality dimensions in a cost-effective manner (e.g. Tangeras 2009). And they can be quite effective (e.g. Nepal and Tooraj 2015 in the context of electricity regulation in Europe).

10.2   A First Conceptual Glimpse at the Complexity of Getting Quality Right

The intuition of the regulatory relevance of quality is quite simple and easily revealed by a model which is a straightforward adaptation of the basic model used in microeconomics textbooks. Suppose that consumers cannot observe the effort of the operator to maintain quality z, but still value it. Their willingness to pay for quantity q is given by the inverse demand function $p(q, \tilde{z})$, where $\tilde{z}$ is the perceived quality. If costs are given by $C(q, z)$, the monopoly, will choose q and z to maximize $\pi(q, z, \tilde{z}) = p(q, \tilde{z})q - C(q, z)$. The problem is that z and $\tilde{z}$ are not always the same. For some types of quality dimensions (i.e., credence attributes), such as those concerning health, it can even be the case that z has no effect on how consumers value $\tilde{z}$. If so, more quality always increases costs without any effect on consumers' willingness to pay: increasing quality would lead to lower profits (i.e., $\frac{\partial \pi}{\partial z} = -\frac{\partial C(q, z)}{\partial z} < 0$). For this type of product the optimal level of quality from the firm's perspective in a world without regulation is $z = 0$.

From the society's perspective, the optimal level of quality is derived from the maximization of social welfare instead, that is, as in Chapter 4, the sum of consumers' net surplus and producers' profit: $W(q, z) = V(q, z) + \pi(q, z)$ Assume that $z = \tilde{z}$, and $\frac{\partial V}{\partial z} > 0$ since a higher quality is valued by consumers, then the desirable level for society is the solution to $\frac{\partial W}{\partial z} \leq 0$. If quality costs are very high, $z = 0$ remains a candidate. However, because we now internalize the beneficial effect to consumers, the solution is most probably $z^* > 0$, given by $\frac{\partial S(q, z^*)}{\partial z} = \frac{\partial C(q, z^*)}{\partial z}$, where $S(q, z)$ is the gross consumer surplus. As we will prove later in the chapter, this only implies that quality z is underprovided if it is not regulated. In this world, the easiest solution is often to impose a minimum standard, provided quality (or quality investments) can be measured by the regulator, and this is what is done in practice for many quality dimensions (Crampes and Hollander 1995).

This basic model also illustrates the importance of the interface between cost and quality, hence between price and quality. In practice, this has long been recognized by all stakeholders in regulated industries as well as by academic research, as illustrated by Box 10.1. However, it is a moving target.

The importance of the interactions between cost and quality has actually been growing as technology and policy are both increasing the quality choices available to consumers. As competition for monopolistic or oligopolistic markets between

Box 10.1 How Does Quality Show Up in the Value of the Assets and in Prices?

The figure illustrates how quality requirements are accounted for in the identification of the revenue requirements of regulated providers. The quality standards imposed must be accounted for in the CAPEX. This is how technological standards, for instance, are reflected ex ante. This clearly influences the value of the regulated asset base and the matching depreciation allowances to determine the maximum allowed revenue.

Downstream, this also influences the maintenance of the assets which eventually will also influence the tariff. Any change to the quality requirements will thus influence the average price. Formally, this comes from the usual formula and quality is hidden in the OPEX and the CAPEX. It is eventually reflected in the firm's asset value at the end of the period.

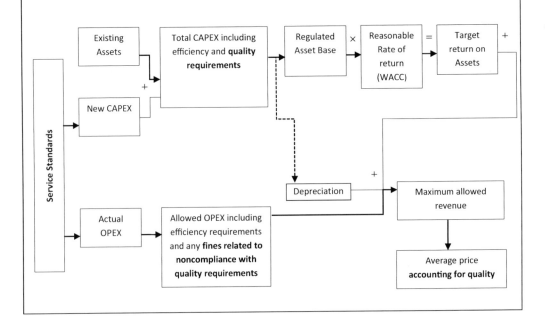

providers of electricity or phone services increases, consumers are indeed being offered much longer menus of options for the service quality they would be willing to pay for. Quality has become one of the main tools used by service providers to differentiate products and services. There has been considerable creativity in enlarging the menu of options. Consumers now get to decide how fast their internet is, how quickly their complaints are addressed or how green their electricity is. And what they choose for each of these dimensions depends on their willingness to pay for quality.

Bundling access to a service with a wide range of quality levels which a consumer can pick from is in principle a desirable situation if there is a clear understanding of what the options are and a willingness to pay for them. The problem is that many of the actual costs and risks of the various options are much better known to the regulated provider than to the users (and taxpayers). Indeed, information asymmetries also show up in the discussion of quality regulation.

When cost information is not as transparent as it should be and the actual quality is not as verifiable as would be desirable, it is reasonable to expect regulated firms to make strategic decisions on the supply of quality. The core regulatory questions are then to figure out when higher quality is unnecessary but provides higher profits and when the quality is insufficient, and how efficient and fair the quality price is.

To provide a robust answer to this question, it is also necessary to account for the demand for quality. This is necessary to link the willingness to pay with the specific quality options offered by the service providers. Would most train riders prefer to pay less even though it takes a bit longer to get to their destination? Are electricity consumers willing to pay more for renewable energy? Any of these questions can be answered by conducting surveys and these have become important tools in regulation. Even if some of the surveys have been criticized for producing subjective rankings, all stakeholders do them. Regulated firms do surveys for obvious business-related reasons since it helps them target demand. Regulators do them, sometimes also to audit firms' claims on the nature and level of demand.

As for the supply side, the challenge is just as data-intensive. Quality must be costed as precisely as possible to ensure that the required revenue computations account for the expenditures the firm needs to make to comply with quality-of-service obligations and/or demand. Are the levels of maintenance consistent with the commitments made when the investment decision was made?[2] Are they consistent with the need to minimize or eliminate the risk of catastrophes such as train derailment, bridges collapsing or the health effects of serious water or air pollution? Most of these questions can be modelled quite precisely to produce costings to be used in regulatory pricing decisions.

Conceptually, all this simply reflects the need for regulators to ensure ex ante that, first, the quality supplied matches the users' willingness and ability to pay and, second, this is costed properly to reduce some of the most predictable sources of information asymmetry. How thorough this diagnostic must be is subject to debate. Clearly, quality covers a broad range of concerns directly related to the service provider. But there may be other quality dimensions indirectly impacted by the regulated service. For instance, regulators increasingly also need to account for environmental and other externalities, even when many consumers and producers would prefer not to have to deal with them. Unfortunately, the handling of these other quality dimensions is too often not accounted for explicitly in the design of the economic regulation mandate assigned to sector regulators. They tend to be left to

---

[2] It is useful to remember that ex ante, when the cost–benefit analysis of a project is conducted, it assumes that for as long as the asset lives it will be maintained according to the expected standards. If during its life the maintenance expenditures are cut, it is likely that the asset life will be lower and the service not as expected. Think of potholes on highways. They signal a lack of maintenance and the resulting damage to cars and trucks reduces the return to the initial investment since it increases the costs to society of using the investment.

specialized regulators and the interactions between the two groups of regulators are not always ideal, as discussed in Chapter 14 on institutions.

Despite the difficulties hinted at in this brief overview of the challenges, the scope for action is significant as the sources of difficulty are reasonably predictable. But how well this can be done depends on the size of the regulatory budget assigned to the job. The multidimensional nature of quality makes its monitoring quite expensive and demands significant budgets. For example, in electricity, quality includes technical dimensions which are easy to control such as the voltage. But it also covers the odds of outages, the safety of the technologies, their impact on the environment or the degree of client orientation (e.g. the clarity of the bills and the rapidity of intervention in case of emergency). Additionally, service failures can originate at the generating plants, or in the transmission and distribution grid, or even at the consumption location because the supplier has signed a contract poorly adapted to requirements. Under vertical divesture, it can be difficult to identify which agent is guilty. This is quite a heterogeneous agenda for any regulator to deliver.

The quality of regulation also depends on the extent to which quality can be verified by any of the stakeholders, whether ex ante or ex post. For instance, it is a lot easier for a regulator to check if a road is full of potholes than to assess the quality of the gravel that has been used to construct the road. Similarly, it is a lot easier to have a sense of water pressure issues than of the extent to which water consumed at home meets the desirable health standards. This explains why the regulation contracts often rely exclusively on some indices easily verifiable ex post, such as SAIDI and SAIFI (mentioned in Chapter 6) for the electricity industry.

The non-verifiability of some quality dimensions is one of the major determinants of the scope for operators to inflate or cut costs as needed, depending on context and opportunities. The lower the regulator's and consumers' ability to verify quality, the higher the operator's leverage and the higher the rent the operator can capture. This translates into higher risks that consumers will be less well-off or that operators will capture an unfairly large share of the efficiency gains that can be achieved from improvements in the quality of assets used to deliver the services. And this is why the effectiveness with which quality is built into the design of regulation is so important.

10.3   Categorizing Quality

Because of the multidimensionality of quality, economic analysts rely on various types of categorizations designed to identify the main issues on which regulators need to focus. Theory has been quite useful to guide these categorizations and assess their policy implications. But before getting to a more technical overview of the ways in which theory helps us think through regulation, it may be useful to start with a more intuitive discussion based on four broad measures:

• Objective versus subjective attributes.
• Vertically versus horizontally differentiable attributes.

- Degree of verifiability.
- Timing of verifiability (ex ante versus ex post).

Objective versus subjective attributes. Quality attributes can be categorized based on the extent to which they can easily be measured objectively or not. Objective measures of quality include durability, safety, reliability, frequency, speed and any other technical characteristics that can be ranked based on performance indices applied and measured in a similar way anywhere. They tend to be relatively easy to obtain and to benchmark. And this accessibility is continuously improving in most regulated industries. Indeed, the digitalization of regulated industries is making many of these measures increasingly precise and, in principle, it should also make quality performance more easily available to all stakeholders, unless regulated companies are allowed to create a new informational rent from their privileged access to all the smart measures allowed by digitalization.

Subjective measures are usually based on perceptions or preferences and to dimensions that may not lead to unanimity. They include, for instance, assessments of the extent to which customer services are responsive to complaints or concerns, the perceived degree of competence or kindness demonstrated during interactions or happiness with the breadth of the menu of options available for technical characteristics (e.g. not enough choice or too much). These subjective measures tend to focus on service quality instead of technical quality. Despite the possibility of biases, they are quite useful in practice, in particular when objective measures are not available. Many subjective dimensions of quality are hard to cost (what's the value of a smile to an unhappy customer?). Thanks to smartphone applications, it is now easier for any consumer of a public service to rate the perceived quality, from 'unsatisfactory' to 'excellent'. Subjective quality can also be a matter of perceived fairness. Even though consumers are considered correctly on objective grounds, they can feel discriminated against when they compare themselves to other groups.

Vertical versus horizontal differentiation of quality. When quality can be unanimously ranked from low to high, it is said to be vertically differentiated. All consumers prefer high quality at the top of the vertical scale to low quality at its bottom. For example, in the electricity industry, a steady frequency (50 Hz in Europe, 60 Hz in the United States) is considered by all users as a highly valuable quality of energy provision. Most regulated firms produce objective indicators that can be differentiated vertically as they are useful from a management perspective. And in some cases, these indicators are audited or produced by regulators themselves, in particular when health or safety risks are relevant concerns.

In contrast, horizontal differentiation reflects differences in preferences across people, then differences in choices among some quality dimensions, even when their prices are equal. In other words, in their assessments of the valuation of quality, regulators must internalize the fact that there is no natural ranking between the dimensions such as design of website, colour or shape of terminals in consumers' houses, too little or too much choice in service type, train schedule. Horizontal differentiation also covers spatial concern. Future users will most likely disagree on objective questions such as where to install a new hospital or a new post office. In transport, if a railway line goes from A to C through B, deciding on how many trains should be direct and how many should stop at B depends on the relative number of potential passengers living at each node as well as the additional costs due to stopping at B (additional wagons, longer journey). Horizontal differentiation is implicit in many of the debates on individual commitments to environmental friendliness when picking transport modes or energy suppliers for instance. In most of these cases, the valuation of quality ends up being a political rather than an economic decision.

From a regulator perspective, what matters is the extent to which the quality measure of interest to consumers can be ranked unanimously or not, because it makes a difference to the way it can be corrected and priced. If the price of two vertically differentiated services is the same, all consumers buy the best-quality one. The same does not hold for horizontally differentiated services.

Most technical quality dimensions can be costed (lower outage risks, better water pressure or more frequent trains have a cost that can be computed). Differences in the ability to cost quality have an impact on the ability to internalize quality in price-setting mechanisms, as we will discuss in Section 10.6.

Verifiable versus non-verifiable quality. A third type of categorization quite relevant in the context of regulation focuses on the extent to which quality attributes can be verified by consumers and regulators. This makes a difference to the ability of regulators to spell out explicit rules on what is expected. More conceptually, when quality is verifiable, a regulator can write an explicit contract on the expected quality to be implemented by the operator. When quality is not verifiable, the regulator cannot contract upon it and the firms have more freedom to manipulate it. This leads to a moral hazard problem such as those discussed in Chapter 5.

Ex ante versus ex post verifiability. A final common way of looking at quality is defined by the timing at which consumers can assess the quality of the commodities they purchase. The approach suggests a distinction between search, experience and credence attributes (Nelson 1970; Darby and Karni 1973). *Search* attributes are those for which consumers can assess the quality or qualities *before* purchasing a commodity. Typical examples are external physical attributes. In the context of transportation, this will typically be the design of the stations or airports, and of buses, trains or airplanes. In the case of electricity, water or gas delivery, very few dimensions of the service are search attributes. One exception is the design of the utility website, and more generally of the marketing policy, such as advertising. *Experience* attributes are those for which consumers can only assess the quality *after* they have used the service or the commodity. Typical examples are system functionality, performance or productivity (e.g. frequency of interruption of service, delay in transportation services, quality of communication). Customer services such as clarity of the bills are other examples. Assessing their quality requires trying the service. Finally, *credence* attributes are those for which consumers cannot assess the quality attributes before or after purchase and use. Typical cases refer to the environmental impact at the production stage, or to health-and-safety-related attributes. For instance, most users have no way to know whether the electricity they consume comes from renewable or fossil energy.

Each one of these categories is useful in the context of regulation. But when considering the importance of information asymmetries in the design of regulation, it is useful to investigate the extent to which quality is verifiable and the cost of producing a specific level or type of quality is known.

10.4 What to Do When Quality Is Verifiable and Production Costs Are Known?

To start with the simplest case, let's focus first on what the regulator can do when quality is verifiable and see what happens in the case of vertically differentiated commodities, since many parts of the services provided by public utilities fit into this category (e.g. pressure of water, reliability of transport services or of electricity provision). In this context, regulators tend to deal with at least two broad quality categories: technical quality and customer service orientation. This dual focus is interesting because it makes it easy to highlight the consequences of a differentiated commitment to monitor quality across dimensions.

At the technical level, regulators are usually primarily concerned with the safety, reliability and continuity of the service provision. Most users agree on these characteristics or trust the guidance they are given on which quality is good and which is bad. And many users tend to trust that regulators will monitor this quality well enough. With respect to customer services (website accessibility, hotline service, clarity of the bills, timeliness of intervention in case of problems, etc.), there is less certainty that regulators will make an equivalent effort to monitor ex ante and ex post quality. The rationale for a lower regulatory involvement is the fact that many of these dimensions correspond to commercial services that users can readily assess. However, they impact on the cost function of regulated public service providers and might lead to moral hazard problems if left unchecked. In what follows we consider both technical and commercial dimensions, although our main focus is on the safety, reliability and continuity of the service provision, i.e. the technical part.

When quality is verifiable, it can be included in a 'regulatory contract' exactly like a quantity, as mentioned earlier. Let $z \geq 0$ denote the verifiable quality of the service. The gross surplus of the users from the consumption of $q \geq 0$ units of the commodity of quality $z \geq 0$ is $S(z,q) = \int_0^q p(z,x)dx$, where the function S is strictly increasing and concave in both arguments and $p(z,q)$, which is the consumers' propensity to pay for q units of the good or service of quality z, is increasing in z and decreasing in q and strictly concave in (z,q). The net consumer surplus is therefore $V = S(z,q) - p(z,q)q$.

The regulated firm's rent is $\pi = t + p(z,q)q - C(z,q)$, where $C(z,q)$ is the cost function and t a subsidy. To keep the exposition simple, assume that the cost function to produce $q \geq 0$ units of the commodity of quality $z \geq 0$ is $C(z,q) = cq + z$. This implies that $\pi = t + p(z,q)q - (cq + z)$.

In this example, the cost function is separable so that the cost of quality investment does not depend upon the regulated quantity. This corresponds to investments in quality that are either independent of the production process, such as commercial investments (e.g. advertising, marketing, customers' services), or fixed cost, such as investments in infrastructure that increase the quality of the service without impacting on the core production process (e.g. upgrading track for railways, maintenance cost for distribution networks). It can also be interpreted as the amount of money allocated to increasing the capacity of the system above the level required to operate in normal conditions. The higher it is, the smaller the probability of an interruption of service.

For instance, in electricity, the reliability of the system boils down to the capacity for ensuring that the consequences of the loss of any single generating unit, transmission circuit or transformer are unnoticed by users. This service quality is essentially achieved through investment in excess capacity. The reliance on global overbuilding to ensure quality is generally true for all infrastructure industries. It is the most common way in which authorities tend to minimize the risks of disruption, bottlenecks or delays.[3]

Overinvesting to achieve quality is not free and the regulator needs to account for this in the decisions on how much quality to aim at. The regulator's objective function, which is used to assess the social value of quality, can be expressed as follows: $W = V + \pi - (1 + \lambda)t$, which is equivalent to $W = S(z, q) - (cq + z) - \lambda t$ where t is the subsidy to the operator and λ is the opportunity cost of public funds defined in Chapter 4.

The only difference compared to the benchmark case studied in Chapter 4 is that now the regulator needs to choose two variables: the quantity q and the quality z. Since $\lambda > 0$, t is to be set at its lowest value, which is $t = cq + z - p(z, q)q$, leaving no rent to the monopoly. Substituting this value of t in W yields $W = S(z, q) - (1 + \lambda)(cq + z) + \lambda p(z, q)q$. Then, under complete information, the quantity that maximizes W is $q^*(z)$, solution to:

$$\frac{p - c}{p} = \frac{\lambda}{1 + \lambda} \frac{1}{\varepsilon(z, q)} \qquad (10.1)$$

where $p = p(z, q)$ and $\varepsilon(z, q) = -\frac{p(z,q)}{qp_q(z,q)}$ is the price elasticity of demand for a given level of quality z, with p_q denoting the partial derivative of the inverse demand with respect to quantity. This is an upgraded version of the standard Ramsey–Boiteux formula in Equation (4.15) studied in Chapter 4. And the optimal quality $z^*(q)$ solves:

$$S_z(z, q) + \lambda p_z(z, q)q = 1 + \lambda \qquad (10.2)$$

where the subscript denotes the partial derivative with respect to z.

The optimal level of quality, the $z^*(q)$ solution to Equation (10.2), is achieved when the social marginal cost of providing it, $1 + \lambda$, is equal to its social marginal benefit, $S_z(z, q) + \lambda p_z(z, q)q$. This is the adaptation of the usual result in economics reflecting the relevance of the cost–benefit assessment of the decision to change quality requirements in the context of regulation.

---

[3] A complementary approach is to rely on dynamic pricing, i.e. to try to reduce effective demand when the installed capacity cannot meet the notional demand.

In the simple setup used here, the social marginal cost of providing quality $1 + \lambda$ is the same whatever the marginal cost of the firm because the cost is linear and separable in c, q and z, and the social benefit of quality does not depend upon which type of firm, identified by c, provides it. The level of quality depends, however, on the total output q^* solution to Equation (10.1), so that $z^* = z^*(q^*)$. Totally differentiating Equation (10.2) shows that from a social perspective, quality and quantity are complementary: larger quantities produced should lead to higher investment in quality: $dz^*(q)/dq > 0$.[4] This is not a surprising result when all the information is transparent.

How does this optimal level compare to the quality level chosen by a non-regulated private monopoly? For a given q, the quality $z^M(q)$ chosen by a monopoly is the one that maximizes its rent $\pi = t + p(z, q)q - cq - z$. Then $z^M(q)$ is the solution to:

$$p_z(z, q)q = 1 \tag{10.3}$$

Quality will be increasing with output, like it is at first best[5]. What this means for consumers can be assessed from their marginal net surplus with respect to quality z: $V_z = S_z(z, q) - p_z(z, q)q$. If $V_z \geq 0$, consumers value better quality more than the monopoly can reap in sales through a higher price and, reciprocally, if $V_z \leq 0$. Unsurprisingly, the monopoly undersupplies quality when $V_z \geq 0$ and oversupplies it when $V_z \leq 0$.

10.5   What to Do with Quality If It Is Verifiable but Costs Are Unknown?

What happens if the regulators cannot observe production costs easily, even if they can observe quality? Consider the possibility that costs can be low or high, that is $c \in \{c^l, c^h\}$, and $c = c^l$ is occurring with probability ν and $c = c^h$ is occurring with probability $1 - \nu$.

Since the regulators can verify quality, they can allow prices to cover the costs of investment in quality and control its level accurately. However, since the firm can still get a rent by lying about its variable production cost, the regulator needs to add incentive compatibility constraints to the optimization problem. As was shown in Chapter 5, these constraints come down to:

(i) $t^h = c^h q^h + z^h - p(q^h, z^h)q^h$
(ii) $t^l = c^l q^l + z^l - p(q^l, z^l)q^l + q^h \Delta c$
(iii) $q^l \geq q^h$

---

[4] Totally differentiating Equation (10.2) yields $\frac{dz^*}{dq} = \frac{-\left[(1+\lambda)p_z(z,q)+\lambda p_{zq}(z,q)q\right]}{S_{zz}(z,q)+\lambda p_{zz}(z,q)q} \geq 0$, as s and p are strictly concave in (z, q) and p is strictly increasing in z (see Auriol 1998).

[5] Totally differentiating Equation (10.3) yields: $\frac{dz^M}{dq} = \frac{p_z(z,q)+p_{zq}(z,q)q}{-p_{zz}(z,q)}$. Since $p(z, q)$ is strictly concave in (z, q), this is positive if $p_z(z, q) + p_{zq}(z, q)q > 0$, which is true if p_{zq} is not too large (if negative), as $p(z, q)$ is increasing in z.

so that the high-cost firm just breaks even whereas the low-cost firm keeps a rent $q^h \Delta c$ with $\Delta c = c^h - c^l$. Neglecting for now condition (iii), the regulator solves after substituting t^h and t^l by their values from conditions (i) and (ii) in the expected welfare function:[6]

$$EW = v\left(S(q^l, z^l) + \lambda p(q^l, z^l)q^l - \lambda \Delta c q^h - (1+\lambda)(c^l q^l + z^l)\right) \\ + (1-v)\left(S(q^h, z^h) + \lambda p(q^h, z^h)q^h - (1+\lambda)(c^h q^h + z^h)\right)$$ (10.4)

Maximizing EW with respect to quality z^i (i.e. stating $\partial EW / \partial z^i = 0$) yields the following result, for $i = l, h$:

$$S_z(z^i, q^i) + \lambda p_z(z^i, q^i)q^i = 1 + \lambda$$ (10.5)

For a given quantity, the quality formula, $z(q)$, is the same as under complete information, i.e. Equations (10.2) and (10.5) are identical. This is because the observable quality investment does not directly depend on the productive efficiency of the firm, so that $z(q) = z^*(q)$. It depends on production efficiency only indirectly through the production level q.

As for the output, for the low-cost firm, the solution to this problem is the solution to $\partial EW / \partial q^l = 0$. Then it is the same as in the benchmark case of complete information (see Equation 10.1):

$$\frac{p^l - c^l}{p^l} = \frac{\lambda}{1+\lambda} \frac{1}{\varepsilon(z^l)}$$ (10.6)

Moreover, since for a given quantity the quality is the same as under complete information, we can deduce that for the low-cost firm $z^l = z^{l*}$ and $q^l = q^{l*}$. This is a reminiscence of the 'no distortion at the top' result studied in Chapter 5.

However, the solution for the high-cost firm given by $\partial EW / \partial q^h = 0$ is distorted:

$$\frac{p^h - c^h}{p^h} = \frac{\lambda}{1+\lambda} \frac{1}{\varepsilon(z^h)} + I$$ (10.7)

where $I = \frac{\lambda}{1+\lambda} \frac{v}{1-v} \frac{\Delta c}{p^h} > 0$ is the information rent (see Equation 5.10). Since I is positive, everything else being equal, the price p^h in Equation (10.7) is now higher than under complete information, which implies that the demand is lower, compared to our benchmark case.

Since we have established that $z'(q) > 0$, we deduce that at the second-best optimum, the quality supplied by the low-cost firm will be superior to the quality supplied by the high-cost firm, i.e. $z^l = z^{l*} \geq z^{h*} \geq z^h$. This also means that, in equilibrium, the price p^h is not only higher than under full information, it is also higher than the price that would prevail under incomplete information if quality were exogenously fixed, as in Equation (5.10) in Chapter 5. Moreover, since the quality z^l is higher than z^h, condition (iii) is satisfied: $q^l \geq q^h$.[7] In other words, quality and quantity are both favoured by lower costs and both penalized by higher costs.

---

[6] Recall that $W = V + \pi$, with $\pi = pq - C + t$ and $V = S - pq - (1+\lambda)t$.
[7] For more on this see the proof in Auriol (1998).

As should sound familiar, the asymmetrical information between the regulator and the service providers will end up favouring the latter. An efficient firm can always pretend to be inefficient – a claim impossible to verify under the assumptions discussed here – and enjoy a high price to cover its inflated costs. The difference between its claimed and its true cost is the informational rent. This rent is a function of the production levels required from high-cost producers. What is peculiar is that the rent does not depend on the quality outcome. But this is the result of the assumed separability in cq and z in the cost function. This means that under verifiable quality and separable cost, the optimal quality level depends upon the total quantity produced and not upon the firm providing it, or the market structure per se. Quality is lower with high-cost providers, not because they are less efficient in providing quality than low-cost providers, but simply because they produce less and quality and quantity are complementary. Under asymmetric information (i.e. when the regulator does not conduct detailed cost audits to distinguish between high- and low-cost ones), if the market is catered to by a high-cost firm the service quality will end up being even lower since its quantities are distorted for rent extraction.

10.6   What Happens When Quality Cannot Be Verified?

We have now established that quality is lower than it should be in common cases in which firms know more about their costs than the regulators, even when regulators can verify quality. The next concern must be the extent to which the poor verifiability of quality can make things worse (see Laffont and Maskin 1987). Intuitively, it is likely that unverifiable quality is particularly challenging to regulate. How difficult it is depends on whether or not quality is observable by consumers.

If consumers can observe quality through use, then the regulator can exploit their knowledge to improve their regulation. Assume that the quality of the delivered product can be observed by the consumers and the supplier but is not verifiable by any third party. The regulator can only monitor prices, subsidies and quantities but not quality. Conceptually, the regulator faces both (and jointly) an adverse-selection problem on the value of c and a moral-hazard problem on the value of quality z.

The regulator's limited ability to control quality means that the firm now freely chooses its investment in quality, based on the regulatory requirements which include a quantity and a subsidy as a function of its stated marginal cost $\hat{c}$. To find out what will happen to quality, it is useful to try to understand why the service provider picks a specific quality level. Conceptually, this means solving the problem backwards (i.e. starting from the observed quality level at the end of the decision process).

We have seen in the previous section that the non-regulated level of quality for a given q is $z^M(q)$, the solution to $p_z(z,q)q = 1$, and that quality is increasing with output.

Then, comparing the incentive of the firm to provide unverifiable quality with what we found for the verifiability case shows that the level of quality provided by the monopoly is lower (respectively higher) than its social optimum if $V_z \geq 0$ (respectively if $V_z \leq 0$):

$$z^M(q) \leq z^*(q) \Leftrightarrow V_z \geq 0 \qquad (10.8)$$

Concretely, this result shows the difficulty for regulators to decide on any intervention when key cost drivers are hard to verify. The optimal regulatory decision depends on the extent to which the consumers gain more in surplus than the provider gains in gross profits. Focusing on gross profit on sales only would be misguided. The demand side is just as important as the supply side, even when cost uncertainty is constraining. In other words, as long as the social gain of an improvement in quality exceeds the willingness to pay for it, regulators should favour more quality. In regulated industries, this happens typically for quality attributes such as longevity or reliability. This is a case where quality is likely to be undersupplied.

The main risk, and hence regulatory concern, should be that the demand is not met. This could arise when a monopoly, unable to capture the whole social gain generated by the quality outcome, is tempted to underprovide the specific type of quality. Without regulatory intervention, a monopoly will have no incentive to internalize the non-monetary benefit of its investment.

In contrast, if the monopolist manages to capture a large share of the surplus (i.e. when $V_z \leq 0$), it tends to overprovide quality as an increase in quality raises its gross profit on sales more than it increases the gross surplus of consumers. This is typically the case with commercial efforts (e.g. advertising boosts sales more than gross consumer surplus): V tends to be decreasing with quality when quality is of the marketing type. This is a case where quality is likely to be oversupplied.

To address these risks, the regulator needs to factor a new constraint into its evaluation of the optimum regulatory strategy. The regulator maximizes EW, defined in Equation (10.4), with respect to quantity q, accounting for the constraint that the regulated firm chooses quality $z^M(q)$, defined in Equation (10.3). The solutions to this problem for the low- and high-cost firms are discussed in detail in Auriol (1998): compared to the situation where quality is verifiable, to minimize the risks of over- and underprovision of quality the regulator needs to fine-tune the regulatory requirements by working on non-quality dimensions. As quality cannot be controlled directly, one option is to work on price regulation and set prices to simultaneously reduce the informational rent and control quality. Prices should be set to achieve these two, sometimes conflicting, goals.

This works as follows. When the monopoly tends to underprovide quality (i.e. when $V_z \geq 0$), the production must be increased to improve quality, but increasing it too much will also increase the cost of asymmetric information. There is a trade-off between rent extraction and quality provision. The optimal regulated monopoly production level depends upon the relative force of these two concerns. It may be either smaller or bigger than in the verifiable quality case. What these models show is that the production of the most efficient firm tends to be distorted upwards (i.e. it produces more than under the first-best solution where quality was verifiable). This is because, under informational constraints, when the firm has a larger market it cares more about quality, as quantity and quality are complementary in its profit function, and therefore it provides more of it.

When the monopoly tends to overprovide quality (i.e. when $V_z \leq 0$), the production must be decreased to avoid the excess investment in quality. The two effects play in the same direction and the optimal regulated monopoly production is reduced across the board compared to the case of verifiable quality. Contrary to the standard 'no distortion at the top result', the production of the efficient firm is also distorted to partially correct for the overinvestment in quality.

One case where this type of production fine-tuning will be ineffective at influencing quality provision is for credence goods and services, defined earlier in Section 10.2. These are goods and services for which some or all quality attributes cannot be observed by the consumer, either before or after purchase, making it difficult to assess the match with preferences for a specific quality level. The regulation of these services is particularly important because their providers understand that many users are willing to pay a premium for what they perceive to be safe, reliable, durable or environmentally friendly services, but many of these dimensions are not observable to them. Therefore, regulators need to come up with credible assessments of the degree to which the expected quality standards are met. This is also why problems can arise linked to the possibility for consumer deception and, more generally, to the inefficiency of signalling of the credence attributes of public utilities services.

One way of minimizing deception and quality underprovision is to rely on regulatory certification. Certification may be defined as a process whereby an unobservable quality level of some product is made known to the consumers through some labelling system, usually issued by an independent third party. There are both product and process certification, the first linked mostly to consumption, the second linked mostly to production. It can be quite effective, but it can also have unexpected impacts on the regulated market.

This is illustrated by certificates guaranteeing the environmental friendliness of energy supply, one of the most common schemes used in regulated industries. From 2010 and 2015, the United Kingdom experimented with the Green Energy Supply Certification Scheme, which was supposed to provide assurance to consumers that certified green tariffs were indeed consistent with the regulator's principles used to define green energy. This was fully in line with the role assigned by theory to certification processes. In practice, it did not work out that way. The scheme was eventually dropped because the willingness to pay for certification was not enough to stimulate the supplier to retain a permanent certified green tariff in their core offer. The failure illustrated the crucial importance of accounting for both the supply and the demand side when one tries to address quality concerns in regulated industries.

The various experiments with certification around the world have provided additional regulatory insights. First, a major concern with certification is consumer confidence, which depends on the credibility of the certification process. It must be done by an authority that is above suspicion. A second concern, which is directly linked to the first one, is that to signal quality with certainty or with little uncertainty, certification is costly and may indeed be very costly in some cases. The assessment of a meltdown risk at a nuclear plant, of the probability of an accident in a dangerous segment of the railways infrastructure, of biophysical, biochemical and microbiological hazard in water usually requires costly equipment and highly trained and highly paid personnel. In addition, such assessments take time.

For regulators keen on certification, the next challenge is to deal with its financing requirements. There are two ways to finance the fixed and variable costs of certification and the controls that it entails. They can be financed either by taxpayers or by users (or a mix of both). The optimal choice between privately funded certification and publicly funded certification depends on λ, the value of the shadow cost of public funds. For a low value of λ, public funding is less distorting than a fee levied on the certified product. However, when λ increases it becomes more and more costly to rely on public funds. The regime based on a user fee becomes preferable.

10.7   What Does All This Mean in Practice for Price Regulation?

We saw earlier that the two main approaches to average price regulation are rate-of-return regulation and price-cap regulation. You may remember that the main difference is that the rate-of-return regulation produces an incentive to inflate costs while price-cap produces an incentive to cut costs. This is important to keep in mind when trying to anticipate the most likely attitude of service providers with respect to quality, in particular when the level and cost of quality are relatively easy to verify ex ante or ex post.

Under rate-of-return regulation, the service providers will have an incentive to oversupply quality if quality has a verifiable cost and all costs are guaranteed to be recovered. Excess quality is thus likely to be linked to excessive prices and possibly affordability problems for some users. In contrast, under a price cap, quality is likely to be undersupplied, in particular the quality dimensions hard to verify by the regulators and/or the consumers. Insufficient quality linked to poorly designed price caps is expected to make services less sustainable or less safe than they should be. One of the highest-profile examples is the 2001 California electricity crisis when retail prices had been capped at levels that ended up being below the wholesale cost of energy. Service providers could not afford to buy electricity on the wholesale market and there were recurring power outages until the government ended up paying for the financing gap.

Where price caps continue to be popular among regulators because of their desirable effects on cost-efficiency, many regulators have come up with a service-quality adjustment factor built into the design of price caps. The intuition is simple. Service providers undersupplying quality verified ex post are allowed a lower average price in the next pricing review and those investing in quality can be rewarded through higher average prices to compensate for their efforts to make the right investments in quality. It remains to fix the appropriate quality target. One way of closing the information gap between regulators and service suppliers is to rely on benchmarking. Identifying a set of comparable providers in similar countries or regions, this can help provide a sense of the quality, offering a solid base for a factual approach to decision-making with regard to setting specific targets for performances.

Formally, under price-cap regulation, the firm's period t prices are required to satisfy

$$p_t \leq p_{t-1}(1 + RPI - X + Z) \tag{10.9}$$

where RPI is the inflation rate, X is the efficiency gain expected to be passed on to consumers. The novelty is Z, a service-quality adjustment factor ensuring that the firm's allowed price is positively correlated with changes in quality.

Note that since quality has a cost, it needs to be accounted for in the computation of the required return of the regulated company. And it is important to account for all the dimensions impacted by changes in quality requirements. Quality has an impact on both investment costs (CAPEX) and on operational and maintenance costs (OPEX). But it can also have an impact on the duration of the assets' life. And the sum of these three effects represents how quality adjustments impact on the financial rate of return computed from the net present value calculation of the regulated business, as discussed in Chapter 7 on the role of finance in the implementation of regulation.

Accounting for this financial dimension is of course essential and it is a reasonably well-accepted practice. But it can be misleading as it does not reflect some of the environmental costs and benefits associated with the regulated activity. Most public service regulators only mention compliance with environmental quality standards as one of the obligations of providers. This is because, in most countries, environmental quality regulation, monitoring and enforcement are typically assigned to a distinct regulator focusing on environmental issues only. This implies that the financial rate of return can be misleading and underestimate or overestimate the quality payoffs of any production activity. Ideally, the impact of quality concerns should be assessed against both the financial and the economic/social rate of return. In practice, this is seldom done.

The challenge of quality does not stop with environmental concerns. One of the most underestimated yet relevant dimensions is the need to account for interactions between projects conducted simultaneously (see Besanko et al. 1998). In many cases, sector regulators omit to look at the aggregate level of the multiple projects implemented by the firms they supervise. The regulators tend to focus on the quality dimensions, project by project, as they are expected to improve following a project-specific due diligence. The sum of the impact across projects, accounting for old capital stocks and technologies, is mostly only assessed ex post when ambient air, water or noise indicators point to a problem. When corrections to the initial costing mistakes are needed, they are often anchored in fines (see Box 10.2 on the design and role of fines).

The upshot is that there is a case for authorities to do better at recognizing that many dimensions of quality have an impact on the financial and economic return produced by many, if not most, regulated activities. This awareness seems to be conceptually quite solid. But it should be just as clear in practice. It is because of their impact on costs that all these dimensions need to be identified and measured as precisely as possible, often both ex ante and ex post. This costing process is needed if regulators stand a chance of getting producers and consumers to internalize quality

---

Box 10.2 On the Design of Penalties and Fines

The specification of the punishment for non-compliance with any type of obligations has long been studied in economics (e.g. Becker 1968). It has continued to progress in the context of anti-trust discussions (e.g. Polinsky et al. 1994; Wils 2006; Heimler and Mehta 2012; Bageri et al. 2013). This research easily extends to non-compliance with service obligations.

According to Wils (2006), there are two schools of thought on picking the right penalty level. The first is utilitarian. It suggests that the optimal fine is the one that produces deterrence at the lowest cost. The second is more legalistic and more morally oriented. It focuses on the retributive view of punishment ensuring that a violation is penalized in proportion to the impact of the wrongdoing. In practice, these two perspectives lead to a punishment made up of two parts: a penalty anchored in the legal vision and a fine that reflects the utilitarian concern for deterrence.

The penalty should aim at offsetting any cost savings or profit increases linked to the violation of obligations. In theory, it would also have to be reimbursed to the users or taxpayers. The estimation of these savings or profit increases can be relatively easily computed for a wide range of predictable possible violations in many of the regulated industries. They should either reflect the excess illegal gains (approximated by excess profits or cost savings) from cheating or an estimation of the pecuniary losses to users resulting from non-compliance (e.g. compensating for all the electronic equipment destroyed as a result of a power outage linked to poor maintenance). If these estimations are too complex to compute, it is common to rely on an approximation based on a set or negotiated percentage of sales, accounting for the duration of the infringement. For instance, the penalty for train delays could be estimated by simply multiplying the delay by the average salary by the number of passengers impacted.

The fine is a punishment for misbehaviour. Its optimal level is more arbitrary but should be picked to ensure it fits the crime. For example, involuntary non-compliance should be subject to lower fines than obviously intended violations. Similarly, repeated offenders are expected to suffer from a harsher punishment than first-time offenders.

The debates on the right design of punishment are, however, not really settled. For instance, the relative importance of the severity and probability of punishment is still debated (e.g. Anderson and Stafford 2003; Bruner 2009). Similarly, there are many debates on the optimal penalty structure, which, according to Becker (1968), should be either flat or declining (e.g. Anderson et al. 2017).

---

concerns and to manage to formulate an optimal regulatory design to do so. This includes the adoption of transitional solutions when changes in quality concerns have significant impacts on the purchasing power of some of the consumers.

Costing quality is much more complex and challenging than the simple, sometimes naïve, theoretical approaches imply. And, in practice, some key dimensions are often left out in sector-specific regulatory costing exercises, most notably some of the more damaging externalities (e.g. look at the carbon prices). But theory has been and continues to be useful in conceptualizing the many incentive issues that result from the difficulty of measuring quality and its costs properly. Both theory and practice are convincingly arguing that more can be done, and better, to fix the failures of many purely market-based solutions to deliver key quality dimensions in a way that accounts for their significant impacts on a wide range of costs to users and society.

Ultimately, accounting for the many limitations discussed in the chapter, the main effort the regulators should focus on is to make quality 'actionable'. Since any deviation from the regulatory requirements has an impact on the financial and economic rate of return, the regulator needs to be able to act on deviation with respect to any dimensions of quality. This demands an effort to turn all the relevant dimensions into measurable dimensions, whether objectively or subjectively. And this measurement makes quality actionable and possibly 'contractable'. This is, in turn, what makes regulatory requirements enforceable. This is how its costs and the degree of compliance can be reflected in the average price of a regulated service, ensuring its financial viability. But as already discussed, the average price is only part of the challenge. It is also important to keep in mind that the pricing structure can help providers and regulators strive to be efficient, while complying with the financial sustainability requirements of regulation.

10.8 How Creative Pricing Addresses Quality Issues: The Case of Congestion

Getting the average price right in the practice of regulation is only one of the dimensions of regulatory practice. It may be the easiest one since it boils down to getting the financial side of a business right. But this drives the business constraints of the regulatory problem. The other challenge, possibly the most difficult one, is to get the incentives for producers and consumers right. And this essentially means coming up with creative pricing structures that produce a reasonable return for the public or private operators of the regulated business while delivering the right signals to all stakeholders.

This is nicely illustrated by the regulation of mobility, for which the main quality indicator is the degree of congestion. By 2050 the world's population will be about 10 billion people and over two-thirds will live in cities.[8] By then, road and rail traffic should have at least doubled. One of the major related quality issues globally is the deterioration in the ability of transport networks to allow mobility at reasonable speed and comfort. As of 2017, congestion (defined as a speed below 65% of the free-flow speed) is an obvious challenge around the world according to the INRIX 2017 Traffic Scorecard, the largest detailed study of congestion to date, covering 1,360 cities in 38

---

[8] United Nations, Department of Economic and Social Affairs, 'World Population Prospects 2019', www.undp.org/content/oslo-governance-centre/en/home/sustainable-development-goals/goal-11-sustainable-cities-and-communities.html

countries. For their cities sample, drivers spend an average of 9% of their travel time in traffic at an average traffic speed of 8.9 miles per hour (14.4 km/h).

This deterioration in the quality of services provided by transport infrastructures (and its enormous economic cost in terms of wasted time) has become one of the main regulatory challenges of city management, in particular in view of the limited ability of cities to finance the expansion of infrastructure investment to match the fast-growing demand for mobility. In this context, fiddling with road and public transport pricing is one of the most frequently recurring options considered to manage the congestion. This illustrates the potential use of price-differentiation techniques discussed at the end of Chapter 8. They can be used to smooth consumption and infrastructure use in time while simultaneously increasing the self-financing ability of the sector. Asking road users to pay to enter city centres and charging different prices for public transportation at peak and off-peak times is widely considered as an option and, conceptually, these are straightforward applications of peak-load pricing and state-contingent pricing.

Let's focus on how peak-load pricing can help address the transport-quality issue. When demand starts regularly using up all the installed capacity of an infrastructure, it needs to be managed to reduce the risks of decreases in the quality of service, in the case of transport, the risk of congestion, or worse, in the case of electricity, disruption of services. This comes down to the management of peaks, since these are the main threat to service quality. In the power sector, we have seen that electricity must be produced at the very same time it is consumed, which requires large investment in capacity that remains idle most of the time. As shown at the end of Chapter 8, peak-load pricing or congestion pricing is the answer to these sorts of situations since it induces decreases or shifts in demand. Similar issues arise in transport. In urban transport, rush hours – when office hours are about to start or the workday has just finished – are the main drivers of peaks. This impacts on congestion but also on quality indicators. For instance, rail commuters know that there is a good chance they will have to stand in the train. In intercity transport, holidays are highly correlated with peaks on highway use. Real-time pricing is the most efficient solution on economic grounds: access fees should be higher at peak periods. However, individual car drivers associate traffic jams with poor quality and poor quality with low prices. It is then a political challenge to implement high dissuasive prices at peak hours, in particular because whereas all drivers contribute to congestion, the poorest will be excluded from highways at peak hours and might suffer worse traffic congestion on alternative routes.

10.9   Summing Up

- Because quality is multidimensional with costs sometimes hard to measure and because many attributes can be quite difficult to verify, both ex ante and ex post, there is a role for a specific intervention on quality of service in regulated industries.
- The main role of regulation is to minimize the risks of underinvestment (typically in reliability of service) and overinvestment (typically in marketing) in quality and to ensure that pricing is efficient, fair and financially sustainable.

- Since some of the risks of mistargeting quality are linked to the specific choice of price regulation, biases built into regulation must be explicitly accounted for.
- High-powered regimes such as price caps are likely to lead to underinvestment while low-powered regimes such as cost-plus or rate-of-return regulation are likely to lead to overinvestment in quality.
- To minimize the risks of mistargeting intervention, regulators have several predictable decisions to take.
  - Budgets allocated to quality control and audits have to match the monitoring and enforcement requirements.
  - To reduce information asymmetries, multiple options are available, including benchmarking, certification and quality assessments produced from user surveys.
  - Fines and penalties to reduce the incentives to cheat must be set to ensure that cost savings linked to non-compliance with quality obligations are at least wiped out.
- Policymakers and regulators need to decide how much they want to account for all dimensions of quality, including environmental and other externalities which typically are not accounted for.
- There are a few techniques to improve the signalling role of prices to account for quality, including congestion, as is the case with price differentiation techniques, such as peak-load pricing.

11 On the Regulation of Investment

Stimulating the right level and composition of investments (and ensuring that they are operated and maintained adequately) is one of the most common regulatory mandates across countries. It is needed to achieve regulation's efficiency and equity objectives. Yet there are many examples of insufficient or mis-targeted investments in regulated industries that leave them with insufficient or outdated assets to deliver their services.

Underinvestments are obvious in developing countries with low access rates to some basic public services (see Abrardi et al. 2016). In those countries, the poor tend to be the victims of failed investment policies. Rich countries also suffer from misguided investment policies. For instance, the actual investments towards a transition to cleaner and safer energy sources fail to match the multiple political commitments to address climate change concerns in many, if not most, countries.

Overinvestment level can also be a problem. White elephants such as roads to nowhere or regional airports with hardly any traffic are quite common. Often, also, investments are much more costly than necessary because their costing is one of the instruments of a broader corruption problem allowing some firms to be favoured in the award of contracts in exchange for bribes to politicians or to the bureaucrats allocating investment contracts.[1] In all cases, they correspond to a waste of money, usually financed by taxpayers, with a high opportunity cost, in particular in countries with tight fiscal constraints.[2] Schools or hospitals are not built because someone can be influenced to allocate the fiscal resources to the wrong assets.

Often the wrong investment level can be linked, at least partially, to regulation.[3] This chapter summarizes the main theoretical and policy lessons on the interactions

---

[1] Morales and Morales (2019) show that Odebrecht, a Brazilian construction giant, provides a widely publicized example of how firms can distort investment decisions on a large scale through bribes. Its management admitted corrupting high-level officials, including heads of state, in various Latin American countries, Angola and Mozambique in exchange for large projects. There are similar cases associated with construction or infrastructure firms around the world. Ferrando-Gamir (2015), shows for Spain, for instance, Mr. Correa, a businessman connected with conservative politicians, conspired for about twenty years with local politicians to rig decisions on public contracts. This case, known as the Gurtel case, ended up costing a conservative Prime Minister (Mr. Rajoy) his job.

[2] See, for instance, Albalate et al. (2019) for a recent detailed discussion of the interactions between investment choices and politics in the context of white elephants.

[3] See, for instance, Burns and Reichman (2004) for a general discussion and Dobbs (2011) for an explicit discussion of the role of the choice of the allowed rate of return in defining the investment level and its welfare consequences.

between regulation and the investment decisions of regulated firms. This is a relatively narrow focus on the sequence of processes driving investment decisions. In regulated industries, they often start with political visions anchored in measures and/or perceptions of gaps and needs. These visions can be influenced by incumbents, potential entrants or by users' demands. In countries keen on due diligence, the political or business commitments to regulated investment are usually supported by fairly technical cost–benefit analyses. And increasingly these technical assessments are followed by a discussion with civil society. All these steps are important, but they go beyond the main focus of this book.

Here, we focus on how investment decisions can be influenced by characteristics under the control of regulators or the ministries they are affiliated with. We discuss the evidence of biases built into these investment decisions linked to regulatory decisions, market structures and sectoral governance only. Academic research has contributed technical solutions to many of the challenges imposed by the investment decision processes. It has also raised many controversies on the optimal design of regulation. For example, Vogelsang (2010) questions the compatibility of incentive regulation and efficient investment. He considers that incentive regulation for regular infrastructure investments needs periodic updating based on rate-of-return regulation criteria.

Ultimately, despite the increasing precision produced by the insights of economic analysis, the key decisions on investments continue to be mostly political. Often, the best economists can do is to highlight trade-offs in more precise ways to ensure that the political process is able to make the most of the complex technical economic discussions. To provide some concrete sense of these tensions, and of where regulation theory and experience can help, we start with a brief discussion of the dimensions to consider when designing regulation to smooth the energy transition needed to address the concerns over climate change. It provides a reasonably encompassing discussion of the complexity of coming up with a regulatory framework capable of producing the right investment at the right time.

11.1 On the Complexity of Investment Regulation: The Energy Sector Transformation

The Paris Agreement signed by a majority of countries in 2016 defines a common global vision of what they should aim at to address climate change concerns. The common goal adopted in the agreement is to limit the rise in average global temperatures to below 2°C (above pre-industrial levels) by 2100. If that is to be achieved, investment in energy will have to change in both type and level. More and cleaner investments should be able to deliver 90% of global emission reductions needed in the energy sector, according to the International Renewable Energy Agency. The cost will not be modest. This Agency estimates that the necessary cumulative investment in renewable energy needs to reach US$27 trillion in the 2016–50 period (IRENA 2019).

This implies a significant commitment by many stakeholders. The multiplicity of actors involved necessitates a complex institutional organization. In practice, regulation will be an important factor in the management of this complexity and in the contribution to the funding needed. How regulators deal with the problems will have a major impact on investment incentives in regulated industries and it will influence the demand for investments as users adjust to the new organization of the sector. The challenge will not be an easy one to tackle as the adoption of renewable energy sources (RES) is forcing regulators to rethink the regulation of electricity markets. Of particular concern is the need to address new types of uncertainties in the design of markets and in their regulation. And this uncertainty matters to the evolution of investment.

Investors internalize the uncertainties associated with RES in their evaluation of the attractiveness of the sector. For instance, they account for the effectiveness with which regulation addresses flexibility needs to modify electricity production (or consumption) in response to random or predicted variability. One of their main concerns is the extent to which incentives are designed clearly and predictably enough to justify developing the assets. Regulation is at the core of the provision of these incentives.[4]

Designing a regulation that addresses the new investors' concerns to stimulate the development of RES has proven to be quite a politically sensitive challenge for many countries. Consumers do not want to have to deal with higher bills. Historical investors want to fully recover their old investments.

In many countries, regulators also need to account for the fact that energy markets are increasingly associated with supranational investments. Countries trade in electricity and this leads to other types of regulatory concerns. Different sectoral governance structures adopted by the various countries imply different degrees of flexibility and hence of risks. In some countries, the electricity sector is still totally or partially vertically integrated (i.e. the production, transmission, distribution and supply of electricity are controlled by a single firm). In others, it has been partially or totally unbundled, with some segments open to competition. The allocation of the costs associated with the joint facility across activities and actors becomes a crucial component of the incentive regimes at both the national and supranational level when countries trade in energy.

Coordination needs become much more complex with efforts to adopt rules aiming at increasing the role of RES in the sector. Any uncertainty with respect to these rules, and their coherence across countries when supranational projects are involved, implies a risk for investors which is reflected in the expected rate of return, which influences investment decisions. For instance, according to DiaCore (2016), in Europe in 2014 the risk perceptions by potential investors of onshore wind projects led to a cost of equity for these projects ranging from 6% in Germany to over 15% in Estonia, Greece, Latvia, Lithuania, Romania and Slovenia. Risks were perceived to be low in

---

[4] The intermittency of RES can be technically addressed by installing storage plants where energy is injected when photovoltaic panels and wind turbines produce in excess of demand and is withdrawn when there is an energy shortage (see Ambec and Crampes 2019; Schmalensee 2020). However, energy storage is not yet economically identified. When Tesla applied to install batteries in the United Kingdom (spring 2020), the only thing the regulator (Ofgem) could grant was a generation licence.

Germany because of the existence of the renewable energy law anchoring regulation while in the other countries, renewable energy had not yet been embedded into reliable legal support. For the United States Krupa and Harvey (2017) and for Africa Sweerts et al. (2019) provide similar insights.

The debates on how to get the incentives right on the supply side are all happening at a time when the global demand for energy continues to grow. This demand is unlikely to fall as the middle class of emerging economies is adopting consumption standards already adopted by those in developed economies. Moreover, the increased addiction to information technologies of a growing share of the world's population further fuels the need to consider the regulatory importance of the management of the demand side of the energy market, which poses its own regulatory and political challenges.[5] This means that regulation will also have to address growing concerns regarding congestion management associated with the uncertainty of renewable energy policy. In doing so, regulators will also have to keep track of an essential trade-off between various generations of users. Lower prices protect current consumers but fail to guarantee a protection of future generations. Moreover, they fail to reflect the costs associated with the longer-term risks taken by investors supporting efforts to improve the environmental sustainability of the sector. Unless prices reflect these costs as well as the need to implement the energy transition, short-term overconsumption is the most likely outcome. The trade-off is not really a fair one: today's consumers vote, tomorrow's consumers don't vote yet.

With so much complexity, is it possible to get the investment types and levels right to address the climate concerns?[6] The design of regulation for such a complex investment challenge is still subject to academic and policy debates. Regulatory specialists are still far from understanding all the dimensions of the regulatory uncertainty associated with the energy transition, the increased role of RES, the stranding of assets and the political risks associated with demand response (see Ambec and Crampes 2021).

For now, those concerned with future generations tend to focus on identifying incentives for supporting a faster move towards sustainability. The speed and timing of investment has become as important as the composition and the level. But decision processes are slower than theoretical papers usually assume. These processes fail to account for the time it takes to build new facilities, even if this is an issue that practitioners and some academics keep voicing.

In Belgium, for instance, where the government has been committed for some time to close nuclear power stations by 2025, the process of building substitute sources of energy had not even started by the end of 2019. It takes at least a year to organize the

---

[5] According to the International Energy Agency (2017), the entire information technology sector, from powering internet servers to charging smartphones, is on course to consume as much as 20% of the world's electricity by 2030. As of 2017, it was already estimated to have the same carbon footprint as the aviation industry's fuel emissions.

[6] We have left out of the discussion the need to ensure the financing of the operation and maintenance of the assets created through investment. These are often quite significant as well, but raise other issues that we will not be able to address here. The basic dynamic constraint of participation was discussed in Chapter 7.

procurement and validate the investment projects. It takes another four to six years to implement the construction phase. And there is nothing the regulator can do because the process has been taken over by governments with a high turnover rate and majorities changing their views on the environmental agenda. Whoever will be in government in 2025 will be blamed for not delivering and it is likely that regulators will share the blame. Yet the delay should be blamed on the difficulty of coming up with a robust regulatory mandate to implement a political decision. Regulating investment decisions has proved to be a problem in the implementation of the energy transition in Belgium, as in many other countries around the world. This inability to commit is one of the themes academics have identified as a reason why it is hard to get the investment levels and types at the right level and at the right speed. But commitment failures are not the only type of failure covered by academic research, as discussed in the following sections.

11.2 On the Multiple Sources of Investment Regulation Failures

The academic literature and the media are replete with examples of failed investment projects by regulated firms.[7] There are many explanations for these failures, including fiscal, institutional, political and, of course, regulation. There are many ways in which regulation can be associated with the wrong investment level or type. The main ones include:

- The specific choice and design of the price regulation mechanism.[8]
- The margin given to incumbents to manipulate the timing of investment.[9]
- A mismatch of the choice of price regulation and complementary obligations with the characteristics of the market to be served by the investment.
- A mismatch of the commitments made by the regulator with their long-term credibility.
- An underestimation of the risk premia expected to compensate for regulatory uncertainty.

The most basic way to bias the investment decision is the specific approach adopted to regulate prices. The rule of thumb many analysts work with is that the specific form of price regulation adopted can be used to predict the extent to which over- or

---

[7] See, for instance, Keep (2021) for the British case, Bel et al. (2015) for the Spanish transport sector or Flyvbjerg (2014) for an overview of the common global mistakes noted in investment decisions in infrastructure.

[8] Dalen (1998) develops a theoretical model to show that yardstick competition increases the incentives for firm-specific investment over individual regulation of firms. If instead investment is industry-specific, incentives to invest are reduced by yardstick competition.

[9] Evans and Guthrie (2012) show that when there are economies of scale in investment, price-regulated firms take less advantage of scale economies than a planner would, investing in smaller, more frequent, increments. Adding quantity regulation exacerbates this behaviour but enhances welfare. The reduced scale dominates the increased frequency, so that on average regulated firms expand capacity more slowly than the regulator would like.

underinvestment is likely to happen. This rule reflects the intuition developed from a long record of academic literature arguing that cost-plus/rate-of-return regulation will tend to lead to overinvestment since it tends to reward large costs or large asset bases. This form of regulation distorts both static and dynamic efficiency.[10] This is essentially the Averch–Johnson effect we discussed in Box 5.4. The incentive to inflate investment quantity or quality in some circumstances has indeed long been correlated with excessive cost levels which explained excessive average price levels. This concern is what stimulated the development of incentive-based regulation to reduce or eliminate that bias.

Practice is more complex of course. Price or revenue cap regulation may be quite effective at increasing the incentive to cut costs but one of its drawbacks is that this effort to cut costs can also lead to underinvestment in either quantity or quality or in both dimensions. When pushing for cost reductions, unless this is controlled through other regulatory tools, incentive-based regulation gives enough margin to the regulated firms to decide *how* to cut costs. It could come from improved efforts to reduce cost padding and to improve the performance of the available assets. But it could also lead to lower maintenance efforts and lower investment in quantity and in quality. Incentive-based regulations may favour static efficiency, but it could do so at the cost of dynamic efficiency.

In practice, the inability of regulation to address short-term static efficiency concerns jointly with dynamic efficiency goals is one of the common ways in which it can impact on the performance of a regulated firm or sector. This is more complex when the regulation must focus on the use of an asset controlled by a single firm but which could be needed by multiple users to develop their own activities. The operators of airports, rail tracks, electricity transmission lines, gas pipelines or optical fibre networks typically enjoy at least some monopoly power as they control access to the facilities they own or operate. Getting regulation wrong can lead these monopolies to underinvest or overinvest for several predictable reasons. And the odds of making mistakes increase with the size of the information gaps a regulator faces. The underlying issue is thus the difficulty of controlling the market power enjoyed by the owner of the asset. The failure of regulation to deal with market power leads to rents captured by the poorly regulated monopolies or oligopolies controlling the investment decisions.

A second way in which regulation may fail to deliver the optimal investment decision is in the monitoring of the strategic use of the timing of the investment decision, as we discussed in the context of the design of regulation to speed up the energy transition. Temporary underinvestment can result from delays in the investment decision or implementation by the regulated monopolistic operator. Slowing investment can be used for example to create bottlenecks which can be exploited to produce rents. These rents are produced by the allocation of access rights to the bottleneck. Control of the access rights can also be used to control the market share

---

[10] In addition to providing an incentive to inflate costs, this form of regulation distorts investment decisions by making it easy for multi-product firms to arbitrarily allocate costs and assets to minimize the effectiveness of regulation focusing on products' subsets.

of potential competitors. Therefore, the regulation of access is an important issue to address in this chapter. More generally, the regulator can use pricing tools to accelerate the launching of investments that firms would like to delay, as illustrated in Box 11.1.

Box 11.1 On Regulation through Price Caps and the Timing of Investments
Investment is not just a matter of volume and content. Its timing is also essential. Regulation, if properly designed, can influence the timing of investment. The basic elements can be presented in the following model.

At period $t = 0$, a firm endowed with capital K can invest I to increase its production capacity irreversibly up to $K + k$ starting from $t = 0$ or it can wait until $t = 1$ to take the decision. Depending on the investment decision, at each future period the revenue net of operating costs will be either $R_s(K)$ or $R_s(K + k)$, where s identifies the state of nature in all future periods, still unknown at $t = 0$: demand will be high $(s = H)$ with probability ρ or low $(s = L)$ with probability $1 - \rho$.

The crucial assumption is that investment will be profitable only in state $s = H$: $R_H(K + k) > R_H(K)$. In state $s = L$, the new assets will remain idle and provoke disturbances in the short-run management: $R_L(K + k) < R_L(K)$.

The trade-off is then between investing at $t = 0$ with the risk of having an excess capacity if demand is low and waiting until $t = 1$ to invest under perfect information on demand, but then to miss the high sales at $t = 1$.

If the firm invests at time $t = 0$, its expected market value discounted at rate $r > 0$ over the infinite horizon is:

$$\Pi_0 = -I + \frac{\rho}{r} R_H(K + k) + \frac{1 - \rho}{r} R_L(K + k).$$

If it waits until period $t = 1$, the market value discounted at date $t = 0$ over the infinite horizon is:

$$\Pi_1 = \frac{\rho}{1 + r}\left(-I + R_H(K) + \frac{R_H(K + k)}{r}\right) + (1 - \rho)\frac{R_L(K)}{r}.$$

Then the firm invests at $t = 0$ if $\Pi_0 > \Pi_1$, i.e. after regrouping:

$$\frac{\rho}{1 + r}(R_H(K + k) - R_H(K)) > I\left(1 - \frac{\rho}{1 + r}\right) + \frac{1 - \rho}{r}(R_L(K) - R_L(K + k))$$

The term on the left-hand side is the discounted expected gain from early investment at period 1 when demand is high. On the right-hand side, first is the additional cost of an immediate investment as compared with a delayed decision, followed by the perpetual losses due to an excess capacity due to a low demand.

To see the impact of regulation on the timing decision, assume that the inequality is reversed so that the unregulated firm prefers to delay investment, whereas, for any reason, the regulator would like an immediate investment. How can the regulator convince the investor to invest earlier?

Box 11.1 (*cont.*)

Let $p(q)$ be the demand function so that the firm's short-term net revenue is $R(q) = p(q)q - C(q)$ and assume that the regulator relies on a price cap. For the policy to be effective, the regulator has to fix the cap $\hat{p}$ such that $max\{p_H(K+k), p_L(K)\} < \hat{p} < p_H(K)$. This increases the left-hand side of the profitability inequality since it leaves $R_H(K+k)$ unchanged and decreases $R_H(K)$, while it has no effect on the right-hand side.

The idea is that the price cap should not be binding when demand is low, and should be binding when demand is high only if the firm has not yet invested.

Source: Based on Dobbs (2004) and Guthrie (2006).

A third way in which regulation can impact on the investment decision is simply the adoption of design that does not match the characteristics of the market or that ignores the need to offset some of the weaknesses built into the price regulation adopted. In practice, it is often essential to complement price or revenue caps with service obligations and to clarify the rules of access to shared facilities as well as the definition of property or financial rights to the shared facility.[11] Weak regulation can give enough margin to allow the firm controlling the shared facility to underinvest or to adopt cream-skimming strategies, to allow predatory practices against potential competitors and/or exclusionary practices against consumers with limited abilities to pay.[12]

Some regulators have been actively trying to correct initial biases. For instance, in 2010 the British energy regulator introduced the RIIO (Revenue–Incentives–Innovation–Output) model, in which prices are set for a period of eight years. It added specific output obligations for regulated firms and some margin to stimulate innovation by allowing revenue to be used for experimentation (OFGEM 2010). This new vision has recently been upgraded to RIIO-2 to reduce the risks of mistargeting investment obligations, among other novelties. What is particularly relevant to this chapter is that, in most cases, the concern for investment is leading to the adoption of hybrid forms of regulation in which output or investment targets are increasingly well specified to reduce the scope for strategic choices by the regulated operators.

A fourth common explanation for underinvestment is a lack of credibility of regulatory commitments. When regulatory processes are open to political interference, which can reverse commitments to recover costs over a long period, underinvestment becomes a rational strategy for the sector operators. This is the outcome of the lack of credibility of the commitments made by regulatory authorities to firms investing in assets that will last long enough to go through multiple political cycles. When

---

[11] For instance, Petropoulos and Willems (2017) show that dynamic efficiency does not require the existence of physical rights for accessing an electric transmission line. The financial rights on receiving the scarcity revenues generated by the transmission equipment are enough.

[12] This exclusion of some low-income regions within a country from the initial investment plans for shared facilities is still common in developing economies.

governments change, it is not unusual to see them reassess regulatory commitments made by their predecessors, which can result in stranded assets, as explained in Box 11.2. This lack of sustained coherence is one [13] of the main drivers of the dynamic inefficiency of regulation in the real world.

A final way in which regulation may hurt investment decisions is when it underestimates the risk premia associated with the uncertainty of regulatory commitments. When regulators are unable to commit to the timescale of investment because they do

---

Box 11.2 Stranded Assets

When firms invest large amounts of resources it is in the hope of reaping profits in addition to recouping their initial bet. They know that all investments are risky, and the result can be well below their expectations. In unregulated industries, this is just the way it should be: losses must be endured by shareholders. By contrast, when firms are regulated, their investments are endorsed, if not imposed, by the regulatory authority. Then it raises the question of what to do if there is an economic downturn or new regulations that prevent a regulated firm from taking advantage of its investment. Should the costs stranded by the new environment be fully recovered? The question was highly controversial during the 1990s when many countries decided to open telecoms and energy industries to competition. New entrants were not burdened by inherited expenses and their production and pricing strategies could prevent the utilities from recovering their costs (Joskow 1996). In the electricity sector, cost recovery can be achieved by means of an 'access charge' to be imposed on every electricity customer,[13] an 'entrance fee' to be paid by every current and new competitor of the utility, and an 'exit fee' to be paid by any customer that stops purchasing electricity from the utility (Baumol and Sidak 1995). When the stranded assets are an essential facility like the electricity transmission network, stranded costs will be recouped by the access fee.

Since there is a trade-off between the social gains from the entry of competitors and the incentives for incumbents to invest in a reliable regulatory framework, the best solution is, as expected, a mixed one: full recovery of a firm's costs that are stranded by competition is not generally socially optimal (Beard et al. 2003).

The question arises again with the ecological transition. After having required the electricity incumbents to invest enough to achieve an almost uninterrupted energy supply, at the beginning of the millennium public authorities decided to subsidize renewables with the objective to speed up the decommissioning of thermal plants and, in some countries, nuclear plants. To compensate investors for this subsidized entry, almost all countries have created capacity mechanisms (direct payments or specific markets), where an extra cost is passed through to final consumers to compensate for the 'missing money'.

---

[13] For example, in Spain, the law passed in 1997 entitled the incumbent generators to some additional payments to compensate them for their stranded costs, i.e. the difference (possibly negative) between the value of the standard costs and the expected payments that each of them would have in the marketplace. These payments were referred to as 'Competition Transition Costs'. See Crampes and Fabra (2005) for details.

not have the autonomy to do so, uncertainty becomes a major influence on the incentives to invest and/or to maintain the assets. Academic research has a long record of warning about the investment implications of a regulation that does not deal with uncertainty.[14] In practice, this uncertainty increases the expected cost of capital in the best-case scenarios and this is likely to influence the investment levels or quality as well. The risks can be high enough to violate the firm's participation constraint and the investment does not take place. Alternatively, the regulator matches the perceived risks with a higher allowed cost of capital, and the consumers end up paying more than they could have for the investment. Taxpayers may also be impacted when the added costs are financed through subsidies. In many countries, the strategy to slow price increases is to extend the amortization period needed to recover the investment costs, which implies that the ability to raise funds to finance the replacement or upgrade of existing assets is reduced. This, in turn, usually leads to delay in investments.

11.3 On the Welfare Costs of the Failures to Regulate Investment

While insufficient access rates are obvious indicators of the undesirable social welfare effects of the distortions associated with regulation, there are others which are also important, although sometimes somewhat more challenging to anticipate.

When regulation is biased towards overinvestment in quantity or quality, there is a risk of preference for excessively capital-intensive technologies. This bias has at least three broader social welfare implications. First, it creates incoherence between the capital–labour ratio that would maximize profit and the one that would minimize costs when the return allowed is larger than the actual cost of capital. It is thus reasonable to expect that overinvestment resulting from a regulatory bias will not lead to cost minimization. Second, it may distort the investment composition. Indeed, when regulation ignores the difference between quantity and quality of investment, it may favour oversupply of quality rather than expansion of service coverage. This means that it may be rational for the investor to pick technologies that are unnecessarily expensive while ignoring access gaps. When demand is inelastic, it also implies that consumers with access will pay more than they would want to get a specific service. This is one of the implications of what is known as gold-plating, i.e. the decision to inflate the cost level and the asset base value on which the return is computed without necessarily improving investment quantity. A third welfare effect is becoming an increasing source of concern in countries with high unemployment rates. New investments often imply replacing workers with machines, and policies designed to stimulate investments can bias the investment decisions towards overinvestment.[15]

---

[14] See for instance, Dobbs (2004), Guthrie (2006), Gautier and Mitra (2006), Armstrong and Sappington (2007), Roques and Savva (2009) and, more recently, Willems and Zwart (2018).

[15] Estache and Kouevi Gath (2019) show that reductions in corporate income taxes in Europe lead to an increase in unemployment as many firms use the lower cost of capital resulting from the tax cut to upgrade or modernize their assets and in the process adopt less labour-intensive technologies.

In countries with high underemployment levels, as is the case for many of the poorest countries, or with high unemployment levels, as is increasingly the case in emerging economies, this bias raises concerns. When the design of regulation ignores this dimension, social tensions are likely to emerge. These tensions are also increasingly present in developed economies where the policy debates on the possibility that machines will replace workers have been a recurrent topic.

These welfare costs also show up when regulation results in underinvestment. Social welfare costs can be quite high when the failure to invest maintains bottlenecks. This has long been a concern for competition agencies rather than regulatory agencies. For instance, the European Commission Competition Directorate has a long record of monitoring the risks of a lack of energy transmission or transport capacities. In the process, it has highlighted the creativity of firms in the way they can restrict access when it is in their interest. For instance, in the late 2000s, the Commission identified several cases in which incumbents were overbooking their use of a shared facility they controlled to prevent competitors from gaining access to this facility in time to reach their own clients. This strategy reduces market entry despite the potential gains that entry would entail to consumers.[16] Unless regulation works, bottlenecks lead to market power for some actors, then to inefficiencies and inequities from the exclusion of some users and some producers. In most cases, a big part of the technical solution is in improving the design of access prices and rules.

11.4   How Sensitive Is the Investment Decision to Access Prices and Rules?

Access rules and prices are essential regulatory tools to avoid price discrimination in the use of a facility that could be shared by several users but is owned and/or operated by a monopoly. The question is how to regulate the decision to invest in new transmission lines, water treatment facilities, railway lines, ports or airports to make sure these investments are at the right level and time, and using the right technology. These are investments in essential facilities that need to be supported by transparent, efficient and fair pricing and access rules that will ensure recovery of the costs, including the financing and operating costs. The revenue to be generated by these investments has to cover the costs in net present value, as discussed in Chapter 7. In environments in which the use of the facilities created by these investments is shared by an incumbent and its actual or potential competitors, the revenue produced by access prices is often a significant share of the total revenue associated with the investment. This is one of the reasons why access rules and investment decisions are often closely related, as discussed in this chapter. It impacts on the scope for

---

[16] The European Commission monitoring of Gaz de France (GDF, now Engie), the owner of the largest gas transmission networks in France showed that most of the available capacities at the main entry points into the French gas transmission network had been booked on a long-term basis by a unit of GDF. For more details, see DG Competition (2007).

competition, as potential entrants will be influenced by access prices and rules. It also influences the investment decision itself.

If the price is not right, unless there are clear subsidies, no firm will take the decision to invest. Moreover, if the price is not set to ensure that the sources of the investment get their money back, the investment will not be financed and hence the project will not be started since typically at least some of the financing needs to be secured before the construction phase starts. To a large extent, the details of the access prices and rules are a determinant of the ability of a firm to rely on enough financing for any investment in a regulated activity.

The signalling role of these access prices and rules is thus essential, but many potential users of these shared assets will expect regulators to balance the desire to increase the incentive to invest by setting prices generous enough with the need to protect users from abuses of the de facto significant leverage the owner/operator of the facility will have on the various potential users competing for access. Although theory can come up with some precise guidelines, as we will discuss next, it should be clear that, in practice, it is very likely that the rules will end up distorting the development of some of the upstream and downstream markets. In increasingly complex and fast-evolving markets, incomplete or simply biased rules can indeed be instrumentalized by the regulated operators of the shared facility to discriminate.[17] They can for instance be used to discourage specific entrants and in the process reduce the ability of a sector to cater to future demand at reasonable prices.

It is quite intuitive to assume that, when regulatory authorities are keen to promote both investment and effective competition in at least some segments of a network industry, they need to anticipate the risk of abuses in the control of access to the essential facility. Without the proper combination of incentives, the operator of the shared facility will often have an incentive to set the investment at a level that makes it easy to create artificial bottlenecks to produce rents and/or exclude some potential upstream or downstream entrants.[18]

The main risk in the design of access rules and prices is to favour some stakeholders too much rather than ensure a proper balance in the way all of them are treated. This problem is reinforced when the entrants in a market formerly controlled by a vertically integrated monopoly (VIM) are foreigners. Governments tend to favour their national champions over foreign-based competition (see Auriol and Biancini 2015). If the sector is going to get the investment it needs to meet future demand, the investor needs to get a fair return on the commitment made to finance assets that tend to be quite long-lived. If the current users are to be protected, the rules must be such that the short-term market power allowed by the nature of the investment is kept under control.

---

[17] Laffont and Tirole (1986, p. 263) already argued that 'as the number of market imperfections grows, the access pricing rule is bound to respond to an increasing number of concerns, ceteris paribus, and more instruments are needed if access prices are not able to arbitrate efficiently among conflicting goals'.

[18] Access pricing is usually seen as part of the anti-trust concern of market foreclosure (the 'essential facility doctrine' covered by the US legislation) and is associated with many competition policy issues, including quantity discounts, cross-subsidies, exclusive dealing or predatory pricing. For more on essential facilities, see Sidak and Lipsky (1999).

11.5   How Complex Is It to Set Rules Balancing Short- and Long-Term Concerns?

In practice, the identification of the desirable access rules that send the right investment signal without penalizing any stakeholder in the short run is a technical matter.[19] It is beyond the scope of this book to get into these details, but it is important to get a feeling for the main drivers of the trade-offs between short-term and long-term concerns. To this end, it is helpful to go through a simplified representation of the potential regulatory challenges. The electricity sector provides a good pedagogical illustration with much broader implications.

The electricity you get at home is first produced in a power plant (generated, in the terminology of the sector specialists), then it is transported in high voltage (transmitted, in the sector terminology) to your city or region and then it is distributed in low voltage and sold to all individual users. In many countries, these four stages are performed by a vertically integrated firm. But in many of these countries, there are potential entrants in the generation segment of the industry that would like to be able to rely on the transmission lines owned by the vertically integrated incumbent to sell the energy produced to final consumers. The potential entrants are unlikely to invest in new transmission lines since they are aware of the financial unsustainability of duplicating an essential facility. Moreover, in most cases, duplication of lines is socially unprofitable. The regulator should not allow it, as it is a waste of resources. This component of the network is a textbook example of a *natural monopoly*. Nevertheless, the incumbent is often interested in allowing access because transmission is subject to economies of scale and the higher its usage, the lower the average costs, as long as the total use remains below total transmission capacity.

Note that the inefficiency of facilities duplication can be a short-sighted argument. By encouraging new entrants to use the existing infrastructure, open access reduces their incentives to innovate, which is detrimental for long-run efficiency. Since entrants do not bear the sunk costs paid by the incumbent, there is an asymmetric allocation of risk and return, which is generally not properly accounted for in the pricing of network services (Pindyck 2004). The recognition of this risk was eventually internalized in 2002 by the American national electricity regulator, the Federal Energy Regulatory Commission (FERC), which had long required vertically integrated owners of pipelines to provide non-discriminatory open access to competitors in the US liquefied natural gas (LNG) industry. Under pressure from the US LNG industry representatives, who had been arguing that the FERC's open access requirements had a deterrent effect on investment in new LNG facilities, the regulation changed. The FERC abandoned the obligation of unbundling and open access for new import terminals and determined that LNG terminals should be treated like any other source of natural gas supply (Knowles 2003).

---

[19] For the case of railways, see for instance: https://ppp.worldbank.org/public-private-partnership/ppp-sector/transportation/railways/railway-laws-and-regulations/track-access-laws-and-regulations/tr

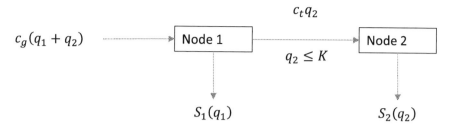

Figure 11.1 A one-line/two-nodes model of the electricity industry

To see the various ways in which access rules and prices can matter, a simple model suffices (see Crampes 2007). Consider an economy in which the electricity industry is composed of three elements: (i) a western 'node' (labelled 1), where electricity is produced and consumed locally; (ii) an eastern 'node' (labelled 2), where electricity needs to be brought from the western node to supply local consumers and (iii) a transmission line bringing the electricity from node 1 to node 2.

Figure 11.1 provides a visual description of this simple economy. All production q is done at node 1 at cost $c_g q$. To simplify further, we assume that c_g is the long-run marginal cost, which includes fixed costs. Consumption takes place at each node $i = 1, 2$. When consumers are provided with the quantity q of electricity, they enjoy utility $S_i(q)$, which is increasing at a decreasing rate. The transmission of a quantity q from node 1 to node 2 has a constant unit cost c_t, a linear approximation of thermal losses. The energy flow on the line cannot be greater than the fixed capacity K. The maintenance of the transportation system has a cost F that mainly depends on K. Consequently, in this short-run model F is also fixed.

Basic theory suggests that all consumers should pay the marginal costs of the electricity they consume. But since there are economies of scale in the transmission of electricity, embodied in the fixed cost F, we know from Chapter 2 that the first-best pricing rules are not financially sustainable. Marginal-cost pricing would not allow the recovery of the investment costs in transmission.[20] A regulator would have to rely on second-best pricing options to make sure that the participation constraint does not prevent the firm from investing. But the specific regulation adopted would also need to ensure that there is no bias built into the access charge in favour of or against new entrants that would need to use the transmission line to be able to compete on the production and retail segments of the industry.

To see what the regulator needs to think through in this simple context, assume that potential entrants, generically denoted e, want to install production capacity at node

[20] The first-best allocation is the solution to max $S_1(q_1) + S_2(q_2) - c_g(q_1 + q_2) - c_t q_2 - F$ subject to the capacity constraint $q_2 \leq K$. Assuming that consumption is strictly positive at both nodes, the optimal allocation is given by $S'_1(q_1) = c_g$ and $S'_2(q_2) = c_g + c_t + \eta$, where η is the congestion shadow price which kicks in when the capacity constraint is binding. It shows that the difference in nodal marginal costs is due to the transportation cost (thermal losses) plus the congestion cost when the capacity constraint is binding. This solution can be implemented by nodal prices $p_1 = c_g$ and $p_2 = c_g + c_t + \eta$. It is not financially viable if $\eta q_2 < F$.

1 to sell q_e to node 2's consumers and thus need access to the transmission line.[21] These potential entrants are competing perfectly with each other so that their net profit can be assumed to be equal to zero. Under these assumptions, to be able to compute the optimal access charge, the regulator would have to go through a simple optimization exercise which accounts for a wide range of costs and should reveal how these costs interact and drive entry (and eventually investment) decisions.[22]

Let us denote by c_e the entrants' long-term generation cost, a the access price and $p_e = c_e + a$ the competitive equilibrium price for the entrants' services. Given c_e, the regulator is indifferent between fixing p_e or a. As shown in Box 11.3, the access fee that should be paid by entrants is:

$$a^0 = c_t + \frac{\eta}{1+\lambda} + \frac{\lambda}{1+\lambda}\frac{p_e}{\bar{\varepsilon}_e}$$

This complex expression is quite insightful from a regulatory policy perspective. It shows that an entrant demanding access to a network operated by a vertically integrated firm should pay a unit access charge that accounts for three different types of costs: (i) the transport variable costs, c_t;[23] (ii) the associated congestion cost, $\frac{\eta}{1+\lambda}$, which is nil when the transmission capacity is not binding and (iii) as in Chapter 4, the costs of using the fixed facility, $\frac{\lambda}{1+\lambda}\frac{p_e}{\bar{\varepsilon}_e}$. This is quite a general insight that drives many of the discussions on the design of access charges in any industry in which there is a shared or common facility that can be used by various competitors. But the actual cost drivers computed here are specific to the assumed initial market structure.

Note that there are many subtler insights produced by this optimization exercise. The first insight to keep in mind is that, at node 2, the products sold by the incumbent and the entrants are not necessarily perfect substitutes. For example, entrants target industrial consumers with specific needs. Another possibility is when entrants are producers using renewable sources of energy and selling their production with a green label, even though at the consumption nodes it is impossible to know where electricity comes from, since the grid transmits energy according to the physical Kirchhoff's laws. The retail contract conditions are different for 'green energy' and energy from thermal plants.[24]

The possibility that the products of the entrants and the product of the incumbent are not perfect substitutes is important because it highlights one flaw of the efficient component pricing rule (ECPR) discussed in Chapter 13. According to the ECPR,

[21] This entry option without dismantling the incumbent is the third-party access (TPA) to the grid (Bier 1999; Pollitt 2019).

[22] The model used here is akin to the one developed by Laffont and Tirole (1994, 2000c) for the telecommunications industry.

[23] This is the only component many entrants claim they should have to pay for, arguing that the infrastructure already exists and will be maintained anyway by the incumbent for its own business.

[24] In many countries, to satisfy the environmental concerns of consumers, each MWh produced from renewable sources is sold accompanied with one green certificate, i.e. a tradable commodity that guarantees its origin. The consumers who sign green contracts accept to pay a higher price even though the electricity they consume is not directly coming from a green source: they do so because they want to participate in the greening of the industry (Council of European Energy Regulators 2018).

Box 11.3 Access Pricing in the Third-Party Access Framework

The profit of the incumbent can be written as:

$$\pi(p_1, p_2, a) = p_1 q_1 + p_2 q_2 + a q_e - c_g(q_1 + q_2) - c_t(q_2 + q_e) - F \quad (11.1)$$

and to highlight the various profit centres for the incumbent, using $a = p_e - c_e$ this can be rewritten as:

$$\pi(p_1, p_2, p_e) = (p_1 - c_g)q_1 + (p_2 - c_g - c_t)q_2 + (p_e - c_e - c_t)q_e - F \quad (11.2)$$

To get to the second-best pricing policy (i.e. the set of prices p_1, p_2 and p_e), sustaining entry in a sector which is operated by a VIM, the regulator would have to conduct the following welfare optimization exercise that accounts for the net consumer surplus[25] $V(p) = S(p) - pq(p)$ at each node and for the profits of the incumbent obliged to share the use of a common facility it had invested in originally to cater to its own business:[26]

$$\max V_1(p_1) + V_2(p_2, p_e) + \pi(p_1, p_2, p_e) \quad (11.3)$$

$$\text{subject to} \quad \pi(p_1, p_2, p_e) \geq 0 \quad (\lambda)$$
$$q_2 + q_e \leq K \quad (\eta)$$
$$q_1 \geq 0, q_2 \geq 0, q_e \geq 0$$

where $q_1 = q_1(p_1)$, $q_2 = q_2(p_2, p_e)$, $q_e = q_e(p_2, p_e)$, $V_2(p_2, p_e) = S_2(q_2(p_2, p_e), q_e(p_2, p_e)) - p_2 q_2(p_2, p_e) - p_e q_e(p_2, p_e)$.

Solving this optimization problem, as proven in the appendix to this chapter, the electricity provided by the entrants should be sold at node 2 at the implicit price:

$$p_e = c_e + c_t + \frac{\eta}{1 + \lambda} + \frac{\lambda}{1 + \lambda} \frac{p_e}{\bar{\varepsilon}_e} \quad (11.4)$$

where η is the congestion shadow price and $\bar{\varepsilon}_e$ stands for the super-elasticity of demand for the energy sold by the entrants at node 2.[27]

Combining this result with the entrants' equilibrium price $p_e = c_e + a$ leads to the following access charge:

$$a^0 = c_t + \frac{\eta}{1 + \lambda} + \frac{\lambda}{1 + \lambda} \frac{p_e}{\bar{\varepsilon}_e} \quad (11.5)$$

[25] The net consumer's surplus has been defined in Chapter 2 as the difference between the gross surplus $S(.)$ and the expenditure $p \times q$. Alternatively, it is the integral of the demand function between the price paid by the consumer and the maximal price they are willing to pay, that is $V(p) = \int_p^{+\infty} q(x)dx$, where $q(x)$ is the quantity demanded at price x.

[26] It should also account for the entrants' profit but, by the assumption $p_e = c_e + a$, it is nil.

[27] A super-elasticity includes all the direct and indirect relative changes in demands q_2 and q_e due to a 1% variation in price p_2 or p_e. Its formal definition is in the appendix.

the access fee should just compensate the incumbent for the sales lost because of entry. Hence, given the second-best pricing of the incumbent determined in the appendix, the access fee should be $p_2 - c_g = c_t + \frac{\eta}{1+\lambda} + \frac{\lambda}{1+\lambda} \frac{p_2}{\varepsilon_e}$. The first two terms are the same as in Equation (11.5) but the last one is different, except in the case where the entrants and the incumbent sell exactly the same product to the same consumers.

The greening of a sector and the associated regulatory uncertainty are not the only challenges to consider when designing policies to stimulate investment. Increasingly, technological innovation is also changing the nature of markets, and with them the number and types of users of the investments. For instance, the fact that new technologies allow the entry of firms that are not traditional actors of a specific regulated sector has an impact on its operations. The most obvious example is the growing digitalization of the energy sector. It is characterized by the entry of firms that are not traditional energy suppliers such as ICT service providers. These new actors intend to use the electric power line for transmitting data from sensors to a hub thanks to the 'power line communication' technology. What is unusual about them in this context is that they will not compete against the incumbent on the energy market. They will even complement energy provision with services such as metering and demand flexibility. On the positive side, they use the facility to add value and can contribute to its financing. On the negative side, they use existing capacity with associated congestion risks. In addition to these risks, there are institutional risks resulting from the fact that the ICT firms and the traditional energy actors are regulated by different regulators. In almost any institutional context, the coordination of these regulators can be quite challenging. And this is more likely to be the case when institutions are weak and assignments unclear.

11.6 How Do Access Prices and Investment Interact in Evolving Markets?

The relationship between investment and access prices can go both ways. First, access prices influence the incentive to invest. This is because they are an essential revenue source for the owner of the facility to be shared with competitors on a market relying on that facility to deliver a service. For instance, a vertically integrated railway company owning the tracks and competing for passengers or freight with other railways operators using the tracks will want to make sure it recovers its fair share of the cost of investing in these tracks and their maintenance costs. These costs are the main focus of the rules adopted to set access prices. They are central to the ex ante assessments of the financial viability of new projects and hence of the ex ante incentive to invest in increasingly competitive environments.

Access prices are often critical to the decision by lenders, equity investors and an incumbent operator to agree to finance an investment in a facility that they will have to share with other users. Unless rivals generate enough revenue for the incumbent that can more than compensate for some of the revenue losses associated with the stronger competition, investment is unlikely to be financed. Getting the access prices wrong can thus have a negative effect on investment if the incumbent is not allowed to make a profit on access provision in this competitive environment.[28]

Second, access prices themselves can actually be influenced by investment decisions. To see in equation (11.5), consider the effects of a decision to increase the transmission capacity K in the electricity sector. The first effect is *technical*: the investment will alleviate congestion, then decrease the shadow price of the transmission constraint, η. The second effect is *financial*. With a larger fixed cost to recover, the dual value of the budget constraint, λ, will increase. Overall, for the second term of the equation, this implies an unambiguous decrease. The effect on the third term is less clear. Since the regulator controls the three prices p_1, p_2 and a, they all will be used to rebalance the additional fixed cost. The ratio $\frac{\lambda}{1+\lambda}$ increases when λ increases (and converges to 1 when the constraint is severely binding). Consequently, the incumbent's retail prices p_1 will unambiguously increase. What happens to p_2 and a depends on whether product 2 and the product offered by the entrant e are substitutes or complements.

If product 2 and product e are *substitutes*, their super-elasticities are positive, so that both p_2 and a are also expected to increase as they commonly participate in the financing of the infrastructure. How much they should increase depends on the elasticity coefficients as shown in Chapter 2, Section 2.2.

If, instead, the entrants sell products that *complement* the incumbent's products, and ignoring for now the congestion problems (i.e. assuming that η is negligible), it would be efficient both privately and socially to charge entry below the transmission cost c_t. This is because of a negative (super-)elasticity: with more complements (e.g. energy services), consumers' willingness to pay for the incumbent's final product (e.g. energy supply), p_2, increases so that it is profitable to invest in a larger capacity. Then for the producers of complementary products, investment will most likely be accompanied by a lower access fee.

It is thus the relative value of the technical and the financial effects that will lead investment to result in a decrease or increase of the optimal access fee. This relative importance thus also determines the final level of entry and hence the number of firms in the sector.

11.7   How Does the Original Sectoral Organization Matter to Investment Decisions?

Pricing is not the only determinant of the investment decisions. Governance matters as well. The same sector can be organized in different ways in different countries. This is one more reason why it is quite difficult to compare the investment-incentive effects of access charges across countries. To illustrate this point, consider again the electricity sector. We just derived an expression, the third-party-access option, showing what a regulator would have to consider in a context in which the sector remains operated by

---

[28] In telecommunications, Kotakorpi (2005) finds that regulation can lower the investment incentives.

a vertically integrated firm. What would happen to investment incentives if the industry was initially characterized by an unbundled structure in which the ownership of electricity production and of transmission is separated?

When the ownership of the 'transmission' company is separated from the producer's/seller's ownership, any producer/seller, old or new, is a user of the network in the same way as the final consumers at each of the two nodes. Identifying the optimal access rule under this market organization is less straightforward than in the case of the vertically integrated structure, in particular because the independent operator can be exclusively in charge of energy transmission, or have the responsibility for both transmission and system operation, or be also a mandatory go-between for producers and sellers. In the latter case, one of the drivers of this complexity is that, in an unbundled structure, the independent transmission system operator (TSO) has only one source of revenues (access fees), whereas in the integrated structure the monopoly also has revenues from energy sales.

To make the discussion as simple as possible, assume that the TSO is also the system operator controlling access to its assets as a middleman between producers and consumers. It buys electricity from the generators at price p^g and sells it to consumers at price p^w. This is the single-buyer option (Bier 1999; Pollitt 2019) that we consider hereafter. Assume also that all the producers sell jointly in an aggregate way and the industry's cost function to produce energy is an increasing convex function $C(q)$.[29] Finally, entrants and the incumbent produce perfect substitutes for consumers at node 2.

As shown in Box 11.4, in this framework the second-best unit access price is:

$$\hat{a} = c_t + \frac{\eta}{1+\lambda} + \frac{\lambda}{1+\lambda}\left(\frac{p_2^w}{\varepsilon_2^w} + \frac{p^g}{\varepsilon^g}\right)$$

We see that despite a quite different organization, the second-best access charge $\hat{a}$ has some similarities with the third-party access charge a^0: the two first terms are identical. The third one is different, but similar rules apply in its computation. Indeed, when social efficiency is only constrained by financial concerns (i.e. $\eta = 0$ *and* $\lambda > 0$), second-best pricing rules command price discrimination based on users' elasticities. In the third-party access case, the utility was making some profit by selling its own electricity on top of charging entrants, whereas in the second-best structure, all its revenues are coming from the access fee complemented by the local gains at node 1, $p_1^w - p^g$.

Note that this complement does not exist for a pure TSO, which can only rely on the transmission fee. Since the fixed cost to cover is the same (F), this means that a higher access fee has to be charged to consumers at node 2. This should be a regulatory concern because of the development of out-of-grid solutions that result in an increase in transmission fees. The consumers who can install photovoltaic panels on their house's roof to bypass the grid and lower their energy bills are, on average,

---

[29] This cost function is a useful approximation of the stepwise merit order of heterogeneous technologies such as those noted in the electricity sector (i.e. solar, nuclear, thermal).

Box 11.4 Access Pricing in the Single-Buyer Framework

Given the prices fixed by the TSO, the network users maximize their net surplus and net profit. At node $i = 1,2$, the consumers' demand function is $q_i^w = q_i(p_i^w)$; then their net surplus as a function of the price is:

$$V_i^w(p_i^w) = \int_{p_i^w}^{+\infty} q_i(x)dx. \tag{11.6}$$

At node 1, producers solve $\max\ pq - C(q)$, which gives the supply function $q^g(p^g)$ and the aggregate profit of producers is:

$$\pi^g(p^g) = p^g q^g(p^g) - C(q^g(p^g)). \tag{11.7}$$

If the transmission company is a private firm, it will fix the prices at the two ends of the line to maximize its profit from the transmission of q_2^w, which is the so-called merchandising surplus:

$$MS = p_2^w q_2^w - p^g q_2^w - c_t q_2^w - F. \tag{11.8}$$

However, from a social point of view, the objective function should also include the energy traded at node 1 (even though it does not transit through the line), the net surplus from consumption at nodes 1 and 2 and the profit of producers. Let $q_1^w + q_2^w \le q^g$. In this perspective, the generalized merchandising surplus is:

$$MS(p_1^w, p_2^w, p^g) = p_1^w q_1^w + p_2^w q_2^w - p^g q^g - c_t q_2^w - F \tag{11.9}$$

The second-best pricing policy in this organizational structure is the set of prices p_1^w, p_2^w, p^g, solving:

$$\max\ V_1(p_1^w) + V_2(p_2^w) + \pi^g(p^g) + MS(p_1^w, p_2^w, p^g) \tag{11.10}$$

$$\text{subject to} \quad \begin{aligned} q_2^w &\le K & (\eta) \\ MS &\ge 0 & (\lambda) \\ q_1^w + q_2^w &\le q^g & (\mu) \end{aligned}$$

where η, λ and μ respectively are the shadow prices of the transmission constraint, the TSO's budget constraint and the energy constraint. As shown in the appendix, the resulting Ramsey prices are:

$$p_1^w = \frac{\mu}{1+\lambda} + \frac{\lambda}{1+\lambda}\frac{p_1^w}{\varepsilon_1^w}, \quad p_2^w = c_t + \frac{\eta+\mu}{1+\lambda} + \frac{\lambda}{1+\lambda}\frac{p_2^w}{\varepsilon_2^w}, \quad p^g = \frac{\mu}{1+\lambda} - \frac{\lambda}{1+\lambda}\frac{p^g}{\varepsilon^g} \tag{11.11}$$

where $\varepsilon^g = \frac{dq^g}{dp^g}\frac{p^g}{q^g}$ is the price elasticity of supply and $\varepsilon_i^w = -\frac{dq_i^w}{dp_i^w}\frac{p_i^w}{q_i^w}$ is the demand elasticity at node $i = 1, 2$.

As compared with the case in which the firm operating the shared facility is vertically integrated (third-party access), in the single-buyer framework there is an additional distortion. Because price discrimination is efficient, the regulator focusing on maximizing social welfare would discriminate between consumers and

Box 11.4 (*cont.*)

producers at node 1, even though they do not use the transmission line since they are both located at the same node. The uniqueness of price at one node is lost as $p_1^w - p^g = \frac{\lambda}{1+\lambda}\left(\frac{p_1^w}{\varepsilon_1^w} + \frac{p^g}{\varepsilon^g}\right) > 0$. It is socially efficient to ask consumers at node 1 to pay a share of the transmission cost because they are members of the same electricity system.

If the main goal of regulation is to maximize social welfare and to provide incentives to invest, the regulator needs to compute the access fees to be charged to the users of the common facility accounting for the results derived so far. One simple way to do this is to assume that there are traders that are allowed to buy electricity at node 1 and sell it to consumers at node 2 after paying the access fee, a. Their unit profit would be $p_2^w - (p^g + a)$. When the trading activity is perfectly competitive, at equilibrium the traders cannot extract rent, which means that the access fee should be fixed at the value $\hat{a}$ such that $\hat{a} = p_2^w - p^g$.

Using the energy Ramsey prices determined above, we obtain:

$$\hat{a} = c_t + \frac{\eta}{1+\lambda} + \frac{\lambda}{1+\lambda}\left(\frac{p_2^w}{\varepsilon_2^w} + \frac{p^g}{\varepsilon^g}\right) \qquad (11.12)$$

richer than those who have no house to do the same. Then the resulting transmission fee increase has a negative social consequence for captive energy consumers.

While this discussion may seem quite technical, it is important from a policy perspective and relevant to many real-life situations in which investment signals are not clear enough to stimulate investment. This will penalize future generations of users and taxpayers. In particular, it shows that whether regulators and policymakers are considering a third-party access, a single-buyer framework or a TSO organizational form, the discussions and concerns on the relationship between access price and investment have to follow very similar logics and address similar concerns. But institutional details matter.

More generally, this discussion shows that the desirable structure and value of the tariff to access an infrastructure depends on the specific institutional framework of the industry. This is one more illustration of the importance of recognizing that one size does not fit all when it comes to deciding on the optimal level and type of regulation. There are some common dimensions across market structures of course. The most obvious is the necessity to pay for variable costs, congestion and fixed costs. For the two cases we have discussed, it is also clear that the price elasticity of demand (or the super-elasticity, if available) should be a key ingredient for the computation of access charges. But differences matter. In an unbundled sector structure (single-buyer), the access fee should be based on both the demand elasticity and the supply elasticity of the users of the line. This relevance of the specific institutional details has become one of the main topics in empirical assessments of the effectiveness of access regulation and, more generally, of the interactions between regulation and investments. It is sometimes harder to 'sell' in political circles where the concept of discrimination is often associated with other interpretations.

11.8   What Does the Evidence Add to Theory?

Evidence accumulated over fifty years confirms that regulation impacts on the incentive to invest, as argued by theoretical research, but it also suggests that it may not do so as simply as suggested by theory. This evidence confirms that regulation has a role in explaining the access gaps and the wrong technological choices. It also identifies more specific dimensions to consider in the design of regulation that may have been overlooked by theory contributing to the ineffectiveness of options adopted by regulators. It is, for instance, quite common for theoretical papers analysing the regulation of investment to forget the relevance of the institutional environment in which the investment decision is made. Yet there is ample evidence now that this environment makes a difference to the optimal choice of regulation when investment is a core regulatory concern.

'Institutional details matter' may be one of the most policy-relevant insights offered by Guthrie's (2006) initial stock-taking survey of the key dimensions to consider when assessing the interactions between regulation and investment. In addition, he emphasized the relevance of more precise dimensions such as the degree of irreversibility of the investment, the nature and intensity of information asymmetries on costs or the level and distribution of risks between the various stakeholders.[30] Other missing variables identified by later research include the characteristics of the firm (i.e. size, product specialization), the industry's organization (i.e. the degree of unbundling and the level of competition), the financing strategy, the governance of the firms (e.g. board composition) and the governance of the sector (including the ability to commit, the quality of regulation and the degree of corruption). The long-lasting omission of these variables by mainstream theoretical research partially explains some of the differences in conclusions reached by theoretical and empirical research.[31]

This empirical research is also useful in showing the similarity of reactions to some of the incentives effects of regulation on investment across sectors. For instance, Egert (2009) analysed the effect of the overall regulatory framework on sectoral investments in four industries (energy, water, rail and telecommunications) of the OECD. His main result was that investments are positively influenced by the adoption of both incentive-based regulation and the introduction of an independent regulator. His results are particularly insightful because they link the adoption of a regulatory agency separated

---

[30] From an econometric perspective, these discussions deal with omitted control variables to consider which could bias results and hence policy conclusions.

[31] For a review challenging the received wisdom on the validity of the Averch–Johnson effect, see Joskow (2005) for an early criticism and Joskow (2014) or Law (2014) for more recent critical surveys of the accumulated evidence.

from the sector Ministry, such as will be discussed in Chapter 14, to the strengthening of the regulatory certainty needed to stimulate investments. This was implicit in the discussions of lack of commitment and regulatory uncertainty identified by theoretical assessments. In practice, these results imply that uncertainty, and the higher risks associated with regimes such as price or revenue caps, could be mitigated by accounting for the institutional constraints and designs (e.g. is the regulator independent or not?). This includes making the most of competition opportunities, which Egert (2009) emphasizes by advocating for lower barriers to entry in regulated sectors.

Some of these general results are validated by sector-specific evaluations, although this literature has tended to be dominated by research on the telecommunications sector where the emphasis is on the need to invest to adjust to fast-evolving technologies (e.g. Greenstein et al. 1995 or Ai and Sappington 2002 for evidence on the US experience). In a nutshell, this sector-specific research confirms that incentive-based regulation can be as effective as predicted by theory in stimulating the right investment levels and composition at the lowest possible cost. It also shows that the specific design of regulation must account explicitly for the institutional and governance dimensions that could reduce or reinforce these incentives. Most importantly maybe, it provides quite convincing evidence that interactions between all the key policy variables also have to be considered when designing regulation to stimulate investment in specific regulated activities.

Many of these lessons have been internalized in actual regulatory policy since the early-to-mid 2000s. For instance, they have been adapted to the assessment of investment in broadband, fibre or high-speed internet. In most countries, regulators have had to find ways to stimulate telecoms operators to replace their old copper networks with fibre-optic technology, known as the 'next generation access broadband networks' (NGA). In that context, the empirical ex post evaluations of the effectiveness of regulatory policies in providing the right investment incentives to speed up the development of these NGAs provides important detailed insights relevant to other sectors. First, it shows that design details matter. The specific design of the access prices to these new infrastructures combined with the specific nature of the competitors influences the level and speed of investment (e.g. Briglauer and Gugler 2013 or Bourreau et al. 2019).[32] Second, it highlights the effectiveness of subsidies in stimulating investment in some contexts (e.g. Bourreau et al. 2015, 2018; Briglauer et al. 2015, 2018). Third, increasing competition can help, but only for a while, as its impact fades as markets become more mature (e.g. Nardotto et al. 2015). Moreover, its impact depends on the specific nature of the competitive threat on the incumbent (Calzada et al. 2018). Finally, market specificities make a difference to the effectiveness of instruments in stimulating investment. The effects of investment incentives on the

---

[32] Some of the most policy-relevant discussions of this literature emphasize the need to be creative in the design of access prices or rules to match the concerns for speeding up investments and the need to account for the specific market structure in which the decision has to be taken. For instance, Bourreau et al. (2015) assess geographically differentiated regulation imposed on fibre infrastructure as a potential regulatory tool to improve the trade-off between more intense retail competition and more infrastructure investment.

firms' decisions vary with the size and the nature of the national or regional markets, such as old versus young population, urban versus rural, low versus high unemployment (Calzada et al. 2018).

Many of the results on the relative importance of the various insights summarized by Guthrie (2006), Egers (2009) and the large volume of research on the telecoms sector have been validated between 2010 and 2019 by Cambini and Rondi of the Torino Polytechnic University and their co-authors for other sectors in Europe. They validated some of the most basic theoretical insights on the relative effectiveness of incentive-based regimes and cost-plus/rate-of-return-based regimes (Cambini and Rondi 2010). For a sample of twenty-three European electric and gas utilities, they showed that incentive regulation led firms to invest significantly between 1997 and 2007, but that the investments were to improve efficiency rather than to expand capacity. This illustrated the importance of the distinction between the quality and the quantity of investment identified by the theoretical papers.

Cambini and Rondi (2010) also illustrate other basic theoretical results. First, they show the relevance of the cost of capital in the investment decision discussed in Chapter 7 since, for their sample, they find that the investment rate is positively correlated to the cost of capital allowed by regulators. The result is important, but it does not allow for assessing whether the permitted return is higher than needed or not. Yet this is a common policy concern, as discussed in Chapter 6, for instance. Second, they confirm the existence of an interaction between investment and the choice of the efficiency factor (the X-factor) in the design of incentive-based regulation such as price or revenue caps. More specifically, they show that when the requested efficiency gain is perceived to be too high, firms chose to increase their asset base since expected large efficiency gains reduce their expected returns on any cost-saving investment. Firms do make the most of the margins allowed by incentive-based regulation, as suggested by theory.

Finally, this very pedagogical paper also tests some of the impact of more institutional dimensions argued to be relevant by theoretical research and already demonstrated to be so empirically for the telecommunications sector. Of particular interest is the absence of statistically significant evidence of a difference between public and private utilities in their investment decisions for a given type of regulation. Similar conclusions on the irrelevance of ownership for the investment decision were reached by Cullman and Niewand (2016) for a detailed assessment of the behaviour of 109 German electricity distribution companies.[33] Somewhat surprisingly, there is not a lot of evidence on the interaction between ownership, regulation and investment for developing countries where the debates on privatization have been quite intensive (e.g. Leighland 2018). The evidence has tended to focus on the extent to which private

---

[33] Poudineh and Jamasb (2014) study the economic and technical determinants of investment in Norwegian electricity distribution networks using a panel dataset of 126 companies. The factors that might affect investment behaviour are the number of network stations, energy density, cost of energy loss, number of leisure homes and depreciation.

investment has been a complement or a substitute to public investment. And that debate is not settled either.

Many of these results were re-tested and validated by Abrardi et al. (2018). They extend the Cambini and Rondi (2010) sample to 2013 and account explicitly for the increased use of hybrid regulatory schemes in the European electricity sector, one of the main regulatory changes noted during the 2010s. In addition, this update allows an evaluation of the extent to which regulators had to deal with the consequences of the Great Recession that started in 2008.

Somewhat reassuringly, the main results did not change despite the evolving context. Incentive-based regulation and a higher allowed return on capital both continued to stimulate investments as suggested by theory. But a few significant new results emerged. First, the increased role of hybrid regimes has made the nature of the investment (cost saving versus asset expansion) more difficult to predict. Second, despite the lesser predictability of the impact of incentives, the evaluation of the experience covered by this sample suggests that: (i) the negative effect of a high X-factor imposed by regulators has become less statistically significant as a result of the growing role of hybrid regimes; (ii) in contrast to what theory suggests, for a given risk level, the impact of the cost of capital on the investment decision is weaker for utilities under incentive regulation than for those under hybrid regimes or under rate-of-return regulation (although this could also be interpreted as implying that the allowed rate of return had been set at levels high enough to cover most risks anticipated by firms).

Of particular interest in an environment in which the financing of regulated industries is increasingly dependent on financial market actors is the result that, for this sample, in recent years the cost of capital has been a stronger driver of investments than the choice of the X-factors. They offer two possible explanations. First, X-factors have already played their role in the early part of the period when the sector was restructured in many countries. Second, regulatory priorities have changed. For instance, increasing the importance of quality or innovation-oriented considerations linked to environmental concerns has been common in many countries, and since this requires large investments, it has motived a switch to hybrids. These new regulatory approaches have allowed an increased commitment to permit firms to recover the associated expenditures.

This brief overview confirms that the empirical research on the interactions between regulation and investment validates many of the most basic theoretical results, but it also adds important caveats on the limits of the basic theory to guide policy. The evidence across sectors and regions reveals the many dimensions often ignored by theory that are relevant to the practice of regulation. Context, market structure, size and nature, institutional governance and capacity, and interactions between these different dimensions matter more than some of the older mainstream theoretical results suggests. We will see in Chapter 14 that these dimensions are progressively being accounted for by theoretical researchers keen on helping refine the robustness of policy advice through additional assessments of the trade-offs and complementarities suggested by experience. But most of these new results have not yet made it to the policy agenda.

11.9   Summing Up

- Underinvestment, overinvestment or mistargeted investment are quite common across sectors at all development stages.
- The losers are reasonably predictable:
  - Underinvestment tends to:
    - penalize the poorest when it slows down increase in access rates;
    - penalize all users when it leads to congestion, environmental impacts or low quality.
  - Overinvestment or mistargeted investment tends to:
    - penalize users and taxpayers as their costs are passed on to final prices or subsidies.
- Regulation is often part of the problem because:
  - Cost-plus/rate-of-return regulation tends to stimulate overinvestment.
  - Price/revenue cap regulation tends to result in underinvestment.
  - Too much leeway on the choice of investment by regulated firms can lead to underinvestment designed to exclude potential entrants.
  - Regulatory designs focusing only on prices and omitting to include service obligations and/or access rules lessen incentives to invest.
  - Unrealistic or non-credible regulatory commitments lead to underinvestment.
- Any regulatory failure or uncertainty tends to increase the risk premia built into the financing cost of investment, contributing to further underinvestment or investment delays.
- Regulation can be part of the solution to stimulate investment decisions for the sake of improving social welfare and a fair distribution of the gains.
  - The adoption of hybrid price regulation approaches can be more effective at stimulating investment than pure price caps or rate-of-return regulation.
  - Access prices and rules are a key to determining investment.
  - The specific design of access rules must be adapted to the industrial structure of the regulated sector.
- Empirical evidence highlights the many dimensions that are ignored by theoretical research, notably key institutional and contextual variables that explain why similar investment incentives built into regulation do not work as effectively in all countries, all sectors and/or all investment types.

Appendix On Access Prices and Market Structures

1 Access Price When the Incumbent Is Vertically Integrated (Third-Party Access)

To solve $\max_{p_1,p_2,p_e} \; V_1(p_1) + V_2(p_2,p_e) + \pi(p_1,p_2,p_e)$

$$s.t. \quad \pi(p_1,p_2,p_e) \geq 0 \qquad (\lambda)$$
$$q_2 + q_e \leq K \qquad (\eta)$$
$$q_1 \geq 0, \; q_2 \geq 0, \; q_e \geq 0$$

we write the Lagrange function:

$$L = V_1(p_1) + V_2(p_2,p_e) + (1+\lambda)\pi(p_1,p_2,p_e) + \eta \cdot \left(K - q_2(p_2,p_e) - q_e(p_2,p_e)\right)$$

where λ is the shadow price of public funds and η is the congestion shadow price.

Using $\frac{\partial V}{\partial p_i} = -q_i$, the first-order conditions of the second-best problem with entrants are:

$$-q_1 + (1+\lambda)\left[q_1 + (p_1 - c_g)\frac{dq_1}{dp_1}\right] = 0$$

$$-q_2 + (1+\lambda)\left[q_2 + (p_2 - c_g - c_t)\frac{dq_2}{dp_2} + (p_e - c_e - c_t)\frac{dq_e}{dp_2}\right] - \eta\left(\frac{dq_2}{dp_2} + \frac{dq_e}{dp_2}\right) = 0$$

$$-q_e + (1+\lambda)\left[q_e + (p_2 - c_g - c_t)\frac{dq_2}{dp_e} + (p_e - c_e - c_t)\frac{dq_e}{\partial p_e}\right] - \eta\left(\frac{dq_2}{dp_e} + \frac{dq_e}{dp_e}\right) = 0$$

Jointly with the complementary slackness conditions derived from the financial and technical constraints, these equations allow us to compute the shadow prices λ, η and the energy prices p_1, p_2, p_e. The system of equations is solved for the margins extracted from the three activities of the incumbent: $p_1 - c_g$ for local consumers, $p_2 - c_g - c_t - \eta/(1+\lambda)$ for remote consumers, and $p_e - c_e - c_t - \eta/(1+\lambda)$ for access to entrants. The Lerner indices are then:

$$\frac{p_1 - c_g}{p_1} = \frac{\lambda}{1+\lambda}\frac{1}{\varepsilon_1}, \quad \frac{p_2 - \left(c_g + c_t + \dfrac{\eta}{1+\lambda}\right)}{p_2} = \frac{\lambda}{1+\lambda}\frac{1}{\bar{\varepsilon}_e}, \quad \frac{p_e - \left(c_e + c_t + \dfrac{\eta}{1+\lambda}\right)}{p_e}$$

$$= \frac{\lambda}{1+\lambda}\frac{1}{\bar{\varepsilon}_e} \quad \text{where } \bar{\varepsilon}_e = \frac{\varepsilon_e\varepsilon_2 - \varepsilon_{e2}\varepsilon_{2e}}{\varepsilon_2 - \varepsilon_{e2}}, \bar{\varepsilon}_2 = \frac{\varepsilon_2\varepsilon_e - \varepsilon_{2e}\varepsilon_{e2}}{\varepsilon_e - \varepsilon_{2e}}, \varepsilon_i = -\frac{dq_i p_i}{dp_i q_i} \quad \text{and}$$

$$\varepsilon_{ij} = \frac{\partial q_i}{\partial p_j} \frac{p_j}{q_i} \quad i = 1, 2, e, \ i \neq j.$$

2   Access Price under Ownership Unbundling (Single-Buyer)

In order to solve $\underset{p^g, p_1^w, p_2^w}{Max} \ V_1\left(p_1^w\right) + V_2\left(p_2^w\right) + \pi^g\left(p^g\right) + MS\left(p_1^w, p_2^w, p^g\right)$

$$\text{s.t.} \quad \begin{array}{ll} q_2^w \leq K & (\eta) \\ MS \geq 0 & (\lambda) \\ q_1^w + q_2^w \leq q^g & (\mu) \end{array}$$

we build the Lagrange function: $\quad L = V_1\left(p_1^w\right) + V_2\left(p_2^w\right) + \pi^g\left(p^g\right) + (1 + \lambda)$
$MS\left(p_1^w, p_2^w, p^g\right) + \eta.\left(K - q_2^w\left(p_2^w\right)\right) + \mu.\left(q^g\left(p^g\right) - q_1^w\left(p_1^w\right) - q_2^w\left(p_2^w\right)\right)$

The first-order conditions are:

$$\frac{\partial L}{\partial p_1^w} = -q_1^w + (1 + \lambda)\left[q_1^w + p_1^w \frac{dq_1^w}{dp_1^w}\right] - \mu \frac{dq_1^w}{dp_1^w} = 0$$

$$\frac{\partial L}{\partial p_2^w} = -q_2^w + (1 + \lambda)\left[q_2^w + p_2^w \frac{dq_2^w}{dp_2^w} - c_t \frac{dq_2^w}{dp_2^w}\right] - \eta \frac{dq_2^w}{dp_2^w} - \mu \frac{dq_2^w}{dp_2^w} = 0$$

$$\frac{\partial L}{\partial p^g} = q^g - (1 + \lambda)\left[q^g + p^g \frac{dq^g}{dp^g}\right] + \mu \frac{dq^g}{dp^g} = 0$$

From these equations and the slackness conditions, one can derive the Ramsey prices for energy:

$$\frac{p_1^w - \dfrac{\mu}{1+\lambda}}{p_1^w} = \frac{\lambda}{1+\lambda}\frac{1}{\varepsilon_1^w}, \quad \frac{p_2^w - \left(c_t + \dfrac{\eta+\mu}{1+\lambda}\right)}{p_2^w} = \frac{\lambda}{1+\lambda}\frac{1}{\varepsilon_2^w}, \quad \frac{p^g - \dfrac{\mu}{1+\lambda}}{p^g} = -\frac{\lambda}{1+\lambda}\frac{1}{\varepsilon^g}$$

where $\varepsilon^g = \frac{dq^g}{dp^g}\frac{p^g}{q^g}$ and $\varepsilon_i = -\frac{dq_i^w}{dp_i^w}\frac{p_i^w}{q_i^w} \ i = 1, 2.$

12   Regulating Multi-Product Oligopolies

The demand for regulation has had to evolve with the changes in the global economy since the mid-1980s because new structures and actors have emerged in the markets traditionally served by regulated monopolies. As we discussed in Chapters 1 and 2, in the last thirty to forty years, many countries have adopted structural economic reforms intended to increase competitive options and to reduce the need to regulate. The massive efforts to deregulate were paired with policies designed to increase the relative importance of the private sector across industries traditionally operated by public enterprises. The changes were supposed to achieve efficiency gains to the benefit of consumers and taxpayers. They did not, or at least not as much as initially expected. Improvements in quantity, quality or prices were disappointing for significant shares of the population, in particular in developing and emerging economies and subsidies to finance investments and sometimes operational expenditures ended up being much higher than promised by the reformers.[1] Moreover, these reforms ended up resulting in high rates of return at low risk levels, as evidenced by the returns earned by investors in infrastructure funds in Australia, Europe or North America.[2]

One of the reasons for the high returns is that the reforms often led to a switch from over-regulated public monopolies to under-regulated oligopolistic markets. Competition *in* the market was not a realistic option if countries were to make the most of increasing returns to scale. And competition *across* markets or *for* the markets was a good option conceptually, but in practice it did not reduce the risks of ex post abuses of market power when compared to the monopolistic structure. Regulating these oligopolistic markets often proved to be more complex than regulating a monopoly.[3]

The optimal design of regulation for these new structures and their new actors is one of the main focuses of this chapter. We review some of the pros and cons about 'deregulation' conceptually and illustrate the implications for infrastructure and public utilities. We also discuss the importance of the residual regulatory requirements and

---

[1] See Estache (2020a) for a survey of the academic quantitative evidence on the effects of infrastructure privatizations.

[2] For the twenty-year period that ended in 2019, the Bloomberg database suggests that the median annual return on infrastructure funds was around 8%, about 15% less than the median return on global equity funds but less than half the dispersion (i.e. half the variance).

[3] For a more detailed discussion, see Motta (2004).

how they can be designed to make the most of the opportunities to reduce production and information asymmetry costs in these new oligopolistic market structures.

The chapter also addresses the impact on the design of regulation of the fact that many of the active and potential operators are involved in multi-product activities. For example, railway companies offer transport for passengers and freight services. This implies that these firms should be regulated, taking into account the cost and demand interdependencies between the different sub-markets they supply. This problem becomes more complex with the liberalization of the public service industries. Because of the widespread deregulation, these traditionally vertically integrated struc-tures now face the entry of competitors to their final products (e.g. passenger transport, electricity) with the obligation to let them use the infrastructure already installed and the one they must develop (e.g. railways, transmission lines). They become de facto multi-product, selling both a final product to consumers and an intermediary product (i.e. access to the infrastructure) to their competitors.

While the chapter does not do full justice to all the issues raised by these recent evolutions, it focuses on those that regulators are most likely to have to address in practice. These include the simultaneous regulation of the prices of the multiple products delivered by the regulated firms, the risks of anticompetitive cross-subsidies of some of the products and pricing of access to backbone infrastructures used by multiple competing firms. We start with an example to illustrate how many of these issues come about in practice in oligopolistic market structures.

12.1   The Challenge of Regulating an Oligopolistic Market in Practice: The Eurostar Case

The railways sector offers a particularly concrete illustration of the challenges of regulation in multi-product markets in oligopolistic structures.[4] To make the example as focused as possible, let's consider the evolution of the operation of Eurostar, the high-speed passenger train that directly links the United Kingdom to France and Belgium via an exclusive 50.45-kilometre tunnel constructed under the North Sea (since 1994).[5]

From a regulatory viewpoint, it is useful to start with a sense of the business perspective on the main characteristics of the oligopolistic markets in which Eurostar

---

[4] For some of the captive shippers, the sector can be considered as a monopoly – for users who have no alternative, for instance because their freight cannot be loaded on trucks (e.g. coal or most raw minerals) and only one railway company serves their region.

[5] The tunnel actually also supports the Eurotunnel Shuttle for road vehicles loaded onto trains and international goods trains. Timetables are shared between these three services. In retrospect, the overall traffic forecasts that justified ex ante the construction of the tunnel were overestimated, notably as a result of the explosion of budget airlines (e.g. Anguera 2006). But biases in demand forecast can also be influenced by random shocks such as the impact of the Covid crisis on travel intensity or changes in policies, such as the impact on transport modal choice resulting from increasingly tight environmental restrictions on airlines.

is a key actor. The most obvious one is that running Eurostar trains relies on a complex technical infrastructure that should not be duplicated (i.e. tracks, signalling systems, stations and depots, in addition to the construction and maintenance of the tunnel). Its cost characteristics are such that it is easy to define this part of the business as a natural monopoly (with the usual cost characteristics leading to scale, scope and density economies[6]). Getlink is the monopoly in charge of operating and maintaining the tunnel.[7] Since 2015, it is jointly regulated by the French multimodal transport regulator (ARAFER) and the British Office of Rail and Road, which set the terms and price of access to the tunnel. They assess the contractual conditions offered to new entrants and their impact on existing users of the tunnel, the mechanisms for allocating the use of the tunnel's capacity, the scheduling and coordination procedures, and the applicable charges for incumbents and entrants.[8]

The second main dimension to deal with is that this facility has many different types of potential users. The simplest distinction is to separate passengers and freight users but the passenger business operated by Eurostar dominates the market. The company focuses on the operation of the rolling stock to deliver passenger transport services (i.e. trains) to two types of users: business and non-business passengers. The fact that each group has a very different willingness to pay for different levels of services is also important to remember.

The third relevant fact concerns the evolution of the ownership of the activities of the regulated firms. Until 2010, Eurostar was operated jointly by the French and Belgian national (public) railway companies (SNCF and SNCB) and Eurostar Ltd, a subsidiary of London and Continental Railways, which also owned the high-speed infrastructure and stations on the British side. In September 2010, Eurostar was incorporated as a single corporate entity called Eurostar International Limited owned by SNCF and SNCB (with 55% of the shares), Caisse de dépôt et placement du Québec (30%) and other smaller investors (adding up to 15%). In many businesses the evolution of ownership can have an impact on the management and operational behaviour, which may be of relevance to regulatory decisions (i.e. impact on dividend policies or on frequency of maintenance).

The fourth relevant dimension is the need to deal with the evolution of the number of operators to regulate. The adoption of a railways sector liberalization policy by the European Commission in 2010 has led the various actors to diversify their activities.[9]

---

[6] Economies of density differ from economies of scale because they are related to spatial properties. The spatial proximity of suppliers and/or consumers allows synergies in service provision leading to lower unit costs. For instance, mail and parcel delivery in urban zones is less costly than in rural areas.

[7] Getlink is a private monopoly based in France and listed on both the Euronext London and Euronext Paris markets.

[8] For an example of the sort of opinions issued by the regulators and their exchanges, see, for instance, https://orr.gov.uk/__data/assets/pdf_file/0010/27694/orr-eurotunnel-network-statement-2019.pdf

[9] Historically, European railways have been public vertically integrated monopolies or VIMs. From the 1980s onwards a process of horizontal and vertical restructuring has been taking place. The 2001 First Railway Package introduced requirements for horizontal separation between the passenger and freight operations, a system for access charges, independent capacity allocation and licensing processes, and technical specifications for interoperability. In 2003–04, the second railway package focused on reducing

The infrastructure company, Getlink, now owns shares in the rail business as well, and in various firms delivering ferry services offering alternatives to transport through the tunnel. Thanks to deregulation, competitors to Eurostar can now enter its market, although as of 2020 travellers still have no other option but to go through the tunnel as Eurostar travellers. The main impact on Eurostar so far has been its decision to diversify its own services. It now also runs seasonal trains to the South of France in summer and to the French and Swiss Alps in the winter and, throughout the year, connections to many destinations across Europe. All this means that, in practice, both firms, Eurostar and Getlink, have become multi-product firms competing with other producers in the oligopolistic segment of their market, but still anchored in a de facto monopoly for Eurostar and a natural monopoly for Getlink for the backbone infrastructure.

So, how should all of these dimensions be internalized in the design of regulation? The first dimension is the obvious relevance of the monopolistic nature of the tunnel in this specific market and the awareness of the extent to which this limits choices. Travelling from London to Amsterdam, Brussels or Paris, the last thing a Eurostar traveller looking outside sees just before entering the tunnel is a sign stating 'Euro Tunnel – the vital link'. This highlights the keen awareness of the potential market power of the owners of the tunnel.

The second striking dimension is the need to account for the nature of the businesses operated by Getlink, the tunnel operator. It not only operates a tunnel but it also runs a car-and-truck shuttle through the tunnel. Furthermore, it is now also considering a discount high-speed service that would challenge Eurostar. This implies that the pricing of the tunnel could become a much more complex regulatory challenge as a result of the diversification of activities taken on by the tunnel operator, the natural monopolist.

A third observation of interest is the extent to which regulation of prices accounts for the risks of abuses of market power since the owner of the common facility (i.e. the tunnel) could impose 'non-price barriers' to potential competing rail service providers. Barriers are not always complex or tricky. They can boil down to a 'refuse to deal' decision by Getlink. And this is something the English regulators have been trying to track systematically, as evidenced by discussions in their various annual reports.

Fourth, the regulator will also have to internalize the possibility that some of the users are captive to the service, i.e. they have no transport alternative than this one. These captive shippers require a more focused treatment in regulation to protect them from the market power of the tunnel operator, which can exploit their captivity to set abusive access prices.

---

barriers to entry and promoted the harmonization of technical and safety standards, and liberalized freight services. In 2007, the third railway package gave passenger railway companies the right to compete on international routes. New international operators also began to compete with the incumbent on short sections of national networks. In 2016, the fourth package removed the remaining barriers to the creation of a single European rail area by the adoption of structural and technical reforms designed to lead to higher levels of safety, inter-operability and reliability in the European rail network.

Finally, a neutral regulator would have to assess whether the fact that Eurostar is partially owned by public companies is not raising conflicts of interest in the implementation of regulatory decisions. Politics matters in regulation and can often influence some decisions which should be smoother if handled only at the technical level. In this specific case, it is not unreasonable to wonder whether the slow progress in seeing entry of competitors in the market may not be explained by political interferences since state-owned companies are key stakeholders.

This list of concerns is not exhaustive, but it provides a reasonably clear picture of the complexity of the regulatory responsibilities in this new type of market structure. To see how these concrete concerns could change the guidelines to adopt in the regulation of the pricing and non-pricing behaviour followed by the players, it is useful, once again, to step back and see what theory has to offer to structure the discussion of the regulatory options.

12.2 Choosing between an Oligopolistic and a Monopolistic Market Structure

The Eurostar example shows that direct or indirect competition is something regulators need to worry about for services that were traditionally considered to be unavoidable monopolies. Indeed, in some sectors, thanks to innovation and lower economies of scale, such as mobile telecommunications, competition has become the norm rather than the exception. In these cases, the formerly monopolistic structure takes the explicit or implicit form of an oligopolistic structure. The new possibility of competition, *in* the market or *across* markets, is also changing the way regulation needs to be designed and implemented.

The global scale of the reforms since the mid-1980s reflects a widespread conviction that making the most of the scope for competition in the industries that had traditionally been controlled by vertically integrated monopolies would yield better outcomes than those observed until then. The benefit of an increased sample of producers from which to choose would reduce variable costs ex post. It would also yield the possibility to rely on some form of yardstick competition between the firms because of the correlation of firms' private information, and hence to reduce the cost of asymmetric information. Having an alternative choice to rely on for service provision also meant that the regulator would be less dependent on any specific regulated firm. All this would be achieved while avoiding the problem of decreasing returns to scale once the major fixed costs have been incurred. In many cases these benefits did indeed outweigh the duplication of the fixed costs.

Thinking through the scope for change in a market structure, and what it means for regulation, involves more than new technological opportunities. It is also linked to a regulator's ability (or lack of it) to behave in the public interest. An inability to tackle the information asymmetries discussed earlier may indeed justify a more radical approach to the assessment of costs and benefits of various degrees of market concentration. It may be rational to give up on some of the potential gains from scale economies to buy more effective regulation of the size of the rent in the market and a fairer sharing of this rent with consumers thanks to increased competition, even if that competition occurs among just a few providers.

There are costs to this strategy. An oligopolistic structure often leads to a duplication of fixed costs that would have been avoided by a monopoly. When deregulation allows various rail service companies to compete, they usually share the same rail tracks rather than duplicate the tracks. But even where there are shared facilities, there is some duplication. In most airports, every airline company has its own sales office. Similarly, most mobile-phone companies tend to rely on their own antennas, shops and repair crews, even if they share major communications infrastructure. So, there are extra costs, but these may be in the public interest. Where consumers had been hostage to a single provider, deregulation (and technology) can offer choice among different providers competing to increase their market share, thereby potentially compensating for higher investment costs. And this is when the oligopolistic structure becomes politically and economically attractive.

In order to understand the specific nature of these benefits, it is again useful to rely on theory. To keep the exposition as simple as possible, we focus on the choice between a monopoly and a duopoly, but the arguments can be generalized to more than two firms. The choice between a monopoly and duopoly amid information asymmetry then arises from the trade-off between economies of scale and the costs of regulating a monopoly. This trade-off is best measured in terms of the efficiency levels that can be achieved and in terms of the extent to which any efficiency gain can be shared fairly. To provide some guidance on how to think through the choice, this section summarizes the most common situations in which the duplication of fixed costs incurred under an oligopolistic structure may be justified by the social gain produced, as initially shown by Auriol and Laffont (1992) and Auriol (1998). These gains can come from at least four different effects: complementarity, increasing marginal costs, benchmarking and sampling. We consider them in turn.

The complementarity effect appears because an oligopolistic market structure allows the delivery of a greater variety of goods and services, for instance, in terms of quality or pricing options. More choice may increase consumers' surplus (by satisfying a larger array of preferences) much more than the imperfect regulation of a monopoly can achieve. The division of production between different firms may also be a much more effective way to enlarge the menu of services than imposing a similar diversification obligation on a monopoly. Experience suggests that under a monopoly the menu of services tends to shrink, leaving consumers with fewer options.

The increasing marginal cost effect defines the second common situation in which it may be useful to consider adopting an oligopolistic structure. It arises when the oligopolistic structure can lower variable production costs. This happens when the firms have increasing marginal costs, due for example to transportation costs or organizational diseconomies of scale. To minimize the *variable cost* functions, production should be split between firms, and the more productive firm should receive a greater share of the market.

The benchmarking/yardstick competition effect is a third reason why an oligopolistic structure may be better than a monopoly. It arises when this structure can be used to set the type of benchmarking we discussed in Chapter 6. This might include a relatively precise assessment of the information rents operators are trying to maintain by hiding some of their relevant cost information. Since the costs of the various firms are correlated, cost reports may be compared across firms. This is especially useful where there are several reasonably comparable *local or regional monopolies*. Collecting the information on these different firms and using it as a basis for firms' compensation helps address, at least partially, the problem of asymmetric information. Firms' information rents are lowered, and their production levels come closer to the first-best level.[10]

The sampling effect of the adoption of an oligopolistic market structure appears in situations in which there are technical uncertainties that need to be resolved as the sector is looking at a possible technological transformation. This is, for instance, the case where sectors are experimenting with renewable or new transport technologies. In that context, the duplication of fixed costs may be socially valuable during research and development (R&D) phase, before production can take place at full scale. Adding some measure of competition at the development phase yields the benefit of an increased sample of producers from which to choose and this tends to reduce future variable costs. An oligopoly not only provides a larger sample of producers than a monopoly, but it can also reduce expected costs when the most efficient technology or design is chosen for final production. The optimal market structure thus results from a trade-off between the duplication of the fixed costs of R&D and the higher variable surplus generated by either a better design/product or more efficient technology (i.e. smaller variable costs). Where a regulator's access to information is asymmetric, it is not always the most efficient firm that is the optimal producer. This is, then, the result of a trade-off between variable costs and information costs instead. We next discuss this in more detail in the context where the regulator needs to stimulate the regulated firm to develop new technologies.

12.3   Should the Need for R&D Influence the Optimal Market Structure?

In the electricity industry, research on renewables has been mainstreamed. For the water sector, it is research on the desalinization of seawater to reduce shortages that is attracting a lot of resources. In railways, some of the focus is on very high-speed vacuum-tube trains that would rely on magnetic levitation lines using partly evacuated tubes or tunnels.[11] In any of these situations, regulated firms are expected to invest in a great deal of R&D.

---

[10] See Auriol (2000) for a more formal modelling of this idea.

[11] Cutting air resistance could allow trains to travel with relatively little energy consumption at up to six times the speed of sound at sea level.

More generally, R&D is needed for any new system that requires the development of prototypes. But these are costly, and the public authority must choose how many R&D teams should work on a project. This decision is not without effects, since this number will shape the future structure of the market. A simple way of modelling the relevance of uncertainty is to focus on the timing of the discovery by the operators of the exact cost of their technologies. Again, the regulator must decide how many firms should be authorized to work on the project without their full knowledge of the future technology. That is, it must choose the market structure before firms discover their future cost structure.

Theory suggests that the first factor to consider in choosing between two market structures is the extent to which costs are uncertain before the market structure is decided. If the costs are unknown, betting on a duopoly can be desirable. Dual sourcing is in fact quite common in this type of situation. In large and ambitious infrastructure projects, it is very common for the public authority to organize a contest where different teams compete for the best design to reduce costs and increase system efficiency. At the end of the contest phase, the best project is generally selected and implemented. In contrast, a monopoly may be a better choice when the cost characteristics are relatively certain at the time a decision on the market structure must be made (i.e. for standardized technologies).

In sum, the choice between a monopolistic or duopolistic structure boils down to the following trade-off: The duopoly implies paying the R&D sunk cost twice but with the expectation of a lower marginal cost (i.e. the sampling effect) considering that a duopoly will enlarge the set of technologies from which to choose. Since the regulator needs to select the market structure before the technological uncertainties have been solved, it bases its decision on expected values, comparing the expected social surplus with a monopoly and the expected social surplus with a duopoly. Under symmetric information, everything else being equal (in particular for a given quantity), a duopoly is more likely to be optimal when the technical uncertainty is great. In this case, marginal costs are likely to be smaller with two firms conducting R&D than with only one. In contrast, for standardized services there is basically no variance in production costs and so dual sourcing is inefficient.

Under asymmetric information, the case is less clear-cut. The regulator must pay informational rent, in addition to production costs, which tend to favour the duopoly. If the firm is in a monopoly position, this rent is maximal as the regulator has no alternative to serve the market. They can just encourage the firm to reveal its true cost by relying on incentive compatible contracts (i.e. allowing an informational rent). Since it breaks the monopoly power of the firm, the duopolistic structure reduces the informational cost. This is especially true if the firms' costs are correlated, as is the case with common technology. The regulator can then implement some benchmarking under asymmetric information (i.e. yardstick competition). This substantially reduces the cost of asymmetric information. If the costs are not correlated, the regulator must abandon some informational rent (i.e. to the most efficient firm if it chooses only one to implement the best technology, or to all if they all produce) but the total informational cost is still lower with a duopoly than with a monopoly.

Because of this additional cost, under asymmetric information, the optimal market structure depends on the technological uncertainties and on the elasticity of demand. For instance, if the demand is not elastic, so that the quantity to be purchased is fixed, then the situation of asymmetric information favours the duopolistic structure. When the regulator has established a single producer at the pre-contract phase, the monopoly power of this firm at the time of contracting is very high if the quantity is not flexible. Since the regulator has no way to protect consumers from the abusive power of the monopoly by lowering its order in case of a high acquisition cost, having a choice between two suppliers is crucial. This would avoid the distortions possibly created by a monopoly. By contrast, if there are some good substitutes for the product, or if demand is very elastic, then asymmetric information costs are not such a big problem. The quantities purchased from the regulated firm will be drastically reduced ex post if they are too costly. This flexibility effect favours the monopoly structure.

12.4   What If the Oligopolies Are neither Purely Private nor Purely Public?

Until now we have focused on symmetrical firms, all of them under either private or public control. However, in practice it is quite common to have private alongside public firms in regulated industries. For historical, social and/or political reasons, in sectors such as energy, telecommunications, water, airlines and railroads, as well as postal services, private firms compete with publicly owned ones (De Fraja 2009). Public 'ownership' can take quite different forms. For instance, in their case studies of the energy sector, Haney and Pollitt (2010) identify various forms, ranging from mutual ownership (in Northern Ireland), consumer trusts (in New Zealand), state ownership (in Chile and Finland) and municipal ownership (in Great Britain).

The economists have analysed the *mixed oligopoly* structure (i.e. a public firm competing with one or several private companies) as a policy instrument to improve resource allocation in imperfectly competitive markets (Cremer et al. 1989, 1991). In terms of industrial policy, the question can be addressed from two different points of view. First, is it socially optimal for the government to nationalize some private firms and to instruct them to maximize social welfare, or even to create some new public operators? Second, would it be socially advantageous to privatize some existing public firms? Clearly, efficiency concerns are not the only driver of government decisions when choosing the optimal mix of firms (Escrihuela-Villar and Gutiérrez-Hita 2019). However, from the regulation point of view, it raises an essential question: should a private firm facing a public firm be regulated like a private firm competing with a peer?

At first sight, the answer is unambiguous: the market power of a private firm (name it A) is mitigated by the activity of the public firm (B_W). This is because B_W is supposed to internalize other objectives than mere profit maximization. In particular, it is supposed to internalize the consumers' well-being on top of its own gains. This should lead the public firm to produce more than its profit-maximizer alternative (B_π). Since B_W would serve a larger market share than the share that would be supplied by a profit maximizer, B_π, when A faces B_W, (i) it produces less than if competing with B_π, and (ii) the price is lower. In the electricity industry, for example, Fiorio and Florio (2013) show that public ownership is associated with lower residential net-of-tax prices in Western Europe. Consequently, at first glance, the regulation of the private firm in a mixed oligopoly does not need to be as tight as when all firms are private.

However, this is true only insofar as the private firm B_π and the public structure B_W differ in terms of their objective functions, *ceteris paribus*. Actually, they will probably also differ in other dimensions, such as their productivity, the total wage bill they must pay, the financial sources they can rely on, the social obligations they must satisfy, or the type of product they supply. For example, if the public firm B_W has both lower productivity (weak incentives) and higher costs (strong labour unions) than its private alternative, B_π, then productive inefficiency can offset any benefit of allocative efficiency and, if it is very efficient, A can be better off and make more rents when its rival is B_W rather than B_π.

As a counter-argument, some economists (e.g. Florio 2013b) explain that the alleged internal inefficiency of publicly controlled firms actually reflects the multidimensionality of the objectives forced upon them. Efficiency is not the only one. It is not even the most important one: others are social affordability, environmental sustainability, security of supply, land planning, employment and the like. It means that if a regulator has a mixed oligopoly under their jurisdiction, they cannot use the costs of the public firm to organize any form of yardstick competition since the observed cost differentials are not just the reflection of moral hazard.

An additional difficulty for the regulator is that, because of their different objective functions and social constraints, the public and private competitors may not choose the same quality for their products and services (Cremer et al. 1997). Neglecting this strategy of quality differentiation by the private operators might increase the market power of the private firm since its clients are less sensitive to the lower price proposed by the public firm when the quality differential is large (Laine and Ma 2017). Then, overall, the presence of public firms in a regulated industry does not make things necessarily simpler for the regulator, especially because of the direct intervention of the Ministers that manage those public firms. In this case an alternative to the independent regulation studied so far is what is called 'self-regulation'.

12.5   When Can Self-Regulation Be an Alternative to a Separate Regulator?

The book has so far left out discussions of various forms of regulation adopted by industries that have proven to be useful complements to more traditional forms of direct or indirect controls by formal government regulators. The main such form of regulation is self-regulation. Broadly defined, self-regulation at the industry level is the regulation designed, implemented and enforced by groups of firms that agree on common production or behavioural standards, principles and rules they define jointly as members of an industry or in collaboration with other stakeholders, including users and public authorities.

When they are defined jointly with other stakeholders, it is also known as co-regulation. In some contexts, it is also defined as the degree of autonomy public enterprises are allowed to retain in a context in which the firm would otherwise be subject to regulatory supervision by a Ministry or a separate regulatory agency but this form of self-regulation has been much less common since the reforms of regulated industries launched in the 1990s.

One of the most common justifications for self-regulation at the industry level is its lower enforcement cost resulting from the fact that these associations have better access to information than an external regulator would. Others include better compliance levels and lower monitoring costs resulting from the fact the regulations are self-defined and imposed, with greater flexibility to adapt as needed to changing context. Critics raise various concerns, including the risks of collusion and conflicts of interests at all stages of the design and implementation process, resulting in exposing consumers and other members of society to uncertain risks. The lack of independent accountability mechanisms is one of the main drivers of these risks. The limited ability to process information (i.e. assessing probabilities of impact) and to relate it to non-industry-specific risk factors (i.e. general state of health) is another concern. These risks are also quite sensitive to the economic and social context and the overall governance state of the countries in which the tool is being considered. Baldwin et al. (2012) and OECD (2015c) provide a more detailed discussion of the conceptual discussions of the approach.

The case for self-regulation may have to be reassessed occasionally, as is the case for any form of regulation. In the context of regulated public service industries, this case is emerging as a result of the growing role of digitalization and of big data. The risks of abusive interpretations of the use of information initially agreed upon by all stakeholders can become a source of conflict between some stakeholders, as illustrated by the use of data collected by smart meters or by the growing role of big data in the investment decisions of the large pharmaceutical firms. In addition to the risks associated with various forms of online piracy and to the concerns for the commercialization of the information against consumers' preferences, self-regulation anchored in different market and technological structures may become obsolete or open the door to new forms of self-regulation as the structures continue to evolve. Just like any form of regulation, self-regulation needs to have the ability, including the resources, to adapt.

Until now, countries have allowed service providers, search platforms and users or producers of generated-content sites to define their own rules. They essentially regulate themselves on the use of the information collected and the collection processes. In many cases, they are not to be held legally liable for illegal use of which they are unaware. This is likely to change as technology evolves, as data use evolves and as the understanding by stakeholders of their specific rights and obligations becomes clearer to all of them. Self-regulation does indeed have its limits, and the evolution of technology increases the case for independent audits of self-regulation, just as the reforms of the 1990s imposed a questioning of the extent to which public enterprises could continue to be self-regulated.

12.6   What About Regulation by Contract? The Case of Public–Private Partnerships

A final form of regulation not discussed so far is regulation by contract.[12] In this approach, the government defines a specific mandate and, usually, organizes an auction to identify the winner. In many cases, the number of bidders tends to be quite limited. The government then signs a detailed contract with a private provider to spell out the expected performance of the service provider (usually private but sometimes public). It defines the right and obligations of all parties to the contract (and allows hardly any voice to other potential stakeholders within the regulatory regime). This contract becomes the main regulatory tool. For instance, it defines the standards of service, the investment type and speed, the tariff-setting mechanisms or the rules of remuneration for the operator. The popularity of this form of regulation among some administrations has been one of the by-products to the growth of public–private partnerships (PPPs) in regulated industries.[13] There are many types of PPPs (and there are many ways of classifying them).

The various types of PPPs may be categorized in three main groups. First, there are management contracts, which are used for service externalization, such as public transportation or waste management, and involve short periods (three to eight years) to allow competition for the market. Second are leasing or affermage contracts, which combine public ownership of the infrastructure with private management and operation of the asset. They are typically used in the water sector and run for longer periods (ten to eighteen years) as the financial commitment by the private sector is higher. Finally, there are concession or build–operate–transfer contracts, which involve substantial private investment and long periods of exploitation (thirty-five to ninety-nine years). BOT contracts and their variations (BOOT, BOO, DBF)[14] are typically used to finance transport infrastructure such as highways, tunnels, airports, ports, bridges, canals and railways. They are also frequently used to finance projects in power generation, water supply, dams, irrigation, sewerage and, to a lesser extent, telecommunications. The attractiveness of BOT concessions to politicians stems from the possibility to limit government spending, and therefore public debt, by shifting (at least in the short run) investment costs to private investors. Historically, the first BOT concessions were hence granted for the construction of turnpike roads in England in 1660, at a time of industrial expansion and embryonic public finances (see Auriol and Picard 2011). PPP were also used to finance ambitious international infrastructures such as the Suez Canal or, more recently, Eurotunnel.

---

[12] For some of the clearest discussions with illustrations, see Gomez-Ibanez (2006) and Cunha Marques (2018).

[13] In practice, since the contracts tend to be incomplete, they are to be complemented by other tools which can be implemented by a regulator or a government agency. For useful recent examples of the challenges they represent in practice see Saussier and de Brux (2018) or Bel et al. (2017), and for a detailed illustration in the case of toll roads, see Athias and Saussier (2018).

[14] The acronyms mean respectively build–operate–transfer, build–own–operate–transfer, build–own–operate, design–build–finance–operate (European Commission 2003).

To induce private investors to sink their capital into expensive and risky infrastructure projects, governments must leave at least some rent to the concession holders during their activities. This is consistent with the insights we saw in Chapters 4–6, which have a very concrete application in this context. Ensuring that the rent is internalized in the design of the contracts is indeed one of the main regulatory challenges of the decision by a government to rely on a PPP. But this rent has to be consistent with the distribution of risk associated with the PPP between the public and the private partners. This is not an easy exercise and experience suggests that it is often done in an imperfect way. But it was not always that complicated: in the seventeenth and eighteenth centuries they were simply given unrestricted monopoly rights over their infrastructure.

The modern versions of PPPs are more challenging. This is best seen in the context of BOTs. Nowadays, a distinctive feature of BOT contracts lies in the transfer of operational responsibilities and profits to a private concession holder for a well-defined time period. Concession periods should vary in function of the estimated time required to recover the costs of the facilities (see Auriol and Picard 2009, 2013). Another important aspect lies in the way the technical and commercial risk of building and managing the infrastructure is shared between the private and the public sector. In 'bad' PPPs all the risk lies on the public side, so that they are debt contracts in disguise. 'Good' PPPs share the risks between the private and the public in such a way that the private sector has an interest in the profitability of the investment. This leads to complex contracts, which typically are 100 pages long. The economic literature, which analyses the main incentive issues in PPPs and the shape of optimal contracts, provides guidance for their efficient design (see Engel et al. 2014; Estache et al. 2015; Iossa and Martimort 2015; Saussier and de Brux 2018).

The evidence suggests mixed outcomes of the use of PPPs, in particular in the water and transport sectors. On the one hand, PPPs can be beneficial each time they lead to the creation of an infrastructure or service that would not have otherwise existed. They can also be beneficial when private management is able to reduce costs substantially and the contract is well designed so that the efficiency gain is shared with the users and the taxpayers. On the other hand, PPPs have often resulted in higher prices for users, which has led to popular unrest and renegotiation worldwide (e.g. Estache 2020a). The European Court Auditors conducted an analysis of the use of European Union funds in the context of 'blended PPPs', a class of PPPs combining EU funding with private investment. They found, for the projects audited, that PPPs had suffered delays, cost increases and were under-used, resulting in over 5% of the funds allocated being misused (European Court of Auditors 2018). For developing countries, the evidence has recently been summarized by Estrin and Pelletier (2018) and Estache (2020a) and it is best defined as mixed. This accumulation of deceiving outcomes helps explain the decision by many local and national administrations to re-nationalize some of the PPPs, as reviewed by Bel (2020) in the context of the water sector, for instance.

In general, the more technical diagnostics covered by these reviews suggests: (i) no significant systematic difference between PPPs and public provision in terms of efficiency, except with respect to cost-efficiency as a result of lower employment and more recent technologies adopted by private operators; (ii) short-term fiscal payoffs, usually offset by longer-term increases in subsidies resulting from contract renegotiations, in particular for the water and transport sectors; (iii) uncertain effects on the quality of governance, with the possibility that it can reduce or increase corruption, depending on the context and (iv) significant risks of exclusions of the poor resulting from a tolerance for cream-skimming built into policy or regulation. There are many success stories, but there are also many failures to get PPPs to deliver on their promises, in particular in regulated industries. In most cases of failure, ex post evaluations at the project level tend to blame poor preparation, poor procurement, incompetent technical teams or political interference. Since many of these issues have been recognized for over twenty years and are still present in the latest audits, it seems reasonable to argue that the conceptual attractiveness of the tool is still far from delivering on its promises. It is a potentially useful tool, but maybe not one for all contexts, notwithstanding its continuous popularity in some policy circles.

12.7   What If a Regulated Firm Offers Multiple Products?

The deconcentration reforms of the 1990s and the widespread use of PPPs have also forced regulatory practice to recognize the relevance of the increase in the diversity of services provided by regulated companies. A telecommunications company enjoying a monopoly over fixed line services can sell phones, internet or entertainment services and similar equipment also available from other suppliers. Electricity distribution companies are increasingly also selling consulting services to learn how to manage energy efficiency opportunities in addition to their traditional services. For each of these products or services, a regulated firm faces different types and number of competitors and users. Yet most basic textbooks dealing with regulation make the convenient assumption that regulated firms specialize in a single product or service.

   This diversity of products and services has very concrete regulatory implications that often demand upgrades of the traditional forms of regulation. This is because it involves a risk of pricing distortions and hence inefficient and/or inequitable outcomes. This risk depends on several characteristics relatively easy to identify. Are the various products and services complements or substitutes on the demand side or are they unrelated? Do the multiple products compete for the same inputs? Does the pricing of the various products give some leeway to engage in anticompetitive cross-subsidies between them (i.e. to make those with a high demand elasticity appear to be cheaper than they really are if they were charged alone)? Do the regulated firms control shared facilities that need to be used by some of their competitors?

   Any of the answers influences regulation. For instance, it has an impact on the extent to which the Ramsey–Boiteux pricing rule discussed in earlier chapters is still relevant. This is why academics, regulators and competition agencies have long been interested in these issues – and not just for regulated industries. Conceptually, the analysis has usually focused on the case of regulated monopolists delivering multiple products or services. Theory has focused on three broad approaches. The first is the case of monopolists selling several products or services, including some in competitive markets. This is known in the literature as the horizontal multi-product monopolist (HMM). A second situation in which monopolists deliver multiple products or services arises when a vertically integrated monopoly (VIM) competes on some markets while maintaining a full monopoly in others. And third is the case in which technological and policy changes may end up transforming the market historically catered to by the monopoly into an oligopoly in which the monopolistic incumbent needs to compete with new firms.

All three approaches are relevant in practice. All three can also be as challenging to regulate in the real world as they are in theory. Simply weighting the uncertain efficiency gains from a monopoly unwilling to share information against the possible efficiency gains from some degree of competition allowed by a more diversified market structure is not very useful to drive regulatory decisions. Efficiency gains in some markets may be used to further distort parts of the less efficient markets and penalize some of the users and producers. Tracking down these distortions requires tools we have not discussed so far. These tools help address the challenges of environments in which the regulator and the firms do not have equal access to key information, as we discuss in the following sections.

12.8 How Different Should Regulation Be When Regulated Firms Diversify Their Supply?

Academic research has been quite creative in trying to assess how regulation of monopolies focusing on single products should be adapted when these monopolies start producing multiple products. A few key papers define the benchmark from which a lot of research still used today in policy diagnostics is evolving. Sappington (1983), Laffont and Tirole (1990a, 1990b, 1990c, 1993), Armstrong and Rochet (1999) focused on the cost side, Iossa (1999) and Armstrong and Vickers (2000) dealt with the demand side. They all accounted for information asymmetries between the regulator and the monopoly and discussed how much residual pricing discretion a regulator should allow a multi-product firm. More recently, Armstrong and Vickers (2018) provide a synthesis of the earlier literature used to suggest new pricing and regulatory guidelines.

Since multi-product monopolies sell products which may be related to each other, either on the demand side or on the production side, it is useful to distinguish the various relevant situations because regulation must adjust to the specific context. Four cases are possible:

- Products can be *complements in demand*, i.e. an increase in the quantity sold of one will bring about an increase in the quantity sold of the other.
- Products can be *substitutes in demand*, i.e. an increase in the quantity sold of one will bring about a decrease in the quantity sold of the other.

- Products can be *complements in production*, i.e. all products are produced from one set of inputs or can be produced jointly in fixed proportions.
- Products can be *substitutes in production*, i.e. products compete for resources – using resources to produce one product takes those resources away from producing other products.

We deal first with the situations in which the key variable is the characterization of demand. The modelling is similar whether the products are complements or substitutes in demand. The discussion of the situations in which the characterization of the supply side is somewhat more complex. More details are needed to eventually discuss the scope for cross-subsidies and its implications for regulation. The literature on each of these topics is quite broad. We limit the discussion of the research on each of these types of situations to the main results of interest to the design of regulation.

12.9   The Case of Dependent Demands: Complement and Substitute Products

When a regulated firm is multi-product, regulation should be different according to whether the products sold are complements or substitutes.

Let's start with an example. Imagine the situation in which an electricity supplier is a monopoly catering to two markets. It sells both kilowatt-hours (service 1) and energy-efficiency advisory services (service 2).[15]

If it is regulated, assuming symmetric information about the firm's costs, the regulator will decide on the prices of the two services according to the result of the following optimization based on a generalization of Equation (4.7) to the multi-product case where $\pi = 0$:

$$\max{}_{q_1,q_2} W(q_1,q_2) = S(q_1,q_2) + \lambda p_1(q_1,q_2)q_1 + \lambda p_2(q_1,q_2)q_2 - (1+\lambda)C(q_1,q_2)$$

$$(12.1)$$

where q_i is the demand for service i when its price is p_i and p_j is the price of service j $(i, j = 1,2)$. The optimal quantity for service i is derived from the first-order condition for good i, which can be rewritten as follows:[16]

$$\frac{p_i - C_{mi}}{p_i} = \frac{\lambda}{1+\lambda}\frac{1}{\varepsilon_{ii}} + \frac{\lambda}{1+\lambda}I_{ji} \qquad (12.2)$$

where $I_{ji} = \frac{\varepsilon_{ji}}{\varepsilon_{ii}}\frac{p_j q_j}{p_i q_i}\frac{p_j - C_{mj}}{p_j}$, C_{mi} is the marginal cost of producing service i, $\varepsilon_{ii} = -\frac{p_i}{q_i}\frac{\Delta q_i}{\Delta p_i}$ is the direct price-elasticity of the demand for service i (discussed in detail in Chapter 2) and $\varepsilon_{ji} = \frac{p_i}{q_j}\frac{\Delta q_j}{\Delta p_i}$ is the cross-elasticity of demand for good j with respect to

---

[15] To make the analysis as simple as possible, we will assume that costs are separable, i.e. if the regulated firm produces quantities q_1 and q_2 of goods 1 and 2, the cost function satisfies $C(q_1,q_2) = C_1(q_1) + C_2(q_2)$.

[16] Alternatively, the margins can be written in terms of the super-elasticities defined in the appendix to Chapter 11.

the price of good i. The cross-elasticity of demand or cross-price elasticity of demand needs to be accounted for because the quantity demanded for a good or a service may respond to a change in the price of another good or service. This holds for regulated services as much as for any other unregulated good or service.

If goods i and j are complements (say electric heaters and electricity), more j is demanded when the price of good i decreases, $\frac{\Delta q_j}{\Delta p_i} < 0$, so that $\varepsilon_{ji} < 0$ and $I_{ji} < 0$. The opposite stands for substitutes (say electric and gas heaters), i.e. $\varepsilon_{ji} > 0$ and $I_{ji} > 0$.

If demands are independent, the cross-price elasticities are nil $\varepsilon_{ji} = 0$ so that $I_{ji} = 0$, and Equation (12.2) shows that the pricing strategy followed by the regulated monopoly is the same that would be observed with two independent mono-product monopolies – i.e. the Ramsey-Boiteux rule again.[17] In this case, Equation (12.2) implies that, with independent products, the regulator doesn't need to distort the price structure to try to extract rents. It simply needs to focus on the rate of return the firm is allowed to achieve.

However, when the two products are related (i.e. they are either complementary, so that $\varepsilon_{ji} < 0$, or substitutes, so that $\varepsilon_{ji} > 0$), the situation is somewhat more complex. The technical details are discussed in Box 12.1 but the policy intuition is simple. When $\varepsilon_{ji} \neq 0$, the regulator of a multi-product monopoly will want to set the individual prices at levels different to those that would have been adopted for the two independent monopolies. The good news is that the sign of the difference with the standard pricing rule is predictable.

In the case of substitutes so that $I_{ij} > 0$, the prices will be higher, i.e. the monopolist's margin is higher than with independent goods. This is because the regulated multi-product monopoly 'internalizes' the negative externality resulting from the substitution between the two goods. Then the regulator increases the prices of both goods relative to a situation where the two goods are treated separately. More specifically, if p_1 increases, q_2 increases and this gives an incentive to increase p_2

In the case of complementary products or services, since $I_{ij} < 0$, the regulator of the monopoly sets lower prices than she would for two independent monopolies. This is because she internalizes the positive externality resulting from the complementarity between the two goods: when p_1 decreases, q_1 increases and therefore q_2 also increases since the two goods are complements. This gives an incentive to decrease p_1. The regulatory risk is that if there is a strong complementarity between the two goods sold, it may be optimal for the unregulated monopolist to sell one of the goods, say good 1, below its marginal cost in order to increase the demand for good 2. This dumping is against the law.

To sum up, a multi-product monopolist will have an incentive to set lower (higher) prices than separate monopolists when the products are complements (substitutes) and when there are (dis)economies of scope. If, as in the case of the single-product monopoly, the regulator knows the demands for all the products then these distortions can easily be corrected for. The optimal regulation of a multi-product monopoly is not

---

[17] This is the same result obtained in third-degree price discrimination, except that here the products or services are different while in third-degree price discrimination they were identical but sold to distinct groups of consumers.

Box 12.1 Measuring Basic Economic Dimensions for Multiple-Product Firms

Consider a monopoly producing two goods 1 and 2 in quantities q_1 and q_2.

Demand side: Given unit prices p_1, p_2, the demand for good $i = 1, 2$ is $q_i(p_1, p_2)$ and total revenue is $R = R_1 + R_2 = p_1 q_1(p_1, p_2) + p_2 q_2(p_1, p_2)$.

When one price changes, the marginal revenue of each product is influenced by the sales of the other product, i.e. $R_{mi} = \Delta R / \Delta p_i = \Delta R_i / \Delta p_i + \Delta R_j / \Delta p_i$ with $i, j = 1, 2$ and $j \neq i$. R_{mi} thus accounts for the interactions between the two products. If the two products are substitutes, $\frac{\Delta R_j}{\Delta p_i} = p_j \frac{\Delta q_j}{\Delta p_i} > 0$, so that $R_{mi} > \frac{\Delta R_i}{\Delta p_i}$. If they are complements, $\frac{\Delta R_j}{\Delta p_i} = p_j \frac{\Delta q_j}{\Delta p_i} < 0$, so that $R_{mi} < \frac{\Delta R_i}{\Delta p_i}$.

In the case of a separable cost function, this implies that the usual markup rule has to be adjusted as follows: $(p_i - C_{mi})/p_i = (1/\varepsilon_{ii}) + I_{ji}$, where I_{ji} is a positive term for substitutes and a negative term for complements. The usual rule thus serves as a lower bound for substitutes and an upper bound for complements. The key piece of information on the extent to which they are complements or substitutes comes from the estimation of the cross-price elasticities. This is relatively easy to estimate for settled markets. It is more challenging when new products or services are involved.

Supply side: An additional difficulty comes from the supply side. Indeed, in many cases, the cost function is not additively separable. In particular, there are some cost savings from producing two goods at the same place or within the same organization. These savings are called *economies of scope*. Information about economies of scope comes from the assessment of the cost function, as explained in Chapter 2. Once the cost function has been estimated, the scope economies C_{co} are computed as $C_{co} = [C(q_1, 0) + C(0, q_2) - C(q_1, q_2)]/C(q_1, q_2)$. If $C_{co} > 0$, there are economies of scope since producing the two goods together is less costly than producing them separately. If $C_{co} < 0$ there are diseconomies of scope. In case of independent cost functions, $C_{co} = 0$. When economies of scope are at work, marginal costs will most likely be affected: an increase in the production of good i will reduce (increase) the marginal cost of good j if the two goods are complements (substitutes) on the supply side.

Note that defining the average cost for a firm producing multiple products is usually quite challenging, and yet this cost measure may often be necessary in regulatory diagnostics. One common approach is to rely on what is known as the ray average cost (*RAC*). *RAC*s describe the behaviour of the cost function as output is expanded proportionally along a ray starting at the origin, as discussed in Baumol et al. (1982). To do so, we need to assume that the products are produced in fixed proportions. In a two-product example, this would be expressed as $q_1 = \alpha_1 q$ and $q_2 = \alpha_2 q$ (with $\alpha_1 + \alpha_2 = 1$) and the ray average cost is: $RAC(q) = C(\alpha_1 q, \alpha_2 q)/q$.

In actual regulatory processes, however, the task imposed by the measurement and interpretation of economies of scale and of scope is complex, especially when the regulator needs to identify their specific sources and contribution to a particular product, as is sometimes needed in regulatory conflict or diagnostic.

the sum of the independent regulation of the different products. The regulator must internalize the additional consumer surplus generated by the products' complementarity/substitutability. The optimal regulated prices are higher than in the separate regulation case when the products are substitutes and lower when they are complements.

These results have institutional implications. They suggest that (geographically and technically) integrated regulation agencies with broad mandates might be a better alternative than narrowly focused ones when regulated firms diversify into multiple products. Not only the cost of duplicating highly qualified staff is saved, but these super-regulation agencies are better able to address the challenges posed by the transformation of markets due to economic integration and innovations, the transition to green technologies, or to monitor the actions of multinational firms.

The regulation of multi-product monopolies is typically not straightforward to enforce, as discussed by Wilson and Wolak (2018) in the case of the US railways for instance. Railroad companies can sell a wide range of services and it can be quite challenging to split the large share of common costs in the railroad's total production cost. Even assuming that the regulator is able to estimate the multi-product cost function of the regulated operator, it will still be a challenge to come up with a robust and specific assessment of what is an excessive price for a specific service or product. This analytical approach may help, but it is only a part of a negotiation process rather than the anchor to rule-based price-setting.

The uncertainty regulators face in practice does not help identify a reasonable threshold for an excessive price. For some products, this may make the price-setting negotiations particularly challenging. This is the case for captive shippers, for instance. For users without any viable alternative such as mining companies needing to transport their products to ports to deliver to their export markets, rail is the only option. The demand elasticity is close to 0. As explained again by Wilson and Wolak (2018), a mechanical implementation of the Ramsey–Boiteux pricing rules would imply that they would need to bear what could be an unaffordable share of the recovery of common costs. And this is unlikely to happen, implying that the rules cannot be implemented blindly.

Whether implemented mechanically or fine-tuned through negotiation, these rules are, however, not the end of the line for regulatory decisions. Indeed, they beg for an obvious follow-up question in the context of regulation. Should the regulator focus on a rate of return for each product line or on a global one that accounts for all business lines jointly? For regulators concerned with the need to track the redistribution of efficiency gains towards consumers (or taxpayers) and relying on price caps, for instance, this implies having to pick between multiple caps (i.e. one for each product) and a basket cap (i.e. one for the average price, weighted to account for the relative importance of each product line).

A single cap allows the monopoly to distribute the tariff changes among the different products and services it delivers. It lets the firm rely on demand elasticities to make the most of its (constrained) leverage to increase the price over costs and/or to control supply to induce prices to be higher than required. The main risk associated with this popular option among regulators is that it may deter entry. But this risk tends to be offset if regulation can be designed to improve efficiency by allowing firms to respond to costs and demand while ensuring that this is not used to discriminate across users. This requires the regulators to make an explicit effort to document costs (through audits or benchmarking exercises) and demand (through surveys). When there is a concern for discrimination, the instruments discussed in Chapter 9 on social issues can be quite helpful to minimize excessive biases in efficiency–equity trade-offs in favour of efficiency concerns.

Considered globally, this intuitive interpretation of the policy-relevance of basic academic results is both reassuring and frustrating. It is reassuring because it shows that theory has been helpful in providing simple rules of thumb to generate markup levels in multi-product markets. It is also frustrating because it shows that even in simple cases, the rules need to be refined to match the diversity of contexts observed in the real world as well as the diversity of policy preferences. We'll discuss this more in Chapter 14. For now, it suffices to keep in mind that the matching of context and regulatory choice has an impact on the trade-offs between efficiency and equity concerns. As is often the case, a more careful look at the details of the regulatory challenge associated with this type of market leads to issues policymakers and regulators must address, but are ignored by the theory.

12.10   The Case of Dependent Costs: On the Relevance of Scope and Scale Economies

The situation in which multi-product regulated firms sell products which may be related to each other on the production side is just as common as the one in which the dependency is on the demand side. Products are complements in production if they are produced more efficiently jointly from the same resource or input, typically in fixed proportions.[18] Products are substitutes in production if they draw on the same set of inputs at the expense of the others.[19]

When the costs of multiple products are interdependent, the level of markup will be influenced by the level and distribution of costs across products. In practice, it is almost impossible to precisely separate a firm's total costs into components that can be assigned to each product, a task assigned to specialists of cost accounting. There are common costs and complementarities in production techniques. Analytically, the total cost of production covers the specific cost of each activity as well as their joint costs.

---

[18] In transport, the complementarity in production of various modal options has anchored the development of multimodal approaches to mobility. For freight, it justifies the establishment of logistics centres and production centres. The same core infrastructure can be used by different modes and this, in turn, can be used to make the most of the complementarity between various related services.

[19] This is discussed in many environmental economics classes. The usual example involves the use of a river to allow fish to prosper and feed local populations and the use of the same river to dump the dirty waste from a local factory. The two activities become substitutes since the fishing activity and the 'dirty' factory cannot use the river simultaneously.

These in turn may depend, or not, on the total quantities produced. For these reasons, regulators need to rely on simplifying assumptions before being able to assess an operator's efficiency performance well enough to be able to engage in discussions with the firm. Each of these assumptions will influence the optimal design of regulation.

To see this formally, let's focus on the example of two products or services that are unrelated in demand (i.e. the cross-elasticity of demand is nil). In this context, the regulatory challenge lies in devising a rule to allocate the total cost between products or service 1 and product or service 2. One way of organizing the decision-making process is to start with a given list of products for which costs have been clearly identified and then assess the additional cost resulting from the introduction of a new line of activity. This is called the *incremental cost*. For instance, $C(q_1, q_2) - C(q_1, 0)$ is the incremental cost of q_2 production.

Incremental cost measures are useful to assess the possibility of observing economies of scope. Indeed, if there are economies of scope, the incremental cost of q_2 is lower than the *stand-alone cost* of q_2, that is $C(0, q_2) > C(q_1, q_2) - C(q_1, 0)$. They are also useful to assess the sources of scale economies in the context of a multi-product firm, in particular whether the scale economies are global or specific to a given product. The rule of thumb to keep in mind is that these scale economies are *specific* to a product if its incremental cost is declining. They are *global* if a simultaneous 1% increase in all outputs is expected to result in a less than 1% increase in cost.

Quantifying these incremental cost measures is particularly important when major changes are taking place or expected to take place in a multi-product regulated industry such as in the context of mergers and acquisition or when considering the unbundling of a vertically integrated monopoly. Whenever a regulated firm wishes to become multi-product, to acquire a competitor, or other firms already producing goods or services in a competitive context, the evaluation of the request has to be anchored in a quantitative assessment of the cost implications. These measures are also necessary to assess the relative importance of economies of scale and scope when there is a desire to reduce the control of a market by a single vertically integrated firm by opening competition on at least some of the segments of its activities.

Incremental costs are also essential to assess how cross-subsidies financed by the regulated services can hurt competitors in the non-regulated products and services the regulated firm is interested in. The extent to which cross-subsidies should be a source of regulatory concern is one of the most frequently recurring themes for regulated utilities and transport companies. How to address these concerns is discussed next.

12.11   How Much Should Regulators Worry about Cross-Subsidies?

As discussed by Fjell (2001), there are many definitions of cross-subsidization used in policy debates because they arise in many types of situations. Two are more common in regulated industries. The first is observed when a firm faces common costs (e.g. overheads) in the delivery of different products or in the service to different consumer groups. As the firm decides to allocate these common costs across consumers or products, it may end up favouring some and penalizing others. This is usually controlled in regulatory accounting guidelines which define the specific cost allocation rules to be adopted.[20] The second describes the most general case in which a firm catering to several markets shifts some of the costs from high-cost activities to low-cost activities. This is harder to deal with and is the main focus of this section.

We focus here on the decision by the regulated firm to price a product or a service above its costs to subsidize the loss from pricing a different product or service below its cost. Conceptually, in the case of a firm delivering two products, a cross-subsidy arises when a firm sells product 1 at a price below marginal cost to hurt its competitors in market 1, while compensating these losses through prices above marginal costs in market 2, in which the firm is protected from competition. This is, for instance, the case of countries in which there is competition for electricity supply or telecoms services in low-cost urban areas but none in high-cost rural areas where it is more expensive to provide services because of distances and the service is provided by a single firm under a regulatory mandate to do so.

In addition to their anticompetitive effects, these cross-subsidies raise more specific efficiency concerns since those paying less than the costs they represent will tend to overconsume and vice versa. They also raise distributional concerns in environments in which all consumers have comparable capacities to pay but some pay more to allow others to pay less. We just ignore here the cases in which cross-subsidies are allowed to compensate for a fiscal inability of the government to support the needs of the poorest consumers, as we saw in Chapter 9.

Cross-subsidization has been quite commonly used in regulated markets and has often been blamed for various sources of inefficiencies. For instance, Faulhaber (2005) reviews many examples in which historical incumbents tried to blockade entry by pricing below cost in liberalized segments. One of the concerns with the growing trend of traditionally well-focused mono-product regulated companies to diversify their activities is that it will help them distort markets. But this risk needs to be balanced against the possibility that the diversification could also be justified based on scale and/or scope economies. For a regulator in this scenario, the challenge is to come up with an assessment of the level at which the pricing strategy is desirable or not.

The intuitive way to do this would be to compare the price with the average stand-alone cost. A price below the average stand-alone cost (i.e. $p_1 < [C(q_1,0)/q_1]$) would seem to be anticompetitive since it impedes the entry of a competitor into market 1. But one of the main insights of theoretical research on this pricing approach is that focusing only on the extent to which prices are below average stand-alone costs could be misleading. What is needed is an approach that accounts for the fact that cross-

---

[20] In regulation, the three most common ways of allocating costs are based on: (i) outputs (common costs are shared as a proportion of production or sales); (ii) other inputs (common costs are shared based on the share of other known inputs such as number of employees or wage bills) and (iii) value-based factors such as prices, revenues or consumers' willingness to pay.

subsidies may be the result of a rational choice if there are economies of scope between activities.

And this is where incremental cost measurements can be, again, a handy regulatory tool. Indeed, it seems a lot more rational to focus on the incremental cost rather than the stand-alone costs in this 'cost–benefit' analysis of cross-subsidies. If the price is not below the incremental average cost, the strategy is acceptable. The rule of thumb usually followed to ensure that the pricing strategy is free from cross-subsidies is that the price complies with the following rule:

$$[C(q_1, q_2) - C(0, q_2)]/q_1 < p_1 < C(q_1, 0)/q_1 \qquad (12.3)$$

which is only feasible if there are economies of scope. In other words, the price of good or service 1 can be below its average stand-alone cost, but it must exceed its average incremental cost. In practice, the extent to which a product or service contributes to revenue more or less than the *incremental* cost to the firm of delivering it has to be assessed in net present value terms. Regulators make this assessment with the forward-looking discount cash-flow model discussed in Chapter 7.

There are many more precise insights emerging from this research, but the discussion so far already provides enough intuition to think through common issues in regulated industries. Ultimately, this discussion suggests that the net cost or the net benefit of cross-subsidies or of uniform pricing constraints is an empirical matter. The evaluation of cross-subsidies in a world of very imperfect markets and institutions needs to be done quantitatively, rather than ideologically as is quite often the case. The goal should be to assess the relative importance of the various incentives.

Many regulators decide to live with cross-subsidies for social reasons when they have no other option to help some groups of consumers, as discussed in Chapter 9. In other cases, when regulators are concerned with some of their negative efficiency and/ or equity effects, they often impose uniform pricing. When prices are the same for everyone, the pie may be smaller, but all users are treated equally. The extent to which the pie may be smaller needs to be assessed as carefully as possible in practice, often from a combination of accounting and billing data. This is needed to increase the transparency of the costs and benefits of uniform pricing options as compared to those produced by cross-subsidies. As in so many other dimensions in regulation, the ultimate decision is often political. But the costs and benefits of the political decision can be measured and made transparent when politicians decide so.

12.12   Limits to Deconcentration

The chapter has shown that 'deregulation' does not mean ceasing to regulate, or ceasing to deal with regulatory trade-offs. Many of the deregulation reforms anticipated the fact that intensified rivalry should result in greater efficiency, reduced cost and price, and increased quality and product variety. But depending on the industry characteristics, some of these goals were and continue to be inherently conflicting.

For instance, interconnection to a common facility, which is often needed to achieve competition and make the most of economies of scale, complicates operations. It ties the different producers into a system where each individual action has a repercussion on every other member of the network. This physical unity is what differentiates interconnected systems from other systems of distribution of goods and services (Crampes 1999). For example, in the electricity industry incidents affect blindly all users connected to the grid. In this context, opening the market to competition yields a free-rider problem, which depresses quality provision when quality has public-good-like features and is not contractible (Auriol 1998). In electricity, reliability is achieved by excess capacity, but private firms want to operate at full scale. This illustrates why assessing the downside of deregulation on reliability of the public utilities services and on investment in public-good components of the networks are just as important as assessing the payoffs to deregulation.

More generally, the analysis covered in this chapter shows that, contrary to common perceptions, notably among conservative politicians, regulation is not superfluous and certainly not any easier in the absence of a monopoly. The US telecommunications regulators learned this very quickly after the first steps toward deregulation were taken in the mid-1980s. The end of the AT&T monopoly was enabled by technological progress. But the sector continued to be concentrated despite the increase in the number of providers, and collusion and other forms of distortions to competition took place. It turned out that the increase in the number of service providers ended up requiring additional monitoring efforts. These additional efforts are typically the mandate of the competition agency/authority rather than the regulatory authorities. Who does what in a given context depends on available technical and financial capacity as well as legal traditions and preferences. What matters is the monitoring of abuses – or their risk – and the organization of enforcement capacity in the interest of consumers. As will be discussed in Chapter 14, several institutional arrangements can achieve this.

Ultimately, in a world of asymmetric access to information, the choice between a monopoly and an oligopoly to deliver services depends on many factors. Regulators need to update and upgrade the tools they once used to supervise regulated services because they must interact with different companies, often characterized by different technologies, different financing options, and sometimes different market segments. This is clearly not a simple exercise in practice, as the deregulation reforms have led to an increase in complexity. But the theory summarized in this chapter, combined with many of the insights discussed in the rest of the book, should help regulators and antitrust authorities to make the right choices.

Overall, considering the numerous distortions and limitations to the assessment of abuses in regulated industries, there is a clear case for a more complex conceptual analytical framework that integrates new technologies, heterogeneity of product quality, the dynamic evolution of industries, including mixed-oligopolies, the financial risks associated with investments in PPPs, often justified by the financial needs of the State, and the social risks and constraints to be accounted for. But in practice, this framework will usually lag the creativity of real market players. In the end, a certain amount of imperfect competition will always remain. It may sometimes be desirable when the risks of regulatory failures are higher than those resulting from market failures in this dynamic context, as discussed next in Chapter 13. Ideally, questions as to 'how much' and 'how to get things done' could be solved analytically, focusing on the long-term payoffs to society. In practice, they are often answered politically: that is, based on concerns for re-election or other non-economic considerations with potentially significant long-term costs.

12.13   Summing Up

- Regulated industries decreasingly look like single-product monopolies and increasingly like multi-product monopolies or like oligopolies, and this has implications for the optimal design of regulation.
- In many regulated industries, at some point, usually as a result of the evolution of technology or of preferences, the regulator may have to choose between a monopoly and an oligopoly.
  - An oligopolistic structure will be preferred if it makes it easier for regulation to cut and share information rents and if these gains offset the loss of gains from scale economies.
  - These rent cuts come from sampling effects, yardstick competition, a complementarity effect and marginal cost effects.
  - In mixed oligopolies, differences in the objectives and constraints of public and private competitors make the regulation tasks more complex and limit the possibility of implementing yardstick competition.
- When the regulator wants to stimulate R&D in a regulated industry, oligopolistic and monopolistic market structures need to be compared:
  - If the costs are unknown, a duopoly leads to lower marginal costs despite the need to duplicate the R&D sunk costs because it can reduce the informational rent to be paid to a monopoly; this is particularly clear when the cost of the two firms are correlated (as in the case of common technology).
  - If the costs are relatively well known (i.e. standardized technologies), a monopoly may be a better choice as there is basically no variance in production costs and so dual sourcing is useless.
  - Overall, the extent to which the market-size impact of a duopoly and of a monopoly offsets the impact of uncertainty on cost (which depends on the elasticity of demand and on the availability of close substitutes) will determine the optimal choice.
- When private firms operate alongside public firms in a regulated industry – in the case of mixed oligopolistic market structures – the extent and the way in which regulation needs to be adjusted depends on the extent to which the two types of firms differ in terms of their objectives and on the relative importance of the increased productive inefficiencies and the gains in allocative efficiency.

- In oligopolistic industries, self-regulation and regulation by contract offer alternatives to regulation by a specialized regulatory agency.
  - Public–private partnership (PPP) contracts often serve as a key regulatory instrument that can be used to define regulatory rights and obligations of the parties to the contract while allocating risks across them.
  - Their track record is, however, far from perfect, in particular in the water and transport sector.
- For a multi-product monopolist, the regulatory adjustment to the authorized optimal pricing strategy also follows a few predictable rules of thumbs:
  - For products or services unrelated on the demand side, the relative prices are the same as those observed when the regulator faces two independent mono-product monopolies – the Ramsey-Boiteux rule.
  - For substitutes on the demand side, the prices will be higher, i.e. the monopolist's margin is higher than with independent goods in order to internalize the negative externality of the price-driven substitution effects.
  - For complements on the demand side, prices will be lower in order to internalize the positive externality of the complementary effects resulting from price changes.
- The challenge is to decide whether to set a rate of return for each product sold by the regulated firm or for its overall business.
  - Under a global regulation, the risks are that the monopolist can easily manipulate the economies of scale and scope to secure rents.
  - The odds of manipulation can be reduced if the regulator tracks the sources of the incremental costs to ensure that consumer's welfare is accounted for in product differentiation and pricing.

13 Abuse of Market Power in (De)Regulated Industries

This chapter strengthens the message that regulation can be desirable not only when the market is best supplied by a monopolist but also when there is an oligopolistic market structure, as is the case in many regulated industries today. However, it also shows that, as for any policy decision, a cost–benefit analysis is often useful to decide whether the risks of imperfect regulation are stronger or weaker than the risks of market imperfections.

One of the reasons why regulation is a lot harder and less effective in practice than it is in theory and can be imperfect is that actual market structures (and information asymmetries) are more complex to manage than models suggest. And the payoffs can often be harder to assess than implied by theory. For instance, the benefits of deregulation in a context of economic integration depend on the extent to which the larger market makes it is easier for several firms to operate profitably. Benefits may also depend on the extent to which deregulation makes it easier to benefit from innovations that lower return to scale. If these benefits are not easy to capture with some form of regulatory intervention, deregulation may not be the best choice from a social welfare perspective.

The experience suggests that markets are generally adjusting better to changes in size (e.g. because of economic integration), preferences and technology (e.g. because of innovation) than regulators. For example, technology made fixed phone lines obsolete for many users in less than twenty years but in many countries telecoms regulators were slow to pick up the consequences of these changes and to anticipate the investment needs of the new communications technologies. Market structures have evolved quickly over recent decades and regulation seems to have had a hard time adjusting fast enough to this evolution.

Many international corporations have been able to take advantage of this weakness and have made the most of the capital mobility and trade liberalization triggered by the end of the cold war, as discussed in Clifton et al. (2011) and Florio et al. (2018a). They grew from the beginning of the 1990s as a result of a surge in mergers and acquisitions, and in particular global cross-border mergers and acquisitions. Big corporations such as ATT, Gazprom, Emi, UPS or Vinci generate annually an added value which is larger than most countries' GDP. It is thus impossible for an isolated regulator, whether in a developed or a developing country, to monitor these big corporations, as the regulator's mandate normally tends to be restricted to domestic activities even if the firm it is regulating enjoys quite a significant margin to allocate its costs and revenues across borders. Moreover, regulators' budgets seldom match those which these firms can mobilize when regulatory conflicts arise. In a closed economy, a government can always control large firms by nationalizing them. In an open world, controlling multinational firms locally is impossible without international coordination.

With the emergence of these powerful oligopolistic structures, one central, yet often underestimated, tool of sector-specific regulation is anti-trust policy. Numerous case studies show that, in advanced economies, conspiracies by firms are frequent and damaging for consumers. Anti-trust aims at preventing cartelization as well as the abuse of their dominant position by firms operating in non-competitive industries.[1] It is at the heart of the functioning of integrated markets such as the European Union or the United States. Unfortunately, in developing countries this new form of regulation is still embryonic, where it exists at all. Most are unable to set up an effective anti-trust authority due to weak institutional capacities (more on these weaknesses in Chapter 14). Although they are poor, and thus need the lowest prices they can get for their commodities, they are often victims of (international) cartels, and other forms of economic crime such as corruption and collusion. This begs for international regulation and arbitration, which requires new global, or at minimum regional, organizations and institutions. Countries need to agree on these structures and on their missions, which is a challenge but, as the experience of the EU Competition Directorate shows, is not impossible.

All over the world, and especially in developing countries, governments and regulators are recognizing the real risk of abuses. Since the mid-1980s firms' mark-ups have increased on average around the world with and without changes in market power (Diez et al. 2018).[2] This is not the expected outcome from the deregulation wave that started in the 1990s in services traditionally delivered by integrated monopolies. Increasing competition *in* the market where there was scope to do so and adopting competition *for* the market through the organization of auctions (for the right to provide the service) when the need to rely on local or national monopolies continued to prevail have clearly not had the expected impact. And these effects have usually not been smoothed by the steady stream of mergers and acquisitions observed among regulated firms. For instance, according to Guinea and Erixon (2019), postal, air transport, telecommunications, broadcasting and water transport are among the most concentrated markets in Europe. These have long been, and continue to be, a significant source of concern among regulators.

This evolution of market structures is impacting the level, the nature and the distribution of market power between old and new stakeholders. This is largely why

---

[1] The competition commission of the EU has uncovered numerous cartels and collusion agreements over the years (e.g. in trucks, airfreight, vitamins, elevators). For more information, visit https://ec.europa.eu/competition/

[2] There is heterogeneity according to regions, sectors and firm size. But the long-term overall trend seems to be quite clear.

regulators need routinely to fine-tune regulation.[3] They need to deal with the commonly observed negative correlation between the poor quality of regulation and the residual market power in regulated industries. The more damaging effect of this correlation shows up when residual market power is turned into abusive mark-ups over costs.[4] Some of these mark-ups are justified, at least temporarily, but regulators should have a formal way to assess when they are justified and when they are not. The main purpose of this chapter is to show how regulation can be structured to assess the risks of abuses of market power. It also aims to underline the risks associated with a naïve interpretation of the standard tools available.

In the following, we discuss the way market power and its impact are being assessed in the context of regulated industries and how this can be used to identify targeted regulatory interventions. As with many of the tools used in regulation and competition policy, these measures are imperfect tools, but they are useful for regulators to identify the risks that could disincentivize firms to deliver efficient and fair outcomes.

13.1   Evidence on the Risks from Increasing Market Power in Regulation

Before getting into the technical details of the various ways in which market power and its effects are being measured, it may be useful to discuss their political and social relevance.[5] When the actual and/or perceived risk of abuse of market power become strong enough, they can lead to significant political tensions. For instance, when high dividends and high chief executive officer (CEO) salaries are reported in the media, it is quite common to see them depicted as evidence of abuse. The political reaction can be quite strong if this happens when consumers are unhappy with what they pay or with the service quality they get. Whether this data reflects a poor or incomplete coverage of regulation, corruption or incompetence or whether it is a negotiated outcome of a longer-term contract between the operators and the State or the regulator is usually not that relevant. What drives the tensions is its apparent correlation with market power.

The political risks are nicely illustrated by the experience of the first massive deregulation in Europe. It occurred in England and Wales. In December 1990, the twelve regional electricity companies – responsible for the distribution and supply of electricity – were privatized and their market power was assessed as being under

---

[3] For a useful, more detailed discussion of the costs and benefits of regularly fine-tuning regulation, see Beecher (2019).

[4] Chisari et al. (1999) show that in the case of the reforms adopted by Argentina in the early 1990s, the payoffs to effective regulation were equivalent to about 2% of GDP and shared between workers and capital owners. Without good regulation, these payoffs largely became a rent for the capital owners explained by higher markups.

[5] Ennis et al. (2019) show that, for a sample of eight OECD countries, market power increases the wealth of the 10% wealthiest by between 12% and 21% while cutting the income of the poorest 20% by 11% or more.

control thanks to the redesign of the market and the tight regulatory supervision organized to ensure they would get their fair share from increased competition. By 2018, competition did not seem as intense as hoped for and six energy firms enjoyed a market share of around 80%. A similar debate started to take place in the British water and sanitation sector where over 80% of all supply point identifiers were being held by the four biggest companies as of 2017.[6] Concerns with high dividends in regulated industries and high CEO salaries were then being blamed on the regulators' tolerance for excessive market power resulting from strong market concentration. For the English Labour party, this became a topic in the 2019 political debates. Their argument was that, if market concentration was unavoidable and regulators unable to enforce contractual obligations, a nationalization of the sector may be the most desirable social option.[7] This argument has been used to justify nationalization of water services in Uruguay in 2004 and Mali in 2005 when conflicts between private operators and the government led to the departure of these operators.[8] More recently several left-leaning governments (e.g. in Argentina, Venezuela or Bolivia) have chosen to re-nationalize key public utilities for more ideological reasons but the decision has been much more widespread, in particular in the case of local water provision, where re-municipalization has become a relatively common occurrence (Bel 2020).

While not all conflicts end up in such extreme re-nationalization solutions, the concerns for increasing mark-up levels in a wide range of developed and developing countries ended up attracting the interest of leading supranational organizations such as the OECD (2018b), the IMF (2019) and European Commission (2016). This echoes the interest demonstrated by academics, including some who had been arguing that the deregulation waves had only delivered modest welfare improvements (e.g. Fabrizio et al. 2007 for the electricity sector). More recent methodological debates have started to link the deceptive performances of deregulation to the increased concentration within many sectors, in particular regulated utilities and transport (Autor et al. 2017; Diez et al. 2018, 2019; Gutierrez and Philippon 2018, 2019).[9] But it has also provided more subtle insights relevant to regulation.

This strand of research shows that a high concentration should not be a matter of political, economic or social concern as it does not necessarily imply anticompetitive harm. It becomes an issue only when there is evidence that it is accompanied by an increase in the abusive use of this market power.[10] This is why it is essential to track

---

[6] Britton (2019), www.cornwall-insight.ie/2019/01/31/hhi-meopathy-water-market-increasingly-concen trated/

[7] *The Financial Times* was quite effective in organizing discussions on this proposal and this can still be read on its website.

[8] For a more detailed assessment of the motivation of the changes and some of the associated regulatory issues, see Estache and Griffel-Tatje (2013) for Mali and Borraz et al. (2013) for Uruguay.

[9] Although a recent assessment conducted for a sample of five European countries shows no increase in concentration between 2010 and 2015, a period during which concentration has continued to increase in the United States (Valletti 2017).

[10] Furman (2018) argues that this tolerance for an increased market power may also be the result of deliberate policy choices. This may explain the differences between the United States and the United

both concentration and some measure of profit margins. One of the ways in which this is assessed, in a preliminary form at least, is by tracking the evolution of the mark-up charged by firms over some measure of costs (marginal or average depending on the context and data availability). Until recently, this evidence came from specific competition cases focusing on specific firms and relying on detailed cost accounting data. Lately, researchers have also started monitoring the evolution at the macroeconomic level relying on more aggregated data.[11] The empirical evidence they produce implies that the number of cases in which abuses may be taking place is large enough to have an impact at the macroeconomic level. This is what emerged, for instance, when one considers jointly some of the results produced by Autor et al. (2017), De Loecker and Eeckout (2018), Diez et al. (2018, 2019). Similarly, Gutierrez and Philippon (2018) and Valletti (2017) point to long-term positive trends in the profit margins achieved by utilities across a highly heterogeneous sample of countries.[12]

From the viewpoint of this book, the heterogeneity of countries also serves as a reminder that the regulators' supervisory efforts need to be matched with the context in which firms are operating. First, the differences observed across countries revealed by these papers point to the importance of the case-specific approach typically adopted by competition agencies. In Europe, Valletti (2017) shows that the profit margin has been increasing across firms on average from around 20% in the 1980s, to 30% in the 2000s, to 40% in the 2010s. In the United States, it is only the 'superstar' firms that have managed to increase their mark-up that significantly. This is what has driven the increase in the average mark-ups. Second there is a relevant technological context to consider as well. The difference in the degree of digitalization across sectors matters. In a context in which 'smart' public service provision is a recurrent topic, it is useful to note that average mark-up growth has been higher in digitally intensive sectors than in the other sectors. These differences can also be observed within sectors since not all firms digitalize at the same speed. This implies that within a country, there may be good reasons to observe differences in mark-ups across firms within a regulated sector. Finally, research also shows that capital-intensiveness matters to assess the extent to which the sizes of mark-ups should be a matter of concern or not. It could be

---

Kingdom, on the one hand, and many of the continental Europe countries, on the other, as shown by Döttling et al. (2017). Crouzet and Eberly (2018) argue that the increase in intangible investment may provide an alternative explanation for the observed increase in industry concentration and that this may be consistent with both rising productivity and weak investment.

[11] This has revealed a significant scope for creativity in the way markups are measured in macro-studies. Conceptually, a markup, which is supposed to measure the difference between the selling price and the cost, is usually reported as a percentage of the cost. Data availability has often been a key driver of the measures adopted. In the recent literature, markups have been measured as the net operating income expressed in percentage of turnover or as a profit rate adjusted for the user cost of capital (e.g. Basu 2019). They have also been measured as a profit margin focusing on production cost alone or on all operational costs (e.g. De Loecker and Eeckhout 2017; Diez et al. 2018). Each measure leads to a different markup level, but the conclusions tend to be quite similar for comparable data samples. A more technical discussion of the measure of markups is provided later in the chapter.

[12] For Europe, Valletti (2017) notes some variation across countries, with Germany and France seeing small increases, while the United Kingdom saw a reduction. Spain and Italy showed no change, with high profit margins.

argued that short-term mark-up measures may underestimate the need to account for the recovery of fixed costs (and not only marginal costs).[13] In an environment in which firms need to modernize their assets to account for growing environmental concerns, it should not be surprising to see higher mark-ups emerging to allow the firms to cover their fixed costs, including when the technological change reduces variable costs. In that context, higher mark-ups can be observed without changes in profits (e.g. De Loecker et al. 2020). Therefore, the detailed measures of market power and mark-ups need to be analysed thoroughly. That is the focus of this chapter.

13.2   Measuring Market Power

Practitioners rely on various ways of establishing the existence of market power. The first is to show that a more efficient competitor would find it difficult to enter and gain a share of the market, and to spell out the various reasons why this would be the case. A second is to show that an established firm can substantially increase its price and maintain it at that high level for a significant amount of time without losing so many customers that it would begin to lose money. A third approach, useful when there is no statistical evidence of market domination, is to look at how a large firm treats its rivals. Blocking access to essential facilities and inputs prevents more efficient competitors from entering the market. A key indicator in these approaches is the impact on prices.

The two simplest measures of the loss of social efficiency caused by the practices of dominant firms are based on profit margins and market shares. The focus on profit margins follows an approach based mostly on accounting data and financial indicators. It is popular among regulatory agencies. They tend to rely on commercial margins combined with profitability indices. Measuring market shares, by contrast, follows a more complex approach that relies on statistical observations and combines them into concentration indices. This is the method used by anti-trust authorities around the world. The following is an overview of the concepts underlying these two approaches and their policy use. The focus is on the broad picture. Details can be somewhat more complex, as discussed in Box 13.1 with a description of the ways in which the measurement of market power can be particularly challenging in the context of regulated industries.

13.3   On the Challenge of Defining the Relevant Market

Defining the relevant/reference market is an essential step in the process of determining the market power of firms. When this market is large, each firm has a small share of the market, and one can readily infer that there is no risk of abuse of monopolistic power. On the contrary, if a restrictive definition of a firm's activities is adopted, it

---

[13] It is also important to track whether cross-sectoral studies have focused on marginal or average costs to assess markups.

Box 13.1 On the Difficulties of Detecting Market Power in Regulated Industries

Identifying whether mark-ups are evidence of abusive use of market power can be quite challenging for regulated industries. An example is when the production function of a regulated activity does not lead to a smoothly increasing supply curve but to an output curve increasing in steps instead. In electricity, for instance, as demonstrated at the end of Chapter 8 and illustrated in Figure 13.1, at certain hours the merit order of technologies leads the market price of a kilowatt-hour to be higher than the operating cost of the last unit of generation used, as happens when demand is at peak. In this case, the simple statistical observation of a price that is higher than the marginal operating cost does not mean that market power is being exercised. At peak periods, when all generation capacity is fully used, the mark-up can be very high without any abuse by any bidder on the wholesale market.

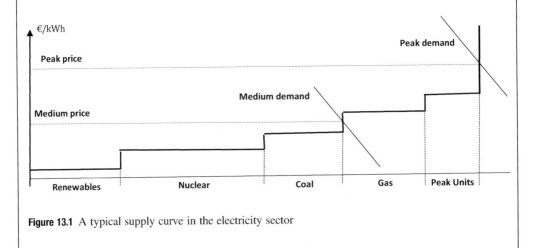

Figure 13.1 A typical supply curve in the electricity sector

would be easy to show that it holds a significant share of the market and, accordingly, that there is (or will be, after some merger) a risk of anticompetitive activity. For example, if one of the global construction companies is accused of anticompetitive behaviour, the firm's response is likely to be that it controls less than 10–20% of the market since there are many other local companies competing with them, whereas the competition authorities may want to argue that it is winning more than 50% of the deals it is competing for in these local markets.[14]

Conceptually, the relevant/reference market of an industry is the set of products or services and points of sale from which demand cannot escape. Or, symmetrically, it is the set within which consumers must satisfy certain specific needs. To establish the limits of this market, the concept of demand elasticity, or rather demand inelasticity, is

---

[14] This would point to a problem with the local procurement processes, which tend to favour large firms over fringe entrants for many of the contracts signed in regulated industries financed by the public authorities (see Estache and Iimi 2011, for instance, for evidence on developing countries).

used implicitly. As discussed earlier, inelastic demand cannot react to changes in price, whereas elastic demand can 'dodge' price increases by lowering consumption and/or substituting other products or services. This tool is thus essential when trying to understand the relevance of the market definition. The definition that the firm will try to adopt comes up with a market for which the demand elasticity is high and the regulator will look for the opposite.

In practice, in regulatory and anti-trust evaluations, the definition of the relevant/reference markets is often the outcome of a negotiation between the various stakeholders. In all cases, it needs to end up with an agreement on the specific products to consider and on the relevant geographical reach of the company under scrutiny. The objective is to identify firms that may limit the freedom of movement of the industry under review, and to prevent them from acting outside the rules of competition law.

The statistical method used to define the relevant market boils down to progressing by trial and error to determine the set of products or services and locations with demand that is sufficiently inelastic to ensure a 'small and non-transitory' price increase (e.g. 5–10%) without defections, with the result that a monopoly in that market could increase its profits substantially.

The test is known as SSNIP: small but significant and non-transitory increase in price. First, the 5% increase is applied to the price of products or services sold by the firm under review. In this initial phase, the firm's competitors are assumed not to react to changes in price. If an increase in profit occurs when the increase is applied to the first product or service, this starting point constitutes the reference market. If it does not, it means that some consumers can escape by buying some close substitutes. Consequently, the relevant market is larger than the market directly served by the firm under scrutiny. This implies that the 5% test has to be applied both to the product initially focused on and its closest substitute. Since demand for the second product or service is less elastic to the price of the first product or service than demand for the first product or service is to its own price, the elasticity of the combined products and/or services decreases. This expansion process is repeated until the smallest group of products and/or services hence defined enables a monopoly to increase its profits through a 5% price increase because consumers can no longer escape. This group constitutes the relevant/reference market for products and services of firms. Once the task of identifying the relevant market has been settled, regulators and anti-trust authorities will use it to assess market concentration. This is crucial to candidates for a merger or to firms suspected of abusing a dominant position.

13.4   Measuring Market Concentration: A First Look

Since it is common to argue that market power is correlated with market concentration, the regulator needs to have a view on the extent to which market concentration is an issue or not. The most common first-order approach is to look at the number of firms active in a market and their relative size. It considers whether the size of one or more participants may be disrupting competition or not. Depending on the focus of the analysis, size may be defined by a regulator in several ways: number of employees, total billings, quantities sold, sales or amounts invested, for example.

When the products or services considered have the same prices because it is imposed by the regulators or because the products and services are homogeneous, it is common to rely on the quantities sold to assess concentration. As explained above, the challenge is then to identify the relevant market for which the estimation is computed. Note that the relevant market can be defined along two dimensions: the product and the geographical dimensions. In both cases, using the SSNIP test, it is the set of products or services and points of sale from which demand cannot escape a specific operator.

To see this more formally, let q_i be the production of firm i and n the number of firms active in the relevant market. The market share of i is measured by:

$$s_i = \frac{q_i}{\sum_{j=1}^{n} q_j} \tag{13.1}$$

Then $0 < s_i \leq 1$. Knowing the vector of the shares $(s_1, s_2, s_3, \ldots, s_n)$, the next step is to construct an index that can provide information about market concentration simply and rapidly.

13.5   Families of Concentration Indices

There are essentially two families of indices: partial indices and composite (or global) indices. Partial indices have the advantage of simplicity and of demanding little data. Composite indices have the advantage of increased precision but demand more data on all firms in the market and suffer from weaknesses as well, albeit different ones, as discussed later in the chapter.

Partial indices use only a part of the statistical information. Typically, after ranking firms so that $s_1 > s_2 > \cdots > s_n$, the index C_x is the sum of the shares of the x largest firms. For example, C_4 measures the cumulative market share of the four largest firms. The choice of x is made by the analyst according to the context in which the analysis is conducted.

The main advantage of these C_x indices is that they are easy to compute and interpret. Their main drawbacks are generally well recognized. First, they are poorly sensitive to the distribution of market shares across firms. The same C_4 can summarize very different markets. For instance, $C_4 = 80$ can be the outcome of $s_1 = 60$, $s_2 = 10$ and $s_3 = s_4 = 5$ or $s_1 = s_2 = s_3 = s_4 = 20$. Second, it may mislead the analyst on the relative importance of some specific actors and in doing so lead to an underestimation of the overall concentration. For instance, in a market in which the top three players share the whole market, i.e. $s_1 = s_2 = s_3 = 33.3$ and $s_4 = 0$, the index C_4 is equal to 100. In contrast, in a market in which two firms dominate the market and two others lag far behind, i.e. $s_1 = s_2 = 49$ and $s_3 = s_4 = 0.25$, the index C_4 is lower, at 98.5. Third, they ignore the possibility of market power of smaller firms on some specific activities such as technological innovations allowing new entry in a market. And fourth, if mergers or acquisitions occur among firms not included in the set of the x largest, and if those operations do not change the ranking of these top x firms, the C_x index does not signal any change.[15]

Composite indices do not have these drawbacks because they use the entire vector of market shares. The most popular is the Herfindahl–Hirschman index (HHI),[16] defined by:

$$HHI = 10^4 \sum_{i=1}^{n} s_i^2 \qquad (13.2)$$

For each exogenous value of the number of active firms, n, this index varies between a minimum of $10^4/n$ when all firms are equal (i.e. $s_i = 1/n$) and a maximum of 10,000 when there is a monopoly. This index defines thresholds often used by competition authorities in the assessment of the anticompetitive effects of mergers.

Markets with an HHI under 1,000 are considered 'not concentrated' and generally do not require further analysis. Markets in which $1,000 < HHI < 1,800$ are 'moderately concentrated', and competition is thought to be threatened if a merger causes the HHI to increase by more than 100 points. Finally, if the HHI exceeds 1,800, the market is defined as 'highly concentrated' and any transaction that causes an increase of the index by more than 50 points (i.e. $\Delta HHI > 50$) calls for further inquiry.

These thresholds seem arbitrary, but they can be explained by considering that since $HHI = 10^4/n$ when n firms are of the same size, the reciprocal value $10^4/HHI$ is a good indicator of the number of firms that play a central role in the market.[17] The two thresholds of the resulting merger guidelines are, respectively, $10^4/1,000 = 10$ firms to define a relatively non-concentrated market and $10^4/1,800 \approx 5$ firms to define a highly concentrated market. An increase of $\Delta HHI = 100$ corresponds to the disappearance of a major firm when the initial value is $HHI = 1,000$. In many countries, the change in the HHI is often used as a filtering system to determine whether a planned merger is cause for concern or not.

Box 13.2 offers an example of the information that can be generated from a comparison of HHI in a specific activity across countries and used to benchmark individual performance. But there are many other uses of the HHI. For instance, some authors suggest interpreting the HHI to measure the distribution of surplus among consumers and firms. When the marginal cost is constant for all firms and the social utility is quadratic, if V is the consumer surplus (gross surplus minus expenditure) and profit π is the producer surplus, Martin and Ocana (1998) show that

---

[15] Article 14 of Spanish law 16/1989 is an example. It states that 'any plan or transaction concerning the concentration of firms must be reported to the Competition Department if the acquisition or increase of market share is equal to or greater than 25% of the domestic market'. Clearly this is a partial index, because it does not refer to all market shares or to the number of competitors.

[16] Other composite measures suggested by research include the entropy index (each market share is weighted by its logarithm) and Rosenbluth index, where each market share is weighted by the rank of the firm: $s_1 + 2s_2 + \cdots + ns_n$ with $s_1 > s_2 > \cdots > s_n$.

[17] $\frac{10^4}{HHI} = n$ only when the market is divided into equal shares. In all other cases, $\frac{10^4}{HHI} < n$.

> **Box 13.2** On the Concentration of the Household Retail Electricity Market in 2016–17
>
> The Council of European Energy Regulators (CEER) tracks several regulatory issues that could be a shared concern across countries. Excessive concentration is one of them. In 2018, it published a comparison of the HHI of the household retail electricity market for a sample of twenty-one EU countries (CEER 2018). The study shows that concentration in 2017 was below the 1,800 threshold for only eight countries. In two countries (Cyprus and Lithuania), the index was at its maximum value since there is only one supplier there. Another seven countries were characterized by an HHI of the household retail electricity market ranging from 3,000 to 8,000. These bad measures increase the relative importance of regulatory activities in the sector. The comparison of the two years for which the index was computed hints at good news from a concentration point of view since it shows a decline in the index for a fair number of countries, notably in Belgium and Bulgaria, where the drop was, respectively, over 1,000 and 2,000 points, and no country had a significant increase.

$\pi/V = 2 \text{ HHI } 10^{-4}$.[18] This relationship suggests that any distribution of the surplus between consumers and producers is directly proportional to the HHI. This insight is an important dimension of the ex post assessments of the effectiveness with which a regulator implements its equity mandate.

Finally, the HHI is an important index used not only by most competition authorities around the world and regulators but also by firms that make complaints against some of their competitors. For instance, in a comment to the 'Inquiry into the Competition and Consumer Amendment (Misuse of Market Power) Bill 2016', Vodafone Hutchison Australia, that controls a mere 16.64% of the Australian mobile market, states that 'the HHI of the Australian mobile market is over 4,000 and has substantially increased from nearly 3,500 in 2004 to well over 4,000 in 2016. Reducing telecommunications oversight in the face of such clear evidence would be illogical'.

Note that, although certainly the most popular, the HHI is not the only index in store. In a market dominated by one or two large firms, a few smaller firms may be able to become more competitive through lower prices, productivity gains, quality improvements and so on, which can benefit consumers. To capture these positive effects of small firms' competition, one option is to rely on indices measuring market imperfections that do not systematically increase when a merger occurs. Specifically, to be useful in this context, the index must increase when the merger involves one or more of the large firms and, on the contrary, must diminish when smaller firms are involved. One index with these properties is the index of domination (ID):

---

[18] This assumes that the market is characterized by Cournot competition, that is, a game where firms decide simultaneously and independently on the quantity they intend to sell and the price is determined by market equilibrium.

$$ID = 10^4 \sum_{i=1}^{n} \frac{q_i^4}{\left(\sum_j q_j^2\right)^2} \tag{13.3}$$

Mergers that prompt a decrease in the ID are not necessarily considered harmful to competition, although practitioners disagree on its usefulness as a rule of thumb.[19]

13.6   Commercial Margins and the Lerner Index, Again

The Lerner index discussed in Chapter 3 is one of the measures used in the theoretical and empirical academic literature on regulation. It is also at the heart of worldwide policies to assess market power, since it measures the extent to which prices distance themselves from marginal cost, i.e. $L_i = (p_i - c_i)/p_i$, where p_i is the observed price and c_i is the estimated marginal cost for firm i. This is used as an approximate measure of competitive distortions resulting from the market power of a firm.

The basic measurement challenge is the estimation of the unit cost, particularly when the firm sells several products and/or services and joint costs are shared among various activities. Electricity retailers today sell electricity but may also sell energy-efficiency equipment, advice or repairs. Rail companies sell both passenger and freight transport as well as, for passenger lines, food. The challenge is often quite hard to overcome but even rough approximations can be reliable enough to help identify some of the big-picture issues that deserve more precise interactions between the regulated firms and the regulator or the competition agency.

When cost data is hard to come by, it is sometimes possible to work with profit data. This data is usually quite easily available from balance sheets reported in the firms' annual reports and from international databases such as Bloomberg, Orbis-Bureau Van Dijck or Thompson-Reuters. Many of these indicators are available from commercial websites producing business valuations. When the companies are not listed publicly, regulators usually have access to fiscal data to produce enough evidence to estimate the total, rather than the marginal, profit level. This allows them to shift the burden of proof on the regulated firm if the firm is unhappy with the estimation. More data needs to be produced by the firm if it wants to make a case for a regulatory treatment differentiated from the treatment of its accounting data.

Practitioners use this information (either fiscal or accounting) to compute a variation of the Lerner index based on average cost that they can use to assess the rents captured by the industry in this market. Conceptually, i's profit is equal to $q_i (p_i - C_{Mi})$, with C_{Mi} representing the average cost (rather than the marginal cost as we discussed in Chapters 3–6). To produce a modified Lerner index, denoted L_{Mi}, anchored into this average measure, the analyst needs to multiply the numerator and

---

[19] Mexico has been using this rule of thumb. In contrast, Spain's Competition Commission has found that arguments based on this index are inadmissible. See www.mineco.es/tdc/, file C54/00, Hidroeléctrica del Cantábrico–Unión Eléctrica Fenosa.

the denominator of the index computed with the average cost by the quantity sold q_i. The modified Lerner index then becomes:

$$L_{Mi} = q_i(p_i - C_{Mi})/q_i p_i = \text{Profit of } i/\text{Sales of } i. \quad (13.4)$$

It is worth noting that, since a firm's average cost is always larger than its marginal cost in increasing return-to-scale industries, L_{Mi} is a lower bound of the actual Lerner index: $L_{Mi} \leq L_i$. It therefore gives an underestimation of the real market power of the firm. If the vector of the modified Lerner indices of all active firms is available, it is easy to calculate a market index based on these individual indices. The simplest average value that can be calculated is the weighted arithmetic mean, with the weights equal to the market shares, that is:

$$L_{MA} = \sum_{i=1}^{n} s_i L_{Mi} \quad (13.5)$$

When n firms sell a homogeneous product, $p_i = p$, it is easy to verify that L_{MA} represents the relationship of the industry's profit to the value of sales:

$$L_{MA} = \sum_i \frac{q_i p - C_{Mi}}{q} \frac{}{p} = \frac{\text{Total profit}}{\text{Total sales}} \quad (13.6)$$

There are no national or international guidelines for setting the thresholds that define a dominant position, as revealed by a profitability index measured by a Lerner index based on average cost. However, it is useful to remember what is lost when working with the average rather than the marginal cost. If the focus is the loss of efficiency linked to the increased concentration, the relative difference between price and marginal cost is a better signal to work with. It reveals the impact of the presence of firms that fail to behave in accordance with the rules of fair competition. Monitoring this difference is one way that regulatory agencies can oversee the actions of large firms. But, as always, it needs to be done carefully and details that go beyond those captured by the data collected to compute the Lerner index may be just as important to identify distortions and market power. A firm can be seen as a low Lerner firm even though it has a strong de facto degree of market power. This happens if it must support high transaction costs to maintain its market power (inefficiency) and/or it is charging a low price because of predatory behaviour.

13.7   Linking HHI and Lerner

Despite the various limitations alluded to, the indicators typically produced to identify market concentration are widely used in practice. In the best-case scenario, they help to establish a simple relationship between a concentration index and a profitability index when there is a suspicion that abuses may be taking place in a market known to suffer from imperfect competition (Encaoua and Jacquemin 1980). The relationship linking concentration to profitability, which is frequently invoked to argue against concentration, is derived below.

The Lerner index discussed in Chapter 3 is one of the measures used in the theoretical and empirical academic literature on regulation. It is also at the heart of worldwide policies to assess market power since it measures the extent to which prices distance themselves from marginal cost, i.e. $L_i = (p_i - c_i)/p_i$, where p_i is the observed price and c_i is the estimated marginal cost for firm i. This is used as an approximate measure of competitive distortions resulting from the market power of a firm. Since marginal costs are not easily uncovered by regulators due to asymmetric information, this index is hard to estimate in practice as explained in the previous section. In contrast, HHI is relatively easy to estimate. The relationship linking concentration (HHI) to profitability (L_i), which is derived below, is therefore often used to assess a sector's profitability. It is also frequently invoked to argue against concentration.

It is useful to start with a discussion of the assumptions needed to establish a relationship between the HHI and the average profitability index, L_A, in a typical regulated oligopolistic market structure in which competing firms make the very same product and choose independently how much of it to produce. This scenario is known as the generalized Cournot model of competition. It offers a reasonable description in any regulated industry in which prices are partially controlled by a public authority and firms need to work with their production decisions to maximize profits. Assuming that the firms cannot collude or form a cartel, and that they make decisions not cooperatively based on their competitors' decisions, the market price is eventually influenced by each firm's output.

Let's see this more formally. If q_i is the production of firm i in this scenario and if the product or service delivered is a homogenous product (a common implicit assumption in the analysis of an anticompetitive threat), the production of the $n - 1$ competitors of i will be represented by $q_{-i} = \sum_{j \neq i} q_j$. The inverse demand function is $p(q)$, with $p'(q) < 0$, where q, the quantity demanded, is defined as $q = q_i + q_{-i}$. At the market equilibrium, supply is equal to demand q. Finally, $C_i(q_i)$ represents the production cost function of firm i, and $C_i' > 0$ is the non-decreasing marginal cost. We assume that the objective of each firm is to maximize its profits, $q_i \, p(q) - C_i(q_i)$, not its market share, by choosing its production volume, q_i.

Under most common functions linking prices and quantities to profits in a regulated industry, the following first-order condition generally characterizes the solution:

$$p(q) + q_i \frac{dp(q)}{dq_i} - C_i'(q_i) = 0 \tag{13.7}$$

By rearranging the terms and dividing both sides by p, we return to the true Lerner index, L_i:

$$\frac{p(q) - C_i'(q_i)}{p(q)} = -\frac{q_i}{p} \frac{dp(q)}{dq_i} \tag{13.8}$$

Now let us consider the right-hand side of Equation (13.8). After some manipulations we can rewrite it to isolate the role of market shares i (i.e. $s_i = q_i/q$) as well as the role of price elasticity of demand ε :[20]

---

[20] The right-hand side of equation (13.8) becomes $-\frac{q_i}{p}\frac{dp(q)}{dq_i} = -\frac{q}{p}\frac{dp(q)}{dq}\left(\frac{d(q_i+q_{-i})}{dq_i}\right)\frac{q_i}{q} = -\frac{1}{\frac{dq}{dp}\frac{p}{q}}\left(1 + \frac{dq_{-i}}{dq_i}\right)$

$\frac{q_i}{q} = \frac{s_i}{\varepsilon}\left(1 + \frac{dq_{-i}}{dq_i}\right)$.

$$-\frac{q_i}{p}\frac{dp(q)}{dq_i} = \frac{s_i}{\varepsilon}\left(1 + \frac{dq_{-i}}{dq_i}\right) \tag{13.9}$$

Firm i's main problem is estimating the term dq_{-i}/dq_i – that is, estimating its competitors' reactions when it changes its own production level. As often in economics, the problem is solved by assumption. In a Cournot oligopoly, this term is assumed to be equal to zero.[21] This yields the basic relationship for each individual firm: $L_i = \frac{s_i}{\varepsilon}$. It shows a positive influence of market share s_i and a negative influence of demand elasticity ε on the market power of i.

If all firms in the sector behave in the same manner, the same relationship applies to each of them. The arithmetic mean (weighted by market shares) of these individual indices gives the market aggregate Lerner index, L_A:

$$L_A = \sum_{i=1}^{n} s_i L_i = \sum_{i=1}^{n} s_i \left(\frac{s_i}{\varepsilon}\right) = \sum_{i=1}^{n} \frac{s_i^2}{\varepsilon} = \frac{HHI}{\varepsilon} 10^{-4} \tag{13.10}$$

Equation (13.10) establishes a positive relationship between the average profitability index, as measured by L_A, and the HHI of concentration. The key new insight, however, is that the relationship is influenced by the demand elasticity ε. With two variables which are relatively easy to measure (HHI and ε), Equation (13.10) suggests that a regulator can have a view on the market profitability in a wide range of settings which tend to be common for regulated industries. The simplicity of such a relationship is attractive but there are several reasons to downplay its general importance once real-world circumstances are accounted for.

Before measuring the HHI, the problem of defining the relevant market was assumed to be solved – the assumption being that in a very small market, the HHI is high and in a very large market it is low. But the market definition has an ambiguous effect on the value of L_A. When a very small relevant market is defined, the index of concentration increases naturally. In addition, the elasticity rises as well, because many competitors are now outside the relevant market and may attract consumers outside that market. Consequently, the average profitability index L_A may increase or decrease as the size of the relevant market changes. Without more information, the relationship is too difficult to use in many regulatory assessments. For instance, it is unrealistic to expect anti-trust authorities to rely exclusively on Equation (13.10) to decide whether to approve a merger between two firms.

Nevertheless, in a regulated market for which the relevant market has been clearly defined, firms behave non-cooperatively and demand elasticity is not too great, Equation (13.10) is a good first step. When these assumptions are not validated, the

---

[21] $dq_{-i}/dq_i \equiv 0$ can be justified in several (non-exclusive) ways. For example, the competitors do not react to i's decision because they are unaware of it (simultaneous decisions), or because their technology does not allow a reaction (technical or contractual inelasticity), or because they do not wish to react (investment in reputation). For its part, firm i may be unable to estimate its reaction or may decide not to take it into account.

equation can easily be overestimated when trying to link concentration with profitability, as discussed next.

13.8 Anticompetitive Behaviour in Deconcentrated Markets

The long record of reliance on the indicators discussed in Section 13.6 (profitability and concentration) has resulted from simple rules that define the common wisdom on the topic. These rules have been translated into popular rules of thumbs. Many are useful but some can be misleading. They deserve some discussion in view of their popularity.

The most popular rule of thumb is that the more concentrated the market, the more likely that the firms operating in that market will behave inefficiently and hurt social welfare. This comes from the idea that concentration leads to inefficiency. Firms with market power tend to raise prices in order to obtain higher profits. Therefore, deconcentration should be a no-brainer policy goal.

Yet the argument does not necessarily hold in the context of regulated public services. First, deconcentration to reduce market power would have to produce efficiency gains that are greater than those achieved from economies of scale or of scope. When losses in scale and scope are costlier than the gains that could be achieved from deconcentration, the assumed link between concentration and prices will not prevail.[22] Second, by equating non-concentration with competition and, reciprocally, concentration with non-competition, the HHI is misleading in markets where the firms do not behave as a Cournot oligopoly. This is quite relevant in many regulated industries. And the empirical evidence shows that since the deconcentration wave of the 1990s, firms' profit margins have indeed been rising (e.g. Valletti 2017, 2018; Valletti and Zenger 2018, 2019, 2021).

In regulated industries in which deregulation has reduced the apparent degree of concentration, there are still harmful anticompetitive behaviours which are not picked up by the HHI. When a leader takes advantage of its position to cause prices to rise, the HHI may fall if small competitors seize the contraction of the leader's supply to increase their own market share. In reality, the margins of all producers increase, so the average Lerner index rises despite the drop in concentration because producers do not necessarily behave independently from each other. This divorce of the indicator of competition (which is increasing) from that of profitability (which, unexpectedly, is also increasing) may derive from the fact that the cost structure of small producers may not enable them to respond to the leader's decrease in output with an equal increase of their own.[23] When this occurs, the aggregate supply decreases and profit margins increase. In electricity markets in England and Spain, regulatory authorities have occasionally accused dominant generators of engaging in this strategy by taking

---

[22] Details have been provided in Chapter 12.

[23] When the firms are not identical, predictions based on symmetric Cournot equilibrium are no longer valid.

some of their production capacity offline during peak periods, specifically some of their hydro-power resources.[24]

Another concern is linked to the risks of collusion. Firms may be similarly rational, which then raises other concerns such as the possibility of coordination between them. If all active producers benefit from a high price in a market where all transactions are made at a single price, collusion may arise. To illustrate the point, let us consider an extreme example, by assuming that firms have a cartel agreement establishing their market shares. Maintaining the assumption that production quantities serve as decision variables, using Equation (13.8) and (13.9), the Lerner index of firm i is expressed as:

$$L_i = \frac{s_i}{\varepsilon}\left(1 + \frac{dq_{-i}}{dq_i}\right) \qquad (13.11)$$

in which, instead of $\frac{dq_{-i}}{dq_i} = 0$, we now have $\frac{dq_{-i}}{dq_i} = \frac{q_{-i}}{q_i}$, because in order to keep its market share unchanged, any change in a firm's output must be proportional to its initial share. It is easy, then, to conclude that $L_i = \frac{s_i}{\varepsilon}\left(1 + \frac{q_{-i}}{q_i}\right) = \frac{s_i}{\varepsilon}\left(\frac{q}{q_i}\right) = \frac{1}{\varepsilon}$.

Therefore, we see that despite the presence of several active firms in the industry, and although the index of concentration may thus be fairly low, each of these firms has market power equal to that of a monopoly as measured by the Lerner index. Clearly, in this sort of situation the index of concentration is meaningless in terms of the distortion of competition. This extreme case also explains why any attempt to set prices in a concerted fashion is explicitly prohibited and penalized by competition authorities.[25]

Finally, the measure of true competition in a sector should not be limited to the responsiveness of demand in the face of existing firms. According to Baumol et al. (1982), supply elasticity, i.e. potential competition, should also be considered. If businesses operating in the sector maximize their profits under the constraint of not encouraging challengers to enter the market, prices may be very low, and the market may be well covered despite the small number of active firms. From this perspective, if the market is contestable or if the firm is predatory, a single firm does not necessarily mean monopolistic rate setting and the extraction of monopolistic rent. That is, a firm can be seen as a low Lerner-index firm even though it has a high de facto degree of market power. This happens if it must support high transaction costs to maintain its market power (inefficiency) and/or it is charging a low price because of predatory behaviour.

Monitoring the difference between concentration and profitability is one way in which regulatory agencies can oversee the actions of large firms. But, as always, it needs to be done carefully and details that go beyond those captured by the data

---

[24] Conceptually, this is like the effects of capacity constraints, which are a common concern in regulated industries.

[25] The explanation for collusive behaviour in terms of non-cooperative game theory involves arguments of repetition. If the firms meet only once, it is in each one's interest to act as a stowaway, i.e. to take any market share left unclaimed. This opportunism is a strong dissuasion for a leader, if there is one, to cut production in order to increase prices. When the game is repeated, the immediate interest of playing the stowaway must be weighed against future reprisals by the other firms in the sector.

collected to compute the Lerner index may be just as important to identify distortions and market power.

13.9   Assessing Risks Associated with Mergers: The Cross-Ownership Case

Despite its faults, the HHI is used in the competition law of many countries. One of its common uses is the assessment of the potential impact of a merger on market concentration and, from there, on the risk of market power abuse. As explained in Section 13.5, the thresholds that trigger a regulatory intervention are generally set at about 1,000 for mergers that would raise the HHI by 100 and about 1,800 − 2,000 for those that would bring an increase of 50. Yet the positive relationship established between the average profitability index L_A and the standard HHI of concentration reflected by Equation (13.10) ignores that the standard HHI concentration measures are based solely on direct market shares. This fails to take into account the increase in profitability derived from financial participation. This is a major concern in regulated industries. This is well illustrated by the British rail industry. There are many companies operating trains in the United Kingdom, including the twenty-three operators of franchised passenger services, officially referred to as train operating companies (TOCs), as distinct from freight operating companies. Yet many of these TOCs are owned by a consortium. For instance, Govia, which was formed in November 1996 as a joint venture between the UK Go-Ahead Group (65%) and the French Keolis (35%), owns Govia Thameslink, London Midland Railway, GTR and South Eastern. The issue of cross-participation is pervasive throughout the European market and in other utilities services. While convenient to get the big picture, in many realistic situations, the HHI is thus once more not that useful for assessing the risks associated with merger.[26]

Mergers come in many shapes and do not simply consist in the full absorption of one firm by another. One of the increasingly common situations in which the basic index may lead to the wrong conclusion concerns the many cases in which there is cross-ownership of firms operating in the same markets. When one firm buys shares in a competitor's assets, it is also a form of (partial) merger. And any acquisition of partial ownership by a firm necessarily leads to a form of distortion. Ignoring the associated risks is one of the ways in which the close relationship with the Lerner index and risks of abusive market power disappears.

To see this, consider the case in which two firms have decided to merge in an already concentrated market. To make it more realistic, assume that the owners of firm 1 also hold a minority share $\alpha \in [0, 0.5)$ of the equity of firm 2, so that the profits to which they are entitled are:

$$\hat{\pi}_1 = q_1 p(q) - C_1(q_1) + \alpha[q_2 p(q) - C_2(q_2)] \tag{13.12}$$

---

[26] For an early discussion of many of insights still relevant today, see Bresnahan and Salop (1986) and O'Brien and Salop (2000).

with $q = q_1 + q_2$. For the sake of comparison with our previous results we assume that the firms still adopt a Cournot-style behaviour. If there are more than two firms in the market, but there are no other cross-ownerships, all the other firms, including firm 2, make their decisions to maximize their profits independently of one another. By contrast, when they maximize Equation (13.12), the owners of firm 1 are trying to account for both the profits generated by firm 1 and firm 2, although in different proportions. The difficulty for them is that control of the variable q_2 depends on the other owners of firm 2 since they only hold a minority interest in that firm.

With this limitation in mind, the rule of thumb to follow by firm 1 owner is simply an adaptation of the usual one. This adaption must account for the impact of their minority interests in firm 2. When they maximize $\hat{\pi}_1$ with respect to q_1, they end up with the following first-order condition: $p + q_1 p' - C_1' + \alpha q_2 p' = 0$. This is useful from a regulator's perspective since it makes it possible to express the Lerner index for firm 1 as:

$$\frac{p - C_1'}{p} = \frac{s_1 + \alpha s_2}{\varepsilon} \tag{13.13}$$

This implies that the production chosen by firm 1 decreases with α, the share of its profits that comes from its minority interests in firm 2. This is what drives the risks of seeing firm 1 not being keen to compete too fiercely with firm 2.

An additional distortion takes place if firm 1's interest in firm 2 is large enough for production decisions at firm 2 to be based on $\hat{\pi}_1$, instead of π_2. This could happen, for instance, in the context of cross-ownership of assets by transport firms committed to multi-modal businesses. It can also be observed in the energy sector when business diversification into renewables is achieved through investments in fast-growing start-ups in the sector. And it is an increasingly common concern associated with the growing role of international investment funds such as BlackRock (one of the world's largest asset management companies). Over the years, they have acquired many shares in regulated infrastructure activities and have become de facto major players in these industries. This situation in which several companies competing in the same markets are partially owned by the same investor or group of investors is known in the literature as common ownership and we will discuss this in Chapter 15 as it is one of the emerging new topics in the practice of regulation.[27]

There are other distortions to consider in the context of increasingly complex ownership structures, but this would get into the topics more typically addressed by competition agencies (e.g. Lopez and Vives 2017; Posner et al. 2017). The brief summary of the recurrent concerns associated with the evolution of the market shows that while simple HHI is useful when assessing mergers and share acquisitions

---

[27] For extremely insightful discussion of the anticompetitive impact of the growing role of institutional investors in the development of common ownership, see Azar and Schmalz (2017) and Schmalz (2018). For a useful discussion of the debates surrounding the relevance of common ownership in the European context, see Burnside and Kidane (2020). For a discussion comparing the US and European perspectives, see Elhauge (2020).

in regulated industries, it is only one of the tools and dimensions to consider in the diagnostic.

13.10 What If Deregulation Maintains Some Vertically Integrated Structures?

Another important issue in most (de)regulated industries is the need to access the backbone infrastructure to be able to serve the consumers. Traditionally, this infrastructure is owned by the historical provider, which is generally vertically integrated. The analysis of the possibility of achieving efficiency gains by allowing a vertically integrated monopolist (VIM) to diversify into products or services already available in upstream or downstream competitive markets leads to its own set of complex regulatory challenges. Think of a vertically integrated electricity company that used to control all of the generation activities and that starts having to deal with competition by producers of renewable sources of energy while at the same time diversifying some of its activities on the retail side by offering activities ranging from energy efficiency advice, for which it competes with small consulting firms, and communication or even banking services, where it competes with much larger regulated providers. The sources of potential gains are quite well understood but so are the risks. This implies that the regulatory decision will have to weigh the benefits and the costs, or risk of costs, associated with the decision to allow the firm to diversify its production activities.[28]

On the benefit side, there are many reasons why it may make sense to consider this heterogeneous market structure anchored in a VIM. The potential benefits from diversification include the efficiency payoffs of the competition effect, the optimization of production cost synergies, including transaction costs, and the incentive to innovate to remain competitive. Both the theoretical and empirical research has shown that welfare gains may be achieved through improved coordination of technical stages and spending economies in any of the traditional regulated industries. But these are not guaranteed because there are risks on the costs side.

The list of cost-related risks is also well known, and it is not short. However, four risks dominate policy diagnostics in the context of regulated industries – and some of them are also relevant to other market structures besides VIMs. The first is that the firm's expansion may distort competition in the unregulated sector. Once again, think of the leverage a large historical incumbent has on users when it competes with small new entrants offering energy-efficiency services. It is not unreasonable that the incumbent will be able to capture a fair market share simply because it enjoys more opportunities to interact with potential clients (e.g. every time you get your electricity bill, they let you know that they are available for other services). Since this is usually fully addressed by the competition agency rather than by the regulators, we will not develop it here.

---

[28] See, for instance, Crew et al. (2005), Reiffen and Ward (2002) and Sappington (2006) for empirical and theoretical reviews of the costs and benefits of vertical divestiture.

The second risk is associated with the increased uncertainty regarding the quality of the regulated services provided. Since quality tends to be part of the regulators' mandate, as discussed in Chapter 9, it is worth summarizing the debates.[29] Under normal circumstances, there are many dimensions of quality that are hard to control. This control becomes even harder when the diversification allows the monopolist to offer several qualities of the same good in order to extract more consumer surplus (e.g. Mussa and Rosen 1978; Besanko et al. 1987). The main risk comes from the capacity of the monopolist to manipulate the quality spectrum and to turn it into a screening device enabling discrimination against potential competitors.

The third risk comes from the social and political consequences of the unfairness in the degree of uncertainty to which different consumer groups may be exposed. For instance, in a context in which there is a continuum of consumers and qualities, the richest consumers, i.e. those with the highest valuation for quality, are provided with the socially optimal quality, while the poorest ones buy a suboptimal quality.[30]

The fourth risk is linked to the specific way regulation is designed to cope with the potential conflicts of interest in the management of the common facility. This risk is largely driven by the extent regulation may change costs for all parties involved, notably by changing scale-and-scope economies at the firm and at the sector level.[31] The main drivers of this risk are the approach to pricing the common facility and the rules of access. Even where their design appears to be clear, its enforcement may be partial, and this is likely to introduce a fair degree of uncertainty. The specific risks stem from the effectiveness with which regulation controls the attempts by the integrated provider to distort prices. Without control, the VIM will have an incentive to charge very low prices for the sale of the homogeneous services for which it faces competition, possibly charging below cost. This gap would then be compensated through high infrastructure access prices charged for the common essential facility. This is yet another way in which cross-subsidies can distort a market. They reduce the odds of entry if access prices are too high and hence increase the residual market power of the regulated incumbent VIM.

This access problem covers all situations arising when a regulated firm sells an essential input to rivals with whom it competes in providing a homogeneous service in an unregulated downstream market. If the regulator gets the access price wrong, it allows the VIM to eliminate competition from the downstream market and this in turn leads to higher prices in this downstream market. In practice, this may be the risk that attracts the most attention in policy discussions, and in theory it has long been, and

---

[29] See Reiffen and Ward (2002) for a more detailed summary of risks associated with efforts to expose the VIM to competition in some of its activities.

[30] See Tirole (1988, p. 150) for a more detailed discussion.

[31] Empirically, the natural tool to track the cost consequences of the multiple activities of the regulated firm and of its competitors is the estimation of multi-product cost functions, since their arguments include output and input prices. But when firms produce two or more outputs utilizing common or joint inputs, the allocation of these common or joint costs will be influenced by the quality of the accounting data available and the measures of aggregate output for the firms to be used in these cost functions.

continues to be, the subject of debates linked to the impossibility of being both fair and efficient in a world of imperfect information, as discussed next.

13.11 How to Set the Access Prices and Rules?

Bottlenecks that require the adoption of access prices and rules are quite common in regulated industries. In telecoms, the bottleneck is the local loop; in electricity, it is the transmission grid; in railways, it includes tracks and stations, for instance. These infrastructures all represent high fixed costs, which somehow must be recovered through markups above marginal cost – or through subsidies.

In solving the access problem in any of these settings, the regulator needs to consider the perspectives of the various stakeholders.[32] The monopolist has a strong incentive to actively oppose any attempt to force an access price which erodes the rent it might earn from its vertically integrated activities. If the access price is set too low, it makes it easier for inefficient firms to enter the market. It also reduces the incentive to build and/or maintain the bottleneck and increases the likelihood of non-price-related actions by the incumbent, such as slowing down access to the common facility, to dissuade entrants. Here also, quality is an adjustment variable and this needs to be addressed by the non-price dimensions of the access rules. On the other hand, if the price is set too high, it creates barriers to entry by efficient entrants and reinforces the incumbent in its monopoly position. It also increases the odds of duplication of the bottleneck.

From the viewpoint of the actual or potential competitors, the expectations are simpler. They want access at prices based on the cost of providing the bottleneck input (i.e. either marginal cost or incremental cost, possibly with some markup). For a regulator interested in achieving an efficient allocation of resources and in ensuring entry by newcomers that can further improve efficiency, the key challenge is thus to come up with efficient and fair access prices and access rules. And this is what makes consumers better off as well.

According to Baumol and Sidak (1994), the efficient price for these essential inputs is equal to the marginal cost of producing that input plus the opportunity cost of the sale to the monopolist. This opportunity cost is the necessary markup. Often, the opportunity cost of the sale to the monopolist is approximated by the forgone profit – that is, the retail price less the cost of producing the retail product less the cost of producing/maintaining the essential input. This is known in the literature as the efficient component pricing rule or ECPR. Using the notations of Box 11.3, it can be expressed as follows:

$$a = c_t + (p_2 - c_2 - c_t) \tag{13.14}$$

---

[32] In Chapter 11, Boxes 11.3 and 11.4 present the second-best approach to access pricing.

where a is the access price, c_t is the marginal cost of operating and maintaining the common essential facility, p_2 and c_2 are respectively the price and the marginal cost of delivering the final service by the incumbent, which are not necessarily equal to the price and cost of delivery by a competitor. Then $p_2 - c_2 - c_t$ is the opportunity cost for the incumbent of not delivering the final service. In the case of the telecoms sector, for instance, c_t is the cost of using the wires needed for the interconnection while the opportunity cost is the net loss to the incumbent due to the fact that the phone call can be billed by a competitor rather than by itself (accounting for the fact that it does not have to pay the interconnection charge).

The formula can be simplified and becomes $a = p_2 - c_2$, which is why it is often known as the margin rule. This highlights the fact that only potential competitors that can charge margins at least as high as the margin achieved by the incumbent will be interested in joining the market. This is attractive from a regulatory perspective because it guarantees productive efficiency. It does not put any pressure on the incumbent since the rule also guarantees no loss of revenue and maintains the rent resulting from information asymmetries. In other words, if the regulated firm was imperfectly regulated to begin with, the ECPR will at best maintain the imperfection of retail prices.

As argued by Armstrong (2001), in his survey of the literature, one of the main virtues of the ECPR is its simplicity. Moreover, it is not very demanding in terms of information since it only relies on the incumbent's retail price and its avoidable costs in the retail segment. But he also explains that this rule is only appropriate in a few specific cases. Usually, it will lead to inefficient outcomes when (i) the competitor's product does not substitute the incumbent's one-for-one or (ii) where competitors have some ability to bypass the incumbent's access service. Despite its limitation, the rule is still frequently quoted and considered in regulatory debates, although seldom used in practice in a pure form. But there are alternatives.

A second option is to rely on Ramsey access prices. These are essentially the prices to be paid by entrants that maximize social welfare under the constraint that the provider of the common essential facility can cover its costs. This approach is developed by Laffont and Tirole (1994) and Armstrong et al. (1996). The price for each service (including the access service) should be set as a markup above marginal cost. They should account for the fact that any increasing returns to scale to the use of the common facility should be internalized as well. Finally, the markup should reflect the elasticity of the demand for the service as usual in the Ramsey pricing strategy. For the specific pricing of the common facility, though, the markup should be adjusted to account for the fact that the sales of the access services are, in a sense, a substitute for sales by the incumbent of retail services.

Ultimately, the regulator deals with two prices. The first price is the regulated retail price which follows the usual Ramsey rule we discussed in Chapters 4 and 8 linking the markup to the elasticity of demand faced by the monopolist. The second is the access price linking the markup to the elasticity of demand for the competitive service, corrected for a factor reflecting the degree of substitutability between the services offered by the regulated incumbent and those offered by the entrants. If they are perfect substitutes, the Ramsey–Boiteux optimal access price is equal to the ECPR.[33] Otherwise, it may be larger or smaller depending on the degree of substitutability. The outcome is a lot more efficient than the simple ECPR rule. But it suffers from the fact that it is more information-intensive.

Laffont and Tirole (2001) offered the most recent main alternative, which also happens to be a more general solution, namely, the global price cap. It is designed to regulate jointly the prices of the retail products or services and the access fee to common facilities. Roughly, it consists in fixing a price cap applied to the weighted average prices of the basket of the regulated products. The access charge, a, is thus not individually but jointly capped with the various goods or services supplied by the operator. For example, if the operator of the facility sells two goods 1 and 2 on top of the access, the global price cap consists in fixing p and letting the firm free to choose a, p_1 and p_2 on condition that:

$$w_0 a + w_1 p_1 + w_2 p_2 \leq p \tag{13.15}$$

This would be the formula adopted, for instance, by a transport regulator who wants to control passengers and freight rail services (services 1 and 2 respectively) but also wants to control the access charges to the tracks and train stations which are owned and operated by one of the rail service operators. The regulator allows the firm to set a, p_1 and p_2 freely and focuses on deciding on the respective weights (w_i, with $i = 0, 1, 2$). Quantifying these weights with precision is one of the challenges of the approach. In practice, it would be based on a moving average of the historical shares of sales. But in a dynamic industry, this could distort decisions quite significantly since market structure is supposed to evolve with entry. Discretionary regulatory control of these weights can, however, be useful if there is a risk that the incumbent operating the common facility tries to rely on inflation of the access charge to be able to practise predatory retail prices while still complying with the global cap. An alternative, suggested by Baumol (1997) and endorsed by Laffont and Tirole (2000b), is to set the access charge at the ECPR level to compute the global cap.

From a strict regulator's viewpoint, the approach is particularly interesting for three reasons. First, the regulator does not need to know the demand functions. Second, it limits the scope for the adoption by the incumbent of non-price strategies to restrict or prevent downstream competition, such as delays in interconnection, refusal to unbundle or imposing costly technical requirements.[34] Laffont and Tirole (2000b) point out that this incentive depends on how much more or how much less strict the final product regulation is than the regulation of the access product. When the access regulation is tighter (looser), the incumbent has a strong (weak) incentive to minimize the risks of entry by competitors downstream. The global price cap corrects this weakness tolerated by the Ramsey approach since the incumbent no longer has any incentive to favour one market over the other. Third, they also argue that, if the

---

[33] In terms of Equation (11.5) in Chapter 11, perfect substitutability between the incumbent's and the entrants' products means that $p_e = p_2$ and $\bar{\varepsilon}_e = \bar{\varepsilon}_2$

[34] This is also known as *foreclosure* in competition policy.

regulator manages to smooth entry in the competitive segment of the business, it may make it easier to rely on performance benchmarking.

The translation of these theoretical results into practical guidelines at the sector level has produced an extraordinarily voluminous literature in the telecommunications sector and to a lesser extent on the pricing of transmission in electricity and on the pricing of access to the various transport infrastructures (airport, rail track and ports). This literature is quite technical because this is what the sector specificities demand. But the sector-specific literature is also producing more general insights. For instance, the ladder of investment theory suggested by Cave et al. (2001) and adopted by many European telecoms regulators in the 2000s as part of the implementation of the unbundling of the sector is highlighting additional options and uses of access pricing and rules. Cave (2007) shows how the access costs of entry can be made to evolve as entrants progressively move from users of a common facility to developers of their own facility. Essentially, in some industries, it is possible to design access rules so that entrants go up the ladder that takes them from users of a shared facility to owners of their own facility. Initially the entrant begins with acquiring access at a level which requires little investment on its part; then, as its client basis increases, its investment needs increase and the regulation is designed to push it to make the necessary investment. The process continues as long as the business grows. From a regulatory perspective, the innovation is that the access charges and rules evolve to get the entrant to make the necessary adjustments as its business evolves. The approach is particularly interesting for industries in which new technologies allow a reduction in the market power of an incumbent, but it takes time to develop the alternative.[35] The energy and transport sectors are natural potential users of these progressive approaches. But there are more ways in which access rules and prices need to adjust. This includes the growing need to deal with two-sided markets analysed in Section 13.13.

13.12   How to Identify the Risk of Abuses: The Debate on Margin Squeezes

Although there can clearly be competitive advantages to unbundling a sector horizontally to increase the scope for direct and indirect competition, we have seen that this does not guarantee efficiency since there are many ways in which incumbents can distort entry and prices. In hybrid market structures in which an incumbent VIM competes in some segments of its business with new or smaller players, the risks of abuse take many forms. For instance, an integrated incumbent may try to set the access price to the essential facility higher than the margin between the retail price and the downstream costs of its competitors to squeeze their margin and eventually get them to exit the retail market. This is known as foreclosing the competitors. It is thus useful to track these margins in regulation.

---

[35] See Bourreau et al. (2012, 2014) for more developed discussion of these transitional issues.

The monitoring of the risks of margin squeezes has a long history of controversial debates. Although margin squeeze assessments formally belong to the competition (anti-trust) toolkit, they come in handy quite often in practice for regulators concerned with hard-to-explain profit margins on one or several of the activities operated by a regulated firm. Bouckaert and Verboven (2004) identify three types of margin squeezes according to the prevailing regulatory regime: (i) regulatory price squeezes (if wholesale and retail prices are regulated); (ii) predatory price squeezes (if only wholesale prices are regulated); and (iii) foreclosure (if no prices are regulated).

Whether regulators or competition agencies should intervene when there is evidence of excessive margin squeeze is not a settled matter (e.g. Gaudin and Matzari 2016). The US approach suggests that unless margin squeezes are linked to a refusal to deal or to predatory pricing, it should be dealt with through access pricing and rules controlled by the sector regulators. Europeans are much more aggressive than the US anti-trust authorities in its use. The European regulation prohibits explicitly VIMs to set the access price above their own retail price (ignoring marginal and common costs). It qualifies the assessment of margin squeeze as a stand-alone tool to test abuse of dominance. In other words, the competition agency can focus on the spread between wholesale and retail prices and does not need to focus on the excessiveness of each individual price.

The main payoff of the European approach is that it reduces the risks of foreclosure, one of the three motivation of price squeezes identified by Bouckaert and Verboven (2004). For instance, it essentially helps ensure that an incumbent vertically integrated energy provider deciding to enter the renewal energy market is not tempted to manipulate the margins to minimize the risk of entry of new smaller players and/or to facilitate the exit of existing competitors. This seems to be a reasonable concern in markets in which changes in preferences and technology are stimulating changes in the number and type of players. But the US position hints at the need also to consider the costs of margin squeeze regulation.

Conceptually, the reduction of the risks of foreclosure from the regulation of margin squeezes could be impacting negatively on the consumer surplus and possibly producer surplus if it penalizes competent incumbents trying to diversify. According to Krämer and Schnurr (2018), in a market structure with two competing VIMs and a non-integrated retailer, margin squeeze regulation is seldom beneficial from a consumer welfare perspective, not even if margin squeeze regulation prevents the foreclosure of the non-integrated retailer. For relatively homogenous goods, the regulation may increase total welfare by increasing overall industry profit, but this would be achieved at the expense of a lower consumer surplus. Krämer and Schnurr (2018) also suggest that it increases the VIMs' incentives to tacitly collude with the new entrants in some of the activities for which there are opportunities to compete.

The debate is still ongoing. Both approaches raise potentially problematic issues, as documented by Gaudin and Matzari (2016). The US regulatory approach underestimates the risks of abuses while the European approach overestimates them, each in different types of circumstances. So, the debate is important because it continues to point to the need for alternative forms of regulation when the risks of abusive behaviour by an incumbent VIM can lead regulators to overreact in a context of uncertain demand and supply. Gaudin and Matzari (2016), for instance, suggest an evaluation of margin squeeze only under adjusted predatory pricing standards which include the easily identifiable opportunity cost due to missed upstream sales in a price–cost comparison test and an explicit assessment of an exclusionary strategy. This is another important policy area that goes beyond the scope of this book.

13.13   Access Issues in Two-Sided Markets

The academic and, in many ways, the policy debate on 'essential facilities' has now switched to two-way network interconnection rules and prices. This is largely what the literature on platform or two-sided markets is all about. These are markets where a firm, the platform operator, serves as a 'match-maker' to bring together two or more sides that all benefit from the existence of the platform. These benefits result from the ability of the platform operator to develop networks on both sides of the market and across the two sides. It turns out that many regulated industries and infrastructure are two-sided.

The usual examples of such operators are the GAFA and credit card companies. Their platforms are anchored in specific operating systems, data, networks, infrastructures and relying on networks of people with specific skills and preferences. The characteristics of these technological platforms are relevant to many regulated industries. For instance, airports or ports are increasingly seen as matchmakers between travellers or freight companies on one side, and transport companies on the other. Airport, train station and port operators are increasingly relying on specific physical and organizational technologies as well as diversification of product and services to cater and develop their respective markets. This includes the development of shops, restaurants, office space within, and logistic support around, the core infrastructure business. These are designed not only to develop the size of the business (travellers do have preferences for specific airports in many countries and shipping companies do have the choice of ports). It also impacts the pricing options. Airports negotiate prices with the airlines, and ports with shipping companies, within the limits set by regulators. And these prices depend on the range of services offered to users on both sides of the market (transport providers and transport users). Similar changes are impacting the energy sector in increasingly creative ways, most notably in developing countries. Digital platforms are now being used to develop off-grid energy delivery in regions long ignored by traditional suppliers. Their financing strategy may be simpler but follows the same logic as those followed by more complex platforms and raises many of the same regulatory issues.

To understand how these platforms are likely to become increasingly helpful in developing regulated markets and to see why they are changing the regulation of access in some markets, it is useful to have a more precise sense of their peculiarities. One of the most obvious is that they organize the matching between users and sellers to turn it into networks. One of the keys to the business model adopted by these platform operators is the effort to maximize network sizes. This is part of their attractiveness to both sides of the market. To increase the size of the market, platforms tend to be multi-product firms with evolving product options (although this does not have to be so). This production heterogeneity helps cater better to the differences in demand by each side of the platform. Some of the matching effectiveness is also linked to the extent to which the value of the products or services delivered by the platform to one side of the platform is impacted by the performance of the platform on its other side. There are thus complex externalities to account for to understand the optimal pricing strategy of these platforms.

From a regulatory perspective, all these characteristics are particularly important because the platform owners and operators enjoy strong leverage on both sides of their market. This leverage could be turned into excessive market power without regulatory supervision. First, their leverage allows the operators to be price setters on both sides. Second, they could easily be tempted to develop the network benefits of their activities through tying and compatibility restrictions designed to control entrants. This is one of the dimensions underlying the debates on the desirability of 'network neutrality' which in practice means the ability of the platform operators to discriminate according to uses (Vogelsang 2018).[36]

Despite its complexity, the dimensions to account for in pricing are reasonably predictable. First, the regulator needs to account for the difference in valuation of the same service on the two sides of the market (think of the value of a restaurant in an airport from the viewpoint of the airline and from that of the passenger). Second, it needs to account for the possible impact of these differences in valuation for the two sides of the market. Third, it needs to account for the fact that it may be rational (i.e. optimal from the firm's perspective to attract more customers) to charge a zero or negative price to some users and to rely on cross-subsidies between the two sides of the market to finance both the OPEX and the CAPEX associated with the development of the platform (i.e. the common facility). Pricing strategies may thus appear to be discriminatory or unfair even though, in practice, they may be welfare enhancing as they allow the financing of the development of the common facility. From a regulatory perspective, the key point is that pricing at marginal cost in every market is no longer optimal and pricing above marginal cost should not be considered as an indication of monopoly power. A subtler implication is that many quality dimensions are endogenous as they need to adjust steadily to the demand of the various actors. And since this will influence costs, it should influence prices.

The pricing policy allowed will have an impact on the development of the two sides of the market and their relative evolution. Allowing a low price (maybe a zero or even a negative price) to be charged on one side increases the number of this side's users, which makes the service more attractive for the other side's users who are ready to pay more. To see this point, assume that the marginal cost of the service is c. Then, taking the collateral effect of price changes into account, it is possible to show that the price

---

[36] The growing role of digital platforms in the delivery of services has been subject to intensive policy and political debates. For a reader-friendly overview of the issues see House of Lords (2019).

p_i to charge for the service to side i when p_j is charged to side j follows the adapted Ramsey rule:[37]

$$\frac{p_i - (c - p_j)}{p_i} = \frac{1}{\varepsilon_i} \tag{13.16}$$

Equation (13.16) clearly shows the complementarity of the two sides. The price paid by side j users decreases the cost of providing the service to side i users. It is this complementarity that regulators need to think through carefully when assessing the scope to redesign access prices in two-sided markets in which the financing of the platform needs to be shared between the two sides. And these two sides now cover a much broader set of actors than the traditional producers and users.

13.14   Moving Forward: How to Improve the Tools Available to Regulators

One of the reasons why price effects may be misread is that regulatory designs are too static. In many countries with weak governance structures, there is a clear need to anchor regulations in predictable rules. In contrast, in sectors in which technology and preferences evolve quickly, this rigidity may be counterproductive. As will be discussed in more detail in Chapter 15 on the emerging challenges for regulators, there is a growing sense that institutional mandates may need to accommodate enough regulatory flexibility to adjust to the risks associated with evolving market structures. This includes changes in the level and nature of concentration, in market power and markup or profit levels at the firm or sector level. This may be necessary to improve the signalling value of the many indexes discussed in this chapter.

Similarly, in a dynamic context, the chances that technical advances will cut costs or improve quality are important. The objection here is Schumpeterian. If a large firm – for finance-related reasons or for reasons of economies of scale in the research process – can bring research and development programmes, or simply much-needed investments, to completion more efficiently or more quickly, society must pay the price of potential temporary inefficiencies. This is the same line of reasoning that justifies the patent system: economic progress comes at the cost of temporary monopolistic positions. This last point shows that the analysis embodied in Equation (13.10) has ignored that the price signal can be affected by variables other than concentration. For instance, if demand increases with quality, as seen in Chapter 10, and if a large firm is likely to offer a better quality of service than smaller ones (more frequent flights, for example, or more reliable service provision because of a higher level of investment), a higher price does not necessarily mean a restriction of the quantity sold. Once more, the assumed simple correlation between concentration and prices is violated.

In the short run, within the scope of their mandates, the main focus of regulators confronted with concerns for abuses of market power should be to use the techniques

---

[37] See the pioneer work of Rochet and Tirole (2006). See also Krueger (2009) for a discussion of the role of elasticity.

discussed in this chapter to shift the burden of proof back to the firms representing a risk for social welfare. In this world of information asymmetry, it should contribute to improve welfare and minimize risks. And it should help curb the long-term increasing trends followed by profit rates in the regulated industries as documented by all the major international organizations.

13.15   Summing Up

- The observed evolution of the risks of abuse of market dominance in regulated multi-firm industries suggests that regulation is not adjusting fast enough to changes in market structure.
- The global sustained increase in markups documented by several studies are not the expected outcome from the deregulation and deconcentration waves that started in the 1990s in services traditionally delivered by integrated monopolies.
- Regulation may not have been effective because actual market structures (and information asymmetries) are more dynamic and complex to manage than theory suggests. This difficulty stems, notably, from the fact that changes in technology and preferences often lead to changes in market structures that could not be anticipated when regulation was designed.
- Since changes impact on market structures and market structures can influence market power, it is essential for regulators to be able to conduct regulatory diagnostics to measure the impact of the evolution of regulated markets and firms on the usual variables of interest.
- In practice, regulators focus on prices and profits when assessing the risks of abuse of market power.
- Risk of abuse diagnostics can be conducted:
  - Ex ante to produce forward-looking 'regulatory risk' assessments (e.g. in the context of merger request ex ante assessments).
  - Ex post assessments of market power abuses (e.g. in the context of standard regulatory assessment of observed markup or profit margins).
- Both the empirical and the more conceptual assessments of the tools available to conduct these diagnostics (e.g. C_x, HHI, markup, profit margins, market reference/relevance definition, price signals) tend to be misleading if the market details are underestimated and/or the necessary accounting data are only partially available.
- Despite the main limitations, these tools are quite commonly used in practice because they allow many regulators to shift the burden of proof onto the suspected 'abusers' in the context of regulatory conflicts.
- The regulation of a VIM participating in a competitive market in some of its production activities can lead to multiple benefits and risks.
  - The potential benefits include the efficiency payoffs of the competition effect, the optimization of production cost synergies, including transaction costs, and the incentive to innovate to remain competitive.

- o The potential risks include a higher uncertainty on quality, social and political outcomes and on the design and the enforcement of access rules and prices, including abusive margin squeezes.
- o Whether the access prices should be based on the global price cap or the efficient component pricing rule approach is still up for debate.
- For two-sided markets, the regulator needs to account for the difference in valuation of the same service on the two sides of the market, the interactive impact of the valuation of the two sides and the possible desirability of cross-subsidies to finance the common facility.

14 On the Relevance of Institutional Quality

So far, we have focused on the proper design of regulation, but we have disregarded the role of the institutions in charge of its implementation and the relevance of their quality for the effectiveness of regulation and for the optimal choice of regulation. We have ignored the relevance of the (lack of) skills of the regulators, of their resource limitations, or of the poor credibility of their pricing commitments to regulated companies to get them to make the necessary investments. And we have overlooked the situations in which the credibility of governments to commit to the right levels and types of subsidies is limited by macroeconomic or political circumstances. Finally, we have overlooked how the risk of corruption could be minimized by the specific choice of regulatory rules and the ways in which the mandate to implement them is distributed between public sector actors or between technocrats and elected authorities. These are all institutional dimensions of regulation.

There is significant evidence that institutions are a critical component of effective regulation in practice. Ignoring these institutional dimensions limits the practical usefulness of some of the important insights from theory on how investors, producers, consumers or governments should reach the right consumption, financing and investment levels.[1] For instance, the ability and willingness of authorities to enforce contracts, laws and regulations are recurring themes in international business environment surveys such as the World Economic Forum Competitiveness Report or the World Bank Doing Business indicators.[2] These surveys suggest that with better institutional quality, it is easier to stimulate investment and improve operational performance. Similar surveys consulting consumers, such as Afrobarometer, Latinbarometer or the European Union consumer surveys, provide similar insights.

The importance of differences in institutional characteristics across countries is reflected in the risk premia we discussed in Chapter 7 on the interactions between finance and regulation. But this is not only about financing costs, ignoring the relevance of institutions also has social implications. At the macroeconomic level, according to Djankov et al. (2018), a 10% improvement in the overall World Bank

---

[1] An early analysis of the importance of institutions for the effectiveness of regulation was provided by Laffont and Tirole (1993) and Levy and Spiller (1994). Most of this early research focused on commitment issues and most of the illustrations were for the telecoms sector. Research has since produced many more insights covered in this chapter. For an overview of the evolution of the role of institutions in the design of infrastructure policy, see Estache (2020b).

[2] www.weforum.org/ and www.doingbusiness.org/

Doing Business indicators, used as a proxy for institutional quality, results in a two percentage point reduction in the poverty headcount.

Besides the insights they offer on financing and social costs, investor and consumer surveys on institutional quality are also useful as they show that the same regulatory instruments and institutions can have very different effects in different countries. So why doesn't the same regulatory tool work just as well anywhere on the planet? The short answer is that differences in effectiveness of a specific instrument may simply reveal a mismatch between the instrument choice and the local institutional context. The long answer is subtler, as we will discuss in this chapter. Matching regulatory choices with institutional constraints is necessary and it has many implications that are easy to forget in broader contexts. For instance, this matching should be a concern in the recurring global effort to harmonize rules and processes across countries in the context of trade agreements or in efforts to create regional electricity transmission networks or rail networks. It should also be a concern when deciding how much to decentralize regulation. The costs and benefits of a standardization of regulatory approaches across countries need to be analysed carefully when their institutional context differs too significantly. For instance, Costa Carvalho and Menezes Bezerra Sampaio (2015) blame underperformance in Brazil on regulatory standardization, insufficient implementation capacity and weak commitment to efficiency.

To structure the discussion on the relevance of institutions, the chapter starts with a case study to provide a sense of what institutional weaknesses and their consequences mean in practice. Then it discusses in very broad terms the most common ways in which countries have assigned the responsibility for most regulatory functions around the world. Next, it summarizes the main sources of institutional weaknesses relevant to regulated industries and some of the most common ways of modelling them. This helps in discussing the optimal form of regulation to be adopted by a country or a sector depending on which weakness is most salient. The chapter concludes with a discussion on the central role of institutions in the effort to harmonize regulation across countries.

14.1   What Does Poor Institutional Quality Mean in Practice?

To anchor the theoretical discussions of the chapter, we start with a case study illustrating the concrete consequences of political interference with regulatory processes and institutions. The event takes place in Spain and starts in 2002. Rodrigo Rato, then Economy Minister of a conservative government, was not happy with the electricity prices resulting from the implementation of rather technical regulatory guidelines designed to ensure the financial sustainability of the sector. He considered that the resulting electricity prices were hurting Spain's industrial competitiveness.[3]

---

[3] Rato eventually became head of the International Monetary Fund from 2004 to 2007, before returning to Spain to chair a Spanish bank (Bankia), which later needed to be rescued by taxpayers. In October 2018, he was sent to jail after a long trial for falsifying information to mislead investors during his tenure as

As a result, he decided to get rid of the inconvenient price adjustment rules and, in the process, de facto took over control of decisions, side-lining regulatory authorities. Rato could overrule the regulatory agency because their autonomy and independence were not guaranteed by the legal system. He then used this leverage to impose a 2% cap on annual electricity price increases, well below the increases in production costs.

Although the cap was supposed to be temporary, subsequent governments, including the socialist government that took over from the conservative administration, did not dare to take on the political costs of allowing prices to catch up (i.e. the political colour does not seem to matter to the strength of the lack of commitment). Nor did they try to change the tariff structures or subsidies to help the poorest because they did not want to discuss the likely fiscal effects of the changes. The Spanish politicians, like most politicians, know that consumers have a strong preference for low electricity prices and that few consumers realize that the costs not recovered through prices end up being recovered through tax-financed subsidies. Since tax financing is less transparent, neither progressive nor conservative political parties were keen on returning to the pricing rules set by regulatory authorities. They seemed to prefer to keep prices as low as possible while subsidizing as needed.

What the successive administrations ignored is that the regulators had designed a price system that was accounting for the need to provide incentives for operators to invest and consumers to adjust their demand to the capacity available. The price freeze broke the balance by allowing demand to increase significantly, while reducing the ability of electricity companies to pay for the investments needed to meet it. Their interference with the regulatory process led to an unsustainable situation.

Until 2005, the financing gap had to be compensated (partially) by debt-financed subsidies. The long-term safeguard offered by an autonomous competent regulatory capacity had been overruled by politicians concerned with a succession of short-term political risks. It is only when these subsidies became fiscally too costly as a result of a lasting increase in the price of oil that regulators were brought back into the picture to come up with a solution. The fiscal damage and the inefficiencies resulting from the weak regulatory institutions were predictable in the young Spanish democracy. But it had been ignored in the design of regulation and in the long-term financing strategy of the sector. With the benefit of hindsight, we know now that the price-setting mechanism should have been designed to account more carefully for these institutional weaknesses. The fiscal burden would have been easier to manage and the inefficiencies minimized. And this is indeed the direction that Spain eventually took. But it was much too late to avoid long-lasting fiscal consequences.

This example illustrates the impact of limited commitment to rule-based regulation and the subsequent political interference with the regulatory process, a very common

Bankia chair. Part of the justification was the excessively loose application of rules in the use of public and private resources by the bank management. Misunderstanding what rules were meant to achieve was part of the argument used by the defence, providing another illustration of the difficulty of relying on rules mismatched with local culture.

challenge in practice.[4] Many countries, developed and developing, have demonstrated similar biases and continue to do so, and this is why the case study is so representative and instructive.[5] But the weakness of institutions comes in many other forms and intensities. The rest of the chapter shows how a fair diagnostic of institutional weaknesses can be helpful in picking the regulatory design minimizing the risks of their undesirable efficiency, equity and fiscal consequences.

14.2   Who Is in Charge of Regulation around the World?

Until the late twentieth century, in most countries, regulation was the responsibility of a Ministry, typically a sectoral Ministry such as telecommunications, transport, public works or energy. All over the world, governments were favouring an implementation of regulation by (central, subnational or local) civil servants subject to direct political control. Very few countries, inspired by the model adopted in the nineteenth century in the United States, had opted for relying on separate regulatory agencies (SRAs). Until the late 1990s, regulation at the Ministry level was the common approach across sectors, and the SRA model was the exception.

The United Kingdom's decision in the 1980s to adopt a model closer to the US model of regulatory institutions triggered a switch in paradigm. The SRA became the dominant model in most sectors after the United Kingdom decided to create sector-specific separate regulators at the same time it was privatizing its major infrastructures.[6] The move from regulation at the Ministry level to separate regulatory agencies essentially shifted the authority to regulate from the direct control of elected officials (the politicians) to appointed technocrats. The latter were expected to be insulated from electoral pressure thanks to the promise of increased autonomy in the way they could decide and implement regulatory interventions.

This corresponded to the first steps of a shift in the role of government in the late 1980s to early 1990s towards what Majone (1994) called the 'regulatory State'.[7] In this new world, rulemaking would become the dominant means of achieving desirable social, economic and environmental outcomes. Table 14.1 shows that it would also seem natural to rely on specialized agencies to design, implement and enforce the new rules. This was rightly perceived by many observers as a massive move away from the interventionist state put in place at the end of World War II to meet the reconstruction needs. Anchored in a Keynesian demand management view of the world, these needs

---

[4] Conceptually, it suggests that politicians, due to re-election concerns, have much larger discount rates (which means much stronger preference in the present) than those used in the evaluation of investments undertaken in regulated industries.

[5] For instance, in Argentina, after a major economic crisis in 2001, the prices of regulated industries were politically controlled in a similar way. This prompted a large number of lawsuits by the private utilities and transport companies arguing that these freezes boiled down to non-compliance with regulatory commitments included in the long-term contractual commitments made by the previous administrations.

[6] For more details, see, for instance, Majone (1994, 1997).

[7] For a political interpretation of the evolution, see Jordana et al. (2011).

Table 14.1 Share of countries with a specific regulator (percentage total in 2016)

	Developed countries	Developing countries	Total
Electricity (%)	74	68	69
(sample size)	(53)	(124)	(177)
Telecoms (%)	100	100	100
(sample size)	(37)	(158)	(195)
Water (%)	46	45	45
(sample size)	(25)	(45)	(70)

Source: Bertomeu-Sanchez and Estache (2017).

justified public ownership of self-regulated or politically regulated utilities (as well as other major industries).

The adoption of the new model has not been as systematic as hinted by Majone's early vision, however. Table 14.1 shows that agency-based regulation has indeed now become the norm in the telecoms sector. And over two-thirds of the countries have created a separate electricity regulator (in a sample of 177 countries). But it has not been as popular for the water and sanitation sector as only 45% of the countries have a separate water regulator (in a sample of 80 countries). While there is no comparable data for transport, the anecdotal evidence suggests that SRAs are much less common in that sector than in the others. Outside of the Anglo-Saxon world, transport is still largely regulated by units anchored in Ministries or public enterprises.

A third option is much less common. It is the decision to rely on a competition agency to sort out conflicts between stakeholders and abuses of market power. In some cases, this competition agency could be assisted by agencies expected to deal with specific market failures such as environmental damage or health risks. This reflects the view that total liberalization anchored in some form of competition is better than any form of regulation. For a service to be provided by a monopoly, competition *in* the market is replaced by competition *for* the market. The right to control a service is awarded through an auction. The idea is that if markets function properly, they will deliver the desired social welfare. The best example of this approach is New Zealand. Other examples include Barbados and Estonia. Note that regulatory agencies and government Ministries also rely on competition for the market to award contracts to service providers they will regulate without interference from a competition agency.

The agency-based approach has until recently been the most popular approach, but it covers a wide range of institutions. These vary in terms of predictable dimensions such as their degree of financial autonomy, in addition to their actual degree of independence from political interference. If institutions are meant to be independent from the risks of political intervention, they need regulatory tools which can be used to ensure the transparency of decisions and hence easy accountability. For new institutions, the mandate should include the development of the tools needed to implement and enforce the rules agreed upon, preferably inspired by the theory we discussed in earlier chapters.

In practice, this is often not the case. But historically, the mainstream view was that separation was desirable and this reform was very effectively 'marketed' by international organizations and many academics.[8] Many countries decided to create these separate agencies, as illustrated by Table 14.1. In most countries it was seen as a major signal to potential investors that their interests would be subject to more transparent and independent treatment than if it were handled within a Ministry, where political interference was supposed to be inevitable. It was expected to cut the return premia linked to regulatory risk claimed by the investors as part of the cost of capital. In Europe, the widespread adoption of the approach in telecoms and energy was, to some extent at least, more ideological. In many ways, it reflected the political goal of European countries to build an integrated market in the EU. This implied breaking down the national monopolies and a rejection of the paternalistic centralized control by a public administration of those sectors that had characterized their management and their regulation since the end of World War II.

The institutional change was not only expected to reduce political interference. It was also expected to limit the excesses of lobbying efforts by 'greedy operators' or at least to increase the transparency of these efforts. Independent regulators were expected to ensure a balance in the treatment of producers and investors on the one hand and of consumers and taxpayers on the other. In many cases, the mandate of the regulators includes an explicit concern for the interests of employees, suppliers and smaller competitors as well as taxpayers when subsidies are given to the service providers.

This does not mean that the regulators are expected to micro-manage the businesses. They are expected to do their best to close the information asymmetries discussed in Chapters 2–6. Their staff is supposed to do so accounting for the interests of all stakeholders and to explain this as part of their decisions announced through administrative texts or decrees. They are expected to deliver public services in sufficient quantity and at an affordable price, without sacrificing the quality and reliability of the service provided and without imposing an unsustainable burden on taxpayers. How well their decisions are justified technically and legally indicate the extent to which regulation reflects technical evaluations accounting for the short- and long-run, rather than political decisions to address concerns relevant to upcoming elections.

The experience suggests that competition agencies, when properly financed and independent, may be less likely to be subject to political interference and to the conflicts of interest linked to opportunities for revolving doors between regulatory positions and jobs in the regulated firms.[9] By contrast, regulations based in a Ministry

---

[8] The role of supranational organizations in the restructuring of institutions is quite a complex topic. The heterogeneity in the way these organizations support the implementation of the reforms they try to stimulate, and sometimes impose, should be a matter of concern since it can help or hurt depending on the quality of the support offered by their staff or the consultants they usually recruit to help in the implementation of the reforms. In developing countries, the role of foreign experts and NGOs should not be underestimated in institutional assessments, even if it is not discussed in this book.

[9] Despite the strong political support of the French and the German governments in favour of the merger between Siemens and Alstom, presented as a future EU champion, the decision by the European Commission to prohibit the merger, on the grounds that it would harm competition in markets for railway

are the most likely to be driven by political concerns inconsistent with the long-term goals assigned to regulation. But there is no zero-risk associated with separate agencies, in particular if they can be overruled, as illustrated by the Spanish case study discussed earlier in the chapter. If the politicians can and choose to interfere with otherwise reasonable goals and rules, there is not much those responsible for regulation can do to deliver on their mandate. In regulation, as in many other fields, the informal authority is often more important and relevant than the formal one. Informal interference with processes is one of the most common institutional weaknesses documented in the context of regulation.

14.3 Which Weaknesses Constrain Institutional Effectiveness?

Corruption and political interference are probably two of the main forms of institutional weakness reducing the effectiveness of regulatory decisions that many people will think of first. They come in various sizes and shapes in the context of regulated industries, including the following: (i) imposing a politician's relative in a top management position; (ii) imposing business partners or relatives to head a regulatory agency in violation of official recruitment policies – as happens in developed as well as developing economies; (iii) tolerance for contributions in cash or in kind to a political party to influence decisions; or (iv) extraction of bribes through threats to expropriate or to introduce new taxes on regulated firms. From a conceptual viewpoint, the scope for corruption is, at least partially, the outcome of the adoption of the wrong processes and rules to implement regulation.

In a democratic political system in which the judicial branch is expected to ensure the proper and effective behaviour of the regulators, it is common to multiply the number of processes and rules to minimize the risks of interference of specific private interests. For any country, it is essential to assess the payoffs to well-intended regulatory complexity aimed at achieving a balanced protection of all stakeholders with their compliance and enforcement costs. Complexity can be counterproductive if not enforceable. In developing countries, where regulatory rules are often included in contracts signed by an operator and the state, it is not uncommon to see the contracts renegotiated because the original authors of the contracts had overestimated the ability of the regulators to enforce excessively ambitious commitments on all parts. In other contexts, the regulators have been excluded from key regulatory decisions despite their ability to have an independent informed view on these decisions. In Belgium, for instance, the energy regulator has regularly been overruled by the executive branch (i.e. the Energy Minister) on standard regulatory matters. This breaks the credibility of decisions made by regulators and of rules supposed to increase the transparency and reliability of decision-making processes. Rules and regulatory diagnostics appear to be politically renegotiable. Recent examples include the quantitative and analytical

signalling systems and high-speed trains, illustrate this independence (https://ec.europa.eu/commission/presscorner/detail/en/IP_19_881).

assessment of the cost and pricing implications of changes in the Belgian energy transition policies which have resulted in a significant concern for power outages during the peaks of cold weather in the 2018–19 winter period.

To structure the discussion of the multiple sources of institutional weaknesses discussed in the literature, we classify them into four broad categories: limited capacity; limited commitment; limited accountability; and limited fiscal efficiency.[10] Their main characteristics can be summarized as follows:

- *Limited capacity.* Regulators can be short of human and/or financial resources. Human resources gaps in quality and in quantity can be an issue when many contracts and rules need to be monitored and enforced simultaneously or when regulations are quite complex. And a lack of financial resources can prevent regulators from recruiting suitably skilled staff or consultants to compensate for skills gaps. This can be a particularly strong challenge in countries with a scarcity of highly educated professionals trained in designing and enforcing regulation, or in a sector or country with an underdeveloped auditing system since data limitations tend to undermine the assessment of many regulatory decisions. But it can also be an issue when funding is deliberately withheld by the government as a means of undermining the regulators' ability to run their diagnostics. This can force regulatory agencies to adopt inadequate salary scales to free resources just to be able to pay for the day-to-day operational needs. This can reduce the ability of regulators to recruit the right people for the key management positions. The skilled regulatory specialists may be more tempted by consulting or management positions in regulated firms if the salary differences are significant enough. At the other extreme, excessively generous salary scales may increase the temptation for political appointments of regulatory staff designed to reward political favours more than skills, in addition to the risks of eroding the resources available for the more operational needs.[11] Capacity can thus often be a matter of finding the right balance in the allocation of the available resources to get the right management skills and operational effectiveness.
- *Limited accountability.* Limited accountability is linked to the tolerance for: (i) a misuse of information available; (ii) efforts to hide information to facilitate private agreements between public sector agents or politicians and specific interest groups, including the service provider; and (iii) unclear assignment of authority across public sector authorities, across government levels in decentralized countries, or across agencies within the same government level when regulatory mandates are shared. Limited accountability is what eases corruption and collusion between the official authorities and various interest groups, including regulated firms. It also explains why incompetent regulators can continue to operate despite evidence of their weakness. Overall, lack of accountability makes it easier for regulators to carry

---

[10] This is the categorization suggested by Estache and Wren-Lewis (2009).

[11] Operational needs cover dimensions as basic as the number of vehicles available to conduct fieldwork, the ability to buy databases to be able to benchmark performance or the cost of training and upgrading the staff skills.

out their own objectives rather than the social objectives they have been entrusted to design and enforce. Limited accountability also makes it easier for regulators, civil servants and politicians to minimize the efforts they make to deliver on their commitments and reduces the odds of seeing them penalized for their failure to deliver on their mandate. This impacts negatively on social welfare because it decreases the likelihood of the social goals being realized and/or tends to increase the costs of the efforts needed to realize them.

- *Limited commitment.* Investment in utilities is particularly vulnerable to public authorities' lack of commitment because their business relies on long-lived and non-transferable investment. Furthermore, if governments cannot commit to enforce contracts, then many of the gains that could be reaped when the investment is initially assessed could be lost in future renegotiations. The evidence suggests that rules, regulations, contracts and sometimes laws do not have the same degree of underlying commitment across countries, at least in infrastructure activities. The difficulty is best illustrated by the prevalence of contract renegotiation mentioned earlier. Guasch et al. (2014) show that in some sectors, notably transport and water, renegotiation is the norm rather than the exception, and often at the request of governments trying to change promises made by earlier administrations. Fear of future renegotiation is a serious impediment to investment financed from private sources. It increases the cost of capital and hence makes the participation constraints more binding. The poor credibility of commitments can be particularly damaging when there is great uncertainty about cost, demand or macroeconomic stability. More recently, Weisman (2019) showed how the optimal design of regulation has to be sensitive to the lack of commitment resulting from the ex post strategic behaviour of regulators. He finds that this strategic behaviour explains the empirical evidence on the efficiency gains from price-cap regulation are often not as clear as suggested by theory.[12]

- *Limited fiscal capacity.* The final source of institutional weakness concerns fiscal institutions. In many contexts, when the ability of consumers to pay for services is limited, subsidies may be needed. If the government is unable to collect adequate revenue to allow direct subsidies, alternatives must be explored. Cross-subsidies are a common option. But when this is limited as well, access or service quality may be less than desired or promised by the authorities. Fiscal inefficiencies impact the speed at which investment can be financed.

Classifying the main institutional issues into these four categories allows use of some relatively standard theoretical models to anticipate the consequences of each of these failures. These models can help assess the extent to which any weakness lowers welfare for the country. They are particularly useful when used to predict the consequences on the key dimensions of interest in any sector diagnostic, i.e. the quantity of service delivered (in terms of both volume and coverage), its quality (which can be either insufficient or excessive), its cost (which can be influenced by the quantity and

---

[12] Weisman (2019) suggests that committing to sharing earnings in addition to capping prices may help offset the risks associated with the ex post strategic behaviour of regulators.

quality choices) and its price (which is related to costs but may also be linked to the specific regulatory regime adopted).

14.4   An Intuitive Discussion of the Modelling of Institutional Weaknesses in Regulation

Before analysing more precisely how any of these institutional weaknesses impact on regulatory effectiveness and how regulatory choices should be influenced by them, it is useful to return to the common basic model of regulation we discussed in Chapter 5. Small adaptations of the model have helped researchers show how welfare changes with the various types of weaknesses. This section focuses on an intuitive introduction to these efforts without going through all the mathematical derivations.[13] We simply present the main results of this literature within our basic model.

The key insight of these models is that they recognize that the regulator and the government are two separate entities, in contrast to the assumption of a single entity with both policy and regulatory functions built into the basic model discussed earlier. In models documenting institutional weaknesses, the regulator is responsible for implementing regulation and the government takes care of policy and regulatory design. It is common for academics to present this as a principal–agent relationship in which the government is the principal and the regulator its agent.[14]

As discussed in detail in Laffont and Martimort (2002), when a principal (i.e. the government) delegates responsibility to an agent (i.e. the regulator), the quality of the information available to the principal is likely to decline, for various reasons. The objectives of the agent and principal may not be perfectly aligned. The specific details of the implicit or explicit regulatory agreements between an operator and a government may become fuzzy. The de facto enforcer (i.e. the regulator) has its own objective function and may control private information. There is not much the government can do to perfectly control regulatory actions in this case. Incentives are much harder to align when the control of information is decentralized.

The challenge is thus to see how the interactions between the principal and the agent influence the effectiveness of the implementation of the regulatory mandate assigned to the agent. Unfortunately, the basic traditional modelling of regulatory choices does not distinguish between governments and regulators and hence needs to be adapted to assess the impact of an increase in the number of public sector actors on the optimal design of regulation.[15]

The first thing to assess is the ability of the public sector to close the information gap with the regulated firm in the interest of users and taxpayers. In most countries, the

---

[13] The interested reader should go back to the original development in Estache and Wren-Lewis (2009).

[14] Note that the analysis that follows does not give a picture of the situation presented at the beginning of the chapter where the regulation agency is installed to prevent short-sighted and egoistic politicians from disregarding welfare maximization. In the following, the government is a welfare-maximizer, and the regulation agency has some private agenda that must be curtailed.

[15] See Laffont and Tirole (1993) or Armstrong and Sappington (2007) for detailed expositions of these models.

collection of information on the regulated firm is assigned to the regulator – for example, through audits or performance benchmarking, which is relatively easy to model. The level and quality of the information collected can be seen as a signal needed to assess the firm's real technological and institutional constraints. The regulator knows the signal will be imperfect as the firm is unlikely to reveal all the necessary information. With some probability, ζ, the signal is enough for the regulator to discover the firm's actual costs, and with the complementary probability, $1 - \zeta$, the regulator receives no information. That is, in this extension of the base model, regulator work is to collect information on $C(q)$ to implement the rules delineated by the government. ζ is the probability that the regulator learns $C(q)$.

The second dimension to account for is the determinant of the regulator's decision on how much of the information collected to share with the government (and implicitly the users and taxpayers). It may share all of it. Or it may have an incentive to hide some or all of it from the government if it has some vested interest to do so, e.g. if obtaining revenue from bribes is a possibility. This creates a new type of information rent controlled by the regulator. Models accounting for these new sources of informational rents resulting from the non-benevolence of the regulator reflect the fact that the regulator could be tempted to report that the signal provides no information on the nature of the firm, even if this were not the case. In other words, to fully understand how regulation could be influenced by an institutional weakness, here non-benevolence, we need to account for the fact that useful information on the regulated firm can be hidden by the regulatory agency from the government. The incentive to hide is linked to the size of the information rent. And this is something well internalized by the regulated firm and drives its efforts to try to lobby or capture the regulator. Ignoring the regulator's incentive to hide or misreport key information to favour a firm will lead to an underestimation of the size of the information rents and hence mislead the design of the optimal level and type of regulation. In practice, governments are usually aware of the possibility that the regulator may be controlling key information and that this can blur the estimation of the size of the information rent. The reaction of the government to this risk also has to be accounted for when assessing a regulatory framework. It might reflect the fact that a government cannot focus only on costs, quality, quantity and prices in defining the mandate assigned to the regulator. It also needs to find an instrument to get the regulator to stick to its mandate.

To close the loop, the modelling needs to recognize that the design of this new instrument must account for the leverage the regulated firm may have on the regulator's decisions. The firm can corrupt the information process by designing a mechanism to share the rent extracted from the government with the regulator. This imposes a cost on users resulting from the higher price the regulated firm will want to collect for its services to finance its ability to influence the regulator, which can be done in a few predictable ways.[16] In most cases, the economic models of corruption in regulation recognize that bribes are the easiest way to distort regulators' decisions illegally. The firm might offer a bribe, or the promise of a job, in exchange for favourable decisions,

---

[16] This is not a recent observation. See Agrell and Gautier (2012), Stigler (1971), Peltzman (1976) and Dal Bó (2006) for an overview of the early literature, as well as Estache (2020b) for a recent update.

which in the context of the model means hiding information that would result in low rents for the firm. The models generally also recognize that there are transactions costs linked to corruption and hence to bribes. Typically, if the regulator, who is self-interested, accepts a bribe it is discounted at $k \leq 1$. Indeed, taking bribes is illegal and immoral. It is risky as it can lead to prosecution and jail time, even the death penalty in some countries. As a result, the regulator prefers to make an income honestly rather than through bribes. The discount rate $k \in [0, 1]$ reflects how easy it is to capture the regulator. When $k = 0$ the regulator is perfectly honest and cannot be corrupted, when $k = 1$, the regulator does not make any distinction between the public legal wage and the bribes from the private sector. The regulator is totally corrupt.

Part of the strategy to be adopted by the government to cut the risks of non-benevolence by the regulator is to increase these transactions costs. This is most effective when the regulatory design accounts for the fact that bribes are not always in cash. For instance, the regulator may be promised a lucrative job in the industry in exchange for favourable decisions. Therefore, a vast literature urges closing what are known as 'revolving doors', including by restricting post-government employment opportunities for regulators.[17] The more effective the government is in increasing the transaction costs between the operator and the regulator (e.g. at decreasing k), the higher the bribe the regulated firm must pay to secure favourable decisions from the regulator. The higher the transaction costs, the lower is the incentive to cheat, for any level of bribe given by the firm, and so the cheaper it is to prevent capture and corruption.

Indeed, one way of modelling the need for laws and regulations to account for the risk of these illegal transactions is to link a regulator's pay to the effectiveness with which it reports the information collected and analysed, that is, to introduce incentive pay (reward for good behaviour). The weaker is the benevolence of the regulator (i.e. the larger is k), and the higher the information rent, the harder it is for the government to fight regulatory capture. To alleviate this problem, the government can try to increase illegal transaction costs and to decrease the informational rent that can be secured by the regulated firms. Indeed, if the information rent is high enough, the regulated firm will be able to offer the regulator more than the government.

This serves as a reminder that the enforcement of anti-corruption laws has a budgetary cost and that any such cost raises its own share of problems from a welfare perspective. Whether the payment is made from government revenues or from user fees levied on the final service to consumers, it adds a distortion to the behaviour of users or taxpayers. Most models assume that this enforcement is tax-financed. Raising taxes imposes a deadweight loss on taxpayers, which is measured by λ. So, each dollar or euro paid with public funds to subsidize the operator or to incentivize the regulator to keep their hands clean, costs taxpayers $1 + \lambda$, as explained in Chapter 4.

---

[17] For a useful overview of evidence in the US context, see Law and Long (2011) and for an example of conceptual modelling, see Salant (1995).

The challenge is thus for the government to find a way to ensure a strong enough incentive to increase benevolence. A common way of ensuring that the right signals are being sent at the lowest possible social cost comes from the design of penalties on the regulator and on the regulated firm (punishment for bad behaviour). The optimal size of the penalty should be linked to the size of the potential bribe a regulator may expect to collect. If the risks of being caught and the penalty are low, one can expect some of the regulated firms to be tempted to cheat.

Ultimately, this discussion shows that to properly model a weak regulatory capacity one needs to account for: (i) the probability that the regulator is likely to provide the right information to the government; (ii) the probability that the regulated firm is actually low cost, since the social payoff to effective monitoring increases with the likelihood that the firm is efficient and (iii) the level and design of the bonuses and fines imposed on the regulator to fight corruption, as well as the fine imposed on the operator in case of corruption. Accounting for all these dimensions in the optimization problem typically yields a complex, non-linear formula. But its interpretation is generally not only quite intuitive, given what we have already discussed on the impact of information asymmetries in policy design, but also quite concrete from a policy perspective.

In most of these models, the optimization tends to show that the government will have to live with a less than efficient outcome at least for a while (i.e. that the firm's costs will be higher than they would be if all information were transparent and all institutions were benevolent and competent). This will last the time it takes for the regulator to document actual costs. What's new is that the outcome will also depend on how far the regulator is willing to go to mispresent reality. In other words, the government should be concerned about the risk associated with the need to minimize non-benevolence. Any rent the low-cost firm receives thanks to the non-benevolence of the regulator is costly to society, since it is paid for through higher, distortive financing options. Minimizing that rent should thus be on the government's agenda.[18] This means distorting the production of the high-cost firm more than would be done if the regulators were benevolent, as shown in more detail in the next section.

Often the best that can be done is to make the most of the information collected to reduce the risk of getting the allowed markup wrong. And this is where the theoretical exercise is so useful. It offers an opportunity to inventory the main incentive issues that are likely to appear, the expected direction and intensity of the associated distortions, and possible tools to mitigate them, including new tools that may be able to get around the data requirements identified so far. For each possible and credible information set collected from the regulated firm, it should be able to get a sense of the upper and lower bounds of the marginal costs, prices and transfers required. Consequently, it should be able to use this information set to assess which type of regulation is less likely to be influenced by specific forms of institutional weaknesses.

---

[18] Note that this rent is equivalent to the rent that arises when the regulator is incompetent rather than corrupt.

14.5   What Does Theory Teach on Institutional Weaknesses in Regulation?

According to the survey conducted by Estache and Wren-Lewis (2009), there are a few predictable insights produced by theory on each type of regulatory weakness listed earlier in the chapter and on the simplest way of modelling them in any context.

Limited regulatory capacity. If we measure regulatory capacity by the ability of a regulator to collect the right information, an improvement in regulatory capacity can be simulated through a higher value of the probability ζ that the regulator is correctly informed. All models tend to suggest that social welfare is increasing in this probability, provided the regulator is honest. In other words, society is better off with a benevolent, better-informed regulator, and reciprocally all countries underestimating the importance of solid and verifiable information in the regulation game tend to be worse off.

The social welfare payoff to more competent or enabled regulators stems from the fact that they are more likely to observe the firm's underlying cost. This increases the expected welfare in two ways, provided they disclose their information honestly. First, welfare is higher from observing the cost because the firm, whatever its value, receives no information rent while it undertakes the efficient amount of effort. This is the result we discussed in the context of the full-information case. Second, even when the cost is not perfectly observed, the government can impose a regulatory contract minimizing distortions for the high-cost type, which sets an upper limit to any margin for a low-cost firm to pretend to be high-cost. For instance, in the Laffont–Tirole case studied in Chapter 5 the effort required from the high-cost producer increases with ζ the probability that the regulator is correctly informed about the firm's cost, while the low-cost firm's effort remains unchanged (no distortion at the top result). That is, with a better-informed regulator, Equation (5.14) becomes:

$$\Psi'\left(e_{\zeta}^{h}\right) = q^{h} - \left(1 - \zeta\frac{\lambda}{1+\lambda}\right)H \tag{14.1}$$

where H is the same function as in Equation (5.14) and $\left(1 - \zeta\frac{\lambda}{1+\lambda}\right)$ is a new term reflecting the regulatory enhancement capacity. We deduce that since $\left(1 - \zeta\frac{\lambda}{1+\lambda}\right) \leq 1$, the solution in effort Equation (14.1) is higher than the solution in Equation (5.14): $e_{\zeta}^{h} \geq e^{h}$. Moreover, e_{ζ}^{h} is increasing in ζ. In other words, as the regulator is able to close the informational gap with probability ζ, it reduces the cost of the extra rent that may go to a low-cost type (i.e. it gets it less often) and therefore the need to make the high-cost contract less appealing by distorting it.

If the payoff is so simple, why are there so many regulators underperforming in their monitoring role? In practice, regulatory agencies are frequently underfunded, and this has several predictable consequences. For instance, insufficient budgets can prevent regulators from relying on suitably skilled staff or monitoring tools or it can slow and limit the number of audits they can conduct. In many countries, an under-developed auditing system and non-specialized judiciary can further limit implementation. Usually, these limitations are the outcome of constraints on a regulator's ability to self-finance. These constraints may be legal when the regulator is not allowed to collect a fee from users or producers. It can also be the result of a shortage of government revenue when the regulatory function is financed through public funds. Sometimes, also, it can reflect a deliberate decision by the government to undermine the agency for strategic reasons, including the desire to engage in corrupt practices without the risk of independent regulatory audits.

The outcome of a poor regulatory capacity as captured by a low ζ is thus welfare-reducing for society for two reasons. First, the regulator has to allow a higher information rent to the firm since it is less able to close the information asymmetry through more cost-effective tools due to a lack of resources. Second, the risk and the costs of corruption are likely to be higher since the monitoring is harder to implement. And this risk is compounded by the possibility that accountability of the public sector agents and the politicians is limited.

Another dimension of regulatory capacity is the ability to design and enforce the regulation mechanism. As for the design, it necessitates specialists in several disciplines, including engineers, economists, lawyers and accountants, with a good knowledge of the sectoral characteristics of the regulated industry. Enforcement powers depend on the legal framework sustaining the agency. The framework can be specific to each sector or common to all but, in most cases, it is quite complex to organize and coordinate as the number of agencies tends to be quite significant. For instance, in France, a 2017 organic law defines the statutes and powers of twenty-six independent administrative authorities and independent public authorities, covering all economic sectors. Some of them (e.g. energy, financial markets, trains) have a committee in charge of dispute settlement and sanctions.

Limited accountability. In the simplest models, limited accountability is modelled in two ways. The first is to assume that better accountability comes down to a reduction in the ease with which the firm can bribe the regulator (i.e. a decrease in the capture rate k). In the simple setting delineated above, introducing corruption implies that Equation (14.1) becomes:

$$\Psi'\left(e_{\zeta k}^h\right) = q^h - \left(1 - \zeta(1 - k)\frac{\lambda}{1 + \lambda}\right)H \qquad (14.2)$$

When the regulator is incorruptible so that $k = 0$, we are back to Equation (14.1). But when k increases, the regulator becomes easier to corrupt. It is costlier to use the regulator's information as the government has to beat the bribers through incentive pay (i.e. it has to give bonuses to the regulator when they report that the firm is low cost). The bonuses increase with the informational rent of the regulated firm, which is positively correlated with the production of the high-cost firm. The government starts to decrease production and effort levels below the optimal level to decrease the rents, and therefore the potential bribes. In the limit when $k = 1$, the regulator is so corrupt as to be useless. The government prefers to entirely bypass the information of the regulator by choosing to implement the solutions we saw in Chapter 5, irrespective of what the regulator learns. This sheds some light on why a rigid set of rules exists in the public procurement office and in regulation. Ruling by the book, with very little freedom for interpretation, or autonomy, is justified when corruption is a serious concern.

To get a full grasp of the payoffs to better accountability modelled this way, it is also necessary to model penalties punishing corrupting operators. They lead to welfare increases in most models for two reasons. First, if they are high enough and the odds of being enforced not too low, it will discourage the operator from trying to bribe the authorities. This has a positive secondary effect on public finances since it implies that the government can also give a smaller transfer to the regulators when they report the truth. Second, an increase in the cost of bribing reduces the incentive of the firm to inflate the information rent. Whether low or high cost, it is more willing to exert effort to reduce its costs, which is likely to lead to a decrease in prices.

A second modelling approach to limited accountability is the possibility that the regulator or government may assign a weight $1 + \gamma \geq 1$ to the producer surplus in the objective function to favour it. This implies that the objective function of regulation defined in Equation (4.7) becomes:

$$W = S(q) + \lambda p(q)q - (1 + \lambda)C(q) - (\lambda - \gamma)\pi \qquad (14.3)$$

where the new parameter $\gamma \geq 0$ measures the degree of capture of public decisions by the industry. If γ decreases, for instance, as a result of the exclusion of a provider too close to the authorities, the government's accountability to users is increased. When $\gamma = 0$, we are back to the basic objective function in equation (4.7) with a benevolent regulator/government. When γ increases, the solution is distorted to favour the firm in the form of higher level of production and higher rents. For instance, when $\gamma = \lambda$, the regulator chooses to implement the full information in Equation (4.24), with the full information quantities solution of Equation (4.23) in the Laffont–Tirole model and of Equation (4.15) in the Baron–Myerson model, which are excessive compared to the optimal solutions under asymmetric information derived in Chapter 5.

More recently, economic models have started to document the impact of unclear allocation of mandates across government levels as a way of creating accountability issues.[19] In practice, the responsibility for some key regulatory decisions can be shared by national and subnational authorities or across various subnational government levels. With uncertain commitment by each of the involved authorities to respect weakly enforceable joint or interrelated contractual obligations, shared mandates can lead to a moral hazard issue. This is well illustrated by Estache et al. (2016), which conducts an assessment of the impact of the shared responsibility for water pollution control in the state of Sao Paulo (Brazil). They show that enforcement of commitments only worked reasonably well when there was political alignment between the various government levels sharing the mandate for sanitation (i.e. when they all belonged to the same party or the same coalition). Joint mandates can reduce

---

[19] Joanis (2014) was one of the first to point to this dimension in the economic literature. But political scientists and public administration specialists have long been arguing that alignment between mandates impacts the provision of adequate local public goods in decentralized economies (e.g. Ostrom et al. 1978 and Weingast 2014).

accountability when the responsibility for failure is shared by distinct/opposed entities. They can play blame games which allow each party to save face.

Limited commitment. In situations in which the regulator cannot credibly commit for the long term, the literature has demonstrated conceptually and empirically the presence of a ratchet effect in the response of regulated firms to this source of uncertainty.[20] The lack of commitment often gets materialized in the form of frequent adjustments made to the design of regulation in response to changes in the general environment or in the observed behaviour by the regulated firms. In principle, in a context of information asymmetry, this is good news since it means that the regulator is able to recapture some of the informational rent controlled by the regulated company. The likely reaction by the regulated firms is a potential source of concern. Indeed, the more the regulator learns and internalizes the new information, the less likely the regulated firms are to make an effort to perform in the interest of users and taxpayers. So the incentive is biased towards looking bad to ensure that the future allowed revenues will continue to be higher than they should be.

To measure the specific importance of commitment and of this ratchet effect, it is useful to consider models accounting explicitly for investment. As mentioned earlier, given that investment decisions are made to cater to future demand, they are influenced by the credibility of promises made by officials to the investors that they will be able to recover their short-term disbursements in the future.

The relevance of commitment to investment decisions can be modelled in many ways. For example, suppose that, rather than the cost being given exogenously, the firm can influence its value by undertaking investment before it is revealed. This investment increases the probability that the firm will be a low-cost type. If the regulator is able to commit to reimbursing a chosen level of investment, the firm will have an incentive to invest according to the potential surplus from additional investment to be achieved by all stakeholders. This, itself, depends on the technological capacity of the regulated firm. If the regulator cannot commit to the firm at the investment stage, then the firm will only consider its private benefits of investing. This will lead to hold-ups and lower investments ex ante.

Lack of commitment damages welfare because the firm will underinvest. Outputs and quality will be lower than they should be, and prices or subsidies required are likely to be higher than needed to meet the usual regulatory goals. In sum, improving commitment increases the odds of getting the firm to account for both current and future users. This is one of the main recurring insights from the investment climate surveys typically run by international agencies and a growing number of private consulting firms.[21] Investments do not take place when authorities are unable to

---

[20] We introduced the general relevance of this ratchet effect in Chapter 5.

[21] Investment climate surveys are questionnaires sent to investors to seek their views on what slows investment and business in a specific country and in specific sectors. They are designed to identify policy and institutional reforms needed to make countries and/or sectors more attractive to local and foreign investors, as well as to identify options to improve productivity.

commit not to renegotiate the agreements reached at the start of their contracts with the regulator.

Limited fiscal capacity. Fiscal weaknesses arise for two reasons. The first is linked to the budgetary constraints which limit the ability of a government to subsidize a sector. This is the case when regulation is assigned to an independent authority with low fiscal power. It is a common concern around the world, especially since the financial crisis of 2008. It is particularly constraining when poverty levels are high and the users' ability to pay for their utilities services is limited. The second way in which the fiscal capacity can be a concern is when the tax system in place is associated with high degrees of distortions in the behaviour of economic agents. In the model from Chapter 4, these sources of limited fiscal capacity are captured by the 'cost of public funds', λ. A greater value of λ implies a lower after-tax consumer surplus since the regulated price is higher and the quantity produced is lower. The distortion becomes worse with asymmetric information, as explained in Chapter 5.

The consumer surplus is impacted by the distortions resulting from the need to rely on tax-financed subsidies in (at least) one more way. To mitigate the cost of public transfers to the regulated firm, for a given service level, an increase of the regulated price is needed. But this only leads to a more efficient outcome if the distortions in the service consumption due to a higher price are lower than those linked to tax financing. This is an empirical matter to be quantified. Auriol and Picard (2009) show that if the consumer surplus is monotonic in λ, the total social surplus, which includes the surplus of the taxpayers, is U-shaped in λ. It initially decreases when λ increases because for the low value of λ the regulator assigns a high weight to the consumer surplus compared to subsidies/taxes. When λ increases, public transfers become costlier, and the regulator starts to distort prices to the detriment of consumers. This initially decreases the social welfare (when the weight put on consumers is still high enough). For large values of λ the regulator focuses on transfers (the objective function is tilted towards the taxpayers). Eventually, as λ becomes very large, the regulator puts no weight on the consumer surplus at all, but simply maximizes the firm's rent and the revenue collected from it, especially if the firm is public, so that the regulated price converges to the laissez-faire monopoly price. In this case, the surplus, assimilated to the firm's rent, increases linearly with λ.

What this analysis shows is that fiscal constraints impact deeply on regulation, not only in the way public utilities and infrastructures are financed, but also in the type of objective it pursues. A government with abundant revenues will ask regulators to focus on the consumer surplus, while a government financially constrained will focus on firms' rents and will therefore behave in a predatory fashion. The recent failed attempt by the Lebanese government to tax the free application WhatsApp is an example of an extreme policy triggered by one of the world's highest debt burdens.[22] A tax reform that reduces the constraints and distortions linked to tax financing thus reduces the need to rely on regulated price increases to finance a service and it helps refocus regulation towards the consumers.

14.6   Institutions Can Be Weak: So What?

In practice, working out the detailed consequences of these various institutional weaknesses through simple models shows that they can impact quite significantly on the effectiveness of price and product regulations. Designing regulations to address the various types of inefficiencies and inequities that can arise in the delivery of public services as a result of the imperfection of markets cannot ignore the context and institutions. When poorly designed, or captured, well-intended regulatory policies may hurt costs, prices or quality. Institutional weaknesses may also affect the degree of competition between firms. For example, they may end up erecting barriers to entry, or place restrictions on product choices. Voluntarily or not, regulators often grant protection to special interest groups, and consequently limit the firms' incentives to be efficient and innovative. Excessively strict regulation may have reduced the dynamism in some industries of continental Europe and reduced their productivity, as suggested by Arnold et al. (2011).

Table 14.2 summarizes the likely impact of institutional weaknesses as identified in the academic literature. This characterization largely focuses on very basic correlations between these weaknesses identified and the outcomes. The correlation is often undetermined as it depends on the specific intensity of the variables discussed earlier. Causality also often generally runs both ways. For instance, high costs may limit the capacity to do more with the limited fiscal resources allocated to the sector. Moreover, interactions between the various types of weaknesses are relevant. It is indeed often useful to account for the fact that a lack of accountability can be a good predictor of a lack of commitment. The lack of accountability makes it easier to fail to deliver deals with desirable investors rather than captured or capturing investors on average. Yet attracting the right type of investors and lenders is really what matters to the ability of the country to attract ethical actors also consistent with the long-term interests of the country rather than those more interested in narrow but very profitable short-term

Table 14.2 How should institutional weaknesses matter to key performance indicators?

Institutional weakness	Costs	Prices	Quantity
Technical or human	?	–	?/–
Commitment	+	+	?/–
Accountability	+	?	–
Fiscal	+	?/+	?/–

Source: Adaptation and update of Estache and Wren-Lewis (2009).
Note: '+' ('–') means that the variable is higher (lower) than it would be if there was no institutional weakness. '?' means that the effect is uncertain.

cream-skimming deals. What this means is that sometimes no deal with a private provider is better than a bad deal.

Table 14.2 does not do full justice to the many insights provided by the observation of the real-world evidence on institutional weaknesses. One of the important but easily underestimated insights is that in most countries or contexts, there are multiple simultaneous reasons why regulatory institutions may be weak. This implies that, in practice, the policy analysts need to identify the dominant source of institutional weakness and use this in the optimal regulatory design. For instance, regulatory capacity limitations argue for higher-powered incentive regulation (i.e. price or revenue caps) since cap-based regulation is, at least initially, less demanding in terms of information requirements. Similarly, price cap tends to do better when the sector is facing a fiscal constraint as caps can be used to put pressure on costs. At the other extreme, commitment or credibility problems argue for low-powered incentive regulation (i.e. cost plus/rate of return) because they demand detailed cost audits, which reduce the risks of cost manipulation and hence increase the accountability of all stakeholders.

The recognition of the multiple dimensionalities of institutional weaknesses and of the importance of matching regulatory design to the dominant source of weakness has other implications which are not always recognized in academia and in policy circles. First, it suggests that standardized approaches adopted because they make things simpler and because there is evidence that they may have worked well elsewhere can be mistaken. The widespread adoption of price caps in the 1990s which ended up being transformed into hybrid forms of regulation in the 2000s following regulatory restructuring or tariff revision provides strong evidence on the fact that one size does not fit all in regulation. Second, the idea that regulatory designs should be aimed at the dominant form of institutional weakness is usually realistic but may sometimes be politically sensitive. This essential role of politics in the specific design of regulation is largely ignored in the modern theory of regulation but may be one of the main challenges for practitioners when they are trying to address regulatory failures.[23]

When institutional weaknesses imply systemic uncertainty in the choice of options, the best is often the enemy of the good. Smaller, simpler scale approaches tend to work better when institutions are weak or in transition, as they are easier to implement and to monitor locally, for instance. And this is also the case in the context of international efforts to coordinate national regulatory approaches to ease international trade in services (see Box 14.1). In practice, the challenge is to match solutions to the institutional constraints rather than to assume away these constraints. But this requires an explicit effort to conduct a serious institutional diagnostic and to internalize its consequences. In some cases, it may also require a willingness to tolerate harsher

---

[23] There is a growing interest among researchers in detailing the relevance of the institutional approaches to regulation and of political preferences. This literature gained a high profile with Besley and Coate (2003) and has since started to produce new insights on the drivers of the design of regulation (e.g. Guerriero 2013).

> **Box 14.1** On the Costs and Benefits of Supranational Regulation of International Market Integration
>
> The idea that the optimal choice of regulatory tools for countries characterized by overlapping and interconnected networks should be influenced by the heterogeneity of the institutional characteristics of the countries involved is not new. Nor is the idea that this heterogeneity should influence the optimal degree of regulatory harmonization. The analytical discussions started with Combes et al. (1997) when they made a robust case for subsidies to a given industry to be differentiated internationally. Calzolari (2004) further strengthened the case for a differentiated but coordinated approach to regulation in the context of multinational companies.
>
> More recently, the harmonization assessment has started to build in the fact that some public service providers are international multinationals able to rely on creative cost allocation techniques across countries in which they operate. These are important insights for the design of regulation. In some ways, the theoretical results produced by Biancini (2011) show that the optimal design of coordination should be influenced by the differences in the cost of public funds across countries. She shows that for the international market integration supported by regulation coordinated across national regulators to be effective: (i) the fiscal costs of regulation have to be lower than the efficiency gains achieved through integration and the reliance on some form of supranational regulation; and (ii) cost correlations across countries and ex ante technological risks have to be accounted for properly. Auriol and Biancini (2015) show that these risks are quite concrete and could lead to underinvestment in interconnection even in a world of benevolent national regulators with national monopolists. Auriol et al. (2018) show that whether supranational regulation is a better option than the coordination of national regulators to stimulate national market integration depends on the risk of seeing supranational regulation being impacted by national institutional weaknesses. The success of efforts to adopt a common regulation to multiple countries characterized by diverse institutional contexts depends on the effectiveness with which the losers of market integration are compensated when national regulation is unlikely to do so.

regulatory decisions as a signal to those with a tendency to abuse institutional weaknesses (e.g. Estache and Foucart 2019).

14.7 What Is the Empirical Evidence on the Impact of Institutional Weaknesses?

Before reviewing the evidence on the impact of institutional weaknesses, it may be useful to get a sense of the international heterogeneity of institutional quality. This information can be seen in international benchmarking exercises. None will provide the necessary details on each of the main sources of weaknesses. But they are usually

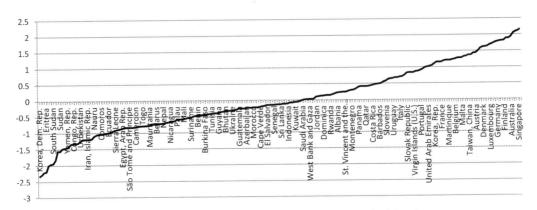

Source: The World Bank (http://info.worldbank.org/governance/wgi/#home)

Figure 14.1 Ranking of countries according to their regulatory quality (2017)
(−2.5 = lowest, 2.5 = highest)
Source: The World Bank (http://info.worldbank.org/governance/wgi/#home).

reliable enough to get a sense of the extent to which regulatory quality is a problem in any given country. The World Bank, for instance, produces, as part of its overall governance indicators, a measure of regulatory quality per country. It ranges from −2.5 (for poor quality) to +2.5 (for great quality). The data for 2017 is reported in Figure 14.1. It shows that the dispersion in regulatory quality is quite large. And, as expected, it is highly correlated with the income per capita of the countries.

One of the purposes of the institutional reforms aiming at improving the quality of regulation is to reduce the spread observed in Figure 14.1. And since the 1990s, the creation of separate regulatory agencies (SRA) may have been the institutional change most commonly adopted to this end. For instance, in the electricity sector, it has been by far the most popular reform, adopted by 70% of the developing countries reviewed in Foster and Rana (2020). It is also one of the reforms most regularly assessed by academics and policymakers, jointly with the adoption of a specific form of price regulation on the performance of a regulated sector (i.e. price cap versus rate of return versus hybrid). Often this has been done in the context of the comparison of the performance of regulated public and private service providers. Often also, as necessary, it has accounted for the unbundling of the production process (e.g. is the electricity provider vertically integrated or is it separated into generation, transmission and distribution? Is the operation of rail tracks and rolling stock separated or not?). Other relevant dimensions are sometimes analysed for countries or sectors for which the data is available. For instance, the extent to which regulatory mandates are shared within government across agencies or across governments and the way they are shared can influence the regulatory effectiveness (e.g. Mookherjee 2015; Estache et al. 2016). When conducting institutional diagnostics, all of these dimensions are important, but their detailed discussion would go beyond the scope of this book. We focus here on the (ir)relevance of the creation of regulatory agencies based on a very simple modelling approach since the importance of agencies is usually measured by the statistical significance of a binary variable (agency yes/no). This is quite imperfect, since there is a wide range of possibilities in terms of the degree of financial, legal and political autonomy that an agency can enjoy, and it has been raised by many authors (e.g. Eberhard 2007; Trillas and Montoya 2011; Vagliasindi 2012).

To get a precise sense of the relevance of regulatory institutions, it is essential to keep in mind their history, the context in which they were adopted and the timing of their adoption. The debate on the desirability of independent regulatory agencies started with the debate on privatization. In Europe, the creation of these agencies was supported by the European Commission legislation aimed at liberalizing markets in network industries. In many ways, this followed the model adopted by England under the Margaret Thatcher administration during the 1980s. In developing countries, the model was largely stimulated during the 1990s by the structural reforms favoured by international organizations. The latter were trying to replicate the British model with the hope of increasing efficiency and private financing. But one of the most frequently recurring justifications was the need to reduce the impact of corruption on decisions taken in regulated industries. This was supposed to be a signal to potential investors that developing and emerging economies were able to improve the quality of their regulation.

Following the initial enthusiasm, the model started being questioned in developing economies in the mid-2000s, even though it has continued to be popular in developed economies. The initial signs that the creation of these agencies was not a safe bet for the effectiveness of regulation emerged from the explosion in the volume of contract renegotiations. According to Guasch et al. (2014), 68% of the large-scale contracts signed with regulated private firms in the 1990s and 2000s were renegotiated within a year. The breakdown is 87% for water contracts, 78% for transport contracts and 41% for electricity contracts. And this took place despite the presence of separate regulatory agencies.

In most cases, the renegotiation was the result of an excessive margin for political interference with regulatory processes. The literature has thus focused on the main drivers of this scope for interference. The first is the inability of a regulatory agency to rely on its own sources of funding (i.e. regulatory fees). Cambini et al. (2016) show that, in Europe, increasing the financial autonomy of regulators increased the odds of a good performance of the sector for a given level of accountability. And increasing accountability improved performance further and minimized the risks of capture of the generated efficiency gains. This was achieved by making regulators accountable to the parliament rather than to the ministries to minimize the risk of interference by politicians or capture by operators. But this accountability was not adopted by many countries. According to Fernández-i-Marín et al. (2015), parliaments have a stronger monitoring role in Europe, in particular in the United Kingdom and Nordic countries, and only a very modest role in developing and emerging countries. This helps explain why the initial goals were not achieved.

But there are other reasons why regulatory agencies have failed to deliver on their mandate. In developing countries, Estache (2020b) shows that one of these reasons is the technical and human capital limitations resulting from the limited funding of these agencies, since these impede the adoption of basic processes in the interactions between regulated firms and regulators. For instance, few countries have adopted cost-accounting rules precise enough to allow regulators to monitor the fairness of cost allocation implemented by regulated companies. Focusing on Brazil, Ferraz and Finan (2008, 2011) show that providing transparent information on costs or on the uses of subsidies improved outcomes. Without data on cost or quality, it is no surprise that the information asymmetries gap is hard to close, whether the regulator is in a developed or a developing country. Initial enthusiasm on the potential of the reforms was slow to fade because details on this weakness were slow to emerge. The data gaps often got closed, at least partially, in conflict situations, when precise audits were implemented. As suggested by Ferraz and Finan (2011) for Brazil, increasing the odds of audits reduced the rents captured by local officials. But once more, only a minority of countries around the world conduct these detailed audits.

Despite these limitations, there are many instances where allowing at least some form of autonomy to regulatory agencies has helped. But this is hard to pick up in many of the studies because they tend to be multi-sectoral or because they extrapolate too much from the experience of the telecoms and energy sector, which have indeed been quite successful, thanks to important innovations. The evidence of the effectiveness of the creation of a separate regulatory agency, SRA, in the water and transport sector is less clear. In these sectors, regulation often has not had the desired investment and operational effects predicted by theory, at least in terms of financing and efficiency.

The European and developing countries' experiences illustrate these insights more generally. In Europe, Cambini and Rondi (2010) rely on a panel of eighty publicly traded EU utilities (including twelve water utilities) over the 1994–2004 period to assess the impact of the creation of SRAs on the investment rate of these utilities. They validate the main theoretical insights related to the creation of SRA, although they find sectoral differences. The energy and telecommunications sectors appear to benefit much more from the presence of SRAs than the water sector, even though a positive impact is also observed for the water sector (public and private). Overall, they conclude that having a SRA may not deliver the expected impacts equally in all sectors because some are more prone to political interference than others. For developing countries, Andrés et al. (2013), Bel et al. (2010), Carvalho et al. (2012), Estache and Wren-Lewis (2010) and Gassner and Pushak (2014) suggest that, in general, SRA does not assure a major improvement in investment, access rates or efficiency. It often improves technical dimensions of service quality however, although not in Sub-Saharan Africa, according to Mande Buafua (2015). This lack of effect in SSA is presumably the result of an unclear mandate and constraints on regulatory monitoring and enforcement capacity. Mande Buafua (2015) for SSA and Guasch et al. (2006), or Martimort and Straub (2009) for Latin America and the Caribbean, suggest that the underperformance of SRA as compared to the promises of theory is largely due to a lack of independence and of competence of the agencies.

However, they also show that the type of contract signed with the operators may matter more than the basic regulation theory has traditionally been focusing on.[24]

The discussion so far points to a multiplicity of results to consider in the evaluation of the design of regulatory agency, of their tools and of their mandate. But there is a simpler takeaway. Indeed, the main insight emerging from the collective efforts of this research is that a good matching of institutional capacity to the type of arrangement makes it easier for a regulatory agency to be effective in designing and delivering on its mandate. Unless the institutional quality discussed earlier is accounted for in the choice of regulation, cross-country surveys will continue to show heterogeneous regulatory outcomes.

In policy circles and in the media, the main source of weakness discussed is corruption. The analysis of the impact of SRAs on the level of corruption in regulated industries yields similar conclusions to those just discussed. There are, however, substantial differences between the electricity and water sectors, further validating the message that one size does not fit all in institutional design. For the Sub-Saharan African electricity sector, Iman et al. (2018) find that the creation of independent regulators combined with privatization efforts has managed to offset the negative effects of corruption on the technical efficiency of the sector and on the efforts to increase access to electricity. Similarly, for the Latin American electricity sector, Wren-Lewis (2015) also finds that independent agencies help reduce the impact of corruption. For the water sector, however, the successes have not been as great, as shown by Bertomeu-Sanchez et al (2018) .

14.8 What Does It All Mean in Practice?

Overall, the econometric studies published in economic journals of the impact of SRAs on the regulatory performance suggest that the outcome depends on relatively easily identifiable institutional factors as well as on the performance indicators of interest. But the practice is often more complex.[25] Political scientists have been keen to point out that many of the economic studies ignore the relevance of key detail. In particular, they focus on the factors determining formal independence (see, for instance, Christensen and Lægrid, 2002; van Kersbergen and van Waarden, 2004; Gilardi, 2007; Gilardi and Magetti, 2011). They all emphasize that the details of the overall institutional configuration matters and that SRAs do not function in a vacuum. For instance, the degree of independence of the agency is important. Independence depends, among other dimensions, on the way regulators are nominated (e.g. they are appointed rather than elected officials), how they are audited (e.g. by parliament, by

---

[24] Athias and Wicht (2014) show, for instance, that French-speaking Switzerland border municipalities are 50% less likely to contract with the private sector for the delivery of public services than their adjacent German-speaking municipalities.

[25] For instance, many regulatory bodies in developing countries work in a risky environment (high crime rate, civil conflict, terrorism, etc.). Although this is essential to account for, it has not yet been studied analytically.

Ministries or by independent auditors) and how they are financed (e.g. tax-financed or financed through regulatory fees paid by users). Differences in any of these dimensions across agencies may explain why the outcomes expected from the creation of an agency may differ across countries or sectors.

The research by political scientists on these details has important policy implications, which could be summarized as follows. The existence of an agency is not a necessary condition for performance improvements. The odds of effectiveness are linked to the degree of independence and competence. But this in turn depends on the credibility and legitimacy of regulation, which depends on the tools used, as well as on the transparency and predictability of the decisions. When institutions are weak, hybrid models that combine traditional visions with more modern approaches can be better to match the local country context, including in terms of governance and capacity. In other words, improvements in regulated sectors can be achieved without creating a new agency, in particular when the business to supervise is specific or narrow enough.

There are several ways to achieve accountable and competent regulation without specific SRAs. In some cases, small units within the Ministries or public enterprises mandated to manage the assets of the State have done just as well as any agency would have done, since the main content of the job is to supervise compliance with a fairly detailed contract. This is illustrated by the regulation of railways in West Africa. The public owners of a rail line joining two countries (the Société Ivoirienne de Patrimoine Ferroviaire, SIPF, in Côte d'Ivoire, and the Société de Gestion du Patrimoine Ferroviaire du Burkina, SOPAFER B, in Burkina Faso) oversee jointly the private rail operators serving the two countries. This allows for more effective coordination of international operations as well as a more effective mutual control of delivery on commitments made to ensure the effectiveness of the service. In practice, this has translated into faster processing of contract preparation and delivery of investment and rehabilitation needs despite the difficulties usually associated with projects involving several countries. In other cases, as suggested by Rouse (2013), the local institutional weaknesses have been compensated by the nomination of a panel of external foreign experts conducting scheduled regulatory audits or settling disputes. In addition to these options typically managed by the public administration, Rouse (2013) suggests that there are other options, which give a voice to consumers, organized or not. Public hearings or consultations are now part of the institutional toolkit of many regulators.

A third option, when concerns for independence are serious, is to rely on NGOs to have a significant monitoring and voice role. The main challenge is to define the limit between a monitoring/watchdog role and the advocacy/activist role that some of these organizations also aim at. Aldashev et al. (2015) argue that not-for-profit organizations can have a role as watchdogs and potential enforcers. As suggested by Baron and Diermeier (2005), NGOs can be quite effective at conducting boycotts or reputation-damaging activism. A downside is that they have their own agenda, which is beyond the control of the other stakeholders.

The implicit, quite rational philosophy in these alternative solutions is to outsource key institutional responsibilities around clear contractual, and 'monitorable', commitments. Such non-traditional solutions can help minimize the negative conse-quences associated with excessive discretionary powers in environments in which traditional arrangements are unreliable or questioned (e.g. Guasch et al. 2014). These approaches are also consistent with Moszoro and Spiller's (2016) concerns that insti-tutional designs should minimize the transaction costs associated with regulation. Ultimately, the most accountable system may also be the most pragmatic solution when countries are trying to resolve their complex institutional environments, reflect-ing weaknesses which often go well beyond the specific sectors.

14.9   Summing Up

- Institutional weaknesses can be classified into four main groups:
  - Limited human and/or financial capacity.
  - Limited accountability.
  - Limited commitment.
  - Limited fiscal capacity.
- Unless regulatory design is matched with the initial institutional capacity, it is unlikely to be effective.
- Ignoring institutional limitations increases the odds of inefficiency (excess demand and underinvestment), undesirable social side effects (increased prices and poverty) and excessive fiscal burden (unsustainable subsidies levels).
- To address some of the limitations, most countries have created specialized separate regulatory agencies (SRAs).
- The SRA model has been less popular for water and transport regulation, which continues to be largely managed by units within ministries or agencies directly controlled by the ministries, than for telecoms and electricity.
- Countries with overlapping and interconnected network facilities are increasingly considering moving part of the regulatory responsibilities to supranational agencies.
- In contrast to the theoretical predictions, the empirical evidence on the effectiveness of the creation of separate regulatory agencies in terms of efficiency, equity, financial/fiscal viability and accountability is mixed.
- The empirical research is also providing increasingly robust evidence that:
  - There is no single perfect institutional solution that applies to all sectors and all countries.
  - The existence of an agency is neither a necessary nor a sufficient condition for performance improvements of a public utility.
  - Hybrid models that combine traditional visions with more modern approaches, which include a role for civil society and for expert panels, can be better to match the local country context, including in terms of governance and capacity.
  - The credibility and legitimacy of regulation depends on the tools and the transparency of their use and of the ensuing decisions.

15 Emerging Regulatory Challenges

Since Chapter 1 included a brief historical perspective on the evolution of the theory and practice of regulation, it seems appropriate to conclude the book with a glimpse at the future of regulation. This chapter focuses on the likely changes in the design, implementation and enforcement of regulation over the next few years. These are the consequences of the evolution of the political, technological and institutional context in which regulation takes place. Unless regulators adapt to this evolution, regulation will become less effective, and probably often less fair, than it already is in many ways, as we saw in Chapter 9.

The most obvious political change with an impact on regulation is the growing and sustained pressure from citizens to address environmental concerns. In many countries, energy policies, and hence regulation, have already modified the mandate of energy regulators. For instance, they have influenced regulated prices through the incentive to use renewables or the design of energy-saving certificates.[1] The long-term environmental agenda is also progressively impacting on the regulation of water and transport industries in equivalent ways. These are important changes, with efficiency, equity and fiscal implications, but most can be dealt with through the tools we have discussed in the book so far.

There are other changes, however, that will impact on regulation, its tools, its financing and its institutions in ways we are still assessing. We will focus on four that we see as the most likely significant changes. Each of them is making its way to the regulatory reform agenda of countries and international organizational working on regulation such as the EU, the OECD, the World Bank or the Inter-American Development Bank. These are:

(1) The growing margin to rely on behavioural economics to improve the effectiveness and targeting of regulation;

---

[1] The agenda faced by regulatory entities to accommodate the renewable sources in the energy mix is very busy. For example, considering that electricity storage is a transmission activity rather than a generation activity is not neutral in terms of regulation (see, for instance, Federal Energy Regulatory Commission 2020). The fact that economic analysis has not been able to provide robust guidance in the evaluation of the challenges raised by the intermittency of renewables is an example of a situation discussed in Chapter 1 in which economic analysis can lag behind practice. As of 2020, it only considers separate solutions such as the flexibility of thermal plants (Crampes and Renault 2019), demand response (Joskow and Wolfram 2012; Crampes and Léautier 2015), and electricity storage (Crampes and Trochet 2019; Junge et al. 2021).

(2) The increasingly pressing role of non-traditional financial actors to get regulators to internalize more systematically financial markets' concerns in the design of regulation in exchange for their willingness to help close the financing gap of many regulated industries;

(3) The exploding dependence on 'big data', algorithms and other data-intensive management and evaluation techniques of both regulated firms and regulators; and

(4) The likely evolution of the institutional environment of regulation to internalize the impact of the data revolution on the distribution of regulatory mandates across countries, across sectors within countries and across agencies.

These changes will lead to new market structures, new market players and new behaviours. They will also result in new technological and financing options for regulated industries and new monitoring and enforcement options for regulators. Some will not always be apparent to the majority of the consumers since many public services will still be delivered in regulated monopolistic or oligopolistic market structures. But they will make a significant difference, as they already have in some sectors where 'smart', i.e. data-intensive, tools are already changing the way business is being done, and hence regulated. Being able to pay our utilities bills from our phone, getting access to banking services through phone or electricity companies, mobilizing private cars as a substitute for public transportation through dedicated applications on our phones would have seemed unrealistic at the end of the twentieth century. They are now common practice around the globe. They will improve the delivery of regulated public services but how much and how fairly so will largely depend on the way regulation, its tools and its institutions are able to adjust to the technological changes.

To be able to measure the impacts over time of these changes, we need baseline measures. These should cover indicators of the main dimensions that regulators aim at improving, such as access, affordability and financing capacity. This is needed to identify failures and successes in the ways regulation is adjusting to the evolving environment in a transparent way. This benchmark should also help define reasonable expectations with respect to the improvement to be delivered by the regulation of the future from the four dimensions of interest. Each are then discussed in some detail.

15.1 What Should the Future of Regulation Deliver?

Taking stock of what has been achieved so far on key regulatory policy objectives may be the simplest, and yet most useful, baseline to start tracking the impact of the changes to come.[2] But this stocktaking of achievements is also important because it puts in evidence the gaps and the failures of the regulatory approaches adopted since the 1990s. In many countries, regions and cities, access, affordability, service quality

---

[2] Estache and Serebrisky (2020) adapt this diagnostic approach to the Latin American context.

and regulatory governance have not improved as fast as needed and as promised when the reforms of the 1990s were launched. This suggests that many of the policy insights discussed in the book have not been internalized globally. Fixing the errors of the past must be an essential component of the expected outcomes of the next generation of regulatory designs. From an ethical perspective, defining a clear baseline to track down social outcomes is seen by many as essential to maximize the odds of policy sustainability. Access and affordability are the most commonly available indicators. They provide a good illustration of the quantitative measures that will have to be tracked to assess the impact of the evolution of regulation.

15.1.1　Benchmarking Access

Access to basic services is generally not an issue in developed economies, but it is the most obvious undelivered promise in developing countries. Remember some of the basic statistics on the sector discussed in Chapter 1 showing that in many parts of the world, people still do not have access to electricity or water services. To make this as concrete as possible, consider the case of Tanzania. It is one of the countries most generously supported by multilateral and bilateral aid donors since the end of the colonies in Africa. Yet, as of 2018, 67% of the population was without access to electricity (83% in rural areas) and many businesses were still rationed in quantity and in quality of electricity. As of 2019, the estimation was that it will take 10–15 years to close the access gap if current investment levels continue to prevail. This is evidence of a major policy and regulatory failure.[3]

Tanzania is not alone in that unhappy situation in the developing world. According to the World Economic Forum (WEF), the worldwide investment needed to close the global gaps in infrastructure and meet the increasing demand is expected to be US$97 trillion by 2040 (about US$3.7 trillion per year). Yet under a business-as-usual scenario the actual investments will only add up to US$79 trillion. Almost three-quarters of this global infrastructure investment gap can be attributed to roads and electricity, two sectors with long asset lives and potentially severe hold-up problems. In most countries, the underinvestment can be blamed on various sources of poor regulatory governance leading to poor technological choices and financing strategies.

15.1.2　Benchmarking Affordability

With respect to affordability, the problem is not just in developing countries, as discussed in Chapter 9. Energy and transport poverty are major issues in many developed economies as well. And in this case also, the problem can be blamed, at least partially, on regulatory weaknesses. The number of task forces in Europe mandated to think through the way regulation should deal with the growing evidence of energy or transport poverty is a good indication that something is not working

---

[3] For more details, see Estache (2019).

properly in regulation. The correlation between poor regulation and affordability problems has been documented for Latin America (De Halleux et al. 2019) and Sub-Saharan Africa (Estache and Wodon 2014). Similar conclusions have been reached for European countries (e.g. Deller and Waddams 2015). How well the regulation of the future will correct these concerns will be one of the indicators of its effectiveness and desirability.

15.1.3   Benchmarking Other Performance Indicators

Many other gaps could be identified in a snapshot of the current performance of the regulated industries. Each should be accounted for in the definition of baselines to be used in the measurement of the effectiveness of regulation. Ideally, these snapshots should be done in some detail at the sector and the country level. But this is not yet a standard mandate assigned to regulatory agencies or to their watchdogs in civil society within countries. International organizations compensate somewhat for this gap as they produce international performance benchmarks. These help get a first order of magnitude of the size and nature of the challenges encountered in almost all countries in the world. Table 15.1 provides an overview of some of the main sources of information on these benchmarks per sector.[4] In some ways, these organizations function as watchdogs and their monitoring should help define the agenda to be assigned to the next generation of regulators and track their progress.

There is thus enough data to set up a baseline anchoring the monitoring of desirable improvements in the delivery of regulated public services along multiple dimensions such as efficiency, equity, financial and governance quality. Not all dimensions are tracked. For instance, there are more data on technical quality than on service quality. Yet quality improvements are part of the hopes associated with the regulation of the future, in addition to improved access and affordability.

We have already established that regulation has not always been able to deliver as expected. This implies that the regulation of the future has some catching up to do on a number of sensitive dimensions. In many ways, regulation will have to change. The degree of change will depend on the extent to which the adjustments to regulation make the most of the opportunities offered by new tools (e.g. behavioural economics), new financing options and new technological solutions offered by the data revolution. Sharing the benefits of the changes fairly across stakeholders will require rethinking the institutions of regulation. Countries need to internalize the consequences and the risks associated with each of these innovations in the interests of *all*, rather than in the interests of a few of these stakeholders. The rest of the chapter discusses the potential role of each of these innovations.

---

[4] One of the commonest questions audiences ask us when we talk about performance is: 'Where can we get data on these dimensions?' Table 15.1 is a minimalist response to that question. There are, of course, more sources, many of them commercial. But this is a good place to start.

Table 15.1 Where to find baseline performance cross-country comparisons for common public services

Sector	Source	Website
		Utilities
Electricity	World Bank	World: https://data.worldbank.org/topic/energy-and-mining Developing countries: http://documents.worldbank.org/curated/en/517781558037625254/pdf/Tracking-SDG-7-The-Energy-Progress-Report-2019.pdf http://rise.esmap.org/
Telecoms	International Telecommunications Union	World: www.itu.int/pub/D-IND-WTID.OL
Water	World Health Organization	World: https://washdata.org/
		Transport (world data)
Air	Airport Council International	https://store.aci.aero/product/2018-airport-key-performance-indicators/
Ports	UNCTAD	www.sft-framework.org/tools/key-performance-indicators
Rail	International Union of Railways	https://uic.org/statistics
Roads	World Road Association International Road Federation	https://rno-its.piarc.org/en/rno-basics-road-user-needs-measuring-performance/performance-indicators www.irf.global/statistics/

15.2   Towards an Increased Adoption of Behavioural Economics in Regulation

Traditional economic analysis of regulation has focused on tools such as prices, taxes, subsidies and quality standards, as discussed in this book. This flows from the vision that consumers and producers are always rational. If this were the case, these tools would indeed incentivize firms and consumers to behave as expected. They have certainly been good to generate cash to get the firms going and to convince investors that the market was worth their long-term commitment in many of the countries.

But as reminded at the beginning of this chapter, investments have been slower than expected and, in many countries, the poor and the lower middle class continue to have a hard time paying for the regulated services they consume, when they have access to them at all. Simultaneously, many are consuming too much because they have not been asked to internalize the environmental consequences of their consumption choices.

These, and many other indicators, should be read as evidence that the price signals sent by the current approach to regulation have not been impacting on the behaviour of producers or consumers as well as they should have. It is sometimes because the prices are ill defined (e.g. the price of water is generally too low for its use in agriculture so there is little incentive to manage consumption). But in many ways, it also shows that the assumption of rationality may lead to a poor reading of what leads people as consumers or as producers to make the right consumption choices. Incentives matter, but not always as assumed by traditional regulatory theory. One of the weaknesses of traditional theory has been the underestimation of the role of behavioural biases in the way producers and consumers, but also regulators, behave. For regulation to be more effective, it needs to be able to deal with various forms of 'irrationality'.

For instance, all of us are more irrational in some basic consumption decisions than we want to recognize. Few of us read all the details of the contracts we agree to with our electricity or water service provider. Not many more look at all of the subscription options we have when we sign up for mobile or internet services. And most of us get confused when we have too many options to pick from anyway. This is why so many consumers end up adopting the default option suggested by the service provider. For similar reasons, many of us fall for basic marketing tricks that get us to consume more or differently than what we really need. These examples are some of the most obvious examples of behavioural biases that are common in any society, but there are many more.

To improve the effectiveness of regulation, the regulatory toolkit will have to evolve. This is where behavioural economics can help, possibly significantly, the regulation of the future. Since in some countries, it has already been tested for some time, there is a solid volume of evidence to assess the scope and limits of new approaches to regulation based on behavioural economics. Lunn (2014) and OECD (2017a) document many experiments conducted since the early 2010s with different ways of changing the behaviour of consumers, producers and investors. These new approaches to regulation try to account for the diversity of cognitive, emotional, cultural or social biases that can explain the ineffectiveness of traditional regulatory instruments. Many of these dimensions are relatively easy to internalize at a low administrative cost. This is because behavioural economists have developed simple methods to identify, analyse and use the relevant non-price dimensions in the design of policies, including regulatory policies. The most popular of these methods is the 'nudge'. Since it is non-technical, it enjoys regular positive media coverage. This also implies that it may be much easier to enjoy political endorsement for the adoption of this tool in the design of the regulation of the future.

The technique is designed to gently push ('nudge') consumers or producers to make the choice that is likely to be best for them as well as for society, without restrictive regulation and usually without income- or price-driven incentives. It is often a complement to the more traditional incentives (e.g. Thaler and Sunstein 2008). It has become one of the most popular ways of using contextual aspects of decision-making to lead people to correct their failure to follow the choices that would have been made if they had been well-informed, competent and rational decision-makers. This includes tricks to remind consumers and producers of social norms.

In regulation, social norms are defined as widely shared beliefs on attitudes about how members of society should behave in the interest of the group rather than the individual. The concept has been used in regulation with a significant degree of success to stimulate efficiency and conservation of resources (OECD 2017a). They have also been used to make the most of the people's sense of fairness to improve the social or financial performance of the sector. It is essential to keep in mind that their design must be sensitive to context and culture as they vary across countries and often within countries (Sunstein et al. 2018). As was already the case for the choices of institutions and standard regulatory tools, one size does not fit all in behavioural regulation.

Advances in technology, including mobile technologies, are making it increasingly easy to reach consumers and monitor producers to improve the effectiveness of regulation in many ways, including through nudges as a complement to traditional forms of regulation. For instance, simple messages delivered through regular and social media targeted to specific concerns and behavioural biases or delivering comparisons between user groups can work. There is evidence showing that they can be designed to make people decide to use less water or energy (OECD 2017a). In some of the experiments conducted, these non-price stimuli achieved consumption reductions equivalent to a significant price increase simply by correcting misperceptions by individuals, making a specific behaviour more salient or raising social awareness on possible actions to take.[5] This does not mean that it always works as expected and the possibility of perverse effects should not be discounted (e.g. Schultz et al. 2007; Ayres et al. 2013; Schubert 2017; Buckley 2020). Nevertheless, in most cases, these new tools are good complements to traditional regulatory instruments, such as prices, and they can be useful substitutes in some others. Given that affordability can be an issue for many users, this is a policy worth considering if it is used in a regulatory toolkit that also preserves the financial viability of the service.[6]

While most of the evidence available on the effectiveness of these tools has been focusing on the richest OECD countries, a growing number of experiments are also taking place in developing or emerging countries. They provide evidence for a wide range of contexts. Peer comparisons were as effective at cutting electricity use by urban customers in India as an increase in tariffs of 12.5% (Sudarshan 2017). Similar peer comparisons allowed water consumption reductions ranging from 3.4% to 5.6% in Costa Rica (Datta et al. 2015). Social information campaigns in Colombia led to a drop in water demand by 6.8% for the targeted population and also a 5.8% drop in the population untargeted by the campaigns, as a result of information spill-overs (Jaime Torres and Carlson 2016). Social nudges have similar effects, although with a stronger difference between targeted and untargeted populations (7% versus 4.4%) for another experiment in Colombia (Lopez 2017).

---

[5] See Nemati and Penn (2018) for a meta-analysis of 117 studies from 1975 to 2017 of the effects of providing non-price information to reduce residential customers' consumption of electricity (ninety-four cases), gas (ten) and water (twenty-three).

[6] The tool can, however, work with some imprecision, as documented by Nauges and Whittington (2019), who identify sources of uncertainty associated with the adoption of social norms when compared to price-based instruments for residential users.

Despite the growing number of successful experiments, as discussed by Brennan (2018) in his evaluation of the role of behavioural economics in regulation, its internalization in the practice of regulation is not fully settled. This is, partially, because it does not yet offer a clear alternative to the full assessment of the costs and benefits of regulatory policies. This is one of the reasons why 'behavioural regulation' is likely to continue to be a complement to more traditional forms of regulation rather than an overall substitute. In that role, it will be particularly useful to point to new factors to consider in the design of more traditional regulation (e.g. Robinson and Hammitt 2011a, 2011b). But regulators should keep in mind that service providers are also quite keen on making the most of the insights of behavioural economics. And this will require additional regulatory monitoring.

One of the lessons for the regulation of the future is that, at the country level, and sometimes at a more local level, scaling up behavioural regulation will demand time. It has to start with trials, initially, to fine-tune the design and the targeting of the tools being considered. And once the choice has been made on the specific design of the new tools, it is often necessary to introduce legal and administrative changes to accommodate the adoption of the new instruments into the general regulatory frame- work (Alemanno and Spina 2014). This will protect citizens from abuses by the private and public users of the data collected through behavioural instruments. This is important because the cognitive, emotional or cultural biases are relatively easy to manipulate for the wrong reasons if the information produced is not ring-fenced.

It is an issue quite like the regulatory risks associated with the increased digitaliza- tion of the information processed in the sector. But this is not the only challenge to the adoption of behavioural regulation. As argued by Trillas (2016), it is also important to account for the fact that regulators are likely to have cognitive, emotional and cultural biases of their own. One of the most common concerns is the possibility of subjective expert biases in the design of regulation and its implementation (Perez 2015).

This brief overview does not do justice to the many insights behavioural economics has to offer to the design of regulation. It does, however, help understand why effective regulation is so often different from formal regulation. Different stakeholders have different biases that make them react differently to constraints, opportunities and other incentive-based regulations. Unless these biases are internalized in the design of regulation (e.g. through the inclusion of nudges in the regulatory toolkits), regulatory achievements will continue to often fail to deliver on goals on at least some dimen- sions. In other words, regulatory tools anchored in behavioural economics can and should help achieve more efficient, fairer and more financially sustainable outcomes than many of the traditional tools have been able to deliver. They will help, but will need to be considered as part of the toolkit rather than the main tool.

15.3   Towards New Financing Strategies

The second major innovation that regulators of public services will have to internalize is the evolution of the private financing options available to the sector. For now, regulators have not been able to adjust fast enough to the resulting evolution in the number and types of essential stakeholders in the management of regulated industries. As discussed in Chapter 7, one of the key weaknesses of regulation in theory and in practice is the underestimation of the growing role of financial actors in the operation of the services. The growing importance of financial markets and their institutional actors is not limited to the regulated industries, but it represents a particular risk in these industries. In many situations, the short-term preferences of the financial sector are incompatible with the long-term needs of public utilities and infrastructure sectors. For instance, the preference for steady flows of high dividends for financial investors interested in the regulated industries is not always consistent with the need to earmark significant amounts of short-term cash to the maintenance of assets when access to alternative financing options is restricted or costly. If the maintenance is cut to favour dividends, the assets deteriorate and the long-run financial attractiveness of the sector should fall, thereby reducing its private financing options as well.

The broader implication of the evolution of private financing sources for the regulators of the future is the need to come up with informed and formal views of the financing strategies of the firms they are supervising. This is not about micro-managing these firms, as some would probably argue. This is about being able to make fair assessments of the use of the market power granted to these operators. Most of the regulation theory suggests focusing on pricing and service obligations as discussed in Chapters 8 and 9. But the practice needs to complement these traditional perspectives with a closer look at the financing side of the business. In Latin America, for instance, the growing role of institutional investors has already changed the governance of the sector and the way financing strategies impact on regulatory outcomes (e.g. Georgoulias et al. 2018).[7] They are less keen on taking on equity and seem more eager to come up with contractual and regulatory arrangements for the long run than more aggressive investors.

The risk stems from the increased complexity of the ways in which finance is impacting on the management of regulated industries and from the lack of transparency in how it influences matching regulatory decisions. One of the main adjustments the regulation of the future will have to make is ensuring that regulators are given the mandate to supervise the evolution of the number and type of actors contributing to the financing of the sector. For instance, over the last few years, institutional investors have been increasingly important sources of financing for infrastructure investments, through bonds or equities, as mentioned in Chapter 7.[8] There is relatively little transparent objective information on the way they influence management decisions in regulated industries, but there is evidence that their presence can be associated with

---

[7] Institutional investors make investments on behalf of individuals or firms expecting their savings to be managed to produce returns higher than those that would be produced by standard bank savings accounts. They include mutual funds, pension funds, insurance companies and specialized funds such as infrastructure or sovereign wealth funds, as well as some commercial banks.

[8] According to IPE Real Assets, as of 2018, the top-100 infrastructure investors had accumulated over $439bn in physical and social (e.g. hospitals, schools) infrastructure assets (see https://realassets.ipe.com/top-100-and-surveys/top-100-infrastructure-investors-2018/10026765.article).

different outcomes on variables such as leverage or prices (Bertomeu-Sanchez 2019). This is likely to be linked to the fact that their concerns and their time horizon are quite different from those credited to traditional lenders (e.g. banks) or investors (e.g. sector-specific operators or construction companies). And this, in turn, is changing risk perceptions and hence the cost of capital. When risks increase, the expected returns and the average prices in the regulated sectors increase as well. Investors are better off on average and consumers and/or taxpayers worse off.

To make the increased 'financialization' of the sector even more transparent, it is useful to recall that several regulated activities, ranging from utilities and transport services to social infrastructure such as hospitals, schools or prisons, are now viewed as a mere asset class by many financial sector specialists. Since they are becoming key actors in the sector, their views on the relevance of size, tangibility, current liquidity and returns on assets matter for the management of the sector. And this ultimately impacts on the availability of the services and the price by the final users or taxpayers.

This transformation of the financing side of the regulated activities is bound to matter to the ability of service providers, whether public or private, to deliver on at least some of their contractual commitments. Finance theory shows that it matters to dividends, borrowing and investment decisions, since the latter adjust to the demand for cash of these new investors. But in practice, it also matters to the risks current and future consumers are exposed to. The regulation of the future will have to do a better job at internalizing the implications of the role of the new types of investors and their ability to influence the corporate financing strategies of the regulated firms. Unless this is done fast, conflicts are likely to be recurrent and renegotiations of contracts to become even more frequent than they currently are. And this will hold for both private and public enterprises as the management of these public enterprises is increasingly commercialized.

In the case of private regulated firms, the risks are well illustrated by recent debates on the level of dividends paid by the water companies in England, where six of the ten companies created at the beginning of the privatization process in 1989 have been de-listed from the British stock market and are now owned by infrastructure funds or financial companies (e.g. Bayliss 2014, 2017).[9] These debates have been extensively covered by all the media in the country and have tended to focus on the inability of the water regulator (OFWAT) to anticipate the opportunity costs of not monitoring dividends properly. More specifically, the criticisms were triggered by the observation that private water companies in England have been increasing their borrowing to raise dividend payments, and to a lesser extent CEO and board members' fees, rather than to finance investment needs. The popular outcry was fuelled by the fact that this happened at a time when investment levels had been lagging behind targets and service quality had been dropping in various dimensions. How could regulated firms

---

[9] See Helm (2018) for a clear description of the debates in the British context and Bertomeu-Sanchez and Estache (2019) for a recent survey of the relevance of omitting the role of dividends in the design of infrastructure regulation.

increase borrowing and raise dividends while simultaneously investing less in quantity and in quality?

A similar pattern emerged in Spain when Endesa, the Spanish electricity company, was taken over by ENEL, an Italian conglomerate. Since 2012, it has been paying high dividends on net ordinary income.[10] Simultaneously, Endesa became the most heavily indebted energy company in Europe while cutting investments and staff (1,000 jobs were lost in Spain in 2013). Yet during the 2015–19 period, it paid out 100% of its earnings to shareholders. Regulators did not have much to say about this because monitoring these changes was not part of their mandate.

These examples illustrate the costly gap between corporate financing and regulatory practice. Many (if not most) large-scale public utilities operators increasingly rely on a model of debt financing anchored in the 'de facto' securitization of revenue flows, similar to those used in the project finance approach to financing investments.[11] Under current regulatory practices, the model has tended to favour shareholders (whether public or private) and financial intermediaries over consumers, by allowing steady dividend payments over time.[12] This bias may explain the growing interest of financial investors for regulated industries. In some countries, the returns are quite high despite the low risks of bankruptcy. This adds to the case made in Chapter 7 for the need to make professional assessments of risks to be accounted for in regulation (and project finance when relevant). The fear of not getting financing is often leading authorities to be too lenient and short-sighted in their non-technical assessments of risks.

The British water and the Spanish electricity examples are quite powerful, and they are not the only ones. Similar combinations of increased dividends and deteriorating performance outcomes along various dimensions have been observed throughout Europe across sectors with private operators of regulated public services (e.g. in the Spanish and French toll roads concessions).[13] Not too long ago, the OECD (2015b) argued that this was part of a more general trend in which high dividends are correlated with weak business investment.

In the OECD, the dividend pay-out ratios for utilities have increased over time and they now tend to be higher than 50%.[14] They also tend to be at the top of the rankings of pay-outs across sectors. This is correlated with the evolution of the ownership of the sector. The growing role of institutional investors, indeed, offers an explanation to the increasing dividend trend as these types of investors are expected to pay higher than average dividends. For instance, the Macquarie Group, a significant global investor in

---

[10] See www.enel.com/investors/investing/dividend-history

[11] It is useful to keep in mind that the trend is also observed for public enterprises. In many ways, because of the guarantees they get from their governments, they can often go further than private firms trying to borrow. In 2015, European Union public enterprises had on average a 40% higher leverage than private firms (European Commission 2016).

[12] In 2018, the Belgian government owned almost 181 million shares of Proximus, the main telecoms company in Belgium (representing roughly a 53.5% stake). It was paid €270 million in dividends.

[13] In France, for instance, high margins and huge dividends by toll road operators have been subject to high-profile debates in the media (Athias and Saussier 2018).

[14] The dividend pay-out or dividend pay-out ratio measures the ratio of the total amount of dividends paid to shareholders in relation to a firm's net income.

regulated industries, advertises ordinary dividend pay-out ratio of 60–80% on its recent annual reports.

An equivalent evolution in the corporate financing strategies of regulated industries has been noted in developing and transition economies. In regions in which the private sector is quite active in these industries, Benavides et al. (2016) and von Eije et al. (2017) show that the target dividend pay-out ratios (and their speed of adjustment) is quite high. These ratios are, for instance, much higher in Latin America than in North America, possibly reflecting differences in longer-term risk perceptions.

These examples also show that the analysis of the corporate financing strategy that regulators should be able to conduct in the future will have to be much more detailed and systematic than it currently is. It will have to account for the fact that high borrowing can be justified by low interest rates available on the financial markets, as long as this financing strategy is used to deliver on quality, investment and other service obligations imposed on regulated industries. A strong commitment to dividends is not necessarily an issue if the business returns are good, but when interest rates are high, it may be more effective to rely on retained earnings as far as possible to finance the obligations. For now, few public service regulators tend to have a formal view on this. The capability to do so in the context of corporate financing decisions should be part of the mandate of the regulators of the future in view of the growing role in operational management decisions of financial actors.

Delivering on this mandate will not be easy because the real stakeholders of the financing will probably be an increasingly moving target as there is a growing secondary market for shares and bonds in the sector. Regulators will have to be able to track these changes or to control their effects on the management of regulated firms. This also demands conducting more systematic assessments of the degree of concentration of ownership and its origin at the firm and the sector level. And, as mentioned in Chapter 13, this implies paying more attention to the extent of cross-ownership in regulated industries. Any of these dimensions will impact on the financial strategy of firms and hence the cost of capital. The less effective regulators are at tracking these changes in concentration and cross-ownership, the greater the capacity of these new players to lobby political and regulatory authorities as well as the management of the regulated firms.

To some readers, it may seem odd that this has not yet been addressed widely. Indeed, the impact on dividend decisions of these new players seems to be predictable. For instance, Gonzalez et al. (2017) show that the dividends paid are higher when the ownership is highly concentrated and the largest owner is based in a common-law country than when ownership is less concentrated.[15] This is the result of the ability of these owners to lobby for a given financing approach. But this lobbying capacity has an impact on the final consumers. For instance, if investors manage to bias corporate financing decisions in favour of borrowing to pay dividends, in a context of rising interest rates (e.g. due to higher risk premia associated with an uncertain political or

---

[15] They show that the opposite holds when the ownership is concentrated in the hands of an individual as the owner tends to extract benefits from minority shareholders instead.

foreign exchange context), the bias will result in higher borrowing costs and further lower the margin to rely on retained earnings to finance CAPEX or even OPEX. This will lead to higher average prices. This is something regulators should be able to deal with in the definition of service or operational obligations. But they need to be given the mandate to do so.

One solution to minimize the risks of undesirable outcomes for consumers in the design of the regulation of the future is to consider capping concentration of ownership by some actors. The payoff to this approach is also implicit in some of the insights provided by Gonzalez et al. (2017). They find that increasing the ownership of the second largest shareholder leads to a decrease in firm dividends and explain this by a stronger monitoring role for this second player. These are interesting but still partial results. In view of the strong role of the State in many countries on the board of regulated enterprises, it would be useful to test if the fact that this second shareholder is private or public makes a difference. This would be particularly important in the context in which adjustments in the number and types of investors are needed to increase the scope for self-financing of a regulated firm (i.e. cutting the need to rely on subsidies).

This is a major concern when the providers are public enterprises. In that case, however, this is less likely to make the headlines because the residual source of financing is the future taxpayer, and this is best measured by the debt level of these firms. This debt is indeed a good indicator of the fairness with which the various generations of stakeholders are being considered by the regulator. The accumulation of debt by regulated public enterprises implies that regulatory decisions tend to favour current taxpayers and consumers over future taxpayers and consumers. Debt financing and debt-financed subsidies are still part of the common strategies adopted to finance public enterprises. And this has not really been internalized by the finance theory used in the practice of regulatory evaluations.

An academic debate on the related international cooperation needs is also taking place to harmonize the monitoring of institutional investors in the financial sector (e.g. Schmaltz 2018). The debate has not yet reached the political and policy arena but the fact that the same investors can be involved (i.e. own shares) in various companies supposed to be competing with each other should be a source of concern as it may limit the scope for global competition in a world of increasingly integrated markets.[16] Under current arrangements, energy, rail, telecoms or water companies may not be competing as much as we think. As discussed in Chapter 13, some experts are warning about the risks associated with excessive tolerance for cross and common ownership in general (Schmaltz 2018; Elhauge 2020).

One approach to control risks (and hence the cost of capital) would be to limit the option to invest by these institutional investors to only one of the firms per sector delivering public services in a given country. In Spain, for instance, where Union

---

[16] Clo et al. (2017) had already raised similar concerns on the limits of competition resulting from the wave of M&A activities between state-owned enterprises that reduced the number of actors in the global market.

Fenosa, Endesa and Iberdrola are supposed to be competing, at least *for* some of the energy markets and *in* some of the markets, investors would be allowed to invest in only one of them. In a more extreme specification of this rule, institutional investors would have to choose one company in which to invest within each industry considering the global markets rather than the national markets. This would stimulate competition for funds and across companies.

Some authors are warning against the risks of overreaction such as the suggestion that there should be a limit on the ownership of shares of multiple firms in oligopolistic industries (Rock and Rubinfeld 2017; Patel 2019). Rock and Rubinfeld (2017) suggest adopting what they label a quasi-'safe harbour'. It would protect investors from the risks of anti-trust liability when: (i) their ownership share is less than 15%; (ii) the investors have no board representation and (iii) they only engage in 'normal' corporate governance activities.

Under any of these solutions, it would also make sense to consider an increased role for supranational authorities to ensure, monitor and enforce consistency across countries. This option has not yet been discussed in the literature, but it is needed. Any evaluation of it would have to assess whether the rules lead to new arbitration between the protection of consumers rights and efficiency gains accounting for the new constraints on financing options, or not.

There is probably a lot more to be said about the impact of the growing role of financial companies in the sector. For now, what is important to retain is that the impact of (largely unsupervised) decisions on leverage, dividend payments and investment has been systematically overlooked in regulatory assessments. The changes in the sources of financing will continue to have implications for highly concrete operational demands in a sector in which the balance between operating and capital expenditures is particularly important to address in regulatory monitoring.

Most of the arguments against the monitoring by regulators of corporate financing strategies turn around the need to avoid micro-management. This concern would be reasonable if it were not for the evidence on the lack of investment and of an insufficient service quality. The decision to penalize ex post non-compliance is the most common practice in the field, but correcting the mistakes takes time. And in an industry highly associated with environmental concerns and strongly committed to make the most of technological improvements, regulatory intervention is generally likely to be slower than needed to adjust to the fast-changing context. And this begs for both an ex ante and an ex post perspective on the corporate financing decisions of firms in the sector. The next generation of regulatory mandates should be able to account for both perspectives.

15.4   Towards a Stronger Role for Big Data

The next major driver of 'the demand for a change' in the regulation of the future, maybe the main driver to consider, is a technological change brought about by the development of information and communication technologies and in particular by the volume of data it is producing. For instance, think of the use of data produced by smart meters and other tracking devices, when you turn on the light or your phone at home or when you turn on your computer in a train. Any of the providers of the regulated services allowing you to connect to the internet while selling you other services are now sitting on a new business, with a market power not very different to the one credited to Google, Facebook or Amazon. This is because there is a market for the information collected by tracking your behaviour and what this reveals about your future needs on a wide range of activities. Should this be regulated? Can it be regulated? If yes, who should be regulating it? Should it be the electricity regulator because it is the consumption of energy that triggers the need to track abuses? Or should it be the telecoms regulator because the abuses will come from the use of data collected through the internet? Or should all of this be done by a new specialized agency? Should it then be a national, regional or a global agency?

For now, the regulation of the use of data by service providers is, at best, only partial in most countries of the world. Many of the firms collecting this data are lobbying hard to keep the control of the new markets derived from a traditionally regulated activity. Their main argument is that it will allow them to provide better quality of service as they will be able to improve the targeting of service to better match demand. The situation deserves a formal political and technical debate. Is this a credible promise? And at what cost? Should the lobbying be controlled as well or is it simply a normal part of a regulatory process that should be accepted as such? Does it matter that this process is growing in complexity in an increasingly fast-evolving technological environment? There is no clear answer to any of these questions so far. But the vast related theoretical and empirical research is already quite helpful to identify the directions the transformation of regulation is likely to go through. This is the focus of the following paragraphs.

The growing volume of sector-specific data collected or produced by international organizations is a good indicator of the growth in the world's ability to produce the type of information that will reduce information asymmetries. More is likely to appear as service providers develop their data-analytical capacity to exploit the growing number of datasets they produce from the monitoring of their clients. Yield-management, that is data-based pricing strategies developed by airlines companies and hotels, is still only the beginning. In early 2012, the corporate vice president at Microsoft, Susan Hauser, argued that: 'Big data absolutely has the potential to change the way governments, organizations, and academic institutions conduct business and make discoveries, and it is likely to change how everyone lives their day-to-day lives.'[17] She was proven right in less than five years. In fact, maybe she underestimated the impact of the evolution of artificial intelligence (AI) based on what we have been able to observe so far.

The explosion of data, the evolution of the role of digitalization, the many applications of AI and the growing role of mobile applications linked to regulated public

---

[17] https://news.microsoft.com/2013/02/11/the-big-bang-how-the-big-data-explosion-is-changing-the-world/

services are having massive measurable consequences in the production and consumption processes of these services.[18] It will also change the way firms and governments use and share information. The potential payoffs have already been well internalized by service providers as more data and a better use of this data can both help cut costs and increase revenue.[19] Smart meters, smart billing or smartphone applications are increasingly becoming part of the standard management tools in regulated industries.[20] And this will lead to changes in the way these sectors can and should be regulated.

Consider first the case of the energy sector. According to the IEA (2017), the world will achieve savings from the digitalization of the sector in the order of US$80 billion per year over 2016–40, or about 5% of total annual power generation costs. About 25% of these gains will be achieved through a drop in OPEX costs (notably thanks to better predictive maintenance). Better efficiency in loss and outage managements will further cut costs. But in the long term, digitalization will also extend the operational lifetime of power plants and network components. On average, cuts in the investment needs of power plants and networks would explain respectively about 42% and 25% of the annual gains. These medium- to long-run benefits impose significant short-run annual investment costs, however. This may explain why global investment in digital electricity infrastructure and software in 2016 already added up to the equivalent of 40% more than investment in gas-fired power generation worldwide. From consumers' perspective, all of this should be good news. Based on the formula we discussed in Chapter 7, most of these changes should eventually lead to lower average prices in the sector and this should be straightforward for regulators to monitor. But in the short run, the investment costs will be part of their bill.

In the water and sanitation sector, many processes are now largely automated. Remote control technology and digital office communication have already been well integrated into best management practice. According to Global Water Intelligence, a specialized commercial research firm, by 2021 the global market for control and monitoring solutions will probably have grown to $30.1 billion.[21] That's almost 7% of the total worldwide investments needs in the sector each year until 2030.

There are no global estimations on cost savings from the changes comparable to those conducted for the energy sector. But the partial information available gives a good sense of where the improvements come from on the demand and the supply side of the market. Digitalization in the water and sanitation sector has already been used to improve the strength of the price signal in the allocation of water across competing uses (from agriculture to final residential consumption). On the supply side, smart integration of information and operational technology is increasingly being used to cut

---

[18] Jorisch et al. (2018) provide many examples of the way technology is also producing environmental payoffs, including in regulated industries.

[19] See Goldfarb and Tucker (2019) for a survey from an economics perspective on the various ways in which costs can be cut thanks to the changes allowed by digitalization.

[20] See Jamasb et al. (2018) for an overview of the spread of smart technologies in the developing countries' electricity sectors.

[21] www.globalwaterintel.com/about-gwi

costs by smoothing the full production chain, ranging from smart 'upstream' supply management at the extraction stage (basins, aquifers, potable reuse or desalination) to 'midstream' such as real-time treatment monitoring, ending with 'downstream' utility operations. At the water utilities level, technological improvements should help reduce the impact of leaks and bursts, which are estimated to be 25–35% of the utilities' water losses. Liemberger and Wyatt (2019) estimate the global volume of unaccounted-for water at about 346 million cubic metres per day, or 126 billion cubic metres per year, which is about US$39 billion per year, if valued at US$0.31 per cubic metre. These potential savings are not minor and many are directly linked to the increased digitalization of the sector.

For the transport sector, the adoption of new AI technologies is progressing also, but at a slower pace (e.g. Opertti 2019). For instance, the electronic exchange of trade-related data has not yet been systemized across regions. To be effective, a more coordinated cross-country approach to new forms of regulation is needed. For now, there is no coherent protection of both traders and consumers (Giordano 2017). As for the other sectors, the expected payoffs are significant and should lead to welfare gains, although not necessarily shared by all stakeholders and not unless some other changes are implemented in the more general sector policies. For public transport, the Global Mobility Report (Sustainable Mobility for All 2017) suggests that the gains from more sustainable mobility services, largely anchored in efficiency gains from an improved use of information, could add up to US$70 trillion by 2050, or about US$2 billion annually. But this demands regulatory authorities to be committed to shared mobility across modes.[22] For freight, PwC (2018), focusing on Europe, suggests that digitalization will lead to a 47% drop in trucking logistics costs by 2030 as compared to 2017. It will also lead to reductions in delivery lead times by 40%. However, there is a catch that policymakers and regulators may not have internalized. Experts believe that the savings will largely be achieved through labour reductions. These are the likely result of the acceleration of automation. The social challenge of possibly massive job destruction must be added to those challenges imposed by the likely increased concentration of the market and the dominant role of large 'tech' companies in the sector.

This brief overview shows that the data-intensive transformation of the regulated sectors is likely to cut many costs. This is something regulators usually know how to internalize into prices. Simultaneously, it is increasing the scope for operational synergies across sectors that need to be addressed by the overall design of regulatory governance. And this is something regulators do not seem to have mastered yet. For instance, joint investment by energy or railways firms with telecoms, financial or insurance companies to collect and use data is becoming increasingly common. How and who should be regulating the distribution of cost savings across businesses and

---

[22] Shared mobility covers (i) shared public and private transportation (with shared financial or physical ownership); (ii) product innovation (next-generation vehicles, transportation equipment relying on data analysis); (iii) real-time customer services (including timetables, fares, travel times) and (iv) data-driven assistance in decision-making (Canales et al. 2017).

the possible risks of collusion and abuse? As regulated firms progressively diversify into non-regulated activities, regulatory issues emerge that need to be internalized in new frameworks. First the odds of observing anticompetitive cross-subsidies and dumping cases increases with diversification, even if significant competition of new specialized entrants can mitigate the risks. Second the assignment of mandates across regulatory institutions and the division of mandates across regulation and competition agencies might become unclear, which might lead to confusion and inefficiency, as discussed later in the chapter.

For regulators to make the most of the cost-cutting opportunities allowed by the increased role of data in the operations of regulated industries, institutions will have to adapt. The mandate and the coordination across sector policies will all have to be reviewed. The changes will also have to address a wide range of practical and ethical dilemmas, as is often the case with disruptive technological changes. If efficiency is likely to improve in many ways, it will probably be achieved at the cost of increased inequity, unless regulators manage to adjust regulation to ensure that the payoffs are shared across stakeholders. It is also likely to raise concerns with respect to the commercial use of private information for which property rights have not been addressed carefully enough by the current regulators. Unless the social mandates of policymakers and regulators are somehow scaled up and refined, the size of the payoffs may not be as high or sustainable as estimated by the experts. And this also should be part of the agenda of the regulation of the future.

15.5   How 'Big Data' Is Already Impacting on Regulation Implementation

The long-term impacts of technological changes on the day-to-day practice of regulation are already quite concrete in many dimensions. Improved data analytics and other more effective AI-driven uses of the growing available data are already observed in many regulated industries.[23] They are leading to smarter and more effective regulation. But the scope for improvement is still significant. For instance, it should make compliance with commitments and obligations by any stakeholder easier to enforce, as illustrated by tax monitoring. Brazil's national public auditor now relies on data-mining tools to audit $5 billion in public spending. In 2015 alone, the unit raised red flags in more than 7,500 cases (Moreno 2017). In the United Kingdom, the tax authorities (Her Majesty's Revenue and Customs, HMRC) relies on predictive analytics to identify high-risk value-added tax (VAT) traders based not only on returns but also on debt information, taxpayers' characteristics and regular audit details.

For regulated industries, achieving this data-processing capacity would require better coordination of data across agencies concerned with regulation. Basic dimensions such as the coordination of websites as a centralized source of information with easy access to all stakeholders in the sector are still lagging. Progress has been

---

[23] For a useful early detailed discussion of the related issues in the context of regulation in general, see Yeung and Lodge (2019).

achieved within agencies, but coordination is still needed to allow faster and cheaper data-sharing across regulators and across jurisdictions. There is still a gap to reach the coordination levels comparable to those achieved in tax policy, for instance. This is the basic anchor to effective regulatory auditing in a world of increasing interactions and overlapping of production and consumption activities.

The potential payoffs are significant, and it is worrying to observe that few regulators have been adapting as fast as the most effective service providers to the opportunities offered by the technological transformations. One indicator of the difference in adjustment speed is the slow reaction of regulators to the increase in dividend payoffs by increasingly digitalized regulated firms without matching improvements in service quality to users or average price reductions (e.g. Bertomeu-Sanchez and Estache 2019). Another (related) indicator is the growing evidence of increased markups in regulated industries associated with digitalization (e.g. Gal et al. 2019). These result from the multiple ways to cut costs thanks to the effective use of AI (e.g. Goldfarb and Tucker 2019) without much reaction so far from regulators. The failure of regulators to track these cost savings or increased profit margins, at least in the short run, suggests that many of the issues of information asymmetries discussed in this book are likely to increase with the increased digitalization of the regulated sectors if the regulators do not catch up with firms.

Consider, for instance, the case of transport regulation to get a better sense of the challenge. The efficiency improvements allowed by the adoption of smart traffic management techniques by many transport companies have been significant. But they have also raised concern that the data produced can be used to manage price discrimination options resulting from a better monitoring of usage. This can be good or bad depending on how it is done, as discussed in Chapter 8, but it is seldom neutral. However, focusing only on the risks associated with price discrimination would be close to a business-as-usual approach. This would ignore the scope for broadening the regulatory agenda allowed by better data availability under a more encompassing regulatory umbrella. Indeed, AI can also help in rethinking the regulation of safety and pollution, for instance, in a much more coordinated way across agencies while controlling for price discrimination. This is in addition to the scope for improvements in the implementation of inter-modality for both passengers and freight. None of these things were on the table in the early 2000s. They are now part of most regulation modernization efforts across the world.

Similar changes will impact on the regulation of prices in more structural term. Digitalization is already changing the nature of markets to be regulated in ways which have not been fully internalized by standard regulation. In electricity, for instance, it is accelerating a shift towards multidirectional distributed energy systems. Demand sources are already increasingly participating actively in balancing supply because improved connectivity makes it easier to link, aggregate and control all energy-production and consumption units. This is changing the traditional distinction between suppliers and consumers built into the traditional forms of price regulation. The owners of solar panels on their rooves are prosumers, sometimes buying energy from the grid, sometimes selling to it. It is very likely to lead to welfare gains but raises concerns as to how to ensure that these gains can be shared between all stakeholders. Actually, subsidies to install photovoltaic panels on the rooves of those who own a house are financed by taxes that inflate the energy bills for all, including low-income consumers.

The growing reliance on algorithmic pricing allowed by the explosion of data adds specific challenges to the redesign of price regulation. In practice, it essentially delegates pricing to AI and software programmers in some markets.[24] The greater reliance on 'machine-based' pricing in regulated industries is linked to the growth of market size allowed by the integration of those markets. Belgium can buy electricity from Germany or France, Niger can buy its electricity in Nigeria, Chile can buy it from Argentina. A similar interconnection is observed in the railways industry and is likely to intensify as integration is not only across countries for a given mode, but also across modes. A ticket from Brussels to Toulouse can be sold by the French or Belgian rail operator or by an independent reseller, even if the trip takes place on the same train. Any of these changes involves absurdly large volumes of information to be handled by operators, which explains the growth of new approaches to pricing. Economic integration and digitalization mean that complexity has increased in the management of these sectors. Once again, the changes are taking place faster than the speed at which regulators can adjust.

Despite its many potential advantages, the likely acceleration in the use of algorithmic pricing has three implications for the future of regulation that still require some fine-tuning to ensure the efficient and fair outcomes expected from this technological revolution. First, it will increase the risks of uncontrolled price discrimination because these complex algorithms are a black box to regulators. Without regulatory monitoring, how the algorithm accounts for both technical (e.g. degree of capacity use) and personal information (e.g. reason for or frequency of travelling based on past behaviour) makes it easier to distort markets, with possible anticompetitive or unfair bias. For instance, demand-response technologies producing consumer-specific, real-time usage data can be used both to improve efficiency and to distort consumption through creative use of neuro-marketing. Second, algorithmic pricing may also ease collusion, including without human interference (e.g. Ezrachi and Stucke 2015). Both issues are more likely to be a concern of competition agencies, but with spill-overs on the evolution of the mandates assigned to regulators. This may include a case to get regulators to test the algorithms more systematically to detect for any built-in bias, as suggested by Harrington (2017). Since these tests can be quite labour- and skill-intensive, and therefore costly to run, the regulators might choose instead to oblige firms that wish to use new algorithms to provide evidence of their unbiasedness (exactly as pharmaceutical companies need to prove the effectiveness and safety of their drugs). For now, not much is done about this in practice. Third is the need to address data privacy concerns. Civil society and academics have been discussing the unclear regulatory framing of the ownership and commercial (or political) use of data

---

[24] Central America and South Asia have particularly benefited from this outsourcing to emerging and developing economies.

> **Box 15.1** How Much Data Generation Should Be Allowed in Regulated Industries?
> The specific decisions shaping the regulation of the future will have an impact on how much can be done with new technologies. Based on the many types of risks just discussed, it could be argued that one of the most basic regulatory decisions to take when the simple fact of consuming produces new data is to assess how much of this data can become a source of rent for an operator. The answer to this question drives the decision for regulation with respect to an opt-in or an opt-out approach to the authorization of data usage by consumers.
>
> The maximum protection is provided by 'opt-in' programmes as they require specific client authorization for certain data to be shared. This is likely to be the preferred solution for most users, i.e. even if there is the possibility of a generation gap on this issue, as older and younger consumers tend to behave differently. In contrast, most firms are likely to prefer 'opt-out' programmes because this allows them to collect data which can be used for pricing and service targeting to maximize profits. The extent to which these decisions are coordinated and regulated across countries will also influence the extent to which firms or consumers are more likely to gain from the 'data explosion'.
>
> In an environment in which the use of the data is uncertain, how the regulator decides on this choice can be quite revealing on its biases in the treatment of stakeholders. But the choice does not have to be binary. There is the possibility of getting clients to self-select in confidentiality options ranging from 'minimal', which would be sufficient to allow essential smart operations (including for regulated prices and quality preferences) to 'full or maximal' within specified ethical limits to be defined by the regulator or the policymakers. The regulator thus has some margin to be as fair as possible to all.

and the loss of control of pricing to AI is likely to make this even harder to manage. How much margin should consumers have to decide on what to do with their data? How much of the data should be confidential (i.e. without any margin for the creation of a market for this data), how well it should be protected (e.g. how much outsourcing on data collection or how much data sharing under which conditions) and who has the property rights on this data are all topics to consider in the redesign of regulation. Any of these questions has regulatory implications, as illustrated by Box 15.1.

For now, this is an unsettled battle as illustrated by the large margin still allowed to the owners and operators of social networks to decide on how to process the data they collect. While in the regulation of public services, there has not yet been any dramatic crisis so far associated with data manipulation, recent examples from the distortion of political processes illustrate how far this can go in biasing outcomes – the equivalent of efficiency and equity in regulatory debates.[25]

---

[25] Between 2015 and 2018, the advisors of conservative politicians such as Ted Cruz or Donald Trump in the United States have been able to use data collected through social networks to manipulate electoral processes. Similar manipulations have allowed the dissemination of fake news in the months that

A final source of concern for regulatory experts is the possible misuse of data stemming from the poor management of cybersecurity risks. It is a regulatory concern because it is linked to the coordination of the use of data and of approaches to cybersecurity across sectors and across countries. These risks are increasing as many of the regulated services are connected to international networks and resource pools. Without harmonization, as in any network, the global level of risk is defined by the weakest link in the interconnected infrastructures. Coordination and the development of common response plans to cyber-attacks have a cost which needs to be internalized in regulation. And just as importantly, it needs to be balanced against the benefits of increasing the reliability of access to regulated services. In the case of energy, for instance, where the diversification of sources is common and international, failing to harmonize is likely to slow the penetration of the wide diversity of renewable energy sources in the menu of supply options possible. This is because unreliability linked to cross-country regulatory differences are likely to increase the odds of outages during the energy transition.

The growing role of AI in regulated industries raises some other politically sensitive and ethical concerns. This is sometimes an underestimated issue in policy debates. Not everyone has a smartphone or a laptop to interact with the service providers. Not everyone has the proper degree of 'technological' literacy. Yet these access problems are generally overlooked in the ways all the stakeholders are expected to interact. Unless this is being controlled by regulators, the risks of discrimination based on access to information may be extremely penalizing for large categories of users, in particular the older populations and the poorest ones.

Just as important, even when access to data is easy and when most actors master the necessary technologies, the evidence shows that some populations are significantly more at risk of being manipulated from poor regulation of the data uses than other. A 2019 PEW survey of eleven emerging economies shows that those with lower levels of education and less intensive use of social media, are less likely to note both the positive and negative impacts of technology. In those countries, consumers are more likely to be sensitive to 'fake news' or marketing manipulation.[26]

In practice, the real challenge is to find a way to regulate without distorting the general potential payoffs to access to more and better data in a wide range of contexts (including political) while protecting the poorest and the weakest links in the data chain. Good regulation should be able to deliver the efficiency and equity payoffs allowed by the access to better and more specific data on regulated industries.[27]

---

preceded the Brexit vote to distort the facts concerning the actual financial and economic interactions between England and the other European Union members. Equivalent distortions were also noted in developing countries. For instance, in India and Indonesia, fake information has been disseminated through social networks to exacerbate nationalist and religious tensions and influence local and global elections. See for instance, https://thediplomat.com/2019/04/fake-news-in-india-and-indonesias-elec tions-2019/

[26] www.pewinternet.org/2019/05/13/publics-in-emerging-economies-worry-social-media-sow-division-even-as-they-offer-new-chances-for-political-engagement/

[27] For an overview of the effects of regulation and competition policy on inequality, including a discussion of when competition is more likely to penalize the poor and how regulation can address this concern, see Baker and Salop (2015).

Regulation is unlikely to be able to do this if it does not develop its capacity to process the data acquired. But the empirical jury is still out, trying to come up with evidence either way.[28]

15.6   Towards a Need to Rethink Regulatory Institutions

The design of regulatory institutions should not be insensitive to the development of new tools, the appearance of new players and the reliance on new data-intensive technologies. Regulation must adapt but so do institutions. The atomization of the sources and uses of data and the multiplication of actors in the production and financing of regulated industries make the risks of inefficiency and unfairness harder to control for predictable reasons.

The first reason flows from the fact that the data used to run electricity, transport or water regulators may be collected from various sources and by a growing number of firms, including some subjected to the regulation of the telecoms regulator rather than any of these sector-specific regulators.[29] This is making the division of regulatory responsibilities between regulators increasingly blurry.

The second reason is the observation that data management is often subcontracted to smaller companies competing on the data markets. The outsourcing of data management and processing further adds to the number of actors to coordinate and monitor. It also adds to the complexity of the institutional adjustments required to deal with the new information management opportunities adopted by regulated industries.

For now, different agencies are responsible for different parts of the interactions between stakeholders, and each regulator tends to focus on relatively narrow dimensions of increasingly diversified activities by service providers. The sector regulators are typically concerned with the price discrimination, quality and service obligations issues, while the competition agencies focus on the associated collusion risks. In most countries, there is a lot of confusion still as to which institution should do what. And the steady evolution of the sources of data relevant to regulatory decisions, and the nature of discrimination and competition is not helping. The risks of a loss of effectiveness of the traditional approaches and tools are increasing as a result. And regulated firms, especially international ones, benefit from the confusion and uncoordinated actions of the various regulators and anti-trust authorities, as their rising profit margins show.

The regulation of the future will need to adjust to the evolving world economic context and to the digital technological revolution in its efforts to address some of the

---

[28] For recent examples in the context of developing countries see Hawthorne and Grzybowski (2019).

[29] Every time you use your phone or your laptop to pay your utilities, even when you manage your cookies actively, you produce information that can be sold back to any of these service providers to characterize you along several consumption dimensions. This information is used to market alternative pricing options. Unless regulators have a common vision on how to manage this, the degree of control of access to data will be determined by the most tolerant of the regulators since the information will eventually find its way to the data market through the least regulated firm.

market failures. It will need to protect consumers from the risk of abuses of market power by an increasing number of actors. And it will have to do so faster than what has been happening recently. For instance, when phone banking leads to abuse, should it be managed by the telecoms regulator or the banking regulator? Unless the mandates are clarified to match the evolution of services allowed by technology, abuses, inefficiencies and conflicts are likely to increase with the evolution of the regulated industries, as they diversify into non-regulated activities anchored in their core business. These should lead to new institutions and practices at the crossroads between regulation and anti-trust. Making the mandate on the supervision of the use of data clear and deciding on who should be expected to enforce this mandate is one of the challenges that need to be addressed in designing the regulatory institutions of the future.

In the short to medium run, the multiplicity of actors can be dealt with in a few ways. First, it could be handled through a strengthening of the current approach to inter-agency coordination adopted by most countries to address common and/or related concerns and to decide when and how to intervene in the regulated markets in a consistent way. The new technological options could be used to develop this improved coordination between sector regulators, competition agencies and procurement agencies (Querbach and Arndt 2017). This could further be complemented by the creation of a dedicated agency which would monitor all data uses. Most OECD countries and various African (e.g. Ghana, South Africa or Tunisia) and Latin American (e.g. Argentina, Brazil or Costa Rica) countries have already adopted data protection agencies. In the United Kingdom, the Parliament has been arguing for the creation of a digital super-regulator to oversee the different bodies charged with safeguarding the internet and its uses, including by businesses (House of Lords 2019). However, none of these agencies have yet exposed (at least publicly) how they will interact with sector-specific agencies in the case of evidence of misbehaviour in the use of data by any of the stakeholders.

Second, the regulation and competition mandates could be consolidated into a single agency. This is the model adopted by several countries already. In 2013 Spain created a 'super-regulator', the National Commission for Markets and Competition. It merged the National Competition Commission and sectoral regulators (i.e. those responsible for telecoms, energy, postal services, audio-visual media, airport services and rail transport).[30] The same year, the Netherlands also moved in that direction, although in a somewhat less ambitious way. It created the Consumer and Market Authority by combining the Dutch Competition Authority, the Consumer Authority and the Independent Post and Telecommunications Authority.

A third solution relevant to some of the regulatory needs would be to internalize the fact that many of the actors are global. Moreover, even when the actors are local on their core business, the use of the data they can produce is global, which is why the national capacity to regulate some of the data-related issues may be hard in the first place. One way of doing this is to increase the role of supranational regulatory

---

[30] The approach is still work in progress and tension on the effective degree of independence of the various regulators continued to prevail five years after the creation of the agency (Otegui Nieto 2018).

agencies on some dimensions. But even for this type of agency, cooperation with national authorities will be essential. This is, for instance, why the European Data Protection Supervisor set up a Digital Clearing House, a voluntary network of contact points in regulatory authorities at national and EU level that are responsible for regulation of the digital sector.

The jury is still out on how best to change the institutional framework to account for the regulatory needs of the future. But it seems clear that a redesign will be essential to the viability of the reforms likely to take place in the sector as a result of the technological changes. This includes the political viability that will depend on how well the State, defined broadly, manages to ensure a fair distribution of the net gains and a minimization of the losses across stakeholders. This also means that it may be important to accept that different countries will have to adopt different institutional arrangements. The world has been experimenting for almost thirty years now with a relatively standardized approach to institutional governance. But as discussed in Chapter 13, this 'one-size-fits-all' approach has not always been as successful as it was expected to be. A minimum of common dimensions must be adopted across countries to meet the international coordination requirements but there is also a need to leave enough margin to allow national specificities to prevail to ensure the matching of the regulatory designs and institutions to the local capacity and governance constraints. The experience shows that excessive institutional standardization will under-deliver. It also shows that the new generation of institutions will need some degree of flexibility to allow their adjustment to fast-evolving sectors.

Overall, this brief discussion of the institutional challenges highlights the diversity of dimensions that should be considered. In practice, addressing the complex related issues is likely to demand ways of simplifying processes and adopting pragmatic approaches without losing the ability to be fair to all stakeholders, the consumers especially, since they tend to be passive actors. It seems clear that simplifications will lead to cutting some corners and that some situations will require a certain capacity for discretion by the regulators to deal with unforeseen contingencies. The experiment, aka the 'regulatory sandbox' depicted in Box 15.2, shows that regulators are already moving in that direction.

Maybe because of the unavoidability of corner-cutting situations, in a simpler institutional framework the regulation of the future will demand an even stronger capacity to regulate in terms of skills and tools. For instance, it is likely to demand an increase in the contribution of data scientists able to assess complex algorithms and other forms of data usage. It will also demand a more systematic analytical approach to decision-making processes to increase the transparency of trade-offs which are too often ignored in current regulatory decisions. And it will demand softer approaches to align the incentives of all stakeholders identified from this increased transparency of trade-offs. A rebalancing of the role of civil society is likely to be part of the equation, but details will have to be context-specific and ideally anchored in a more systematic use of competent and equally well-trained independent watchdogs. Ultimately, all this means that governance and processes are likely to matter even more as complexity resulting from the increased access to data explodes.

Box 15.2 Regulation in the Sandbox

From its very beginning, regulation has followed a top-down process where public authorities are the initiators and designers of constraining mechanisms imposed on big firms. Beginning a couple of decades ago, the hearings of stakeholders before implementation have introduced some form of feedback, but it remains true that regulated incumbents and newcomers have no choice: they must comply with published rules. When technologies and/or preferences evolve very quickly, standard business models and the way they are regulated become obsolete. To avoid slowing down, or even foreclosing, innovations, regulators are now experimenting with a bottom-up mechanism where products, services or business models that do not meet all the established rules can be accepted by the regulator for a limited range and duration. These 'regulatory sandboxes' are now used by many countries in the finance, health care, telecoms and energy industries (Ringe and Ruof 2020; van der Waal et al. 2020). The concept is inherited from computer sciences, where analysts need to run potentially unsafe codes without the risk of infecting the entire system. The social benefits of the sandbox system are the difference between the expected gains from innovations and the potential damage provoked by granted derogations.[31]

15.7 Will the Regulators of the Future Deliver?

Based on the discussion of the theory and evidence on the way regulation has been designed and implemented, the extent to which the regulation of the future will improve social welfare in a fair and sustainable way is likely to depend on the ability of:

(1) *regulators*, to adjust fast enough to the technological evolution in the production, consumption and financing of the regulated services. This means adopting new tools anchored in credible and evidence-based analytical assessments of their robustness and to commit the human and financial resources to enforce them.

(2) *governments and parliaments*, to internalize the knowledge accumulated by regulators and their suggestions to adjust to the evolving regulatory needs resulting from changes in demand, in technology and in supply options. This will require a willingness to adjust the mandate of regulatory agencies to account for the evolution of technology and the resulting changes in the number and nature of stakeholders. This will require a minimization of the risk of capture of the reform agenda by some of the more powerful old and new actors in the production and financing of regulated services.

---

[31] The regulators' websites provide information on their ongoing experiments. See for example www .ofgem.gov.uk/system/files/docs/2020/07/sandbox_guidance_notes.pdf and www.cre.fr/Transition-ener getique-et-innovation-technologique/dispositif-d-experimentation-reglementaire for the British and French energy regulators.

(3) *civil society*, to serve as a watchdog to ensure that the interests of all stakeholders is indeed accounted for in political government and parliamentary decisions on regulatory matters. This will require ensuring the representativeness of NGOs and other equivalent organizations such as consumers' associations but also their accountability to minimize the risk of capture of these stakeholders by special interests more concerned with private than with social welfare. These groups should systematically participate in the hearing rounds organized by regulators.

(4) *academics and policy advisors*, to develop the tools that will correct the mistakes of the past and to address the new issues appearing as regulators adjust to the changes taking place in the markets they monitor. This will require more systematic interactions with all stakeholders to get a better sense of the diversity of concerns on all sides of the regulated markets and minimize the risk of captured research agenda.

(5) *regulated firms*, to understand that they have a long-run interest in sharing information with regulators in a transparent way, even though it can be costly in the short term. This is particularly important in environments in which demand and regulatory uncertainty resulting from evolving political pressure concerning issues such as the need to address climate change are important drivers of financing requirements and options. Unless the regulators have reliable information on cost consequences of these sources of uncertainty, it will be difficult to provide a fair treatment of all regulated firms.

(6) *financial actors* such as banks and investors, to recognize that their commitment to corporate social responsibilities (CSR) imply that their discount rate and dividend expectations may need to be more carefully aligned with the long-term concerns built into these CSR. In regulated industries, this means the adoption of rules such as those linking the return to investors to the performance of the funded infrastructure. This would allow operators to hedge some of the risks associated with the evolution of policies and regulatory decisions without penalizing the investors in the longer term or the consumers and taxpayers in the short term.

An additional driver of the effectiveness of the regulation of the future is the speed at which all these stakeholders will be able to adjust to the evolving regulatory needs. Because of the intensity and the speed of the technological evolution, regulatory research and practice are often lagging a fast-moving target. Regulated firms demonstrated their ability to adapt quite fast to the opportunities offered by technology and new financing options. Unless the various State actors match this ability to adjust, the risk of information asymmetry, their abusive uses by some privileged stakeholders and the welfare costs discussed throughout the book will continue to be a significant social and political problem in the foreseeable future.

15.8   Summing Up

- The environmental concern and its social side effects will be at the core of regulation authorities' agenda on top of short-term efficiency objectives in the foreseeable future.

- The steady growth of 'big data', of digitalization and of the new data-processing technologies will change the way firms and governments use and share information in the design, compliance and enforcement of regulation.
- The institutional environment of regulation will need to evolve to correct institutional mistakes of the past and to internalize the impact of the data revolution on the distribution of regulatory mandates across agencies and across sectors within countries and across countries.
- Non-traditional financial actors will press regulators to internalize more systematically financial markets' concerns in the design of regulation in exchange for their willingness to help close the financing gap of many regulated industries.
- Keeping the right balance between the return on investment objectives of non-traditional financial actors, investment targets, users' needs and taxpayers' benefit is a challenge for the regulators of the future.
- Tools emerging from applied research in behavioural economics will offer new alternative regulatory tools to improve the effectiveness and targeting of regulation.

Bibliography

Abbott, M. and B. Cohen (2017), 'Vertical Integration, Separation in the Rail Industry: A Survey of Empirical Studies on Efficiency', *European Journal of Transport and Infrastructure Research*, 17(2): 207–24.

Abrardi, L., C. Cambini and L. Rondi (2016), 'Investment and Regulation in MENA Countries: The Impact of Regulatory Independence', in A. Rubino, V. Lenzi, I. Ozturk and M. T. Costa Campi, eds., *Regulation and Investments in Energy Markets: Solutions for the Mediterranean*, Amsterdam: Elsevier, 242–73.

Abrardi, L., C. Cambini and L. Rondi (2018), 'The Impact of Regulation on Utilities' Investments: A Survey and New Evidence from the Energy Industry', *De Economist*, 166(1): 41–62.

Aeropuertos Españoles y Navegación Aérea (AENA) (2017), Annual Report, Madrid.

Agrell, P. J. and A. Gautier (2012), 'Rethinking Regulatory Capture', in J. E. Harrington Jr and Y. Katsoulacos, eds., *Chapter 14 in Recent Advances in the Analysis of Competition Policy and Regulation*, Cheltenham: Edward Elgar, 286–302.

Ai, C. and D. E. M. Sappington (2002), 'The Impact of State Incentive Regulation on the U.S. Telecommunications Industry', *Journal of Regulatory Economics*, 22(2): 133–60.

Albalate, D. (2014), *The Privatisation and Nationalisation of European Roads: Success and Failure in Public–Private Partnerships*, Cheltenham: Edward Elgar.

Albalate, D., G. Bel and A. Gragera (2019), 'Politics, Risk, and White Elephants in Infrastructure PPPs', *Utilities Policy*, 58: 158–65.

Aldashev, G., M. Marini and T. Verdier (2015), 'Governance of Non-Profit and Non-Governmental Organizations – within- and between-Organization Analyses: An Introduction', *Annals of Public and Cooperative Economics*, 86(1): 1–5.

Alemanno, A. and A. Spina (2014), 'Nudging Legally: On the Checks and Balances of Behavioral Regulation', *International Journal of Constitutional Law*, 12(2): 429–56.

Alexander, I., C. Mayer and H. Weeds (1996), 'Regulatory Structure and Risk and Infrastructure Firms: An International Comparison', Policy Research Working Paper Series 1698, World Bank.

Alexander, I., A. Estache and A. Oliveri (2000), 'A Few Things Transport Regulators Should Know about Risk and the Cost of Capital', *Utilities Policy*, 9(1): 1–13.

Allcott, H. (2011), 'Social Norms and Energy Conservation', *Journal of Public Economics*, 95 (9–10): 1082–95.

Ambec, S. and C. Crampes (2012), 'Electricity Provision with Intermittent Sources of Energy', *Resource and Energy Economics*, 34(3): 319–36.

Ambec, S. and C. Crampes (2019), 'Decarbonizing Electricity Generation with Intermittent Sources of Energy', *Journal of the Association of Environmental and Resource Economists*, 6(6): 919–48.

Ambec, S. and C. Crampes (2021), 'Real-Time Electricity Pricing to Balance Green Energy Intermittency', *Energy Economics*, 94: 105074.

Amin, S., J. Das and M. Goldstein (2008), *Are You Being Served? New Tools for Measuring Services Delivery*, Washington, DC: World Bank.

Anderson, L. R. and S. L. Stafford (2003), 'Punishment in a Regulatory Setting: Experimental Evidence from the VCM', *Journal of Regulatory Economics*, 24(1): 91–110.

Anderson, L. R., G. DeAngelo, W. Emons, B. Freeborn and H. Lang (2017), 'Penalty Structures and Deterrence in a Two-Stage Model: Experimental Evidence', *Economic Inquiry*, 55(4): 1833–67.

Andrés, L., J. L. Guasch and S. Straub (2007), 'Do Regulation and Institutional Design Matter for Infrastructure Sector Performance?', World Bank Policy Research Working Paper Series, No. 4378.

Andrés, L. A., J. Schwartz and J. L. Guasch (2013), *Uncovering the Drivers of Utility Performance: Lessons from Latin America and the Caribbean on the Role of the Private Sector, Regulation, and Governance in the Power, Water, and Telecommunication Sectors*, Washington, DC: World Bank.

Angel-Urdinola, D. F. and Q. Wodon (2006), 'Do Utility Subsidies Reach the Poor? Framework and Evidence for Cape Verde, Sao Tome, and Rwanda', *Economics Bulletin*, 9(4): 1–7.

Angel-Urdinola, D. F. and Q. Wodon (2012), 'Does Increasing Access to Infrastructure Services Improve the Targeting Performance of Water Subsidies?', *Journal of International Development*, 24(1): 88–101.

Anguera, R. (2006), 'The Channel Tunnel – An Ex Post Economic Evaluation', *Transportation Research Part A: Policy and Practice*, 40(4): 291–315.

Armstrong, M. (2001), 'The Theory of Access Pricing and Interconnection', MPRA Paper 15608.

Armstrong M. (2006), 'Price Discrimination', MPRA Paper 4693.

Armstrong, M. and J.-C. Rochet (1999), 'Multi-Dimensional Screening: A User's Guide', *European Economic Review*, 43(4–6): 959–79.

Armstrong, M. and D. Sappington (2007), 'Recent Developments in the Theory of Regulation', in M. Armstrong and R. Porter, eds., *The Handbook of Industrial Organization*, Vol. 3, Amsterdam: Elsevier, 1557–700.

Armstrong, M. and J. Vickers (2000), 'Multiproduct Price Regulation under Asymmetric Information', *Journal of Industrial Economics*, 48(2): 137–60.

Armstrong, M. and J. Vickers (2018), 'Multiproduct Pricing Made Simple', *Journal of Political Economy*, 126(4): 1444–71.

Armstrong, M., S. Cowan and J. Vickers (1994), *Regulatory Reform: Economic Analysis and British Experience*, Boston, MA: MIT Press.

Armstrong, M., C. Doyle and J. Vickers (1996), 'The Access Pricing Problem: A Synthesis', *Journal of Industrial Economics*, 44(2): 131–50.

Arnold, J., G. Nicoletti and S. Scarpetta (2011), 'Regulation, Resource Reallocation and Productivity Growth', *EIB Papers, European Investment Bank*, 16(1): 90–115.

Asian Development Bank (2017). *Meeting Asia's Infrastructure Needs*. Manila: ADB.

Athias, L. and S. Saussier (2018), 'Are Public Private Partnerships That Rigid? and Why? Evidence from Price Provisions in French Toll Road Concession Contracts', *Transportation Research Part A: Policy and Practice*, 111: 174–86.

Athias L. and P. Wicht (2014), 'Cultural Biases in Public Service Delivery: Evidence from a Regression Discontinuity Approach', Chaire EPPP, IAE Panthéon-Sorbonne, Discussion Paper 2014–14.

Auriol, E. (1998), 'Deregulation and Quality', *International Journal of Industrial Organization*, 16: 169–94.

Auriol, E. (2000), 'Concurrence par Comparaison: un point de vue normatif', *Revue Économique*, 51: 621–34.

Auriol, E. and S. Biancini (2015), 'Powering Up Developing Countries through Economic Integration', *World Bank Economic Review*, 29(1): 1–40.

Auriol, E. and A. Blanc (2009), 'Capture and Corruption in Public Utilities: The Cases of Water and Electricity in Sub-Saharan Africa', *Utilities Policy*, 17(2): 203–16.

Auriol, E. and J.-J. Laffont (1992), 'Regulation by Duopoly', *Journal of Economics and Management Strategy*, 1(3): 507–33.

Auriol, E. and P. Picard (2009), 'Government Outsourcing: Public Contracting with Private Monopoly', *Economic Journal*, 119(540): 1464–93.

Auriol, E. and P. Picard (2011), 'A Theory of BOT Concession Contracts', *Journal of Economic Behavior & Organization*, 89(1): 187–209.

Auriol, E. and P. Picard (2013), 'A Theory of BOT Concession Contracts', *Journal of Economic Behavior and Organization*, 89: 187–209.

Auriol, E. and M. Warlters (2005), 'Taxation Base in Developing Countries', *Journal of Public Economics*, 89(4): 'Special Issue: Cornell – ISPE Conference on Public Finance and Development', April: 625–46.

Auriol, E. and M. Warlters (2012), 'The Marginal Cost of Public Funds and Tax Reform in Africa', *Journal of Development Economics*, 97(1): 58–72.

Auriol, E., A. Estache and L. Wren-Lewis (2018), 'Can Supranational Infrastructure Regulation Compensate for National Institutional Weaknesses?', *Revue Economique*, 69(6): 925–48.

Austen-Smith D. and J. S. Banks (1996), 'Information Aggregation, Rationality, and the Condorcet Jury Theorem', *American Political Science Review*, 90: 34–45.

Autor, D., D. Dorn, L. F. Katz, C. Patterson, and J. van Reenen (2017), 'Concentrating on the Fall of the Labor Share', *American Economic Review*, 107(5): 180–85.

Averch, H. and L. L. Johnson (1962), 'Behavior of the Firm under Regulatory Constraint', *American Economic Review*, 52: 1059–69.

Ayres, I., S. Raseman, and A. Shih (2013), 'Evidence from Two Large Field Experiments That Peer Comparison Feedback Can Reduce Residential Energy Usage', *Journal of Law, Economics, and Organization*, 29(5): 9921022.

Azar, J. and M. C. Schmalz (2017), 'Common Ownership of Competitors Raises Antitrust Concerns', *Journal of European Competition Law & Practice*, 8(5): 329–32.

Bageri, V., Y. Katsoulacos and G. Spagnolo (2013), 'The Distortive Effects of Antitrust Fines Based on Revenue', *Economic Journal*, 123(572): 545–57.

Bagnoli, L., S. Bertomeu-Sanchez and A. Estache (2018), 'Infrastructure Affordability in Developed and Developing Economies: Rules of Thumbs and Evidence', *Working Papers ECARES 2018-02*, Université Libre de Bruxelles.

Bagnoli, L., S. Bertomeu-Sanchez and A. Estache (2020), 'Are the Poor Better Off with Public or Private Utilities? A Survey of the Academic Evidence on Developing Economies', *Working Papers ECARES, 2020-24*, Université libre de Bruxelles.

Baker, J. B. and S. C. Salop (2015), 'Antitrust, Competition Policy, and Inequality', *Georgetown Law Journal Online*, 104(1): 1–28.

Baldwin, R., M. Cave and M. Lodge (2012), *Understanding Regulation: Theory, Strategy, and Practice*, 2nd edition, Oxford: Oxford University Press.

Barde, J. A. and P. Lehmann (2014), 'Distributional Effects of Water Tariff Reforms: An Empirical Study from Lima, Peru', *Water Resources and Economics*, 6: 30–57.

Baron, D. and D. Diermeier (2005), 'Strategic Activism and Nonmarket Strategy', *Stanford GSB Research Paper* No. 1909, August.

Baron, D. and R. Myerson (1982), 'Regulating a Monopolist with Unknown Costs', *Econometrica*, 50: 911–30.

Basu, S. (2019), 'Are Price-Cost Markups Rising in the United States? A Discussion of the Evidence', *Journal of Economics Perspectives*, 33(3): 3–22.

Baumol, W. J. (1997), 'Competitive Neutrality Via Differential Access Pricing: Preservation of Desired Cross Subsidies Under Competitive Entry', Working Papers 97-40, C. V. Starr Center for Applied Economics, New York University.

Baumol, W. J. and J. G. Sidak (1994), 'The Pricing of Inputs Sold to Competitors', *Yale Journal on Regulation*, 11(1): 171–202.

Baumol, W. J. and J. G. Sidak (1995), 'Stranded Costs', *Harvard Journal of Law & Public Policy. Summer 95*, 18(3): 835–49.

Baumol, W. J., J. C. Panzar and R. D. Willig (1982), *Contestable Markets and the Theory of Industry Structure*, San Diego, CA: Harcourt Brace Jovanovich.

Bayliss, K. (2014), 'The Financialization of Water', *Review of Radical Political Economics*, 46 (3): 292–307.

Bayliss, K. (2017), 'Material Cultures of Water Financialisation in England and Wales', *New Political Economy*, 22(4): 383–97.

Beard, R. T., D. L. Kaserman and J. W. Mayo (2003), 'Regulation, Competition, and the Optimal Recovery of Stranded Costs', *International Journal of Industrial Organization*, 21: 831–48.

Becker, G. S. (1968), 'Crime and Punishment: An Economic Approach', *Journal of Political Economy*, 76: 169–217.

Beecher, J. A. (2019), 'Does Regulation Fail or Do We Fail Regulation?', *Competition and Regulation in Network Industries*, 7 August, OnlineFirst.

Beecher, J. A. and S. G. Kihm (2016), *Risk Principle for Public Utilities Regulators*, East Lansing: Michigan State University Press.

Bel, G. (2006), 'Retrospectives: The Coining of "Privatization" and Germany's National Socialist Party', *Journal of Economic Perspectives*, 20(3): 187–94.

Bel, G. (2011), 'The First Privatisation: Selling SOEs and Privatising Public Monopolies in Fascist Italy (1922–1925)', *Cambridge Journal of Economics*, 35(5): 937–56.

Bel, G. (2020), 'Public versus Private Water Delivery, Remunicipalization and Water Tariffs', *Utilities Policy*, 62: 100982.

Bel, G., X. Fageda and M. E. Warner (2010), 'Is Private Production of Public Services Cheaper than Public Production? A Meta-regression Analysis of Solid Waste and Water Services', *Journal of Policy Analysis and Management*, 29(3): 553–77.

Bel, G., A. Estache and R. Foucart (2014), 'Transport Infrastructure Failure: Mismanagement and Incompetence or Political Capture', in T. Søreide and A. Williams, eds., *Corruption, Grabbing and Development: Real World Challenges*, Cheltenham: Edward Elgar, 129–39.

Bel, G., F. A. Gonzalez-Gomez and J. Picazo-Tadeo (2015), 'Does Market Concentration Affect Prices in the Urban Water Industry?', *Environment and Planning C*, 33(6): 1546–65.

Bel, G., P. Bel-Piñana and J. Rosell (2017), 'Myopic PPPs: Risk Allocation and Hidden Liabilities for Taxpayers and Users', *Utilities Policy*, 48: 147–56.

Benavides, J., L. Berggrun and H. Perafan (2016), 'Dividend Payout Policies: Evidence from Latin America', *Finance Research Letters*, 17: 197–210.

Berg, S. V. and J. Tschirhart (1988), *Natural Monopoly Regulation: Principles and Practice*, Cambridge: Cambridge University Press.

Bertomeu-Sanchez, S. (2019), 'On the Effects of the Financialization of Private Utilities: Lessons from the UK Water Sector', ECARES Working Papers 2019-29, Universite Libre de Bruxelles.

Bertomeu-Sanchez, S. and A. Estache (2017), 'Infrastructure Regulatory Agencies around the World', mimeo, ECARES, Université libre de Bruxelles.

Bertomeu-Sanchez, S. and A. Estache (2019), 'Should Infrastructure Regulators Regulate Dividends? Hints from a Literature Survey', ECARES Working Papers 2019-18, Université libre de Bruxelles.

Bertomeu-Sanchez, S., D. Camos and A. Estache (2018), 'Do Economic Regulatory Agencies Matter to Private-Sector Involvement in Water Utilities in Developing Countries?', *Utilities Policy*, 50(C): 153–63.

Besanko, D., S. Donnenfeld and L. White (1987), 'Monopoly and Quality Distortion: Effects and Remedies', *Quarterly Journal of Economics*, 102: 743–68.

Besanko, D., S. Donnenfeld and L. White (1988), 'The Multiproduct Firm, Quality Choice, and Regulation', *Journal of Industrial Economics*, 36(4): 411–29.

Besley, T. and S. Coate (2003), 'Elected versus Appointed Regulators: Theory and Evidence', *Journal of the European Economic Association*, 1(5): 1176–206.

Bevan, G. and D. Wilson (2013), 'Does "Naming and Shaming" Work for Schools and Hospitals? Lessons from Natural Experiments following Devolution in England and Wales', *Public Money & Management*, 33(4): 245–52.

Bier, C. (1999), 'Network Access in the Deregulated European Electricity Market: Negotiated Third-Party Access vs. Single Buyer', CSLE Discussion Paper, No. 99-06.

Biancini, S. (2011), 'Market Integration with Regulated National Champions', in O. Falck, C. Gollier and L. Woessmann, eds., *Industrial Policy for National Champions*, CESinfo Seminar Series, Boston, MA: MIT Press, 155–76.

Boiteux, M. (1956), 'Sur la gestion des monopoles publics astreints a l'equilibre budgetaire', *Econometrica*, 24(1): 22–40.

Boiteux, M. (1960), 'Peak Load Pricing', *Journal of Business*, 33(2): 157–79.

Bolton, P. and M. Dewatripont (2004), *Contract Theory*, Boston, MA: MIT Press.

Borenstein, S. and J. Bushnell (2015), 'The US Electricity Industry after 20 Years of Restructuring', *Annual Review of Economics*, 7(1): 437–63.

Borraz, F., N. Pampillón and M. Olarreaga (2013), 'Water Nationalization and Service Quality', *World Bank Economic Review*, 27(3): 389–412.

Bortolotti, B. and M. Faccio (2009), 'Government Control of Privatized Firms (August 2009)', *Review of Financial Studies*, 22(8): 2907–39.

Bortolotti, B., C. Cambini, L. Rondi and Y. Spiegel (2011), 'Capital Structure and Regulation: Do Ownership and Regulatory Independence Matter?', *Journal of Economics & Management Strategy*, 20(2): 517–64.

Bouckaert, J. and F. Verboven (2004), 'Price Squeezes in a Regulatory Environment', *Journal of Regulatory Economics*, 26(3): 321–51.

Bourreau, M., C. Cambini and P. Dogan (2012). 'Access Pricing, Competition, and Incentives to Migrate from "Old" to "New" Technology', *International Journal of Industrial Organization*, 30: 713–23.

Bourreau, M., P. Dogan and R. Lestage (2014), 'Level of Access and Infrastructure Investment in Network Industries', *Journal of Regulatory Economics*, 46: 237–60.

Bourreau, M., C. Cambini and S. Hoenig (2015), 'Geographical Access Markets and Investments in Next Generation Networks', *Information Economics and Policy*, 31: 13–21.

Bourreau, M., C. Cambini and S. Hoenig (2018), 'Cooperative Investment, Access, and Uncertainty', *International Journal of Industrial Organization*, 56: 78–106.

Bourreau, M., L. Grzybowski and M. Hasbi (2019), 'Unbundling the Incumbent and Deployment of High-Speed Internet: Evidence from France', *International Journal of Industrial Organization*, 67: 102526, DOI:10.1016/j.ijindorg.2019.102526.

Bremberger, F., C. Cambini, K. Gugler and L. Rondi (2016), 'Dividend Policy in Regulated Network Industries: Evidence from the EU', *Economic Inquiry*, 54(1): 408–32.

Brennan, T. J. (2018), 'The Rise of Behavioral Economics in Regulatory Policy: Rational Choice or Cognitive Limitation?', *International Journal of the Economics of Business*, 25(1): 97–108.

Bresnahan, T. F. and S. C. Salop (1986), 'Quantifying the Competitive Effects of Production Joint Ventures', *International Journal of Industrial Organization*, 4: 155–75.

Briglauer, W. and K. Gugler (2013), 'The Deployment and Penetration of High-Speed Fiber Networks and Services: Why Are EU Member States Lagging Behind?', *Telecommunications Policy*, 37(10): 819–35.

Briglauer, W., S. Frübing and I. Vogelsang (2015), 'The Impact of Alternative Public Policies on the Deployment of New Communications Infrastructure – A Survey', ZEW – Centre for European Economic Research Discussion Paper No. 15-003.

Briglauer, W., C. Cambini and M. Grajek (2018), 'Speeding Up the Internet: regulation and Investment in the European Fiber Optic Infrastructure', *International Journal of Industrial Organization*, 61, 613–52.

Brown, S. and D. Sibley (1986), *The Theory of Public Utility Pricing*, Cambridge: Cambridge University Press.

Bruner, D. (2009), 'Changing the Probability versus Changing the Reward', *Experimental Economics*, 12(4): 367–85.

Buckley, P. (2020) 'Prices, Information and Nudges for Residential Electricity Conservation: A Meta-analysis', *Ecological Economics*, 172, 106635.

Bulow, J. and P. Klemperer (1996), 'Auctions versus Negotiations', *American Economic Review*, 86: 180–94.

Burns, P. and C. Riechmann (2004), 'Regulatory Instruments and Investment Behavior', *Utilities Policy*, 12(4): 211–19.

Burns, P., R. Turvey and T. G. Weyman-Jones (2003), 'The Behaviour of the Firm under Alternative Regulatory Constraints', *Scottish Journal of Political Economy*, 45(2): 133–57.

Burns, P., C. Jenkins, C. Riechmann and M. Mikkers (2006), 'The Role of the Policy Framework for the Effectiveness of Benchmarking in Regulatory Proceedings', *Competition and Regulation in Network Industries*, 1(2): 287–306.

Burnside, A. J. and A. Kidane (2020), 'Common Ownership: An EU Perspective', *Journal of Antitrust Enforcement*, 8(3): 456–510.

Bustos, A. and A. Galetovic (2002), 'Regulación por Empresa Eficiente: ¿Quién es Realmente Usted?', *Centro de Estudios Públicos*, 86: 145–82.

Bustos, A. and A. Galetovic (2006), 'Monopoly Regulation, Chilean Style: The Efficient Firm Standard in Theory and Practice', in O. Chisari, ed., *Regulatory Economics and Quantitative Methods: Evidence from Latin America*, Cheltenham: Edward Elgar, 55–86.

Busuioc, M. (2009), 'Accountability, Control and Independence: The Case of European Agencies', *European Law Journal*, 15(5): 599–615.

California Public Utilities Commission (CPUC) (2018), Actions to Limit Utility Costs and Rates, Public Utilities Code Section 913.1, Annual Report to the Governor and Legislature, May, SB 695 Report 2018 FINAL.pdf (ca.gov)

Calzada, J., B. García-Mariñoso, J. Ribé, R. Rubio and D. Suárez (2018), 'Fiber Deployment in Spain', *Journal of Regulatory Economics*, 53(3): 256–74.

Calzolari, G. (2004), 'Incentive Regulation of Multinational Enterprise', *International Economic Review*, 45: 257–82.

Cambini, C. and L. Rondi (2010), 'Incentive Regulation and Investment: Evidence from European Energy Utilities', *Journal of Regulatory Economics*, 38: 1–26.

Cambini, C. and L. Rondi (2017), 'Independent Agencies, Political Interference and Firm Investment: Evidence from European Union', *Economic Inquiry*, 55(1): 281–304.

Cambini, C., E. Fumagalli and L. Rondi (2016), 'Incentives to Quality and Investment: Evidence from Electricity Distribution in Italy', *Journal of Regulatory Economics*, 49(1): 1–32.

Canales, D., S. Bouton, E. Trimble, J. Thayne, L. da Silva, S. Shastry, S. Knupfer and M. Powell (2017), *Connected Urban Growth: Public–Private Collaborations for Transforming Urban Mobility*, London, DC: Coalition for Urban Transitions, http://newclimateeconomy.net/content/cities-working-papers

Carvalho, P., R. C. Cunha Marques and S. Berg (2012), 'A Meta-Regression Analysis of Benchmarking Studies on Water Utilities Market Structure,' *Utilities Policy*, 21: 40–49.

Cave, M. (2007), 'Broadband Regulation in Europe – Present and Future', *Competition and Regulation in Network Industries*, 8(4): 405–24.

Cave, M., S. Majumdar, H. Rood, T. Valletti and I. Vogelsang (2001), 'The Relationship between Access Pricing Regulation and Infrastructure Competition', Report to OPTA and DG Telecommunications and Post, www.opta.nl/download/relationship_accesspricing_infrastructure_260301.pdf

Cherchye, L., B. De Rock, A. Estache and M. Verschelde (2018), 'Efficiency Measures in Regulated Industries: History, Outstanding Challenges and Emerging Solutions', in E. Grifell-Tatje, K. Lovell and R. Sickles, eds., *Handbook of Productivity and Efficiency Measures*, Oxford: Oxford University Press, 493–522.

Cervero, R. (2011), 'State Roles in Providing Affordable Mass Transport Services for Low-Income Residents', International Transport Forum, Discussion Paper, 2011-17, Paris: Organisation for Economic Co-operation and Development (OECD).

Chisari, O., ed. (2007), *Regulatory Economics and Quantitative Methods*, Cheltenham: Edward Elgar.

Chisari, O., A. Estache and C. Romero (1999), 'Winners and Losers from the Privatization and Regulation of Utilities: Lessons from a General Equilibrium Model of Argentina', *World Bank Economic Review*, 13(2): 357–78.

Christensen, J. G. and P. Lægreid (2002), 'New Public Management: Puzzles of Democracy and the Influence of Citizens', *Journal of Political Philosophy*, 10(3): 267–96.

Clifton, J., F. Comín and D. Diaz Fuentes (2006), 'Privatizing Public Enterprises in the European Union 1960–2002: Ideological, Pragmatic, Inevitable?', *Journal of European Public Policy*, 13(5): 736–56.

Clifton, J., P. Lanthier and H. Schröter (2011), 'Regulating and Deregulating the Public Utilities 1830–2010', *Business History*, 53(5): 659–72.

Clifton, J., D. Diaz-Fuente and M. Warner (2016), 'The Loss of Public Values When Public Shareholders Go Abroad', *Utilities Policy*, 40: 134–43.

Clifton, J., M. Warner, R. Gradus and G. Bel (2019), 'Re-municipalization of Public Services: Trend or Hype?', *Journal of Economic Policy Reform*: 1–12.

Coelli, T., A. Estache, S. Perelman and L. Trujillo (2003), *A Primer on Efficiency Measurement for Utilities and Transport Regulators*, Washington, DC: World Bank Institute.

Colombo, S. (2018), 'Behavior- and Characteristic-Based Price Discrimination', *Journal of Economics and Management Strategy*, 27(2): 237–50.

Combes, P., B. Caillaud and B. Jullien (1997), 'Common Market with Regulated Firms', *Annals of Economics and Statistics*: 65–99.

Contreras, S., A. Gómez-Lobo and I. Palma (2018), ' Revisiting the Distributional Impacts of Water Subsidy Policy in Chile: A Historical Analysis from 1998–2015', *Water Policy*, 20: 1208–26.

Costa Carvalho, A. E. and L. Menezes Bezerra Sampaio (2015), 'Paths to Universalize Water and Sewage Services in Brazil: The Role of Regulatory Authorities in Promoting Efficient Service', *Utilities Policy*, 34: 1–10.

Council of European Energy Regulators (2018), 'Status Review of Renewable Support Schemes in Europe for 2016 and 2017', Ref: C18-SD-63-03, December, www.ceer.eu/documents/104400/-/-/80ff3127-8328-52c3-4d01-0acbdb2d3bed

Crampes, C. (1999), 'Network Industries and Network Goods', *European Economy*, 4: 81–89.

Crampes, C. (2007) 'Access Pricing and Unbundling in the Electricity Industry', TSE Working Papers, August, www.tse-fr.eu/publications/access-pricing-and-unbundling-electricity-industry

Crampes, C. and N. Fabra (2005), 'The Spanish Electricity Industry: Plus ça Change...', *Energy Journal*, 26, Special Issue: European Electricity Liberalisation: 127–53.

Crampes, C. and A. Hollander (1995), 'Duopoly and Quality Standards', *European Economic Review*, 39(1): 71–82.

Crampes, C. and M. Laffont (2014), 'Connection Pricing and Universal Service Obligations in Distribution Networks', *Competition and Regulation in Network Industries*, 15(1): 32–58.

Crampes, C. and M. Laffont (2016), 'Retail Price Regulation in the British Energy Industry', *Competition and Regulation in Network Industries*, 17(3–4): 204–25.

Crampes, C. and T.-O. Léautier (2015), 'Demand Response in Adjustment Markets for Electricity', *Journal of Regulatory Economics*, 48(2): 169–93.

Crampes, C. and J. M. Lozachmeur (2014), 'Tarif progressif, efficience et équité', *Revue d'Économie Industrielle*, 148: 133–60.

Crampes, C. and J. Renault (2019), 'How Many Markets for Wholesale Electricity When Supply Is Partially Flexible?', *Energy Economics*, 81: 465–78.

Crampes, C. and J.-M. Trochet (2019), 'Economics of Stationary Electricity Storage with Various Charge and Discharge Durations', *Journal of Energy Storage*, 24: 100746.

Cremer, H., M. Marchand and J.-F. Thisse (1989), 'The Public Firm as an Instrument for Regulating an Oligopolistic Market', *Oxford Economic Papers* 41, 283–301.

Cremer, H., M. De Rycke and A. Grimaud (1997), 'Service Quality, Competition and Regulatory Policies in the Postal Sector', *Journal of Regulatory Economics*, 11: 5–19.

Crew, M. A. and P. R. Kleindorfer (2012), 'Regulatory Economics and the Journal of Regulatory Economics: A 30-Year Retrospective', *Journal of Regulatory Economics*, 41(1): 1–18.

Crew, M. A. and D. Parker, eds. (2006), *International Handbook on Economic Regulation*, Cheltenham: Edward Elgar.

Crew, M. A., P. Kleindorfer and J. Sumpter (2005), 'Bringing Competition to Telecommunications by Divesting the RBOCs', in M. A. Crew and M. Spiegel, eds., *Obtaining the Best from Regulation and Competition*, New York: Kluwer Academic Publishers, 21–40.

Crouzet, N. and J. Eberly (2018), 'Intangibles, Investment, and Efficiency', *AEA Papers and Proceedings*, 108: 426–31.

Cubbin, J. and J. Stern (2006), 'The Impact of Regulatory Governance and Privatization on Electricity Industry Generation Capacity in Developing Economies', *World Bank Economic Review*, 20(1): 115–41.

Cullman, A. and M. Nieswand (2016), 'Regulation and Investment Incentives in Electricity Distribution: An Empirical Assessment', *Energy Economics*, 57: 192–203.

Cunha Marques, R. (2018), 'Regulation by Contract: Overseeing PPPs', *Utilities Policy*, 50: 211–14.

Dal Bo, E. (2006), 'Regulatory Capture: A Review', *Oxford Review of Economic Policy*, 22(2): 203–25.

Dalen, D. M. (1998), 'Yardstick Competition and Investment Incentives', *Journal of Economics & Management Strategy*, 7(1): 105–26.

Damodaran, A. (2020), 'Risk Premiums: Determinants, Estimation and Implications - The 2020 Edition', New York University, Stern School of Business, https://ssrn.com/abstract=3550293 or http://dx.doi.org/10.2139/ssrn.3550293

Darby, M. and E. Karni (1973), 'Free Competition and the Optimal Amount of Fraud', *Journal of Law and Economics*, 16(1): 67–88.

Datta, S., J. J. Miranda, L. Zoratto, O. Calvo-Gonzalez, M. Darling and K. Lorenzana (2015), 'A Behavioral Approach to Water Conservation: Evidence from Costa Rica', *World Bank Policy Research Working Paper*, No. 7283.

Decker, C. (2014), *Modern Economic Regulation: An Introduction to Theory and Practice*, Cambridge: Cambridge University Press.

De Fraja, G. (2009), 'Mixed Oligopoly: Old and New', University of Leicester, Working Paper no. 09/20, September.

De Halleux, M., A. Estache and T. Serebrisky (2019), 'How Much Does Technology Impact the Management of Latin American Cities?', IDB Technical Note 1497, Inter-American Development Bank.

De Loecker, J. and J. Eeckhout (2017), 'The Rise of Market Power and the Macroeconomic Implications', NBER Working Paper 23687.

De Loecker, J. and J. Eeckhout (2018), 'Global Market Power', NBER Working Paper w24768.

Den Hertog, J. A. (2012), 'Economic Theories of Regulation', in R. J. van den Berg and A. M. Pacces, eds., *Regulation and Economics*, Cheltenham: Edward Elgar, 25–96.

De Witte, K. and D. Saal (2009), 'Is a Little Sunshine All We Need? On the Impact of Sunshine Regulation on Profits, Productivity and Prices in the Dutch Drinking Water Sector', *Journal of Regulatory Economics*, 37(3): 219–42.

DG Competition (2007), Final Report on Energy Sector Inquiry, 10.1.2007 ('Sector Inquiry Report'), http://ec.europa.eu/competition/sectors/energy/inquiry/full_report_part1.pdf

DiaCore (2016), 'The Impact of Risks in Renewable Energy Investments and the Role of Smart Policies', Final Report to the European Commission, http://diacore.eu/images/files2/WP3-Final%20Report/diacore-2016-impact-of-risk-in-res-investments.pdf

Dierker, D. (1991), 'The Optimality of Boiteux–Ramsey Pricing', *Econometrica*, 59(1): 99–121.

Diez, F. J., J. Fan and C. Villegas-Sánchez (2019), 'Global Declining Competition', IMF Working Paper No. 19/82.

Diez, F. J., D. Leigh and S. Tambunlertchai (2018), 'Global Market Power and Its Macroeconomic Implications', IMF Working Paper No. 18/137.

Djankov, S., D. Georgieva and R. Ramalho (2018), 'Business Regulations and Poverty', *Economics Letters*, 165(C): 82–87.

Dobbs, I. M. (2004), 'Intertemporal Price Cap Regulation under Uncertainty', *Economic Journal*, 114: 421–40.

Dobbs, I. M. (2011), 'Modeling Welfare Loss Asymmetries Arising from Uncertainty in the Regulatory Cost of Finance', *Journal of Regulatory Economics*, 39(1): 1–28.

Döttling, R., G. Gutierrez Gallardo and T. Philippon (2017), 'Is There an Investment Gap in Advanced Economies? If So, Why?', Proceedings of the ECB Forum on Central Banking: Investment and Growth in Advanced Economies, Sintra, Portugal.

Dunkerley, F., C. Rohr and A. Daly (2016), *Road Traffic Demand Elasticities: A Rapid Evidence Assessment*, Santa Monica, CA: RAND Corporation.

Eberhard, A. A. (2008), 'A Re-assessment of Independent Regulation of Infrastructure in Developing Countries: Improving Performance through Hybrid and Transitional Models', in J.-M. Chevalier, J. H. Frison-Roche, J. H. Keppler and P. Noumba Um, eds., *Droit et économie des infrastructures essentielles* (perspectives dans les pays en voie de développement, Paris: Lextenso-editions, 185–216.

Egert, B. (2009), 'Infrastructure Investment in Network Industries: The Role of Incentive Regulation and Regulatory Independence', *OECD Economics Department Working Papers*, No. 688, Paris: OECD Publishing.

Elhauge, E. (2020), 'How Horizontal Shareholding Harms Our Economy – And Why Antitrust Law Can Fix It', *Harvard Business Law Review*, 10(2) 207–86.

Encoua, D. and A. Jacquemin (1980), 'Degree of Monopoly, Indices of Concentration and Threat of Entry', *International Economic Review*, 21(1): 87–105.

Engel, E., R. Fisher and A. Galetovic (2014), *The Economics of Public–Private Partnerships: A Basic Guide*, Cambridge: Cambridge University Press.

Ennis, S. F., P. Gonzaga and C. Pike (2019), 'Inequality: A Hidden Cost of Market Power', *Oxford Review of Economic Policy*, 35(3): 518–49.

Escrihuela-Villar, M. and C. Gutiérrez-Hita (2019), 'On Competition and Welfare Enhancing Policies in a Mixed Oligopoly', *Journal of Economics*, 126: 259–74.

Estache, A. (2014), 'Infrastructure and Corruption: A Brief Survey', *Working Papers ECARES* 2014-37, Université Libre de Bruxelles.

Estache, A. (2019), Comments on C. Godinho and A. Eberhard, 'Power', chapter 7, Tanzania Institutional Diagnostics, https://edi.opml.co.uk/resource/tanzania-institutional-diagnostic-chapter-7/

Estache, A. (2020a), 'Infrastructure "Privatization": When Ideology Meets Evidence', ECARES Working Papers, No. 2020-28, Université Libre de Bruxelles.

Estache, A. (2020b), 'Institutions for Infrastructure in Developing Countries: What We Know and the Lot We still Need to Know', in J. M. Baland, F. Bourguignon, J. P. Platteau and T. Verdier, eds., *The Handbook of Economic Development and Institutions*, Princeton, NJ: Princeton University Press, 634–88.

Estache, A. and R. Foucart (2019), 'The Scope and Limits of Accounting and Judicial Courts Intervention in Inefficient Public Procurement', *Journal of Public Economics*, 157: 95–106.

Estache, A. and M. Goldstein (2009), 'Subsidies', in A. Estache and D. Leipziger, eds., *Stuck in the Middle: Is Fiscal Policy Failing the Middle Class?*, Washington, DC: Brookings Institution.

Estache, A. and E. Grifell-Tatjé (2013), 'How (Un) Even Was the Distribution of the Impacts of Mali's Water Privatization across Stakeholders?', *Journal of Development Studies*, 49(4): 483–99.

Estache, A. and A. Iimi (2011), *The Economics of Infrastructure Procurement: Theory and Evidence*, London: CEPR. Centre for Economic Policy Research

Estache, A. and B. Kouevi Gath (2019), 'Corporate Income Taxes and (Un-)Employment in the OECD', ECARES Working Papers, No. 2019-11, Université Libre de Bruxelles.

Estache, A. and D. Martimort (2000), 'Transaction Costs, Politics, Regulatory Institutions and Regulatory Outcomes', in L. Manzetti, ed., *Regulatory Policy in Latin America: Post-Privatization Realities*, Miami, FL: North–South Press Center at the University of Miami.

Estache, A. and S. Saussier (2014), 'Public–Private Partnerships and Efficiency: A Short Assessment', *CESifo DICE Report* 3/2014 (September): 8–13.

Estache, A. and T. Serebrisky (2020), 'Updating Infrastructure Regulation for the 21st Century in Latin America and the Caribbean', IDB Technical Note, TN 01856, January.

Estache, A. and Q. Wodon (2014), *Infrastructure and Poverty in Sub-Saharan Africa*, New York: Palgrave Macmillan.

Estache, A. and L. Wren-Lewis (2009), 'Towards a Theory of Regulation for Developing Countries: Following Jean-Jacques Laffont's Lead', *Journal of Economic Literature*, 47: 729–70.

Estache, A., and L. Wren-Lewis (2010), 'Regulation in Developing Economics: A Survey of Theory and Evidence', in R. Baldwin, M. Cave and M. Lodge, eds., *Oxford Handbook of Regulation*, Oxford: Oxford University Press, 371–406.

Estache, A., V. Foster and Q. Wodon (2002), *Accounting for Poverty in Infrastructure Reform – Learning from Latin America's Experience*, Washington, DC: World Bank Institute Publications, Studies in Development Series.

Estache, A., J. J. Laffont and X. Zhang (2006), 'Universal Service Obligations in LDCs: The Effect of Uniform Pricing on Infrastructure Access', *Journal of Public Economics*, 90(6–7): 1155–79.

Estache, A., T. Serebrisky and L. Wren-Lewis (2015), 'Financing Infrastructure in Developing Countries', *Oxford Review of Economic Policy*, 31(3–4): 279–304.

Estache, A., G. Garsous and R. Seroa da Motta (2016), 'Shared Mandates, Moral Hazard and Political (Mis)alignment in a Decentralized Economy', *World Development*, 83: 98–110.

Estrin, S. and A. Pelletier (2018), 'Privatization in Developing Countries: What Are the Lessons of Recent Experience?', *World Bank Research Observer*, 33(1): 65–102.

European Commission (2003), *Guidelines for Successful Public–Private Partnerships*, March, https://ec.europa.eu/regional_policy/sources/docgener/guides/ppp_en.pdf

European Commission (2016), 'State-Owned Enterprises in the EU: Lessons Learnt and the Way Forward in the Post-Crisis Context', *European Economy Institutional Papers* No. 31.

European Court of Auditors (2018), *Public Private Partnerships in the EU: Widespread Shortcomings and Limited Benefits*, www.eca.europa.eu/en/Pages/DocItem.aspx?did=45153

Evans, L. and G. Guthrie (2012), 'Price-Cap Regulation and the Scale and Timing of Investment', *RAND Journal of Economics*, 43(3): 537–61.

Ezrachi, A. and M. E. Stucke (2015), 'Artificial Intelligence and Collusion: When Computers Inhibit Competition', Oxford Legal Studies Research Paper No. 18/2015, University of Tennessee Legal Studies Research Paper No. 267.

Fabrizio, K., N. Rose and C. Wolfram (2007), 'Do Markets Reduce Costs? Assessing the Impact of Regulatory Restructuring on US Electric Generation Efficiency', *American Economic Review*, 97(4): 1250–77.

Fallah-Fini, S., K. Triantis and A. L. Johnson (2013), 'Reviewing the Literature on Non-Parametric Dynamic Efficiency Measurement: State-of-the-Art', *Journal of Productivity Analysis*, 41: 1–17.

Färe, R. and S. Grosskopf (1996), *Intertemporal Production Frontiers: With Dynamic DEA*, New York: Springer.

Faulhaber, G. R. (2005), 'Cross-Subsidy Analysis with More than Two Services', *Journal of Competition Law and Economics*, 1(3): 441–48.

Fay, M., L. Andres, E. C. J. Fox, G. Ulf Narloch, S. Straub and M. A. Slawson (2017), *Rethinking Infrastructure in Latin America and the Caribbean: Spending Better to Achieve More*, Washington, DC: World Bank.

Federal Energy Regulatory Commission (2020), *Midcontinent Independent System Operator, Inc.; Supplemental Notice of Technical Conference*, [Docket No. ER20-588-000], www.govinfo.gov/content/pkg/FR-2020-05-07/pdf/2020-09751.pdf

Fernandez, P. (2019), 'WACC and CAPM According to Utilities Regulators: Confusions, Errors and Inconsistencies', University of Navarra – IESE Business School, https://ssrn.com/abstract=3327206 or http://dx.doi.org/10.2139/ssrn.3327206

Fernández-i-Marín, X., J. Jordana and A. Biancully (2015), 'Varieties of Accountability Mechanisms in Regulatory Agencies', in A. Bianculli, J. Jordana, X. Fernández-i-Marín, eds., *Accountability and Regulatory Governance: Audiences, Controls and Responsibilities in the Politics of Regulation*, New York: Palgrave Macmillan.

Ferrando-Gamir, A. (2015), 'Spain Case Study: Mapping High-Level Corruption in Spanish Public Procurement', Corruption Research Center, Budapest, February.

Ferraro, P. J. and M. K. Price (2013), 'Using Nonpecuniary Strategies to Influence Behavior: Evidence from a Large-Scale Field Experiment', *Review of Economics and Statistics*, 95(1): 64–73.

Ferraz, C. and F. Finan (2008), 'Exposing Corrupt Politicians: The Effects of Brazil's Publicly Released Audits on Electoral Outcomes', *Quarterly Journal of Economics*, 123(2): 703–74.

Ferraz, C. and F. Finan (2011), 'Electoral Accountability and Corruption: Evidence from the Audits of Local Governments', *American Economic Review*, 101(4): 1274–311.

Finger, M. and C. Jaag, eds. (2016), *The Routledge Companion to Network Industries*, London: Routledge.

Fiorio, C. V. and M. Florio (2013), 'Electricity Prices and Public Ownership: Evidence from the EU15 over Thirty Years', *Energy Economics*, 39: 222–32.

Fjell, K. (2001), 'A Cross-Subsidy Classification Framework', *Journal of Public Policy*, 21(3): 265–82.

Florio, M. (2013a), *Network Industries and Social Welfare: The Experiment that Reshuffled European Utilities*, Oxford: Oxford University Press.

Florio, M. (2013b), 'Rethinking on Public Enterprise: Editorial Introduction and Some Personal Remarks on the Research Agenda', *International Review of Applied Economics*, 27(2): 135–49.

Florio, M., M. Ferraris and D. Vandone (2018a), 'Motives of Mergers and Acquisitions by State-Owned Enterprises: A Taxonomy and International Evidence', *International Journal of Public Sector Management*, 31(2): 142–66.

Florio, M., V. Morretta and W. Willak (2018b), 'Cost–Benefit Analysis and European Union Cohesion Policy: Economic versus Financial Returns in Investment Project Appraisal', *Journal of Benefit–Cost Analysis*, 9(1): 147–80.

Florio, M., M. Ferraris and D. Vandone (2018c), 'State-Owned Enterprises: Rationales for Mergers and Acquisitions', CIRIEC Working Papers 1801, CIRIEC – Université de Liège.

Flyvbjerg, B. (2008), 'Curbing Optimism Bias and Strategic Misrepresentation in Planning: Reference Class Forecasting in Practice', *European Planning Studies*, 16: 3–21.

Flyvbjerg, B. (2014), 'What You Should Know about Megaprojects and Why: An Overview', *Project Management Journal*, 45(2): 6–19.

Flyvbjerg, B. (2017), *Oxford Handbook of Megaproject Management*, Oxford: Oxford University Press.

Flyvbjerg, B., N. Bruzelius and W. Rothengatter (2003), *Megaprojects and Risk: An Anatomy of Ambition*, Cambridge: Cambridge University Press.

Ford, J. and G. Plimmer (2018), 'Returning the UK's Privatised Services to the Public', *Financial Times*, 26 February.

Foster, V. and A. Rana (2020), *Rethinking Power Sector Reform in the Developing World: Sustainable Infrastructure*, Washington, DC: World Bank.

Foster, V., S. Witte, S. G. Banerjee and A. Moreno (2017), 'Charting the Diffusion of Power Sector Reforms across the Developing World', Policy Research Working Paper No. 8235, Washington, DC: World Bank.

Fouquet, R. (2014), 'Long-Run Demand for Energy Services: Income and Price Elasticities over Two Hundred Years', *Review of Environmental Economics and Policy*, 8(2): 186–207.

Furman, J. (2018), 'Antitrust in a Changing Economy and Changing Economics', *Promarket*, Stigler Center of the Economy and the State, Chicago University Booth School of Business, 30 November.

Gal, P., G. Nicoletti, T. Renault, S. Sorbe and C. Timiliotis (2019), 'Digitalisation and Productivity: In Search of the holy Grail – Firm-Level Empirical Evidence from EU Countries', OECD *Economics Department Working Papers* 1533.

Garcia-Sierra, M., J. van den Bergh and C. Miralles-Guasch (2015), 'Behavioural Economics, Travel Behaviour and Environmental-Transport Policy', *Transportation Research Part D: Transport and Environment*, 41: 288–305.

Gassner, K., A. Popov and N. Pushak (2009), *Does Private Sector Participation Improve Performance in Electricity and Water Distribution?*, Washington, DC: World Bank.

Gassner, K., and Pushak, N. (2014), '30 Years of British Utility Regulation: Developing Country Experience and Outlook', *Utilities Policy*, 31: 44–51.

Gaudin, G. and D, Mantzari (2016), 'Margin Squeeze: An Above-Cost Predatory Pricing Approach', *Journal of Competition Law & Economics*, 12(1): 151–79.

Gautier, A. and M. Mitra (2006), 'Regulating a Monopolist with Limited Funds', *Economic Theory*, 27(3): 705–18.

Georgoulias, A., G. Giovanni, L. Frisari, H. Meller, M. C. Ramirez, T. Serebrisky and G. Watkins (2018), 'Attractors of Institutional Investment in Latin American Infrastructure Lessons from Envision Project Case Studies', *Technical Note* No. IDB-TN-1386, Inter-American Development Bank.

Gifford, D. J. and R. T. Kudrle (2010), 'The Law and Economics of Price Discrimination in Modern Economies: Time for Reconciliation?', *UC Davis Law Review*, 1235: 1241–42.

Gilardi, F. (2007), 'The Same, but Different: Central Banks, Regulatory Agencies, and the Politics of Delegation to Independent Authorities', *Comparative European Politics*, 5(3): 303–27.

Gilardi, F. and M. Maggetti (2011), 'The Independence of Regulatory Authorities', in D. Levi-Faur, ed., *Handbook on Regulation*, Cheltenham: Edward Elgar, 201–14.

Giordano, P., ed. (2017), *Trade and Integration Monitor 2017: Beyond the Recovery: Competing for Market Share in the Digital Era*, Washington, DC: Inter-American Development Bank.

Goldfarb, A. and C. Tucker (2019), 'Digital Economics', *Journal of Economic Literature*, 57(1): 3–43.

Gomez-Ibanez, J. A. (2006), *Regulating Infrastructure: Monopoly, Contracts, and Discretion: Monopoly, Contracts and Discretion*, Cambridge, MA: Harvard University Press.

Gomez-Lobo, A. (2003), 'Determinación de la eficiencia operativa en la regulación de monopolios naturales: el uso de información de consultores versus competencia por comparaciones', Universidad de Chile, Departamento de Economía, Documento de Trabajo no. 204.

Gómez-Lobo, A. (2006), 'Bottom-Up or Top-Down Benchmarking in Natural Monopoly Regulation: The Case of Chile and the United Kingdom', in O. Chisari, ed., *Regulatory Economics and Quantitative Methods*, Cheltenham: Edward Elgar.

Gomez-Lobo, A. (2011), 'Affordability of Public Transport: A Methodological Clarification', *Journal of Transport Economics and Policy*, 45(3): 473–56.

Gómez-Lobo, A. and M. Vargas (2002), 'La regulación de las empresas sanitarias en Chile: una revisión crítica', *Perspectivas*, 6(1): 79–109.

Gonzalez, M., C. Molina Manzano, E. Pablo and J. W. Rosso (2017), 'The Effect of Ownership Concentration and Composition on Dividends: Evidence from Latin America', *Emerging Markets Review*, 30(C): 1–18.

Greenstein, S., S. McMaster and P. Spiller (1995), 'The Effect of Incentive Regulation on Infrastructure Modernization: Local Exchange Companies' Deployment of Digital Technology', *Journal of Economics and Management Strategy*, 4(2): 187–236.

Grifell-Tatje, E. and C. A. Knox Lovell (2003), 'The Managers versus the Consultants', *Scandinavian Journal of Economics*, 105(1): 119–38.

Grifell-Tatje E., K. Lovell and R. Sickles, eds. (2018), *The Oxford Handbook of Productivity Analysis*, Oxford: Oxford University Press.

Guasch, J. L., D. Benitez, I. Portabales and L. Flor (2014), 'The Renegotiation of PPP Contracts: An Overview of Its Recent Evolution in Latin America', *International Transport Forum Discussion Papers* No. 2014/18, OECD.

Guasch, J. L., J. J. Laffont and S. Straub (2016), 'Renegotiation of Concession Contracts: A Theoretical Approach', *Review of Industrial Organization*, 29: 55–73.

Guasch, J. L., D. Benitez, I. Portabalesi and L. Flor (2017), 'The Renegotiation of Public–Private Partnership Contracts: An Overview of the Recent Evolution in Latin America', in *Public Private Partnerships for Transport Infrastructure: Renegotiation and Economic Outcomes*, Paris: Éditions OCDE.

Guerriero, C. (2013), 'The Political Economy of Incentive Regulation: Theory and Evidence from the U.S. States', *Journal of Comparative Economics*, 41: 91–107.

Gugler, K., M. Liebensteiner and S. Schmitt (2017), 'Vertical Disintegration in the European Electricity Sector: Empirical Evidence on Lost Synergies', *International Journal of Industrial Organization*, 52: 450–78.

Guinea, O. and F. Erixon (2019), 'Standing Up for Competition: Market Concentration, Regulation, and Europe's Quest for a New Industrial Policy', ECIPE Occasional Paper 01/2019, European Center for International Political Economy.

Guthrie, G. (2006), 'Regulating Infrastructure: The Impact on Risk and Investment', *Journal of Economic Literature*, 44(4): 925–72.

Gutierrez, G. and T. Philippon (2018), 'How EU Markets Became More Competitive than US Markets: A Study of Institutional Drift', Working Paper 24700, National Bureau of Economic Research.

Gutierrez, G. and T. Philippon (2019), 'Fading Stars', *AEA Papers and Proceedings*, 109: 312–16.

Hagerman, R. and B. Ratchford (1978), 'Some Determinants of Allowed Rates of Return on Equity to Electric Utilities', *Bell Journal of Economics*, 9(1): 46–55.

Haney, A. B. and M. Pollitt (2010), 'New Models of Public Ownership in Energy', *International Review of Applied Economics*, October, https://doi.org/10.1080/02692171.2012.734790

Harberger, A. C. (1954), 'Monopoly and Resource Allocation', *American Economic Review*, 44 (2), Papers and Proceedings of the Sixty-sixth Annual Meeting of the American Economic Association): 77–87.

Harrington, J. E. (2017), 'Developing Competition Law for Collusion by Autonomous Agents', The Wharton School, University of Pennsylvania.

Hawthorne, R. and L. Grzybowski (2019), 'Benefits of Regulation vs. Competition Where Inequality Is High: The Case of Mobile Telephony in South Africa', *CESifo Working Paper* No. 7703.

Heimler, A. and Mehta, K. (2012) 'Violations of Antitrust Provisions: The Optimal Level of Fines for Achieving Deterrence', *World Competition*, 35 (1): 103–19.

Helm, D. (2018), 'The Dividend Puzzle: What Should Utilities Pay Out?', www.dieterhelm.co.uk/regulation/regulation/the-dividend-puzzle-what-should-utilities-pay-out/

Heymans, C., K. Eales and R. Franceys (2014), *The Limits and Possibilities of Prepaid Water in Urban Africa: Lessons from the Field*, Washington, DC: World Bank.

Hobman, E. V., E. R. Frederiks, K. Stenner and S. Meikle (2016), 'Uptake and Usage of Cost-Reflective Electricity Pricing: Insights from Psychology and behavioural Economics', *Renewable and Sustainable Energy Reviews*, 57: 455–67.

House of Lords (2019), *Select Committee on Communications Regulating in a Digital World*, 2nd Report of Session 2017–19 – published 9 March 2019 – HL Paper 299, https://publications.parliament.uk/pa/ld201719/ldselect/ldcomuni/299/29902.htm

Imam, M. I., T. Jamasb and M. Llorca (2018), 'Sector Reforms and Institutional Corruption: Evidence from Electricity Industry in Sub-Saharan Africa', Working Papers EPRG 1801, Energy Policy Research Group, Cambridge Judge Business School, University of Cambridge.

International Energy Agency (2017), *Digitalization and Energy*, Paris: IEA.

International Monetary Fund (IMF) (2019), 'World Economic Outlook – Growth Slowdown, Precarious Recovery', April, Washington, DC.

International Renewable Energy Agency (IRENA) (2019), *Global Energy Transformation: A Roadmap to 2050*, Abu Dhabi: International Renewable Energy Agency.

Iossa, E. (1999), 'Informative Externalities and Pricing in Regulated Multiproduct Industries', *Journal of Industrial Economics*, 47(2): 195–219.

Iossa, E. and D. Martimort (2015), 'The Simple Microeconomics of Public–Private Partnerships', *Journal of Public Economic Theory*, 17(1), Special Issue on Public–Private Partnerships: 4–48.

Ito, K. (2014), 'Do Consumers Respond to Marginal or Average Price? Evidence from Nonlinear Electricity Pricing', *American Economic Review*, 104(2): 537–63.

Jaime Torres, M. M. and F. Carlsson (2016), 'Social Norms and Information Diffusion in Water-Saving Programs: Evidence from a Randomized Field Experiment in Colombia', University of Gothenburg, Department of Economics, *Working Papers in Economics*, No. 652.

Jamasb, T., T. Triptar and B. Baidyanath (2018), 'Smart Electricity Distribution Networks, Business Models, and Application for Developing Countries', *Energy Policy*, 114(C): 22–29.

Joanis, M. (2014), 'Shared Accountability and Partial Decentralization in Local Public Good Provision', *Journal of Development Economics*, 107: 28–37.

Jordana, J. and D. Levi-Faur (2004), 'The Politics of Regulation in the Age of Governance', in J. Jordana and D. Levi-Faur, eds., *The Politics of Regulation*, Cheltenham: Edward Elgar, 1–30.

Jorisch, D., C. Mallin, M. Accurso, A. Garcia Zaballos and E. Iglesias Rodríguez (2018), *Technology for Climate Action in Latin America and the Caribbean: How ICT and Mobile Solutions Contribute to a Sustainable, Low-Carbon Future*, Washington, DC: Inter-American Development Bank.

Joskow, P. L. (1996), 'Does Stranded Cost Recovery Distort Competition?', *Electricity Journal*, 9(3): 31–45.

Joskow, P. L. (2005), 'Regulation and Deregulation after 25 Years: Lessons Learned fir Research in Industrial Organization', *Review of Industrial Organization*, 26(2): 169–93.

Joskow, P. L. (2007), 'Regulation of Natural Monopoly', in A. M. Polinsky and S. Shavell, eds., *Handbook of Law and Economics*, Amsterdam: Elsevier, Vol. 2: 1227–348.

Joskow, P. L. (2014), 'Incentive Regulation in Theory and Practice: Electricity Distribution and Transmission Networks', in N. Rose, ed., *Economic Regulation and Its Reform: What Have We Learned?*, Boston: National Bureau of Economic Research, 291–344.

Joskow P. L. and C. D. Wolfram (2012), 'Dynamic Pricing of Electricity', *American Economic Review: Papers & Proceedings*, 102(3): 381–85.

Junge C., D. Mallapragada and R. Schmalensee (2021), 'Energy Storage Investment and Operation in Efficient Electric Power Systems', MIT CEEPR Working Paper 2021-001, January.

Keep, M. (2021), 'Infrastructure Policies and Investment', Briefing Paper 6594, March, London: House of Commons Library.

Kelsey, J. B. and G. Smith (2015), 'Pay as You Go: Prepaid Metering and Electricity Expenditures in South Africa', *American Economic Review*, 105(5): 237–41.

Kenny, C. (2010), 'Publishing Construction Contracts and Outcome Details', Policy Research Working Paper Series 5247, World Bank.

Kenny, C. and Musatova, M. (2011), '"Red Flags of Corruption" in World Bank Projects: An Analysis of Infrastructure Contracts', in S. Rose-Ackerman and T. Søreide, eds., *International Handbook on the Economics of Corruption*, Vol. 2, chapter 18, Cheltenham: Edward Elgar, 499–527.

Knowles, G. L. (2003), 'Liquefied Natural Gas: Regulation in a Competitive Natural Gas Market', *Energy Law Journal*, 24(2): 293–319.

Kotakorpi, K. (2005), 'Access Price Regulation, Investment and Entry in Telecommunications', *International Journal of Industrial Organization*, 24(5): 1013–20.

Krämer, J. and D. Schnurr (2018), 'Margin Squeeze Regulation and Infrastructure Competition', *Information Economics and Policy*, 45(C): 30–46.

Krueger, M. (2009), 'The Elasticity Pricing Rule for Two-Sided Markets: A Note', *Review of Network Economics*, 8: 271–78.

Krupa, J. and D. Harvey (2017), 'Renewable Electricity Finance in the United States: A State-of-the-Art Review', *Energy*, 135(C): 913–29.

Küfeoglu, S., M. Politt and K. Anaya (2018), 'Electric Power Distribution in the World: Today and Tomorrow', *EPRG Working Paper* 1826, Cambridge Working Paper in Economics.

Laffont, J. J. and D. Martimort (1999), 'Separation of Regulators against Collusive Behavior', *RAND Journal of Economics*, 30(2): 232–62.

Laffont, J. J. and D. Martimort (2002), *The Theory of Incentives: The Principal–Agent Model*, Princeton, NJ: Princeton University Press.

Laffont, J. J. and E. Maskin (1987), 'Monopoly with Asymmetric Information about Quality: Behavior and Regulation', *European Economic Review*, 31(1–2): 483–89.

Laffont, J. J. and J. Tirole (1986), 'Using Cost Observation to Regulate Firms', *Journal of Political Economy*, 94(3): 614–41.

Laffont, J. J. and J. Tirole (1990a), 'The Politics of Government Decision Making: Regulatory Institutions', *Journal of Law, Economics, and Organization*, 6(1): 1–31.

Laffont, J. J. and J. Tirole (1990b), 'The Regulation of Multiproduct Firms: Part I: Theory', *Journal of Public Economics*, 4(1): 1–36.

Laffont, J. J. and J. Tirole (1990c), 'The Regulation of Multiproduct Firms: Part II: Applications to Competitive Environments and Policy Analysis', *Journal of Public Economics*, 43 (1): 37–67.

Laffont, J. J. and J. Tirole (1993), *A Theory of Incentives in Procurement and Regulation*, Cambridge, MA: MIT Press.

Laffont, J. J. and J. Tirole (1994), 'Access Pricing and Competition', *European Economic Review*, 38(9): 1673–710.

Laffont, J. J. and J. Tirole (1995), 'Using Cost Observation to Regulate Firms', in K. Hartley and T. Sandler, eds., *The Economics of Defense*, series 'International Library of Critical Writings in Economics', Vol. II, Cheltenham: Edward Elgar, 239–66.

Laffont, J. J. and J. Tirole (2000a), 'Using Cost Observation to Regulate Firms', in P. L. Joskow, ed., *Economic Regulation*, series 'Critical Ideas in Economics', Cheltenham: Edward Elgar, 310–37.

Laffont, J. J. and J. Tirole (2000b), 'The Regulation of Multiproduct Firms: Part I: Theory', in P. L. Joskow, ed., *Economic Regulation*, Cheltenham: Edward Elgar, series 'Critical Ideas in Economics', 94–115.

Laffont, J. J. and J. Tirole (2000c), *Competition in Telecommunications*, Boston, MA: MIT Press.

Laine, L. T. and C. T. A. Ma (2017), 'Quality and Competition between Public and Private Firms', *Journal of Economic Behavior & Organization*, 140: 336–53.

Lambrecht, A., K. Seim, N. Vilcassim, A. Cheema, Y. Chen, G. S. Crawford, K. Hosanagar, R. Iyengar, O. Koenigsberg, R. Lee, E. J. Miravete and O. Sahin (2012), 'Price Discrimination in Service Industries', *Marketing Letters*, 23(2): 423–38.

Landes, W. W. and R. A. Posner (1981), 'Market Power in Antitrust Cases', *Harvard Law Review*, 94(5): 937–96.

Law, S. M. (2014), 'Assessing the Averch–Johnson–Welliz Effect for Regulated Utilities', *International Journal of Economics and Finance*, 6(8): 41–67.

Law, M. T. and C. X. Long (2011), 'Revolving Door Laws and State Public Utility Commissioners', *Governance and Regulation*, 5: 405–25.

Leautier, T.-O. (2019), *Imperfect Markets and Imperfect Regulation: An Introduction to the Microeconomics and Political Economy of Power Markets*, Boston, MA: MIT Press.

Leibenstein, H. (1966), 'Allocative Efficiency vs. "X-Efficiency"', *American Economic Review*, 56(3): 392–415.

Leigland, J. (2018), 'Public–Private Partnerships in Developing Countries: The Emerging Evidence-based Critique', *The World Bank Research Observer*, 33(1): 103–34.

Lerner, A. (1934), 'The Concept of Monopoly and the Measurement of Monopoly Power', *Review of Economic Studies*, 1(3): 157–75.

Levi-Faur, D., ed. (2011), *Handbook on the Politics of Regulation*, Cheltenham: Edward Elgar.

Levy, B. and P. Spiller (1994), 'The Institutional Foundations of Regulatory Commitment: A Comparative Analysis of Telecommunications Regulation', *Journal of Law, Economics, & Organization*, 10(2): 201–46.

Liemberger, R. and A. Wyatt (2019), 'Quantifying the Global Non-Revenue Water Problem', *Water Supply*, 19(3): 831–37.

Litman, T. (2010), *Transportation Elasticities How Prices and Other Factors Affect Travel Behavior*, Victoria, BC: Transport Policy Institute.

Littlechild, S. (1983), Regulation of British Telecommunications Profitability, Technical Report, Department of Industry, London.

Lodge, M. and K. Wegrich (2012), *Managing Regulation: Regulatory Analysis, Politics and Policy*. Basingstoke: Palgrave.

Lopez, A.-L. and X. Vives (2017): 'Overlapping Ownership, R&D Spillovers, and Antitrust Policy', IESE Business School WP-1140.37.

Lopez, J. D. (2017), 'Spreading the Word: Effects of a Nudge on Residential Water Conservation. A Field Experiment in Small Urban Villages in Colombia', *LACEEP Working Paper Series*, No. 96, August.

Lu, L., D. Deller and M. Hviid (2019), 'Price and Behavioural Signals to Encourage Household Water Conservation: Implications for the UK', *Water Resources Management*, 33: 475–91.

Lunn, P. (2014), *Regulatory Policy and Behavioural Economics*, Paris: OECD.

Macho-Stadler, I. and D. Pérez-Castrillo (2018), 'Moral Hazard: Base Models and Two Extensions, in L. C. Corchón and M. A. Marini, eds., *Handbook of Game Theory and Industrial Organization,* Vol. 1, Cheltenham: Edward Elgar.

Mack, E. A. and S. Wrase (2017), 'A Burgeoning Crisis? A Nationwide Assessment of the Geography of Water Affordability in the United States', *PLoS ONE* 12(1), e0169488, https://doi.org/10.1371/journal.pone.0169488

Mande Buafua, P. (2015), 'Efficiency of Urban Water Supply in Sub-Saharan Africa: Do Organization and Regulation Matter?', *Utilities Policy*, 37: 13–22.

Majone, G. (1994), 'The Rise of the Regulatory State in Europe', *West European Politics*, 17: 77–101.

Majone, G. (1996), *Regulating Europe*, London: Routledge.

Majone, G. (1997), 'From the Positive to the Regulatory State: Causes and Consequences of Changes in the Mode of Governance', *Journal of Public Policy*, 17(2): 139–67.

Martimort, D. and S. Straub (2009), 'Infrastructure Privatization and Changes in Corruption Patterns: The Roots of Public Discontent', *Journal of Development Economics*, 90(1): 69–84.

Martin, M. J. and C. Ocaña (1998), 'Competencia practicable y regulación', Moneda y crédito, Fundación Central Hispano, no. 206, 89–111.

McKinsey Global Institute (2016), 'Bridging Global Infrastructure Gaps', Report prepared by J. Woetzel, N. Garemo, J. Mischke, M. Hjerpe and R. Palter, www.mckinsey.com/business-functions/operations/our-insights/bridging-global-infrastructure-gaps#

Meyer, R. (2012a), 'Vertical Economies and the Costs of Separating Electricity Supply: A Review of Theoretical and Empirical Literature', *Energy Journal*, 33(4): 161–85.

Meyer, R. (2012b), 'Economies of Scope in Electricity Supply and the Costs of Vertical Separation for Different Unbundling Scenarios', *Journal of Regulatory Economics*, 42(1): 92–114.

Modigliani, F. and M. H. Miller (1958), 'The Cost of Capital, Corporation Finance, and the Theory of Investment', *American Economic Review*, 48(3): 61–97.

Mookherjee, D. (2015), 'Political Decentralization', *Annual Review of Economics*, 7: 231–49.

Morales, S. and O. Morales (2019), 'From Bribes to International Corruption: The Odebrecht Case', *Emerald Emerging Markets Case Studies*, 9(3): 1–13.

Moreno, L. A. (2017), 'How Tech Can Fight Corruption in Latin America and the Caribbean', World Economic Forum, www.weforum.org/agenda/2017/12/how-technology-is-becoming-a-powerful-ally-in-the-fight-against-corruption-in-latin-america-and-the-caribbean

Morin, R. A. (1994), 'Regulatory Finance – Utilities Cost of Capital', Public Utilities Reports, Arlington, Virginia.

Motta, M. (2004), *Competition Policy: Theory and Practice*, Cambridge: Cambridge University Press.

Mundell, R. A. (1962), 'Review of L. H. Janssen's Free Trade, Protection, and Customs Union', *American Economic Review*, 52: 621–2.

Musacchio, A. and S. G. Lazzarini (2014), *Reinventing State Capitalism: Leviathan in Business, Brazil and Beyond*, Cambridge, MA: Harvard University Press.

Mussa, M. and S. Rosen (1978), 'Monopoly and Product Quality', *Journal of Economic Theory*, 18: 301–17.

Nag, B. (2013), 'Public Procurement – Case Study of the Indian Railways', *Journal of Institute of Public Enterprise*, 36(1–2): 45–69.

Nardotto, M., T. Valletti and F. Verboven (2015), 'Unbundling the Incumbent: Evidence from UK Broadband!', *Journal of the European Economic Association*, 13(2): 330–62.

National Audit Office (2018), PFI and PF22 – Report by the Comptroller and Auditor General, London, www.nao.org.uk/wp-content/uploads/2018/01/PFI-and-PF2.pdf

Nauges, C. and D. Whittington (2017), 'Evaluating the Performance of Alternative Municipal Tariff Designs: Quantifying the Trade-Offs between Equity, Economic Efficiency, and Cost Recovery', *World Development*, 91: 125–43.

Nauges, C. and D. Whittington (2019), 'Social Norms Information Treatments in the Municipal Water Supply Sector: Some New Insights on Benefits and Costs', *Water Economics and Policy*, 5(3): 1–40.

Nelson, P. (1970), 'Information and Consumer Behavior', *Journal of Political Economy*, 2: 311–29.

Nemati, M. and J. Penn (2018), 'The Impact of Social Norms, Feedback, and Price Information on Conservation Behavior: A Meta-Analysis', 2018 Annual Meeting, 5–7 August, Washington, DC, Agricultural and Applied Economics Association.

Nepal, R. and J. Tooraj (2015), 'Incentive Regulation and Utility Benchmarking for Electricity Network Security', *Economic Analysis and Policy*, 48(C): 117–27.

Newbery, D. M. (2000), *Privatization, Restructuring and Regulation of Network Utilities*, Cambridge, MA: MIT Press.

O'Brien, D. and S. Salop (2000), 'Competitive Effects of Partial Ownership: Financial Interest and Corporate Control', *Antitrust Law Journal*, 67(3): 559–614.

O'Brien, D. P. and K. Waehrer (2017), 'The Competitive Effects of Common Ownership: We Know Less than We Think', *Antitrust Law Journal*, 81: 729–76.

OECD (2015a), *Guidelines on Corporate Governance of State-Owned Enterprises*, Paris: OECD Publishing.

OECD (2015b), *Corporate Investment and the Stagnation Puzzle, OECD Business and Finance Outlook*, Paris: OECD Publishing.

OECD (2015c), 'Industry Self Regulation: Role and Use in Supporting Consumer Interests', OECD *Digital Economy Papers*, No. 247, OECD Publishing, Paris, http://dx.doi.org/10.1787/5js4k1fjqkwh-en

OECD (2017a), *Behavioural Insights and Public Policy: Lessons from around the World*, Paris: OECD Publishing.

OECD (2017b), *The Size and Sectoral Distribution of State-Owned Enterprises*, Paris: OECD Publishing.

OECD (2018a), *Ownership and Governance of State-Owned Enterprises: A Compendium of National Practices*, Paris: OECD Publishing.

OECD (2018b), *Economic Outlook*, Issue 2, Paris: OECD Publishing.

OECD (2019), *Better Regulation Practices across the European Union*, Paris: OECD Publishing.

Office of Gas and Energy Markets (OFGEM) (2010), 'RIIO: A New Way to Regulate Energy Networks; Final Decision', Technical Report, OFGEM.

Office of the Rail Regulator (2017), *Rail Finance-2016–17 – Annual Statistical Release*, United Kingdom.

Opertti, F. (2019), *Trade Globalization and Digitalization*, https://blogs.iadb.org/integration-trade/en/trade-globalization-digitalization/

Ostrom, E., R. B. Parks, G. P. Whitaker and S. L. Percy (1978), 'The Public Service Production Process: A Framework for Analyzing Police Services', *Policy Studies Journal*, 7(s1): 381–89.

Otegui Nieto, J. N. (2018), 'Competition in Crisis – Challenges to Spanish Enforcement Performance', https://ssrn.com/abstract=3208268 or http://dx.doi.org/10.2139/ssrn.3208268

Ovtchinnikov, A. V. (2010), 'Capital Structure Decisions: Evidence from Deregulated Industries', *Journal of Financial Economics*, 95(2): 249–74.

Ovtchinnikov, A. V. (2016), 'Debt Decisions in Deregulated Industries', *Journal of Corporate Finance*, 36(C): 230–54.

OXERA (2015), 'Which WACC When? A Cost of Capital Puzzle', www.oxera.com/wp-content/uploads/2018/07/Which-WACC-when_a-cost-of-capital-puzzle.pdf.pdf

Parker, D. and C. Kirpatrick (2012), 'Measuring Regulatory Performance: The Economic Impact of Regulatory Policy: A Literature Review of Quantitative Evidence', *OECD Expert Paper*, No. 3.

Patel, M. S. (2019), 'Common Ownership and Antitrust: Eight Critical Points to Guide Antitrust Policy', https://ssrn.com/abstract=3377720

Peltzman, S. (1976), 'Toward a More General Theory of Regulation', *Journal of Law & Economics*, 19(2): 211–40.

Perez, O. (2015), 'Can Experts Be Trusted and What Can Be Done about It? Insights from the Biases and Heuristics Literature', in A. Alemanno and A.-L. Sibony, eds., *Nudge and the Law: A European Perspective*, Oxford: Hart, 115–38.

Petropoulos, G. and B. Willems (2017), 'Providing Efficient Network Access to Green Power Generators: A Long-Term Property Rights Perspective', *TSE Working Paper*, 17-770.

Piga, G. (2011), 'A Fighting Chance against Corruption in Public Procurement', in S. Rose-Ackerman and T. Soreide, eds., *International Handbook on the Economics of Corruption*, Vol. 2, Cheltenham: Edward Elgar, 141–84.

Pindyck, R. (2004), 'Mandatory Unbundling and Irreversible Investment in Telecom Networks', *NBER Working Papers*, No. 10287, February.

Polinsky, A. M. and S. Shavell (1994), 'Should Liability Be Based on the Harm to the Victim or the Gain to the Injurer?', *Journal of Law, Economics, and Organization*, 10(2): 427–37.

Pollitt, M. G. (2019), 'The European Single Market in Electricity: An Economic Assessment', *Review of Industrial Organization*, 55(1): 63–87.

Posner, E. A., F. Scott Morton and E. Glen Weyl (2017), 'A Proposal to Limit the Anti-Competitive Power of Institutional Investors', *Antitrust Law Journal*, 81(3), 669–89.

Poudineh, R. and T. Jamasb (2014), 'Determinants of Investment under Incentive Regulation: The Case of the Norwegian Electricity Distribution Networks', *Energy Economics*, 53(C): 193–202.

PwC (2018), *The Era of Digitized Trucking: Charting Your Transformation to a New Business Model*, www.strategyand.pwc.com/de/en/insights/2018/digitized-trucking.html

PwC and Ecorys (2013), *Identifying and Reducing Corruption in Public Procurement*, https://ec.europa.eu/anti-fraud/sites/antifraud/files/docs/body/identifying_reducing_corruption_in_public_procurement_en.pdf

Querbach, T. and C. Arndt (2017), 'Regulatory Policy in Latin America: An Analysis of the State of Play', *OECD Regulatory Policy Working Papers*.

Ramsey, F. P. (1927), 'A Contribution to the Theory of Taxation', *Economic Journal*, 37: 47–61.

Ramsey, F. P. (1928), 'A Mathematical Theory of Saving', *Economic Journal*, 38(152): 543–59.

Rawls, J. (1971) *A Theory of Justice*, Cambridge, MA: Belknap Press.

Reiffen, D. and M. R. Ward (2002), 'Recent Empirical Evidence on Discrimination by Regulated Firms', *Review of Network Economics*, 1(1): 39–53.

Reynaud, A. (2016), 'Assessing the Impact of Full Cost Recovery of Water Services on European Households', *Water Resources and Economics*, 74: 65–78.

Ringe, W.-G. and C. Ruof (2020), 'Regulating Fintech in the EU: The Case for a Guided Sandbox', *European Journal of Risk Regulation*, March, Published online by Cambridge University Press.

Robinson, C. (2007), *Utility Regulation in Competitive Markets: Problems and Progress*, London: Insitute of Economic Affairs.

Robinson, L. A. and J. K. Hammitt (2011a), 'Behavioural Economics and Regulatory Analysis', *Risk Analysis*, 31(9): 1408–22.

Robinson, L. A. and J. K. Hammitt (2011b), 'Behavioral Economics and the Conduct of Benefit–Cost Analysis: Towards Principles and Standards', *Journal of Benefit–Cost Analysis*, 2(2): 1–51.

Rock, E. B. and D. L. Rubinfeld (2017), 'Defusing the Antitrust Threat to Institutional Investor Involvement in Corporate Governance', *NYU Law and Economics Research Paper*, No. 17-05.

Rodriguez Pardina, M., R. Schlirf Rapti and E. Groom (2008), *Accounting for Infrastructure Regulation: An Introduction*, Washington, DC: World Bank, https://openknowledge.worldbank.org/handle/10986/6426

Roques, F. and N. Savva (2009), 'Investment under Uncertainty with Price Ceilings in Oligopolies', *Journal of Economic Dynamics & Control*, 33(2): 507–24.

Rose, N. L., ed. (2014), *Economic Regulation and Its Reform: What Have We Learned?*, Boston: NBER.

Rose-Ackerman, S. and T. Søreide, eds. (2011), *International Handbook on the Economics of Corruption*, Vol. 2, Cheltenham: Edward Elgar.

Rochet, J. C. and J. J. Tirole (2006), 'Two-Sided Markets: A Progress Report', *RAND Journal of Economics*, 37: 645–67.

Rouse, M. (2013), *Institutional Governance and Regulation of Water Services: The Essential Elements*, 2nd edition, London: IWA Publishing.

Rovine, A. W. (2014), *Contemporary Issues in International Arbitration and Mediation: The Fordham Papers*, The Hague: Martinus Nijhoff.

Saal, D. S., P. Arocena, A. Maziotis and T. Triebs (2013), 'Scale and Scope Economies and the Efficient Vertical and Horizontal Configuration of the Water Industry: A Survey of the Literature', *Review of Network Economics*, 12(1): 93–129.

Salant, D. (1995), 'Behind the Revolving Door: A New View of Public Utility Regulation', *RAND Journal of Economics*, 26(3): 362–77.

Salling, K. B. and S. Leleur (2015), 'Accounting for the Inaccuracies in Demand Forecasts and Construction Cost Estimations in Transport Project Evaluation', *Transport Policy*, 34: 8–18.

Sappington, D. (1983), 'Optimal Regulation of a Multiproduct Monopoly with Unknown Technological Capabilities', *Bell Journal of Economics*, 14(2): 453–63.

Sappington, D. (2005), 'Regulating Service Quality: A Survey', *Journal of Regulatory Economics*, 27(2): 123–54.

Sappington, D. (2006), 'Regulation in Vertically-Related Industries: Myths, Facts, and Policy', *Review of Industrial Organization*, 28(1): 3–16.

Saussier, S. and J. de Brux, eds. (2018), *The Economics of Public-Private Partnerships. Theoretical and Empirical Developments*, Paris: Springer International.

Schmalensee, R. (2020), 'Competitive Energy Storage and the Duck Curve', July, MIT-CEEPRv WP 2020-012.

Schmaltz, M. C. (2018), 'Common-Ownership Concentration and Corporate Conduct', in P. Bolton, ed., *Annual Review of Financial Economics*, 10, December.

Schmitz Jr, J. A. (2012), 'New and Larger Costs of Monopoly and Tariffs', *Federal Reserve Bank of Minneapolis, Staff Report* 468, July.

Schubert, C. (2017), 'Green Nudges: Do They Work? Are They Ethical?', *Ecological Economics*, 132(C): 329–42.

Schultz, P. W., J. M. Nolan, R. B. Cialdini, N. J. Goldstein and V. Griskevicius (2007), 'The Constructive, Destructive, and Reconstructive Power of Social Norms', *Psychological Science*, 18(5): 429434.

Sebri, M. (2014), 'A Meta-Analysis of Residential Water Demand Studies', *Environment, Development and Sustainability*, 16: 499–520.

Serebrisky, T., A. Gómez-Lobo, N. Estupiñán and R. Muñoz-Raskin (2009), 'Affordability and Subsidies in Public Urban Transport: What Do We Mean, What Can Be Done?', *Transport Reviews*, 29(6): 715–39.

Sherman, R. (2008), *Market Regulation*, New York: Pearson.

Sidak, J. G. and A. P. Lipsky (1999), 'Essential Facilities', *Stanford Law Review*, 51(5): 1187–249.

Silva, H. (2017), 'Input Third-Degree Price Discrimination in Transport Markets', *Documento de Trabajo IE-PUC*, No. 499.

Skou Nicolaisen, M. and P. A. Driscoll (2014), 'Ex-Post Evaluations of Demand Forecast Accuracy: A Literature Review', *Transport Review*, 34(4): 540–57.

Sonenshine, R. (2016), 'Effect of Utility Deregulation and Mergers on Consumer Welfare', American University, Economics Department, Working Paper Series, 2016-08.

Soreide, T. (2014), *Drivers of Corruption: A Brief Review*, Washington, DC: World Bank.

Spiegel, Y. (1994), 'The Capital Structure and Investment of Regulated Firms under Alternative Regulatory Regimes', *Journal of Regulatory Economics*, 6(3): 297–319.

Spiegel, Y. and D. F. Spulber (1994), 'The Capital Structure of a Regulated Firm', *RAND Journal of Economics*, 25(3): 424–40.

Spiegel, Y. and D. F. Spulber (1997), 'Capital Structure with Countervailing Incentives', *RAND Journal of Economics*, 28(1): 1–24.

Spiller, P. (2010), 'Transactions Cost Regulation', *California Management Review*, 52(2): 147–58.

Spiller, P. (2011), 'Basic Economic Principles of Infrastructure Liberalization: A Transaction Cost Perspective', in M. Finger and R. W. Kunneke, eds., *Handbook of Network Industries – The Liberalization of Infrastructure*, Cheltenham: Edward Elgar.

Spiller, P. and M. Moszoro (2016), 'Coase and the Transaction Cost Approach to Regulation', in C. Ménard and E. Bertrand, eds., *The Elgar Companion to Ronald H. Coase*, Cheltenham: Edward Elgar, chapter 19, 262–75.

Stigler, G. (1971), 'The Theory of Economic Regulation', *Bell Journal of Economics and Management Science*, 2(1): 3–21.

Sudarshan, A. (2017), 'Nudges in the Marketplace: The Response of Household Electricity Consumption to Information and Monetary Incentives', *Journal of Economic Behavior & Organization*, 134(C): 320–35.

Sunstein, C. R., L. A. Reisch and J. Rauber (2018), 'A Worldwide Consensus on Nudging? Not Quite, but Almost', *Regulation & Governance*, 12: 3–22.

Sustainable Mobility for All (2017), Global Mobility Report 2017: Tracking Sector Performance, Washington DC, License: Creative Commons Attribution CC BY 3.0.

Sweerts, B., F. Dalla Longa and B. van der Zwaan (2019), 'Financial De-risking to Unlock Africa's Renewable Energy Potential', *Renewable and Sustainable Energy Reviews*, 102: 75–82.

Tangeras, T. (2009), 'Yardstick Competition and Quality', *Journal of Economics & Management Strategy*, 18(2): 589–613.

Thaler, R. H. and C. R. Sunstein (2008), *Nudge: Improving Decisions about Health, Wealth, and Happiness*, New Haven, CT: Yale University Press.

Thatcher, M. (2002), 'Regulation after Delegation: Independent Regulatory Agencies in Europe', *Journal of European Public Policy*, 9(6): 954–72.

Thatcher, M. (2011), 'The Creation of European Regulatory Agencies and Its Limits: A Comparative Analysis of European Delegation', *Journal of European Public Policy*, 18 (6): 790–809.

Tirole, J. (1988), *The Theory of Industrial Organization*, Cambridge, MA: MIT Press.

Tirole, J. (2015), 'Market Failures and Public Policy', *American Economic Review, American Economic Association*, 105(6): 1665–82.

Tirole, J. (2017), *Economics for the Common Good*, Princeton, NJ: Princeton University Press.

Torero, M. (2015), 'The Impact of Rural Electrification: Challenges and Ways Forward', *Revue d'économie du développement*, 23(HS): 49–75.

Train, K. (1991), *Optimal Regulation: The Economic Theory of Natural Monopoly*, Cambridge, MA: MIT Press.

Trillas, F. (2016), 'Behavioral Regulatory Agencies', *Working Papers wpdea1606*, Department of Applied Economics at Universitat Autonoma of Barcelona.

UNSW City Futures Research Centre (2019), Australia's Household Infrastructure Bill, Analysis Report, 4 April, www.infrastructureaustralia.gov.au/publications/australian-infrastructure-audit-2019

Vagliasindi, M. (2012), 'The Role of Regulatory Governance in Driving PPPs in Electricity Transmission and Distribution in Developing Countries: A Cross-Country Analysis', World Bank, Policy Research Working Paper 6121.

Valletti, T. (2017), 'Concentration Trends in Europe', PPT of the Presentation at the CRA Annual Brussels Conference: Economic Developments in Competition Policy, December, https://ecp.crai.com/wp-content/uploads/2017/12/Valletti-Concentration_Trends_TV_CRA-002.pdf

Valletti, T. (2018), 'Après moi, le déluge: Tech Giants in the Digital Age', PPT of the presentation at the CRA Annual Brussels Conference: Economic Developments in Competition Policy, December, https://ecp.crai.com/wp-content/uploads/2018/12/Tommaso-Valletti-2018.pdf

Valletti, T. and H. Zenger (2018), 'Should Profit Margins Play a More Decisive Role in Merger Control? A Rejonder to Jorge Padilla', *Journal of European Competition Law and Practice*, 9: 336–42.

Valletti, T. and H. Zenger (2019), 'Increasing Market Power and Merger Control ',*Competition Law & Policy Debate*, 5(1): 26–35.

Valletti T. and H. Zenger (2021), 'Mergers with Differentiated Products: Where Do We Stand?', *Review of Industrial Organization*, 58: 179–212.

Van der Waal, E. C., A. Das and T. van der Schoor (2020), 'Participatory Experimentation with Energy Law: Digging in a 'Regulatory Sandbox' for Local Energy Initiatives in the Netherlands', *Energies*, 13(2): 1–21.

Van Kersbergen, K. and F. van Waarden (2004), '"Governance" as a Bridge between Disciplines: Cross-Disciplinary Inspiration Regarding Shifts in Governance and Problems of Governability, Accountability and Legitimacy', *European Journal of Political Research*, 43(2): 143–71.

Villadsen, B., M. J. Vilbert, D. Harris and A. L. Kolbe (2017), *Risk and Return for Regulated Industries*, Amsterdam: Elsevier.

Viscusi, W. K., J. E. Harrington, Jr. and D. E. M. Sappington (2018), *Economics of Regulation and Antitrust*, 5th edition, Boston, MA: MIT Press.

Vogelsang, I. (2002), 'Incentive Regulation and Competition in Public Utility Markets: A 20-Year Perspective', *Journal of Regulatory Economics*, 22(1): 5–27.

Vogelsang, I. (2010), 'Incentive Regulation, Investments and Technological Change', *CESifo Working Paper Series*, No. 2964.

Vogelsang, I. (2018), 'Net Neutrality Regulation: Much Ado about Nothing?', *Review of Network Economics*, 17: 225–43.

Von Eije, H., A. Goyal and C. Muckley (2017), 'Flexible Firm-Level Dividends in Latin America', *Finance Research Letters*, 23: 133–36.

Waddams, C. and D. Deller(2015), 'Affordability of Utilities' Services: Extent, Practice, Policy', Centre for Regulation in Europe (CERRE) report, Brussels.

Weingast, B. R. (2014), 'Second Generation Fiscal Federalism: Political Aspects of Decentralization and Economic Development', *World Development*, 53: 14–25.

Weisman, D. L. (2019), 'The Power of Regulatory Regimes Re-examined', *Journal of Regulatory Economics*, 56(2–3): 125–48.

Weitzman, M. L. (1980), 'The "Rachet Principle" and Performance Incentives', *Bell Journal of Economics*, 11(1): 302–8.

Willems, B. and G. Zwart (2018), 'Optimal Regulation of Network Expansion', *RAND Journal*, 19(1): 23–42.

Wils, W. P. J. (2006), 'Optimal Antitrust Fines: Theory and Practice', *World Competition*, 29 (2): 183–208.

Wilson, R. (1993), *Nonlinear Pricing*, Oxford: Oxford University Press.

Wilson, W. W. and F. A. Wolak (2018), 'Benchmark Regulation of Multiproduct Firms: An Application to the Rail Industry', NBER Working Papers 25268, National Bureau of Economic Research.

Whittington, D., C. Nauges, D. Fuente and X. Wu (2015), 'A Diagnostic Tool for Estimating the Incidence of Subsidies Delivered by Water Utilities in Low- and Medium-Income Countries, with Illustrative Simulations', *Utilities Policy*, 34(C): 70–81.

World Bank (1996), *Argentina – Reforming Provincial Utilities: Issues, Challenges and Best Practice*, http://documents.worldbank.org/curated/en/365271468740396874/Argentina-Reforming-provincial-utilities-issues-challenges-and-best-practice

Wren-Lewis, L. (2015), 'Do Infrastructure Reforms Reduce the Effect of Corruption? Theory and Evidence from Latin America and the Caribbean', *World Bank Economic Review*, 29(2): 353–84.

Wright, S., P. Burns, R. Mason, D. Pickford and A. Hewitt (2018), 'Estimating the Cost of Capital for Implementation of Price Controls by UK Regulators: An Update on Mason, Miles and Wright (2003)', www.bbk.ac.uk/ems/faculty/wright/wrightburnsmasonpickford2018.pdf

Yeung, K. and M. Lodge, eds. (2019), *Algorithmic Regulation*, Oxford: Oxford University Press.

Index

Abbott, M., 13
Abrardi, L. C., 274
access and social outcomes
    artificial intelligence and, 383–84
    benchmarking, 355–59, 365
    beneficiaries of regulation and, 212–14
    coverage gaps, 11–12
    defined, 212–14
    market evolution and investment effects, 266–67
    problems and limitations of, 221–24
    quality issues and, 223–24
    subsidy design and, 218–19
access rules
    deregulated vertical integration and, 323–24
    guidelines for setting, 325–28
    investment decisions and, 260–61
    margin squeezes and, 328–30
    regulation and, 17–18, 271–74
    sector organization and, 267–71
    single-buyer framework, 267–71, 277
    third-party access framework, 265
    two-sided markets, 330–32
accountability, institutional limits on, 341–44, 349–51
accounting practices
    adverse selection and, 108
    moral hazard and, 109–10, 117–23
    price-cap regulation formula and, 141–44
    production and technology benchmarking and, 48–49
    public monopoly cost manipulation and, 94–98
    quality of regulation and, 123–27
adverse selection
    accounting and benchmarking and, 123–27
    asymmetric information and price regulation, 154–56
    Baron–Myerson private monopoly regulation model and, 90–94
    cap-based price regulation and, 145
    incentive compatibility constraints in, 112–15
    information gaps and, 107–11
    Laffont–Tirole monopoly regulation framework, 94–98
    participation constraint in, 111–17

pricing regulation and, 138–39
    risk model for, 111–17
    yardstick competition price regulation and, 146–49
affordability
    basic principles of, 214–16
    of benchmarking, 364–65
    beneficiaries of regulation and, 212–14
    income elasticity and, 44–45
    limits of regulation and, 224–26
algorithmic pricing, 381–82
allowed rate of return
    financial/fiscal viability assessment and, 160
    weighted average cost of capital and, 176–79
alternative sources, demand forecasting and, 160–63
Andrés, L., 101
Angel-Urdinola, D. F., 218–19
anti-trust regulation
    access pricing rules and, 261n.21
    importance of, 17–18
    margin squeezes and, 328–30
    oligopolistic structures and, 304–6
    relevant/reference markets and, 309–11
Armstrong, M., 292–93, 308–26
assets
    common- and cross-ownership risk and, 322–23
    depreciation of, 158–60
    historical cost of, 161n.12
    investment regulation and role of, 253n.6
    rehabilitation, 109–10
    stranded assets, 258
asymmetric information. *See* informational
    constraints
Auriol, E., 62, 242–44, 282–84, 308, 355
Autor, D. D., 308
average profitability index, 316–18
Averch–Johnson effect, 127, 139–41, 254–58

Baldwin, R. M., 287–88
Barde, J. A., 208–9
Baron, D., 80–84, 90–94
Baron–Myerson monopoly regulation model, 90–94
    adverse selection in, 90–94, 108, 111–17
    Laffont–Tirole framework compared to, 94–98
Bastos C. M., 145–50